Neural Models
of Plasticity

Neural Models of Plasticity

Experimental and Theoretical Approaches

Edited by

John H. Byrne

Department of Neurobiology and Anatomy
University of Texas Medical School at Houston
Houston, Texas

William O. Berry

Air Force Office of Scientific Research
Bolling Air Force Base
Washington, D.C.

Academic Press, Inc.
Harcourt Brace Jovanovich, Publishers
San Diego   New York   Berkeley   Boston
London   Sydney   Tokyo   Toronto

ACADEMIC PRESS, INC.
San Diego, California 92101

United Kingdom Edition published by
ACADEMIC PRESS LIMITED
24-28 Oval Road, London NW1 7DX

Library of Congress Cataloging-in-Publication Data

Neural models of plasticity : experimental and theoretical approaches
/ John H. Byrne and William O. Berry.
    p.   cm.
  Includes index.
  ISBN   0-12-148955-8   (hardcover) (alk. paper)
  ISBN   0-12-148956-6   (paperback) (alk. paper)
    1. Neuroplasticity—Congresses.   2. Neuroplasticity—Mathematical
models—Congresses.   3. Learning—Congresses.   4. Learning-
-Mathematical models—Congresses.   5. Memory—Congresses.
  6. Memory—Mathematical models—Congresses.   I. Byrne, John H.
II. Berry, William O.
QP372.6.N49   1988
153.1—dc19   88-12124
                                                       CIP

PRINTED IN THE UNITED STATES OF AMERICA
89 90 91 92   9 8 7 6 5 4 3 2

Contents

7 Classical Conditioning Phenomena Predicted by a Drive-Reinforcement Model of Neuronal Function
A. Harry Klopf

8 Olfactory Processing and Associative Memory: Cellular and Modeling Studies
A. Gelperin, D. W. Tank, and G. Tesauro

9 Neural Circuit for Classical Conditioning of the Eyelid Closure Response
Richard F. Thompson

Contributors

Numbers in parentheses indicate the pages on which the authors' contributions begin.

DAVID G. AMARAL (208), The Salk Institute and The Clayton Foundation for Research–California Division, San Diego, California 92138

DIANE E. J. BLAZIS (187), Department of Psychology, University of Massachusetts, Amherst, Massachusetts 01003

THOMAS H. BROWN[1] (266), Department of Cellular Neurophysiology, Division of Neurosciences, Beckman Research Institute of the City of Hope, Duarte, California 91010

JOHN H. BYRNE (58), Department of Neurobiology and Anatomy, The University of Texas Medical School, Houston, Texas 77225

THOMAS J. CAREW (22), Departments of Psychology and Biology, Yale University, New Haven, Connecticut 06520

TERRY CROW[2] (1), Department of Physiology, University of Pittsburgh, School of Medicine, Pittsburgh, Pennsylvania 15261

F. EDWARD DUDEK (378), Mental Retardation Research Center, University of California at Los Angeles, Los Angeles, California 70024

ALAN H. GANONG (266), Department of Cellular Neurophysiology, Division of Neurosciences, Beckman Research Institute of the City of Hope, Duarte, California 91010

A. GELPERIN (133), AT&T Bell Laboratories, Murray Hill, New Jersey 07974

KEVIN J. GINGRICH (58), Department of Neurobiology, The University of Texas Medical School, Houston, Texas 77225

RICHARD GRANGER (329), Center for the Neurobiology and Anatomy of Learning and Memory, University of California, Irvine, California 92717

[1]Present address: Yale University, New Haven, Connecticut 06520.
[2]Present address: Department of Neurobiology and Anatomy, The University of Texas Medical School, Houston, Texas 77225.

RICHARD GRAY (307), Department of Neurology and Departments of Physiology and Molecular Biophysics, Baylor College of Medicine, Houston, Texas 77030

STEVEN M. GREENBERG (47), Howard Hughes Medical Institute, Center for Neurobiology and Behavior, Columbia University, New York, New York 10032

ROBERT D. HAWKINS (74), Center for Neurobiology and Behavior, College of Physicians and Surgeons of Columbia University, New York, New York 10032

J. J. HOPFIELD (363), AT&T Bell Laboratories, Murray Hill, New Jersey 07974, and Divisions of Chemistry and Biology, California Institute of Technology, Pasadena, California 91125

WILLIAM F. HOPKINS (307), Neurology Research, Veterans Administration Medical Center, Portland, Oregon 97201

MASAO ITO (178), Department of Physiology, Faculty of Medicine, University of Tokyo, Tokyo 113, Japan

DANIEL JOHNSTON (307), Department of Neurology, Baylor College of Medicine, Houston, Texas 77030

EDWARD W. KAIRISS (266), Department of Biological Sciences, University of Illinois at Chicago, Chicago, Illinois 60680

CLAUDE L. KEENAN (266), Department of Biological Sciences, University of Illinois at Chicago, Chicago, Illinois 60680

STEPHEN R. KELSO (266), Department of Biological Sciences, University of Illinois at Chicago, Chicago, Illinois 60680

A. HARRY KLOPF (104), Air Force Wright Aeronautical Laboratories, Wright-Patterson Air Force Base, Ohio 45433

JOHN LARSON (329), Center for the Neurobiology of Learning and Memory, University of California, Irvine, California 92717

GARY LYNCH (329), Center for the Neurobiology of Learning and Memory, University of California, Irvine, California 92717

JOHN W. MOORE (187), Department of Psychology, University of Massachusetts, Amherst, Massachusetts 01003

EDMUND T. ROLLS (240), Department of Experimental Psychology, University of Oxford, Oxford OX1 3UD, England

JAMES H. SCHWARTZ (47), Howard Hughes Medical Institute, Center for Neurobiology and Behavior, Columbia University, New York, New York 10032

TERRENCE J. SEJNOWSKI (94), Department of Biophysics, The Johns Hopkins University, Baltimore, Maryland 21218

ARTHUR P. SHIMAMURA (208), Veterans Administration Medical Center, San Diego, California 92161 and Department of Psychiatry, University of California, San Diego, La Jolla, California 92093

LARRY R. SQUIRE (208), Veterans Administration Medical Center, San Diego, California 92161 and Department of Psychiatry, University of California, San Diego, La Jolla, California 92093

D. W. TANK (133, 363), AT&T Laboratories, Murray Hill, New Jersey 07974

GERALD TESAURO[3] (94, 133), Center for Complex Systems Research, University of Illinois, Champaign-Urbana, Illinois 61820

RICHARD F. THOMPSON (160), Department of Psychology, University of Southern California, Los Angeles, California 90089

ROGER D. TRAUB (378), IBM, Thomas J. Watson Research Center, Yorktown Heights, New York 10598 and Department of Neurology, College of Physicians and Surgeons of Columbia University, New York, New York 10032

ROBERT S. ZUCKER (403), Department of Physiology-Anatomy, University of California at Berkeley, Berkeley, California 94720

[3]Present address: Research Division, International Business Machines Corporation (IBM), Thomas J. Watson Research Center, Yorktown Heights, New York 10598.

Preface

Two separate approaches, one theoretical and the other empirical, are being used currently to explore the role of neuronal plasticity in learning, memory, and complex brain functions. The theoretical approach attempts to simulate and synthesize brain function with mathematical models based on known and hypothesized principles of neural function. The empirical approach attempts to delineate the detailed biochemical and biophysical properties of neurons, the rules that determine their connectivity, and the mechanisms through which their properties and connections are modified during learning. While these two approaches have traditionally been used independently, there is a growing realization among neurobiologists, psychologists, and adaptive systems theorists that progress in understanding the brain is dependent upon a combined use of both approaches.

Neural Models of Plasticity is an outgrowth of a conference that was held at Woods Hole, Massachusetts, in the spring of 1987. The purpose of that conference was to review recent developments in both areas and to foster communication between those researchers pursuing theoretical approaches and those pursuing more empirical approaches. We trust that this volume will serve a similar purpose. We have solicited chapters from individuals who represent both ends of the spectrum of approaches as well as those using a combination of the two. As these chapters indicate, our knowledge of the plastic capabilities of the nervous system is accelerating rapidly. This is so both because of the rapid advances in the understanding of basic subcellular and molecular mechanisms of plasticity and because of the computational capabilities and plastic properties that emerge from neural networks and assemblies. We believe that the acceleration of knowledge will continue and be driven by the mutually reinforcing effects that these complementary "wet" and "dry" approaches have on each other. The theorists and modelers help identify new hypotheses to test experimentally, while the empiricists provide new data for the improvement of the models, progressively leading to more substantial understanding of neuronal plasticity and its relationship to learning and memory and information processing.

J. H. Byrne
W. O. Berry

1

Associative Learning, Memory, and Neuromodulation in *Hermissenda*

Terry Crow

I. Introduction

Learning mechanisms derived from recent studies of cellular and synaptic plasticity have a number of fundamental differences in the way that the basic neural processes that underly learning and memory are produced by experience. However, regardless of the different cellular mechanism(s) underlying learning, theories of learning must provide an explanation for the role played by motivation and rewards in learning. There is considerable evidence that learning and memory in both experimental animals and humans are influenced by treatments that affect brain function when administered during or shortly after training (for review, see McGaugh, 1983). In addressing the question of the role of motivation in learning and memory, it is attractive to speculate that motivation and rewards may influence learning through the action of neuromodulators. Recent physiological studies have identified a number of neuromodulators in the central nervous system whose actions produce profound effects on the electrical excitability of target neurons. These studies of neuromodulators have been carried to the cellular and subcellular level, where second-messenger systems have been identified and specific membrane conductances affected by the modulators have been examined (for review see Kaczmarek and Levitan, 1987). Since the effects of neuromodulation may depend on activity in target cells and since changes in the excitability of target cells are typically long-lasting, modulators provide for both a primary role in associative processes and the possibility of enhancing an associative change produced by the action of another neurotransmitter. Secondary effects could be expressed by co-release of a neuromodulator and classical neurotransmitter, or by extrinsic input from another neural pathway. Since neuromodulators are ubiquitous in the nervous system of both vertebrates and invertebrates, it is attractive to propose a role for a neuromodulator in associative learning of the marine mollusk *Hermissenda*, the subject of this review. Before discussing the evidence for neuromodulation, the organization of the central pathways mediating conditioning in *Hermissenda* and the behavior that is modified by conditioning will be described.

II. Organization of the Central Nervous System

The central nervous system of the Pacific nudibranch *Hermissenda* consists of a ring of ganglia surrounding the esophageous. A diagram of the dorsal surface of the circumesophageal nervous system is shown in Fig. 1. The circumesophageal nervous system contains several thousand neurons and consists of the paired pedal ganglia and the paired cerebropleural ganglia (see Fig. 1). The two sensory systems that have received a great deal of attention in studies of conditioning are the visual system and a primitive vestibular organ or gravity-detecting organ called the statocyst. An example of the location of the eyes and statocysts in the isolated nervous system is shown in the photomicrograph in Fig. 2(1a). As shown in Figs. 1 and 2, these two sensory systems are located bilaterally on the dorsal surface of the nervous system between the pedal and cerebropleural ganglia. Both of these sensory systems are independent and central; thus the two independent sensory systems remain intact following the surgical isolation of the central nervous system. This feature allows for the study of the synaptic interaction of cells both within

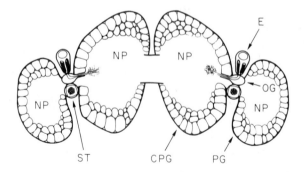

Figure 1.
Diagram of the dorsal surface of the circumesophageal nervous system of *Hermissenda crassicornis*. Two type-B photoreceptor somata, black areas in each eye, their axons and terminal processes are drawn schematically. Photoreceptors receive synaptic input from other photoreceptors at their terminal endings in the neuropil. Key: E, eye; OG, optic ganglion; NP, neuropil; ST, statocyst; CPG, cerebropleural ganglia; PG, pedal ganglia. [Adapted from Crow *et al.* (1979).]

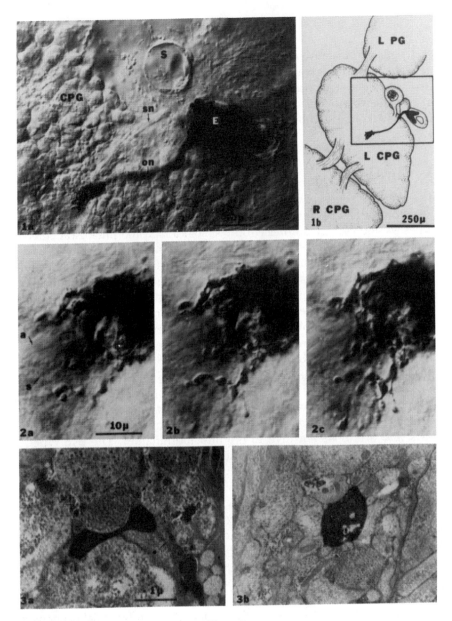

Figure 2.

Optical section ×240 of the portion of the circumesophageal ganglia of *Hermissenda crassicornis* indicated (at ×90) by the box in 1b. The primary features are the eye (E) and optic nerve (on) in which one axon has been stained with HRP, and the statocyst (S) and the static nerve (sn). Key: L PG, left pedal ganglion; L CPG, left cerebropleural ganglion; R CPG, right cerebropleural ganglion. Parts 2a–c: Three sequential optical sections, separated by 1-μm intervals, of the branched region in part 1, now magnified ×1500. A greater sense of continuity and depth may be obtained by viewing them pairwise in stereo. Note en passant and terminal swellings. Part 3: Electron micrographic cross sections (×13,500) of swellings as seen in part 2. Note that the labeled swellings in both parts 2 and 3 are on the order of 1–2 μm in diameter, but that small processes are also seen in the electron micrographs. [From Senft *et al.* (1982).]

each sensory structure and between the two sensory systems and other neurons in the ganglion. The synaptic organization of neurons in these two sensory systems in an isolated nervous system has been examined in considerable detail using electrophysiological and anatomical techniques (Alkon, 1973a,b, 1975a,b; Alkon and Fuortes, 1972; Crow et al., 1979).

A. Visual System

The eyes of *Hermissenda* are relatively simple: each eye contains five photoreceptors. The photoreceptors within each eye can be divided into two types (A and B), based on electrophysiological and morphological criteria (Alkon and Fuortes, 1972; Dennis, 1967). The three type-B photoreceptors are located in the posterior region of the eye, are spontaneously active in the dark (generate action potentials), and are most sensitive to dim illumination (Alkon and Fuortes, 1972). The B photoreceptors exhibit intrinsic plastic changes produced by conditioning that have been the focus of recent neurophysiological and biochemical studies (Acosta-Urquidi et al., 1984; Alkon et al., 1982, 1983; Bridge and Crow, 1986; Crow, 1985b,c; Crow and Alkon, 1980; Neary et al., 1981). Of the three type-B photoreceptors, two can be identified according to their position in the eye and are termed the medial and lateral B, respectively. The two type-A photoreceptors are located in the anterior part of the eye near the lens (see Fig. 1). The A-type photoreceptors are not typically active in the dark and are most sensitive to brighter illumination. The two type-A photoreceptors can be further identified by position, such as medial A and lateral A. Type-A photoreceptors also exhibit neural correlates in conditioned animals that are intrinsic to the photoreceptors (Richards and Farley, 1984; T. Crow and M. S. Bridge, unpublished observations). In both types A and B photoreceptors, action-potential generation and synaptic interactions take place near the distal region of the axon in the neuropil approximately 60–70 μm from the cell bodies. Phototransduction occurs near the cell bodies where the rhabdomeres abut the lens. This spatial separation of function allows for the isolation of photoreceptors by axotomy, which results in a photoreceptor that is isolated from both normal synaptic input and the active region of action potential generation (Alkon and Fuortes, 1972). However, axotomized photoreceptors respond to light with normal depolarizing generator potentials. Second-order neurons in the visual system are located in the optic ganglion, an egg-shaped structure directly posterior to the eyes (Fig. 1). The axons of the five photoreceptors converge at the base of each eye to form the optic nerve, which projects through the optic ganglion to terminate in a series of secondary processes after entering the neuropil of the cerebropleural ganglion (see Fig. 2). The visual system of *Hermissenda* is not an image-forming system, but functions primarily as an intensity discriminator for detecting changes in illumination.

B. Vestibular System

The paired gravity-sensing statocysts of *Hermissenda* are spherical fluid-filled structures containing a mass of discrete particles called statoconia, which interact with the tips of cilia projecting from the hair cells lining the lumen (Alkon, 1975a; Alkon and Bak, 1973; Detwiler and Alkon, 1973; Detwiler and Fuortes, 1975). Statocysts of this type, common in gastropod molluscs, are generally considered to be mechanoreceptors. Each statocyst consists of 12–13 hair cells whose axons project into the cerebropleural ganglion. The axons of the hair cells make up the static nerve, which follows a course roughly parallel to the optic nerve before projecting to the same region of the neuropil where photoreceptors terminate (see Fig. 2). An appreciation for the convergence between the two independent sensory systems can be gained by examining the photomicrograph in Fig. 2. The development of the conditioning procedure used to modify behavior of *Hermissenda* was guided by the organization of these two independent sensory systems.

III. Conditioning Procedure

A. Phototactic Behavior

Both in the open field and in a restricted experimental chamber such as a glass tube filled with seawater, *Hermissenda* displays a robust phototaxis (Alkon, 1974; Crow, 1983, 1985a,b; Crow and Alkon, 1978; Crow and Harrigan, 1979, 1984; Crow and Offenbach, 1979, 1983; Harrigan and Alkon, 1985). Various measures of phototactic behavior have been used to assess visually guided behavior (for review, see Crow, 1984, 1988). These measures include the time taken to initiate locomotion in the presence of light, the time taken to locomote into an illuminated area that is the brightest area of a light gradient of increasing intensity, and the time that animals remain in the brightest part of a light gradient after entering the illuminated area. All of the different measures of phototactic behavior are consistent, indicating that *Hermissenda* are positively phototactic.

B. Suppression of Phototaxis

The various components of phototactic behavior described in Section III,A can be modified by a classical conditioning procedure. The conditioning paradigm was developed to stimulate the two independent sensory systems described in Section II, which were analyzed in the isolated nervous system. Pairing light, the conditioned stimulus (CS), with high-speed rotation, the nominal unconditioned stimulus (US), produced a long-term suppression of the normal positive phototactic response of *Hermissenda* (Crow, 1983, 1985a,b; Crow and Alkon, 1978; Crow and Offenbach, 1979, 1983; Harrigan and Alkon, 1985; Tyndale and Crow, 1979). The conditioning was expressed by a significant increase in the time to initiate locomotion in the presence of light and the time taken to locomote into the brightest area of a light gradient (Crow and Alkon, 1978; Crow and Offenbach, 1979, 1983). The suppression of normal positive phototactic behavior by conditioning shows stimulus specificity, since locomotion is affected only by the presence of the CS; behavior in the dark is not significantly changed (Crow and Offenbach, 1979). Various control groups, including groups that received unpaired presentations of the CS and US or groups that received presentations of the CS and US programmed on independent random schedules, do not show long-term suppression of phototaxis as shown in Fig. 3 (Crow and Alkon, 1978). Collectively, the results of various behavioral studies of conditioning in *Hermissenda* exhibit most of the parametric features of conditioning that have been described in studies of conditioning in vertebrates. The suppression of normal positive phototaxis is specific to pairing of the CS and US and is dependent on the presence of the CS during testing (Crow and Offenbach, 1979). The behavior that is modified exhibits extinction, savings, and long-term retention.

The results of initial studies of conditioning of *Hermissenda* indicated that normal positive phototactic behavior could be suppressed for several days following 3 days of 50 CS–US pairings each day (see Fig. 3). However, the conditioning procedure has been shown recently to produce substantially longer retention of phototactic suppression. Increasing the number of training trials to 100 each day for 6 days results in suppressed phototactic behavior for 18 days (Harrigan and Alkon, 1985). Since *Hermissenda* is a subannual species, the 18-day retention period for phototactic suppression represents a substantial period in the life cycle of this preparation.

————— IV. Associative and Nonassociative —————
Contributions to Phototactic
Suppression

An issue that has received considerable attention is the relationship of sensitization or nonassociative forms of learning to classical conditioning, an associative form of learning (for review, see Carew *et al.*, 1984). Do these different examples of learning represent a single underlying process where associative learning is an elaboration or amplification of nonassociation learning? A prerequisite for addressing this question is an experimental preparation where it is feasible to study associative and nonassociative learning at both the cellular and behavioral level in the same animal. In *Hermissenda* progress has been made on the analysis of the nonassociative components contributing to the phototactic suppression produced by conditioning (Crow, 1983). However, the cellular analysis of this example of a nonassociative modification of behavior has only recently been initiated for *Hermissenda* in experiments examining cellular correlates in B photoreceptors detected shortly after (1 hr) the presentation of a conditioning analog consisting of light paired with serotonin (5-HT) (Forrester and Crow, 1987; also see Section V,C). Presentation of

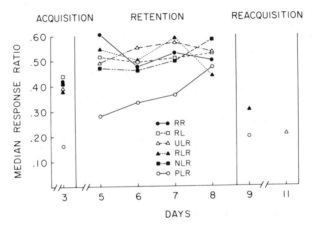

Figure 3.

Acquisition, retention, and reacquisition of phototactic behavior suppressed by a conditioning procedure in *Hermissenda*. The median values on the ordinate represent the measure of learning where the behavioral response to light before conditioning is compared to behavior after conditioning in the form of a ratio $A/A + B$. The ratio is computed from the response to light before training *(A)* and the response following 3 days of training *(B)*. A response ratio of < 0.50 indicates that conditioning produced a suppression of normal phototactic behavior, a ratio > 0.50 indicates an enhancement of phototactic behavior, and values of 0.50 signify that the conditioning procedure did not affect phototactic behavior. Key: (RR) random rotation, (RL) random light, (ULR) unpaired light and rotation, (RLR) random light and rotation, (NLR) light and rotation not presented, (PLR) light paired with rotation. The results for the group data consisted of two independent replications for all the control groups and three independent replications for the group that received light paired with rotation. All of the control groups exhibit a transient nonassociative suppression of phototactic behavior when tested immediately after day 3 of training. During the reacquisition phase the group that had previously received light paired with rotation followed by an extinction procedure exhibited significantly greater phototactic suppression after one training session as compared to a control that received the same amount of training. This result is an indication of "savings." [From Crow and Alkon (1978).]

the conditioning analog results in an enhanced light-evoked generator potential recorded from axotomized B photoreceptors from both the paired and unpaired groups. While it is interesting that nonassociative correlates can be observed in B photoreceptors after the presentation of the conditioning analog, the relationship between the short-term neural correlates produced by the conditioning analog and short-term nonassociative components of phototactic suppression has not been established.

The initial studies of conditioning in *Hermissenda* revealed that all control groups exhibited some phototactic suppression when tested immediately after the conclusion of 3 days of training (Crow and Alkon, 1978; also see Fig. 3). The nonassociative contribution to suppression of phototaxis was short-term, since the behavior of all control groups was close to baseline pretest scores when the animals were tested 48 hr after the conclusion of training as shown in Fig. 3. Subsequent behavioral studies have shown that nonassociative effects on phototactic suppression depend on the time of testing following conditioning and the number of training trials used to condition the *Hermissenda*. Five and 10 conditioning trials produce nonassociative effects when posttraining tests are conducted 15 and 30 min after conditioning (Crow, 1983). Single-session training (50 trials) and multiple-session training (150 trials) both produce nonassociative effects on phototactic behavior observed 30 min after training; however, the effects are short-term and decrement during the 1-hr period after training (Crow, 1983). These results indicate that nonassociative effects are expressed early in conditioning, decrement rapidly, and do not increase significantly over the course of multiple session training. Since the nonassociative and associative effects of conditioning on phototactic suppression have different time courses, the underlying mechanisms in *Hermissenda* may be independent; that is, the mechanism for the associative effect is not an elaboration of the nonassociative mechanism. Consistent with this proposal is the finding that short-term enhancement of the B photoreceptor generator potential produced by the conditioning analog is not pairing-specific. Moreover, the long-term pairing-specific change in the light response of B photoreceptors produced by the conditioning analog is expressed by a decrease in adaptation to sustained illumination and not by an overall enhancement of the amplitude of the generator potential, as observed for paired and unpaired groups 1 hr after the presentation of the conditioning analog (Forrester and Crow, 1987). At present, any similarity in the mechanism(s) of nonassociative and associative learning has not been established for *Hermissenda*. Perhaps the analysis of the influence of a neuromodulator such as 5-HT to conditioning in *Hermissenda* may help to elucidate the differences in mechanisms underlying associative and nonassociative contributions to phototactic suppression.

V. Neuromodulation:
Possible Contribution to Conditioning

In general neuromodulation refers to the consequences of synaptic or hormonal stimulation upon the electrical excitability of neurons. In the best documented examples of modulation the altered excitability of neurons produced by a neuromodulator is coupled by a number of intracellular biochemical changes that involve second messengers (for review, see Kaczmarek and Levitan, 1987). Of the various neuromodulators that have been examined in invertebrates, a number of biogenic amines have received considerable attention (Abrams *et al.*, 1984; Benson and Levitan, 1983; Boyle *et al.*, 1984; Brunelli *et al.*, 1976; Gelperin, 1981; Jacklet and Acosta-Urquidi, 1985; Kandel *et al.*, 1983; Kistler *et al.*, 1985; Klein and Kandel, 1978; Klein *et al.*, 1982; Lloyd *et al.*, 1984; Mackey and Carew, 1983; Ocorr *et al.*, 1985; Pellmar and Carpenter, 1980).

Both dopamine and serotonin (5-HT) have been identified as putative transmitters and neuromodulators in identified molluscan neurons (for review, see Gershon, 1977; Kupfermann, 1979), and in particular have been shown to have physiological effects on a number of invertebrate photoreceptors including *Hermissenda* (Adolph and Tuan, 1972; Barlow *et al.*, 1977; Corrent *et al.*, 1978; Crow and Bridge, 1985; Eskin *et al.*, 1984; Farley and Auerbach, 1986; Kass and Barlow, 1984; Sakakibara *et al.*, 1987; Wu and Farley, 1984). The possibility that a neuromodulator mediated by a second messenger system may play a prominent role in learning in *Hermissenda* was not seriously considered in the initial proposals for cellular mechanisms of associative learning. However, recently several putative neuromodulators have been implicated in conditioning of *Hermissenda*, with the primary focus on catecholamines and 5-HT.

A. Catecholamines

The evidence for a possible physiological role for a catecholamine such as dopamine in the circumesophageal nervous system of *Hermissenda* comes from early studies using histofluorescence techniques (Heldman *et al.*, 1979). This study reported a cell in the optic ganglion whose green fluorescence revealed by the Falck–Hillarp method indicated the presence of a catecholamine. In addition, more recent studies using the modified glyoxylic acid method (Tritt *et al.*, 1983) indicated that the nervous system contained catecholaminergic neurons, axons, and fine processes in the neuropil of both the cerebropleural and pedal ganglia (P. W. Land and T. Crow, unpublished observations). The catecholamine identified in the nervous system is most likely dopamine, since norepinephrine is not found in *Hermissenda* or other related gastropod molluscs (Heldman and

Alkon, 1978). In addition, previous work with labeled precursors indicated that the *Hermissenda* nervous system synthesizes both dopamine and 5-HT but not norepinephrine (Heldmann and Alkon, 1978). However, dopamine is not a good candidate for the action of a neuromodulator involved in learning in *Hermissenda*, since it does not produce reliable changes in the photoresponse of type B photoreceptors similar to previously reported neural correlates of conditioning (Alkon, 1984), or mimic conditioning effects on phototactic behavior (Crow and Forrester, 1986). Another catecholamine may be involved, since both clonidine (an α_2 agonist) and norepinephrine produce reductions in the two K^+ currents (I_A and $I_{K,Ca}$) that are reduced by the conditioning procedure (Alkon, 1984; Sakakibara *et al.*, 1984). In addition, clonidine mimics some aspects of conditioning induced plasticity since it produces an enhancement of the amplitude of light-evoked generator potentials in B photoreceptors (Crow and Bridge, 1985; Sakakibara *et al.*, 1987). However, clonidine is not a neurotransmitter and, as previously mentioned, norepinephrine is not found in *Hermissenda*. Taken collectively these results indicate that if a catecholamine is a modulator involved in learning in *Hermissenda*, it is presently unidentified.

B. Serotonin

The evidence for a possible physiological role for serotonin (5-HT) in the *Hermissenda* nervous system, both as a neuromodulator and a contributor to conditioning, is more convincing. First, 5-HT is synthesized in the nervous system (Heldman and Alkon, 1978) and is released by stimulation of the isolated nervous system (Auerbach *et al.*, 1985). The amplitude of the generator potential of B photoreceptors is enhanced by 5-HT (Crow and Bridge, 1985), and a conditioning analog consisting of light paired with 5-HT produces both short-term and long-term changes in the light-evoked photoresponse of type B-photoreceptors (Crow and Forrester, 1987; Forrester and Crow, 1987) (see Section VI). An example of serotonergic modulation of light responses of B photoreceptors is shown in Fig. 4. Additional evidence for a physiological role for 5-HT comes from voltage-clamp studies that have shown that both I_A and $I_{K,Ca}$ are effected by 5-HT (Collin and Alkon, 1987, 1988; Farley and Auerbach, 1986; Wu and Farley, 1984). If 5-HT acts as a neuromodulator in the visual system of *Hermissenda*, is there evidence for a source of 5-HT in neurons that is presynaptic to the photoreceptors? Histofluorescence studies have shown that 5-HT is contained in cell bodies and fine processes in the neuropil of the pedal and cerebropleural ganglia (Heldman *et al.*, 1979; P. W. Land and T. Crow, unpublished observations). In addition, the results of a recent immunohistochemical study revealed serotonergic immunoreactive fibers and varicosities near the optic nerve and in the synaptic region in the neuropil near the photoreceptor synaptic terminals (Land and Crow, 1985). An example of serotonergic immunoreactive processes in the nervous system of *Hermissenda* is shown in Fig. 5. Previous studies employing injections of lucifer yellow and horseradish peroxidase (HRP) into photoreceptors have shown that synaptic interactions between photoreceptors and neurons that are pre- and postsynaptic take place near the terminal processes in the neuropil (Crow *et al.*, 1979). As shown in the sections through the optic ganglion in Fig. 5, serotonergic immunoreactivity is not found in the optic ganglion. In addition, an examination of whole mounts did not reveal the presence of 5-HT in the eyes of *Hermissenda* (Land and Crow, 1985). However, immunoreactive processes and varicosities are found around the distal portion of the optic nerve and in the neuropil where photoreceptors,

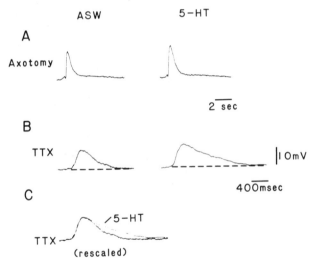

Figure 4.
Modulation of type-B photoresponses by 5-HT. (A) Effect of 10^{-4} M 5-HT on type-B photoresponses. In normal artificial seawater (ASW) a light flash evokes a depolarizing generator potential in a preparation where the photoreceptor was surgically isolated by cutting the optic nerve (axotomy). In the presence of ASW containing 5-HT the amplitude and duration of the photoresponse evoked by the brief light flash was increased. (B) Examples of type-B photoresponses showing the effects of 5-HT in a preparation where sodium spike activity in the photoreceptors and circumesophageal nervous system was blocked with 30 μM tetrodotoxin (TTX). Note the 400-msec time scale in B. (C) Superimposed records from recordings in B before and after 5-HT application photographically rescaled so that the amplitudes are the same, revealing the prolonged decay of the response. [Adapted from Crow and Bridge (1985).]

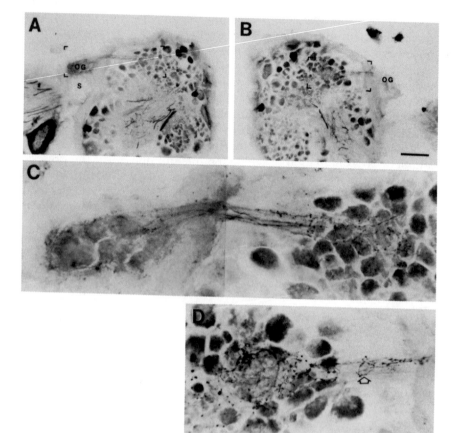

Figure 5.
Patterns of serotonergic immunoreactivity (IR) in *Hermissenda* visual pathways. Photomicrographs (A) and (B) show low magnification of horizontal sections through the CPG of two specimens at the level of the optic ganglia (OG). The optic nerves can be seen passing through the left OG, in (A), and right OG, in (B), to enter the neuropil of the CPG. Note that OG neurons show only background reactivity compared with the CPG triplet visible at the top right and top left, respectively, of (A) and (B). Regions enclosed by boxes are shown at high magnification in (C) and (D). (C) High magnification of area enclosed by box in (A). Note fine, varicose IR axons in photoreceptor synaptic region, at right of photomontage, and along distal portion of optic nerve. Fewer stained processes are evident nearer the OG. (D) High magnification of area enclosed by box in B. In addition to the delicate IR axons in the photoreceptor synaptic region (left), note stained processes (e.g., open arrow) that appear to encircle the optic nerve in its course through the CPG. Bar in B = 100 μm for A and B; bar in D = 25 μm for C and D; S, statocyst. [From Land and Crow (1985).]

optic ganglion cells, and statocyst hair cells terminate (see Fig. 5). While these results indicate that 5-HT is not contained in neurons in the visual system of *Hermissenda*, a possible serotonergic pathway that could modulate activity of photoreceptors is provided by the serotonergic immunoreactive inputs near the optic nerve and terminal processes. Although the exact source of the 5-HT found near the optic nerve is not known, it is attractive to suggest that the most likely sources for the serotonergic immunoreactivity are the two clusters of serotonergic neurons found in the cerebropleural ganglion, termed the CPG triplets as shown in Fig. 5A. If these neurons receive synaptic input from statocyst hair cells and in turn provide direct input to photoreceptors, then 5-HT could act as both a transmitter and modulator in the pathway activated by the unconditioned stimulus (US).

C. Behavior

If the hypothesis that 5-HT acts a modulator in the US pathway and thus is involved in conditioning is correct, then substitution of normal rotational stimulation of the US pathway (statocyst) with 5-HT applied directly to the nervous system should produce similar changes in behavior. This was shown recently by the application of a conditioning analog consisting of pairing light (CS) with direct application of 5-HT to the exposed nervous system of otherwise intact *Hermissenda* (Crow and Forrester, 1986). One 5-min training session consisting of the CS paired with 5-HT produced significant suppression of phototactic behavior when the *Hermissenda* were tested 24 hr after the end of the training session (see Fig. 6). As a control for nonspecific effects, two other putative neuromodulators were tested. Both dopamine and octopamine were paired with the CS and the behavioral tests were conducted 24 hr after the application of the putative neuromodulators. Only the *Hermissenda* that received the CS paired with 5-HT showed significant suppression of phototactic behavior, as shown in Fig. 6A. If the CS and 5-HT pairings are analogous to the conditioning procedure used to modify phototactic behavior of *Hermissenda*, then the change in behavior should be dependent on the temporal pairing of the CS and 5-HT. Pairing specificity was shown by comparing the group that received the CS paired with 5-HT to a group that received the CS and 5-HT unpaired, and to a group that only received 5-HT. Only the group that received the CS paired with 5-HT showed phototactic suppression when tested the next day (see Fig. 6B). As an additional control, one control group that had initially received the unpaired CS with 5-HT was tested again after receiving the application of the CS paired with 5-HT (Fig. 6c). Following the paired CS and 5-HT procedure, the *Hermissenda* showed behavioral suppression when tested 24 hr later.

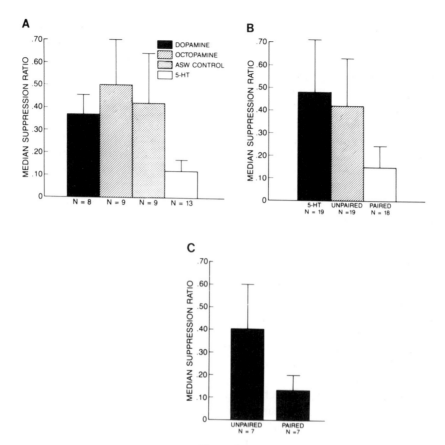

Figure 6.
Conditioning analog consisting of substitution of normal activation of the US pathway with the direct application of neuromodulators to the exposed nervous system. (A) Different groups of *Hermissenda* received light (CS) paired with several putative neurotransmitters/neuromodulators applied to the nervous system. Animals were tested before training and 24 hr after the application of the conditioning analog to assess suppression of phototactic behavior. The ordinate represents the measure of learning, median suppression ratio ± semi-interquartile range. Only the group that received the light (CS) paired with 5-HT exhibited significant suppression of phototactic behavior. (B) Pairing-specific effect of light and 5-HT. Light paired with 5-HT results in suppression of phototactic behavior when tested 24 hr after training with the conditioning analog. Unpaired light and 5-HT and 5-HT applied in the dark do not produce statistically significant suppression of phototactic behavior. (C) Within-group comparison of the effects on behavior of unpaired light and 5-HT, and paired light and 5-HT. The unpaired group represents the behavior of a control group that initially received unpaired light and 5-HT. When the group that had previously received the unpaired control procedure were trained with light paired with 5-HT, a significant suppression of phototactic behavior was observed. [From Crow and Forrester (1986).]

VI. Short- and
Long-Term Plasticity

The original conditioning procedure used to modify phototactic behavior of *Hermissenda* consisted of 3 days of training followed by several tests of phototactic suppression (Crow and Alkon, 1978). This procedure did not allow for a trial-by-trial assessment of behavioral acquisition or an analysis of the time course for induction of plastic changes in the photoreceptors. Recent studies have attempted to overcome this problem by stimulating the isolated nervous system with a conditioning analog consisting of light paired with depolarization of caudal hair cells produced by the passage of extrinsic current (Farley and Alkon, 1987). However, while such studies report short-term pairing specific changes in B photoreceptors following stimulation of the isolated nervous system, the interpretation of the behavioral relevance of such a procedure is flawed since short-term changes in behavior have strong nonassociative components (Crow, 1983; also see Section IV). The development of the conditioning analog that can be applied to intact *Hermissenda* capable of expressing behavior provided an opportunity to analyze over time the induction of plasticity in the B photoreceptors and in addition to examine phototactic suppression at different time periods following the application of light and 5-HT.

The finding that pairing light and 5-HT can mimic the effects of conditioning on phototactic behavior provides evidence for a possible role of 5-HT in associative learning in *Hermissenda*. However, the question can be raised concerning neural correlates produced by the conditioning analog and the relationship between the correlates and behavior.

A. Cellular Neurophysiological Correlates

Neural correlates produced by the conditioning analog have been the focus of recent cellular neurophysiological studies. For these experiments *Hermissenda* were trained in one session using the conditioning analog and neural correlates were examined in isolated B photoreceptors at two time periods following the training, 1 hr and 24 hr (Forrester and Crow, 1987). Pairing light (CS) with 5-HT produced both short-term (1 hr) and long-term (24 hr) cellular correlates in identified B photoreceptors. The conditioning analog resulted in an enhanced generator potential when B photoreceptors were examined 1 hr after training. However, photoreceptors from both the paired and unpaired control groups showed an enhanced generator potential, indicating that the neural correlate was not specific to pairing the CS with 5-HT. In contrast to the short-term changes, *Hermissenda* tested 24 hr after training did show a pairing-specific effect of the CS paired with 5-HT. Recordings from one type of B photoreceptor, termed the lateral B, exhibited an enhancement of the steady-state phase of the generator potential only for the group that received the CS paired with 5-HT.

Taken collectively, the electrophysiological and behavioral results suggest that a neuromodulator such as 5-HT may play a role in learning in *Hermissenda*. However, 5-HT may operate in parallel with neurons in the previously identified CS and US pathways to amplify conditioning-induced changes in membrane currents that have been previously identified. As an alternative, 5-HT may play a more direct role in learning in *Hermissenda* by interacting with light- and/or voltage-dependent processes in photoreceptors activated by the CS to induce long-term changes in membrane conductances produced by conditioning.

B. Role of Protein Synthesis

Since the conditioning analog produces both short- and long-term cellular changes, it is now feasible to study cellular mechanisms underlying the induction of both short-term and long-term neural correlates produced by conditioning in *Hermissenda*. Are the same mechanisms responsible for the induction of both short- and long-term memory in *Hermissenda*? In addition, since both short-term and long-term cellular changes can be detected in identical B photoreceptors, it is possible to study the cellular mechanisms of time-dependent processes related to both short- and long-term memory produced by this procedure in *Hermissenda*. Historically, it has been proposed that short- and long-term memory represent different components of memory with distinct qualitative and quantitative features. Previous studies of memory in vertebrates suggested that long-term memory requires protein synthesis while short-term memory is not dependent on protein synthesis (for a review see Davis and Squire, 1984). Consistent with this hypothesis are the recent finding that inhibitors of protein synthesis blocked long-term facilitation of the sensory and motor connection of cultured *Aplysia* neurons (Montarolo *et al.*, 1986). In addition, Montarolo *et al.* (1986) reported that short-term facilitation was not blocked by inhibitors of protein synthesis or RNA synthesis.

In *Hermissenda*, presenting the conditioning analog in the presence of the protein synthesis inhibitor anisomycin did not block the short-term cellular correlates. This was shown recently by the finding that enhanced generator potentials produced by light and 5-HT were recorded from isolated B photoreceptors, and were detected 1 hr following the conditioning session carried out in the presence of anisomycin (Crow and Forrester, 1987). In contrast to the results showing that protein synthesis inhibition is ineffective in blocking short-term neural correlates produced by the conditioning analog, long-term changes in adaptation of the generator potential were blocked if the conditioning session occurred in the presence of the protein synthesis inhibitor anisomycin

(Crow and Forrester, 1987). As a control procedure a derivative of anisomycin, deacetylanisomycin, which is inactive in inhibiting protein synthesis, was shown to not block the long-term cellular correlates produced by the conditioning analog. The protein synthesis inhibitor by itself did not result in a change in the amplitude of the generator potential. Consistent with other studies (Montarolo *et al.*, 1986), protein synthesis inhibition was only effective when applied during the presentation of the CS and 5-HT. When the protein synthesis inhibitor was applied 1 hr after the conditioning session, typical long-term cellular correlates were detected in the lateral B photoreceptors, and the correlates were identical to those produced when the CS was paired with 5-HT without anisomycin.

These results suggest that long-term memory induced by pairing light and 5-HT requires the expression of gene products that are not essential for the expression of short-term memory in the B-photoreceptors of *Hermissenda*. The processes related to converting memory into a more enduring form (long-term memory) may depend on additional biochemical steps that are distinct from the mechanisms responsible for the induction of associative learning and short-term memory. However, the same modulatory transmitters such as 5-HT and intracellular messengers that act to initiate short-term memory may also initiate long-term memory, as suggested by Goelet and Kandel (1986).

_____ VII. Discussion and Conclusions _____

There is now a considerable amount of indirect evidence that a neuromodulator may play a role in conditioning of *Hermissenda*. Of the various modulators that have been proposed, the strongest case can be made for the neuromodulator 5-HT. A number of different laboratories have now reported that application of 5-HT to the isolated nervous system produces changes in the amplitude of various components of the generator potential of B photoreceptors evoked by light (Crow and Bridge, 1985; Farley and Auerbach, 1986; Forrester and Crow, 1987; Sakakibara *et al.*, 1987; Wu and Farley, 1984). In addition, 5-HT has been reported to reduce a number of K^+ currents (I_A, $I_{K,Ca}$) that have been reported to be reduced by the conditioning procedure (Farley and Auerbach, 1986), although the results are controversial since 5-HT has been reported to also enhance the same K^+ currents (I_A and $I_{K,Ca}$) (Collin *et al.*, 1986). Histofluoroscence and immunohistochemical studies have identified serotonergic neurons and neural processes in the cerebropleural and pedal ganglia (Land and Crow, 1985). Of particular interest from the results of the Land and Crow (1985) study is the observation that serotonergic-immunoreactive fibers and varicosities terminate near the optic nerve and in the synaptic region of the neuropil near the photoreceptors' synaptic terminals. This provides a potential presynaptic source for serotonergic modulation of type B photoreceptors that may contribute to conditioning by interacting with the effects of the CS through activation of the pathway mediating the US. However, the serotonergic neurons that provide input to the visual system have not been identified and it is not known whether these neurons receive input from the statocyst hair cells.

The possibility that 5-HT contributes to learning in *Hermissenda* is also supported by the results of the conditioning analog experiments. Pairing light and 5-HT in one session produces significant phototactic suppression (mimics conditioning effects) when the *Hermissenda* are tested 24 hr after the session. The effect of the conditioning analog is pairing-specific and specific to 5-HT; for example, octopamine and dopamine do not produce a similar effect (Crow and Forrester, 1986). In addition to changes in phototactic behavior, the conditioning analog produces both short- and long-term changes in the B photoreceptors that can be detected at 1 hr and 24 hr following the conditioning session. The short-term changes that can be detected at 1 hr following the application of light and 5-HT are not pairing-specific, since both paired and unpaired groups exhibit an enhanced light response (Forrester and Crow, 1987). These electrophysiological results show an interesting parallel with behavioral studies that have examined the time course of nonassociative changes in phototactic suppression (Crow, 1983). In the behavioral studies that employed the standard conditioning procedure, nonassociative changes in phototactic behavior were observed soon after the conclusion of conditioning and exhibited a rapid decrement (Crow, 1983).

The long-term changes observed in B photoreceptors following the application of the conditioning analog were detected in only the lateral B photoreceptor and were expressed by a change in adaptation of the generator potential to sustained illumination. However, neural correlates have been identified in both medial and lateral B photoreceptors following 3 days of conditioning where light (CS) was paired with rotation (US) (Crow, 1985b; Crow and Alkon, 1980). Those results suggest that the conditioning analog and standard conditioning procedure are similar in that both procedures result in changes that are intrinsic to the sensory neurons of the pathway mediating the CS. However, since multiple-session training (standard conditioning procedure) and the conditioning analog produce correlates in different B photoreceptors, the relationship between the neural correlates that have been detected following both procedures and the behavior has not been established. Regardless of the differences in neural correlates produced by multiple-session training and the conditioning analog, the conditioning analog is a useful tool because it provides a system for the study of molecular mechanisms of the induction of both short- and long-term memory in an identified neuron in *Hermissenda*. This is supported by the observation that the expression of long-term plasticity produced by light paired with 5-HT can be blocked by inhibiting protein synthesis, while short-term plasticity is unaffected.

Taken collectively, the available evidence suggests that 5-HT may play some role in associative learning in *Hermissenda*. However, the precise nature of the role of a neuromodulator such as 5-HT contributing to associative learning in *Hermissenda* will require the identification of the neural circuit controlling locomotion and, further, the identification of the source of serotonergic input to the sensory system, both of which are currently under investigation.

Acknowledgments

I thank J. Forrester for assistance with the illustrations, T. Hodgson for reading an earlier draft of the manuscript, and C. Staley for typing the manuscript. This work was supported by National Institutes of Health grant HD 15793 and National Institute for Mental Health grant MH 40860.

References

Abrams, T. W., Castellucci, V. F., Comardo, J. S., Kandel, E. R., and Lloyd, P. E. (1984). *Proc. Natl. Acad. Sci. U.S.A.* **81,** 7956–7960.

Acosta-Urquidi, J., Alkon, D. L., and Neary, J. T. (1984). *Science* **224,** 1254–1257.

Adolph, A. R., and Tuan, F. J. (1972). *J. Gen. Physiol.* **60,** 679–697.

Alkon, D. L. (1973a). *J. Gen. Physiol.* **61,** 444–461.

Alkon, D. L. (1973b). *J. Gen. Physiol.* **62,** 185–202.

Alkon, D. L. (1974). *J. Gen. Physiol.* **64,** 70–84.

Alkon, D. L. (1975a). *J. Gen. Physiol.* **65,** 385–397.

Alkon, D. L. (1975b). *J. Gen. Physiol.* **66,** 507–530.

Alkon, D. L. (1984). *Science* **226,** 1037–1045.

Alkon, D. L., and Bak, A. (1973). *J. Gen. Physiol.* **61,** 619–637.

Alkon, D. L., and Fuortes, M. G. F. (1972). *J. Gen. Physiol.* **60,** 631–649.

Alkon, D. L., Lederhendler, I., and Shoukimas, J. J. (1982). *Science* **215,** 643–645.

Alkon, D. L., Acosta-Urquidi, J., Olds, J., Kuzma, G., and Neary, J. T. (1983). *Science* **219,** 303–306.

Auerbach, S., Grover, L., and Farley, J. (1985). *Soc. Neurosci. Abstr.* **11,** 481.

Barlow, R. B., Jr., Chamberlain, S. C., and Kaplan, E. (1977). *Biol. Bull. (Woods Hole, Mass.)* **153,** 414.

Benson, J. A., and Levitan, I. B. (1983). *Proc. Natl. Acad. Sci. U.S.A.* **80,** 3522–3525.

Boyle, M. B., Klein, M., Smith, S., and Kandel, E. R. (1984). *Proc. Natl. Acad. Sci. U.S.A.* **81,** 7642–7646.

Bridge, M. S., and Crow, T. (1986). *Soc. Neurosci. Abstr.* **12,** 861.

Brunelli, M., Castellucci, V. F., and Kandel, E. R. (1976). *Science* **194,** 1178–1181.

Carew, T. J., Abrams, T. W., Hawkins, R. D., and Kandel, E. R. (1984). *In* "Primary Neural Substrates of Learning and Behavioral Change" (D. L. Alkon and J. Farley, eds.), pp. 169–183. Cambridge Univ. Press, London and New York.

Collin, C. E., and Alkon, D. L. (1987). *Soc. Neurosci. Abstr.* **13,** 389.

Collin, C. E., Harrigan, J., and Alkon, D. L. (1986). *Soc. Neurosci. Abstr.* **12,** 1153.

Corrent, G., McAdoo, D. J., and Eskin, A. (1978). *Science* **202**, 977–979.

Crow, T. (1983). *J. Neurosci.* **3**, 2621–2628.

Crow, T. (1984). *In* "Neuropsychology of Memory" (L. R. Squire and N. Butters, eds.), pp. 608–621. Guilford Press, New York.

Crow, T. (1985a). *J. Neurosci.* **5**, 209–214.

Crow, T. (1985b). *J. Neurosci.* **5**, 215–223.

Crow, T. (1985c). *Soc. Neurosci. Abstr.* **11**, 794.

Crow, T. (1988). *Trends Neurosci.* **11**, 136–142.

Crow, T., and Alkon, D. L. (1978). *Science* **201**, 1239–1241.

Crow, T., and Alkon, D. L. (1980). *Science* **209**, 412–414.

Crow, T., and Bridge, M. S. (1985). *Neurosci. Lett.* **60**, 83–88.

Crow, T., and Forrester, J. F. (1986). *Proc. Natl. Acad. Sci. U.S.A.* **83**, 7975–7978.

Crow, T., and Forrester, J. F. (1987). *Soc. Neurosci. Abstr.* **13**, 389.

Crow, T., and Harrigan, J. F. (1979). *Brain Res.* **173**, 179–184.

Crow, T., and Harrigan, J. F. (1984). *Behav. Brain Res.* **12**, 81–85.

Crow, T., and Offenbach, N. (1979). *Biol. Bull. (Woods Hole, Mass.)* **157**, 364–365.

Crow, T., and Offenbach, N. (1983). *Brain Res.* **271**, 301–310.

Crow, T., Heldman, E., Hacopian, V., Enos, R., and Alkon, D. L. (1979). *J. Neurocytol.* **8**, 181–195.

Davis, H. P., and Squire, L. R. (1984). *Psychol. Bull.* **96**, 518–559.

Dennis, M. J. (1967). *J. Neurophysiol.* **30**, 1439–1465.

Detwiler, P. B., and Alkon, D. L. (1973). *J. Gen. Physiol.* **62**, 618–642.

Detwiler, P. B., and Fuortes, M. G. F. (1975). *J. Physiol. (London)* **251**, 107–129.

Eskin, A., Young, S. J., and Kass, M. R. (1984). *Proc. Natl. Acad. Sci. U.S.A.* **81**, 7637–7641.

Farley, J., and Alkon, D. L. (1987). *J. Neurophysiol.* **57**, 1639–1668.

Farley, J., and Auerbach, S. (1986). *Nature (London)* **319**, 220–223.

Forrester, J. F., and Crow, T. (1987). *Soc. Neurosci. Abstr.* **13**, 618.

Gelperin, A. (1981). *In* "Serotonin Neurotransmission and Behavior" (B. Jacobs and A. Gelperin, eds.), pp. 288–304. MIT Press, Cambridge, Massachusetts.

Gershon, M. D. (1977). *In* "Handbook of Physiology" (E. R. Kandel, ed.), Sect. 1, Vol. II, pp. 573–623. Am. Physiol. Soc., Bethesda, Maryland.

Goelet, P., and Kandel, E. R. (1986). *Trends Neurosci.* **9**, 492–499.

Harrigan, J. F., and Alkon, D. L. (1985). *Biol. Bull. (Woods Hole, Mass.)* **168**, 222–234.

Heldman, E., and Alkon, D. L. (1978). *Comp. Biochem. Physiol.* **59**, 117–125.

Heldman, E., Grossman, Y., Jerussi, T. P., and Alkon, D. L. (1979). *J. Neurophysiol.* **42**, 153–165.

Jacklet, J. W., and Acosta-Urquidi, J. (1985). *Cell. Mol. Neurobiol.* **5**, 407–412.

Kaczmarek, L. K., and Levitan, I. B. (1987). *In* "Neuromodulation: The Biochemical Control of Neuronal Excitability" (L. K. Kaczmarek and I. B. Levitan, eds.), pp. 3–17. Oxford Univ. Press, London and New York.

Kandel, E. R., Abrams, T., Bernier, L., Carew, T. J., Hawkins, R. D., and Schwartz, J. H. (1983). *Cold Spring Harbor Symp. Quant. Biol.* **48**, 821–830.

Kass, L. and Barlow, R. J., Jr. (1984). *J. Neurosci.* **4**, 908–917.

Kistler, H. B., Hawkins, R. D., Koester, J., Steinbusch, H. W. M., Kandel, E. R., and Schwartz, J. H. (1985). *J. Neurosci.* **5**, 72–80.

Klein, M., Comardo, T. and Kandel, E. R. (1982). *Proc. Natl. Acad. Sci. U.S.A.* **79**, 5713–5717.

Klein, M., and Kandel, E. R. (1978). *Proc. Natl. Acad. Sci. U.S.A.* **75**, 3512–3516.

Kupfermann, I. (1979). *Annu. Rev. Neurosci.* **2**, 447–666.

Land, P. W., and Crow, T. (1985). *Neurosci. Lett.* **62**, 199–205.

Lloyd, P. E., Kupferman, I., and Weiss, K. R. (1984). *Proc. Natl. Acad. Sci. U.S.A.* **80**, 3522–3525.

Mackey, S., and Carew, T. J. (1983). *J. Neurosci.* **3**, 1469–1477.

McGaugh, J. L. (1983). *Am. Psychol.* **38,** 161–174.

Montarolo, P. G., Goelet, P., Castellucci, V. F., Morgan, J., Kandel, E. R., and Schacher, S. (1986). *Science* **234,** 1249–1254.

Neary, J. T., Crow, T. J., and Alkon, D. L. (1981). *Nature (London)* **243,** 658–660.

Ocorr, K. A., Walters, E. T., and Byrne, J. H. (1985). *Proc. Natl. Acad. Sci. U.S.A.* **82,** 2548–2552.

Pellmar, T., and Carpenter, D. (1980). *J. Neurophysiol.* **44,** 423–439.

Richards, W., and Farley, J. (1984). *Soc. Neurosci. Abstr.* **10,** 623.

Sakakibara, M., Alkon, D. L., Lederhendler, I., and Heldman, E. (1984). *Soc. Neurosci. Abstr.* **10,** 950.

Sakakibara, M., Collin, C., Kuzirian, A., Alkon, D. L., Heldmann, E., Naito, S., and Lederhendler, I. (1987). *J. Neurochem.* **48,** 405–416.

Senft, S. L., Allen, R. D., Crow, T., and Alkon, D. L. (1982). *J. Neurosci. Meth.* **5,** 153–159.

Tritt, S. H., Lowe, I. P., and Byrne, J. H. (1983). *Brain Res.* **259,** 159–162.

Tyndale, C. L., and Crow, T. J. (1979). *IEEE Trans. Biomed. Eng.* **BME-26,** 649–655.

Wu, R., and Farley, J. (1984). *Soc. Neurosci. Abstr.* **10,** 620.

2

Developmental Assembly of Multiple Components of Learning and Memory in *Aplysia*

Thomas J. Carew

I. Introduction

A fundamental question that has long captured the imagination of scholars in such diverse fields as psychology, biology, and computer science concerns the mechanisms that underly the remarkable ability of animals to learn and remember. This question has often been translated into an analysis of the cellular and molecular events that occur when particular forms of learning are acquired and stored in the nervous system. One approach to this type of analysis that has proved to be quite powerful in recent years is the use of a "simple-systems" strategy. Several vertebrate and invertebrate preparations have now been developed in which it is possible to specify the neural circuitry involved in learning, and in some cases it has been possible to specify aspects of the biophysical and molecular mechanisms underlying different forms of learning (for reviews, see Alkon, 1983; Quinn, 1984; Carew and Sahley, 1986; Hawkins *et al.*, 1987; Byrne, 1987).

Another strategy in the analysis of learning and memory that has been quite profitable is a developmental approach. This type of analysis involves investigating the way in which different learning and memory processes emerge and become integrated during ontogeny. The advantage of this approach is that it permits the delineation of relationships between the emergence of particular forms of learning and the emergence of specific neural structures, circuits, and networks. This approach has usually been applied to altricial mammalian species, which are born with relatively immature nervous systems and are thus well suited for such analyses (for reviews, see Campbell and Spear, 1972; Campbell and Coulter, 1976; Amsel and Stanton, 1980).

In recent years, my colleagues Dave Cash, Emilie Marcus, Thomas Nolen, Catharine Rankin, Mark Stopfer, and I have combined the power of a simple-systems approach with the advantages of a developmental

22

strategy, by examining the developmental assembly of different forms of learning in the marine mollusk *Aplysia californica*. *Aplysia* is an excellent preparation for such an analysis for several reasons. First, the animal exhibits a variety of both nonassociative and associative types of learning that can exist in both short-term and long-term forms (for review, see Carew, 1987). Second, the cellular and molecular mechanisms of many forms of learning have been extensively examined in *Aplysia* (for reviews, see Carew, 1987; Hawkins *et al.*, 1987; Byrne, 1987; see also Chapters 3, 4, and 5, this volume). Finally, the development of *Aplysia* is quite well understood, and throughout behaviorally relevant developmental stages the animal is amenable to behavioral, cellular, and biochemical analysis (for reviews, see Kandel *et al.*, 1980; Rankin *et al.*, 1987).

Our developmental investigation of learning in *Aplysia* has allowed us to identify several important features of the functional assembly of learning and memory in this animal. For example:

1. Several forms of nonassociative learning, as well as their cellular analogs, emerge according to very different developmental timetables.

2. In addition to facilitatory processes known to exist in the adult, novel inhibitory processes have been revealed using a developmental analysis.

3. One important form of learning, sensitization, emerges simultaneously in several different response systems, suggesting the developmental expression of a general process.

4. A dramatic increase in neuronal number throughout the central nervous system (CNS) accompanies the emergence of sensitization, raising the possibility that some aspect of the developmental trigger for neuronal proliferation may also trigger the expression of this form of learning.

In this chapter I will first review some of the evidence that my colleagues and I have obtained that supports the conclusions described above. I will then conclude by discussing our developmental approach in the broader context of this volume, which provides a common ground for theoretical and empirical approaches to the analysis of neuronal plasticity.

II. Different Forms of Learning in *Aplysia* Emerge According to Different Developmental Timetables

Before discussing the development of learning in *Aplysia*, it would be useful to provide a brief introduction to the general development of the animal, which has been extensively analyzed by Kriegstein *et al.* (1974) and Kriegstein (1977a). In their studies they divided the life cycle of *Aplysia* into five phases: (1) *embryonic* (about 10 days); (2) *planktonic* (about 34 days); (3) *metamorphic* (about 2–3 days); *juvenile* (at least 90 days); and (5) *adult*. Kriegstein (1977b) further divided these phases into 13 stages, each defined by a specific set of morphological criteria. Our work has focused on the relatively long juvenile phase of development (stages 9–12) because many of the behavioral systems that we are interested in first emerge then. In the juvenile phase, under our laboratory conditions, stage 9 lasts about 4–7 days, stage 10 about 7–10 days, and stages 11 and 12 about 40–50 days each (Kriegstein, 1977b; Rankin *et al.*, 1987).

Much of our work has focused on the gill and siphon withdrawal reflex in *Aplysia*. This is a very useful system for a developmental analysis of learning, since it exhibits a variety of forms of learning and memory, its neural circuitry has been extensively analyzed in the adult, and the cellular and molecular mechanisms of learning in this reflex have been studied in detail (for reviews, see Carew, 1987; Hawkins *et al.*, 1987). An added advantage of this response system is that gill and siphon withdrawal can be reliably elicited and quantitatively studied as soon as the organs emerge during development.

The preparation we used to study the gill and siphon withdrawal reflex is shown in Fig. 1. Animals were viewed through a stereomicroscope fitted with a video camera. The animal was restrained above the substrate with three suction micropipettes, one on each parapodium and one on the tail. The reflex was triggered by delivering a brief water jet to the siphon. An electrical stimulus applied through the suction electrode on the tail was used to produce dishabituation and sensitization (see below). The reflex response amplitude was quantified by computing the percent reduction in siphon area (Fig. 1B and C) (Rankin and Carew, 1987a). Using this reflex system we have studied the development of three forms of nonassociative learning: habituation, dishabituation, and sensitization. I will discuss each of these in turn.

A. Habituation

Habituation involves the progressive decrement in magnitude of a behavioral response produced by the repeated elicitation of that response. In our first set of experiments we investigated the developmental timetable for habituation in the siphon withdrawal component of the reflex (Rankin and Carew, 1987a). We found that habituation of siphon withdrawal was present in very early stages of juvenile development; however, it existed in an immature form. In the youngest animals significant habituation could be produced only with very short interstimulus intervals (ISIs). However, as the animals continued to develop, significant habituation could be produced in response to progressively longer ISIs. Thus, in stage 9, significant habituation occurred in response to only a

1-sec ISI, but not to 5- or 10-sec ISIs; in stage 10, to 1- and 5-sec ISIs, but not to a 10-sec ISI; and in stage 11, to all three ISIs. Moreover, even in later juvenile stages, further maturation of habituation was evident. For example, in response to a 30-sec ISI, stage-12 animals show significantly less habituation than did adult animals to this same ISI. The early emergence of habituation and its gradual convergence to the adult range of effective ISIs are depicted in Fig. 2.

Although I have discussed the development of habituation in the context of learning, our results may also provide some preliminary insights into the development of memory as well. The ISI function for habituation, for example, can provide a rudimentary tool with which to assess a form of short-term memory. In order for an animal to habituate to a particular stimulus, its nervous system must somehow register and store the information indicating that a prior stimulus has occurred. Thus, the interval between stimuli that gives rise to habituation can provide a measure of the temporal holding capacity (memory) of that system. Using the ISI function as such an index, it appears that this form of short-term memory in *Aplysia* progressively develops throughout the entire juvenile period into the adult stage.

B. Dishabituation

Dishabituation involves the facilitation of previously habituated responses by the presentation of a novel or noxious stimulus. Interestingly,

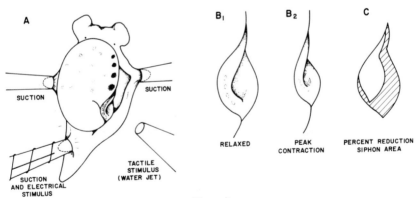

Figure 1.
Experimental preparation for the study of the siphon withdrawal reflex in juvenile *Aplysia*. (A) A juvenile animal is restrained with three suction pipettes. The reflex is evoked with a brief tactile stimulus (water jet) to the siphon. For dishabituation and sensitization training, a train of electric shocks is delivered through the pipette on the tail. (B, C) Quantification of the reflex contraction: (B1) Enlarged view of the relaxed siphon 1 sec prior to stimulation. (B2) Peak of the contraction following tactile stimulation. (C) Superimposed outlines of (B1) and (B2). Reduction in siphon area (hatched portion) is used as a measure of response amplitude.

although habituation was present at the earliest stage of development studied, we found that dishabituation was not (Rankin and Carew, 1987a). Specifically, whereas significant dishabituation in response to tail shock was evident in stages 10 and 11, it was completely absent in stage 9. This result has subsequently been confirmed and extended by Rankin and Carew (1987b), who examined a range of tail shock intensities. In all cases the same pattern emerged: habituation was present in early juvenile development (stage 9) and dishabituation emerged approximately 1 week later in a distinct and later stage (stage 10; Fig. 2).

C. Sensitization

Sensitization, like dishabituation, involves response facilitation; however, it differs from dishabituation in that it involves the facilitation of *nonde-*

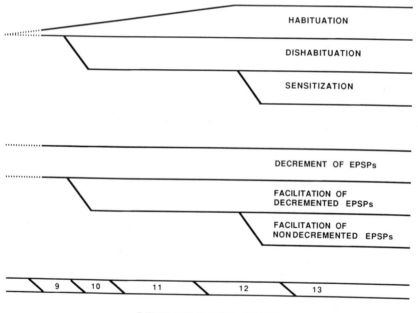

DEVELOPMENTAL STAGE

Figure 2.
Comparison of the developmental timetables of behavioral habituation, dishabituation and sensitization and their cellular analogs. Several forms of nonassociative learning emerge in the gill and siphon withdrawal reflex at different times during juvenile development. Habituation and its cellular analog (homosynaptic decrement of EPSPs) emerge by stage 9; dishabituation and its analog (facilitation of decremented EPSPs) emerge in stage 10. Sensitization and its cellular analog (facilitation of non-decremented EPSPs) emerge much later (approximately 60 days), in mid to late stage 12.

cremented responses by the presentation of a strong or noxious stimulus. Until recently, dishabituation and sensitization had commonly been considered to reflect a single underlying facilitatory process. This view was supported by the general observation that both nondecremented and decremented responses were simultaneously facilitated by the presentation of a single strong or noxious stimulus. The most parsimonious explanation for this kind of result was that a noxious stimulus initiated a general arousal-like process that was widespread in the nervous system, facilitating habituated and nonhabituated responses alike (Groves and Thompson, 1970; Carew *et al.*, 1971). Although both reasonable and logically consistent, this explanation did not rule out the possibility that dishabituation and sensitization could reflect separate facilitatory processes that are activated in *parallel* by a strong stimulus. In fact, direct cellular evidence for two separate facilitatory processes has recently been provided by Hochner and colleagues (1986a,b), who first suggested that dishabituation and sensitization in adult *Aplysia* may be produced, at least in part, by different cellular mechanisms.

One way to behaviorally address the question of whether dishabituation and sensitization reflect a unitary process is to examine them as they emerge during development. If a single process is involved, both forms of learning must be expressed at the same time ontogenetically. Alternatively, if more than one process is involved, one might emerge before the other; thus it might be possible to separate them developmentally.

Since we had established that dishabituation emerged in stage 10, in the next series of experiments we examined when sensitization emerged during development. To address this question we examined the effects of tail shock on both decremented and nondecremented responses in developmental stages 11, early 12, and late 12 (Rankin and Carew, 1988). In each stage two groups of animals were examined. One group received *dishabituation training:* habituation followed by tail shock. The other received *sensitization training:* several baseline stimuli were delivered at an ISI too long to produce response decrement, followed by a tail shock identical to that of the dishabituation group. Both groups were then tested for response facilitation resulting from tail shock.

In all stages, habituated animals showed significant facilitation of response amplitude following tail shock. Thus, confirming previous results (Rankin and Carew, 1987a), dishabituation was present in each of the developmental stages examined. In contrast, the results for animals that received sensitization training showed a strikingly different pattern: sensitization was completely absent in stage 11 and early stage 12. In these stages, the same animals that exhibited dishabituation lacked sensitization. Moreover, sensitization was absent regardless of the intensity of siphon stimulation used to elicit the reflex, or of the intensity of tail shock (in fact, as I will discuss below, in these early stages in which sensitization was absent, tail shock produced a modest but significant *depression* of response amplitude). However, in late stage 12, tail shock did, indeed, produce sensitization of the reflex (Fig. 2).

As stated above, dishabituation and sensitization have often been considered to reflect a unitary facilitatory process. Our behavioral results, however, showing that dishabituation and sensitization emerge as separate behavioral processes according to very different developmental timetables (separated by at least 60 days), stand in contrast to a unitary process view (see below).

III. Cellular Analogs of Learning Have the Same Developmental Timetables as Their Respective Behavioral Forms of Learning

The developmental separation of different learning processes in the gill and siphon withdrawal reflex of *Aplysia* that I have described above affords the opportunity to examine the unique contributions of different cellular and molecular mechanisms to each form of learning. A first step in this analysis is to establish that cellular analogs of these forms of learning can be identified and analyzed in the central nervous system of juvenile *Aplysia* at the same stages of development that those forms of learning are first behaviorally expressed. The neural circuit in the abdominal ganglion that controls siphon and gill withdrawal is well understood in adult *Aplysia,* but it has not yet been mapped in juvenile animals. However, the giant mucus motor neuron R2, also found in the abdominal ganglion, can provide an excellent system in which to explore cellular analogs of learning. This neuron is readily identifiable as a unique individual throughout juvenile development (Kriegstein, 1977a). In addition, R2 receives significant afferent input from the siphon (Kandel and Tauc, 1964; Rayport, 1981). Thus R2 can serve as a cellular vantage point to monitor plastic changes that emerge in the reflex pathways for gill and siphon withdrawal.

A. Synaptic Depression

The cellular analog of habituation in the gill and siphon withdrawal reflexes of *Aplysia* is synaptic depression, which can be seen as a progressive decrement in complex excitatory postsynaptic potentials (EPSPs) produced by repeated afferent input. These EPSPs can be measured with intracellular electrodes either in motor neurons for the reflex (Kupfermann *et al.*, 1970; Carew *et al.*, 1971) or in the giant neuron R2 (Kandel and Tauc, 1964; Rayport, 1981; Rayport and Camardo, 1984). The development of the cellular analog of habituation in R2 was first examined by Rayport (1981) and Rayport and Camardo (1984). They found that synaptic decrement was evident in R2 very early in juvenile development in stage 9 (Fig. 2). Thus these observations are consistent with our subsequent behavioral observations that habituation in the siphon withdrawal reflex is present as early as stage 9, when the siphon first emerges as an effector organ (Rankin and Carew, 1987a; Rankin *et al.*, 1987).

B. Facilitation of Decremented Synaptic Potentials

The cellular analog of dishabituation can be seen as the facilitation of *previously decremented* complex EPSPs, produced by electrical stimulation of the pleuro-abdominal connectives, which carry facilitating input to the abdominal ganglion from the head and tail (Kandel and Tauc, 1964; Kupfermann *et al.*, 1970; Carew *et al.*, 1971). Rayport (1981) and Rayport and Camardo (1984) found that the cellular analog of dishabituation in R2 was not present in stage 9 of juvenile development; rather it emerged about 1 week later in stage 10 (Fig. 2). Thus, these cellular observations are also consistent with our subsequent behavioral results showing that dishabituation of the reflex did not emerge until stage 10. Also consistent with both the cellular results of Rayport and Camardo (1984) and the behavioral results of Rankin and Carew (1987a) were the findings of Nolen *et al.* (1987), who showed that habituation and dishabituation in the gill withdrawal component of the reflex was present in juvenile stage 11. This was shown both in behavioral studies directly measuring gill withdrawal and in cellular analog studies measuring the evoked neural discharge in an efferent nerve innervating the gill.

C. Facilitation of Nondecremented Synaptic Potentials

The cellular analog of sensitization can be seen as the facilitation of *nondecremented* complex EPSPs by connective stimulation (Carew *et al.*, 1971). Since behavioral studies indicated that sensitization emerged during stage 12, we focused on this stage for our studies of the developmental emergence of the cellular analog of sensitization (Nolen and Carew, 1988). While recording intracellularly from R2, brief electrical pulses were delivered to the siphon nerve, which evoked a complex EPSP in R2. A train of electrical pulses was delivered to the pleural–abdominal connective to produce facilitation. The analog of sensitization was examined by analyzing the ability of connective stimulation to facilitate nondecremented complex EPSPs in R2. In previous behavioral studies stage 12 was divided into two substages, early stage 12 and late stage 12; sensitization was absent in early stage 12, but present in late stage 12. To permit greater resolution of the temporal emergence of the analog of sensitization, for the cellular analyses we divided stage 12 into three substages: early, mid, and late stage 12.

As would be predicted on the basis of the behavioral findings, the analog of sensitization was clearly present in late stage 12 animals. Specifically, connective stimulation produced significant facilitation of nondecremented EPSPs. Moreover, in mid stage 12 animals, connective stimulation also produced clear facilitation of nondecremented EPSPs. Thus, the analog of sensitization was present in both late and mid stage 12 of juvenile development. However, in contrast, connective stimulation produced no significant facilitation of nondecremented EPSPs in early stage 12. Thus the analog of sensitization was absent in this early stage (Fig. 2). In fact, at this early stage the connective stimulation actually produced significant *depression* of EPSP amplitude (see below). These cellular results therefore show a clear developmental trend in the emergence of the cellular analog of sensitization and support the behavioral observation that sensitization is absent in early stage 12 of juvenile development (Rankin and Carew, 1988).

A summary and comparison of the developmental timetables for behavioral habituation, dishabituation, and sensitization and their cellular analogs is shown in Fig. 2. Habituation is present as early as we can study the siphon, in stage 9, and continues to develop in terms of the ISI that produces habituation throughout the juvenile life of the animal. Dishabituation emerges approximately 4 days later in stage 10. Finally, sensitization emerges several weeks after dishabituation, during stage 12. A clear parallel is apparent between each of these forms of learning and its respective cellular analog: habituation and its analog, synaptic decrement, are present in stage 9 (Rayport and Camardo, 1984), the earliest stage tested; dishabituation and its analog, facilitation of decremented EPSPs, emerge in stage 10 (Rayport and Camardo, 1984; Nolen et al., 1987); and sensitization and its analog, facilitation of nondecremented EPSPs, emerge considerably later, during stage 12 (Rankin and Carew, 1987b; Nolen and Carew, 1988). The developmental parallel between the emergence of each form of learning and its respective cellular analog is striking, and suggests that gaining an understanding of the cellular mechanisms underlying the expression of synaptic plasticity we have observed may contribute importantly to an understanding of the mechanisms underlying the expression of the learning processes themselves.

IV. Analysis of Nondecremented Responses Prior to the Emergence of Sensitization Reveals a Novel Inhibitory Process

A. Behavioral Studies

In our behavioral experiments examining the developmental emergence of sensitization, we assessed the effects of tail shock on nondecremented responses in three juvenile stages: stage 11, early stage 12, and late stage 12. This analysis revealed an unexpected result. In early developmental stages (stage 11 and early stage 12) a modest but consistent inhibitory effect of tail shock became evident. Then, between early and late stage 12, there was a dramatic transition after which tail shock could produce its facilitatory effect (Rankin and Carew, 1988). This transition is illustrated in Fig. 3. In any single group of animals the inhibitory effect of

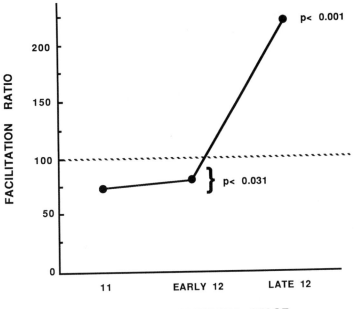

Figure 3.
Developmental transition from inhibition to facilitation of nondecremented responses following tail shock. A composite facilitation ratio was computed for each stage. In stage 11 and early stage 12, tail shock produces significant reflex inhibition (p < 0.031, two-tailed). In contrast, in late stage 12 tail shock produces significant facilitation ($p < 0.001$, two-tailed).

tail shock was modest, but it was quite consistent; in six out of six different experiments in stage 11 and early stage 12 animals, the mean of the first postshock response was lower than the mean of the preshock responses. Thus, significant response inhibition was seen in early stages, whereas significant facilitation was seen in the later stage (Rankin and Carew, 1987a,b, 1988).

In quite recent studies, further examining this inhibitory process, Rankin and Carew (1987b) examined the effects of different intensities of tail shock (very weak and very strong) on the amplitude of siphon withdrawal in stage 11 and early stage 12 animals. Confirming previous studies, sensitization was completely absent in these stages. Moreover, not surprisingly, they found that greater inhibition was produced by the strong tail shock than by the weak shock. In fact the magnitude of inhibition appeared to be a linear function of the magnitude of tail shock. However, counterintuitively, they found that significantly *less* dishabituation was produced by strong tail shock than by weak tail shock. Specifically, the magnitude of dishabituation was an inverted U-shaped function of the magnitude of tail shock. (A similar finding has recently been obtained in adult *Aplysia* as well; Marcus *et al.*, 1987, 1988.) This observation is consistent with the hypothesis that the inhibition produced by the strong tail shock actually competes with the expression of a facilitatory process (dishabituation) that is present in the early developmental stages. Taken collectively, these data suggest the hypothesis that two antagonistic processes, one facilitatory (dishabituation) and the other inhibitory, emerge early in development, and that at a later stage another facilitatory process (sensitization) emerges as well.

B. Cellular Studies

As described above, there are striking parallels between the developmental emergence of three different forms of nonassociative learning and their respective cellular analogs. This parallel between behavioral and cellular results was also observed in our analysis of the inhibitory process. Specifically, Nolen and Carew (1988) identified a cellular analog of the behavioral depressive effect of tail shock (Fig. 3) prior to the emergence of sensitization. They found that in early stage 12, nondecremented complex EPSPs in R2 were actually significantly *depressed* by connective stimulation. Thus the effect of connective stimulation showed a pronounced developmental transition from depression to synaptic facilitation in mid and late stage 12 (Fig. 4). Therefore, our combined behavioral and cellular studies show that early in development, prior to the emergence of sensitization, a novel inhibitory process is present.

C. Dishabituation, Sensitization, and Inhibition
Can Be Behaviorally Dissociated in Adult *Aplysia*

The behavioral separation of dishabituation and sensitization (Fig. 2), as well as the identification of an inhibitory process (Figs. 3 and 4) in developing juvenile *Aplysia,* raised the important question of whether these processes can be behaviorally identified and dissociated in adult animals as well. Recent experiments by Marcus *et al.*, (1987, 1988) show that they can (Fig. 5). By examining a range of stimulus intensities of tail shock, several relatively weak intensities were identified that produced significant dishabituation of the siphon withdrawal reflex, but produced *no* sensitization. Sensitization was only produced by strong

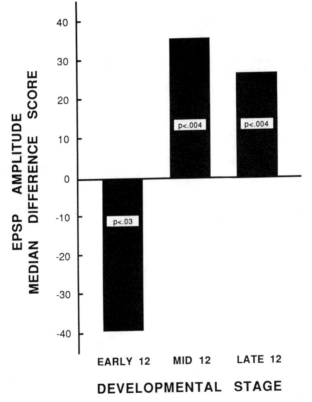

Figure 4.
Emergence of the cellular analog of sensitization in *Aplysia.* The median difference in EPSP amplitude (percent post minus pre) in the mucus motor neuron R2 is shown for each developmental substage. While significant facilitation was present in middle ($N = 8$) and late stage 12 ($N = 13$), significant inhibition was present in early stage 12 ($N = 8$).

A

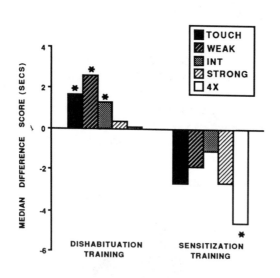

B

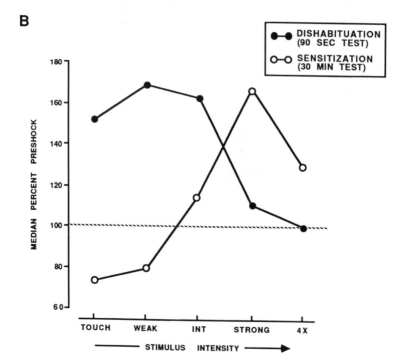

tail shock (Fig. 5B). Moreover, dishabituation and sensitization differed in their time of onset: dishabituation was evident early (90 sec) after shock, whereas sensitization was not evident at 90 sec (Fig. 5A). Sensitization did not appear until significantly later (20–30 min) after shock. Finally, soon (90 sec) after tail shock, nondecremented responses showed significant *inhibition* of reflex amplitude in response to very strong (4×) shock (Fig. 5A).

Thus, the behavioral processes of dishabituation and sensitization can be dissociated not only in juvenile animals on the basis of their differential developmental emergence, but also in adult animals on the basis of their differential time of onset and their differential sensitivity to stimulus intensity. In addition, we have been able to identify an *inhibitory* behavioral process in adult animals. Similar tail shock-induced inhibition in adult *Aplysia* has also been recently described by Mackey *et al.* (1987) and Krontiris-Litowitz *et al.* (1987). Thus, the inhibitory process that we have identified in juvenile animals appears to persist into adult life in *Aplysia.*

D. Reevaluation of a Dual-Process Model of Nonassociative Learning

As I described earlier, until recently a commonly held view was that habituation, dishabituation, and sensitization could be accounted for by two opponent processes: a single decrementing process that produces habituation, and a single facilitating process that produces *both* dishabituation and sensitization (for reviews, see Groves and Thompson, 1970; Carew *et al.,* 1971; Carew and Kandel, 1974). Four lines of evidence suggest that this view requires revision.

First, on theoretical grounds, Wagner (1976) suggested that dishabituation may reflect a distracter-like process, which could be triggered

---

Figure 5.

Behavioral dissociation of dishabituation, sensitization, and inhibition in adult *Aplysia.* (A) *Time of onset:* The effects of a range of stimulus intensities on habituated and nonhabituated responses (dishabituation and sensitization training, respectively) in a test 90 sec after tail shock are shown. Data are presented as median difference scores of posttests minus prescores. Significant dishabituation is evident at several intensities (asterisks), whereas sensitization is not seen at any intensity; in all cases tail shock produced suppression of nondecremented responses, with the strongest stimulus producing significant inhibition (asterisk). (B) *Sensitivity to stimulus intensity:* Reflex magnitude as a function of tail shock intensity for dishabituation and sensitization is summarized. The dashed line through 100% indicates baseline. Maximal dishabituation is produced by WEAK stimuli (which produce no significant sensitization) and maximal sensitization is produced by STRONG stimuli (which produce no significant dishabituation). Data from Marcus *et al.* (1988).

by a novel (but not necessarily noxious) stimulus that disrupted the memory for habituation. He further suggested that dishabituation might be dissociable from sensitization on the basis of the stimulus intensity required to produce each process. Whitlow (1975) provided experimental support for this idea by showing that a relatively weak but complex stimulus could facilitate a decremented vasomotor response in rabbits, but that the same stimulus was ineffective in facilitating a nondecremented response. Thus the stimulus produced dishabituation, but not sensitization.

Second, as described previously, Hochner and colleagues (1986a,b) have recently produced cellular evidence in the sensory neurons of adult *Aplysia* that two separate processes are involved in presynaptic facilitation of transmission from the sensory neurons to their follower cells. One process, spike broadening, predominates when synaptic transmission is at a normal (nondecremented) level; the other process, thought to involve transmitter mobilization, predominates when synaptic transmission is decremented. These observations led Hochner and colleagues (1986a,b) to first propose that sensitization and dishabituation in *Aplysia* may, at least in part, involve separate cellular mechanisms. Recently, Gingrich and Byrne (1987) have described a mathematical model that demonstrates that transmitter mobilization in conjunction with spike broadening can account for the physiological results obtained by Hochner and his colleagues (1986a,b).

Third, the recent results of Marcus *et al.* (1987, 1988) show that dishabituation and sensitization can be behaviorally dissociated in adult *Aplysia* in two ways: (1) by their differential time of onset; and (2) by their differential sensitivity to stimulus intensity (Fig. 5). These behavioral observations raise interesting questions about the cellular processes underlying the dissociation of these two forms of learning. One possibility is that, as suggested above, dishabituation and sensitization may reflect different underlying mechanisms. For example, the temporal dissociation between the onset of dishabituation and sensitization in adult animals (Fig. 5A) may reflect the differential activation of two processes, one which turns on rapidly and produces facilitation of decremented responses, and another which turns on gradually and produces facilitation of nondecremented responses. An alternative possibility is that the behavioral dissociation we observe is produced by the inhibitory process initiated by tail shock. For example, nondecremented processes may be more susceptible to inhibition, and thus the delayed onset of sensitization may reflect the gradual wearing off of the inhibitory process which competes with or masks the expression of sensitization. Thus far, our behavioral results cannot distinguish between these possibilities. However, recent progress in elucidating the cellular mechanisms underlying dishabituation and sensitization (Hochner et al., 1986a; Gingrich and Byrne, 1987) as well as inhibition (Mackey et al., 1987; Belardetti et al., 1987;

Piomelli *et al.*, 1987; Wright *et al.*, 1988) suggests that it may soon be possible to understand these behavioral processes at a more fundamental level.

Finally, the work I have discussed thus far in this chapter regarding the development of nonassociative learning in *Aplysia* provides both behavioral and cellular support for the idea that dishabituation and sensitization may reflect separate processes, since they emerge according to very different developmental timetables (Fig. 2).

Thus, the four lines of evidence described above suggest that a dual-process view may not adequately account for habituation, dishabituation, and sensitization. Several processes may potentially contribute to these forms of nonassociative learning. These include (1) a decrementing process underlying habituation, (2) a facilitatory process underlying dishabituation, (3) a possible additional facilitatory process underlying sensitization, and (4) an inhibitory process triggered by tail shock. It will now be important to determine the degree to which these different mechanistic processes can account for the behavioral dissociation that we have observed both developmentally and in adult animals.

V. Sensitization Emerges Simultaneously in Different Response Systems in *Aplysia*

In the work I have presented thus far, the development of learning has been analyzed in the gill and siphon withdrawal reflex. Having established the timetable for the emergence of sensitization in this reflex system, we next asked if the emergence of sensitization was due to the development of a process restricted to the gill and siphon withdrawal circuit, or whether it was due to a more general change in the whole animal. One way to examine this question is to analyze the development of sensitization in other response systems; thus we turned our attention to escape locomotion, a dramatic stereotypic response in which an animal rapidly locomotes away from a source of noxious stimulation. This response offers a variety of advantages for a developmental analysis:

1. It is expressed very early in development (as early as stage 8; Stopfer and Carew, unpublished observations).

2. It is simple to quantify in an unrestrained animal (Hening *et al.*, 1979; Walters *et al.*, 1979).

3. The response in the adult is known to be modulated by several different forms of both nonassociative and associative learning (Walters *et al.*, 1978, 1981; Carew *et al.*, 1981).

4. The neural circuitry underlying escape locomotion in the adult has been examined in some detail (Jahan-Parwar and Fredman, 1978a,b; Hening *et al.*, 1979).

We examined the development of escape locomotion in juvenile stages 10, 11, early 12, and late 12, as well as in adults (Stopfer and Carew, 1988a). For each developmental stage two groups of animals were run: a sensitization group, which received sensitization training (strong electric shocks to the tail), and a control group, which received only a weak tail stimulus. Before and after training, locomotion in response to a weak test stimulus to the tail was assessed in terms of the total distance travelled in a 2-min observation period.

In stage 10, stage 11, and early stage 12 there were no significant differences between animals that received sensitization training and animals that received the control procedure—that is, there was no sensitization in these early juvenile stages. However, in late stage 12 animals there was significant sensitization as a result of strong tail shock. Thus, sensitization of escape locomotion emerged some time between early and late stage 12 of juvenile development.

The emergence of sensitization of escape locomotion in late stage 12 is strikingly similar to the timetable for sensitization in the siphon withdrawal reflex (Fig. 2). This result is quite interesting because the gill and siphon withdrawal reflex and escape locomotion represent very different classes of response systems: siphon and gill withdrawal are graded responses that involve a restricted effector organ system (the mantle organs: gill, siphon, and mantle shelf), whereas escape locomotion involves a widespread effector organ system (involving virtually the entire body, including the head and neck, the whole foot, the bilateral body walls, and the two parapodia). In addition, the two response systems have very different underlying neural circuits: the gill and siphon withdrawal reflex is mediated by a relatively simple circuit located in the abdominal ganglion (for review, see Hawkins *et al.*, 1987), whereas escape locomotion is mediated by more complex circuitry involving the coordination of triggering, oscillatory, and effector circuits in the cerebral, pleural, and pedal ganglia (Jahan-Parwar and Fredman, 1978a,b; Hening *et al.*, 1979).

It is intriguing that, despite several differences in ontogeny, response topography, and underlying circuit complexity, both the escape locomotion system and the gill and siphon withdrawal reflex begin to express the capacity for sensitization in the same late stage of juvenile development. This suggests the possibility that sensitization may emerge as a single unified process during development, and thus may be expressed in a variety of response systems simultaneously. We are currently investigating the development of sensitization in other response systems in *Aplysia*, such as tail withdrawal (Stopfer and Carew, 1988b) as well as head withdrawal, and feeding (Stopfer and Carew, in progress), to further test this hypothesis.

VI. Widespread Proliferation of Central Neurons Occurs in the Same Developmental Stage as the Emergence of Sensitization

The emergence of sensitization in different response systems in stage 12 of juvenile development, as described above, could imply the presence of a general developmental trigger occurring in that stage that promotes the expression of sensitization. A recent study examining the development of central neurons throughout all juvenile stages in *Aplysia* has also suggested the presence of an important developmental trigger occurring in stage 12. Cash and Carew (1987) counted the number of neurons present in each ganglion (discrete anatomical regions) in the CNS of *Aplysia* in each stage of juvenile development: stage 9, 10, 11, early 12, late 12, and adult. They found that the pattern of cell proliferation was remarkably similar in each pair of ganglia (buccals, cerebrals, pleurals, and pedals), as well as in the unpaired abdominal ganglion. Thus examining the pattern of total cell number throughout the entire CNS provides an accurate picture of the developmental pattern within each ganglion. The results expressed in this fashion are shown in Fig. 6, which reveals a highly nonlinear pattern of addition of neurons throughout juvenile development. There is little change in cell number in stages 9, 10, and 11 (a period of approximately 60 days). However, in stage 12 there is a dramatic proliferation of neurons: in early stage 12 there is an approximate doubling of neurons in all ganglia, and in late stage 12 there is a further tripling of neurons (Fig. 6). Thus in stage 12, within approximately 60 days, there is roughly a sixfold increase in neuronal cell number, with the greatest increase occurring in the last half of this stage.

Such a dramatic increase in cell number throughout the entire CNS at a specific developmental stage implies the possible presence of a specific developmental trigger for neuronal proliferation. Interestingly, this proliferation occurs at the same stage of development as the emergence of sensitization in at least two different behavioral response systems (the siphon withdrawal reflex and escape locomotion), as well as emergence of the cellular analog of sensitization in one of them (siphon withdrawal). This raises the intriguing possibility that some common aspect of the developmental trigger for neuronal proliferation (e.g., either a general hormonal signal or the emergence of a particular class of facilitating circuitry) could also participate in the developmental expression of sensitization. If this were the case, characterization of such a signal or trigger

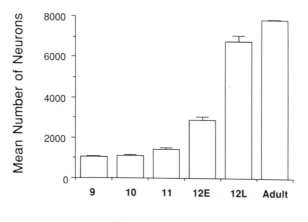

Developmental Stages

Figure 6.
Increase in neuronal number throughout juvenile development. The mean
number of neurons in the entire CNS is shown for each stage of juvenile
development. In stages 9, 10, and 11, there is relatively little change in cell
number. However, in early and late stage 12 there is a dramatic
proliferation of neurons that tapers off in the early adult stage.

might permit experiments in which the process of sensitization could,
in the limit, be developmentally triggered at will. This in turn could
provide the unique opportunity to gain direct experimental control over
the expression of a specific form of learning in identified circuits within
the nervous system. This possibility is, of course, entirely speculative
at the moment. But the notion is sufficiently attractive, both experimentally and theoretically, to warrant further exploration.

VII. Concluding Remarks

In this chapter I have reviewed recent work that my colleagues and I
have carried out examining the developmental assembly of different
forms of learning in *Aplysia*. Using this approach we have been able to
dissect seemingly very simple forms of nonassociative learning into a
number of underlying interactive components, on both behavioral and
cellular levels. We are currently extending these studies in three principal
directions. First, thus far we have only focused on nonassociative learning
processes. However, *Aplysia* exhibits several forms of associative learning,
including fear conditioning (Walters *et al.*, 1981), differential classical
conditioning (Carew *et al.*, 1983), operant conditioning (Cook and Carew,
1985, 1986, 1988; Hawkins *et al.*, 1985), and higher-order features of conditioning such as context conditioning (Colwill, 1985) and contingency

effects (Hawkins *et al.*, 1986). It will be extremely interesting to determine the developmental timetables for these different forms of associative learning and compare them to those already established for nonassociative processes.

Second, we have focused our studies thus far only on short-term memory. However, many forms of both nonassociative and associative learning can exist not only in a short-term form, lasting hours, but also in a long-term form, lasting days to weeks (Carew *et al.*, 1972, 1981; Pinsker *et al.*, 1973). It will be of considerable importance to determine the developmental timetable for the expression of long-term memory in *Aplysia*, and to compare the ontogeny of long-term memory in different forms of learning. For example, habituation and sensitization emerge during development separated by 60–70 days. It will be of great interest to ask whether long-term memory for *each* form of learning emerges, perhaps at some time later, but in temporal register with the time of emergence of the capacity for learning itself, or whether long-term memory emerges as a general process, independent of any particular form of learning. Such an analysis could provide important insights into the theoretically interesting issue of the relationship between the processes that underlie learning and those that underlie memory.

Finally, it will be of obvious importance to specify the cellular and molecular mechanisms that are expressed in particular neural circuits that give rise to the developmental expression of different forms of learning and memory. The cellular and molecular mechanisms underlying a variety of forms of learning and memory in adult *Aplysia* have been extensively investigated, and in some cases are quite well understood (for review, see Carew, 1987; Hawkins *et al.*, 1987; Byrne, 1987; see also the chapters by Byrne, Hawkins and Schwartz in this volume). Using a developmental approach, it will be possible, by the appropriate timing of cellular experiments, to study aspects of the cellular mechanisms underlying some forms of learning in developmental isolation from other, later-emerging mechanisms. Thus it may be possible to gain unique insights into the substrates underlying learning and memory by studying their developmental assembly.

In the work discussed in this chapter, my colleagues and I have used a developmental approach to study issues of relevance to learning and memory in *Aplysia*. In conclusion, I would like to raise the possibility that this approach might also be useful in the broader context of this volume, which has focused on issues of relevance to interfacing theoretical and empirical approaches to the analysis of neuronal plasticity. For any theoretical or quantitative computational analysis to have direct relevance to an actual, operational neuronal system (whether it be in an invertebrate ganglion or in the hippocampus or cerebellum), it is important to be able to specify the critical cellular and network parameters involved in the actual functioning of that neural system. An important question then is, how do we choose among the vast array of possible parameters, those that are of critical (perhaps unique) importance in the network?

A developmental approach such as the one that we are using in *Aplysia* could be of value in addressing this question. Specifically, using such an approach, it might be possible to obtain important clues as to critical parameters in the operation of a neural network, by examining the way the behavior of that network changes as particular neuronal characteristics mature or particular circuit elements are added during ontogeny. For example, if the input/output characteristics of a particular neuronal network changed dramatically, or plasticity within that network first appeared, with the developmental emergence of a specific class of membrane currents or the emergence of particular inhibitory or facilitating circuit elements, this could be of considerable value in helping to focus on the specific neuronal features or circuit properties that should be incorporated into a comprehensive computational model of that system and its plasticity. As discussed earlier, a number of different response systems in *Aplysia* exhibit interesting forms of behavioral plasticity, and many of these systems are at least partly understood in terms of their underlying neuronal circuitry. Since all of these response systems are amenable to the developmental strategy that I have outlined, it is possible that this general approach may be useful not only for an empirical analysis of cellular and molecular mechanisms of learning, but also for quantitative and theoretical approaches to the analysis of neuronal plasticity.

Acknowledgments

I wish to thank my colleagues Emilie Marcus, Thomas Nolen, William Wright, and Mark Stopfer for their helpful comments and suggestions, and Kent Fitzgerald for his help in preparation of the manuscript. I am also very grateful to the Howard Hughes Medical Institute for their continued and generous support in supplying juvenile *Aplysia*. This work has been supported by National Institutes of Health CDA Award 7-K02-MH00081-09, by National Institutes of Health BRSG grant 507-RR-0750 15, by National Science Foundation grant BNS 8614961, and by Office of Naval Research contract N00014-87-K-0381.

References

Alkon, D. L. (1983). Learning in a marine snail. *Sci. Am.* **249**, 70–84.

Amsel, A., and Stanton, M. (1980). Ontogeny and phylogeny of paradoxical reward effects. *Adv. Study Behav.* **2**, 227–274.

Belardetti, F., Kandel, E. R., and Siegelbaum, S. A. (1987). Neuronal inhibition by the peptide FMRFamide involves opening of S K^+ channels. *Nature,* **325,** 153–156.

Byrne, J. H. (1987). Cellular analysis of associative learning. *Physiol. Rev.* **67**(2), 329–439.

Campbell, B. A., and Coulter, X. (1976). The ontogenesis of learning and memory. *In* "Neural Mechanisms of Learning and Memory" (M. R. Rosenzwieg and E. L. Bennett, eds.), pp. 71–74. MIT Press, Cambridge, Massachusetts.

Campbell, B. A., and Spear, N. E. (1972). Ontogeny of memory. *Psychol. Rev.* **79**(3), 215–236.

Carew, T. J. (1987). Cellular and molecular advances in the study of learning in *Aplysia*. *In* "The Neural and Molecular Basis of Learning" (J. P. Changeaux and M. Konishi, eds.), pp. 177–204. Wiley, New York.

Carew, T. J., and Kandel, E. R. (1974). A synaptic analysis of the interrelationship between different behavioral modifications in *Aplysia*. *In* "Synaptic Transmission and Neuronal Interaction" (M. V. L. Bennett and E. R. Kandel, eds.), pp. 187–215. Raven Press, New York.

Carew, T. J., and Sahley, C. L. (1986). Invertebrate learning and memory: From behavior to molecules. *Ann. Rev. Neurosci.* **9**, 435–487.

Carew, T. J., Castellucci, V. F., and Kandel, E. R. (1971). An analysis of dishabituation and sensitization of the gill-withdrawal reflex in *Aplysia*. *Int. J. Neurosci.* **2**, 79–98.

Carew, T. J., Pinsker, H. M., and Kandel, E. R. (1972). Long-term habituation of a defensive withdrawal reflex in *Aplysia*. *Science* **175**, 451–454.

Carew, T. J., Walters, E. T., and Kandel, E. R. (1981). Associative learning in *Aplysia*: Cellular correlates supporting a conditioned fear hypothesis. *Science* **211**, 501–504.

Carew, T. J., Hawkins, R. D., and Kandel, E. R. (1983). Differential classical conditioning of a defensive withdrawal reflex in *Aplysia californica*. *Science* **219**, 397–400.

Cash, D., and Carew, T. J. (1987). A quantitative analysis of the development of the CNS in juvenile *Aplysia*. *Soc. Neurosci. Abstr.* **13**, 816.

Colwill, R. M. (1985). Context conditioning in *Aplysia californica*. *Soc. Neurosci. Abstr.* **11**, 796.

Cook, D. G., and Carew, T. J. (1985). Operant conditioning of head-waving in *Aplysia*. *Soc. Neurosci. Abstr.* **11**, 796.

Cook, D. G., and Carew, T. J. (1986). Operant conditioning of head-waving in *Aplysia*. *Proc. Natl. Acad. Sci. U.S.A.* **83**, 1120–1124.

Cook, D. G., and Carew, T. J. (1988). Operant conditioning of identified neck muscles and individual motor neurons in *Aplysia*. *Soc. Neurosci. Abstr.* **14**, 607.

Gingrich, K. J., and Byrne, J. H. (1987). Mathematical model of two cellular mechanisms contributing to dishabituation and sensitization in *Aplysia*. *Soc. Neurosci. Abstr.* **13**, 597.

Groves, P. M., and Thompson, R. F. (1970). Habituation: A dual process theory. *Psychol. Rev.* **77**, 419–450.

Hawkins, R. D., Clark, G. A., and Kandel, E. R. (1985). Operant conditioning and differential classical conditioning of gill withdrawal in *Aplysia*. *Soc. Neurosci. Abstr.* **11**, 796.

Hawkins, R. D., Carew, T. J., and Kandel, E. R. (1986). Effects of interstimulus interval and contingency on classical conditioning of the *Aplysia* siphon withdrawal reflex. *J. Neurosci.* **6**, 1695–1701.

Hawkins, R. D., Clark, G. A., and Kandel, E. R. (1987). Cell biological studies of learning in simple vertebrate and invertebrate systems. *In* "Handbook of Physiology Section I: The Nervous System" Vol. 6, pp. 25–83 (F. Plum, ed.). Bethesda, Maryland.

Hening, W. A., Walters, E. T., Carew, T. J., and Kandel, E. R. (1979). Motorneuronal control of locomotion in *Aplysia*. *Brain Res.* **179**, 231–253.

Hochner, B., Klein, M., Schacher, S., and Kandel, E. R. (1986a). Action-potential duration and the modulation of transmitter release from the sensory neurons of *Aplysia* in presynaptic facilitation and behavioral sensitization. *Proc. Natl. Acad. Sci. U.S.A.* **83**, 8410–8414.

Hochner, B., Klein, M., Schacher, S., and Kandel, E. R. (1986b). Additional component in the cellular mechanism of presynaptic facilitation contributes to behavioral dishabituation in *Aplysia*. *Proc. Natl. Acad. Sci. U.S.A.* **83**, 8794–8798.

Jahan-Parwar, B., and Fredman, S. M. (1978a). Control of pedal and parapodial movements in *Aplysia*. I. Proprioceptive and tactile reflexes. *J. Neurophysiol.* **41**, 600–608.

Jahan-Parwar, B., and Fredman, S. M. (1978b). Control of pedal and parapodial movements in *Aplysia*. II. Cerebral ganglion neurons. *J. Neurophysiol.* **41**, 609–620.

Kandel, E. R., and Tauc, L. (1964). Mechanism of prolonged heterosynaptic facilitation. *Nature (London)* **202**, 145–147.

Kandel, E. R., Kriegstein, A. R., and Schacher, S. (1980). Development of the central nervous system of *Aplysia* in terms of the differentiation of its specific identified cells. *Neuroscience* **5**, 2033–2063.

Kriegstein, A. R. (1977a). Development of the nervous system of *Aplysia californica*. *Proc. Natl. Acad. Sci. U.S.A.* **74**, 375–378.

Kriegstein, A. R. (1977b). Stages in the post-hatching development of *Aplysia californica*. *J. Exp. Zool.* **199**, 275–288.

Kriegstein, A. R., Castellucci, V. F., and Kandel, E. R. (1974). Metamorphosis of *Aplysia californica* in laboratory culture. *Proc. Natl. Acad. Sci. U.S.A.* **71**, 3654–3658.

Krontiris-Litowitz, J. K., Erickson, M. T., and Walters, E. T. (1987). Central suppression of defensive reflexes in *Aplysia* by noxious stimulation and by factors released from body wall. *Soc. Neurosci. Abstr.* **13**, 815.

Kupfermann, I., Castellucci, V. F., Pinsker, H., and Kandel, E. R. (1970). Neuronal correlates of habituation and dishabituation of the gill-withdrawal reflex in *Aplysia*. *Science* **167**, 1743–1745.

Mackey, S. L., Glanzman, D. L., Small, S. A., Dyke, A. M., Kandel, E. R. and Hawkins, R. D. (1987). Tail shock produces inhibition as well as sensitization of the siphon-withdrawal reflex of *Aplysia*: Possible behavioral role for presynaptic inhibition mediated by the peptide Phe-Met-Arg-Phe-NH_2. *Proc. Nat. Acad. Sci.*, **84**, 8730–8734.

Marcus, E. A., Nolen, T. G., Rankin, C. H., and Carew, T. J. (1987). Behavioral dissociation of dishabituation, sensitization and inhibition in the siphon withdrawal reflex of adult *Aplysia*. *Soc. Neurosci. Abstr.* **13**, 816.

Marcus, E. A., Nolen, T. G., Rankin, C. H. and Cares, T. J. (1988). Behavioral dissociation of dishabituation, sensitization and inhibition in *Aplysia*. *Science* **241**, 210–213.

Nolen, T. G., and Carew, T. J. (1988). The cellular analog of sensitization emerges at the same time in development as behavioral sensitization in *Aplysia*. *J. Neurosci.* **8**, 212–222.

Nolen, T. G., Marcus, E. A., and Carew, T. J. (1987). Development of learning and memory in *Aplysia*. III. Central neuronal correlates. *J. Neurosci.* **7**, 144–153.

Pinsker, H., Carew, T. J., Hening, W., and Kandel, E. R. (1973). Long-term sensitization of a defensive withdrawal reflex in *Aplysia californica*. *Science* **182**, 1039–1042.

Piomelli, D., Volterra, A., Dale, N., Siegelbaum, S. A., Kandel, E. R., Schwartz, J. H. and Belardetti, F. (1987). Lipoxygenase metabolites of arachidonic acid as second messengers for presynaptic inhibition of *Aplysia* sensory cells. *Nature*, **328**, 38–43.

Quinn, W. G. (1984). Work in invertebrates on the mechanisms underlying learning. *In* "Biology of Learning" (P. Marler and H. Terrace, eds.), pp. 197–246. Dahlem Konferenzen, Berlin.

Rankin, C. H., and Carew, T. J. (1987a). Development of learning and memory in *Aplysia*. II. Habituation and dishabituation. *J. Neurosci.* **7**, 133–143.

Rankin, C. H., and Carew, T. J. (1987b). Analysis of the developmental emergence of sensitization in *Aplysia* reveals an inhibitory effect of a facilitatory stimulus. *Soc. Neurosci. Abstr.* **13**, 816.

Rankin, C. H., and Carew, T. J. (1988). Dishabituation and sensitization emerge as separate processes during development in *Aplysia*. *J. Neurosci.* **8**, 197–211.

Rankin, C. H., Stopfer, M., Marcus, E. A., and Carew, T. J. (1987). Development of learning and memory in *Aplysia*. I. Functional assembly of gill and siphon withdrawal. *J. Neurosci.* **7**, 120–132.

Rayport, S. G. (1981). Development of the functional and plastic capabilities of neurons mediating a defensive behavior in *Aplysia*. Ph.D. Thesis, Columbia University, New York.

Rayport, S. G., and Camardo, J. S. (1984). Differential emergence of cellular mechanisms mediating habituation and sensitization in the developing *Aplysia* nervous system. *J. Neurosci.* **4**, 2528–2532.

Stopfer, M., and Carew, T. J. (1988a). Development of sensitization in the escape locomotion system of *Aplysia. J. Neurosci.* **8,** 223–230.

Stopfer, M. and Carew, T. J. (1988b). Developmental dissociation of dishabituation and sensitization in the tail-withdrawal reflex of *Aplysia. Soc. Neurosci. Abstr.* **14,** 841.

Wagner, A. R. (1976). Priming in STM: An information-processing mechanism for self-generated or retrieval-generated depression of performance. *In* "Habituation: Perspectives from Child Development, Animal Behavior, and Neurophysiology" (T. J. Tighe and R. N. Leaton, eds.), pp. 95–128. Erlbaum, Hillsdale, New Jersey.

Walters, E. T., Carew, T. J., and Kandel, E. R. (1978). Conflict and response selection in the locomotor system of *Aplysia. Soc. Neurosci. Abstr.* **4,** 209.

Walters, E. T., Carew, T. J., and Kandel, E. R. (1979). Classical conditioning in *Aplysia californica. Proc. Natl. Acad. Sci. U.S.A.* **76,** 6675–6679.

Walters, E. T., Carew, T. J., and Kandel, E. R. (1981). Associative learning in *Aplysia:* Evidence for conditioned fear in an invertebrate. *Science* **211,** 504–506.

Whitlow, J. W. (1975). Short-term memory in habituation and dishabituation. *J. Exp. Psychol., Anim. Behav. Processes* **1,** 189–206.

Wright, W. G., Marcus, E. A., Thaker, H., and Carew, T. J. (1988). A cellular analysis of tail-shock induced inhibition in the siphon withdrawal reflex of *Aplysia. Soc. Neurosci. Abstr.* **14,** 841.

3

Turtles All the Way Down: Some Molecular Mechanisms Underlying Long-Term Sensitization in *Aplysia*

James H. Schwartz and Steven M. Greenberg

A promise of contemporary neuroscience is to explain the molecular basis of memory. Underlying this promise is the idea that the biochemical reactions that cause memory occur in the nerve cells that mediate the behavior which is altered by learning. The specific working hypothesis is that many simple forms of learning and memory are mediated by identifiable neurons through cellular processes that operate either to increase or decrease the amounts of transmitter substances released at the synapses of those neurons. With the abundant material available in the nerve cells of invertebrates, the sensitive techniques of modern biochemistry can now measure changes in metabolites and macromolecules that occur during the physiologically relevant time periods, and the technology of recombinant DNA promises to make changes in even smaller cells available for measurement.

Demonstration of a molecular change does not in itself guarantee that the altered process actually *causes* the change in synaptic activity presumed to underlie the change in behavior that constitutes memory and learning. Might not a change that takes place in one molecular process actually be secondary to some other, more fundamental mechanism? It is quite likely that many biochemical changes occur in a neuron as a consequence of training that might only reinforce the obligatory molecular events underlying synaptic plasticity. At worst, such a change in biochemical properties might be functionally gratuitous. The task then is not only to detect biochemical changes in nerve cells that occur during learning, but also to arrange those changes in order of functional relevance.

_____ I. Molecular Components _____
Underlying Sensitization

Transient elevation of cAMP with activation of cAMP-dependent protein kinase results in brief closure of a special K^+ channel in terminals of *Aplysia* mechanosensory neurons, which is thought to account for the neurophysiological correlates underlying short-term sensitization of the defensive gill- and siphon-withdrawal reflex (Klein and Kandel, 1980; Castellucci *et al.*, 1980, 1982; Bernier *et al.*, 1982). Short-term sensitization lasts only minutes; its brief duration is explained by the transient activation of the protein kinase. Long-term sensitization of these reflexes can also be produced by more extensive training (see Kandel and Schwartz, 1982; Byrne, 1987). There must be some other mechanism to produce memory that endures for hours or longer, well past the time after which the cAMP in sensory neurons has returned to its unstimulated concentration (Bernier *et al.*, 1982).

After reviewing the evidence that activation of cAMP-dependent protein kinase in *Aplysia* sensory neurons produces short-term sensitization, Kandel and Schwartz (1982) suggested that the long-term form of this behavioral modification might be mediated by the induction of an altered kinase molecule. The holoenzyme of the kinase, a tetramer composed of regulatory (R) and inactive catalytic (C) subunits, dissociates when each R binds two molecules of cAMP to release active C monomers:

$$R_2C_2 + 4cAMP \rightleftharpoons (2cAMP \cdot R)_2 + 2C$$

Since Bernier *et al.* (1982) found that cAMP does not remain elevated in sensory cells for extended periods of time after long-term training, it was further suggested that the R subunits of the kinase would be altered in some way so as to be activated at basal concentrations of cAMP. According to this idea, the same protein substrates that cause sensitization in the short term also would be phosphorylated in the long term, but with an enzyme more responsive to the second messenger.

This hypothesis actually consists of two distinct predictions. The first is that the processes that produce the long-term form of sensitization occur at the same locus as that of the short-term form—the synapses between sensory neurons and motor neurons—and use the same biophysical mechanism—inhibition of the K_s^+ channel. The second distinct prediction is that the biochemical difference between a trained and naive sensory neuron is the activity of its cAMP-dependent protein kinase. In trained sensory neurons, more K_s^+ channels would be in the closed state because of greater protein phosphorylation, even though the basal concentrations of cAMP in trained and naive cells would be equivalent. There is substantial neurophysiological evidence for the first idea (Frost *et al.*, 1985; Scholz and Byrne, 1987; Dale *et al.*, 1986). Our task was to determine the molecular mechanisms that would result in the enhanced activity of the kinase.

II. Long-Term Sensitization
Is Accompanied by a Decrease in
Regulatory Subunits

A change in sensitivity of the cAMP-dependent protein kinase in sensory neurons might be produced either by induction of new forms of R subunits with greater affinity for cAMP (as originally proposed by Kandel and Schwartz, 1982) or by a decrease in the ratio of regulatory to catalytic subunits. To examine the effects of training on the enzyme, we, with the collaboration of Dr. Vincent F. Castellucci, assayed kinase subunits in tissue samples enriched in the LE sensory neuron cluster dissected from abdominal ganglia of animals one day after sensitization. Training consisted of four series of tail shocks delivered over a period of 90 min (Frost et al., 1985). Regulatory subunits were measured by the quantitative binding of the cAMP analog $[^{32}P]$-8-N$_3$cAMP. This photoaffinity reagent has previously been used to show that Aplysia neurons contain five distinct R subunits separable by two-dimensional sodium dodecyl sulfate (SDS) polyacrylamide gel electrophoresis (SDS-PAGE) (Eppler et al., 1982, 1986). Upon one-dimensional gel electrophoresis, these appear as three specifically labeled bands with molecular weights of 47,000, 52,000, and 105,000 (Fig. 1A). The training protocol significantly reduced the amounts of R in all of the molecular weight classes and no new photolabeled components appeared (Fig. 1B).

The disappearance of R subunits from the neurons in ganglia of the trained animals was selective. The amounts of catalytic activity—1.7 nmol phosphate incorporated into a synthetic peptide substrate (Kemptide, Sigma) per minute per milligram protein assayed at 23°C as described previously (Greenberg et al., 1987a)—did not change after training. Also, there were no differences in the amounts of tubulin between the samples of neurons from trained and control animals, nor did we detect differences in any of the unidentified protein bands stained with Coomassie blue. The decrease in the ratio did not occur in animals that had been stimulated by a brief train of shocks to the tail, a training procedure that produces only short-term sensitization of the reflex: when tested a day later, the amounts of R in neurons from the short-term sensitized animals were the same as those of naive controls.

III. A Molecular Mechanism
for Enhanced Protein Phosphorylation

Decreasing the amount of R relative to C should increase kinase activity at any subsaturating concentration of cAMP. The dependence of phosphorylating activity on cAMP at several different ratios of R to C is shown in Fig. 2A: the lower the ratio, the lower the concentration of cAMP needed to activate the enzyme. Even the 25% change in the ratio found after training would be expected to promote phosphorylation of proteins in sensory cells after cAMP returns to the basal concentration. In sensory neurons of untrained animals, Greenberg *et al.* (1987a) showed that about 20% of the total binding sites on R subunits in the sensory cells are occupied by cAMP, and that short-term training raises this value to 60% (pathway 1 in Fig. 2B). At the diminished ratio of R to C found in neurons of long-term trained animals, the concentration of cAMP—which is equivalent to the basal concentration (B) in the untrained cells (Bernier *et al.*, 1982)—could activate the kinase to an extent similar to that produced by the elevated concentration of cAMP (S) formed in response to short-term stimulation (Fig. 2B, pathway 2). The change in sensitivity of the kinase predicted by the original hypothesis for long-term training thus could be produced by the decrease in the ratio of R to C subunits.

IV. The Mechanism by Which R Subunits Are Diminished

Increased degradation is a plausible explanation for the disappearance of R that occurs during training. Free R subunits are known to be extremely susceptible to proteolytic cleavage both *in vitro* and *in vivo*. Much evidence from other animals indicates that association with C subunits protects R from proteolytic cleavage (Potter and Taylor, 1980; Beer *et al.*, 1984). In mutant S49 lymphoma cells lacking C, Steinberg and Agard (1981) found a greatly accelerated turnover of R. Uhler and McKnight (1987) have engineered the overexpression of C subunits in mouse cells in culture and found that the amounts of one of the forms of R (R_I) were greatly increased. Messenger RNA for the regulatory subunit was unchanged in these cells, however, suggesting that the amount of R subunits is governed by the amount of C, not by a change in the synthesis of R.

To show that elevating the concentration of cAMP is sufficient to cause selective loss of R subunits, we treated *Aplysia* synaptosomes with 8-(4-chlorophenylthio)-cAMP (CPT-cAMP), a permeating analog effective in *Aplysia* (Weiss *et al.*, 1979). We found that the amounts of R subunits in the synaptosomes decreased with the time of exposure: after 2 hr, a period that approximates the time cAMP would remain elevated in the intact animal after 90 min of training, R was diminished by 20–40% (see Fig. 3), and after 24 hr, by 72%. Treatment with CPT-cAMP affected neither the amount of catalytic activity nor any of the major stained proteins. Similar results were obtained when the synaptosomes were made permeable with saponin and stimulated with 8-N_3 cAMP (Fig. 4, lane 3, 4).

When extracted, R subunits of *Aplysia* and other animals are most readily cleaved at the sensitive hinge region close to the N-terminus of the molecule, producing an M_r 39,500 fragment that retains the ability

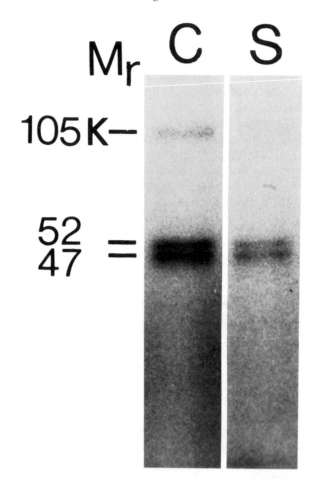

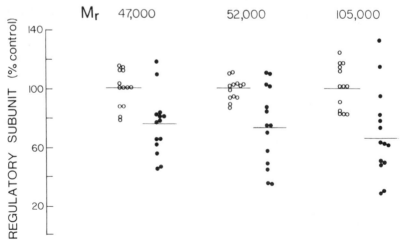

to bind cAMP (Eppler *et al.*, 1982; Corbin *et al.*, 1978; Weber and Hilz, 1979). One feature of the degradation of R in both cAMP-treated synaptosomes and the long-term trained animals was unexpected: neither treatment produced a photolabeled fragment. Both differed in this respect from the proteolytic cleavage of R that occurs when saponin-permeabilized synaptosomes were exposed to Ca^{2+}. Under these conditions, a labeled fragment was generated (Fig. 4, lanes 1 and 2) that is similar in size to the fragment seen when *Aplysia* nervous tissue is extracted in the absence of protease inhibitors and to the fragment derived from R by Ca^{2+}-stimulated cleavage at its protease-sensitive hinge region (Corbin *et al.*, 1978; Beer *et al.*, 1984). The absence of a photolabeled breakdown product in our experiments suggests either that this fragment is degraded as rapidly as it is formed or that the degradation of R *in vivo* does not occur by way of proteolysis at the hinge region. The idea that physiological degradation of R may not involve cleavage at the hinge in other animals is supported by experiments with S49 cells in which R subunits with mutations that render the hinge regions highly sensitive to proteolysis are not turned over at an accelerated rate (R. A. Steinberg, personal communication).

Figure 1.

Effect of long-term sensitization on cAMP-dependent protein kinase R subunits. (A) Autoradiographs of labeled samples of tissue containing sensory cells with equal amounts of protein, one from a control (C), the other from a sensitized (S) animal. Size markers (M_r) in thousands. (B) Summary of results with trained animals. Each point represents a radiolabeled component from a single naive (○) or trained (●) animal. Means are marked by a horizontal line. Values for each species of regulatory subunit in samples from the trained animals were significantly lower than those for the controls [for the M_r 47,000 species (left), $p < 0.02$; for the 52,000 (middle) and 105,000 (right) species, $p < 0.01$, two-tailed Student's t-test]. The amounts measured in trained animals varied more than in controls, perhaps reflecting the variation in aptitude often observed in behavioral experiments with *Aplysia*. Methods are described in Greenberg *et al.* (1987b). Briefly, 13 control and 14 trained animals were studied in a total of three separate experiments. Siphon withdrawal times were significantly greater than their pretraining scores. The middle portion of the left half of the abdominal ganglion, which contains the siphon sensory neurons as well as some interneurons and motor neurons, was homogenized and incubated with 1 μM [^{32}P]-8-N$_3$cAMP (ICN) followed by exposure to ultraviolet light. After photolysis, proteins in the samples were separated by SDS-PAGE and detected by autoradiography. Radiolabeled proteins were quantified by densitometric scanning. Values were normalized to the amount of protein applied. Control experiments with added [^{32}P]-8-N$_3$cAMP showed the cAMP bound to R subunits exchanges completely under the conditions used. The [^{32}P]-8-N$_3$cAMP labels R subunits in *Aplysia* [as in other animals (Rangel-Aldao *et al.*, 1979; Kerlavage and Taylor, 1982; Walter *et al.*, 1979; Bubis and Taylor, 1985)] with a stoichiometry of 1 : 1. [From Greenberg *et al.* (1987b).]

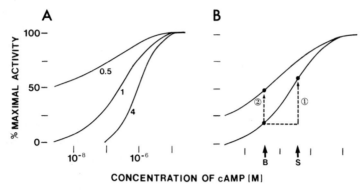

CONCENTRATION OF cAMP (M)

Figure 2.
Model for the effect of short-term and long-term training on phosphorylation by the C subunit. (A) Each curve is designated according to the stoichiometric ration of R-to-C subunit that it represents. The curves showing 4 : 1 and 1 : 1 ratios are drawn from published results (Schwechheimer and Hofmann, 1977); the other is calculated assuming that catalytic activity is proportional to the amount of C subunits not associated with R. (B) Curves for the 1 : 1 and 0.75 : 1 ratios are used to illustrate the effect of a 25% loss of R. We have not yet determined the actual effects, which would depend on the different affinities of the cAMP-binding sites of the various R subunits (Greenberg et al., 1987a) as well as on the activity of any endogenous kinase inhibitors. [From Greenberg et al. (1987b). Reprinted by permission from Nature **329**, 62–65. Copyright © 1987 Macmillan Journals Limited.]

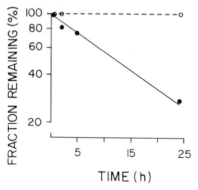

TIME (h)

Figure 3.
Time course of loss of regulatory subunit in CPT-cAMP-treated synaptosomes. Synaptosome fractions prepared according to Chin et al. (1989) were incubated in the presence (closed circles, solid line) or absence (open circles, dashed line) of CPT-cAMP for the time indicated, then washed, photolabeled, electrophoresed, and quantitated (Greenberg et al., 1987b). The data shown represent the sum of all three molecular-weight classes of regulatory subunit. Results are calculated as the amount of R remaining (amount prior to incubation set at 100%) and drawn on a logarithmic scale.

Proteolysis has frequently figured in explanations of memory and other forms of cellular regulation (Lynch and Baudry, 1984; Beer et al., 1984; Baldassare et al., 1985; Melloni et al., 1986). These explanations make use of Ca^{2+}-dependent neutral proteases that are abundant in neurons. Our results suggest that cAMP-dependent loss of regulatory subunits can occur within the cell by a mechanism that does not involve Ca^{2+}-dependent proteases, however, although it is possible that elevated intracellular Ca^{2+} might potentiate the effect of cAMP (Fig. 4, compare lanes 2 and 4).

We propose that the elevation of cAMP produced in sensory neurons by long-term training (Bernier et al., 1982) promotes the proteolysis of regulatory subunits, a posttranslational mechanism. Loss of R subunits need not require protein synthesis, since it occurs in synaptosomes that

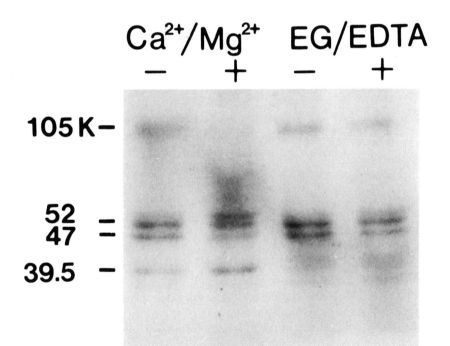

Figure 4.
Loss of regulatory subunit in synaptosomes made permeable with saponin. Synaptosomal pellets were permeabilized by resuspension in 5 μl 0.2% saponin (Fisher), 5 mM EGTA, 5 mM EDTA, and 100 mM Tris-HCl (pH 8.0), and incubated either with ($+$) or without ($-$) 2 μM [^{32}P]-8-N$_3$cAMP for 2 hr. In the left-hand pair of lanes, EDTA and EGTA in the incubation buffer were replaced with 1 mM CaCl$_2$ and 1 mM MgCl$_2$. Samples were photolabeled at a final concentration of 2 μM [^{32}P]-8-N$_3$cAMP. In addition to the three classes of intact regulatory subunits, a distinct proteolytic fragment is indicated in the left-hand pair of lanes at M_r 39,500. (A band appearing at M_r 57,000 in the second lane from the left is artifactual; its labeling is undiminished by adding an excess of cAMP.)

do not make protein. Crick (1984), Lisman (1985), and Miller and Kennedy (1986) have suggested that specific stimulus-induced posttranslational modifications of a protein kinase molecule could result in prolonged or even permanent memory without changes in gene expression. We have previously reviewed how specific proteolysis, autophosphorylation, and changes in subcellular distribution can affect the three major multifunctional protein kinases (Schwartz and Greenberg, 1987). These posttranslational modifications, produced through receptor-mediated mobilization or synthesis of second messenger, can prolong the action of a kinase. As with the degradation of R that we find with the cAMP-dependent protein kinase described above, this class of modification renders the enzyme less dependent on the presence of the original stimulating second messenger; in the limit, the modified kinase can become fully autonomous. As a consequence of being modified, the altered enzyme continues to phosphorylate protein substrates even when the concentration of stimulating second messenger falls back to basal levels. The regulation of the cAMP-dependent protein kinase in long-term trained sensory neurons appears to be another example of this family of posttranslational control mechanisms.

V. Role of Synthesizing New Proteins for Long-Term Memory: The Mechanism behind the Other Mechanisms?

Protein synthesis has convincingly been shown not to be required for short-term forms of synaptic plasticity (in *Aplysia*) (Schwartz *et al.*, 1971; reviewed by Goelet *et al.*, 1986). This lack of dependence was to be expected, since the biochemical mechanisms underlying these forms have been found to involve transient, posttranslational modifications of existing proteins. To the contrary, common sense and many highly suggestive but still inconclusive experiments indicate that synthesis of new proteins is obligatory for retention of memories. In the instance of long-term sensitization of the gill- and siphon-withdrawal reflex in *Aplysia*, two sets of experiments are particularly indicative. Bailey and Chen (1983, 1986), using serial reconstruction of identified sensory neurons in the abdominal ganglion, found that long-term training resulted in an increase in the number, size, and vesicle content of varicosities. These observations show that the training produces structural changes at sensory neuron synapses, and changes in structure suggest changes in protein synthesis. The second set of experiments was performed on cultured sensory and motor neurons, which establish synaptic contact. Montarolo *et al.* (1986) found that five applications of the facilitatory transmitter, serotonin, over a period of 90 min resulted in long-term facilitation that lasted longer than 24 hr. Inhibition of protein and messenger RNA synthesis blocked the acquisition of the long-term facilitation. The requirement that protein must be synthesized in order to establish long-term memory, suggested by these experiments, need not be inconsistent with the posttranslational mechanisms that we describe.

We suggest that a posttranslational proteolytic mechanism that results in a persistently active protein kinase operates during the period intermediate between the dissipation of short-lived second messengers and the expression of new proteins and their distribution to synaptic endings. Gene induction and axonal transport are relatively slow. If, as behavioral and neurophysiological studies suggest (Montarolo *et al.*, 1986; Frost *et al.*, 1985; Scholz and Byrne, 1987; Dale *et al.*, 1986), short-term and long-term sensitization are continuous, there must be a distinct intermediate molecular mechanism for enhancing release of transmitter before the postulated new gene products arrive from the cell body (Schwartz and Greenberg, 1987). The cAMP-dependent proteolysis of R subunits at synapses is a molecular process that could underlie sensitization long after cAMP has returned to basal concentrations.

Short-term, intermediate, and long-term memory may all be produced by the same final biochemical process: protein phosphorylation catalyzed by the cAMP-dependent protein kinase. How long the memory lasts, however, would be governed by a cascade of mechanisms: persistence for intermediate time periods, by posttranslational modifications; kinase activity that endures for longer periods might depend on formation of new protein. The duration of the memory might be sustained in the long term if the altered subunit ratio becomes dependent on newly induced gene products arriving at the nerve terminals. What sort of new protein might be needed to maintain the decreased R-to-C ratio? The new protein might be a specific protease (DeLotto and Spierer, 1986), an isoform of regulatory subunit more susceptible to cleavage by existing proteases (Rogers *et al.*, 1986), or a DNA-binding protein (Goelet *et al.*, 1986) that represses the gene expression of R.

VI. Turtles All the Way Down: An Indian Story

Can memory be understood in molecular terms? Only if the biochemical reactions are arranged in some functional order. Will the ordered arrangement of mechanisms lead to an ultimate understanding of a phenomenon as complex as memory? Clifford Geertz (1973) tells the following enlightening story:

There is an Indian story—at least I heard it as an Indian story—
about an Englishman who, having been told that the world rested on a
platform which rested on the back of an elephant which rested in turn on

the back of a turtle, asked . . . what did the turtle rest on? "Another turtle." And that turtle? "Ah, Sahib, after that it's turtles all the way down."

Acknowledgments

We thank Hagan Bayley for his helpful and critical discussion. Steven Greenberg was supported by National Institutes of Health Training Grant GM07367.

References

Bailey, C. H., and Chen, M. (1983). *Science* **220**, 91–93.

Bailey, C. H., and Chen, M. (1986). *Soc. Neurosci. Abstr.* **12**, 860.

Baldassare, J. J., Bakshian, S., Knipp, M. A., and Fisher, G. T. (1985). *J. Biol. Chem.* **260**, 10531–10535.

Beer, D. G., Butley, M. S., and Malkinson, A. M. (1984). *Arch. Biochem. Biophys.* **228**, 207–219.

Bernier, L., Castellucci, V. F., Kandel, E. R., and Schwartz, J. H. (1982). *J. Neurosci.* **2**, 1682–1691.

Bubis, J., and Taylor, S. S. (1985). *Biochemistry* **24**, 2163–2170.

Byrne, J. H. (1987). *Physiol. Rev.* **67**, 329–439.

Castellucci, V. F., Kandel, E. R., Schwartz, J. H., Wilson, F. D., Nairn, A. C., and Greengard, P. (1980). *Proc. Natl. Acad. Sci. U.S.A.* **77**, 7492–7496.

Castellucci, V. F., Nairn, A., Greengard, P., Schwartz, J. H., and Kandel, E. R. (1982). *J. Neurosci.* **2**, 1673–1681.

Chin, G. J., Shapiro, E., Vogel, S. S., and Schwartz, J. H. (1989). *J. Neurosci.* (in press).

Corbin, J. D., Sugden, P. H., West, L., Flockhart, D. A., Lincoln, T. M., and McCarthy, D. (1978). *J. Biol. Chem.* **253**, 3997–4003.

Crick, F. (1984). *Nature (London)* **312**, 101.

Dale, N., Kandel, E. R., and Schacher, S. (1986). *Soc. Neurosci. Abstr.* **12**, 1339.

DeLotto, R., and Spierer, P. (1986). *Nature (London)* **323**, 688–692.

Eppler, C. M., Palazzolo, M. J., and Schwartz, J. H. (1982). *J. Neurosci.* **2**, 1692–1704.

Eppler, C. M., Bayley, H., Greenberg, S. M., and Schwartz, J. H. (1986). *J. Cell Biol.* **102**, 320–321.

Frost, W. N., Castellucci, V. F., Hawkins, R. D., and Kandel, E. R. (1985). *Proc. Natl. Acad. Sci. U.S.A.* **82**, 8266–8269.

Geertz, C. (1973). "The Interpretation of Cultures: Selected Essays," pp. 28–29. Basic Books, New York.

Goelet, P., Castellucci, V. F., Schacher, S., and Kandel, E. R. (1986). *Nature (London)* **322**, 419–422.

Greenberg, S. M., Bernier, L., and Schwartz, J. H. (1987a). *J. Neurosci.* **7**, 291–301.

Greenberg, S. M., Castellucci, V. F., Bayley, H., and Schwartz, J. H. (1987b). *Nature (London)* **329**, 62–65.

Kandel, E. R., and Schwartz, J. H. (1982). *Science* **218**, 433–443.

Kerlavage, A. R., and Taylor, S. S. (1982). *J. Biol. Chem.* **257**, 1749–1754.

Klein, M., and Kandel, E. R. (1980). *Proc. Natl. Acad. Sci. U.S.A.* **77**, 6912–6916.

Lisman, J. E. (1985). *Proc. Natl. Acad. Sci. U.S.A.* **82**, 3055–3057.

Lynch, G., and Baudry, M. (1984). *Science* **224**, 1057–1063.

Melloni, E., Pontremoli, S., Michetti, M., Sacco, O., Spartore, B., and Horrecker, B. L. (1986). *J. Biol. Chem.* **261**, 4101–4105.

Miller, S. G., and Kennedy, M. B. (1986). *Cell (Cambridge, Mass.)* **44**, 861–870.

Montarolo, P. G., Goelet, P., Castellucci, V. F., Morgan, J., Kandel, E. R., and Schacher, S. (1986). *Science* **234**, 1249–1254.

Potter, R. L., and Taylor, S. S. (1980). *J. Biol. Chem.* **255**, 9706–9712.

Rangel-Aldao, R., Kupiec, J. W., and Rosen, O. M. (1979). *J. Biol. Chem.* **254**, 2499–2508.

Rogers, S., Wills, R., and Rechsteiner, M. (1986). *Science* **234**, 364–368.

Scholz, K. P., and Byrne, J. H. (1987). *Science* **235**, 685–687.

Schwartz, J. H., and Greenberg, S. M. (1987). *Annu. Rev. Neurosci.* **10**, 459–476.

Schwartz, J. H., Castellucci, V. F., and Kandel, E. R. (1971). *J. Neurophysiol.* **34**, 939–953.

Schwechheimer, K., and Hofmann, F. (1977). *J. Biol. Chem.* **252**, 7690–7696.

Steinberg, R. A., and Agard, D. A. (1981). *J. Biol. Chem.* **256**, 10731–10734.

Uhler, M. D., and McKnight, G. S. (1987). *J. Biol. Chem.* **262**, 15202–15207.

Walter, U., Costa, M. R. C., Breakefield, X. O., and Greengard, P. (1979). *Proc. Natl. Acad. Sci. U.S.A.* **76**, 3251–3255.

Weber, W., and Hilz, H. (1979). *Biochem. Biophys. Res. Commun.* **90**, 1073–1081.

Weiss, K. R., Mandelbaum, D. E., Schonberg, M., and Kupfermann, I. (1979). *J. Neurophysiol.* **42**, 791–803.

4

Mathematical Model of Cellular and Molecular Processes Contributing to Associative and Nonassociative Learning in *Aplysia*

John H. Byrne and Kevin J. Gingrich

I. Introduction

From empirical studies on simple forms of learning performed in a variety of vertebrate and invertebrate model systems, at least four general principles are emerging (for review, see Byrne, 1987). First, learning involves changes in existing neural circuits. Second, there is not just a single locus for learning, since expression of learned behavior can be at the sensory, interneuronal, or motor levels. Third, plasticity at one site or locus involves multiple subcellular processes that act in a coordinated way to alter the effectiveness of synaptic connections. Fourth, learning involves the activation of second-messenger systems.

Given this diversity of possible loci and processes, a fundamental question is to what extent a proposed collection of loci and mechanisms can quantitatively account for a particular behavior. One way of addressing this issue is to formulate mathematical descriptions of the proposed processes, mechanisms, and their interactions and examine whether a simulation of the resultant model can account for features of the behavior. Modeling and simulation studies have additional benefits as they provide a concise formulation of current hypotheses regarding complex interactions between multiple subcellular systems and processes. This approach facilitates understanding of the consequences of those interactions. In addition, models make predictions that can be subsequently tested at the cellular and behavioral level, which helps to identify critical parameters that warrant experimental examination in greater detail. Finally, models of simple forms of learning at the cellular level can be used as "building blocks" for incorporation into neural networks.

NEURAL MODELS OF PLASTICITY

This synthetic and more theoretical approach provides the opportunity to examine the ability of such networks to exhibit complex features of learning and computational capabilities. In this chapter we review some of our attempts to mathematically model the cellular and subcellular processes contributing to nonassociative and associative learning in the marine mollusc *Aplysia*. Chapter 5 (this volume) describes some of the consequences of incorporating single-cell models into a network consisting of multiple plastic cells.

Recent studies on *Aplysia* indicate that a cellular mechanism called activity-dependent neuromodulation (Hawkins *et al.*, 1983; Walters and Byrne, 1983a) may contribute to classical conditioning observed on a behavioral level (Carew *et al.*, 1983; Hawkins *et al.*, 1986). A proposed general cellular scheme of activity-dependent neuromodulation is illustrated in Fig. 1A. Two sensory neurons (1 and 2) make weak subthreshold connections to a response system (e.g., a motor neuron). Delivering a reinforcing or unconditioned stimulus (US) alone has two effects. First, the US activates the response system and produces the unconditioned response (UR). Second, the US activates a diffuse modulatory system that nonspecifically enhances transmitter release from all the sensory neurons. This nonspecific enhancement contributes to sensitization, an example of nonassociative learning. Temporal specificity, characteristic of associative learning, occurs when there is pairing of the CS, spike activity in one of the sensory neurons (sensory neuron 1), with the US, causing a selective amplification of the modulatory effects in that specific sensory neuron (Hawkins *et al.*, 1983; Walters and Byrne, 1983a). Unpaired activity does not amplify the effects of the US in sensory neuron 2. The amplification of the modulatory effects in the paired sensory neuron leads to an enhancement of the ability of that sensory neuron to activate the response system and produce the conditioned response (CR).

Experimental analyses of sensitization of defensive reflexes in *Aplysia* have shown that the neuromodulator released by the reinforcing stimulus acts, at least in part, by reducing potassium currents in the sensory neurons. Consequently, action potentials elicited after the reinforcing stimulus are broader (due to less repolarizing K^+ current) causing an enhanced influx of Ca^{2+} (Klein and Kandel, 1978, 1980; for reviews, see Byrne, 1985, 1987; Kandel and Schwartz, 1982). Enhanced influx of Ca^{2+} triggers greater release of transmitter from the sensory neurons, which causes increased activation of motor neurons and thus sensitization of the reflex. The effects of the natural modulatory transmitter released by sensitizing stimuli (Bernier *et al.*, 1982; Ocorr *et al.*, 1986) can be mimicked by application of serotonin (5-HT) (Bernier *et al.*, 1982; Brunelli *et al.*, 1976). This agent exerts its effects on action potential duration and transmitter release through changes in the level of the intracellular second messenger cAMP (Bernier *et al.*, 1982; Ocorr and Byrne, 1985). In addition to enhancing influx of Ca^{2+}, it has also been suggested that the neuromodulator released by the reinforcing stimulus leads to mobilization of transmitter in the sensory neurons (Gingrich and Byrne, 1984, 1985, 1987; see also Hochner *et al.*, 1986). Empirical evidence indicates that pairing specificity is due to an enhancement of cAMP levels beyond that produced by the modulator alone (Abrams *et al.*, 1984; Ocorr *et al.*, 1983, 1985). Furthermore, it appears that influx of Ca^{2+} associated with the CS (spike activity) amplifies the US-mediated modulatory effect (Abrams *et al.*, 1983) by interacting with a Ca^{2+}-sensitive component of the adenylate cyclase (Abrams *et al.*, 1985).

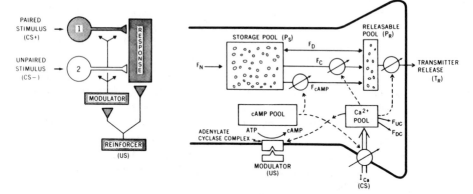

Figure 1.

Cellular models for associative learning. (A) Network model. Two sensory neurons (1 and 2) make subthreshold connections to a response system. Reinforcing stimuli (US) cause direct activation of response system and also activate a diffuse modulatory system. Pairing of CS and US (indicated by stippling) enhances the modulatory effects over that of unpaired stimulation. (B) Single-cell model. The CS (spike activity) increases the level of intracellular Ca^{2+}, which triggers transmitter release (T_R) and mobilization of transmitter (F_C) from a storage pool (P_S) to a releasable pool (P_R), and primes the adenylate cyclase complex. The Ca^{2+} is removed from the Ca^{2+} pool by F_{UC}, active uptake, and by F_{DC}, passive diffusion. The term F_D represents diffusion of vesicles between the storage and releasable pools. The US activates adenylate cyclase to increase cAMP levels that enhance mobilization of transmitter (F_{cAMP}) and increase Ca^{2+} influx (I_{Ca}). Increased Ca^{2+} influx is achieved indirectly through changes in duration of the action potential. Association of CS and US occurs when Ca^{2+} levels are high at the time of the US. Paired application of the CS and US results in increased levels of cAMP due to Ca^{2+} priming of the adenylate cyclase complex. The elevated cAMP triggers increased mobilization of transmitter and subsequent enhanced Ca^{2+} influx and transmitter release with the next test stimulus. The circles with arrows through their center represent elements of the model which are positively modulated by other variables. [Modified from Gingrich and Byrne (1987).]

In addition to the nonassociative neuronal modifications contributing to sensitization and the associative neuronal modifications contributing to classical conditioning, which occur in the sensory neurons (see above), the connections between the sensory neurons and their follower cells also exhibit a number of nonassociative plastic properties including synaptic depression and posttetanic potentiation.

II. Subcellular Model for Associative and Nonassociative Learning

In order to account for many of the features of synaptic plasticity exhibited by the sensory neurons, we found it necessary to construct a rather complex model of the sensory neuron. This model includes descriptions of a variety of subcellular processes. Details of the equations are described in Gingrich and Byrne (1985, 1987). A general overview is presented below.

The approach was to begin with generally accepted principles of neuronal function, transform these into mathematical formalisms, and, where possible, determine the values of constants using available experimental data. Components of the model were then linked together as a system of equations to describe the overall function of a sensory neuron. Figure 1B illustrates some of the major components of the model and their interactions. The model contains equations describing two pools of transmitter, a readily releasable pool (P_R) and a storage pool (P_S). Vesicles move from one pool to the other via three fluxes, one driven by diffusion (F_D), another driven by Ca^{2+} (F_C), and the third driven by levels of cAMP (F_{cAMP}). There are also equations describing the regulation of the levels of cAMP and Ca^{2+}. Action potentials lead to influx of Ca^{2+} (I_{Ca}), release of transmitter (T_R), and accumulation of Ca^{2+}. Application of the US leads to increased synthesis of cAMP, which leads to mobilization of transmitter (F_{cAMP}) and modulation of the spike parameters such that subsequent action potentials are broader, thus allowing for greater influx of Ca^{2+} and enhanced release of transmitter. When the CS (a burst of spikes) preceeds the US, the elevated levels of Ca^{2+} regulate the adenylate cyclase complex such that when a subsequent US is delivered, there is greater synthesis of cAMP.

A. Ca^{2+} Channel and Regulation of the Levels of Ca^{2+}

The pool of Ca^{2+} in Fig. 1B actually contains two volumes called the submembrane and interior compartments. The submembrane compartment represents the fraction of the cytosol lining the membrane with a thickness of a few vesicle diameters. The interior compartment represents the larger fraction of the cytosol interior to the submembrane compartment, which contains cellular organelles and systems that affect intracellular Ca^{2+}. During an action potential, Ca^{2+} (I_{Ca}) enters the submembrane compartment through voltage-dependent Ca^{2+} channels and rapidly diffuses into the larger interior compartment. Here the processes responsible for Ca^{2+} uptake and buffering exert their effect. These processes are represented as fluxes that remove Ca^{2+} from the interior compartment in accordance with two equations. One equation represents a flux (F_{UC}) that removes Ca^{2+} from the interior compartment by active processes in organelles such as the endoplasmic reticulum. A second equation represents removal of Ca^{2+} from the interior compartment due to diffusion (F_{DC}).

The concentration of Ca^{2+} (C_{Ca}) is determined by solving the differential equation

$$(1) \quad \frac{dC_{Ca}}{dt} = (I_{Ca} - F_{UC} - F_{DC})(1/V_C)$$

where I_{Ca} is the membrane Ca^{2+} current, F_{UC} the Ca^{2+} removed by active processes, F_{DC} the Ca^{2+} removed by diffusion, and V_C the volume of the interior compartment.

In the model, the duration of the action potential is modulated as a function of cAMP levels. While the details of this relationship are not fully understood, we assume, as a first approximation, that spike duration is a linear function of the concentration of cAMP:

$$(2) \quad \text{Spike duration} = 0.003 + K_{DC} \times C_{cAMP} \quad (\text{sec})$$

where K_{DC} is a constant and C_{cAMP} is the concentration of cAMP. The unmodified spike duration is 3 msec.

B. Regulation of cAMP

The model also includes equations describing the concentration of cAMP and its effects on the release of transmitter from the sensory neuron. The cAMP cascade is a sequence of multiple events, which includes the binding of a modulatory transmitter such as 5-HT to receptors, activation and decay of the activity of adenylate cyclase, synthesis and hydrolysis of cAMP, and protein phosphorylation and dephosphorylation. While many steps are involved, some evidence indicates that the rate-limiting step is the decay of adenylate cyclase activity (Castellucci et al., 1982; Schwartz et al., 1983). As a first approximation, we therefore assumed that the concentration of cAMP (C_{cAMP}) is described by a single lumped-parameter dynamic equation. We simulated the effects of the CS (a burst of spikes) on the level of cAMP by making the concentration of cAMP dependent on the intracellular concentration of calcium (C_{Ca}). During the US

(3) $\dfrac{dC_{cAMP}}{dt} = (-C_{cAMP}/\tau_{cAMP}) + K_{SC} + (K_{EC}C_{Ca}).$

Where τ_{cAMP} is the overall time constant for the regulation of cAMP levels (primarily decay of the activity of adenylate cyclase), K_{SC} is a constant that describes the degree of activation of the cAMP cascade in the presence of resting levels of intracellular Ca^{2+} during application of the US, K_{EC} is a constant that describes the additional activation of the cAMP cascade in the presence of intracellular Ca^{2+} (C_{Ca}) beyond resting level, and C_{Ca} represents the Ca^{2+} concentration of the interior compartment [see Eq. (1)]. The first term in Eq. (3) describes the decay of cAMP levels, while the remaining terms describe the activation of the adenylate cyclase during application of the US. In the absence of the US,

(4) $\dfrac{dC_{cAMP}}{dt} = (-C_{cAMP}/\tau_{cAMP})$

A simplifying assumption is that intracellular Ca^{2+} does not by itself lead to significant stimulation of adenylate cyclase (Ocorr et al., 1985). Thus, Eq. (4) also applies when the level of intracellular Ca^{2+} is altered as a result of test stimuli or CS presentations in the absence of the US. Mechanisms for intermediate and long-term memory (see Chapter 3, this volume) have not been included in the model.

C. Release, Storage, and Mobilization of Transmitter

The releasable pool (P_R) contains vesicles that are in close proximity to release sites where Ca^{2+} promotes vesicle fusion and exocytosis of transmitter (transmitter release, T_R). As a consequence of release this pool is depleted, and in order to offset depletion there is delivery of transmitter to the depleted releasable pool, a process that is referred to as mobilization.

Mobilization may occur by the synthesis or translocation of transmitter. It seems likely that these diverse processes may have different kinetics and be regulated by multiple biochemical mechanisms. Given that mobilization occurs, it is reasonable to assume that a storage pool (P_S) acts as a reservoir from which vesicles can be removed to replenish the releasable pool. In our model, the storage pool also undergoes depletion, which is replenished slowly by synthesis of new vesicles or transport from other storage pools (flux F_N in Fig. 1B).

1. Transmitter Release and Determination of Excitatory Postsynaptic Potentials

The influx of Ca^{2+} (I_{Ca}) during an action potential causes the release of transmitter (T_R). We assume that release is a function of the product of number of vesicles available for release and the submembrane concentration of Ca^{2+}. An equation that reflects these principles is

$$(5) \quad T_R = N_R(I_{Ca}K_R)$$

where T_R is the instantaneous rate of release, N_R the number of vesicles in the releasable pool, and K_R a constant. The product of I_{Ca} and K_R is proportional to the Ca^{2+} concentration in the submembrane compartment (see above). Therefore, the release of transmitter is a function of the number of vesicles in close proximity to release sites (the releasable pool) and the concentration of Ca^{2+}.

At present there is little information concerning the relationship between transmitter release and the subsequent potential that is produced in the postsynaptic neuron. We assume that the excitatory postsynaptic potential (EPSP) is proportional to the total amount of transmitter that is released during an action potential in the sensory neuron. The differential equation describing this relationship is

$$(6) \quad \frac{d(EPSP)}{dt} = T_R$$

where T_R is determined from Eq. (5).

2. Other Functions

The term F_D is a flux of vesicles due to a difference in the concentration of vesicles in the storage pool and releasable pool. The magnitude of this current is a linear function of the concentration difference.

The Ca^{2+}-mediated mobilization of vesicles from the storage to the releasable pool is represented by F_C. The term F_C actually represents two Ca^{2+}-dependent fluxes, one that is fast in its response to changes in intracellular Ca^{2+} concentration and a second that is slower (see Gingrich and Byrne, 1985, for details).

The term F_N represents the delivery of vesicles to the storage pool from unmodeled sources and results from transport from other storage pools or synthesis triggered by depletion of the storage pool. F_N replenishes the storage pool slowly because it is small relative to the volume of the pool. Its magnitude is proportional to the difference between the initial and instantaneous concentration of vesicles in the storage pool.

In the model, US-stimulated increases in the level of cAMP modulate transmitter release in two ways. First, cAMP closes resting K^+ channels (Klein et al., 1982; Shuster et al., 1985; Siegelbaum et al., 1982), which results in spike broadening and prolonged influx of Ca^{2+} with subsequent action potentials [see above and Eq. (2)]. Second, cAMP enhances mobilization of vesicles (F_{cAMP}) from the storage pool to the releasable pool (Gingrich and Byrne, 1984, 1985, 1987; see also Hochner *et al.*, 1986):

$$(7) \quad F_{cAMP} = KC_S C_{cAMP}$$

where K is a constant, C_S represents the concentration of vesicles in the storage pool, and C_{cAMP} is the concentration of cAMP. A role for mobilization of transmitter during synaptic facilitation is suggested by recent experimental work (see below).

With the individual fluxes specified, it is possible to write differential equations describing the concentration of vesicles in both pools. For the storage pool (P_S), the differential equation is

$$(8) \quad \frac{dC_S}{dt} = (F_N - F_C - F_{cAMP} - F_D)(1/V_S)$$

where C_S is the concentration of vesicles in P_S and V_S is the volume of P_S.

For the releasable pool (P_R), the differential equation is

$$(9) \quad \frac{dC_R}{dt} = (F_{cAMP} + F_C + F_D - T_R)(1/V_R)$$

where C_R is the concentration of vesicles in P_R and V_R is the volume of P_R.

The parameters in the various equations were adjusted by a combination of nonlinear parameter estimation and by trial and error to obtain an optimal fit to some of the available experimental data.

III. Simulation and Predictions of the Model

The model not only simulated the data on which it was based but also qualitatively predicted other features of nonassociative plasticity that it was not designed to fit. These included features of synaptic depression with high and low levels of transmitter release, posttetanic potentiation (PTP), a steep relationship between action potential duration and transmitter release, and enhanced release produced by broadening the sensory neuron action potential (presynaptic facilitation) (Gingrich and Byrne, 1985). In the model, synaptic depression is due primarily to depletion of the readily releasable pool. PTP is due to enhanced Ca^{2+} influx with the tetanus triggering mobilization of transmitter from the storage pool to the releasable pool. Presynaptic facilitation is due to the fact that broadened spikes lead to more Ca^{2+} influx and greater release of transmitter from the releasable pool.

Figure 2 illustrates the ability of the model to simulate the empirical data on associative neuronal plasticity. Figure 2A shows the results of a previous experimental analysis (Walters and Byrne, 1983a) and Fig. 2B shows the results of the computer simulation of the model. In both the experimental and simulation study a three-phase test–train–test procedure was utilized. The first test phase consisted of initiating single action potentials in a sensory neuron at 5-min intervals and monitoring the baseline EPSP (B in Fig. 2A and B). Three training conditions were simulated: paired CS and US with the CS occurring 600 msec before the US (CS +), explicitly unpaired CS and US with the CS occurring 2 min after the US (CS −), and presentation of the US alone (SENS). The CS was simulated with a 400-msec train (25 Hz) of spikes in the sensory neuron, and the US was applied for 200 msec. The training phase was repeated five times at 5-min intervals. During the training phase the single test stimuli were still delivered but 4 min after the US. After the training phase, the delivery of single test action potentials was continued to

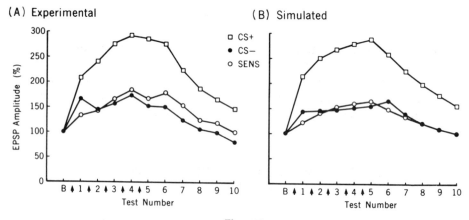

Figure 2.
Associative modifications of transmitter release. (A) Experimental data, using a three-phase test–train–test procedure for paired training (CS +, CS precedes US by 600 msec), explicitly unpaired training (CS −, CS follows US by 2 min), and US alone (SENS) training. The B on the abscissa is the baseline EPSP evoked in a motor neuron in response to a test stimulus (single action potential in a sensory neuron). Training trials occur between test stimuli B and 5 at the arrows. EPSPs produced by the training trials are not shown. Test numbers 5–10 represent the posttraining period. Paired training (CS +) results in significant enhancement of the test EPSP compared to unpaired (CS −) and US alone (SENS) training. (B) Simulation of experimental data. Simulation captures salient qualities of empirical data of part (A). [From Gingrich and Byrne (1987).]

monitor the effectiveness of conditioning. Each of the conditioning procedures (CS+, CS−, SENS) produced enhancement of transmitter release. The CS+ group, however, is enhanced beyond that of the CS− and SENS groups, while there is little difference between the CS− and SENS groups (Fig. 2).

Changes in some of the variables of the model in response to paired and explicitly unpaired presentations of the CS and US for the first training trial are illustrated in Fig. 3. Two test pulses, one prior to pairing (at 1440 sec) and one after pairing (at 1740 sec), are also illustrated. Thus,

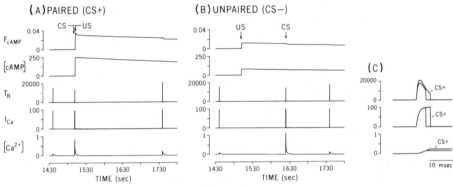

Figure 3.

Model variables during paired and unpaired stimulation. The term F_{cAMP} is cAMP-mediated mobilization of transmitter, [cAMP] is the concentration of cAMP, T_R is the transmitter release, I_{Ca} is the influx of Ca^{2+}, and $[Ca^{2+}]$ is the concentration of Ca^{2+}. (A) Paired stimulation. Prior to pairing spike activity with the US, five test stimuli (single 3-msec spikes) at 5-min intervals were generated in order to obtain stable responses. The response at 1440 sec was the fifth baseline response. At 60 sec after the fifth control response the CS (a train of action potentials) was applied (first arrow). This was followed 600 msec later by application of the US (second arrow). The resultant elevation of Ca^{2+} levels by the CS at the time of the US caused increased synthesis of cAMP, which resulted in increased mobilization (F_{cAMP}) and spike widening. (B) Unpaired stimulation. The CS was delivered 120 sec after the US. cAMP levels are not enhanced by Ca^{2+}, and they are smaller than the levels achieved with the paired stimulation shown in (A). Consequently, the enhancement of transmitter release (T_R) (at 1740 sec) is less than that resulting from paired presentations of the CS and US. Note that for both (A) and (B) the peak of T_R is less during the CS than for the preceding test stimuli at 1440 sec, which results from depletion of transmitter by the test stimulus at the time of the CS. For the case of CS−, there is greater Ca^{2+} influx and rise of $[Ca^{2+}]$ with the first CS because of cAMP-mediated broadening of spikes, which was induced by the preceding US. (C) Superimposed responses from parts A and B to test stimuli at 1740 sec are displayed on an expanded time base. Transmitter release is greater (increased magnitude and duration of T_R) for paired training due to enhanced mobilization and spike broadening. [Modified from Gingrich and Byrne (1987).]

Fig. 3 is a representation in continuous time spanning the first two values of the abscissa (test numbers B and 1) in Fig. 2. Paired presentations of the CS and US (Fig. 3A) lead to greater levels of cAMP than unpaired presentations (Fig. 3B) because the influx of Ca^{2+} preceding the US has amplified the synthesis of cAMP. Increased levels of cAMP cause greater spike broadening and mobilization of transmitter than that produced by unpaired presentations and thus greater facilitation of transmitter release [compare the transmitter release (T_R) at 1740 sec in Fig. 3C].

As illustrated in Fig. 2, a characteristic of the acquisition phase of the learning is that the amplitude of the EPSPs for the paired group increases as a function of trials and approaches an asymptote at approximately 300% of control. The results of the simulation suggest that the rising phase of the acquisition process is due to increasing levels of cAMP, while the asymptote is a result of the establishment of a steady-state level of cAMP.

A characteristic feature of associative learning is the requirement for a close temporal association between the CS and US for effective conditioning. For conditioning of many simple reflex responses, the optimal interstimulus interval (ISI) is generally about 400 msec. Longer ISIs are less effective and presentations of the CS after the US (backward conditioning) are generally ineffective. We were therefore interested in determining whether the model could demonstrate a dependence on ISI similar to that observed in conditioning studies in *Aplysia* and other animals (Clark, 1984; Hawkins *et al.*, 1986; Hull, 1943, 1952; Smith *et al.*, 1969). Figure 4 illustrates the results. An ISI of 170 msec is optimal, while longer or shorter ISIs are less effective. The optimal ISI is affected by both changes in spike frequency and duration of the CS and the duration of the US. Backward conditioning (negative ISIs) is ineffective. The ISI function in the model is a direct consequence of the kinetics of the buffering of intracellular Ca^{2+}. When the ISI is short, high levels of Ca^{2+} are present at the time of the US and therefore the CS-mediated amplification of the effects of the US are greatest. As the interval between the CS and US increases, Ca^{2+} levels are buffered; consequently with longer ISIs, there is less amplification of the effects of the US. Thus, the elevation of intracellular Ca^{2+} levels produced by the CS serves as a "trace" that becomes associated with a closely paired US.

IV. Discussion

We have used formalisms to describe complex processes such as the regulation of cAMP levels, spike broadening, and mobilization of transmitter that are necessarily simplifications of the actual processes. While the descriptions of these subcellular processes are rather coarse, we believe that these descriptions provide for a more substantial biological underpinning for models of learning than has heretofore been feasible (Gluck and Thompson, 1987; Hawkins and Kandel, 1984; Sutton and Barto, 1981).

The model demonstrates that associative learning at the single-cell level can be produced by a simple elaboration of mechanisms that contribute to nonassociative learning (sensitization). The fact that this particular mathematical formulation leads to a fit of empirical data it was designed to fit does not validate the model. However, the utility of the model is demonstrated by its predictive value and its ability to account for empirical data not addressed during its construction. For example, recent experimental work (Bailey and Chen, 1988) supports an assumption in the model, the involvement of depletion of neurotransmitter in the plasticity of this synapse.

Additional studies will be necessary to determine the extent to which the proposed processes play a physiological role in synaptic plasticity of the sensory neuron and obtain independent measurements of the parameters. One critical component of the model is the Ca^{2+}-triggered amplification of US-mediated synthesis of cAMP. If Ca^{2+}-dependence is

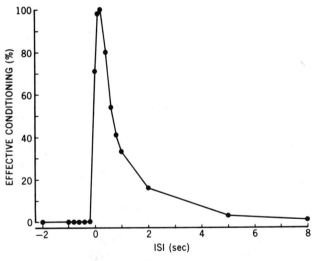

Figure 4.
Interstimulus interval (ISI) function for model. The effective conditioning is the normalized difference between responses to the second test pulse after training in paired (CS+) and explicitly unpaired (CS−) simulations as a function of the time period (ISI) between paired CS and US applications. In this simulation 10 training trials were presented so that the changes in transmitter release reached asymptotic levels. The relationship between the effectiveness of conditioning and the CS–US interval is due to the time course of the accumulation and buffering of Ca^{2+} in the cytoplasm. [From Gingrich and Byrne (1987).]

deleted from the model, the associative effect is abolished. Evidence supporting the interaction of Ca^{2+} with adenylate cyclase is provided by studies of vertebrate neural tissue where a Ca^{2+}/calmodulin-dependent activation of neuotransmitter-stimulated adenylate cyclase has been demonstrated (Brostrom et al., 1978; Gnegy et al., 1984; Gnegy and Treisman, 1981; Malnoe et al., 1983). Recent evidence indicates the presence of a Ca^{2+}-sensitive cyclase in Aplysia as well (Abrams et al., 1985; Schwartz et al., 1983; Weiss and Drummond, 1985). A critical role for Ca^{2+}-stimulated cyclase is also provided by studies of Drosophila, where it has been shown that the particulate adenylate cyclase of a mutant deficient in associative learning exhibits a loss of Ca^{2+}/calmodulin sensitivity (Aceves-Pina et al., 1983; Dudai, 1985; Livingstone, 1985). A major unresolved issue that must be examined, however, is whether the proposed interaction of Ca^{2+}/calmodulin with the adenylate cyclase complex has intrinsic temporal specificity such that increases in levels of Ca^{2+} after modulation by the US (backward conditioning) do not amplify cAMP production. Temporal specificity, if not intrinsic to the cyclase, could be achieved by a second messenger-mediated down-regulation of Ca^{2+}/calmodulin effects. Alternatively, interneurons in the circuit, which inhibit the sensory neurons, may help endow the system with temporal specificity (Cleary and Byrne, 1986; Hawkins et al., 1981; Walters and Byrne, 1983b).

While our mathematical model is capable of predicting some features of associative learning, it cannot predict aspects of associative learning that depend on an interplay of multiple stimuli at different sites or on more than one stimulus modality. This limitation, however, is due to the fact that the model is based only on a single neuron. By incorporating the present single-cell model into a circuit that includes multiple sensory neurons as well as modulatory or facilitatory interneurons, it will be possible to test its ability to predict more complex features of associative learning (see Chapter 5, this volume; Byrne et al., 1988; Gluck and Thompson, 1987; Hawkins and Kandel, 1984; Sutton and Barto, 1981). Indeed, much theoretical work by others has shown that artificial neural networks based on relatively simple learning rules have rather interesting computational properties. An intriguing question that we hope to pursue is, what new properties might emerge as both the learning rules and the circuitry are made more physiological?

Acknowledgments

This research was sponsored by the Air Force Office of Scientific Research, Air Force Systems Command, USAF, under grants AFOSR 84-0213 and 87-0274, and by National Institute of Mental Health Award K02 MH00649.

References

Abrams, T. W., Carew, T. J., Hawkins, R. D., and Kandel, E. R. (1983). *Soc. Neurosci. Abstr.* **9,** 168.

Abrams, T. W., Bernier, L., Hawkins, R. D., and Kandel, E. R. (1984). *Soc. Neurosci. Abstr.* **10,** 269.

Abrams, T. W., Eliot, L., Dudai, Y., and Kandel, E. R. (1985). *Soc. Neurosci. Abstr.* **11,** 797.

Aceves-Pina, E. O., Booker, R., Duerr, J. S., Livingston, M. S., Quinn, W. G., Smith, R. F., Sziber, P. P., Tempel, B. L., and Tully, T. P. (1983). *Cold Spring Harbor Symp. Quant. Biol.* **48,** 831–840.

Bailey, C. H., and Chen, M. (1988). *J. Neurosci.* **8,** 2452–2459.

Bernier, L., Castellucci, V. F., Kandel, E. R., and Schwartz, J. H. (1982). *J. Neurosci.* **2,** 1682–1691.

Brostrom, M. A., Brostrom, C. O., Breckenridge, B. M., and Wolff, D. J. (1978). *Adv. Cyclic Nucleotide Res.* **9,** 85–99.

Brunelli, M., Castellucci, V., and Kandel, E. R. (1976). *Science* **194,** 1178–1181.

Byrne, J. H. (1985). *Trends Neurosci.* **8,** 478–482.

Byrne, J. H. (1987). *Physiol. Rev.* **67,** 329–439.

Byrne, J. H., Buonomano, D., Corros, I., Patel, S., and Baxter, D. A. (1988). *Soc. Neurosci. Abstr.* **14,** 840.

Carew, T. J., Hawkins, R. D., and Kandel, E. R. (1983). *Science* **219,** 397–400.

Castellucci, V. F., Nairn, A., Greengard, P., Schwartz, J. H., and Kandel, E. R. (1982). *J. Neurosci.* **2,** 1673–1681.

Clark, G. A. (1984). *Soc. Neurosci. Abstr.* **10,** 268.

Cleary, L. J., and Byrne, J. H. (1986). *Soc. Neurosci. Abstr.* **12,** 397.

Dudai, Y. (1985). *Trends Neurosci.* **7,** 18–21.

Gingrich, K. J., and Byrne, J. H. (1984). *Soc. Neurosci. Abstr.* **10,** 270.

Gingrich, K. J., and Byrne, J. H. (1985). *J. Neurophysiol.* **53,** 652–669.

Gingrich, K. J., and Byrne, J. H. (1987). *J. Neurophysiol.* **57,** 1705–1715.

Gluck, M. A., and Thompson, R. F. (1987). *Psychol. Rev.* **94,** 176–191.

Gnegy, M. E. and Treisman, G. (1981). *Mol. Pharmacol.* **219,** 256–263.

Gnegy, M. E., Muirhead, N., Roberts-Lewis, J. M., and Treisman, G. (1984). *J. Neurosci.* **4,** 2712–2717.

Hawkins, R. D., and Kandel, E. R. (1984). *Psychol. Rev.* **91,** 375–391.

Hawkins, R. D., Castellucci, V. F., and Kandel, E. R. (1981). *J. Neurophysiol.* **45,** 304–314.

Hawkins, R. D., Abrams, T. W., Carew, T. J., and Kandel, E. R. (1983). *Science* **219,** 400–405.

Hawkins, R. D., Carew, T. J., and Kandel, E. R. (1986). *J. Neurosci.* **6,** 1695–1701.

Hochner, B., Klein, M., Schacher, S., and Kandel, E. R. (1986). *Proc. Natl. Acad. Sci. U.S.A.* **83,** 8794–8798.

Hull, C. L. (1943). "Principles of Behavior." Appleton, New York.

Hull, C. L. (1952). "A Behavior System." Yale Univ. Press, New Haven, Connecticut.

Kandel, E. R., and Schwartz, J. H. (1982). *Science* **218,** 433–443.

Klein, M., and Kandel, E. R. (1978). *Proc. Natl. Acad. Sci. U.S.A.* **75,** 3512–3516.

Klein, M., and Kandel, E. R. (1980). *Proc. Natl. Acad. Sci. U.S.A.* **77,** 6912–6916.

Klein, M., Camardo, J., and Kandel, E. R. (1982). *Proc. Natl. Acad. Sci. U.S.A.* **79,** 5713–5717.

Livingstone, M. S. (1985). *Proc. Natl. Acad. Sci. U.S.A* **82,** 5992–5996.

Malnoe, A., Stein, E. A., and Cox, J. A. (1983). *Neurochem. Int.* **5,** 65–72.

Ocorr, K. A., and Byrne, J. H. (1985). *Neurosci. Lett.* **55,** 113–118.

Ocorr, K. A., Walters, E. T., and Byrne, J. H. (1983). *Soc. Neurosci. Abstr.* **9,** 169.

Ocorr, K. A., Walters, E. T., and Byrne, J. H. (1985). *Proc. Natl. Acad. Sci. U.S.A.* **82,** 2548–2552.

Ocorr, K. A., Tabata, M., and Byrne, J. H. (1986). *Brain Res.* **371**, 190–192.

Schwartz, J. H., Bernier, L., Castellucci, V. F., Plazzolo, M., Saitoh, T., Stapleton, A., and Kandel, E. R. (1983). *Cold Spring Harbor Symp. Quant. Biol.* **48**, 811–819.

Shuster, M. J., Comardo, J. S., Siegelbaum, S. A., and Kandel, E. R. (1985). *Nature (London)* **313**, 392–395.

Siegelbaum, S. A., Camardo, J. S., and Kandel, E. R. (1982). *Nature (London)* **299**, 413–417.

Smith, M. C., Coleman, S. R., and Gormezano, I. (1969). *J. Comp. Physiol. Psychol.* **69**, 226–231.

Sutton, R. S., and Barto, A. G. (1981). *Psychol. Rev.* **88**, 135–170.

Walters, E. T., and Byrne, J. H. (1983a). *Science* **219**, 405–408.

Walters, E. T., and Byrne, J. H. (1983b). *Brain Res.* **280**, 165–168.

Weiss, S., and Drummond, G. I. (1985). *Comp. Biochem. Physiol. B* **80B**, 251–255.

5

A Simple Circuit Model for Higher-Order Features of Classical Conditioning

Robert D. Hawkins

A long-standing issue in psychology is how different forms of learning are related at the mechanistic level. Evidence obtained over the last several years indicates that a mechanism of classical conditioning in *Aplysia* appears to be an elaboration of the mechanism of a simpler form of learning, sensitization (Hawkins *et al.*, 1983; Walters and Byrne, 1983; Abrams *et al.*, 1985). This finding suggests the hypothesis that yet more complex forms of learning may in turn be generated by putting together combinations of the mechanisms of these elementary forms of learning (Hawkins and Kandel, 1984). The higher-order features of classical conditioning, including second-order conditioning, blocking, and the effect of contingency, provide an attractive area in which to investigate this hypothesis, for two reasons. First, these features of conditioning have a cognitive flavor (in the sense that the animal's behavior is thought to depend on a comparison of current sensory input with an internal representation of the world) and may therefore provide a bridge between basic conditioning and more advanced forms of learning (Kamin, 1969; Rescorla, 1978; Wagner, 1978; Mackintosh, 1983; Dickinson, 1980). Second, some of these features of conditioning have been demonstrated in invertebrates, where a cellular analysis of their mechanisms may be feasible (Sahley *et al.*, 1981; Colwill, 1985; Hawkins *et al.*, 1986; Farley, 1987).

In a theoretical paper, Hawkins and Kandel (1984) suggested how several of the higher-order features of conditioning could be accounted for by combinations of the mechanisms of habituation, sensitization, and classical conditioning in the basic neural circuit for the *Aplysia* gill-withdrawal reflex. Since the arguments in that paper were entirely qualitative, however, quantitative modeling seemed desirable. In this chapter, I describe quantitative modeling based on the ideas Kandel and I presented earlier. As in our previous paper, I have restricted myself to cellular processes and circuitry that are known to exist in *Aplysia*, rather than using hypothetical "neuron-like" elements or algebraic learning rules. Although this decision is somewhat arbitrary, I feel that it is important,

73

since the ultimate goal of neuroscientists is to understand how real neurons and circuits generate complex behaviors.

On the cellular level, my model is very similar to the single-cell model for conditioning of Gingrich and Byrne (1987; see also Chapter 4, this volume). Basically, I have attempted to plug a simplified version of Gingrich and Byrne's single-cell model into a very simple neural circuit, to see whether the resulting circuit properties could account for higher-order features of classical conditioning. Unlike Gingrich and Byrne, I have not tried to fit a particular set of empirical data, since some of the features of conditioning addressed have not yet been tested in *Aplysia*. Rather, my goal is to show that these higher-order features of classical conditioning could in principle be generated in the manner I suggest.

I. Behavioral and Cellular Studies of Learning in *Aplysia*

Studies of learning in *Aplysia* have focused on the defensive withdrawal reflexes of the external organs of the mantle cavity. In *Aplysia* and in other mollusks, the mantle cavity, a respiratory chamber housing the gill, is covered by a protective sheet, the mantle shelf, which terminates in a fleshy spout, the siphon. When the siphon or mantle shelf is stimulated by touch, the siphon, mantle shelf, and gill all contract vigorously and withdraw into the mantle cavity. This reflex is analogous to vertebrate defensive escape and withdrawal responses, which can be modified by experience. Unlike vertebrate withdrawal reflexes, however, the *Aplysia* withdrawal reflex is partly monosynaptic—siphon sensory neurons synapse directly on gill and siphon motor neurons (Fig. 1). Nonetheless, this simple reflex can be modified by two forms of nonassociative learning, habituation and sensitization, as well as by a form of associative learning, classical conditioning.

A. Habituation

In habituation, perhaps the simplest form of learning, an animal learns to ignore a weak stimulus that is repeatedly presented when the consequences of the stimulus are neither noxious nor rewarding. Thus, an *Aplysia* will initially respond to a tactile stimulus to the siphon by briskly withdrawing its gill and siphon. But with repeated exposure to the stimulus, the animal will exhibit reflex responses that are reduced to a fraction of their initial value. Habituation can last from minutes to weeks, depending on the number and pattern of stimulations (Carew *et al.*, 1972; Pinsker *et al.*, 1970).

At the cellular level, the short-term (minutes to hours) form of habituation involves a depression of transmitter release at the synapses that the siphon sensory neurons make on gill and siphon motor neurons and interneurons (Castellucci and Kandel, 1974; Castellucci et al., 1970). This depression is thought to involve a decrease in the amount of Ca^{2+} that flows into the terminals of the sensory neurons with each action potential (Klein et al., 1980). Since Ca^{2+} influx determines how much transmitter is released, a decrease in Ca^{2+} influx would result in decreased release (Fig. 2A). Recent evidence suggests that habituation may also involve depletion of releasable transmitter pools (Bailey and Chen, 1985; Gingrich and Byrne, 1985).

B. Sensitization

Sensitization is a somewhat more complex form of nonassociative learning in which an animal learns to strengthen its defensive reflexes and to respond vigorously to a variety of previously weak or neutral stimuli after it has been exposed to a potentially threatening or noxious stimulus. Thus, if a noxious sensitizing stimulus is presented to the neck or tail, the siphon and gill withdrawal reflexes will be enhanced, as will inking, walking, and other defensive behaviors (Pinsker et al., 1970; Walters et al., 1981). This enhancement persists from minutes to weeks, depending on the number and intensity of the sensitizing stimuli (Pinsker et al., 1973).

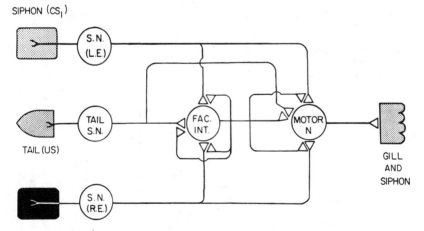

Figure 1.
Partial neuronal circuit for the *Aplysia* gill- and siphon-withdrawal reflex and its modification by tail stimulation. Mechanosensory neurons (S.N.) from the siphon (LE cluster), mantle (RE cluster), and tail excite gill and siphon motor neurons. The sensory neurons also excite facilitator interneurons, which produce presynaptic facilitation at all of the terminals of the sensory neurons.

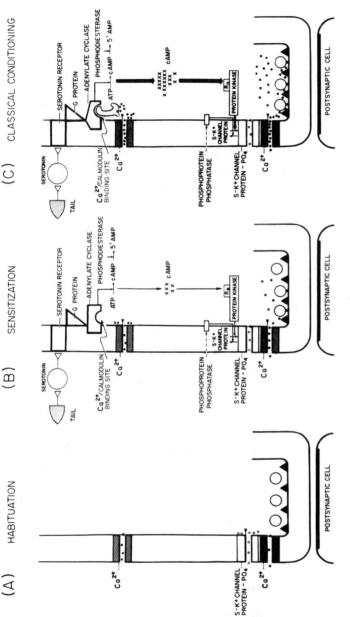

Figure 2.

Cellular mechanisms of habituation, sensitization, and classical conditioning of the *Aplysia* gill- and siphon-withdrawal reflex. (A) Habituation. Repeated stimulation of a siphon sensory neuron, the presynaptic cell in the figure, produces prolonged inactivation of Ca^{2+} channels in that neuron (represented by the closed gates), leading to a decrease in Ca^{2+} influx during each action potential and decreased transmitter release. (B) Sensitization. Stimulation of the tail produces prolonged inactivation of K^+ channels in the siphon sensory neuron through a sequence of steps involving cAMP and protein phosphorylation. Closing these K^+ channels produces broadening of subsequent action potentials, which in turn produces an increase in Ca^{2+} influx and increased transmitter release. (C) Classical conditioning. Tail stimulation produces amplified facilitation of transmitter release from the siphon sensory neuron if the tail stimulation is preceded by action potentials in the sensory neuron. This effect may be due to priming of the adenyl cyclase by Ca^{2+} that enters the sensory neuron during the action potentials, so that the cyclase produces more cAMP when it is activated by the tail stimulation.

The short-term (minutes to hours) form of sensitization involves the same cellular locus as habituation, the synapses that the sensory neurons make on their central target cells, and again the learning process involves an alteration in transmitter release—in this case an enhancement in the amount released (Castellucci and Kandel, 1976; Castellucci et al., 1970). But sensitization uses more complex molecular machinery. This machinery has at least five steps (Figs. 1 and 2B):

1. Stimulating the tail activates a group of facilitator neurons which synapse on or near the terminals of the sensory neurons and act there to enhance transmitter release. This process is called *presynaptic facilitation.*

2. The transmitters released by the facilitator neurons, which include serotonin and a small peptide (SCP), activate an adenylate cyclase, which increases the level of free cyclic AMP in the terminals of the sensory neurons.

3. Elevation of free cyclic AMP, in turn, activates a second enzyme, a cAMP-dependent protein kinase.

4. The kinase acts by means of protein phosphorylation to close a particular type of K^+ channel and thereby decreases the total number of K^+ channels that are open during the action potential.

5. A decrease in K^+ current leads to broadening of subsequent action potentials, which allows a greater amount of Ca^{2+} to flow into the terminal and thus enhances transmitter release (Kandel and Schwartz, 1982; Klein and Kandel, 1980; Siegelbaum et al., 1982; Castellucci et al., 1982; Bernier et al., 1982; Hawkins et al., 1981; Kitler et al., 1985; Abrams et al., 1984; Mackey et al., 1986).

Recent evidence suggests that sensitization may also involve mobilization of transmitter to release sites, perhaps through Ca^{2+}/calmodulin- or Ca^{2+}/phospholipid-dependent protein phosphorylation (Gingrich and Byrne, 1985; Hochner et al., 1986a,b; Boyle et al., 1984; Sacktor et al., 1986).

C. Classical Conditioning

Classical conditioning resembles sensitization in that the response to a stimulus to one pathway is enhanced by activity in another. In classical conditioning an initially weak or ineffective conditioned stimulus (CS) becomes highly effective in producing a behavioral response after it has been paired temporally with a strong unconditioned stimulus (US). Often a reflex can be modified by both sensitization and classical conditioning. In such cases, the response enhancement produced by classical conditioning (paired presentation of the CS and US) is greater and/or lasts longer than the enhancement produced by sensitization (presentation of the US alone). Moreover, whereas the consequences of sensitization are broad and affect defensive responses to a range of stimuli, the effects of classical conditioning are specific and enhance only responses to stimuli that are paired with the US.

In conditioning of the *Aplysia* withdrawal response, the unconditioned stimulus is a strong shock to the tail and produces a powerful set of defensive responses; the conditioned stimulus is a weak stimulus to the siphon and produces a feeble response. After repeated pairing of the CS and US, the CS becomes more effective and elicits a strong gill and siphon withdrawal reflex. Enhancement of this reflex is acquired within 15 trials, is retained for days, extinquishes with repeated presentation of the CS alone, and recovers with rest (Carew et al., 1981). The siphon withdrawal reflex can also be differentially conditioned using stimuli to the siphon and mantle shelf as the discriminative stimuli. Using this procedure, we have found that a single training trial is sufficient to produce significant learning, and that the learning becomes progressively more robust with more training trials (Carew et al., 1983). We also found significant conditioning when the onset of the CS preceded the onset of the US by 0.5 sec, and marginally significant conditioning when the interval between the CS and the US was extended to 1.0 sec. In contrast, no significant learning occurred when the CS preceded the US by 2 sec or more, when the two stimuli were simultaneous, or, in backward conditioning, when US onset preceded the CS by 0.5 sec or more (Hawkins et al., 1986). Thus, conditioning in *Aplysia* resembles conditioning in vertebrates in having a steep ISI function, with optimal learning when the CS precedes the US by approximately 0.5 sec (e.g., Gormezano, 1972).

What cellular processes give classical conditioning this characteristic stimulus and temporal specificity? Evidence obtained over the past several years indicates that classical conditioning of the withdrawal reflex involves a pairing-specific enhancement of presynaptic facilitation. In classical conditioning the sensory neurons of the CS pathway fire action potentials just before the facilitator neurons of the US pathway become active. Using a reduced preparation we have found that if action potentials are generated in a sensory neuron just before the US is delivered, the US produces substantially more facilitation of the synaptic potential from the sensory neuron to a motor neuron than if the US is not paired with activity in the sensory neuron. Pairing spike activity in a sensory neuron with the US also produces greater broadening of the action potential in the sensory neuron than unpaired stimulation, indicating that the enhancement of facilitation occurs presynaptically. Thus, at least some aspects of the mechanism for classical conditioning occur within the sensory neuron itself. We have called this type of enhancement *activity-dependent amplification of presynaptic facilitation* (Hawkins et al., 1983).

Similar cellular results have been obtained independently by Walters and Byrne (1983), who have found activity-dependent synaptic facilitation in identified sensory neurons that innervate the tail of *Aplysia*. By contrast, Carew *et al.* (1984) have found that a different type of synaptic plasticity first postulated by Hebb (1949), which has often been thought to underlie learning (see Sejnowski and Tesauro, Chapter 6, this volume), does *not* occur at the sensory neurnon–motor neuron synapses in the siphon withdrawal circuit.

These experiments indicate that a mechanism of classical conditioning of the withdrawal reflex is an elaboration of the mechanism of sensitization of the reflex: presynaptic facilitation caused by an increase in action potential duration and Ca^{2+} influx in the sensory neurons. The pairing specificity characteristic of classical conditioning results because the presynaptic facilitation is augmented or amplified by temporally paired spike activity in the sensory neurons. We do not yet know which aspect of the action potential in a sensory neuron interacts with the process of presynaptic facilitation to amplify it, nor which step in the biochemical cascade leading to presynaptic facilitation is sensitive to the action potential. Preliminary results suggest that the influx of Ca^{2+} with each action potential provides the signal for activity, and that it interacts with the cAMP cascade so that serotonin produces more cAMP (Fig. 2C). Thus, brief application of serotonin to the sensory cells can substitute for tail shock as the US in the cellular experiments, and Ca^{2+} must be present in the external medium for paired spike activity to enhance the effect of the serotonin (Abrams, 1985; Abrams *et al.*, 1983). Furthermore, serotonin produces a greater increase in cAMP levels in siphon sensory cells if it is preceded by spike activity in the sensory cells than if it is not (Kandel *et al.*, 1983; see also Occor *et al.*, 1985, for a similar result in *Aplysia* tail sensory neurons). Finally, experiments on a cell-free membrane homogenate preparation have shown that the adenyl cyclase is stimulated by both Ca^{2+} and serotonin, consistent with the idea that the cyclase is a point of convergence of the CS and US inputs (Abrams *et al.*, 1985).

II. A Quantitative Model for Conditioning

The quantitative model I have developed to simulate various aspects of conditioning incorporates the neural circuit shown in Fig. 1 and the cellular processes diagrammed in Fig. 2. The cellular processes in the model were made as simple as possible to reduce both free parameters and computation time, and are therefore only rough approximations of reality. In particular, in the version described in this paper, habituation is assumed to be due solely to Ca^{2+} channel inactivation and sensitization to spike broadening, although experimental evidence suggests that transmitter depletion and mobilization are also involved. This choice was not critical, however, since an alternate version based solely on trans- mitter handling produced similar results for all of the features of con- ditioning discussed except partial reinforcement and latent inhibition. Free parameters in the model were adjusted by trial and error so that one set of parameters would produce strong conditioning with all of the higher-order features addressed. None of the parameter values appeared to be critical within a factor of 2, although this point was not investigated systematically.

Time is modeled as a series of discrete units, which are conceived of as being the same length as the stimulus durations. No attempt has been made to model events (such as the interstimulus interval function) with a greater time resolution. In each time unit, CS1, CS2, the US, or any combination of these stimuli can occur. A stimulus produces one or more action potentials in the corresponding sensory neuron. Stimulus strength is coded by the number of action potentials produced—in the simulations shown (except overshadowing), CS1 and CS2 each produce one action potential, and the US produces six action potentials. Synaptic depression is assumed to be independent of the number of action po- tentials produced (this is approximately true since the depression is par- tially offset by a homosynaptic facilitatory process not modeled here— see Gingrich and Byrne, 1985). Thus, if a sensory neuron is activated, the number of available calcium channels in that neuron (N) decreases by a fixed percentage:

(1) $\Delta N = -C_1 \times N$

and this number recovers by another fixed percentage during each time unit:

(2) $N(t + 1) = N(t) + C_2[N_{max} - N(t)]$

The duration of each action potential in a sensory neuron is assumed to be proportional to the cAMP level in that neuron plus one:

(3) $Dur = 1 + C_3 \times cAMP$

and calcium influx per action potential is proportional to the action po- tential duration times the number of available calcium channels:

(4) $Ca = Dur \times (N/N_{max})$

Transmitter release from each sensory neuron is assumed to be linear with calcium influx, and the resultant PSP in both the motor neuron and the facilitator neuron is linear with the total transmitter released by all of the sensory neurons:

(5) $PSP = C_4 \times \Sigma\, Ca$

The facilitator neuron fires a number of action potentials equal to the difference between the PSP and a threshold:

(6) $Spikes = \begin{cases} PSP - Thresh & \text{if } PSP > Thresh \\ 0 & \text{otherwise} \end{cases}$

The facilitator neuron threshold is variable, and is set equal to a fraction of the PSP level during the *previous* time unit:

(7) $Thresh(t) = C_5 \times PSP(t - 1)$

This has the effect of causing accommodation of facilitator neuron firing during a prolonged input. Spikes in the facilitator release transmitter, which causes an increase in cAMP levels in the sensory neurons according to the following equation:

(8) $\Delta cAMP = C_6 \times Spikes \times [1 + C_7 \times Ca(t - 1)]$

where $Ca(t - 1)$ represents the calcium influx in that sensory neuron during the *previous* time unit. cAMP levels then decay by a fixed percentage during each time unit:

(9) $cAMP\,(t + 1) = C_8 \times cAMP(t)$

In the simulations shown in this paper, the initial values are

$$N = N_{max} \qquad Thresh = 0$$
$$cAMP = 0 \qquad\qquad Ca = 0$$

and the parameter values are as follows:

$$\begin{aligned} C_1 &= 0.15 & C_5 &= 0.9 \\ C_2 &= 0.005 & C_6 &= 0.002 \\ C_3 &= 1 & C_7 &= 15 \\ C_4 &= 7.5 & C_8 &= 0.9975 \end{aligned}$$

To minimize computation time, the time unit is 10 sec (very similar results were obtained in Fig. 3 with a 1-sec unit, which is more realistic). With these parameters, the time constant for decay of cAMP levels is approximately 1 hr, and the time constant for recovery from calcium channel inactivation is approximately 30 min.

III. Simulations of Basic Features of Conditioning

Figure 3 shows a simulation of acquisition and extinction of a conditioned response by the model described in the previous section. In this hy-

82   R. D. Hawkins

pothetical experiment there are a pretest, five paired trials with the CS preceding the US by one time unit, five extinction trials, and a posttest. The intertrial interval is 5 min. The ordinate shows the amplitude of the PSP produced in the motor neuron each time a stmulus (CS or US) occurs. At the level of the motor neuron, conditioning produces an enhancement of a preexisting response to the CS. However, if there were a threshold PSP amplitude for producing a behavioral response (of, for example, 15 mV), conditioning would lead to the development of a new response to the CS at the behavioral level.

The acquisition function produced by this model is S-shaped. The initial acceleration is due to positive feedback in the calcium priming process: the first conditioning trial produces broadening of the action potential and hence an increase in calcium priming of the cAMP cascade on the second conditioning trial [Eqs. (3), (4), and (8)]. This produces greater broadening of the action potential and greater calcium priming on the third trial, etc. The deceleration in acquisition occurs as the response evoked by the CS approaches that evoked by the US. This leads to decreased effectiveness of the US due to accommodation in the facilitator neuron (see the discussion of blocking, below), so that the re-

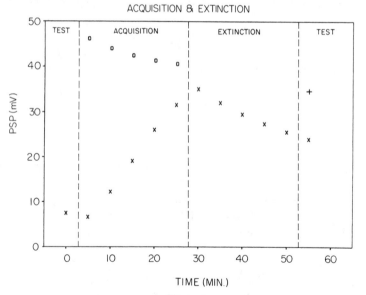

Figure 3.
Simulation of acquisition and extinction. The ordinate shows the amplitude of the PSP produced in the motor neuron each time a stimulus (CS or US) occurs in a hypothetical conditioning experiment. Key: o, US; X, CS; +, response to the CS at that time if the five extinction trials are omitted.

sponse to the CS assymptotes at approximately the level of the response to the US.

Extinction in this model is assumed to have the same cellular mechanism as habituation—synaptic depression. Any stimulus (CS or US) tends to activate two competing processes in the sensory neurons: depression, which is intrinsic to those neurons, and facilitation, which is caused by excitation of the facilitator neuron. The net result depends on the balance of these two processes. The parameters in these simulations were chosen so that depression would predominate with repetition of either the CS or the US by itself, leading to gradual extinction or habituation of responding.

Control procedures are necessary to demonstrate that an increase in responding to the CS is associative in nature. Simulations with the CS and US occurring either by themselves or explicitly unpaired produce little or no increase in responding to the CS. Paired training with the CS and US occurring simultaneously or with the US preceding the CS by one time unit also produces no conditioning. Figure 4 shows another type of control procedure, differential conditioning. In this experiment, two CSs that activate different sensory neurons are used. During training, one CS is paired with the US and the other CS is given unpaired with the US. The response to the paired CS shows a large increase, whereas the response to the unpaired CS shows none, demonstrating the associative nature of the learning. In real conditioning, there is frequently

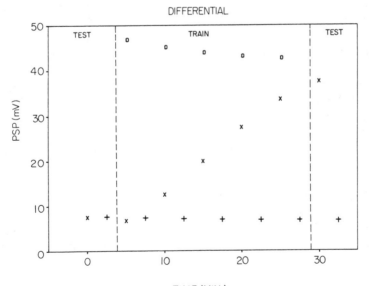

Figure 4.
Simulation of differential conditioning. Key: o, US; X, CS1; +, CS2.

also some increase in responding to the unpaired CS, which is attributable to the nonassociative process of sensitization (e.g., Hawkins *et al.*, 1986). An interesting result of the model is that the relative contributions of conditioning and sensitization depend entirely on the priming factor, C_7.

IV. Simulations of Higher-Order Features of Conditioning

In addition to the features described above, classical conditioning has higher-order features that are thought to have a cognitive flavor. In this section I will describe possible neural mechanisms for several of these, including second-order conditioning, blocking, the effect of contingency, and latent inhibition.

A. Second-Order Conditioning

A second-order conditioning experiment has two stages: in stage I CS1 is paired with the US, and then in stage II a second CS (CS2) is paired with CS1. As Pavlov (1927) noted, this procedure can lead to an associative increase in responding to CS2. Thus, in effect, as a result of the conditioning in stage I, CS1 acquires the ability to act as a US in stage II.

Second-order conditioning might be explained by two features of the neural circuit shown in Fig. 1. First, in addition to being excited by the US, the facilitator neuron is also excited by the CS sensory neurons. Second, the facilitator neuron produces facilitation not only at the synapses from the sensory neurons to the motor neurons but also at the synapses from the sensory neurons to the facilitator neuron itself. This fact has the interesting consequence that the sensory-facilitator synapses (unlike the sensory-motor synapses) act like Hebb synapses (see Chapter 6, this volume). That is, firing a sensory neuron just before firing the facilitator produces selective strengthening of the synapse from that sensory neuron to the facilitator. As a result, during stage I conditioning, CS1 acquires a greater ability to excite the facilitator, allowing it to act as a US in stage II.

Figure 5 shows a simulation of second-order conditioning. During stage II, the response to CS2 increases while CS1 undergoes extinction. As controls, CS2 does not condition in stage II if CS1 is presented unpaired with the US in stage I, or if CS2 is presented unpaired with CS1 in stage II.

B. Blocking and Overshadowing

Like a second-order conditioning experiment, a blocking experiment has two stages. In stage I, CS1 is paired with the US as usual. In stage II,

CS2 is added to CS1 and the compound stimulus CS1/CS2 is paired with the US. As Kamin (1969) noted, this procedure generally produces little conditioning of CS2, even though good conditioning of CS2 occurs if CS1 is omitted in stage II or if CS1 was not previously conditioned in stage I. Thus, simultaneous presentation with a previously conditioned stimulus (CS1) "blocks" conditioning of a naive stimulus (CS2).

The discovery of blocking was very influential in thinking about conditioning, because it demonstrates that animals may *not* acquire a conditioned response despite many pairings of the CS and US. This result suggests that conditioning is not a simple result of stimulus pairing, but may instead involve cognitive processes. For example, Kamin (1969) proposed that an animal forms expectations about the world, compares current input with those expectations, and learns only when something unpredicted occurs. Because CS1 comes to predict the US in the first stage of training, in the second stage the compound CS1/CS2 is not followed by anything unexpected and, therefore, little conditioning occurs.

Rescorla and Wagner (1972) have formalized this explanation by suggesting that the strength of a CS subtracts from the strength of a US with which it is paired. In the neural model, this subtraction function is accomplished by accommodation of firing in the facilitator neuron [Eqs. (6) and (7)]. Thus, as the synapses from CS1 to the facilitator become strengthened during stage I training the facilitator fires progressively more during CS1 and less during the US, due to accommodation caused by CS1. This process reaches an assymptote when there is just enough

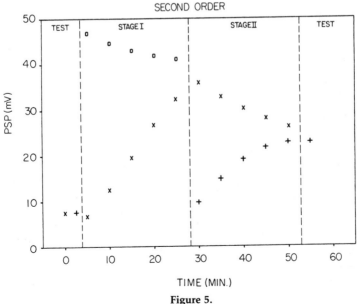

Figure 5.
Simulation of second-order conditioning. Key as in Fig. 4.

firing left during the US to counteract CS1 habituation. When training with the compound stimulus CS1/CS2 starts in the second stage of training, CS2 is followed by very little firing in the facilitator neuron and therefore does not become conditioned. Firing of the facilitator neuron at the onset of CS2 does not produce activity-dependent facilitation, because that process requires a delay between CS onset and the onset of facilitation [Eq. (8)].

Figure 6 shows a simulation of blocking. Following stage II training there is very little conditioning of CS2, while CS1 retains the associative strength it acquired in stage I. As controls, CS2 undergoes substantially more conditioning during stage II if CS1 occurs unpaired with the US in stage I, or if CS1 occurs separately from CS2 and the US during stage II.

Gluck and Thompson (1987) have reported some difficulty in simulating blocking with a quantitative model based on the ideas suggested by Hawkins and Kandel (1984). Although the Gluck and Thompson model is basically similar to the one described here, it differs in many details. In particular, it is formulated at the level of algebraic synaptic learning rules rather than molecular processes. Gluck and Thompson (1987) note that blocking is much more successful in their model if they assume an S-shaped acquisition function, rather than a decelerating acquisition function (which was their initial assumption). This observation

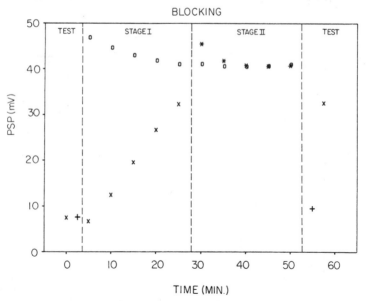

Figure 6.
Simulation of blocking. Key as in Fig. 4. Asterisk indicates simultaneous occurrence of CS1 and CS2.

may explain why the model described here simulates blocking with little difficulty. An S-shaped acquisition function is a natural consequence of the molecular processes (in particular, calcium priming of the cAMP cascade) upon which this model is based.

Overshadowing is phenomenologically similar to blocking, but involves training with CSs that differ in salience rather than previous association with the US. As Pavlov (1927) noted, if CS1 is more salient (stronger) than CS2 and the compound stimulus CS1/CS2 is paired with the US, there will tend to be little conditioning of CS2, even though good conditioning of CS2 occurs if it is paired with the US by itself. Thus, a strong CS "overshadows" a weaker CS when they are presented simultaneously, preventing conditioning of the weak CS.

Figure 7 shows a simulation of overshadowing. The explanation of this effect is similar to the explanation proposed for blocking: CS1 conditions more rapidly than CS2 initially (due to greater calcium priming of the cAMP cascade), and conditioning of both CSs decelerates as their combined strengths approach the US strength. In the simulation this occurs by the second paired trial, before there has been much conditioning of CS2. As training continues, the CS strengths actually habituate slightly, with the response to CS1 remaining near assymptote and the response to CS2 remaining at a low level.

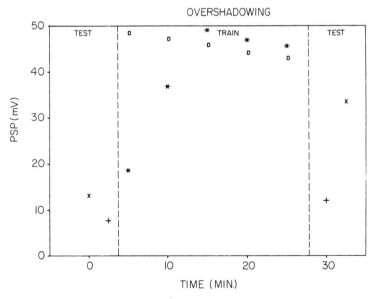

Figure 7.
Simulation of overshadowing. Key as in Fig. 4. CS1 strength = 1.75, CS2 strength = 1.00. Asterisk indicates simultaneous occurrence of CS1 and CS2.

C. Effect of Contingency

Like blocking, the effect of contingency illustrates that animals do not simply learn about the pairing the events, but also learn about their correlation or contingency—that is, how well one event predicts another. Rescorla (1968) demonstrated this effect by showing that adding additional, unpaired CSs or USs to a conditioning procedure decreases learning, although the animals receive the same number of pairings of the CS and US. A similar effect of extra USs has been demonstrated for conditioning of gill- and siphon-withdrawal in *Aplysia* (Hawkins et al., 1986).

Rescorla and Wagner (1972) proposed that the effect of extra USs could be explained by an extenion of the argument they advanced for blocking, by including in the analysis the stimuli that are always present in the experimental situation (the background stimuli). Hawkins and Kandel (1984) suggested that a simpler mechanism, habituation of US effectiveness, might also contribute. Thus, just as CS effectiveness habituates with repeated presentations of the CS, so might US effectiveness habituate with repeated presentations of the US. Adding additional, unpaired USs would therefore cause greater habituation of the US, leading to decreased US effectiveness on the paired trials and decreased learning.

The neuronal model includes US habituation, since the US pathway is not treated any differently than the CS pathways. Figure 8 shows a

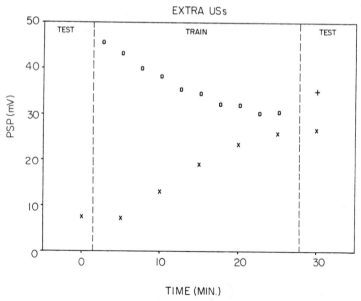

Figure 8.
Simulation of extra USs (partial warning). Key: o, US; X, CS. Plus indicates response to the CS at that time if the five extra USs are omitted.

simulation of an experiment in which additional, unpaired USs are presented during training. This procedure causes extra US habituation and decreased conditioning of the CS.

Presenting additional, unpaired CSs during training (partial reinforcement) also decreases conditioning, as shown in Fig. 9. This effect has two explanations: extinction (CS habituation) caused by the unpaired CSs, and a consequent decrease in calcium priming of the cAMP cascade on the paired trials. As might be expected, presenting both additional USs and CSs causes an even greater decrease in conditioning than either procedure by itself (simulation not shown).

D. Latent Inhibition and US Preexposure

Learning can be disrupted by presenting extra, unpaired stimuli *before* paired training, as well as during it. For example, presentation of unpaired CSs in stage I of an experiment causes a retardation of conditioning during paired training in stage II. This effect, which is referred to as "latent inhibition," has a formal similarity to the effect of partial reinforcement described above, and it may have a similar neural explanation. Figure 10 shows a simulation of latent inhibition in which inactivation of Ca^{2+} current during stage I leads to a decrease in Ca^{2+} priming of the cAMP cascade and hence decreased conditioning in stage II.

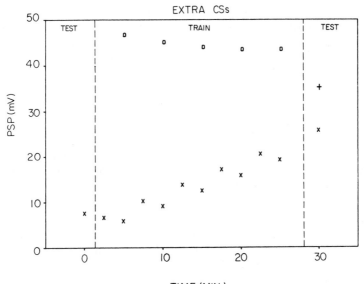

Figure 9.
Simulation of extra CSs (partial reinforcement). Key: o, US; X, CS. Plus indicates response to the CS at that time if the five extra CSs are omitted.

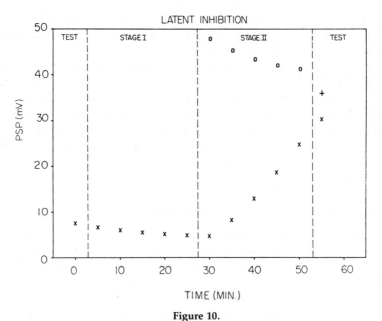

Figure 10.
Simulation of latent inhibition. Key: o, US; X, CS. Plus indicates response to the CS at that time if stage I training is omitted.

For reasons similar to those described above for the effect of extra USs, presentation of unpaired USs in stage I (US preexposure) also decreases conditioning during paired training in stage II. Furthermore, unpaired presentation of both CSs and USs in stage I produces an even greater decrease in conditioning than presentation of either stimulus by itself (simulations not shown).

V. Discussion

In this chapter I have attempted to demonstrate how several higher-order features of classical conditioning might be generated from combinations of the cellular mechanisms used in simpler forms of learning. The model I have presented, which is based on known *Aplysia* physiology and neural circuitry, is similar in many respects to psychological models proposed by modern behaviorists to account for the same phenomena. In particular, it provides a neuronal version of a concept central to many of those models, which is that learning depends on the degree to which the US is surprising or unpredicted (e.g., Rescorla and Wagner, 1972; Wagner, 1978, 1981; Mackintosh, 1975). The model differs from most psychological models, however, in that it utilizes the mechanism of habituation, synaptic depression, for all negative learning. The relative success of this model demonstrates that habituation may contribute to a wider range of learning phenomena than has generally been appreciated. Habituation cannot account for conditioned inhibition and related learning phenomena, however, since the lowest habituation can go is zero. To explain those phenomena, it will presumably be necessary to add inhibitory interneurons to the neuronal circuit shown in Fig. 1. Neurons that produce inhibition in this circuit have been identified, and their properties are currently being investigated (Hawkins *et al.*, 1981; Mackey *et al.*, 1987).

Although the model I have described successfully simulates the basic phenomena of acquisition, extinction, differential conditioning, second-order conditioning, blocking, overshadowing, the effect of contingency, latent inhibition, and US preexposure, it also has distinct limitations. In particular, several of the behavioral phenomena addressed have not yet been tested in *Aplysia*, so the relevance of *Aplysia* physiology and circuitry to those phenomena is not demonstrated. Also, the model does not explain several other important phenomena in conditioning, such as sensory preconditioning and the nature of the conditioned response. A virtue of the model is that it should be testable on the neuronal level by recording from the relevant neurons during behavioral conditioning. Whether or not the results of those tests support the details of the model, however, the success of the simulations described in this chapter do support the more general hypothesis stated at the outset: that relatively advanced types of learning may result from combinations of known cellular processes in simple neural circuits.

Acknowledgments

I am grateful to Kathrin Hilten and Louise Katz for preparing the figures and to Harriet Ayers for typing the manuscript. Preparation of this article was supported by a grant from the National Institute of Mental Health (MH-26212).

References

Abrams, T. W. (1985). *Cell. Mol. Neurobiol.* **5**, 123–145.
Abrams, T. W., Carew, T. J., Hawkins, R. D., and Kandel, E. R. (1983). *Soc. Neurosci. Abstr.* **9**, 168.
Abrams, T. W., Castellucci, V. F., Camardo, J. S., Kandel, E. R., and Lloyd, P. E. (1984). *Proc. Natl. Acad. Sci. U.S.A.* **81**, 7956–7960.
Abrams, T. W., Eliot, L., Dudai, Y., and Kandel, E. R. (1985). *Soc. Neurosci. Abstr.* **11**, 797.
Bailey, C. H., and Chen, M. (1985). *Soc. Neurosci. Abstr.* **11**, 1110.
Bernier, L., Castellucci, V. F., Kandel, E. R., and Schwartz, J. H. (1982). *J. Neurosci.* **2**, 1682–1691.
Boyle, M. B., Klein, M., Smith, S. J., and Kandel, E. R. (1984). *Proc. Natl. Acad. Sci. U.S.A.* **81**, 7642–7646.

Carew, T. J., Pinsker, H. M., and Kandel, E. R. (1972). *Science* **175,** 451–454.

Carew, T. J., Walters, E. T., and Kandel, E. R. (1981). *J. Neurosci.* **1,** 1426–1437.

Carew, T. J., Hawkins, R. D., and Kandel, E. R. (1983). *Science* **219,** 397–400.

Carew, T. J., Hawkins, R. D., Abrams, T. W., and Kandel, E. R. (1984). *J. Neurosci.* **4,** 1217–1224.

Castellucci, V. F., and Kandel, E. R. (1974). *Proc. Natl. Acad. Sci. U.S.A.* **71,** 5004–5008.

Castellucci, V. F., and Kandel, E. R. (1976). *Science* **194,** 1176–1178.

Castellucci, V., Pinsker, H., Kupfermann, I., and Kandel, E. R. (1970). *Science* **167,** 1745–1748.

Castellucci, V. F., Nairn, A., Greengard, P., Schwartz, J. H., and Kandel, E. R. (1982). *J. Neurosci.* **2,** 1673–1681.

Colwill, R. M. (1985). *Soc. Neurosci. Abstr.* **11,** 796.

Dickinson, A. (1980). "Contemporary Animal Learning Theory." Cambridge Univ. Press, London and New York.

Farley, J. (1987). *Behav. Neurosci.* **101,** 13–27.

Gingrich, K. J., and Byrne, J. H. (1985). *J. Neurophysiol.* **53,** 652–669.

Gingrich, K. J., and Byrne, J. H. (1987). *J. Neurophysiol.* **57,** 1705–1715.

Gluck, M. A., and Thompson, R. F. (1987). *Psychol. Rev.* **94,** 176–191.

Gormezano, I. (1972). *In* "Classical Conditioning II: Current Research and Theory" (A. H. Black and W. F. Prokasy, eds.), pp. 151–181. Appleton, New York.

Hawkins, R. D., and Kandel, E. R. (1984). *Psychol. Rev.* **91,** 375–391.

Hawkins, R. D., Castellucci, V. F., and Kandel, E. R. (1981). *J. Neurophysiol.* **45,** 315–326.

Hawkins, R. D., Abrams, T. W., Carew, T. J., and Kandel, E. R. (1983). *Science* **219,** 400–405.

Hawkins, R. D., Carew, T. J., and Kandel, E. R. (1986). *J. Neurosci.* **6,** 1695–1701.

Hebb, D. O. (1949). "Organization of Behavior." Wiley, New York.

Hochner, B., Braha, O., Klein, M., and Kandel, E. R. (1986a). *Soc. Neurosci. Abstr.* **12,** 1340.

Hochner, B., Klein, M., Schacher, S., and Kandel, E. R. (1986b). *Proc. Natl. Acad. Sci. U.S.A.* **83,** 8794–8798.

Kamin, L. J. (1969). *In* "Punishment and Aversive Behavior" (B. A. Campbell and R. M. Church, eds.), pp. 279–296. Appleton, New York.

Kandel, E. R., and Schwartz, J. H. (1982). *Science* **218,** 433–443.

Kandel, E. R., Abrams, T., Bernier, L., Carew, T. J., Hawkins, R. D., and Schwartz, J. H. (1983). *Cold Spring Harbor Symp. Quant. Biol.* **48,** 821–830.

Kistler, H. B., Jr., Hawkins, R. D., Koester, J., Steinbusch, H. W. M., Kandel, E. R., and Schwartz, J. H. (1985). *J. Neurosci.* **5,** 72–80.

Klein, M., and Kandel, E. R. (1980). *Proc. Natl. Acad. Sci. U.S.A.* **77,** 6912–6916.

Klein, M., Shapiro, E., and Kandel, E. R. (1980). *J. Exp. Biol.* **89,** 117–157.

Mackey, S. L., Hawkins, R. D., and Kandel, E. R. (1986). *Soc. Neurosci. Abstr.* **12,** 1340.

Mackey, S. L., Small, S. A., Dyke, A. M., Hawkins, R. D., Glanzman, D. L., and Kandel, E. R. (1987). *Proc. Natl. Acad. Sci. U.S.A.* **84** 8730–8734

Mackintosh, N. J. (1975). *Psych. Rev.* **82,** 276–298.

Mackintosh, N. J. (1983). "Conditioning and Associative Learning." Oxford Univ. Press, London and New York.

Ocorr, K. A., Walters, E. T., and Byrne, J. H. (1985). *Proc. Natl. Acad. Sci. U.S.A.* **82,** 2548–2552.

Pavlov, I. P. (1927). "Conditioned Reflexes: An Investigation of the Physiological Activity of the Cerebral Cortex" (Trans by G. V. Anrep). Oxford Univ. Press, London and New York.

Pinsker, H. M., Kupfermann, I., Castellucci, V., and Kandel, E. R. (1970). *Science* **167,** 1740–1742.

Pinsker, H. M., Hening, W. A., Carew, T. J., and Kandel, E. R. (1973). *Science* **182,** 1039–1042.

Rescorla, R. A. (1968). *J. Comp. Physiol. Psychol.* **66,** 1–5.

Rescorla, R. A. (1978). *In* "Cognitive Processes in Animal Behavior" (S. H. Hulse, H. Fowler, and W. Honig, eds.), pp. 15–50. Erlbaum, Hillsdale, New Jersey.

Rescorla, R. A., and Wagner, A. R. (1972). *In* "Classical Conditioning II: Current Research and Theory" (A. H. Black and W. F. Prokasy, eds.), pp. 64–99. Appleton, New York.

Sacktor, T. C., O'Brian, C. A., Weinstein, J. B., and Schwartz, J. H. (1986). *Soc. Neurosci. Abstr.* **12,** 1340.

Sahley, C., Rudy, J. W., and Gelperin, A. (1981). *J. Comp. Physiol.* **144,** 1–8.

Siegelbaum, S. A., Camardo, J. S., and Kandel, E. R. (1982). *Nature (London)* **299,** 413–417.

Wagner, A. R. (1978). *In* "Cognitive Processes in Animal Behavior" (S. H. Hulse, H. Fowler, and W. Honig, eds.), pp. 177–209. Erlbaum, Hillsdale, New Jersey.

Wagner, A. R. (1981). *In* "Information Processing in Animals: Memory Mechanisms" (N. E. Spear and R. R. Miller, eds.), pp. 5–47. Erlbaum, Hillsdale, New Jersey.

Walters, E. T., and Byrne, J. H. (1983). *Science* **219,** 405–408.

Walters, E. T., Carew, T. J., and Kandel, E. R. (1981). *Science* **211,** 504–506.

6

The Hebb Rule for Synaptic Plasticity: Algorithms and Implementations

Terrence J. Sejnowski and Gerald Tesauro

Terrence J. Sejnowski and Gerald Tesauro

———————————— I. Introduction ————————————

In 1949 Donald Hebb published "The Organization of Behavior," in which he introduced several hypotheses about the neural substrate of learning and memory, including the Hebb learning rule or Hebb synapse. At that time very little was known about neural mechanisms of plasticity at the molecular and cellular levels. The primary data on which Hebb formulated his hypotheses was Golgi material, provided mainly by Lorente de Nó, and psychological evidence for short-term and long-term memory traces. Hebb's hypotheses were an attempt to understand the development and the organization of behavior based on the antamomical and physiological data available to him, though they did not constitute a model for learning or memory in a formal sense.

Some 40 years later we now have solid physiological evidence, verified in several laboratories, that long-term potentiation (LTP) in some parts of the mammalian hippocampus follows the Hebb rule (Kelso *et al.*, 1986; Levy *et al.*, 1983; McNaughton *et al.*, 1978; Wigstrom and Gustafsson, 1985; McNaughton and Morris, 1987; Brown *et al.*, 1988; see Chapter 14 in this volume). However, Hebb was primarily concerned with cerebral cortex, not the hippocampus. The relevance of Hebbian plasticity in the hippocampus to Hebb's original motivation for making the hypothesis is not obvious, although LTP may well be found under somewhat different circumstances in cerebral cortex (Artola and Singer, 1987; Komatsu *et al.*, 1988).

The Hebb rule and variations on it have also served as the starting point for the study of information storage in simplified "neural network"

94

models (Sejnowski, 1981; Kohonen, 1984; Rumelhart and McClelland, 1986; Hopfield and Tank, 1986). Many types of networks have been studied—networks with random connectivity, networks with layers, networks with feedback between layers, and a wide variety of local patterns of connectivity. Even the simplest network model has complexities that are difficult to analyze.

In this chapter we will provide a framework within which the Hebb rule and other related learning algorithms serve as an important link between the implementation level of analysis, which is the level at which experimental work on neural mechanisms takes place, and the computational level, on which the behavioral aspects of learning and perception are studied. In particular, it will be shown how the Hebb rule can be built out of realistic neural components in several different ways.

II. Levels of Analysis

The notion of an algorithm is central in thinking about information processing in the nervous system. An algorithm is a well-defined procedure for solving a problem. It can be as formal as a set of mathematical equations for finding the area under a curve or as informal as a step-by-step recipe for baking a cake. What is common to all algorithms is a level of abstraction beyond the details that must be specified in order to actually solve a particular problem. For example, the formulas for finding the area under a curve could be programmed into a digital computer or implemented by someone using a slide rule. When a cup of sugar is required in a recipe, the exact brand is not specified, nor is the actual method for estimating volume.

Hebb's proposal for the neural substrate of learning has some elements that make it implementational, inasmuch as he specified the conditions under which synapses are to be modified. However, he did not specify exactly which synapses, nor precisely how the modifications should be made. Hence, Hebb's proposal is more like an algorithmn, or, more accurately, one of the components of an algorithm. As such, there are many possible ways that it could be implemented in the brain, and several examples will be given in the next section.

Underlying the notion of an algorithm is the assumption that there is a problem to solve. Marr (1982) called the level at which problems are specified the computational level, and he emphasized the importance of this level of analysis for understanding how the brain processes information. If we could specify precisely what these problems are, algorithms could be devised that could solve the problem, and implementations of the algorithms could be looked for in the nervous system.

One problem with this top-down approach is that our intuition about the computational level is probably not very reliable, since the brain is the product of evolution and not designed by an engineer; second, even when a problem can be identified, there are too many possible algorithms to explore, and again our intuition may not lead us to the right ones. Finally, there are many structural levels of organization in the brain, and it is likely that there is a corresponding multiplicity of algorithmic and computational levels as well (Churchland and Sejnowski, 1988).

What computation does the Hebb algorithm perform? Hebb saw his postulate as a step toward understanding learning and memory, but there are many different aspects of learning and memory that could be involved (see Chapter 12, this volume). Examples of several forms of learning that could be based on algorithms using the Hebb rule include associative learning, classical conditioning, and error-correction learning (see Sejnowski and Tesauro, 1988, for a review).

III. Implementations of the Hebb Rule

Before considering the various possible ways of implementing the Hebb rule, one should examine what Hebb (1949, p. 62) actually proposed: "What an axon of cell A is near enough to excite cell B or repeatedly or persistently takes part in firing it, some growth process or metabolic change takes place in one or both cells such that A's efficiency, as one of the cells firing B, is increased."

This statement can be translated into a precise quantitative expression as follows. We consider the situation in which neuron A, with average firing rate V_A, projects to neuron B, with average firing rate V_B. The synaptic connection from A to B has a strength value T_{BA}, which determines the degree to which activity in A is capable of exciting B. (The postsynaptic depolarization of B due to A is usually taken to be the product of the firing rate V_A times the synaptic strength value T_{BA}.) Now the statement by Hebb above states that the strength of the synapse T_{BA} should be modified in some way that is dependent on both activity in A and activity in B. The most general expression which captures this notion is

(1) $\Delta T_{BA} = F(V_A, V_B)$

which states that the change in the synaptic strength at any given time is some as yet unspecified function F of both the presynaptic firing rate and the postsynaptic firing rate. Strictly speaking, we should say that $F(V_A, V_B)$ is a functional, since the plasticity may depend on the firing rates at previous times as well as at the current time. Given this general form of the assumed learning rule, it is then necessary to choose a particular form for the function $F(V_A, V_B)$. The most straightforward interpretation of what Hebb said is a simple product:

(2) $\Delta T_{BA} = \varepsilon V_A V_B$

where ε is a numerical constant usually taken to be small. However, we wish to emphasize that there are many other choices possible for the function $F(V_A, V_B)$. The choice depends on the particular task at hand. Equation (2) might be appropriate for an simple associative memory task, but for other tasks one would need different forms of the function $F(V_A, V_B)$ in Eq. (1). For example, in classical conditioning, as we shall see in the following section, the precise timing relationships of the presynaptic and postsynaptic signals are important, and the plasticity must then depend on the rate of change of firing, or on the "trace" of the firing rate (i.e., a weighted average over previous times), rather than simply depending on the current instantaneous firing rate (Klopf, 1982). Once the particular form of the learning algorithm is established, the next step is to decide how the algorithm is to be implemented. We shall describe here three possible implementation schemes. This is meant to illustrate the variety of schemes that is possible.

The first implementation scheme, as shown in Fig. 1a, is the simplest way to implement the proposed plasticity rule. The circuit consists solely of neurons, A and B, and a conventional axo-dendritic or axo-somatic synapse from A to B. One postulates that there is some molecular mechanism that operates on the postsynaptic side of the synapse, that is capable of sensing the rate of firing of both cells, and that changes the strength of synaptic transmission from cell B to cell A according to

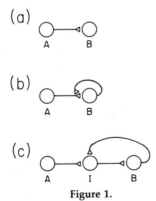

Figure 1.
Three implementations of the Hebb rule for synaptic plasticity. The strength of the coupling between cell A and cell B is strengthened when they are both active at the same time. (a) Postsynaptic site for coincidence detection. (b) Presynaptic site for coincidence detection. (c) Interneuron detects coincidence.

the product of the two firing rates. This is in fact quite similar to the recently discovered mechanism of associative LTP that has been studied in rat hippocampus (Brown et al., 1988; this volume). [Strictly speaking, the plasticity in LTP depends not on the postsynaptic firing rate, but instead on the postsynaptic depolarization. However, in practice these two are usually closely related (Kelso et al., 1986).] Even here, there are many different molecular mechanisms possible. For example, even though it is hard to escape a postsynaptic site for the induction of plasticity, the long-term structural change may well be presynaptic (Dolphin et al., 1982).

A second possible implementation scheme for the Hebb rule is shown in Fig. 1b. In this circuit there is now a feedback projection from the postsynpatic neuron, which forms an axo-axonic synapse on the projection from A to B. The plasticity mechanism involves presynaptic facilitations: one assumes that the strength of the synapse from A to B is increased in proportion to the product of the presynaptic firing rate times the facilitator firing rate (i.e., the postsynaptic firing rate). This type of mechanism also exists and has been extensively studied in *Aplysia* (Carew et al., 1983; Kandel et al., 1987; Walters and Byrne, 1983). Several authors have pointed out that this circuit is a functionally equivalent way of implementing the Hebb rule (Hawkins and Kandel, 1984; Gelperin et al., 1985; Tesauro, 1986; Hawkins, Chapter 5 this volume).

A third scheme for implementing the Hebb rule, one that does not specifically require plasticity in individual synapses, is shown in Fig. 1c. In this scheme the modifiable synapse from A to B is replaced by an interneuron, I, with a modifiable threshold for initiation of action potentials. The Hebb rule is satisfied if the threshold of I decreases according to the product of the firing rate in the projection from A times the firing rate in the projection from B. This is quite similar, although not strictly equivalent, to the literal Hebb rule, because the effect of changing the interneuron threshold is not identical to the effect of changing the strength of a direct synaptic connection. A plasticity mechanism similar to the one proposed here has been studied in *Hermissenda* (Farley and Alkon, 1985; Alkon, 1987) and in models (Tesauro, 1988).

The three methods for implementing the Hebb rule shown in Fig. 1 are by no means exhaustive. There is no doubt that nature is more clever than we are at designing mechanisms for plasticity, especially since we are not aware of most evolutionary constraints. These three circuits can be considered equivalent circuits, since they effectively perform the same function even though they differ in the way that they accomplish it. There also are many ways that each circuit could be instantiated at the cellular and molecular levels. Despite major differences between them, we can nonetheless say that they all implement the Hebb rule.

Most synapses in cerebral cortex occur on dendrites where complex spatial interactions are possible. For example, the activation of a synapse might depolarize the dendrite sufficiently to serve as the postsynaptic signal for modifying an adjacent synapse. Such cooperativity between synapses is a generalization of the Hebb rule in which a section of dendrite is considered the functional unit rather than the entire neuron (Finkel and Edelman, 1987). Dendritic compartments with voltage-dependent channels have all the properties needed for nonlinear processing units (Shepherd *et al.*, 1985).

IV. Conditioning

The Hebb rule can be used to form associations between one stimulus and another. Such associations can be either static, in which case the resulting neural circuit functions as an associative memory (Steinbuch, 1961; Longuet-Higgins, 1968; Anderson, 1970; Kohonen, 1970), or they can be temporal, in which case the network learns to predict that one stimulus pattern will be followed at a later time by another. The latter case has been extensively studied in classical conditioning experiments, in which repeated temporally paired presentations of a conditioned stimulus (CS) followed by an unconditioned stimulus (US) cause the animal to respond to the CS in a way that is similar to its response to the US. The animal has learned that the presence of the CS predicts the subsequent presence of the US. A simple neural circuit model of the classical conditioning process that uses the Hebb rule is illustrated in Fig. 2. This circuit contains three neurons: a sensory neuron for the CS, a sensory neuron for the US, and a motor neuron, R, that generates the unconditioned response. There is a strong, unmodifiable synapse from US to R, so that the presence of the US automatically evokes the response. There is also a modifiable synapse from CS to R, which in the naive untrained animal is initially weak.

One might think that the straightforward application of the literal interpretation of the Hebb rule, as expressed in Eq. (2), would suffice

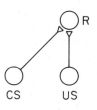

Figure 2.
Model of classical conditioning using a modified Hebb synapse. The unconditioned stimulus (US) elicits a response in the postsynaptic cell (R). Coincidence of the response with the conditioned stimulus (CS) leads to strengthening of the synapse between CS and R.

to generate the desired conditioning effects in the circuit of Fig. 2. However, there are a number of serious problems with this learning algorithm. One of the most serious is the lack of timing sensitivity in Eq. (2). Learning would occur regardless of the order in which the neurons came to be activated. However, in conditioning we know that the temporal order of stimuli is important—if the US follows the CS, then learning occurs, while if the US appears before the CS, then no learning occurs. Hence Eq. (2) must be modified in some way to include this timing sensitivity. Another serious problem is a sort of "runaway instability" that occurs when the CS–R synapse is strengthened to the point where activity in the CS neuron is able to cause by itself firing of the R neuron. In that case, Eq. (2) would cause the synapse to be strengthened upon presentation of the CS alone, without being followed by the US. However, in real animals we know that presentation of CS alone causes a learned association to be extinguished; that is, the synaptic strength should decrease, not increase. The basic problem is that algorithm 2 is only capable of generating positive learning, and has no way to generate zero or negative learning.

It is clear then that the literal Hebb rule needs to be modified to produce desired conditioning phenomena (Tesauro, 1986). One of the most popular ways to overcome the problems of the literal Hebb rule is by using algorithms such as the following (Klopf, 1982; Sutton and Barto, 1981):

$$(3) \quad \Delta T_{BA} = \varepsilon \overline{V}_A \dot{V}_B$$

Here $\overline{V}_A$ represents the stimulus trace of V_A, that is, the weighted average of V_A over previous times, and $\dot{V}_B$ represents the time derivative of V_B. The stimulus trace provides the required timing sensitivity so that learning only occurs in forward conditioning and not in backward conditioning. The use of the time derivative of the postsynaptic firing rate, rather than the postsynaptic firing rate, is a way of changing the sign of learning and thus avoiding the runaway instability problem. With this algorithm, extinction would occur because upon onset of the CS, no positive learning takes place due to the presynaptic trace, and negative learning takes place upon offset of the CS. There are many other variations and elaborations of Eq. (3), which behave in a slightly different way, and which take into account other conditioning behaviors such as second-order conditioning and blocking, and for the details we refer the reader to Sutton and Barto (1981), Sutton (1987), Klopf (1988), Gluck and Thompson (1987), Tesauro (1986), and Gelperin et al. (1985); see also Chapters 4, 5, 7, 9, 11, this volume. However, all of these other algorithms are built upon the same basic notion of modifying the literal Hebb rule to incorporate a mechanism of timing sensitivity and a mechanism for changing the sign of learning.

_____ **V. Conclusions** _____

The algorithmic level is a fruitful one for pursuing network models at the present time for two reasons. First, working top-down from computational considerations is difficult since our intuitions about the computational level in the brain may be wrong or misleading. Knowing more about the computational capabilities of simple neural networks may help us gain a better intuition. Second, working from the bottom up can be treacherous, since we may not yet know the relevant signals in the nervous system that support information processing. The study of learning in model networks can help guide the search for neural mechanisms underlying learning and memory. Thus, network models at the algorithmic level are a unifying framework within which to explore neural information processing.

Hebb's learning rule has led to a fruitful line of experimental research and a rich set of network models. The Hebb synapse is a building block for many different neural network algorithms. As experiments refine the parameters for Hebbian plasticity in particular brain areas, it should become possible to begin refining network models for those areas. There is still a formidable gap between the complexity of real brain circuits and the simplicity of the current generation of network models. As models and experiments evolve the common bonds linking them are likely to be postulates like the Hebb synapse, which serve as algorithmic building blocks.

It is curious that the Golgi studies of Lorente de Nó should have led Hebb to suggest dynamic rules for synaptic plasticity and dynamic processing in neural assemblies. Ramón y Cajál, too, was inspired by static images of neurons to postulate many dynamical principles, such as the polarization of information flow in neurons and the pathfinding of growth cones during development. This suggests that structure in the brain may continue to be a source of inspiration for more algorithmic building blocks, if we could only see as clearly as Cajál and Hebb.

References

Alkon, D. L. (1987). "Memory Traces in the Brain." Oxford Univ. Press, London and New York.

Anderson, J. A. (1970). Two models for memory organization using interacting traces. *Math. Biosci.* **8**, 137–160.

Artola, A., and Singer, W. (1987). Long-term potentiation and NMDA receptors in rat visual cortex. *Nature* **330**, 649–652.

Brown, T. H., Chang, V. C., Ganong, A. H., and Keenan, C. L., Kelso, S. R., (1988). Biophysical properties of dendrites and spines that may control the induction and expression of long-term synaptic potentiation. *In* "Long-Term Potentiation: From Biophysics to Behavior" (P. W. Landfield and S. A. Deadwyler, eds.) pp. 201–264. Alan R. Liss, Inc., New York.

Carew, T. J. Hawkins, R. D., and Kandel, E. R. (1983). Differential classical conditioning of a defensive withdrawal reflex in *Aplysia californica*. *Science* **219**, 397–400.

Churchland, P. S., and Sejnowski, T. J. (1988). Neural representations and neural computations. *In* "Neural Connections and Mental Computation" (L. Nadel, ed.). MIT Press, Cambridge, Massachusetts.

Dolphin, A. C., Errington, M. L., and Bliss, T. V. P. (1982). Long-term potentiation of perforant path *in vivo* is associated with increased glutamate release. *Nature (London)* **297**, 496.

Farley, J., and Alkon, D. L. (1985). Cellular mechanisms of learning, memory and information storage. *Annu. Rev. Psychol.* **36**, 419–494.

Finkel, L. H., and Edelman, G. M. (1987). Population rules for synapses in networks. *In* "Synaptic Function" (G. M. Edelman, W. E. Gall, and W. M. Cowan, eds.), pp. 711–757. Wiley, New York.

Gelperin, A., Hopfield, J. J., and Tank, D. W. (1985). The logic of Limax learning. *In* "Model Neural Networks and Behavior" (A. I. Selverston, ed.), 237–261. Plenum, New York.

Gluck, M. A., and Thompson, R. F. (1987). Modeling the neural substrates of associative learning and memory: A computational approach. *Psychol. Rev.* **94**, 176–191.

Hawkins, R. D., and Kandel, E. R. (1984). Is there a cell-biological alphabet for simple forms of learning? *Psychol. Rev.* **91**, 375–391.

Hebb, D. O. (1949). "The Organization of Behavior." Wiley, New York.

Hopfield, J. J., and Tank, D. W. (1986). Computing with neural circuits: A model. *Science* **233**, 625–633.

Kandel, E. R., Klein, M., Hochner, B., Shuster, M., Siegelbaum, S. A., Hawkins, R. D., Glanzman, D. L., and Castellucci, V. F. (1987). Synaptic modulation and learning: New insights into synaptic transmission from the study of behavior. *In* "Synaptic Function" (G. M. Edelman, W. E. Gall, and W. M. Cowan, eds.), pp. 471–518. Wiley, New York.

Kelso, S. R., Ganong, A. H., and Brown, T. H. (1986). Hebbian synapses in hippocampus. *Proc. Natl. Acad. Sci. U.S.A.* **83**, 5326–5330.

Klopf, A. H. (1982). "The Hedonistic Neuron: A Theory of Memory, Learning, and Intelligence." Hemisphere, New York.

Klopf, A. H. (1988). A neuronal model of classical conditioning. *Psychobiology* **16**, 85–125.

Kohonen, T. (1970). Correlation matrix memories. *IEEE Trans. Comput.* **C-21**, 353–359.

Kohonen, T. (1984). "Self-Organization and Associative Memory." Springer-Verlag, Berlin and New York.

Komatsu, Y., Fujii, K., Maeda, J., Sakaguchi, H., and Toyama, K. (1988). Long-term potentiation of synaptic transmission in kitten visual cortex. *J. Neurophysiol.* **59**, 124–141.

Levy, W. B., Brassel, S. E., and Moore, S. D. (1983). Partial quantification of the associative synaptic learning rule of the dentate gyrus. *Neuroscience* **8**, 799–808.

Longuet-Higgins, H. C. (1968). Holographic model of temporal recall. *Nature (London)* **217**, 104–107.

Marr, D. (1982). "Vision." Freeman, San Francisco, California.

McNaughton, B. L., and Morris, R. G. (1987). Hippocampal synaptic enchancement and information storage within a distributed memory system. *Trends Neurosci.* **10**, 408–415.

McNaughton, B. L., Douglas, R. M., and Goddard, G. V. (1978). *Brain Res.* **157**, 277.

Rumelhart, D. E., and McClelland, J. L., eds. (1986). "Parallel Distributed Processing: Explorations in the Microstructure of Cognition," Vol. 1. MIT Press, Cambridge, Massachusetts.

Sejnowski, T. J. (1981). Skeleton filters in the brain. *In* "Parallel Models of Associative Memory" (G. E. Hinton and J. A. Anderson, eds.), pp. 189–212. Erlbaum, Hillsdale, New Jersey.

Sejnowski, T. J., and Tesauro, G. (1988). Building network learning algorithms from Hebbian synapses. *In* "Brain Organization and Memory: Cells, Systems and Circuits" (J. L. McGaugh, N. M. Weinberger, and G. Lynch, eds.). Oxford University Press, New York.

Shepherd, G. M., Brayton, R. K., Miller, J. P., Segev, I., Rinzel, J., and Rall, W. (1985). Signal enhancement in distal cortical dendrites by means of interactions between active dendritic spines. *Proc. Natl. Acad. Sci. U.S.A.* **82,** 2192–2195.

Steinbuch, K. (1961). Die lernmatrix. *Kybernetik* **1,** 36–45.

Sutton, R. S. (1987). A temporal-difference model of classical conditioning. *GTE Lab. Tech. Rep.* **TR87-509.2.**

Sutton, R. S. and Barto, A. G. (1981). Toward a modern theory of adaptive networks: Expectation and prediction. *Psychol. Rev.* **88,** 135–170.

Tesauro, G. (1986). Simple neural models of classical conditioning. *Biol. Cybernet.* **55,** 187–200.

Tesauro, G. (1988). A plausible neural circuit for classical conditioning without synaptic plasticity. *Proc. Natl. Acad. Sci. U.S.A.* **85,** 2830–2833.

Walters, E. T., and Byrne, J. H. (1983). Associative conditioning of single sensory neurons suggests a cellular mechanism for learning. *Science* **219,** 405–408.

Wigstrom, H., and Gustafsson, B. (1985). *Acta Physiol. Scand.* **123,** 519.

7

Classical Conditioning Phenomena Predicted by a Drive-Reinforcement Model of Neuronal Function

A. Harry Klopf

I. Introduction

Pavlov (1927) and Hebb (1949) were among the first investigators to extensively analyze possible relationships between the behavior of whole animals and the behavior of single neurons. Building on Pavlov's experimental foundation, Hebb's theoretical analyses led him to a model of single-neuron function that continues to be relevant to the theoretical and experimental issues of learning and memory. There had been earlier attempts to develop such neuronal models. Among them were the models of Freud (1895), Rashevsky (1938), and McCulloch and Pitts (1943), but to this day the neuronal model proposed by Hebb has remained the most influential among theorists. Current theorists who have utilized variants of the Hebbian model include Anderson *et al.* (1977), Kohonen (1977), Grossberg (1982), Levy and Desmond (1985), Hopfield and Tank (1986), and Rolls (1987); (see Chapters 6, 11, 13, 14, and 16 in this volume).

In this chapter, I will suggest several modifications to the Hebbian neuronal model. The modifications yield a model that will be shown to be more nearly in accord with animal learning phenomena that are observed experimentally. The model to be proposed is an extension of the Sutton–Barto (1981) model.

After defining the neuronal model, first qualitatively and then mathematically, I will show, by means of computer simulations, that the neuronal model predicts a wide range of classical conditioning phenomena. The model offers a way of defining drives and reinforcers at a neuronal level such that a neurobiological basis is suggested for animal learning. In the theoretical context that the neuronal model provides, I will suggest that *drives*, in their most general sense, are simply *signal levels in the nervous system,* and that *reinforcers,* in their most general sense, are simply *changes in signal levels.* The result will be a theoretical framework based on what I propose to call a drive-reinforcement model of single neuron function.

II. The Neuronal Model

A. Qualitative Description

I will begin by defining the drive-reinforcement neuronal model in qualitative terms. It will be easiest to do this by contrasting the model with the Hebbian model. Hebb (1949) suggested that the efficacy of a plastic synapse increased whenever the synapse was active in conjunction with activity of the postsynaptic neuron. Thus, Hebb was proposing that learning (i.e., changes in the efficacy of synapses) was a function of correlations between approximately simultaneous pre- and postsynaptic levels of neuronal activity.

I wish to suggest three modifications to the Hebbian model:

1. Instead of correlating pre- and postsynaptic levels of activity, *changes* in presynaptic levels of activity should be correlated with *changes* in postsynaptic levels of activity. In other words, instead of correlating signal levels on the input and output sides of the neuron, the first derivatives of the input and output signal levels should be correlated.

2. Instead of correlating approximately simultaneous pre- and postsynaptic signal levels, earlier presynaptic signal levels should be correlated with later postsynaptic signal levels. More precisely and consistent with (1), earlier *changes* in presynaptic signal levels should be correlated with later *changes* in postsynaptic signal levels. Thus, sequentiality replaces simultaneity in the model. The interval between correlated changes in pre- and postsynaptic signal levels is suggested to range up to that of the maximum effective interstimulus interval in delay conditioning.

3. A change in the efficacy of a synapse should be proportional to the current efficacy of the synapse, accounting for the initial positive acceleration in the S-shaped acquisition curves observed in animal learning.

One refinement of the model may be noted at this point. The ability of the neuronal model to predict animal learning phenomena is improved if, instead of correlating positive and negative changes in neuronal inputs with changes in neuronal outputs, only *positive* changes in inputs are correlated with changes in outputs. To clarify this, positive changes in inputs refer to increases in the frequency of action potentials at a synapse, whether the synapse is excitatory or inhibitory. Negative changes in inputs refer to decreases in the frequency of action potentials at a synapse, whether the synapse is excitatory or inhibitory. Furthermore, the changes in frequencies of action potentials I am referring to will be relatively abrupt, occurring within about a second or less. It is hypothesized that more gradual and long-term changes in the frequency of action potentials at a synapse do not trigger the neuronal learning mechanism.

After the neuronal model has been defined precisely and the results of computer simulations have been presented, it will be seen that this model of neuronal function bears the following relationship to models of whole animal behavior. In general, changes in presynaptic frequencies of firing will reflect the onsets and offsets of conditioned stimuli. In general, changes in postsynaptic frequencies of firing will reflect increases or decreases in levels of drives (with drives being defined more broadly than has been customary in the past). In the case of the neuronal model, changes in the levels of drives (which will usually manifest as changes in postsynaptic frequencies of firing) will be associated with reinforcement. With regard to the behavior of whole animals, the notion that changes in drive levels constitute reinforcement has been a fundamental part of animal learning theory since the time of Hull (1943) and Mowrer (1960). Here, I am taking the notion down to the level of the single neuron. Changes in signal levels, which play a fundamental role in the neuronal model being proposed, have long been recognized to be of importance. For example, Berlyne (1973, p. 16) notes that "many recent theorists have been led from different starting points to the conclusion that hedonic value is dependent above all on changes in level of stimulation or level of activity. They include McClelland *et al.* (1953), Premack (1959), Helson (1964), and Fowler (1971)."

Before concluding this introduction to the drive-reinforcement neuronal model, the relationship of the model to earlier models from which it derives will be discussed. As has already been indicated, the drive-reinforcement model is an extenstion of the Sutton–Barto (1981) model. The Sutton–Barto model, in turn, can be viewed as a temporally refined extension of the Rescorla–Wagner (1972) model. The drive-reinforcement model is an example of a *differential learning mechanism*, a class of learning mechanisms that correlates earlier derivatives of inputs with later derivatives of outputs. This class of learning mechanisms was independently discovered by Klopf (1986), coming from the directions of neuronal modeling and animal learning, and by Kosko (1986), coming from philosophical and mathematical directions.

I will show that the drive-reinforcement model eliminates some shortcomings of the Rescorla–Wagner and Sutton–Barto models. Both of the latter models predict strictly negatively accelerated acquisition or learning curves. The Rescorla–Wagner model also predicts extinction of conditioned inhibition. Consistent with the experimental evidence, it will be seen below that the drive-reinforcement model predicts (a) an acquisition curve that is initially positively accelerating and subsequently negatively accelerating and (b) conditioned inhibition that does not extinguish. In addition, the drive-reinforcement model solves some problems with conditioned stimulus duration effects that arise in the case of the Sutton-Barto model.

B. Mathematical Specification

The drive-reinforcement neuronal model may be defined precisely as follows. The input–output relationship of a neuron will be modeled in a fashion that is customary among neural network modelers. Namely, it will be assumed that single neurons are forming sums of their weighted excitatory and inhibitory inputs and then thresholding the sum. If the sum equals or exceeds the threshold, the neuron fires. Such a model of a neuron's input–output relationship can be based on the view that neuronal signals are binary (a neuron fires or it does not) or on the view that neuronal signals are real-valued (reflecting some measure of the frequency of firing of neurons as a function of the amount by which the neuronal threshold is exceeded). Here, the latter view will be adopted. Neuronal input and output signals will be treated as frequencies. This approach to modeling neuronal input-output relationships is consistent with experimental evidence reviewed by Calvin (1975).

Mathematically, then, the neuronal input–output relationship may be specified as follows:

$$(1) \qquad y(t) = \sum_{i=1}^{n} w_i(t)x_i(t) - \theta$$

where $y(t)$ is a measure of the postsynaptic frequency of firing at discrete time t; n is the number of synapses impinging on the neuron; $w_i(t)$ is the efficacy of the ith synapse; $x_i(t)$ is a measure of the frequency of action potentials at the ith synapse; and θ is the neuronal threshold. The synaptic efficacy, $w_i(t)$, can be positive or negative, corresponding to excitatory or inhibitory synapses, respectively. Also, $y(t)$ is bounded such that $y(t)$ is greater than or equal to zero and less than or equal to the maximal output frequency $y'(t)$ of the neuron. Negative values of $y(t)$ have no meaning as they would correspond to negative frequencies of firing.

To complete the mathematical specification of the neuronal model, the learning mechanism described earlier in qualitative terms remains to be presented. The learning mechanism may be specified mathematically as follows:

$$(2) \qquad \Delta w_i(t) = \Delta y(t) \sum_{j=1}^{\tau} c_j \mid w_i(t-j) \mid \Delta x_i(t-j)$$

where $\Delta w_i(t) = w_i(t+1) - w_i(t)$, $\Delta y(t) = y(t) - y(t-1)$, and $\Delta x_i(t-j) = x_i(t-j) - x_i(t-j-1)$. If $\Delta x_i(t-j)$ is less than zero, $\Delta x_i(t-j)$ is set equal to zero for the purposes of Eq. (2). The term $\Delta w_i(t)$ represents the change in the efficacy of the ith synapse at time t, yielding the adjusted or new efficacy of the synapse at time $t+1$. The term $\Delta x_i(t-j)$ represents a presynaptic change in signal level, and $\Delta y(t)$ represents the postsynaptic change in signal level. Further, τ is the longest interstimulus interval, measured in discrete time steps, over which delay conditioning is effective, and c_j is an empirically established learning-rate constant that is proportional to the efficacy of conditioning when the interstimulus interval is j. The remaining symbols are defined as in Eq. (1). A diagram of the neuron modeled by Eqs. (1) and (2) is shown in Fig. 1.

Like Hebb's model, the drive-reinforcement model is an example of a *real-time learning mechanism*. Real-time learning mechanisms emphasize the *temporal* association of signals: each critical event in the sequence leading to learning has a time of occurrence associated with it, and this time plays a fundamental role in the computations that yield changes in the efficacy of synapses. This is in contrast to *non-real-time*

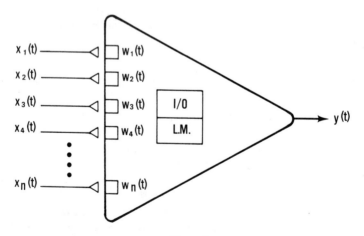

Figure 1.
A model of a single neuron with n synapses. Presynaptic frequencies of firing are represented by $x_i(t)$, synaptic efficacies by $w_i(t)$, and the postsynaptic frequency of firing by $y(t)$. The input–output (I/O) relationship is specified by Eq. (1) and the learning mechanism (L.M.) is specified by Eq. (2) in the text.

learning mechanisms such as the perceptron (Rosenblatt, 1962), adaline (Widrow, 1962), or back propagation (Werbos, 1974; Parker, 1982, 1985; Rumelhart *et al.*, 1985, 1986) learning mechanisms for which error signals follow system responses and only the order of the inputs, outputs, and error signals is important, not the exact time of occurrence of each signal, relative to the others. It should be noted that "real time" in this context does not mean continuous time as contrasted with discrete time, nor does it refer to a learning system's ability to accomplish its computations at a sufficient speed to keep pace with the environment within which it is embedded. Rather, a real-time learning mechanism, as defined here, is one for which the time of occurrence of each critical event in the sequence leading to learning is of fundamental importance with respect to the computations the learning mechanism is performing. For additional discussions of real-time learning mechanism models, see Klopf (1972, 1975, 1979, 1982), Moore and Stickney (1980), Sutton and Barto (1981, 1987), Wagner (1981), Grossberg (1982), Gelperin *et al.* (1985), Blazis *et al.* (1986), Tesauro (1986), and Donegan and Wagner (1987). Proposals for real-time models that give especially careful attention to neurobiological constraints are those of Hawkins and Kandel (1984) and Gluck and Thompson (1987).

Generally, in interpreting and working with Eq. (2), I have adopted the following assumptions, consistent with what is known of learning involving the skeletal reflexes. I usually consider each discrete time step t to be equal to 0.5 sec. This is a meaningful interval over which to obtain measures of the pre- and postsynaptic frequencies of firing, $x_i(t)$ and $y(t)$. Also, it is probably a reasonable interval of time with respect to the learning processes underlying changes in synaptic efficacy. For example, the optimal interstimulus interval for classically conditioning a skeletal reflex is nominally 0.5 sec [optimal interstimulus intervals vary from about 200 to 500 msec depending on the species and the response system within the species (see review by Woody, 1982)], and very little or no conditioning is observed with intervals approaching zero or exceeding 3 sec (Frey and Ross, 1968; McAllister, 1953; Russell, 1966; Moore and Gormezano, 1977). Thus, in Eq. (2), indexing starts with j equal to 1 because c_0 is equal to zero, reflecting the fact that no conditioning is observed with an interstimulus interval of zero. The term c_1 is assigned the maximal value, reflecting the fact that 0.5 sec is (approximately) the optimal interstimulus interval. Then c_{j+1} is less than c_j for the remaining c values, reflecting the decreasing efficacy of conditioning as the interstimulus interval increases beyond 0.5 sec. The term τ is normally set equal to 5, because when $j = 6$ (corresponding to an interstimulus interval of 3 sec) little or no conditioning would occur so c_6 would be approximately equal to zero.

A lower bound is set on the absolute values of the synaptic weights, $w_i(t)$. The bound is near but not equal to zero because synaptic weights appear as factors on the right side of Eq. (2). It can be seen that the learning mechanism would cease to yield changes in synaptic efficacy for any synapse whose efficacy reached zero; that is, $\Delta w_i(t)$ would henceforth always equal zero. A lower bound on the absolute values of synaptic weights results in excitatory weights always remaining excitatory (positive) and inhibitory weights always remaining inhibitory (negative); that is, synaptic weights do not cross zero. This is consistent with the known physiology of synapses (Eccles, 1964). A nonzero lower bound on the efficacy of synapses is also consistent with evidence suggesting that potential conditioned stimuli are weakly connected to unconditioned responses prior to conditioning (Gould, 1986; Schwartz, 1978; Pavlov, 1927). Also, a nonzero lower bound on the efficacy of synapses models the notion that a synapse must have some effect on the postsynaptic neuron in order for the postsynaptic learning mechanism to be triggered. That learning mechanisms are postsynaptic, at least in phylogenetically advanced organisms, has been well argued by McNaughton *et al.* (1984). In the case of the mammalian central nervous system, Thompson *et al.* (1983b) note that what little evidence now exists is perhaps more consistent with the hypothesis of postsynaptic rather than presynaptic learning mechanisms.

In general, it is expected that the efficacy of synapses, $w_i(t)$, is variable and under the control of the neuronal learning mechanism. However, some synapses can be expected to have fixed weights, that is, weights that are innate and unchangeable. This may be true for many or most synapses in the autonomic nervous system. In the somatic nervous system, it is likely that many more synapses and perhaps most are variable or "plastic." In the case of the drive-reinforcement neuronal model, it will be assumed that synapses mediating conditioned stimuli have variable weights and that synapses mediating unconditioned stimuli have fixed weights. The innately specified synaptic weights that are assumed to mediate unconditioned stimuli are expected to reflect the evolutionary history of the organism.

Let us now stand back and look at what is happening in Eq. (2). As the specification of the learning mechanism for the drive-reinforcement neuronal model, Eq. (2) suggests how the efficacy of a synapse changes as a function of four factors: (1) learning-rate constants c_j that are assumed to be innate; (2) the absolute value $|w_i(t - j)|$ of the efficacy of the synapse at time $t - j$, when the change in presynaptic level of activity occurred; (3) the change in presynaptic level of activity, $\Delta x_i(t - j)$; and (4) the change in postsynaptic level of activity, $\Delta y(t)$.

One way of visualizing either the Hebbian or the drive-reinforcement learning mechanism is in terms of a temporal window that slides along the time line as learning occurs, changing the efficacy of synapses as it moves along. In the case of the Hebbian model, the learning mechanism employs a temporal window that is, in effect, only one time step wide. The learning mechanism slides along the time line, modifying the efficacy of synapses proportional to (1) a learning-rate constant, (2) the presynaptic level of activity, and (3) the postsynaptic level of activity. (The Hebbian model will be presented in mathematical form later.) In the case of the drive-reinforcement model, the learning mechanism employs a temporal window that is $\tau + 1$ time steps wide. The learning mechanism slides along the time line modifying the efficacy of synapses proportional to (1) learning-rate constants, (2) the efficacy of synapses, (3) changes in presynaptic levels of activity, and (4) changes in postsynaptic levels of activity. It can be seen that the Hebbian learning mechanism correlates approximately simultaneous signal levels and the drive-reinforcement learning mechanism correlates temporally separated derivatives of signal levels. (In the case of the drive-reinforcement model, I am not suggesting that a neuron would have to compute anything as refined as a first derivative. A first-order difference will suffice, as will be demonstrated later.) The differences in the behavior of the Hebbian and the drive-reinforcement learning mechanisms will be examined below when the results of computer simulations of both models are presented.

C. Properties of the Model

The drive-reinforcement neuronal model suggests that what neurons are learning to do is to anticipate or predict the onsets and offsets of pulse trains. By pulse trains, I mean sequences or clusters of action potentials in axons. The drive-reinforcement neuronal model learns to predict the onsets and offsets of pulse trains representing unconditioned stimuli, utilizing the onsets of pulse trains representing conditioned stimuli. This will become evident when the results of computer simulations of the model are presented. It will be seen that the learning mechanism moves the onsets and offsets of pulse trains to earlier points in time. Fundamentally, the learning mechanism is a shaper of pulse trains. The efficacy of a synapse changes in a direction such that the neuron comes to anticipate the unconditioned response; that is, the conditioned stimulus comes to produce the conditioned response prior to the occurrence of the unconditioned stimulus and the unconditioned response. The way the drive-reinforcement neuronal learning mechanism shapes pulse trains in illustrated in Fig. 2. Earlier investigators have pointed to the anticipatory or predictive nature of conditioning phenomena. Noteworthy in this regard is the work of Kamin (1968, 1969), Rescorla and Wagner (1972), Dickinson and Mackintosh (1978), and Sutton and Barto (1981).

_____ III. Predictions of the Model _____

Classical conditioning phenomena are basic to learning. By means of computer simulations, it will be demonstrated that the drive-reinforcement neuronal model predicts a wide range of classical conditioning phenomena.

The neuronal model that was simulated is shown in Fig. 3. The input–output (I/O) relationship assumed for the neuron was that of Eq. (1). The neuronal learning mechanism (L.M.) was that of Eq. (2) with the refinement noted earlier: whenever $\Delta x_i(t - j)$ was less than zero, $\Delta x_i(t - j)$ was set equal to zero for the purpose of calculating $\Delta w_i(t)$. In the computer simulations, a conditioned stimulus (CS) or unconditioned stimulus (UCS) that was presented to the neuron had an amplitude that ranged between zero and one and a duration that was specified in terms

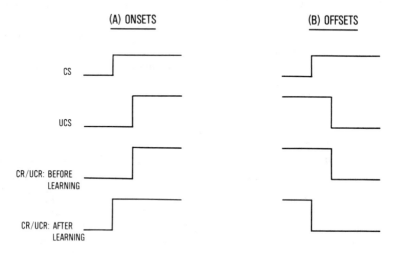

Figure 2.

Examples of how the drive-reinforcement learning mechanism alters the onsets and offsets of pulse trains for a single theoretical neuron. Panels (A) and (B) show the effects of UCS onset and offset, respectively. In each example, the conditioned stimulus (CS) is followed by an unconditioned stimulus (UCS), both of which represent presynaptic signals. The two presynaptic signals are assumed to be mediated by separate synapses, with the CS-mediating synapse having a variable efficacy (weight) under the control of the neuronal learning mechanism. The conditioned and unconditioned response (CR and UCR) before and after learning (i.e., before and after a number of presentations of the CS–UCS pair) are shown below the waveforms for the CS and UCS pulse trains. The conditioned and unconditioned response (CR/UCR) represents the postsynaptic frequency of firing of the neuron. In panels (A) and (B), it is seen that the onset and offset of firing, respectively, occurs earlier in time after learning. Thus, in each case, the neuron has learned to anticipate the unconditioned response by learning to start firing earlier (A) or stop firing earlier (B).

of the times of stimulus onset and offset. In the figures showing results of the computer simulations, each CS–UCS configurations is graphed so the reader may see the relative amplitudes and durations of stimuli at a glance. (For exact values for any of the parameters for the computer simulations, the Appendix should be consulted.)

Each stimulus was presented to the simulated neuron through both an excitatory and an inhibitory synapse so that the neuronal learning mechanism had, for each input, both an excitatory and an inhibitory weight available for modification. The learning mechanism could then choose to modify one or the other weight or both in each time step. In the case of an actual (biological) neuron, if a CS is not represented by both excitatory and inhibitory synapses, the individual neuron will be constrained in terms of what classical conditioning phenomena it can manifest. It will be seen in the simulations below that, for a drive-reinforcement neuron, some classical conditioning phenomena require only excitatory plastic synapses and some require only inhibitory plastic synapses. Those classical conditioning phenomena requiring both excitatory and inhibitory plastic synapses would have to emerge at a higher level if the individual neurons involved had their CSs represented by only excitatory or only inhibitory plastic synapses.

In the discussion that follows, a conditioned or unconditioned stimulus and the associated $x_i(t)$ in Fig. 3 are identical. For example, $x_1(t)$ and $x_2(t)$ are one and the same as CS_1. The weights associated with the

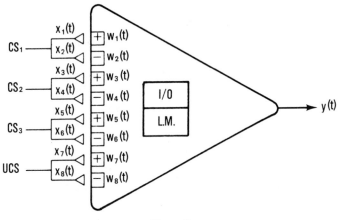

Figure 3.
Drive-reinforcement neuronal model employed in the computer simulations. This is a specific example of the more general model shown in Fig. 1. The description that was given in Fig. 1 applies here. In addition, each CS and UCS is represented by an excitatory (+) and an inhibitory (−) synapse. The efficacies of synapses [i.e., the synaptic weights, $w_i(t)$] are variable (plastic) for synapses mediating CSs and fixed (nonplastic) for synapses mediating UCSs.

synapses carrying the unconditioned stimulus were fixed (nonplastic) and the remaining synaptic weights were variable (plastic).

The conditioned stimulus or unconditioned stimulus that is described should, perhaps, more properly be referred to as a *neuronal* conditioned stimulus or a *neuronal* unconditioned stimulus, because it is the stimulus that is reaching the neuron, not the stimulus that is reaching the whole animal. However, for the sake of simplicity in the discussion, I will refer to these neuronal input signals as conditioned and unconditioned stimuli or, simply, CSs and UCSs. Likewise, the output $y(t)$ of the neuron would more properly be referred to as the *neuronal* conditioned or unconditioned response, but I will usually refer to the neuronal response as the conditioned response (CR) or unconditioned response (UCR). Built into these terminological conventions is the assumption that stimuli and responses external to an animal's nervous system do not differ fundamentally in form from the way stimuli and responses are represented internal to the animal's nervous system. This assumption might not hold up well at higher, cognitive levels of function, but the assumption appears reasonable as a starting point for testing the ability of a neuronal model to predict fundamental learning phenomena.

Just as the range of $x_i(t)$ in the simulations was from zero to one, as was noted when the range of CS and UCS amplitudes was discussed, so the range of $y(t)$, the neuronal output, was from zero to one. Such a range serves to model a finite range of frequencies for neuronal inputs and outputs. Actual frequencies of biological neurons range up to several hundred spikes per second in the case of neocortical neurons firing for brief intervals (Lynch *et al.*, 1977). Therefore, one could multiply the neuronal input and output amplitudes used in the simulations by, say, 300 if one desires to see more realistic numbers. However, for the purposes of the simulations to be reported, the relative magnitudes of the parameters are important, not the absolute magnitudes.

The number of synapses impinging on the simulated neuron was eight, as is indicated in Fig. 3. This corresponded to three possible CSs and one UCS. The absolute values of the plastic synaptic weights mediating the CSs had a lower bound of 0.1 and, when the simulations began, these excitatory and inhibitory weights were set at plus and minus 0.1, respectively. The neuronal threshold was set at zero because at higher values of the neuronal threshold the form of the model's predictions did not change. The only effect of higher thresholds was that more trials were required for the synaptic weights to reach their asymptotic values. For the learning mechanism, the learning-rate constants, c_1–c_5, were set at values such that $c_j > c_{j+1}$. As noted earlier, this is reasonable if one views each time step as being equivalent to 0.5 sec because then c_1 is maximal, corresponding to a nominal optimal interstimulus interval of 0.5 sec. Successive c values then decrease as the interstimulus interval increases. As also noted earlier, c_0 and c_6 were set equal to zero, corresponding to interstimulus intervals of 0 and 3 sec, respectively. Thus, in the simulations, j ranged from 1 to 5; that is, τ was set equal to 5.

What follows are the results of computer simulations of the drive-reinforcement neuronal model for a variety of CS–UCS configurations. Predictions of the model have been demonstrated to be accurate for the following categories of classical conditioning phenomena: delay and trace conditioning, CS and UCS duration and amplitude effects, partial reinforcement effects, interstimulus interval effects including simultaneous conditioning, second-order conditioning, conditioned inhibition, extinction, reacquisition effects, backward conditioning, blocking, overshadowing, compound conditioning, and discriminative stimulus effects (Klopf, 1988). Because of space limitations, results of the computer simulations can be shown for only the following categories of classical conditioning phenomena: delay conditioning, CS duration effects, conditioned inhibition, and extinction.

During a simulation, the CS–UCS configuration was presented once in each trial. The values of the synaptic weights at the end of each trial were recorded and plotted as a function of the trial number. These graphs of synaptic weights versus trials are shown in the figures accompanying the discussion below. In addition, in each figure, the CS–UCS configuration is graphed along with the response of the neuron during the last trial. The neuronal response is labeled "Y," designating a plot of $y(t)$ for the last trial of the simulation. The definition of a trial should be noted. The CS–UCS configuration, or what is referred to in the figures as the "stimulus configuration," defines a trial. Thus, the graphed stimulus configurations in the figures are intended to show not only relative times of onset and offset along with amplitudes of stimuli but also the number of times a stimulus was presented during a trial. What will be seen in the figures is that the behavior of the synaptic weights, as predicted by the drive-reinforcement neuronal model, mirrors the observed behavior of animals as they are learning during classical conditioning experiments.

Before discussing the individual simulations, two remarks are in order regarding the graphs of synaptic weights versus trials. Any synaptic weight that played a significant role for the conditioning phenomenon being discussed is shown in the accompanying graph. Any synaptic weight that played no significant role (typically meaning that the neuronal learning mechanism did not alter the weight at all during the simulation) is not shown, in order to simplify the graphs. Also, data points for the synaptic weight values at the end of each trial are not shown on the graphs because the resulting density of the data points would be excessive and because the data points fall exactly on the (theoretical) curves that have been drawn.

A. Delay Conditioning

Delay conditioning is defined such that CS onset precedes UCS onset and CS offset occurs at the same time as or after UCS onset. An example is the well-known Pavlovian experiment in which a bell (the CS) is paired with food (the UCS). The observed result in such experiments is that conditioned excitation develops. The bell becomes excitatory with respect to the salivary gland. In addition, it is observed that the amount of salivation in response to the bell alone (measured with occasional test probes) increases with increasing trials such that an S-shaped or sigmoid curve results when the amount of salivation is plotted versus the trial number. This is the classic S-shaped acquisition curve of animal learning. The amount of salivation in response to the bell alone, as a function of trials, positively accelerates initially and then negatively accelerates as an asymptotic level of conditioning is approached (Pavlov, 1927). Spence (1956) has observed that the acquisition curves of classical conditioning are always S-shaped, providing that the experiments are done carefully enough to capture the initial positive acceleration and the later negative acceleration. For example, Spence (1956, pp. 68–70) states that acquisition curves that "do not exhibit an initial, positively accelerated phase do not do so either because they do not start at zero level of conditioning or because the conditioning is so rapid that the period of initial acceleration is too brief to be revealed except by very small groups or blocks of trials."

Figure 4 shows the predicted acquisition curves of three neuronal models for delay conditioning. In Fig. 4(a), the results of a simulation of the model proposed by Hebb (1949) are shown. For the Hebbian model, the input–output relationship is the same as for the drive-reinforcement model and is, therefore, specified by Eq. (1). The Hebbian learning mechanism equation may be written as

$$(3) \quad \Delta w_i(t) = c x_i(t) y(t)$$

where c is a learning rate constant and the other symbols are as defined earlier. It can be seen in Fig. 4(a) that if a Hebbian neuron were driving the salivary gland, the amount of saliva produced in response to the bell alone as a function of trials would exhibit an essentially linear relationship because the excitatory synaptic weight associated with the CS varies in an essentially linear fashion with the trial number. Also, it may be noted that the Hebbian learning mechanism does not yield an asymptotic synaptic weight value but, rather, continues to increase the synaptic weight indefinitely or, of course, until an upper bound would be reached.

The results of a simulation of the Sutton-Barto (1981) model are shown in Fig. 4(b). The model's input–output relationship is that of Eq.

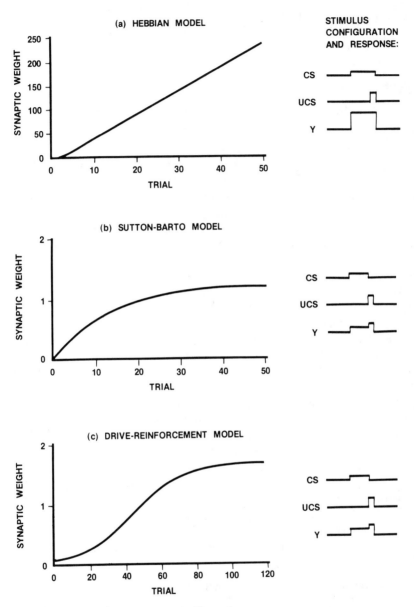

Figure 4.
Results of simulated delay conditioning experiments with (a) Hebbian, (b) Sutton–Barto, and (c) drive-reinforcement neuronal models. The Hebbian model yields an essentially linear acquisition curve. The Sutton–Barto model yields a negatively accelerated acquisition curve. Consistent with the experimental evidence, the drive-reinforcement neuronal model yields an S-shaped acquisition curve. (See text and Appendix for details.)

(1). The Sutton–Barto learning mechanism is specified by the following equation:

(4) $\Delta w_i(t) = c\bar{x}_i(t)\,\Delta y(t)$

where

(5) $\bar{x}_i(t) = \alpha\bar{x}_i(t-1) + x_i(t-1)$

In Eq. (5), α is a positive constant. In Fig. 4(b), the model is seen to predict a negatively accelerated acquisition curve in that the excitatory synaptic weight associated with the CS negatively accelerates with increasing trials. It may be noted that the Rescorla–Wagner (1972) model also predicts a negatively accelerated acquisition curve, as have earlier psychological models [see, for example, a model due to Estes (1950)].

In Fig. 4(c), the results of a simulation of the drive-reinforcement model are shown. The model is seen to predict an S-shaped acquisition curve: conditioned excitation develops, first through a positively accelerating phase and then through a negatively accelerating phase. The drive-reinforcement model is thus seen to be consistent with this aspect of the experimental evidence of delay conditioning.

Some reasons why the drive-reinforcement model yields an S-shaped acquisition curve may be noted. The initial positive acceleration is due to the efficacy of the relevant synapse appearing as a factor on the right side of Eq. (2). Thus, as the learning mechanism increases the efficacy of the synapse, the future rate of change of the efficacy of the synapse is also caused to increase. With continued conditioning, another process comes to dominate, yielding the eventual negative acceleration in the acquisition curve. The negative acceleration is due to $\Delta y(t)$ decreasing with continued conditioning. In effect, $\Delta y(t)$ moves to an earlier point in time with conditioning, becoming $\Delta y(t-j)$ where j is the interstimulus interval. Thus, throughout the conditioning process, increasing values of $w_i(t-j)$ are competing with decreasing values of $\Delta y(t)$ in Eq. (2). Rapidly increasing values of $w_i(t-j)$ prevail initially, and rapidly decreasing values of $\Delta y(t)$ prevail later, yielding the respective positive and negative accelerations in the acquisition curve.

B. Conditioned Stimulus Duration Effects

A careful reader may note that, in Fig. 4, the same CS–UCS configuration is not used for the simulation of each of the models. The Hebbian model's CS offset coincides with the offset of the UCS, whereas the Sutton–Barto and drive-reinforcement model CSs have the offset occuring at the time of UCS onset. I chose those particular CS–UCS configurations because otherwise the Hebbian and Sutton–Barto models would not have predicted the development of conditioned excitation. Both of these models are sensitive to CS durations in a way that is not consistent with the experimental evidence, the models predicting no conditioning or conditioned inhibition for some CS–UCS configurations that, experimentally, are known to yield conditioned excitation. The effect of CS duration is examined systematically in Fig. 5, where each model's predictions are shown for the same set of three CS–UCS configurations. I will specify how the three CS–UCS configurations differ and then discuss each model's predictions for each of the three configurations.

In Fig. 5, CS_1 offset occurs at the time of UCS onset, CS_2 offset occurs at the time of UCS offset, and CS_3 offset occurs one time step after UCS offset. Experimentally, it is known that conditioned excitation (corresponding in the neuronal models to the growth of positive synaptic weights) is observed in all three cases. In general, the efficacy of delay conditioning is a strong function of the time of CS onset and is relatively independent of CS duration (Kamin, 1965).

In Fig. 5(a), it is seen that the Hebbian model predicts conditioned excitation for CS_2 and CS_3 but not for CS_1. In Fig. 5(b), it is seen that the Sutton–Barto model predicts conditioned excitation for CS_1 and strong conditioned inhibition for CS_2 and CS_3. In Fig. 5(c), it is seen that, consistent with the experimental evidence, the drive-reinforcement model predicts conditioned excitation for all three CSs and, in each case, predicts an S-shaped acquisition curve.

In Fig. 5(c), more detailed aspects of the drive-reinforcement model's predictions may be noted. For example, the model predicts a particular ranking of CSs in terms of initial rate of conditioning and asymptotic synaptic weight value as a function of CS duration. The experimental literature does not, at this point, permit the accuracy of these more detailed predictions to be assessed. Furthermore, whole-animal data may be insufficient to test these predictions, in that higher-level attention mechanisms may play a significant role when CS durations are extended beyond the UCS (Ayres et al., 1987). Experiments at the level of the single neuron may be required to test these predictions.

Thus far, the drive-reinforcement neuronal model's predictions have been demonstrated to be accurate for two categories of classical conditioning phenomena: (1) the form of the acquisition curve in delay conditioning and (2) relative insensitivity to CS duration. The predictions of the model for two other CS–UCS configurations will now be examined. While the predictions of the Hebbian and Sutton–Barto models for these CS–UCS configurations will not be shown, it should be noted that the Hebbian model's predictions frequently deviate substantially from experimentally observed behavior, examples of this having already been seen in Fig. 4 and 5. (Of course, it remains a theoretical possibility that biological neurons are Hebbian and that classical conditioning phenomena are emergent, resulting from the interactions of perhaps large numbers of Hebbian neurons.) The predictions of the Sutton–Barto model are similar to those of the drive-reinforcement model, if one is careful,

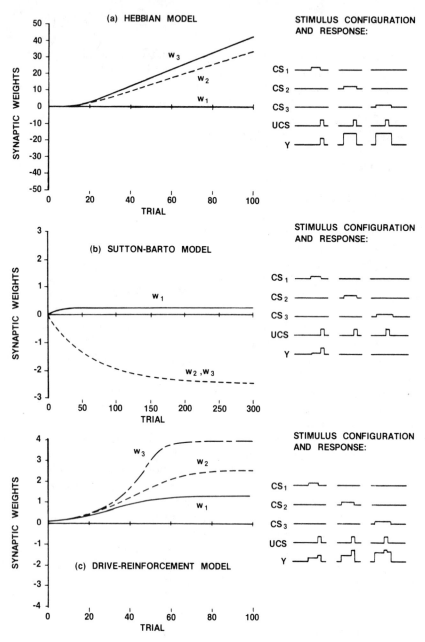

Figure 5.
Results of simulated delay conditioning experiments with (a) Hebbian, (b) Sutton–Barto, and (c) drive-reinforcement neuronal models. The effect of CS duration is examined. CS_1 offset occurs at the time of UCS onset. CS_2 offset occurs at the time of UCS offset. CS_3 offset occurs after UCS offset. The Hebbian model yields conditioned excitation for CS_2 and CS_3 and no conditioning for CS_1. The Sutton–Barto neuronal model yields conditioned excitation for CS_1 and conditioned inhibition for CS_2 and CS_3. Consistent with the experimental evidence, the drive-reinforcement neuronal model yields conditioned excitation for CS_1, CS_2, and CS_3. (See text and Appendix for details.)

in the case of the Sutton–Barto model, not to use substantially overlapping CSs and UCSs and accepting that the Sutton–Barto model's predicted acquisition curves are not S-shaped.

C. Conditioned Inhibition

Delay conditioning yields *conditioned excitation;* that is, the CS comes to excite the conditioned response (CR). An alternative procedure developed by Pavlov (1927) yields what he termed *conditioned inhibition:* a CS would come to inhibit a CR that otherwise would have manifested.

One of Pavlov's procedures for demonstrating conditioned inhibition was as follows. In the first stage of conditioning, Pavlov would utilize a delay conditioning procedure to render CS_1 excitatory with respect to a CR. Then, in a second stage of conditioning, he would continue to reinforce CS_1 with the UCS but he would also present an *unreinforced* CS_1–CS_2 pair to the animal. During the second stage of conditioning, the animal's response to CS_1 unpaired would decrease initially and then return to its original level. The animal's response to the CS_1–CS_2 pair would decrease to zero. Furthermore, Pavlov was able to demonstrate that CS_2 became a conditioned inhibitor in that, after stage-two conditioning, if CS_2 was paired with another CS, say CS_3, that was known by itself to be a conditioned exciter, the CR associated with CS_3 was in general reduced or eliminated.

The drive-reinforcement model predicts this behavior, as can be seen in Fig. 6. In stage one (trials 1–70) of the simulated conditioning, CS_1 is reinforced by a UCS such that conditioned excitation develops, with the progress of the excitatory weight, $w_1(E)$, exhibiting the usual S-shaped acquisition curve. Then, in stage two (trials 71–200), CS_1 unpaired is reinforced by the UCS once in each trial while the CS_1–CS_2 pair is also presented once during each trial and the pair is unreinforced. The model predicts that the excitatory weight associated with CS_1 will decrease initially and then return to its previous level, mirroring the behavior Pavlov observed with his animals. Also, the model predicts that the inhibitory weight, $w_2(I)$, associated with CS_2, will grow stronger as stage two conditioning proceeds, consistent with Pavlov's observation that CS_2 becomes a conditioned inhibitor. (For the notation employed here, an "E" or an "I" in parentheses following "w_i" signifies an excitatory or inhibitory weight, respectively. This notation involves a degree of redundancy in that excitatory weights will always be positive and inhibitory weights will always be negative, so in the graphs excitatory and inhibitory weights for a particular CS could be distinguished on that basis.)

Because the decrease in the excitatory weight associated with CS_1 during the second stage of conditioning and then its subsequent return to the asymptotic level achieved in the first stage of conditioning may seem surprising, a few words of explanation may be in order. The initial

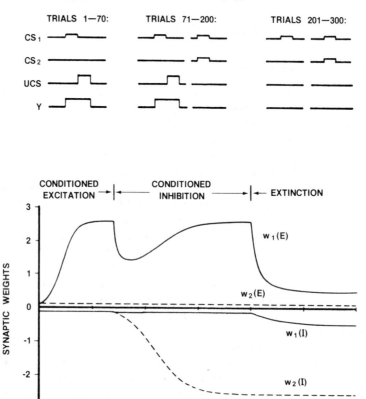

STIMULUS CONFIGURATION AND RESPONSE:

Figure 6.
Results of a simulated classical conditioning experiment modeled after experiments performed by Pavlov (1927). In the simulated experiment, the drive-reinforcement model's predictions are examined for three stages of conditioning. In stage 1 (trials 1–70), a delay conditioning paradigm is utilized and, consistent with the experimental evidence, an S-shaped acquisition curve for the excitatory synaptic weight, $w_1(E)$, associated with CS_1, is predicted. In stage 2 (trials 71–200), Pavlov's conditioned inhibition paradigm is employed and time courses for the CS_1 excitatory synaptic weight, $w_1(E)$, and the CS_2 inhibitory synaptic weight, $w_2(I)$, are predicted consistent with Pavlov's observations that salivation to CS_1 decreased initially and then returned to its previous asymptotic level and that CS_2 became a conditioned inhibitor. In stage 3 (trials 201–300), an extinction paradigm is employed and, consistent with Pavlov's observations and inferences, the behavioral response to CS_1 extinguishes [the sum of $w_1(E)$ and $w_1(I)$ approaches zero]; the CS_1 inhibitory synaptic weight, $w_1(I)$, undergoes a small increase in its absolute value; and the CS_2 inhibitory synaptic weight, $w_2(I)$, does not extinguish. (See text and Appendix for details.)

decrease is due to the occurrence of the unreinforced CS_1–CS_2 pair in that the onset of the CS_1–CS_2 pair yields a positive Δx_1 that is followed by a negative Δy at the time of termination of CS_1 and CS_2. The negative Δy occurs because, with an unreinforced pair, no UCS onset occurs at the time of CS_1–CS_2 offset and thus there is nothing to cause the neuronal response to be sustained. The drive-reinforcement learning mechanism yields negative values of Δw whenever a positive Δx_i is followed within τ time steps by a negative Δy. Thus, the excitatory weight associated with CS_1 decreases initially in stage two of conditioning. Similarly, the inhibitory weight associated with CS_2 is decreasing (i.e., becoming more negative or becoming stronger in terms of its absolute value) because CS_2 onset yields a positive Δx_2 that is followed by a negative Δy at the time of CS_1–CS_2 offset. The excitatory weight associated with CS_1 ceases to decrease and starts increasing when the conditioned inhibition becomes sufficient, such that the positive Δy following the onset of CS_1 unpaired with CS_2 is larger than the negative Δy following the onset of CS_1–CS_2 paired. The inhibitory weight associated with CS_2 continues to decrease (become more strongly inhibitory) because its onset, yielding a positive Δx_2, continues to be followed by a negative Δy until the conditioned inhibition of CS_2 becomes sufficient to cancel the conditioned excitation of CS_1, at which point the CS_2 inhibitory weight, $w_2(I)$, reaches its asymptotic level. At the same time, the CS_1 excitatory weight, $w_1(E)$, approaches its asymptotic level, equal to its prior asymptotic level, because when the CS_2 conditioned inhibition cancels the CS_1 conditioned excitation, the reinforcement of CS_1 unpaired is the only event in each trial that yields a nonzero Δy following a positive Δx. Thus, toward the end of stage-two conditioning, the situation in terms of positive values of Δx followed by nonzero values of Δy is similar to the situation that occurred in stage one.

D. Extinction

When conditioned excitation develops in conjunction with a CS, as was the case for CS_1 at the conclusion of stage one (trials 1–70) and stage two (trials 71–200) of conditioning in Fig. 6, if the CS continues to be presented in a third stage of conditioning, this time without reinforcement, then Pavlov (1927) observed that the CR *extinguishes;* that is, the CR decreases in magnitude, reaching zero with a sufficient number of unreinforced presentations of the CS. In addition, Pavlov inferred that conditioned inhibition developed during the extinction process because he observed "spontaneous recovery" of the CR with time and he also observed more rapid reacquisition of the CR if reinforced presentations of the CS were resumed. The predictions of the drive-reinforcement model are consistent with Pavlov's observations and inferences. Note that in stage three (trials 201–300) of conditioning in Fig. 6, where CS_1

is presented without reinforcement, the CS_1 excitatory weight, $w_1(E)$, declines and the CS_1 inhibitory weight, $w_1(I)$, grows stronger, until they cancel one another, at which time the CR will no longer appear.

Perhaps a few words are in order regarding the phenomenon of spontaneous recovery following extinction. Spontaneous recovery refers to the tendency of an extinguished conditioned response to return after the CS is not presented for some period of time. It seems that spontaneous recovery could be due to the state of the nervous system changing sufficiently with time so that the conditioned inhibition that may develop during the process of extinction becomes less effective. [As noted above, Pavlov (1927) believed that conditioned inhibition developed during the process of extinction. However, Rescorla (1969, p.87) has stated that "There is only meager evidence bearing on this question."] If the hypothesized conditioned inhibition were to become less effective because a change in the state of the nervous system resulted in fewer of the conditioned inhibitory synapses being active, then it would become easier for the conditioned response to manifest again. If this explanation of spontaneous recovery is correct, a neuronal model would not be expected to predict the phenomenon. A *network* model would be required to generate the prediction.

In the third stage of conditioning in Fig. 6, the drive-reinforcement model makes one further prediction that has not yet been discussed. In this simulation, not only was CS_1 presented unreinforced in stage three but the CS_1–CS_2 pair was also presented unreinforced. Pavlov (1927) observed that under these circumstances, the conditioned excitation associated with CS_1 extinguished but the conditioned inhibition associated with CS_2 did not. This is predicted by the drive-reinforcement model. In the third stage of conditioning in Fig. 6, notice that the inhibitory weight, $w_2(I)$, remains unchanged during the unreinforced presentations of the CS_1–CS_2 pair. This prediction of the drive-reinforcement model differs from that of the Rescorla–Wagner model of classical conditioning. As Rescorla and Wagner (1972) point out, their model is inconsistent with the experimental evidence of conditioned inhibition studies in that the model predicts the extinction of conditioned inhibition. The drive-reinforcement model does not make this prediction because the positive Δx occurring at the time of CS_2 onset is not followed by a positive Δy.

E. Drives and Reinforcers

The behavior of the proposed neuronal model may be understood in terms of two processes involving postulated neuronal drives and reinforcers. If weighted presynaptic signal levels are defined to be neuronal drives and changes in weighted presynaptic signal levels are defined to be neuronal reinforcers, then the drive-reinforcement learning mechanism operates such that neuronal drive induction promotes learned excitatory processes and neuronal drive reduction promotes learned inhibitory processes. The interplay between these two processes is seen to yield the categories of classical conditioning phenomena discussed above.

IV. Experimental Tests

By means of computer simulations, the drive-reinforcement neuronal model has been demonstrated to be consistent, in general, with the experimental evidence of classical conditioning. However, such a demonstration involves comparing theoretical predictions of a *neuronal* model with experimental evidence obtained from *whole animals*. To some extent, whole-animal data has to be problematic vis-à-vis the predictions of a neuronal model. The effects of multiple interacting neurons, the effects of the brain's many interacting subsystems, and, in general, the effects of the global architecture of the brain will of course influence whole-animal data. All of these effects, collectively, I will refer to as *network effects* to distinguish them from *neuronal* (meaning single-neuron) *effects*. Network effects will preclude rigorous experimental tests of any neuronal model in terms of whole-animal data. Tests at a neurobiological level will be required. Fortunately, such experimental tests are becoming feasible and, indeed, results to date encourage the notion that classical conditioning phenomena may manifest at the level of the single neuron, as the drive-reinforcement model suggests. See reviews by Kandel and Spencer (1968), Mpitsos et al. (1978), Thompson et al. (1983a), Farley and Alkon (1985), Woody (1986), Carew and Sahley (1986), and Byrne (1987); see also Hawkins and Kandel (1984) and Kelso and Brown (1986). Instrumental conditioning experiments at the level of the single neuron are also becoming feasible (Stein and Belluzzi, 1988).

At this point, perhaps a note is in order regarding the semantics I am adopting. When I suggest that a single neuron may manifest classical conditioning phenomena, the "single neuron" I am referring to includes the synapses that impinge upon it. Those synapses, of course, come from other neurons or from sensory receptors and, in that sense, what I am referring to as a phenomenon involving a "single neuron" is, in fact, a multineuron or neuron and receptor phenomenon. The point, though, is that a single neuron may be undergoing the conditioning, as distinguished from alternative theoretical models that can be envisioned in which whole circuits consisting of many neurons would be the lowest level at which conditioning could occur. An implication of the drive-reinforcement neuronal model is that classical conditioning is not an emergent phenomenon, but rather that the ability to undergo classical conditioning is a fundamental property of single cells.

Actually, the hypothesized drive-reinforcement learning mechanism could be implemented at a lower level than that of the single neuron. Minimally, what would seem to be required would be two synapses interacting such that one synapse would deliver the signal corresponding to $\Delta x_i(t - j)$, reflecting the onset of the CS, and the other synapse would deliver the signal corresponding to $\Delta y(t)$, reflecting the onset or offset of the UCS. Evidence of such interactions between synapses has been obtained in investigations of classical conditioning in *Aplysia*. The learning mechanism appears to involve what is termed activity-dependent amplification of presynaptic facilitation (Hawkins *et al.*, 1983) or activity-dependent neuromodulation (Walters and Byrne, 1983) of sensory neuron terminals (see Chapters 4 and 5 in this volume). The optimal interstimulus interval between activation of the sensory neuron terminal representing the CS and activation of the facilitator neuron terminal representing the UCS has been found to be about 500 msec (Carew *et al.*, 1981; Hawkins *et al.*, 1986). While the evidence for conditioning at a neuronal level in *Aplysia* has been interpreted as suggesting a presynaptic learning mechanism, Farley and Alkon (1985) indicate that the sites of the changes may not be exclusively presynaptic.

Whether presynaptic or postsynaptic processes or both underlie learning is a question that has been investigated theoretically (Zipser, 1986) and experimentally (Carew *et al.*, 1984). In this chapter, I have formulated the drive-reinforcement learning mechanism in terms of postsynaptic processes although, as discussed above, the learning mechanism could be implemented in an exclusively presynaptic form. Apart from activity-dependent amplification of presynaptic facilitation or activity-dependent neuromodulation offering a possible implementation of the drive-reinforcement learning mechanism, other possibilities can be envisioned that would still involve less than a whole neuron. Portions of dendritic trees and their impinging synapses might function in a manner analogous to the model I have envisioned for the whole neuron. Thus there are a range of possibilities for implementation of the drive-reinforcement learning mechanism, extending from what is perhaps a minimal two-synapse interaction on the low end ranging through portions of dendritic trees functioning as a basic unit of learning, up through the level at which a single neuron functions as the basic unit and beyond to the point where the whole organism is treated as a single unit. Variations of the drive-reinforcement model may have relevance at each of these levels, even though the learning mechanism seems to lend itself naturally to implementation at a neuronal level.

Regarding the question of how the drive-reinforcement model can be tested at a neuronal level, synaptic inputs will have to be controlled and monitored precisely for a single neuron while the neuron's frequency of firing is continually monitored. It will be necessary to measure the direction and preferably also the magnitude of the changes in efficacy of affected synapses. Changes in synaptic inputs, as potential CSs, and changes in neuronal outputs, representing potential reinforcement, will have to be tested to determine which, if any, input and output patterns yield changes in the efficacy of synapses. In this way, it can be established whether onsets and offsets of hypothesized neuronal CSs and UCSs determine the efficacy of synapses in the manner specified by the drive-reinforcement model.

V. Summary

A neuronal model of classical conditioning has been proposed. The model is most easily described by contrasting it with a still influential neuronal model first analyzed by Hebb (1949). It is proposed that the Hebbian model be modified in three ways to yield a model more in accordance with animal learning phenomena. First, instead of correlating pre- and postsynaptic levels of activity, *changes* in pre- and postsynaptic levels of activity should be correlated to determine the changes in synaptic efficacy that represent learning. Second, instead of correlating approximately simultaneous pre- and postsynaptic signals, earlier changes in presynaptic signals should be correlated with later changes in postsynaptic signals. Third, a change in the efficacy of a synapse should be proportional to the current efficacy of the synapse, accounting for the initial positive acceleration in the S-shaped acquisition curves observed in animal learning. The resulting model, termed a drive-reinforcement model of single-neuron function, suggests that nervous system activity can be understood in terms of two classes of neuronal signals: *drives* that are defined to be signal levels, and *reinforcers* that are defined to be changes in signal levels. Defining drives and reinforcers in this way, in conjunction with the neuronal model, suggests a basis for a neurobiological theory of learning. The drive-reinforcement model is an example of a real-time learning mechanism, a class of mechanisms that may be fundamental to memory and learning. The proposed neuronal model is an extension of the Sutton–Barto (1981) model, which, in turn, can be seen as a temporally refined extension of the Rescorla–Wagner (1972) model. By means of computer simulations, it has been shown that the proposed neuronal model predicts a wide range of classical conditioning phenomena, including delay and trace conditioning, conditioned and unconditioned stimulus duration and amplitude effects, partial reinforcement effects, interstimulus interval effects including simultaneous conditioning, second-order conditioning, conditioned inhibition, extinction, reacquisition effects, backward conditioning, blocking, overshadowing, compound conditioning, and discriminative stimulus effects. The neuronal model also eliminates some inconsistencies with the experimental evidence that occur with the Rescorla–Wagner and Sutton–Barto models. Experimental tests of the drive-reinforcement neuronal model have been proposed.

Acknowledgments

This research was supported by the Life Sciences Directorate of the Air Force Office of Scientific Research under Task 2312 R1. Jim Morgan is acknowledged for many helpful discussions and for the software he wrote for the single-neuron simulator employed in this research. I am grateful to the following people for comments on an earlier draft of this chapter: Andy Barto, Diana Blazis, Jack Byrne, John Desmond, Bruce Edson, Chuck Hendrix, Joan Klopf, John Moore, Jim Morgan, Libby Patterson, Rick Ricart, and Rich Sutton.

References

Anderson, J. A., Silverman, J. W., Ritz, S. A., and Jones, R. S. (1977). *Psychol. Rev.* **84,** 413–451.
Ayres, J. J. B., Albert, M., and Bombase, J. C. (1987). *J. Exp. Psychol., Anim. Behav. Processes* **13**(2), 168–181.
Berlyne, D. E. (1973). *In* "Pleasure, Reward, Preference" (D. E. Berlyne and K. B. Madsen, eds.), pp. 1–33. Academic Press, New York.
Blazis, D. E. J., Desmond, J. E., Moore, J. W., and Berthier, N. E. (1986). *Proc. 8th Annu. Conf. Cogn. Sci. Soc.* pp. 176–186.
Byrne, J. H. (1987). *Physiol. Rev.* **67**(2), 329–439.
Calvin, W. H. (1975). *Brain Res.* **84,** 1–22.
Carew, T. J., and Sahley, C. L. (1986). *Annu. Rev. Neurosci.* **9,** 435–487.
Carew, T. J., Walters, E. T., and Kandel, E. R. (1981). *J. Neurosci.* **1,** 1426–1437.
Carew, T. J., Hawkins, R. D., Abrams, T. W., and Kandel, E. R. (1984). *J. Neurosci.* **4,** 1217–1224.
Dickinson, A., and Mackintosh, N. J. (1978). *Annu. Rev. Psychol.* **29,** 587–612.
Donegan, N. H., and Wagner, A. R. (1987). *In* "Classical Conditioning" (I. Gormezano, W. F. Prokasy, and R. F. Thompson, eds.), 3rd ed., pp. 339–369. Erlbaum, Hillsdale, New Jersey.
Eccles, J. C. (1964). "The Physiology of Synapses." Academic Press, New York.
Estes, W. K. (1950). *Psych. Rev.* **57,** 94–107.
Farley, J., and Alkon, D. L. (1985). *Annu. Rev. Psychol.* **36,** 419–494.
Fowler, H. (1971). *In* "The Nature of Reinforcement" (R. Glaser, ed.), pp. 151–195. Academic Press, New York.
Freud, S. (1895). *In* "The Standard Edition of the Complete Psychological Works of Sigmund Freud" (J. Strachey, ed.), Vol. 1, pp. 281–387. Macmillan, New York (reprinted 1964).
Frey, P. W., and Ross, L. E. (1968). *J. Comp. Physiol. Psychol.* **65,** 246–250.
Gelperin, A., Hopfield, J. J., and Tank, D. W. (1985). *In* "Model Neural Networks and Behavior" (A. I. Selverston, ed.), pp. 237–261. Plenum, New York.
Gluck, M. A., and Thompson, R. F. (1987). *Psycho. Rev.* **94**(2), 176–191.
Gould, J. L. (1986). *Annu. Rev. Psychol.* **37,** 163–192.
Grossberg, S. (1982). "Studies of Mind and Brain." Reidel, Boston, Massachusetts.
Hawkins, R. D., and Kandel, E. R. (1984). *In* "Neurobiology of Learning and Memory" (G. Lynch, J. L. McGaugh, and N. M. Weinberger, eds.), pp. 385–404. Guilford Press, New York.
Hawkins, R. D., Abrams, T. W., Carew, T. J., and Kandel, E. R. (1983). *Science* **219,** 400–405.
Hawkins, R. D., Carew, T. J., and Kandel, E. R. (1986). *J. Neurosci.* **6,** 1695–1701.
Hebb, D. O. (1949). "The Organization of Behavior." Wiley, New York.
Helson, H. (1964). "Adaptation-Level Theory." Harpers New York.

Hopfield, J. J., and Tank, D. W. (1986). *Science* **233**, 625–633.

Hull, C. L. (1943). "Principles of Behavior." Appleton, New York.

Kamin, L. J. (1965). *In* "Classical Conditioning: A Symposium" (W. F. Prokasy, ed.), pp. 118–147. Appleton, New York.

Kamin, L. J. (1968). *In* "Miami Symposium on the Prediction of Behavior: Aversive Stimulation" (M. R. Jones, ed.), pp. 9–31. Univ. of Miami Press, Miami.

Kamin, L. J. (1969). *In* "Punishment and Aversive Behavior" (B. A. Campbell and R. M. Church, eds.). pp. 279–296. Appleton, New York.

Kandel, E. R., and Spencer, W. A. (1968). *Physiol. Rev.* **48**(1), 65–134.

Kelso, S. R. and Brown, T. H. (1986). *Science* **232**, 85–87.

Klopf, A. H. (1972). "Brain Function and Adaptive Systems—A Heterostatic Theory", Rep. No. 133 (AFCRL-72-0164). Air Force Cambridge Res. Lab., L. G. Hanscom Field, Bedford, Massachusetts (DTIC Report AD 742259 available from the Defense Technical Information Center, Cameron Station, Alexandria, Virginia 22304-6145).

Klopf, A. H. (1975). *Assoc. Comput. Mach. Spec. Interest Group Artif. Intell. Newsl.* No. 52, pp. 11–13.

Klopf, A. H. (1979). *Cognit. Brain Theory Newsl.* **3**(2), 54–62.

Klopf, A. H. (1982). "The Hedonistic Neuron: A Theory of Memory, Learning, and Intelligence." Hemisphere/Taylor & Francis, New York.

Klopf, A. H. (1986). *AIP Conf. Proc.* **151**, 265–270.

Klopf, A. H. (1988). A Neuronal Model of Classical Conditioning. *Psychobiol.*, 16(2), 85–125.

Kohonen, T. (1977). "Associative Memory: A System Theoretic Approach." Springer, New York.

Kosko, B. (1986). *AIP Conf. Proc.* **151**, 277–282.

Levy, W. B., and Desmond, N. L. (1985). *In* "Synaptic Modification, Neuron Selectivity, and Nervous System Organization" (W. B. Levy, J. A. Anderson, and L. Lehmkuhle, eds.), pp. 105–121. Erlbaum, Hillsdale, New Jersey.

Lynch, J. C., Mountcastle, V. B., Talbot, W. H., and Yin, T. C. T. (1977). *J. Neurophysiol.* **40**, 362–389.

McAllister, W. R. (1953). *J. Exp. Psychol.* **45**, 417–422.

McClelland, D. C., Atkinson, J. W., Clark, R. A., and Lowell, E. L. (1953). "The Achievement Motive." Appleton, New York.

McCulloch, W. S. (1965). "Embodiments of Mind," pp. 19–39. MIT Press, Cambridge, Massachusetts.

McCulloch, W. S., and Pitts, W. (1943). *Bull. Math. Biophys.* **5**, 115–137 (reprinted in McCulloch, 1965).

McNaughton, B. L., Barnes, C. A., and Rao, G. (1984). *In* "Neurobiology of Learning and Memory" (G. Lynch, J. L. McGaugh, and N. M. Weinberger, eds.), pp. 466–469. Guilford Press, New York.

Moore, J. W., and Gormezano, I. (1977). *In* "Fundamentals and Applications of Learning" (M. H. Marx and M. E. Bunch, eds.), pp. 87–120. Macmillan, New York.

Moore, J. W., and Stickney, K. J. (1980). *Physiol. Psychol.* **8**(2), 207–217.

Mowrer, O. H. (1960). "Learning Theory and Behavior." Wiley, New York (Krieger/Ed., 1973).

Mpitsos, G. J., Collins, S. D., and McClelland, A. D. (1978). *Science* **199**, 497–506.

Parker, D. B. (1982). "Learning Logic," Invent. Rep. S81-64, File 1. Office of Technology Licensing, Stanford University, Stanford, California.

Parker, D. B. (1985). "Learning-logic", Tech. Rep. 47. Center for Computational Research in Economics and Management Science, Massachusetts Institute of Technology, Cambridge.

Pavlov, I. P. (1927). "Conditioned Reflexes." Oxford Univ. Press, London and New York (Dover Edition, 1960).

Premack, D. (1959). *Psychol. Rev.* **66**, 219–233.

Rashevsky, N. (1938). "Mathematical Biophysics." Univ. of Chicago Press, Chicago, Illinois.

Rescorla, R. A. (1969). *Psychol. Bull.* **72**(2), 77–94.

Rescorla, R. A., and Wagner, A. R. (1972). *In* "Classical Conditioning II: Current Research and Theory" (A. H. Black and W. F. Prokasy, eds.), pp. 64–99. Appleton, New York.

Rolls, E. T. (1987). *In* "The Neural and Molecular Bases of Learning" (J.-P. Changeux and M. Konishi, eds.), pp. 503–540. Wiley, New York.

Rosenblatt, F. (1962). "Principles of Neurodynamics." Spartan Books, New York.

Rumelhart, D. E., Hinton, G. E., and Williams, R. J. (1985). "Learning Internal Representations by Error Propagation", ICS Rep. 8506. Institute for Cognitive Science, University of California, San Diego.

Rumelhart, D. E., Hinton, G. E., and Williams, R. J. (1986). *In* "Parallel Distributed Processing" (D. E. Rumelhart and J. L. McClelland, eds.), Vol. 1, pp. 318–364. MIT Press, Cambridge, Massachusetts.

Russell, I. S. (1966). *In* "Aspects of Learning and Memory" (D. Richter, ed.), pp. 121–171. Basic Books, New York.

Schwartz, B. (1978), "Psychology of Learning and Behavior." Norton, New York.

Spence, K. W. (1956). "Behavior Theory and Conditioning." Yale Univ. Press, New Haven, Connecticut.

Stein, L., and Belluzzi, J. D. (1988). *In* "Quantitative Analyses of Behavior" (M. Commons, R. Church, J. Stellar, and A. Wagner, eds.), Vol. 7. Erlbaum, Hillsdale, New Jersey (in press).

Sutton, R. S., and Barto, A. G. (1981). *Psychol. Rev.* **88**, 135–170.

Sutton, R. S., and Barto, A. G. (1987). "A Temporal-Difference Model of Classical Conditioning," Techn. 87-509.2. GTE Laboratories, Waltham, Massachusetts.

Tesauro, G. (1986). *Biol. Cybernet.* **55**, 187–200.

Thompson, R. F., Berger, T. W., and Madden, J., IV. (1983a). *Annu. Rev. Neurosci.* **6**, 447–491.

Thompson, R. F., McCormick, D. A., Lavond, D. G., Clark, G. A., Kettner, R. E., and Mauk, M. D. (1983b). *Prog. Psychobiol. Physiol. Psychol.* **10**, 167–196.

Wagner, A. R. (1981). *In* "Information Processing in Animals: Memory Mechanisms" (N. E. Spear and R. R. Miller, eds.), pp. 5–47. Erlbaum, Hillsdale, New Jersey.

Walters, E. T., and Byrne, J. H. (1983). *Science* **219**, 405–408.

Werbos, P. J. (1974). Unpublished Doctoral Dissertation, Harvard University, Cambridge, Massachusetts.

Widrow, B. (1962). *In* "Self-Organizing Systems—1962" (M. C. Yovits, G. T. Jacobi, and G. D. Goldstein, eds.), pp. 435–461. Spartan Books, Washington, D.C.

Woody, C. D. (1982). "Memory, Learning and Higher Function." Springer-Verlag, Berlin and New York.

Woody, C. D. (1986). *Annu. Rev. Psychol.* **37**, 433–493.

Zipser, D. (1986). *Behav. Neurosci.* **100**(5), 764–776.

_____ Appendix: Parameter Specifications _____
for the Computer Simulations of the
Neuronal Models

A. Drive-Reinforcement Model

Learning-rate constants: $c_1 = 5.0$, $c_2 = 3.0$, $c_3 = 1.5$, $c_4 = 0.75$, $c_5 = 0.25$ ($\tau = 5$)

CS initial synaptic weight values [i.e., $w_i(t)$ at $t = 0$]: $+0.1$ (excitatory weights), -0.1 (inhibitory weights).

UCS (nonplastic) synaptic weight values: $+1.0$ (excitatory weight) and 0.0 (inhibitory weight).

Lower bound on synaptic weights: $| w_i(t) | \geq 0.1$

Neuronal output limits: $0.0 \leq y(t) \leq 1.0$

Neuronal threshold: $\theta = 0.0$

CS amplitudes (measured relative to zero-level baseline): 0.2

UCS amplitudes (measured relative to zero-level baseline): 0.5

CS and UCS timing: See Table I for times of onset and offset of CSs and UCSs within a trial. Also specified in Table I are the trials during which each CS and UCS was present. For all of the CS–UCS configurations, the time of onset of the first stimulus was arbitrarily chosen to be 10. *Onset* of a stimulus at time step t means that the stimulus was on during time step t and was not on during the previous time step. *Offset* of a stimulus at time step t means that the stimulus was off during time step t and was not off during the previous time step.

Table I.

Timing of the CS–UCS Configurations in Figs. 4–6.

Figure number	CS and UCS timing (time step of onset/time step of offset/trials during which stimulus was present)			
	CS_1	CS_2	CS_3	UCS
4(a)	10/15/1–50	—	—	14/15/1–50
4(b)	10/14/1–50	—	—	14/15/1–50
4(c)	10/14/1–120	—	—	14/15/1–120
5(a)	10/13/1–100	20/24/1–100	30/35/1–100	13/14/1–100
				23/24/1–100
				33/34/1–100
5(b)	10/13/1–300	20/24/1–300	30/35/1–300	13/14/1–300
				23/24/1–300
				33/34/1–300
5(c)	10/13/1–100	20/24/1–100	30/35/1–100	13/14/1–100
				23/24/1–100
				33/34/1–100
6	10/13/1–300	20/23/71–300	—	13/16/1–200
	20/23/71–300			

B. Hebbian Model

Where applicable, parameter values were the same as for the drive-re-inforcement model except that $c = 0.5$, the initial synaptic weight values were 0.0, and there was no lower bound on the synaptic weights.

C. Sutton–Barto Model

Where applicable, parameter values were the same as for the drive-re-inforcement model except that $c = 0.5$, $\alpha = 0.9$, the initial synaptic weight values were 0.0, and there was no lower bound on the synaptic weights.

8

Olfactory Processing and Associative Memory: Cellular and Modeling Studies

A. Gelperin, D. W. Tank, and G. Tesauro

I. Introduction

Computational models of collective neural systems (for example, see Hopfield and Tank, 1986; Ullman, 1986; Hildreth and Koch, 1987; Rumelhart and McClelland, 1986, and references therein) are providing new ways to conceptualize the operations of neural networks and stimulating new measurement schemes to test the models. The new computational or connectionist approach represents an attempt to understand the "emergent" properties (Bullock, 1976) of neural networks, which often cannot be predicted or extrapolated from detailed knowledge of individual circuit elements and interconnections (Selverston, 1980). Even though the existing cross-links between computational modeling of the collective properties of neural networks and electrophysiological measurements on actual neural networks are tenuous at this very early stage, we suggest that for understanding the operation of some types of neural circuits, the computational approach is an essential complement to the traditional strategies of cellular analysis.

Olfactory processing systems seem very likely to operate as collective neural systems. Computer simulations have shown that collective networks are particularly adept at classifying patterns of input activity based on imprecise or incomplete data. Based on data in the literature, the spatial and temporal patterns of sensory neuron activity resulting from repeated presentations of a given odor are not likely to be highly specific and thus informationally imprecise from the viewpoint of any particular olfactory sensory cell. The sensory input pattern will be constant only when viewed over the entire ensemble of sensory cells. This view of the sensory code for odors, termed the across-fiber patterning hypothesis, arose because detailed electrophysiological studies of individual olfactory neurons responding to a variety of odorants failed to reveal a clear categorization scheme (Anholt, 1987; Kauer, 1987a; Dethier and Crnjar, 1982). Multisite measurements of odor-induced neural activity patterns are now being made in several olfactory systems (Kauer, 1987b; Freeman and Baird, 1987; Leon, 1987). The vertebrate olfactory system has provided a basis for several computer simulations (Lynch *et al.*, Chapter 16, this volume; Wilson and Bower, 1987).

Our analysis of olfactory processing and associative memory in the mollusk *Limax maximus* is being carried out at several levels. Behavioral experiments define the computational tasks accomplished by the olfactory system. Electrophysiological measurements and anatomical studies delimit the pathways of information flow and constrain the universe of plausible models. Biophysical and biochemical studies on membrane properties and neurotransmitter-stimulated events also aim to both guide the modeling and link our results with the growing body of similar data in other systems, both molluscan and mammalian. The modeling work has the dual role of testing the computational ability of various algorithms to match the animal's behavior and, from the results of computer experiments, suggesting critical new experiments at both the behavioral and cellular levels of analysis. The following sections attempt to make clear the multifaceted nature of the work and the myriad interactions between the various types of analysis.

Olfaction is the dominant sensory modality guiding several kinds of behavior in *Limax* and other pulmonate gastropods (Gelperin, 1974; Croll, 1983; Chase, 1986). Homing behavior, trail following, mate recognition, and food finding all depend critically on the functioning of the noses located at the tips of the superior tentacles. Several of these behaviors involve integrating information about odor quality and intensity with wind direction. The superior nose is extremely sensitive to wind (Chase, 1981; A. Gelperin, unpublished observations). Snails with only one superior nose cannot orient properly to a source of food odor in still air, while they do orient normally to a source of food odor when locomoting in a moving airstream (Chase and Croll, 1981). An understanding of the cellular basis for olfaction in *Limax* must address these computations as well as those involved in associative learning. *Limax* can not only identify and orient to odors but can also learn to alter their meaning (attractive or repellent) based on stimulus events associated with odor stimulation (Gelperin, 1986; Sahley *et al.*, 1987).

A number of higher-order conditioning phenomena such as second-order conditioning and blocking have been described in *Limax* (Sahley, 1984). Memory retention times of at least 126 days were found for post-ingestive learning to avoid diets deficient in essential amino acids (Delaney and Gelperin, 1986). The influence of interevent relations on learning by *Limax* bears striking similarity to their influence on vertebrate conditioning (Sahley *et al.*, 1984; Sahley, 1984). For example, in *Limax* there are two procedures which produce second-order conditioning with different properties. If A^+ and B^+ are innately attractive odors and Q^-

a very aversive taste, the two phases of the second-order conditioning paradigm can be diagrammed as $A^+ + Q^- \rightarrow A^-$ followed by $B^+ + A^- \rightarrow B^-$. If, in the second phase of conditioning, A and B are presented simultaneously, then subsequent extinction of the aversive response to A causes extinction of the aversive response to B. However, if B and A are presented sequentially in the second phase of conditioning, then extinction of the aversive response to A does *not* alter the conditioned aversion to B.

Since many of the behaviors modified by learning involve olfaction and feeding, experimental work has focussed on understanding the basic anatomy and cellular organization of the olfactory and feeding control systems. Our current, rather limited, understanding of the organization of the olfactory system in *Limax* is shown schematically in Fig. 1. The animal has two pairs of noses, the superior noses at the ends of the superior tentacles and the inferior noses at the ends of the inferior tentacles. The sensory receptors sit in a neuroepithelium, sending a distal

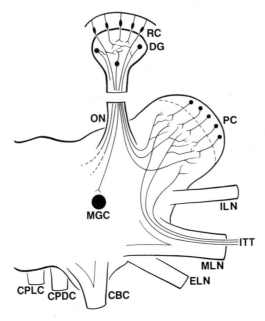

Figure 1.
Diagram of olfactory pathways in *Limax* based on data from *Limax* and other pulmonate gastropods, particularly *Achatina* as described by Chase (1986). CBC, cerebrobuccal connective; CPDC, cerebropedal connective; CPLC, cerebropleural connective; DG, digitate ganglion; ELN, external lip nerve; ILN, internal lip nerve; ITT, inferior tentacle tract; MGC, metacerebral giant cell; MLN, medial lip nerve; ON, olfactory nerve; PC, procerebral lobe; RC, receptor cells.

dendrite to the surface where it terminates in a tuft of cilia. The sensory axons enter a tentacular ganglion situated immediately behind the sensory epithelium. Some sensory axons terminate in the tentacular ganglion, while others pass directly into the olfactory nerve. The superior nose is required for odor recognition beyond a few centimeters from the source, while the inferior nose is utilized for odor recognition within a few millimeters of the source (Gelperin, 1974; Chase and Croll, 1981; Cook, 1985).

Olfactory processing in *Limax maximus* includes a region called the procerebrum (PC), whose anatomy strongly suggests collective computation. The PC is comprised of an enormous number (of order 10^5) of small (7–9 μm) interneurons. This means that $\gtrsim$ 90% of all neurons in the *Limax* nervous system are PC neurons. The PC neuropil is coupled directly to the major nose and its associated tentacular ganglion located at the tip of the superior tentacle through the olfactory nerve (ON) fiber tract (Chase, 1985; Gelperin *et al.*, 1985). We found that the minor nose, located at the tip of the inferior tentacle, also connects with the PC neuropil, as judged by nickel backfills of the branch of the medial lip nerve which innervates the minor nose. Figure 2 shows a silver-intensified preparation of such a backfill. The bilobed topology of the minor nose projection into the PC is striking. Nickel backfills of other, nonolfactory, nerves entering the cerebral ganglion have failed to show nonolfactory sensory projections into the *Limax* PC. Efferent projections from the PC are unknown. Although behavioral data on PC-lesioned animals are a necessary prerequisite to establishing a functional role for the PC in *Limax* olfaction, we have begun to characterize the anatomy and the biochemical and electrophysiological properties of this structure. Figure 3 shows scanning electron microscope (SEM) images of the desheathed surface of the PC. Figure 3A shows the prevalence of fibers in the cell body layer, shown by Zs.-Nagy and Sakharov (1970) to form numerous axosomatic synapses. The close spacing of adjacent neuronal somata is shown by the triplet of neurons in Fig. 3B. The close packing of somata and processes in the *Limax* PC has recently been confirmed by S. Curtis (personal communication, 1987). Individual PC interneurons have very widespread and extensively branched processes in the neuropil (Veratti, 1900), with input and output synaptic specializations evident along single processes (Zs.-Nagy and Sakharov, 1970). The fine-structure analysis reveals a dense matrix of reciprocal chemical synapses between processes in the neuropil (S. Curtis, personal communication, 1987), presumably representing interactions both between PC interneurons and between input and output fibers from outside the lobe and the intrinsic interneurons.

Neurochemical hardware to implement synaptic modification may reside in PC-lobe input fibers containing serotonin and dopamine, both of which are known to modulate synaptic efficacy in other networks

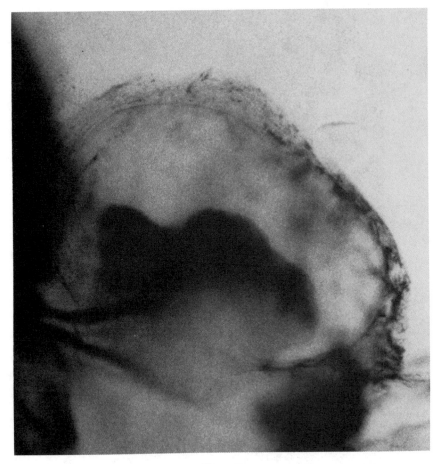

Figure 2.
Photomicrograph of the procerebral lobe projection from the branch of the
medial lip nerve terminating in the minor nose at the tip of the inferior
tentacle. The minor nose nerve was exposed to nickel chloride for 24 hr
and the preparation was developed by exposure to ammonium sulfide. A
silver intensification procedure was then employed.

(Goelet *et al.*, 1986; Dowling, 1986). A third neuromodulator, small cardioactive peptide B (SCP$_B$) (Lloyd *et al.*, 1987), is contained within a small
population of PC-lobe neurons as revealed by immunocytochemistry.
SCP$_B$ increases the responsiveness of feeding motor program to taste
inputs (Prior and Watson, 1988) and has excitatory actions on the *Limax*
heart at $2 \times 10^{-9}\ M$ (Welsford and Prior, 1987). All three of these neuromodulators transiently increase the cAMP level of PC lobes (Yamane
and Gelperin, 1987), and all alter the state of phosphorylation of specific membrane proteins isolated from PC lobes (Yamane *et al.*, 1987).

(A)

(B)

Figure 3.
Scanning electron micrographs of the desheathed surface of the
procerebral lobe of *Limax*. Tissue was fixed in paraformaldehyde,
dehydrated in ethanol, critical-point dried, and coated with gold.
Specimens were examined in a JSM model 840 scanning electron
microscope. The packing density of somata in the procerebral lobe is
much greater than is apparent on the surface of the image in (A).
Calibration bar is 10 μm in (A) and 1 μm in (B).

Figure 4 shows a typical result for serotonin activation of cAMP synthesis in the PC lobe. A group of isolated lobes was exposed to 86.5 μM serotonin. At the times indicated by the data points in Fig. 4, two lobes were removed from the serotonin and used for cAMP determination by radioimmunoassay. Isobutylmethylxanthine (IBMX) even at 3 mM did not dramatically prolong the duration of cAMP elevation. SCP_B also augments cAMP in the PC, and the effects of serotonin and SCP_B are additive (Yamane and Gelperin, 1987). The neuropeptide phe-met-arg-phe-NH_2 (FMRFamide) is also localized within a small population of PC neurons (Cooke and Gelperin, 1988). FMRFamide has an inhibitory effect on the taste input to feeding motor output pathway (Cooke *et al.*, 1985), perhaps

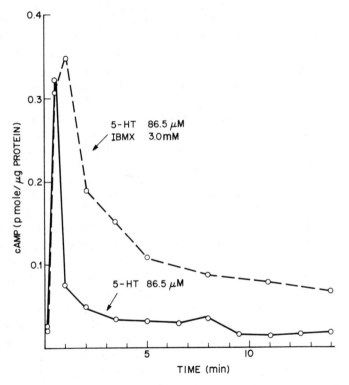

Figure 4.

Serotonin causes a transient elevation in the cAMP content of procerebral neurons. A group of 24 procerebral lobes was exposed to serotonin (5-HT), and at the times indicated, two lobes were subjected to cAMP assay using an extremely sensitive radioimmunoassay. The elevation in cAMP was transient even in the continued presence of serotonin and was not dramatically prolonged even by a high concentration of the phosphodiesterase inhibitor IBMX.

mediated by metabolites of arachidonic acid as recently demonstrated in *Aplysia* (Piomelli *et al.*, 1987). Thus, in addition to its interesting anatomical organization, the PC lobe appears to have biochemical machinery implicated in synaptic plasticity in other systems (Byrne, 1987).

Our initial electrophysiological explorations of the PC lobe were directed toward establishing that an afferent pathway exists from the major nose. A patch electrode for recording extracellular currents was inserted into the desheathed PC lobe. ON shock produced a characteristic multiphasic series of current flows, as shown in Fig. 5A. To differentiate currents due to action potentials in ON input fibers from currents due to postsynaptic events, the ON–PC lobe preparation was bathed in low calcium saline. The current profile due to ON shock during synaptic blockade revealed a clear deficit (Fig. 5B), suggesting that ON shock did activate intrinsic PC synapses. Some loose-patch recordings from surface layer PC neuron somata were obtained during these experiments. Some of the PC cells displayed action potential trains in response to ON shock. Slowly oscillating currents (< 1 Hz) were also recorded. Odorant-containing solutions applied directly to the superior nose elicited action potential trains in the ON but did not produce the large multiphasic potentials in the PC observed with ON shock. Although ON shock leads to PC circuit responses that may not be directly relevant to its computation, the simple system can be used to explore some aspects of the synaptic physiology and pharmacology of the PC in much the same way that fiber tract activation and the elicited population potentials in hippocampus are used to study long-term potentiation (LTP). For example, it will be of great interest to determine the effects of stimulus train parameters, dopamine, serotonin, SCP_B, and FMRFamide on the synaptic currents of the PC lobe. Our observation of synaptic responses in the PC produced by ON shock, the absence of labeled PC cell somata in ON nickel and horseradish peroxidase (HRP) backfills, and the demonstration that odor presentation to the major nose produces increased metabolic activity in the PC (Chase, 1985) provide evidence that odorant information is passed to the PC by afferent fibers in the ON.

To characterize single-cell physiology more fully, a tissue-culture preparation of PC neurons has been developed. Lobes were treated with proteolytic enzyme and mechanically dissociated. The isolated neurons were maintained in culture for periods of several weeks. In a medium of *Limax* saline and bovine serum albumin (BSA) (45 mg/ml) these cells adhered to polylysine-covered substrates and started to regrow processes within 10–12 hr. Cell-attached loose-patch recordings revealed action potentials, suggesting that the cells in the intact PC are spiking interneurons. Action potentials were sometimes spontaneous in the cultured cells and in all cases could be stimulated by K^+ depolarization. Initial experiments have shown that the cells were responsive to dopamine, serotonin, and glutamate, as determined by responses to the transmitter

(A)

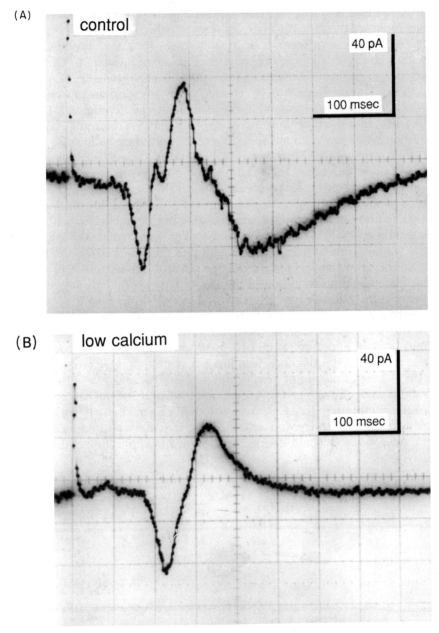

Figure 5.
(A) Multiphasic current flows elicited by olfactory nerve shock when recording from the procerebral lobe neuropil. (B) Same stimulus and recording conditions but preparation now bathed in low-calcium saline to block chemical synaptic transmission.

applied by a pressure pulse from a micropipette positioned near the cell. Serotonin transiently activated cells (Fig. 6), whereas dopamine activated PC cells for tens of seconds or in some cases for a few minutes, often with a characteristic bursting pattern. Glutamate inhibited PC neuron activity, seen most clearly as an interruption of spontaneous PC neuron activity. The connection between electrophysiological and biochemical effects of these transmitters, if any, remains to be determined. It is interesting that the time constant of dopamine and serotonin's activation of membrane ion channels is so different when they both cause a brief (1 min) increase in cAMP levels in PC lobes (Yamane and Gelperin, 1987).

Determining the single-cell physiology of PC neurons will greatly aid the longterm goal of understanding how the activity in the many cells of the PC is related to olfaction and *Limax* behavior. Because the vast majority of PC lobe cells are probably not unique identifiable cells, it is unlikely that single cell electrophysiology in the intact PC will reveal the way that the system operates as a unit. Techniques to monitor the electrical and chemical state of a large set of these neurons will greatly facilitate our understanding of the PC. Initial experiments suggest that the calcium indicator fura-2 can be used as an indirect monitor of action-potential activity. Cultured cells were loaded with fura-2 by soaking them in the acetoxymethylester (AM) derivative, which is membrane-permeant. A 30 min application of 5 μM fura-2 AM was sufficient to load the cells. Cell fluorescence was imaged with a charge-coupled device (CCD) based imaging system (Connor, 1986; Hiraoka *et al.*, 1987). The ratio of images produced by excitation at 340 and 380 nm can be related to the cytoplasmic free Ca^{2+} concentration (Tsien *et al.*, 1985). The depolarization and increased action-potential activity elicited in cultured PC neurons by elevated external potassium and application of dopamine

SEROTONIN

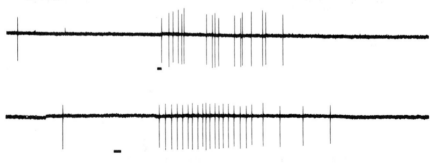

Figure 6.
Serotonin application excites cultured procerebral neurons. The upper trace shows the response of a neuron to a 600-msec puff of 10^{-4} M serotonin from a micropipette located just upstream of the neuron. The bottom trace shows the response to a 1-sec puff of serotonin.

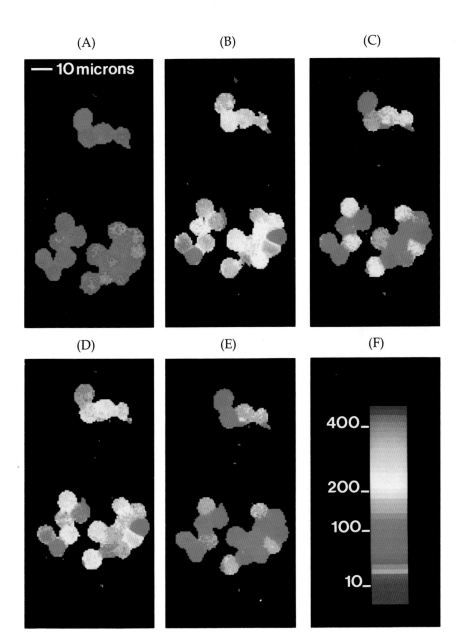

Figure 7

Glutamate lowers intracellular calcium in PC neurons. Digital images of cultured procerebral neurons before, during, and after stimulation with high potassium (20 mM) medium. False-color calibration scale shows calcium concentration in nanomolarity. (A) Normal saline; (B) 10 mM potassium; (C) 10 mM potassium + 0.1 mM glutamate; (D) 10 mM potassium; (E) normal saline; (F) [Ca] nM.

and serotonin was sufficient to produce clear elevations in intracellular calcium levels. Typical responses of intracellular calcium to high (10 mM) potassium depolarization and inhibition by 0.1 mM glutamate are shown in Fig. 7. Simultaneous electrical and optical monitoring will be used to determine just how small an increment in action-potential frequency is detectable by the imaging system. The time resolution of the imaging system is now about 2 frames/sec. Improvements in hardware and software should result in time resolution of a few hundreds of milliseconds between successive images. This should be more than sufficient to follow the temporal and spatial evolution of odor-elicited PC lobe activity patterns using a nose-PC lobe preparation.

II. Feeding Command Neurons

Observations made in a number of systems from mammal (Grillner, 1985) to mollusk (Getting, 1985) suggest that small numbers of interneurons, termed command neurons (Kupfermann and Weiss, 1978), can control the behavioral output triggered by sensory stimulation. Molluscan feeding systems conform to this general scheme (Kovac et al., 1986; Benjamin et al., 1985), so it seemed essential to find and characterize such feeding command neurons in Limax. Learning-related changes have been shown to involve feeding command neurons in the marine slug Pleurobranchaea (Morielli et al., 1986). Using the lip–brain preparation and new techniques for stabilizing the ganglia and visualizing interneurons in the cerebral ganglia, a population of approximately 16 such cells has been identified, and eight of them have been characterized extensively as to their inputs from lip taste and touch, their membrane properties, and their outputs on the feeding motor network (Delaney, 1987). The cells all have an axon in the cerebrobuccal connective between chemosensory integrating areas in the cerebral ganglion and the motor center for ingestive feeding movements in the buccal ganglia; hence the feeding command cells are called cerebrobuccal (CB) interneurons. The CBs are activated by food extracts applied to the lips and have widespread activating affects on the buccal motor centers, including the central pattern generator (CPG) for rhythmic feeding movements. Some individual CBs can initiate fictive feeding, depending on the state of excitation in the feeding network (Fig. 8). Activation of selected pairs of CBs reliably activates fictive feeding independent of the state of background activation of the feeding control system. This observation shows that CB activation is sufficient for producing the feeding motor program. Due to the technical problem of simultaneously and reversibly inactivating a population of cells, only indirect evidence is available indicating that CB activity may be *necessary* for the feeding motor program. If postsynaptic activation by presynaptic input is greatly reduced in the cerebral ganglia by soaking the cerebral

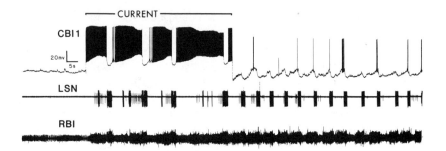

Figure 8.
Induction of feeding motor program by imposed activity in a single
cerebrobuccal (CB) interneuron. Driving CB_1 with transmembrane current
applied via an intracellular electrode causes four bites to be produced by
the motor circuitry of the buccal ganglion at a subnormal frequency. After
the CB is released from activation by transmembrane current, the feeding
rhythm speeds up and regularizes.

ganglia in $3 \times Ca^{2+}$, $5 \times Mg^{2+}$, cobalt-containing saline, then full-
strength food extracts applied to the lips do not trigger the feeding motor
program. A second line of indirect evidence for the necessity of CB activity in triggering fictive feeding comes from experiments in which the
role of acetylcholine (ACh) in triggering feeding motor program was explored (King *et al.*, 1987). Bath application of ACh to the cerebral ganglia
reliably elicits fictive feeding. More to the point, a puff of ACh applied
from a micropipette positioned over a cluster of five CB somata also
triggers fictive feeding, while the same ACh application delivered over
other regions of the cerebral ganglion does not trigger fictive feeding.
Even if activity in the CB interneurons characterized to date does not
prove necessary for activation of fictive feeding when tested more critically, the CBs still provide a very informative site in the feeding circuit
from which to determine how taste stimuli are processed.

Several of the CBs give responses of opposite sign to attractive and
repellent tastes (Fig. 9). The inhibition of CB_1 and CB_4 by quinidine applied to the lip chemoreceptors is clearest when the bitter taste is applied
soon after the excitatory taste of potato (Fig. 9C). It will be of great interest
to measure the synaptic activation of CBs by an innately attractive taste
which has been rendered aversive due to associative conditioning.

The command neurons described thus far activate the motor circuitry for ingestive feeding movements. It is not clear from our behavioral
experiments whether or not these feeding command neurons receive
direct synaptic input from the odor-processing circuit. In most of our
behavioral experiments on learning, animals show oriented locomotion
in response to the odor cues. If command neurons for oriented locomotion were found, they would be the most logical sites to test for synaptic drive from the olfactory system. There is, however, at least one

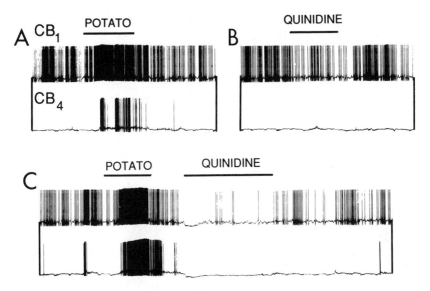

Figure 9.
Responses of two cerebrobuccal (CB) interneurons to (A) attractive and (B) repellent tastes. Taste stimuli were applied to the lip chemoreceptors while recording from the somata of the CBs. The excitatory effect of potato taste is clear in both cells (A). The inhibitory effects of quinidine taste are not always evident when applied alone (B), but can be seen clearly (C) where the quinidine is applied 10 sec after a 20-sec application of potato.

situation in which odors do elicit ingestive feeding movements. Naive food-deprived slugs will ingest plain agar if exposed to food odors while presented with plain agar discs. Nonfood odors do not elicit biting on plain agar discs (Sahley *et al.*, 1982). These data suggest that feeding command neurons may well receive direct synaptic input from the nose.

III. The LIMAX Model

The odor-learning and feeding network of *Limax* has been modeled as a computer simulation called LIMAX (Gelperin *et al.*, 1986). This is *not* a structural simulation (cf. Gingrich and Byrne, 1987; Wilson and Bower, 1987; Traub and Wong, 1982) of the known *Limax* anatomy, but a connectionist model meant to test computational algorithms that produce the observed *Limax* odor-related behavior. A goal of our research is for structural simulations and computational networks to converge as the physiology of *Limax* becomes better understood. The current computational model has sensory processing, categorization, and behavioral control modules (Fig. 10). LIMAX recognizes odors based on activity in an array of 100 chemoreceptors (LIP) and the pattern of activity set up

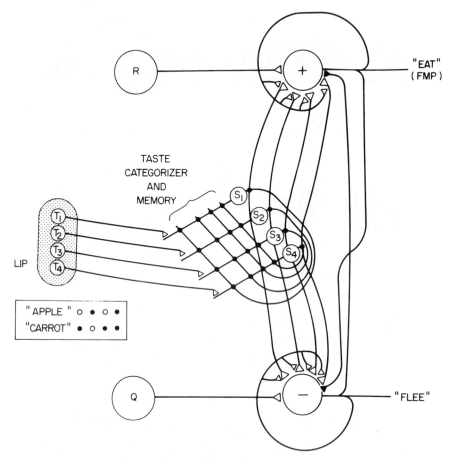

Figure 10.
Diagram of the components of the LIMAX computer simulation. The array
of chemoreceptors labeled "LIP" serves equally well as a nose. The taste
categorizer and memory circuit is the procerebral lobe analog. The "EAT"
command neuron corresponds to the cerebrobuccal interneurons. The
"FLEE" command neuron has yet to be found; Q is the aversive input
pathway and R is the reward input pathway.

in a highly interconnected interneuronal network (TASTE CATEGO-
RIZER) immediately postsynaptic to the chemoreceptor array. The system
therefore represents a cross-fiber olfactory code. Note that the activity
pattern in the taste categorizer has no inherent behavioral meaning.

Activity patterns in the LIMAX categorizer induced by olfactory
input can be made into stable, stored patterns by adjusting the synaptic
strengths between units of the odor categorizer using a Hebb-like learning
rule. The resulting synaptic organization and the dynamics of the odor-
analyzer network are such that if the network is driven to an activity

state close to one of the stored stable activity states, its activity will evolve to match the previously stored pattern and thus the presented input will be recognized as a member of a known odor category. The synaptic structure is that of an associative or content-addressable memory (Anderson and Hinton, 1981; Kohonen, 1987; Hopfield, 1982, 1984).

The behavioral control module is implemented as command-like interneurons whose activity determines which behavioral output, feeding or fleeing, will be selected in response to a sensory input. The command-like interneurons receive from the odor-categorizer network synaptic inputs that modify their strength based on temporal relationships between odor and quinine stimulation (aversive conditioning) or odor and fructose stimulation (appetitive conditioning). This model is able to reproduce some but not all of the conditioning phenomena demonstrated with *Limax*. Even though LIMAX is not complete, the functions accomplished by its modules are likely to be present in *Limax* in some form. LIMAX has encouraged us to explore olfactory coding and processing in the PC lobe and search for command-like interneurons in the feeding control system of *Limax*. The LIMAX model also suggested a set of odor mixture discrimination experiments, which, although they produced results at variance with the prediction of the LIMAX model, revealed that *Limax* possesses another high-order computational ability, configural conditioning, as explained below (Gelperin and J. F. Hopfield, 1988).

IV. Behavioral Aspects of the LIMAX Model

We have found the LIMAX model to be useful both as a guide to the general anatomical organization of *Limax* and as a behavioral model. Although not a structural model, LIMAX makes a number of interesting predictions concerning the anatomical structure of the basic modules, the connectivity between modules, and the kinds of synaptic plasticity mechanisms that are needed to obtain conditioning effects. In this section, we will consider the LIMAX model purely as a behavioral entity. The behavioral phenomenology produced by a neural network model can be of interest independent of its anatomical plausibility. The kinds of behaviors that are addressed in the design and testing of a model are often somewhat different from the behaviors that are usually studied in real animals. Thus a productive interplay can be expected in which animal behaviors suggest goals for theoretical modeling, and novel behaviors found in the models can in turn be sought in animal behavior experiments.

In describing the behavioral properties of the LIMAX model, it will be useful to make a basic distinction between behaviors that are essentially "front-end" effects, and those that are primarily "back-end" effects.

The front end of the model is comprised of the input chemoreceptor array and the categorizer network to which it connects. The back end of the model consists of the behavioral command neurons, including their synaptic inputs and outputs. The back-end behavioral effects result from the particular nature of the plasticity rule governing the synapses from the categorizer neurons to the eat–flee decision units, and do not depend on the detailed nature of the representation of sensory stimuli in the front end of the network. In particular, local representations could be used instead of distributed representations, and the same behavioral phenomena would still be observed. Examples of such phenomena that are discussed below include standard first-order conditioning, extinction of conditioning, the delayed second-order conditioning paradigm, and blocking of conditioning. On the other hand, the LIMAX model also displays behaviors that depend substantially on the nature of the front end used to represent the conditioned stimuli. Examples of these effects include compound conditioning, the simultaneous second-order conditioning paradigm, and certain aspects of blocking phenomena. These are also discussed below.

A. "Front-End" Conditioning Effects

A number of important behaviors of the LIMAX model are primarily due to the nature of the front-end categorizer network. This is most directly tied to the physiology of the olfactory system. The categorizer is a collective circuit, uses nontrival distributed representations of the known food categories, and has the further ability to learn new categories. As a result, a number of behavioral phenomena are obtained that can not be produced with static local representations. The most dramatic of these behavioral results involves aversive conditioning to mixtures, or compound stimuli. One notable success of the LIMAX model of Gelperin *et al.* (1985) was an explanation of the stimultaneous second-order conditioning paradigm by having the categorizer learn the mixture AB as a new category. As a consequence of the sensory representation scheme used, the category AB has a large overlap with A and B, but is separate from both. If food A has been aversively paired with Q, then the response to AB will also be aversive, due to the large overlap with A. When stimulus B is presented, it will tend to evoke the representation of AB, and thus an aversive response will be observed. On the other hand, if aversion to food A is extinguished, this will also have the effect of extinguishing the aversive response to AB. Thus fleeing B will no longer be observed. This kind of effect is critically dependent on the representation and algorithm used to recognize and categorize olfactory information.

Additional effects are generated in the LIMAX model due to the random nature of the representations of food categories. A typical food category is represented by a pattern of activity in about 20% of the categorizer neurons. The particular neurons that comprise this pattern are chosen at random. When a mixture or compound stimulus is presented, the pattern of activity that comes to represent the mixture has a large fraction (~40–50%) of bits in common with each component, but there is a significant variability due to the random nature of the categories. This random variability has important behavioral consequences. For example, in blocking experiments with the modified LIMAX model, the crucial variable that determines the amount of blocking is the degree of initial aversive response to the compound stimulus. The aversive response will be large if the overlap with the aversively trained CS_1 is large, and it will not be as large if the overlap is small. The amount of overlap in the model stimuli can vary greatly due to the random nature of the food categories. The behavioral result is that for some pairs of foods the model displays nearly complete blocking, whereas for other food pairs only partial blocking is obtained. This is expected to be representative of the situation in real animals, although the degree of variability of blocking has not been systematically studied in *Limax*.

A similar effect is obtained in the model for the case of compound conditioning. When a compound stimulus AB is aversively trained, the degree of aversive response to the individual components A and B will depend on the overlap between each component and the mixture. Since these overlaps can vary significantly, substantial variations in the response to the components can result for different food-pair combinations. With the models, we studied responses to the component stimuli after a single compound conditioning trial, using several different food pairs. For some pairs the response to both components is strongly aversive, while for other pairs one component may be strongly aversive and the other may be only weakly aversive. However, in no case would we expect to see a weakly aversive response to both components. This is because the method of defining a pattern of activity for the mixture precludes the possibility of that pattern having a small overlap with both components. Although the food tastes of LIMAX arise from random assignment of chemosensory input lines to various foods, it is likely that the taste inputs from pairs of real foods may be correlated. Thus *Limax* may experience more overlap in sensory representation between some nominally different food categories than does LIMAX.

B. "Back-End" Conditioning Effects

A critical variable in first-order conditioning $(A + Q^- \rightarrow A^-)$ is the interstimulus interval (ISI), that is, the time interval between the presentation of the CS and the presentation of the US. If this interval is negative, so that the US arrives before the CS, no conditioning takes place typically. Learning does take place for positive intervals, and usually there is a smooth transition to no learning as the ISI is reduced. For very large

ISIs there is often once again a transition to zero learning: if the US follows the CS by an extremely long interval, the animal does not learn to make the association between them.

In the modified LIMAX model of Tesauro (1986) there is considerable flexibility as to how the system learns as the ISI is increased to very large values. This is due to the capability of using two fundamentally different types of synaptic plasticity rules: rules that depend on the presynaptic activity, and rules that depend on the time derivative of the presynaptic activity. In the first case, once the CS is presented, the synapse remains eligible for modification as long as the sensory neuron remains active. In the second case, when the CS is presented there is then only a limited window of eligibility in which the synapse may be modified. These two characteristic types of behavior are illustrated in Fig. 11. The learned response to a single first-order conditioning trial is plotted versus ISI for the learning algorithm in which the change in synaptic strength is proportional to the trace of the presynaptic activity. With this learning algorithm, conditioning still takes place for arbitrarily large ISIs. In contrast, the alternative algorithm in which the change in synaptic strength depends on the trace of the derivative of presynaptic activity shows very different behavior. (In this algorithm only positive values

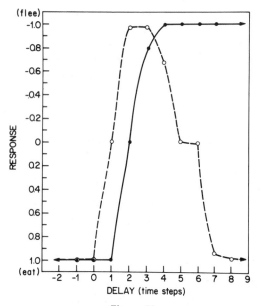

Figure 11.
Behavioral output of modified LIMAX after a single first-order
conditioning trial as a function of CS–US interval. Solid line: synaptic
strength change proportional to presynaptic activity. Dashed line: synaptic
strength change proportional to derivative of presynaptic activity.

of the derivative contribute to the trace.) The derivative trace algorithm qualitatively reproduces the usual inverted-U shape of learning versus ISI curves in real-animal experiments, although the precise shape of the curve appears to be nonstandard. This is because there are really two separate responses ("eat" and "flee") that are being plotted on the same axis. Due to the particular rule by which overall eating or fleeing activity is computed, and the rule for modifying the synapses to "eat," it turns out that the point of zero activity is a relatively stable point, and thus a "kink" appears in the otherwise inverted-U shape of the learning versus ISI curve.

The two kinds of synaptic plasticity algorithms display different types of behavior in extinction of associations formed by first-order conditioning. In the first case, in which the trace of presynaptic activity is used, negative learning will take place as long as the conditioned stimulus is left on (Fig. 12). In the second case, in which the derivative of presynaptic activity is used, only a fixed amount of extinction per trial may be obtained, after which the conditioned stimulus must be taken away and presented again to obtain further extinction.

As stated previously, in the real animal there are two qualitatively different types of second-order conditioning ($A^+ + Q^-$ then $B^+ + A^-$ → B^-), depending on whether or not B is presented before A, or at the same time in the second phase of the conditioning procedure. In the

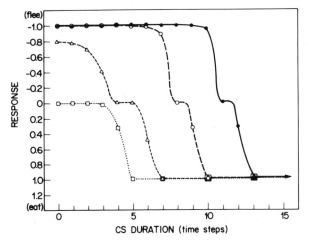

Figure 12.
Behavioral output of modified LIMAX during extinction of previous conditioned responses, using algorithm with synaptic strength change proportional to presynaptic activity. Different curves represent different ISIs in initial training. Curve 1, ISI = 2 (boxes); curve 2, ISI = 3 (triangles); curve 3, ISI = 4 (circles); curve 4, ISI = 5 (dots).

delayed second-order paradigm, extinction of A⁻ does not extinguish the aversive response of B, whereas it does in the simultaneous paradigm. These effects are obtained in the model by utilizing two different learning mechanisms: in the delayed paradigm, learning takes place in the back end—that is, the synapses to the decision units are modified—whereas in the simultaneous paradigm, learning takes place in the front end, by having the categorizer learn the new food category AB. Consider the delayed paradigm. Figure 13 illustrates the response to B after a single pairing with A⁻, as a function of ISI. It is important to note that the plotted responses represent the response after A⁻ has been extinguished. We see that the same basic type of learning curve is obtained as in the first-order conditioning plotted in Fig. 11. The maximal aversive response to B is essentially indistinguishable from the aversive response to A. Note that no learning takes place when the two stimuli are presented simultaneously, or with a very small ISI. This is because the response is observed after A has been extinguished, which has the effect of extinguishing the aversive response that is learned in the simultaneous paradigm. Also in the LIMAX model, the two different kinds of learning

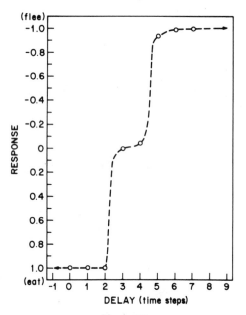

Figure 13.
Response of modified LIMAX to odor B after a single second-order aversive conditioning trial pairing odor B with the previously aversively conditioned odor A as the US. Response is shown after extinguishing the aversive response to odor A, as a function of odor B–odor A interval during the single second-order conditioning trial.

take place on different time scales. To obtain simultaneous second-order conditioning, several trials are required, whereas in Fig. 13 the response is shown after a single trial.

V. Challenges to *Limax* from LIMAX

There are a number of ways in which theoretical neural network models of classical conditioning can be useful to experimentalists studying animal learning and memory. The theoretical design concepts and quantitative properties of the "neurons" and "synapses" in the model can provide a new way of organizing one's thinking about the behavioral phenomena of real animals. In the ideal case, a large body of behavioral data would be simply and concisely explained in terms of a few theoretical principles. Furthermore, novel theoretical concepts often lead to the design of experimental procedures that would not be conceived solely by studying animals at the phenomenological level.

The LIMAX models have indeed suggested a large number of behavioral experiments that could provide new insights into the bases of classical conditioning in *Limax*. Some of these experiments are suggested by the "robust" properties of the LIMAX models, that is, predicted behaviors that are always obtained regardless of the precise details of the model design. For example, it appears that the time scale for identification or categorization of the conditioned stimulus must be significantly faster than the time scale of learning a behavioral response. Serious degradation of the performance of the model occurs if this is not the case. Another robust prediction is that the time scale for conditioning an aversive response is much faster than the time scale for extinguishing such a response. Finally, the model predicts that blocking would eventually fail after a large number of trials. This is because the categorizer would eventually learn the new category AB, which would be aversive because of its large overlap with A^-. All of these predictions can be tested by direct behavioral studies in *Limax*.

Another class of experiments is suggested by certain nonintuitive behavioral "quirks" of the model. One such quirk is what might be called an "autoconditioning" effect: if a food A has been partially conditioned, subsequent presentation of A without being followed by Q could actually lead to a slight increase in the aversive response to A. This would occur if the categorizer neurons representing A turn on at different times after A is presented. The earliest A neurons to respond would receive an increment in their aversive conditioning when the full activation of the A representation caused the transition to flee and synaptic modification was triggered. Another quirk of the model is that it is possible for the second phase of a second-order conditioning procedure ($B^+ + A^- \rightarrow$

B⁻) to cause an increase in the aversiveness of A⁻. This would happen if the extinction rate is low enough, and if the degree of overlap of A and B is higher than normal. Both of these phenomena are usually not seen in animal studies, and it would be most interesting if there were some circumstances under which they could be obtained.

Finally, there are a number of behavioral questions for which the model does not provide an unambiguous answer. Different answers may be obtained by changing, for example, the particular choice of learning algorithm or parameter settings. The most important of these effects has to do with the choice of the function rule or the derivative rule in the learning algorithm. If the function rule is used, then it will be possible to obtain conditioning by leaving the CS on for an arbitrarily long time, and then following it with a US. With real *Limax*, habituation to the CS will limit the effects of prolonged CS exposure and complicate the interpretation of behavioral experiments incorporating prolonged CS exposures. Similarly, when a CS has been aversively trained and is presented without US reinforcement, extinction will occur for as long as the CS is left on. On the other hand, with the derivative rule, there is only a limited window of time in which conditioning can occur after presentation of the CS, and only a fixed amount of extinction per trial can be obtained. This ambiguity could be resolved directly and quickly by carrying out the appropriate experiments in *Limax*. Another ambiguous issue is what happens in multiple-US experiments. For example, if food A is paired with Q_1, and then A and B are presented simultaneously, followed by Q_2, is an aversive response to B generated? Different anatomical connections in the LIMAX model could provide either a yes or no answer, and once again, experimental data from real animals are needed to guide the modeler. The final ambiguity that we mention here is the issue of learning based on the *offsets* of stimuli, or "trace" conditioning. This has been recently studied in *Limax* (Sahley *et al.*, 1988) and *Hermissenda* (Grover and Farley, 1987), although the present models do not address this issue.

VI. Challenges to LIMAX from *Limax*

Configural conditioning is learning to respond differentially to the elements of a compound stimulus presented alone versus the response given to the compound stimulus itself. For example, configural conditioning would be demonstrated if, after aversive training to a compound stimulus A + B, an animal displays a positive response to odor A and odor B presented separately but a negative response to the compound odor stimulus A + B. The initial formulation of the odor coding and processing scheme of LIMAX did not allow configural conditioning, so it was of interest to determine if *Limax* could learn a configural discrimination. Training of *Limax* was carried out using two pure odors, 2-ethyl-3-methoxypyrazine (potato odor) and 1-octen-3-ol (mushroom odor) (Johnson *et al.*, 1971). Concentrations of the pure potato odorant and the pure mushroom odorant were found that were attractive to *Limax* on first exposure and remained attractive over sequential exposures. Odor mixtures were made in one of two ways: by either a physical mixture of the two odor sources, or a closely spaced but physically separate array of odorant stripes. Slugs were trained to avoid the compound odor using either the odor mixture or the odor stripes and then tested for their responses to the elements of the odor compound presented separately and to the compound odor derived from the physical mixture of the potato and mushroom odorants. The prediction was that if *Limax* behaves like LIMAX, training an avoidance response to either compound odor would result in an avoidance response also to the individual components of the compound odor. We found that *Limax* trained to avoid the physical mixture of potato and mushroom odorants would show a clear aversion to the compound odor while retaining a strong positive response to the potato or mushroom odors presented separately (Gelperin and J. F. Hopfield, 1988). The interpretation of this result as configural conditioning depends critically on showing that the odor mixture derived from the physical mixture of odorants is not a unique new odor unrecognizable to slugs trained on the odor stripes, but is recognized and avoided by animals trained to avoid the compound odor derived from odor stripes. We found that slugs trained to avoid the odor stripes did avoid the odor of the physical mixture. This demonstration of configural conditioning by *Limax* necessitates a reconfiguration of the sensory coding scheme used in LIMAX.

VII. Future Directions

The LIMAX model has been extraordinarily useful in clarifying our thinking about the kinds of information processing and control modules that must be present in *Limax* to accomplish the odor-recognition and learning tasks documented to date. Speculations on smell in our system and many others strongly suggest collective circuit properties as the critical parameter for odor recognition. To measure patterns of odor activation of neurons in the PC lobe, we are attempting to use the calcium indicator fura-2 and a digital imaging system that can monitor large areas of the PC lobe. Several synaptic modulators of the PC lobe are known (serotonin, dopamine, SCP_B, FMRFamide), and their actions on PC-lobe activity can be studied. Command-like interneurons with potent synaptic effects on the motor system for ingestive feeding movements can be used to test the categorization of tastes based on the sign of synaptic activation of the identified interneurons. The synaptic activation of interneurons, by providing access to subthreshold events, has already proven much more revealing than past measurements based on the presence or absence of a feeding motor output in studies of inhibitory pathways to feeding arising from foot shock and aversive tastes. Just as the LIMAX model has suggested experiments for *Limax*, the reverse is also true. The configural conditioning result with *Limax* indicates need for revision of the sensory coding scheme of LIMAX. Since *Limax* has very recently been shown capable of inhibitory conditioning (Martin and Sahley, 1986), it will be interesting to see if LIMAX can equal this performance.

Acknowledgments

For permission to include some of their data and helpful comments on the manuscript, we thank M. King, K. Delaney, T. Yamane, P. G. Sokolove, and J. J. Hopfield. E. V. Lenk provided valuable assistance with scanning electron microscopy, as did J. Flores with culturing procerebral neurons. H. J. Chiel and P. Hockberger were valuable discussants during the course of this work.

References

Anderson, J. A., and Hinton, G. E. (1981). Models of information processing in the brain. *In* "Parallel Models of Associative Memory" (G. E. Hinton and J. A. Anderson, eds.), pp. 9–48. Erlbaum, Hillsdale, New Jersey.

Anholt, R. R. H. (1987). Primary events in olfactory reception. *Trends Biochem. Sci.* **12**, 58–62.

Benjamin, P. R., Elliott, C. J. H., and Ferguson, G. P. (1985). Neural network analysis in the snail brain. *In* "Model Neural Networks and Behavior" (A. I. Selverston, ed.), pp. 87–108. Plenum, New York.

Bullock, T. H. (1976). In search of principles of neural integration. *In* "Simpler Networks and Behavior" (J. C. Fentress, ed.), pp. 52–60. Sinauer Associates, Sunderland, Massachusetts.

Byrne, J. H. (1987). Cellular analysis of associative learning. *Physiol. Rev.* **67**, 329–439.

Chase, R. (1981). Electrical responses of snail tentacle ganglion to stimulation of the epithelium with wind and odors. *Comp. Biochem. Physiol. A* **70**, 149–155.

Chase, R. (1985). Responses to odors mapped in snail tentacle and brain by [^{14}C]-2-deoxyglucose autoradiography. *J. Neurosci.* **5**, 2930–2939.

Chase, R. (1986). Lessons from snail tentacles. *Chem. Senses* **11**, 411–426.

Chase, R., and Croll, R. P. (1981). Tentacular function in snail olfactory orientation. *J. Comp. Physiol.* **143**, 357–362.

Connor, J. A. (1986). Measurement of free calcium levels in tissue culture neurons using charge-coupled device (CCD) camera technology. *In* "Imaging Function in the Nervous System. Optical Methods in Cellular Neurobiology" (B. Salzberg, ed.), pp. 14–24. Soc. Neurosci., Washington, D.C.

Cook, A. (1985). Tentacular function in trail following by the pulmonate slug *Limax pseudoflavus* Evans. *J. Molluscan Stud.* **51**, 240–247.

Cooke, I. R. C., and Gelperin, A. (1988). The distribution of FMRFamide-like immuno-reactivity in the nervous system of the slug *Limax maximus*. *Cell Tissue Res.* **253**, 69–76.

Cooke, I. R. C., Delaney, K., and Gelperin, A. (1985). Complex computation in a small neural network. *In* "Memory Systems of the Brain" (N. M. Weinberger, J. L. McGaugh, and G. Lynch, eds.), pp. 173–192. Guilford Press, New York.

Croll, R. P. (1983). Gastropod chemoreception. *Biol. Rev. Cambridge Philos. Soc.* **58**, 293–319.

Delaney, K. R. (1987). Initiation and modulation of fictive feeding by identified interneurons in the terrestrial slug *Limax maximus*. Ph.D. Dissertation, Princeton University, Princeton, New Jersey.

Delaney, K. R., and Gelperin, A. (1986). Post-ingestive food-aversion learning to amino acid deficient diets by the terrestrial slug *Limax maximus*. *J. Comp. Physiol.* **159A**, 281–295.

Dethier, V. G., and Crnjar, R. M. (1982). Candidate codes in the gustatory system of caterpillars. *J. Gen. Physiol.* **79**, 549–570.

Dowling, J. E. (1986). Dopamine, a retinal neuromodulator? *Trends NeuroSci.* **9**, 236–240.

Freeman, W. J., and Baird, B. (1987). Relation of olfactory EEG to behavior. Spatial analysis. *Behav. Neurosci.* **101**, 398–408.

Gelperin, A. (1974). Olfactory basis of homing behavior in the giant garden slug, *Limax maximus*. *Proc. Natl. Acad. Sci. U.S.A.* **71**, 966–970.

Gelperin, A. (1986). Complex associative learning in small neural networks. *Trends NeuroSci.* **9**, 323–328.

Gelperin, A., and Hopfield, J. F. (1988). Differential conditioning to a compound stimulus and its components in the terrestrial mollusc *Limax maximus*. *Behav. Neurosci.*, in press.

Gelperin, A., Hopfield, J. J., and Tank, D. W. (1985). The logic of *Limax* learning. *In* "Model Neural Networks and Behavior" (A. I. Selverston, ed.), pp. 237–261. Plenum, New York.

Gelperin, A., Tank, D. W., and Chiel, H. J. (1986). Cellular and synaptic responses recorded from an olfactory processing circuit. *Soc. Neurosci. Abstr.* **12**, 862.

Getting, P. A. (1985). Neural control of behavior in gastropods. *In* "The Mollusca" Vol. 8, Part 1, (K. M. Wilbur, ed.), pp. 269–334. Academic Press, New York.

Gingrich, K. J., and Byrne, J. H. (1987). Single-cell neuronal model for associative learning. *J. Neurophysiol.* **57**, 1705–1715.

Goelet, P., Castellucci, V. P., Schacher, S., and Kandel, E. R. (1986). The long and the short of long-term memory—A molecular framework. *Nature (London)* **322**, 419–422.

Grillner, S. (1985). Neural control of vertebrate locomotion—Central mechanisms and reflex interaction with special reference to the cat. *In* "Feedback and Motor Control in Invertebrates and Vertebrates" (W. J. P. Barnes and M. H. Gladden, eds.), pp. 35–68. Croom Helm, London.

Grover, L. M., and Farley, J. (1987). Temporal order sensitivity of associative neural and behavioral changes in *Hermissenda*. *Behav. Neurosci.* **101**, 658–675.

Hildreth, E. C., and Koch, C. (1987). The analysis of visual motion. From computational theory to neuronal mechanism. *Annu. Rev. Neurosci.* **10**, 477–533.

Hiraoka, Y., Sedat, J. W., and Agard, D. A. (1987). The use of a charge-coupled device for quantitative optical microscopy of biological structures. *Science* **238**, 36–41.

Hopfield, J. J. (1982). Neural networks and physical systems with emergent collective computational abilities. *Proc. Natl. Acad. Sci. U.S.A.* **79**, 2554–2558.

Hopfield, J. J. (1984). Neurons with graded responses have collective computational abilities. *Proc. Natl. Acad. Sci. U.S.A.* **81**, 3088–3092.

Hopfield, J. J., and Tank, D. W. (1986). Computing with neural circuits. A model. *Science* **233**, 625–633.

Johnson, A. E., Nursten, H. E., and Williams, A. A. (1971). Vegetable volatiles; A survey of components identified. Part II. *Chem. Ind. (London)* pp. 1212–1224.

Kauer, J. S. (1987a). Coding in the olfactory system. *In* "Neurobiology of Taste and Smell"

(T. E. Finger and W. L. Silver, eds.), pp. 205–231. Wiley, New York.

Kauer, J. S. (1987b). Real-time imaging of evoked activity in local circuits of the salamander. *Nature (London)* **331,** 166–168.

King, M. S., Delaney, K., and Gelperin, A. (1987). Acetylcholine activates cerebral interneurons and feeding motor program in *Limax maximus. J. Neurobiol.* **18,** 509–530.

Kohonen, T. (1987). "Content-Addressable Memories," 2nd ed. Springer-Verlag, Berlin and New York.

Kovac, M. P., Matera, E. M., Volk, P. J., and Davis, W. J. (1986). Food avoidance learning is accompanied by synaptic attenuation in identified interneurons controlling feeding behavior in *Pleurobranchaea. J. Neurophysiol.* **56,** 891–905.

Kupfermann, I., and Weiss, K. R. (1978). The command neuron concept. *Behav. Brain Sci.* **1,** 3–39.

Leon, M. (1987). Plasticity of olfactory output circuits related to early olfactory learning. *Trends Neurosci.* **10,** 434–438.

Lloyd, P. E., Kupfermann, I., and Weiss, K. R. (1987). Sequence of small cardioactive peptide A: A second member of a class of neuropeptides in *Aplysia. Peptides* **8,** 179–184.

Martin, K., and Sahley, C. (1986). Analysis of associative learning in *Limax maximus.* Excitatory and inhibitory conditioning. *Soc. Neurosci. Abstr.* **12,** 39.

Morielli, A. D., Matera, E. M., Kovac, M. P., Shrum, R. G., McCormack, K. J., and Davis, W. J. (1986). Cholinergic suppression: A postsynaptic mechanism of long-term associative learning. *Proc. Natl. Acad. Sci. U.S.A.* **83,** 4556–4560.

Piomelli, D., Volterra, A., Dale, N., Siegelbaum, S. A., Kandel, E. R., Schwartz, J. H., and Belardetti, F. (1987). Lipoxygenase metabolites of arachidonic acid as second messengers for presynaptic inhibition of *Aplysia* sensory cells. *Nature (London)* **328,** 38–43.

Prior, D. J., and Watson, W. (1988). The molluscan neuropeptide SCP$_B$ increases the responsiveness of the feeding motor program of *Limax maximus. J. Neurobiol.* **19,** 87–105.

Rumelhart, D. E., McClelland, J. L., eds., and The PDP Research Group (1986). "Parallel Distributed Processing: Explorations in the Microstructures of Cognition," Vols. I and II. MIT Press, Cambridge, Massachusetts.

Sahley, C. L. (1984). Behavior theory and invertebrate learning. *In* "The Biology of Learning" (P. Marler and H. S. Terrace, eds.), pp. 181–196. Springer-Verlag, Berlin and New York.

Sahley, C. L., Hardison, P., Hsuan, A., and Gelperin, A. (1982). Appetitively reinforced odor-conditioning modulates feeding in *Limax maximus. Soc. Neurosci. Abstr.* **8,** 823.

Sahley, C. L., Rudy, J. W., and Gelperin, A. (1984). Associative learning in a mollusc: A comparative analysis. *In* "Primary Neural Substrates of Learning and Behavioral Change" (J. Farley and D. Alkon, eds.), pp. 243–258. Cambridge Univ. Press, London and New York.

Sahley, C. L., Martin, K. A., and Gelperin, A. (1988). Analysis of associative learning in the terrestrial mollusc *Limax maximus.* II. Appetitive learning. Submitted for publication.

Selverston, A. I. (1980). Are central pattern generators understandable? *Behav. Brain Sci.* **3,** 535–571.

Tesauro, G. (1986). Simple neural models of classical conditioning. *Biol. Cybernet.* **55,** 187–200.

Traub, R. D., and Wong, R. K. S. (1982). Cellular mechanism of neuronal synchronization in epilepsy. *Science* **216,** 745–747.

Tsien, R. Y., Rink, T. J., and Poenie, M. (1985). Measurement of cytosolic free calcium in individual small cells using fluorescence microscopy with dual excitation wavelengths. *Cell Calcium* **6,** 145–157.

Ullman, S. (1986). Artificial intelligence and the brain. Computational studies of the visual system. *Annu. Rev. Neurosci.* **9,** 1–26.

Veratti, E. (1900). Ricerche sul sistema nervoso dei *Limax. R. Ist. Lomb. Sci. Lett., Mem.* **18,** 9.

Welsford, I. G., and Prior, D. J. (1987). The effects of SCP$_B$ application and buccal neuron B1 stimulation on heart activity in the slug. *Limax maximus. Am. Zool.* **27,** 138A.

Wilson, M., and Bower, J. (1987). A computer simulation of a three-dimensional model of piriform cortex with functional implications for storage and recognition of spatial and temporal olfactory patterns. *Soc. Neurosci. Abstr.,* **13,** Part 2, 1401.

Yamane, T., and Gelperin, A. (1987). Aminergic and peptidergic amplification of intracellular cyclic AMP levels in a molluscan neural network. *Cell. Mol. Neurobiol.* **7,** 291–301.

Yamane, T., Oestreicher, A. B., and Gelperin, A. (1987). Aminergic and peptidergic modulation of phosphorylation and synthesis of specific proteins in the procerebral lobe of *Limax maximus.* Submitted for publication.

Zs.-Nagy, I., and Sakharov, D. A. (1970). The fine structure of the procerebrum of pulmonate molluscs, *Helix* and *Limax. Tissue Cell* **2,** 399–411.

9

Neural Circuit for Classical Conditioning of the Eyelid Closure Response

Richard F. Thompson

I. Introduction

We have used classical conditioning of the eyelid closure (and nictitating membrane extension) response in rabbits as our basic model paradigm of associative learning and memory, but we and our colleagues have used other behavioral responses and other species as well; our results appear to be general for mammals, including humans.

Our evidence to date demonstrates that the cerebellum is necessary for the learning and memory of eyelid closure and other discrete behavioral responses. When we began this work about 18 years ago, we had no idea that we would be led to the cerebellum as the key structure that appears to store the essential memory trace. With the advantage of hindsight, it is perhaps not so surprising. The conditioned eyelid closure response is a very precisely timed movement—over the entire effective conditioned stimulus–unconditioned stimulus (CS–US) onset interval where learning occurs, from about 100 msec to over 1 sec, the learned response develops such that the eyelid closure is maximal at the time of onset of the US. In this sense it is a maximally adaptive response. It is also a very precisely timed "skilled" movement, perhaps the most elementary form of learned skilled movement. Our results strongly support the general spirit of earlier theories of the role of the cerebellum in motor learning (Albus, 1971; Eccles, 1977; Ito, 1972; Marr, 1969) (see Fig. 2).

Decorticate and even decerebrate mammals can learn the conditioned eyelid response (Norman et al., 1977; Oakley and Russell, 1972). Furthermore, animals (rabbits) that are first trained and then acutely decerebrated (using Halothane anesthesia) robustly retain the learned response (Mauk and Thompson, 1987). The essential memory trace circuit for this form of learning is thus below the level of the thalamus.

Some years ago we adopted the general strategy of recording neuronal unit activity in the trained animal (rabbit eyelid conditioning) as an initial survey and sampling method to identify putative sites of memory storage. A pattern of neuronal activity that correlates with the behavioral learned response, specifically one that precedes the behavioral response in time within trials, predicts the form of the learned response within trials and predicts that the development of learning over trials is a necessary (but not sufficient) requirement for identification of a storage locus.

In the course of mapping the brainstem and cerebellum we discovered localized regions of cerebellar cortex and a region in the lateral interpositus nucleus where neuronal activity exhibited the requisite memory trace properties—patterned changes in neuronal discharge frequency that preceded the behavioral learned response by as much as 60 msec [minimum behavioral conditioned response (CR) onset latency approximately 100 msec], predicted the form of the learned behavioral response (but not the reflex response), and grew over the course of training, that is, predicted the development of behavioral learning (McCormick et al., 1981, 1982a; McCormick and Thompson, 1984a; Thompson, 1986; Thompson et al., 1983 (Fig. 1).

We undertook a series of lesion studies: large lesions of lateral cerebellar cortex and nuclei, electrolytic lesions of the lateral interpositus–

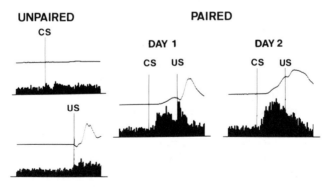

Figure 1.
Neuronal unit activity recorded from the lateral interpositus nucleus during unpaired and paired presentations of the training stimuli. The animal was first given pseudo-randomly unpaired presentations of the tone and corneal airpuff, in which the neurons responded very little to either stimulus. However, when the stimuli were paired together in time, the cells began responding within the CS period as the animal learned the eyeblink response. The onset of this unit activity preceded the behavioral NM response within a trial by 36–58 msec. Stimulation through this recording site yielded ipsilateral eyelid closure and NM extension. Each histogram bar is 9 msec in duration. The upper trace of each histogram represents the movement of the NM, with up being extension across the eyeball. [From McCormick and Thompson (1984b).]

medial dentate nuclear region, and lesions of the superior cerebellar peduncle ipsilateral to the learned response all abolished the learned response completely and permanently, had no effect on the reflex unconditioned response (UR), and did not prevent or impair learning on the contralateral side of the body (Clark et al., 1984; Lavond et al., 1981; Lincoln et al., 1982; McCormick et al., 1981, 1982a,b; Thompson et al., 1984). After our initial papers were published, Yeo, Glickstein, and associates replicated our basic lesion result for the interpositus nucleus, using light as well as tone CSs and a periorbital shock US (we had used corneal airpuff US), thus extending the generality of the result (Yeo et al., 1985).

Electrolytic or aspiration lesions of the cerebellum cause degeneration in the inferior olive—the lesion-abolition of the learned response could be due to olivary degeneration rather than cerebellar damage, per se. We made kainic acid lesions of the interpositus. A lesion as small as a cubic millimeter in the lateral anterior interpositus permanently and selectively abolished the learned response with no attendant degeneration in the inferior olive (Lavond et al., 1985). Additional work suggests that the lesion result holds across CS modalities, skeletal response systems, species, and perhaps with instrumental contingencies as well (Donegan et al., 1983; Polenchar et al., 1985; Yeo et al., 1985). Electrical microstimulation of the interpositus nucleus in untrained animals elicits behavioral responses by way of the superior cerebellar peduncle (e.g., eyeblink, leg flexion), the nature of the response being determined by the locus of the electrode (McCormick and Thompson, 1984b). Collectively, these data build a case that the memory traces are afferent to the efferent fibers of the superior cerebellar peduncle, that is, in interpositus, cerebellar cortex, or systems for which the cerebellum is a mandatory efferent.

The essential efferent CR pathway appears to consist of fibers exiting from the interpositus nucleus ipsilateral to the trained side of the body in the superior cerebellar peduncle, crossing to relay in the contralateral magnocellular division of the red nucleus and crossing back to descend in the rubral pathway to act ultimately on motor neurons (Chapman et al., 1985; Haley et al., 1983; Lavond et al., 1981; Madden et al., 1983; McCormick et al., 1982b; Rosenfield et al., 1985) (see Fig. 2). Possible involvement of other efferent systems in control of the CR has not yet been determined, but descending systems taking origin rostral to the midbrain are not necessary for learning or retention of the CR, as noted above.

Lesion and microstimulation data suggest that the essential conditioned stimulus (CS) pathway includes mossy fiber projections to the cerebellum via the pontine nuclei (see Fig. 2). Thus, sufficiently large lesions of the middle cerebellar peduncle prevent acquisition and immediately abolish retention of the eyelid CR to all modalities of CS (Solomon et al., 1986), whereas lesions in the pontine nuclear region can

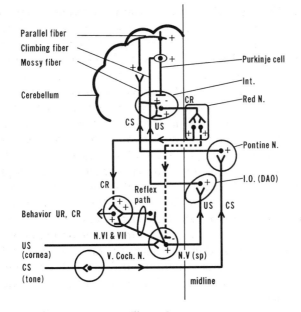

Figure 2.
Simplified schematic of hypothetical memory trace circuit for discrete
behavioral responses learned as adaptation to aversive events. The US
(corneal airpuff) pathway seems to consist of somatosensory projections to
the dorsal accessory portion of the inferior olive (DAO) and its climbing
fiber projections to the cerebellum. The tone GS pathway seems to consist
of auditory projections to the cerebellum. The efferent (eyelid closure) CR
pathway projects from the interpositus nucleus (Int.) of the cerebellum to
the red nucleus (Red N.) and via the descending rubral pathway to act
ultimately on motor neurons. The red nucleus may also exert inhibitory
control over the transmission of somatic sensory information about the US
to the inferior olive (IO), so that when a CR occurs (eyelid closes), the red
nucleus dampens US activation of climbing fibers. Evidence to date is
most consistent with storage of the memory traces in localized regions of
cerebellar cortex and possibly interpositus nucleus as well. Plus symbols
indicate excitatory and minuses inhibitory synaptic action. Additional
abbreviations: N. V (sp), spinal fifth cranial nucleus; N. VI, sixth cranial
nucleus; N. VII, seventh cranial nucleus; V. Coch N., ventral cochlear
nucleus. [From Thompson (1986), reprinted by permission of *Science*.]

selectively abolish the eyelid CR to an acoustic CS (Steinmetz *et al.*, 1986a).
Consistent with this result is current anatomical evidence from our laboratory for a direct contralateral projection from the ventral cochlear nucleus to this same region of the pons (Thompson *et al.*, 1986) and electrophysiological evidence of a "primary-like" auditory relay nucleus in
this pontine region (Logan *et al.*, 1986).

Electrical microstimulation of the mossy fiber system serves as a very effective CS, producing rapid learning, on average more rapid than with peripheral CSs, when paired with, for instance, a corneal airpuff US (Steinmetz *et al.*, 1985a). If animals are trained with a left pontine nuclear stimulation CS and then tested for transfer to right pontine stimulation, transfer is immediate (i.e., one trial) if the two electrodes have similar locations in the two sides, suggesting that at least under these conditions the traces are not formed in the pontine nuclei but rather in the cerebellum, probably beyond the mossy fiber terminals (Steinmetz *et al.*, 1986a). Finally, appropriate forward pairing of mossy fiber stimulation as a CS and climbing fiber stimulation as a US (see below) yields *normal behavioral learning* of the response elicited by climbing fiber stimulation (Steinmetz *et al.*, 1985b). Lesion of the interpositus abolishes both the CR and the UR in this paradigm. All of these results taken together would seem to build an increasingly strong case for localization of the essential memory traces to the cerebellum, particularly in the "reduced" preparation with stimulation of mossy fibers as the CS and climbing fibers as the US. In the normal animal trained with peripheral stimuli, the possibility of trace formation in brainstem structures has not yet been definitively ruled out.

Recordings from Purkinje cells in the eyelid conditioning paradigm are consistent with the formation of memory traces in cerebellar cortex. Prior to training, a tone CS causes a variable evoked increase in frequency of discharge of simple spikes in many Purkinje cells in HVI, Crus I, and Crus II (Donegan *et al.*, 1985; Foy and Thompson, 1986). Following training, the majority of Purkinje cells that develop a change in frequency of simple spike discharge that correlates with the behavioral response, as opposed to being stimulus evoked, show decreases in frequency of discharge of simple spikes that precede and "predict" the form of the behavioral learned response, although increases in "predictive" discharge frequency occur in some cells.

Conjoint electrical stimulation of mossy fibers and climbing fibers can yield normal learning of behavioral responses, as noted above (Steinmetz *et al.*, 1985b). The properties of these learned responses appear identical to those of the same conditioned responses learned with peripheral stimuli (e.g., eyelid closure, leg flexion). The temporal requirements for such conjoint stimulation that yields behavioral learning are essentially identical to those required with peripheral stimuli: no learning at all if CS onset does not precede US onset by more than 50 msec, best learning if CS precedes US by 200–400 msec, and progressively poorer learning with increasing CS precedence (Gormezano, 1972). Further, normal learning occurs if the mossy fiber CS consists of only two pulses, 5 msec apart, at the beginning of a 250-msec CS–US onset interval (Logan *et al.*, 1985). Collectively, the evidence reviewed above demonstrates that the cerebellum is essential for the category of "procedural" memory we have studied. It also builds an increasingly strong case that the essential memory traces are stored in very localized regions of the cerebellum. Our current working hypothesis is that memory traces are formed in regions of cerebellar cortex where CS-activated mossy fiber–granule cell–parallel fiber projections and US-activated climbing fiber projections converge. Similarly, we hypothesize that traces are formed at regions of convergence of mossy fibers and parallel fibers in the interpositus nucleus.

II. The Dorsal Accessory Olive–Climbing Fiber System—The Essential US Reinforcing (Teaching) Pathway?

Small electrolytic lesions in the rostromedial (face) region of the dorsal accessory olive (DAO) have a most interesting effect on the learned eyelid closure response. Following the lesion (contralateral to the trained eye) the animals showed normal behavioral CRs. But with continued paired training (i.e., tone CS, corneal airpuff US) the unconditioned response extinguished in a manner very similar to control animals (with electrodes implanted in the DAO but not lesioned) where the corneal airpuff discontinued and the animals were given conventional CS-alone extinction training (McCormick et al., 1985). The effective DAO lesion has no effect on the unconditioned response (UR) to corneal airpuff stimulation. An example of the behavioral results is shown in Fig. 3. Effective lesions are reconstructed in Fig. 4. Figure 5 is a composite of all ineffective lesions. The lesion was made before training in a separate group of animals. They were unable to learn the conditioned response.

To our knowledge this is the first report of a central brain lesion that produces extinction of the learned behavioral response with continued paired CS–US training in classical conditioning. This result demonstrates that the essential memory trace is not in the inferior olive—the animals performed the normal CR following lesions. The result is also supportive of our hypothesis that the DAO–climbing fiber system is a part of the essential US reinforcing pathway.

Perhaps the most extraordinary result we have obtained to date involves microstimulation of the DAO (Mauk et al., 1986). Such stimulation can elicit a wide range of behavioral responses (e.g., eyelid closure, limb flexion or extension, head turn), the exact location of the stimulating microelectrode determining the nature of the behavioral response, consistent with the organization of somatic sensory projections to the DAO (e.g., Gellman et al., 1983). If this movement-evoking DAO stimulus is now used as a US and paired with a tone CS, the animal learns to perform exactly the same behavioral response (phasic movement) as a conditioned

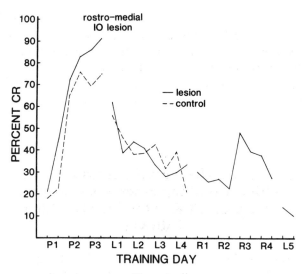

Figure 3.
Effect of lesion of the rostro-medial inferior olive on the percent of trials in which conditioned responses were performed. The animals were first trained (P1–P3) and then received either a lesion that included the rostro-medial inferior olive (lesion) or disconnection of the airpuff (control), followed by 4 days of paired trials to the same eye (L1–L4) for the lesion group or by tone-alone trials for the control group. Subsequent training to the contralateral eye in the lesion group (R1–R4) gave indications of learning, but the percent of responses never rose above 50%. One final day of training on the left (L5) was then performed. Each data point represents the average of half a day of training (McCormick *et al.*, 1985).

response to the tone CS. The time course of learning and the properties of the learned movement appear identical to conditioned responses learned with an aversive peripheral US (e.g., corneal airpuff, paw shock) (see Figs. 6 and 7). Excluding nociceptive components of the somatosensory system, we know of no other system in the brain that can produce this effect. Interestingly, electrical microstimulation of the DAO that serves as an entirely adequate US is not at all aversive to the animal.

Typical stimulus parameters to the DAO are steel microelectrodes of approximately 0.1 MΩ impedance, 0.1-msec pulses delivered at rates from 60 to 400 Hz, train duration 100 msec, and current range from 60 to 400 μA. The lowest current value that elicited a behavioral movement in our studies to date with stimulus trains is 60 μA (60 Hz).

We argue that the effective stimulus to obtain this result is to the cells of origin of climbing fibers projecting to the cerebellum from the DAO. There are, of course, alternative explanations, mostly relating to the possibility of stimulation of fibers of passage. We have completed a number of control procedures and observations in an attempt to rule

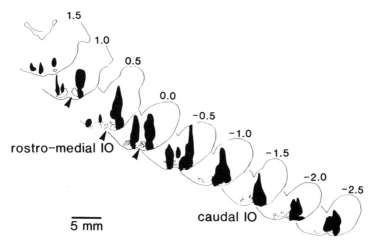

Figure 4.
Histological reconstructions of all seven of the lesions of the rostro-medial inferior olivary complex. Lesions in animals 1, 3, and 7 are found to be entirely contralateral to the trained eye, while in animals 4, 5, and 6 the lesions are bilateral. The lesion in animal 2 was completely ipsilateral. Since the axons of the cells in the IO cross through the contralateral IO, an electrolytic lesion of one IO is expected to cause degeneration of portions of the other IO. Thus, an ipsilateral lesion is in effect bilateral. The number above the sections on the left are the number of millimeters anterior to the lambda bone suture (McCormick *et al.*, 1985).

out these alternatives. We next list alternative hypotheses and summarize our evidences against them.

1. The spontaneous discharge rate of DAO cells is low (e.g., 2/sec) and our stimulus train is at too high a frequency to be physiological.

(a) We have now succeeded in obtaining the DAO–US effect with a single electrical pulse stimulus to the DAO, which is eminently physiological (J. E. Steinmetz and R. F. Thompson, unpublished observations).

2. The effective stimulus is to fibers of passage that do not project to the cerebellum.

(a) Lesion of the interpositus abolishes both the CR *and the UR* elicited by DAO stimulation (Mauk *et al.*, 1986). Lesions of the interpositus *do not* abolish or even alter reflex responses to peripheral USs.

(b) Stimulation of the reticular formation just dorsal to the inferior olive (IO) can also elicit phasic movements but this stimulus does not function as a US; that is, the stimulus-elicited movement cannot be conditioned to a tone CS.

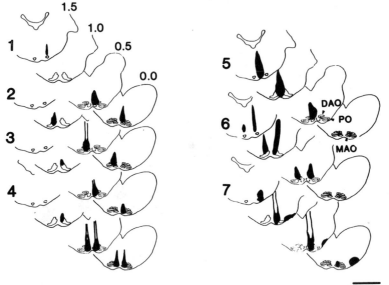

Figure 5.
Cumulative histological reconstruction illustrating lesions that were
ineffective in permanently abolishing the conditioned response or causing
the response to diminish over training. The ineffective lesions are found to
include almost all regions of the IO except for the rostro-medial division.
Large lesions of the reticular formation were also without effect. The
number above each section is the number of millimeters anterior to the
lambda bone suture.

3. The effective stimulus is to afferents from the spinal trigeminal
nucleus, which activate the reflex and hence the normal peripherally
activated US pathway.

(a) In contrast to peripheral USs, the DAO–US is not aversive, as
noted above.

(b) If so, the lesion data re interpositus and DAO noted above indicate that the DAO is still a necessary part of the US pathway; that is,
the same pathway would be anti- and orthodromically activated, thus
activating DAO neurons and their climbing fiber projections to the cerebellum.

4. The DAO stimulus somehow activates mossy fiber projections
to the cerebellum and these serve as the effective US (since the interpositus is essential for the CR and the DAO–UR, the US projection system
must be mossy and/or climbing fibers).

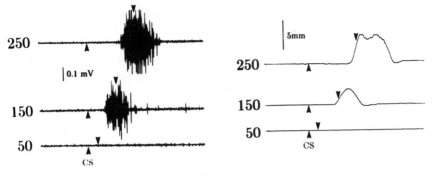

Figure 6.
Microstimulation of the IO as a US. Shown here are eyelid responses from one of the animals in which the effects of ISI was studied. Each electromyogram (EMG) response in the left column is taken from the last day of training using the indicated ISI. (Right) Same eyelid responses as measured with a potentiometer attached to the upper eyelid (upward deflection indicates eyelid closure). In each trace the upward-pointing arrow indicates CS onset, and the downward arrow indicates where the US normally occurs (these are CS-alone trials). Note the robust conditioned responses observed using ISIs of 150 and 250 msec and the absence of responses when the ISI is 50 msec. Also note that the latency of the response varies according to the ISI such that the response peak occurs near US onset. These results are identical to those obtained with a peripheral (corneal airpuff) US from (Mauk *et al.*, 1986).

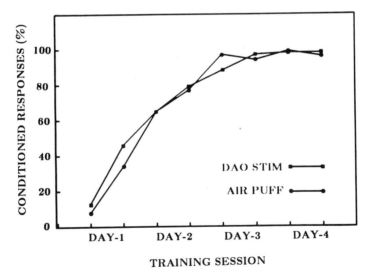

Figure 7.
A comparison of acquisition of conditioned eyelid responses expressed as percent responses for animals trained with stimulation of the DAO (■) or with an airpuff (●) as the US. The four daily training sessions are represented as eight half sessions. The conditioned response criterion was an EMG response of at least 10 μV elicited by the CS.

(a) Simulation of cells of origin of mossy fibers in the pontine nucleus or mossy fibers directly (middle cerebellar peduncle) does not elicit movements and does not serve as an effective US (Steinmetz *et al.*, 1986a).

5. Our DAO–US is not stimulating the DAO or activating climbing fibers to the cerebellum.

(a) The consistent and systematic relationship between electrode placements and the resultant conditioned responses implicates DAO neurons rather than fibers of passage (Fig. 8).

(b) At the time the DAO electrode is implanted, we record the climbing fiber field potential in cerebellar cortex and position the DAO electrode to elicit a lowest threshold field potential (Mauk *et al.*, 1986).

(c) In current studies we are using the 2-deoxyglucose (2DG) technique. In brief, after the animal has been trained with DAO stimulation as a US, the animal is injected with 2DG and the DAO is stimulated with the same stimulus pulse at a low rate (e.g., 4/sec) for 45 min. X-Ray film is exposed to the brain sections and optical density is measured

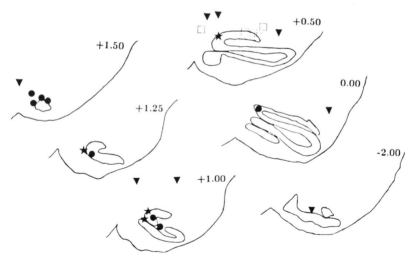

Figure 8.
Schematic representation of the electrode location in all animals.
Placements resulting in conditioned eyelid responses are indicated by
circles; placements resulting in particularly discrete eyelid responses are
indicated by stars. Triangles denote placements in which no conditioned
responses developed, and open squares indicate placements that resulted
in conditioned head movements from (Mauk *et al.*, 1986).

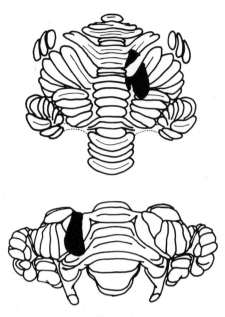

Figure 9.
Regions of cerebellar cortex showing increased optical density (increased 2DG utilization inferred) (relative to controls) following microstimulation of the upper face region of the left DAO for 45 min at 4/sec after systematic injection of 2DG. This stimulus location served as an effective US—the animal learned the conditioned eyeblink response to a tone CS paired with DAO stimulation as a US. Above, dorsal view; below, frontal view (J. E. Steinmetz, Morton, D. G. Lavond, and R. F. Thompson, unpublished observations).

(2DG uptake inferred). Control animals have electrodes implanted in the DAO but are not stimulated. An example is shown in Fig. 9 of the regions of cerebellar cortex differentially activated (stimulated versus control) by stimulation of the left DAO (J. E. Steinmetz, Morton, D. G. Lavond, and R. F. Thompson, unpublished observations). The activated regions correspond closely to the anatomical distribution of climbing fibers from the stimulated region of the IO (Brodal, 1981). There were no other clear differentially activated regions of the brain (many areas, particularly in the auditory system, show considerable uptake but are equivalent for control and stimulated animals). The 2DG method would seem to be an excellent technique to identify or rule out stimulation of fibers of passage versus the neurons at the electrode tip.

Two lines of evidence from electrophysiological recording studies support the notion that the climbing fiber system is the essential US reinforcing pathway. The first involves recording the activity of single Purkinje neurons. As noted above, there are clear and marked changes in the patterns of simple spike discharges of Purkinje neurons (mossy fiber–granule cell–parallel fiber system). But there are also clear and dramatic changes in the patterns of complex spike discharges (climbing fibers from the IO). Prior to training, the onset of the US (corneal airpuff) consistently evokes complex spikes in those Purkinje cells receiving climbing-fiber projections from the region of the IO that is activated by stimulation of the eye region of the face. In well-trained animals, the US onset typically does not evoke complex spikes in the appropriate Purkinje cells (Foy and Thompson, 1986). It appears that as the CR develops, climbing-fiber activation of the Purkinje cells by the US becomes markedly attenuated.

In current studies we have obtained more direct evidence by recording activity of neurons in the dorsal accessory olive activated by the corneal airpuff US onset (Steinmetz et al., 1988). Presentations of US alone consistently evoke a phasic increase in responses of these neurons (US onset-evoked). As the behavioral CR (eyelid response) begins to develop, this US onset-evoked response in dorsal accessory olive neurons becomes markedly attenuated. Indeed, in a well-trained animal, US onset-evoked activity may be completely absent in the dorsal accessory olive on trials where the animal gives a CR. But US *alone* presentations still evoke the same onset response that the US evoked prior to training.

In contrast to the corneal airpuff US-evoked unit response in the DAO, which is marked, the tone CS does not evoke any response in this region of the IO, either before or after training; that is, there is no auditory projection to this region of the IO. This constitutes another line of evidence arguing strongly against the hypothesis that the memory traces are formed in the IO. A site of memory trace formation must have convergent activation by the CS and the US. This region of the IO does not, and it is the only region of the IO that is necessary for acquisition and maintenance of the CR.

It should be noted that an adequate peripheral US (i.e., a somatosensory stimulus) activates both mossy fibers and climbing fibers that converge in their projections to cerebellar cortex. This coactivation (of Purkinje cells) may play a role in classical conditioning for peripheral USs, but the evidence reviewed above argues that climbing fibers alone can serve as an effective US. In the waking animal, a large number of Purkinje neurons (approximately 60% in our recordings from HVI, Crus I, and Crus II) show variable evoked increases in simple spike frequency to the tone CS prior to training (presumed mossy-fiber activation). It is the regions of convergence of the tone-evoked mossy-fiber activation and corneal airpuff-evoked climbing-fiber activation that we hypothesize to be the sites of trace formation.

III. The Nature of Reinforcement in Classical Conditioning and the Role of Climbing Fibers

The most successful mathematical formulation of the process of classical conditioning at the behavioral level is that developed by Rescorla and Wagner (1972):

$$\Delta V_i = \beta \left(\lambda - \sum_s Vs \right)$$

where ΔV_i is the strength of association between CS_i and a given US, β is a rate parameter, λ is the maximum possible level of association strength conditionable with the given US intensity, and $\sum s\ V_s$ is the sum of the association strengths between all elements present on the trial, including CS_i and the US. Insofar as reinforcement is concerned, at the beginning of training, $\sum s\ V_s = 0$ and the amount of associative strength added by a CS–US trial is maximal ($\beta\lambda$). As training continues and association strength accrues, $\sum s\ V_s$ approaches λ and the amount added by a CS–US pairing decreases. When learning is asymptotic and the accrued CS–US associative strength equals the maximum, then $\sum s\ V_s = \lambda$, $\Delta V_i = \beta\ (\lambda - \lambda) = 0$; and no additional associative strength is added by CS–US pairing. This formulation can successfully account for a wide range of phenomena in classical conditioning, including the more complex or "cognitive" features, such as blocking.

The cerebellar circuit we have identified (Fig. 2) is very nicely consistent with the Rescorla–Wagner formulation. The basic requirement for the circuit is that the more the CR develops with a given CS and US, the less effective the US becomes—the less "reinforcing" it is. We make the following assumption: the degree to which the US is reinforcing (i.e., the degree to which it adds associative strength on CS–US trials) is a direct function of the occurrence of a climbing-fiber volley to the cerebellum evoked by the US onset (Donegan *et al.*, 1988).

Since the hypothetical memory trace in the cerebellum must involve a population of Purkinje cells and a population of climbing fibers projecting from the dorsal accessory olive portion of the inferior olive, a simple way to conceptualize reinforcement strength is as the proportion of effective climbing fibers activated by the US (by "effective" is meant all those activated by the particular US prior to training).

Before learning, the tone CS does not result in any increase in the activity of interpositus neurons; that is, the efferent CR pathway from interpositus to red nucleus to motor neurons is not activated (see Fig. 1). As training proceeds, neurons in the interpositus increase their patterns of discharge in the CS period such that they precede and predict the occurrence of the behavioral CR, as noted above (see Fig. 1). In a well-trained animal, activation of neurons in the efferent CR pathway is massive in the CS period (Fig. 1).

Suppose that in addition to driving the behavioral CR, the efferent CR pathway also exerts an inhibitory influence on the essential US pathway. Then as the CR is increasingly well learned, activation of the US pathway by the US is increasingly attenuated. In a well-trained animal, the US pathway might be completely shut down. If so, then additional training will result in no additional associative strength—the US has functionally ceased to occur at the critical regions of memory trace formation in the cerebellum (see Fig. 2).

Recent evidence suggests that activation of the red nucleus can inhibit somatosensory activation of the inferior olive (Weiss *et al.*, 1985). Electrical stimulation of the red nucleus can produce inhibition of activation of IO neurons by tactile stimulation (of the forepaw). Weiss *et al.* (1985) suggest that this inhibition acts at the somatosensory relay in the cuneate nucleus (relaying somatosensory information to the IO and to higher brain structures from the forelimbs). Recent anatomical and physiological evidence also indicates the existence of a powerful inhibitory pathway from interpositus to the inferior olive (Andersson *et al.*, 1987; Nelson and Mugnoini, 1987).

If this descending system inhibiting the IO and somatosensory activation of the IO does in fact exist, then our cerebellar circuit provides the basic architecture for the Rescorla–Wagner formulation. The strong prediction is that as the CR develops to a CS, activation of the essential US pathway in dorsal accessory olive–climbing fibers–cerebellum by the US will decrease, until in a well-trained animal the US no longer activates the essential US pathway at all. This is precisely what we have found in our recordings from Purkinje cells and from neurons in the dorsal accessory olive.

Acknowledgments

Supported by grants from the National Science Foundation (BNS 8117115), the Office of Naval Research (N00014-83), the McKnight Foundation, and the Sloan Foundation.

References

Albus, J. S. (1971). A theory of cerebellar function. *Math. Biosci.* **10,** 25–61.
Andersson, G., Gorwicz, M., and Hesslow, G. (1987). Effects of bicuculline on cerebellar inhibition of the inferior olive. *Abstr. World Congr. Neurosci., 2nd, 1987* p. 5631.
Brodal, A. (1981). *In* "Neurological Anatomy." Oxford University Press, New York.

Brodal, P. (1975). Demonstration of a somatotopically organized projection onto the paramedian lobule and the anterior lobe from the lateral reticular nucleus. An experimental study with the horseradish peroxidase method. *Brain Res.* **95**, 221–239.

Chapman, P. F., Steinmetz, J. E., and Thompson, R. F. (1985). Classical conditioning of the rabbit eyeblink does not occur with stimulation of the cerebellar nuclei as the unconditioned stimulus. *Soc. Neurosci. Abstr.* **11**, 835.

Clark, G. A., McCormick, D. A., Lavond, D. G., and Thompson, R. F. (1984). Effects of lesions of cerebellar nuclei on conditioned behavioral and hippocampal neuronal responses. *Brain Res.* **291**, 125–136.

Donegan, N. H., Lowry, R. W., and Thompson, R. F. (1983). Effects of lesioning cerebellar nuclei on conditioned leg-flexion responses. *Soc. Neurosci. Abstr.* **9**, 331.

Donegan, N. H., Foy, M. R., and Thompson, R. F. (1985). Neuronal responses of the rabbit cerebellar cortex during performance of the classically conditioned eyelid response. *Soc. Neurosci. Abstr.* **11**, 835.

Donegan, N. H., Gluck, M. A., and Thompson, R. F. (1988). Interpreting behavioral and biological models of classical conditioning. *In* "Computational models of learning in simple neural systems (Psychology of Learning and Memory, Vol. 22)" (R. D. Hawkins and G. H. Bower, eds.). Academic Press, New York.

Eccles, J. C. (1977). An instruction-selection theory of learning in the cerebellar cortex. *Brain Res.* **127**, 327–352.

Foy, M. R., and Thompson, R. F. (1986). Single unit analysis of Purkinje cell discharge in classically conditioned and untrained rabbits. *Soc. Neurosci. Abstr.* **12**, 518.

Gellman, R., Houk, J. C., and Gibson, A. R. (1983). Somatosensory properties of the inferior olive of the cat. *J. Comp. Neurol.* **215**, 228–243.

Gormezano, I. (1972). Investigations of defense and reward conditioning in the rabbit. *In* "Classical Conditioning II: Current Research and Theory" (A. H. Black and W. F. Prokasy, eds.), pp. 151–181. Appleton, New York.

Haley, D. A., Lavond, D. G., and Thompson, R. F. (1983). Effects of contralateral red nuclear lesions on retention of the classically conditioned nictitating membrane/eyelid response. *Soc. Neurosci. Abstr.* **9**, 643.

Ito, M. (1972). Neural design of the cerebellar motor control system. *Brain Res.* **40**, 81–84.

Lavond, D. G., McCormick, D. A., Clark, G. A., Holmes, D. T., and Thompson, R. F. (1981). Effects of ipsilateral rostral pontine reticular lesions on retention of classically conditioned nictitating membrane and eyelid response. *Physiol. Psychol.* **9**(4), 335–339.

Lavond, D. G., Hembree, T. L., and Thompson, R. F. (1985). Effect of kainic acid lesions of the cerebellar interpositus nucleus on eyelid conditioning in the rabbit. *Brain Res.* **326**, 179–182.

Lincoln, J. S., McCormick, D. A., and Thompson, R. F. (1982). Ipsilateral cerebellar lesions prevent learning of the classically conditioned nictitating membrane/eyelid response of the rabbit. *Brain Res.* **242**, 190–193.

Logan, C. G., Steinmetz, J. E., Woodruff-Pak, D. S., and Thompson, R. F. (1985). Short-duration mossy fiber stimulation is effective as a CS in eyelid classical conditioning. *Soc. Neurosci. Abstr.* **11**, 835.

Logan, C. G., Steinmetz, J. G., and Thompson, R. F. (1986). Acoustic related responses recorded from the region of the pontine nuclei. *Neurosci. Abstr.* **12**, 754.

Madden, J., IV, Haley, D. A., Barchas, J. D., and Thompson, R. F. (1983). Microinfusion of picrotoxin into the caudal red nucleus selectively abolishes the classically conditioned nictitating membrane/eyelid response in the rabbit. *Soc. Neurosci. Abstr.* **9**, 830.

Marr, D. (1969). A theory of cerebellar cortex. *J. Physiol. (London)* **202**, 437–470.

Mauk, M. D., and Thompson, R. F. (1987). Retention of classically conditioned eyelid responses following acute decerebration. *Brain Res.* **403**, 89–95.

Mauk, M. D., Steinmetz, J. E., and Thompson, R. F. (1986). Classical conditioning using stimulation of the inferior olive as the unconditioned stimulus. *Proc. Natl. Acad. Sci. U.S.A.* **83**, 5349–5353.

McCormick, D. A., and Thompson, R. F. (1984a). Cerebellum: Essential involvement in the classically conditioned eyelid response. *Science* **223**, 296–299.

McCormick, D. A., and Thompson, R. F. (1984b). Neuronal responses of the rabbit cerebellum during acquisition and performance of a classically conditioned nictitating membrane-eyelid response. *J. Neurosci.* **4**, 2811–2822.

McCormick, D. A., Lavond, D. G., Clark, G. A., Kettner, R. E., Rising, C. E., and Thompson, R. F. (1981). The engram found? Role of the cerebellum in classical conditioning of nictitating membrane and eyelid responses. *Bull. Psychon. Soc.* **18,**(3), 103–105.

McCormick, D. A., Clark, G. A., Lavond, D. G., and Thompson, R. F. (1982a). Initial localization of the memory trace for a basic form of learning. *Proc. Natl. Acad. Sci. U.S.A.* **79**, 2731–2742.

McCormick, D. A., Guyer, P. E., and Thompson, R. F. (1982b). Superior cerebellar peduncle lesions selectively abolish the ipsilateral classically conditioned nictitating membrane/eyelid response in the rabbit. *Brain Res.* **244**, 347–350.

McCormick, D. A., Steinmetz, J. E., and Thompson, R. F. (1985). Lesions of the inferior olivary complex cause extinction of the classically conditioned eyeblink response. *Brain Res.* **359**, 120–130.

Nelson, B., and Mugnoini, E. (1987). GABAergic innervation of the inferior olivary complex and experimental evidence for its origin. *In* "The Olivocerebellar System in Motor Control."

Norman, R. J., Buchwald, J. S., and Villablanca, J. R. (1977). Classical conditioning with auditory discrimination of the eyeblink in decerebrate cats. *Science* **196**, 551–553.

Oakley, D. A., and Russell, I. S. (1972). Neocortical lesions and classical conditioning. *Physiol. Behav.* **8**, 915–926.

Polenchar, B. E., Patterson, M. M., Lavond, D. G., and Thompson, R. F. (1985). Cerebellar lesions abolish an avoidance response in rabbit. *Behav. Neural Biol.* **44**, 221–227.

Rescorla, R. A., and Wagner, A. R. (1972). A theory of Pavlovian conditioning: Variations in the effectiveness of reinforcement and non-reinforcement. *In* "Classical conditioning II: Current Research and Theory" (A. H. Black and W. F. Prokasy, eds.), pp. 64–99. Appleton, New York.

Rosenfield, M. E., Devydaitis, A., and Moore, J. W. (1985). Brachium conjunctivum and rubrobulbar tract: Brainstem projections of red nucleus essential for the conditioned nictitating membrane response. *Physiol. Behav.* **34**, 751–759.

Solomon, P. R., Lewis, J. L., LoTurco, J. J., Steinmetz, J. E., and Thompson, R. F. (1986). The role of the middle cerebellar peduncle in acquisition and retention of the rabbit's classically conditioned nictitating membrane response. *Bull. Psychon. Soc.* **24**(1), 75–78.

Steinmetz, J. E., Lavond, D. G., and Thompson, R. F. (1985a). Classical conditioning of the rabbit eyelid response with mossy fiber stimulation as the conditioned stimulus. *Bull. Psychon. Soc.* **23**(3), 245–248.

Steinmetz, J. E., Lavond, D. G., and Thompson, R. F. (1985b). Classical conditioning of skeletal muscle responses with mossy fiber stimulation CS and climbing fiber stimulation US. *Soc. Neurosci. Abstr.* **11**, 982.

Steinmetz, J. E., Rosen, D. L., Chapman, P. F., Lavond, D. G., and Thompson, R. F. (1986a). Classical conditioning of the rabbit eyelid response with a mossy fiber stimulation CS. I. Pontine nuclei and middle cerebellar peduncle stimulation. *Behav. Neurosci.* **100**, 871–880.

Steinmetz, J. E., Rosen, D. J., Woodruff-Pak, D. S., Lavond, D. G., and Thompson, R. F. (1986b). Rapid transfer of training occurs when direct mossy fiber stimulation is used as a conditioned stimulus for classical eyelid conditioning. *Neurosci. Res.* **3**, 606–616.

Steinmetz, J. E., Donegan, N. H., and Thompson, R. F. (1988). In preparation.

Thompson, J. K., Lavond, D. G., and Thompson, R. F. (1986). Preliminary evidence for a projection from the cochlear nucleus to the pontine nuclear region. *Soc. Neurosci. Abstr.* **12**, 754.

Thompson, R. F. (1986). The neurobiology of learning and memory. *Science* **233**, 941–947.

Thompson, R. F., Berger, T. W., and Madden, J., IV (1983). Cellular processes of learning and memory in the mammalian CNS. *Annu. Rev. Neurosci.* **6,** 447–491.

Thompson, R. F., Clark, G. A., Donegan, N. H., Lavond, D. G., Madden, J., IV, Mamounas, L. A., Mauk, M. D., and McCormick, D. A. (1984). Neuronal substrates of basic associative learning. *In* "Neuropsychology of Memory" (L. Squire and N. Butters, eds.), pp. 424–442. Guilford Press, New York.

Weiss, C., McCurdy, M. L., Houk, J. C., and Gibson, A. R. (1985). Anatomy and physiology of dorsal column afferents to forelimb dorsal accessory olive. *Soc. Neurosci. Abstr.* **11,** 182.

Yeo, C. H., Hardiman, M. J., and Glickstein, M. (1985). Classical conditioning of the nictitating membrane response of the rabbit: I. Lesions of the cerebellar nuclei. *Exp. Brain Res.* **60,** 87–98.

10

Long-Term Depression: Possible Cellular Mechanism for Learning Mediated by the Cerebellum

Masao Ito

I. Introduction

Long-term depression (LTD) is unique and characteristic of synaptic plasticity present in the cerebellar cortex, which is presumed to subserve as a memory element for motor learning (see Chapter 9, this volume). The LTD occurs when impulses arrive at a Purkinje cell approximately simultaneously through two distinct afferent pathways: one from cerebellar mossy-fiber afferents through granule cells and their axons (parallel fibers), and the other from olivocerebellar afferent fibers through their climbing-fiber terminals. As contrasted to the long-term potentiation (LTP) prevailing in the hippocampus, LTD is a long-lasting lowering of transmission efficacy at those parallel fiber-Purkinje cell synapses imposed by repetitive conjunctive activation with climbing fibers. Presence of such synaptic plasticity in the cerebellar cortex has long been suggested (Brindley, 1964; Marr, 1969; Grossberg, 1969; Albus, 1971), but experimental evidence for this has started to accumulate only recently (Ito *et al.*, 1982). This chapter introduces data collected in our laboratory in order to characterize the LTD and to get insight into its molecular mechanisms and roles in cerebellar function.

II. Specification of LTD

The LTD has been demonstrated to occur with a variety of stimulating and recording methods. It can be induced by conjunctive stimulation of mossy fibers and climbing fibers, being tested by mossy-fiber stimulation (Ito *et al.*, 1982), or can be induced by conjunctive stimulation of parallel fibers and climbing fibers, being tested by parallel-fiber stimulation (Ekerot and Kano, 1985). Extracellular unit recording from Purkinje cells in *in vivo* preparations has been used for these testings, but intradendritic recording in *in vitro* cerebellar slices has also been successful (Sakurai, 1987). Extracellular recording of mass field potentials in the molecular layer, on the other hand, gives only a poor index of LTD (Ito and Kano, 1982), probably because these have heterogenous origin from Purkinje, stellate, basket, and Golgi cells.

An essential feature of the LTD is that it is induced only by combination of parallel-fiber and climbing-fiber impulses, but not by impulses of parallel fibers or climbing fibers alone. Repetitive stimulation of parallel fibers alone in a cerebellar slice where spontaneous climbing-fiber activity is absent, induces a slight potentiation lasting for 20–50 min, instead of a depression, in parallel-fiber–Purkinje cell transmission. Stimulation of climbing fibers alone neither increases nor decreases parallel-fiber–Purkinje cell transmission efficacy (Ito *et al.*, 1982; Sakurai, 1987).

In the above testing, conjunctive stimulation of parallel fibers and climbing fibers at the rates of 1–4 Hz for 0.5–8 min effectively induced LTD. The timing of parallel-fiber and climbing-fiber stimulations to effectively induce LTD is allowed a relatively wide latitude. Stimulation of parallel fibers during the period between 20 msec prior and 150 msec subsequent to the stimulation of climbing fibers is nearly equally potent in inducing the LTD. Even those occurring 250 msec after a climbing-fiber impulse induced the LTD, though with less predictability (C.-F. Ekerot and M. Kano, personal communication). In this connection, it is pointed out that the critical timing of conjunction postulated by Marr (1969) is not a severe restriction in cerebellar network theories. The LTD may depend on some variable factor such as enhanced correlation between the firing of parallel fibers and that of climbing fibers, as postulated in Fujita's (1982a) adaptive filter theory of the cerebellum. The idea of critical timing of collision with parallel-fiber impulses is unrealistic also in view of the characteristically slow, irregular discharge pattern of climbing fiber impulses (see Ito, 1984).

The LTD induced with electrical conjunctive stimulation of mossy or parallel fibers and climbing fibers usually consists of an initial phase for about 10 min followed by a later phase lasting for 1 hr or more. Because of technical difficulties inherent to extracellular and intradendritic recording from single Purkinje cells, it is not easy to follow the time course of LTD over an hour. In some cases, though, LTD has been followed over 3 hr without recovery. Efforts should be devoted to clarify the whole time course of LTD and its dependence on stimulus conditions. For the present, it is certain that conjunctive activation of parallel fibers and climbing fibers for 0.5–8 min at a physiological range of frequency for climbing-fiber firing (1–4 Hz) produces LTD lasting for hours. It is uncertain, though, whether LTD lasts longer under rigorous stimulating conditions, or whether it eventually becomes a permanent memory trace. These questions are still open to future investigation.

---------- **III. Involvement of Glutamate** ----------
Receptors in LTD

Involvement of postsynaptic glutamate sensitivity of Purkinje cells in LTD was first suggested by the finding that conjunctive iontophoretic application of L-glutamate with electrical stimulation of climbing fibers induced a sustained depression of L-glutamate sensitivity of Purkinje cells (Ito *et al.*, 1982). The depression of L-glutamate sensitivity displayed two phases similar to those of LTD. Since L-glutamate is a putative neurotransmitter of parallel fibers, it is postulated that the LTD in parallel-fiber–Purkinje cell transmission is underlaid by decreased L-glutamate sensitivity of Purkinje cells, presumably at dendritic synaptic sites. This postulate is supported by testing of parallel-fiber–Purkinje cell transmission after conjunctive application of L-glutamate with electrical stimulation of climbing fibers (Kano and Kato, 1987). Parallel-fiber–Purkinje cell transmission at those synapses, where L-glutamate was applied in conjunction with climbing-fiber stimulation, underwent a long-lasting depression equivalent to the LTD in time course and magnitude.

Depression of parallel-fiber–Purkinje cell transmission was also induced by application of quisqualate, a glutamate agonist, in conjunction with climbing fibers, but not by application of either aspartate or kainate, even though these substances also activated Purkinje cells effectively. Since another glutamate agonist, NMDA (N-methyl D-aspartate), does not effectively activate adult Purkinje cells (Dupont *et al.*, 1987; Kano *et al.*, 1988), its involvement in LTD is doubtful. It is concluded that quisqualate-specific glutamate receptors at parallel-fiber–Purkinje cell synapses are responsible for production of LTD.

Iontophoretic application of glutamate or quisqualate alone without conjunctive stimulation of climbing fibers did not affect the glutamate sensitivity of Purkinje cells or parallel fiber-Purkinje cell transmission (Ito *et al.*, 1982; Kano and Kato, 1988). The effect of conjunctive application of glutamate with climbing fiber impulses in inducing LTD was abolished when the excitatory effect of glutamate on a Purkinje cell was blocked by iontophoretic application of kynurenic acid (Kano and Kato, 1988). These observations indicate that the LTD is due to desensitization of glutamate receptors effected under influences of climbing-fiber impulses.

---------- **IV. Involvement of Ca^{2+}** ----------
Inflow in LTD

LTD has been shown to be abolished when climbing-fiber impulses are conditioned with postsynaptic inhibition of Purkinje cell dendrites through stellate cells (Ekerot and Kano, 1985). Since stellate-cell inhibition depresses both the Ca^{2+} spikes and subsequent Ca^{2+}-dependent plateau potentials induced in Purkinje cell dendrites by climbing-fiber impulses, the above observation suggests that Ca^{2+} inflow into Purkinje cell dendrites plays an essential role in inducing LTD. More direct evidence for the role of Ca^{2+} inflow has recently been obtained by intradendritic injection of a Ca^{2+} chelator, EGTA (M. Sakurai, personal communication). Iontophoretic injection of EGTA through an electrode containing EGTA plus potassium acetate abolished the LTD, whereas control injection of acetate ions did not affect the LTD.

It is apparent that LTD is triggered by Ca^{2+} inflow into Purkinje-cell dendrites evoked by climbing fiber impulses and that LTD is eventually effected by desensitization of quisqualate-specific glutamate receptors. Desensitization of acetylcholine receptor molecules due to allosteric conformational changes occurs under direct influence of Ca^{2+} (Changeux and Heidman, 1987). This may provide an excellent model for the LTD, but there is presently no available evidence suggesting that desensitization of glutamate receptors is likewise facilitated by Ca^{2+}. An alternative possibility is that Ca^{2+} ions activate a certain second-messenger process in Purkinje cell dendrites, which in turn facilitates glutamate desensitization.

Desensitization of glutamate receptors in cerebellar synaptosomes is actually facilitated by a relatively high concentration of cyclic GMP (cGMP) (Sharif and Roberts, 1980). cGMP and cGMP-dependent protein kinase are contained specifically in Purkinje cells (Lohmann *et al.*, 1981), and the level of cGMP in Purkinje cells is elevated after activation of climbing fibers (Biggio and Guidotti, 1976). It is also known that Ca^{2+} ions activate guanylate cyclase in cerebellar slices (Ohga and Daly, 1977). The possibility may be suggested that climbing-fiber impulses enhance cGMP content in Purkinje cell dendrites and thereby facilitate desensitization of glutamate receptors at parallel-fiber–Purkinje cell synapses (Ito, 1986). How cGMP facilitates glutamate receptors is unclear, but an analogy may be drawn from the suggestion on acetylcholine receptors that cAMP-dependent kinase phosphorylation of the γ and δ subunits of the receptors is equivalent in terms of desensitization (Steinbach and Zempel, 1987). These possibilities should be subjected to appropriate pharmacological tests.

V. Role of LTD in the Vestibulo-Ocular Reflex

The possibility that LTD plays a key role in cerebellar function has been examined in studies of the flocculo-vestibuloocular system. The flocculus is a phylogenetically old part of the cerebellum and projects Purkinje cell axons to relay cells of the vestibulo-ocular reflex (VOR). These Purkinje cells receive vestibular signals as a mossy-fiber input and visual signals as a climbing fiber input. It seems that the visual climbing-fiber afferents convey "retinal error signals" to the flocculus as to the effectiveness of VOR eye movements compensating for head movements. If these climbing-fiber signals act to modify the signal-transfer character-istics of the vestibular mossy fiber–granule cell–Purkinje cell pathway in the flocculus by producing LTD, modification would then occur in VOR dynamics toward improved visual stability. LTD may act as if it disconnects wrong wiring in the flocculus responsible for errors in VOR performance (for references, see Ito, 1984).

The gain of the horizontal VOR is indeed modified adaptively under mismatched visual–vestibular stimulating conditions, as first demon-strated by Gonshor and Melvill-Jones (1976). It either increases or de-creases toward minimization of retinal error signals under given stim-ulating conditions. Evidence supporting the hypothesis that the flocculus adaptively controls VOR has been collected through two lines of exper-iments (see Ito, 1984). First, the adaptiveness of the VOR is abolished by ablation of the flocculus and also by severance of the visual climbing-fiber pathway to the flocculus. Second, floccular Purkinje cells indeed represent retinal errors with their climbing-fiber activity, and also exhibit changes of mossy-fiber responsiveness to head rotation paralleling adaption of the VOR. Purkinje cells specifically involved in control of the horizontal VOR can be recorded in floccular areas where local stim-ulation through the recording microelectrode induces abduction of the ipsilateral eye. The relationship between the climbing-fiber responses and the change of vestibular mossy-fiber responsiveness supports the assumption that LTD occurs in parallel-fiber–Purkinje cell synapses me-diating vestibular signals when they are conjunctively activated with visual climbing-fiber signals.

Performance of the entire flocculo–VOR system has been computer-simulated (Fujita, 1982b). Fujita's (1982a) adaptive filter model of the cerebellum can manipulate frequency-modulated time analog signals similar to nerve impulses occurring in actual nervous systems. With the adaptive filter model in place of the flocculus, the model of the whole flocculo–VOR system successfully reproduced the performance of human horizontal VOR adapted to the reversal of visual fields with dove prism goggles. Fujita's (1982a) model utilizes a learning principle similar to the Marr (1969) and Albus (1971) models: conjunction of climbing fiber and parallel fiber impulses leads to modification of parallel-fiber–Purkinje cell synapses. Therefore, the success of the simulation study is a strong support for the view that LTD underlies the VOR adaptation.

VI. Discussion

The long-term depression is now established as a special type of synaptic plasticity present in the cerebellar cortex. The characteristic dual inputs to Purkinje cells, one from parallel fibers and the other from a climbing fiber, is the structural basis for this plasticity. In this respect, it differs from the long-term depression reported in the hippocampus, which occurs in a single type of input activated at a low rate (Bramham and Stubro, 1987). Earlier failure in detecting LTD in the cerebellar cortex may be due to several complications. Stellate-cell inhibition might be induced by strong stimulation of parallel fibers and abolish LTD; climbing fibers might be stimulated at too a high frequency beyond their physiological range, and cause general depression of Purkinje cells, thereby disturbing examination of their activity; mass field potentials might be observed, but because of contamination by activities of numerous non-Purkinje cells, these might provide only a poor index of Purkinje cell-specific activity.

When LTD is compared with other types of synaptic plasticity, such as LTP in the hippocampus and sensitization in *Aplysia* (Klein and Kandel, 1980; Byrne, 1987), Ca^{2+} ions commonly play a key role, even though the mechanism for enhancement of Ca^{2+} entry is varied: via NMDA receptor-associated chemically activated Ca^{2+} channels at least in certain parts of the hippocampus, and via electrically activated Ca^{2+} channels in *Aplysia* neurons and Purkinje cells. Molecular processes subsequent to Ca^{2+} entry are also varied; desensitization of glutamate receptors in the postsynaptic membrane occurs in Purkinje cells, whereas an increase in number of effective glutamate receptors in postsynaptic membrane (Lynch and Baudry, 1985) or an increase of glutamate release from presynaptic fibers terminals (Bliss *et al.*, 1986), or both, would occur in hippocampal neurons. Enhanced release of as yet unidentified neurotransmitter accounts for sensitization in *Aplysia*. It is well evidenced that synthesis of cAMP is an essential step in sensitization (see Chapters 3, 4, and 5, this volume), whereas cGMP could be involved in induction of LTD. Thus, the three major types of synaptic plasticity involve similar elementary processes, but in different combinations and with different implications.

Synapses mediating LTP in the hippocampus and those mediating LTD in the cerebellum are both formed on dendritic spines and have Gray's type I asymmetric electronmicroscopic configuration. Both of these synapses are also presumed to utilize L-glutamate as neurotransmitter, and postsynaptic receptors responsible for signal transmission in them are quisqualate-specific. However, corresponding to the differences in physiological and biochemical aspects between the LTP and LTD, there seem to be some differences in the molecular structure of synapses between the cerebrum and cerebellum; 51,000-M_r protein specifically localized in cerebral type I synapses is virtually absent in the cerebellum (Flanagan *et al.*, 1982). The Calpain–glutamate receptor interaction that is assumed to be a key process of LTP in the hippocampus does not seem to apply to the cerebellum (Lynch and Baudry, 1985). Close comparison of ultrastructures and biochemical composition of cerebral and cerebellar spine synapses would help elucidation of molecular mechanisms of LTP and LTD.

While enhancement of transmitter release from presynaptic terminals accounts for sensitization in *Aplysia* and probably also, at least partly, for LTP in the hippocampus, there is no evidence suggesting a presynaptic component of LTD. Nevertheless, parallel fibers in the cerebellum are equipped with $GABA_B$ receptors (Wilkin *et al.*, 1981) and adenosine receptors (Goodman *et al.*, 1983), and hence the parallel-fiber–Purkinje cell transmission would be modulated by GABA (gamma-aminobutyric acid) (Hackett, 1974) and adenosine (Kocsis *et al.*, 1984). On the other hand, postsynaptic glutamate sensitivity of Purkinje cells is reduced by serotonin (Lee *et al.*, 1986) and thyrotropin-releasing hormone (TRH) (Ito and Kano, unpublished), while it is enhanced by norepinephrine (Woodward *et al.*, 1979). Parallel-fiber–Purkinje cell synapses are thus equipped with fairly complex chemical regulatory mechanisms. It is an important future task to elucidate relationships of LTD with these chemical regulatory mechanisms.

Beside these biochemical processes, a mechanical factor might also be involved in LTD. Since the parallel-fiber–Purkinje cell synapses are formed on the top of dendritic spines, constriction of the spine neck would prevent synaptic currents generated at the subsynaptic membrane from spreading to dendritic shafts. A possibility emerges that such mechanical changes account for LTD, or at least for a part of it. This situation is analogous, although opposite in direction, to the shortening of spines that could underlie LTP (Crick, 1982; Koch and Poggio, 1983; Kawato *et al.*, 1984). However, actin filaments present in Purkinje cell spines form a bundle running along the spine shaft (H. Hirokawa, personal communication). Contraction of these fibers would cause shortening, but not constriction, of spines. Hence, there is no evidence for a shape change of Purkinje cell spines related to LTD.

The flocculo–vestibulo-ocular system provides good material for testing the roles of LTD in cerebellar function. Several lines of evidence so far collected conjointly support the view that the flocculus acts as a center of adaptive control of VOR, and that LTD subserves as a memory element for this adaptive control. An observation contradicting this view was reported in VOR adaption of monkeys (Miles and Lisberger, 1981), but the controversy was solved in a later reexamination as due to inadequate selection of floccular Purkinje cells (Watanabe, 1984, 1985). Another controversy has been reported in an experiment on visual fixation of monkeys (Lisberger, 1988), in which visual–vestibular mismatching is assumed to induce an adaptive change in vestibular nuclear neurons, but not in the flocculus. This interpretation, however, is derived from a speculative calculation based on oversimplified neuronal circuit connections, and for the present it lacks support from direct evidence. On the other hand, observation of Purkinje cell behavior in monkeys during adaptation of wrist movements (Gilbert and Thach, 1977) and that in rabbits during classically conditioned eyeblink reflexes (Thompson, 1986) consistently supports the view that LTD in the cerebellum is a central process of adaptive motor performance. The author feels that there is enough justification for maintaining this view.

References

Albus, J. S. (1971). *Math. Biosci.* **10,** 25–61.

Biggio, G., and Guidotti, A. (1976). *Brain Res.* **107,** 365–373.

Bliss, T. V. P., Douglass, R. M., Errington, M. L., and Lynch, M. A. (1986). *J. Physiol. (London)* **377,** 391–408.

Bramham, C. R., and Stubro, B. (1987). *Brain Res.* **405,** 100–107.

Brindley, G. S. (1964). *Int. Brain Res. Organ. Bull.* **3,** 80.

Byrne, J. H. (1987). *Physiol. Rev.* **67,** 329–439.

Changeux, J.-P., and Heidman, T. (1987). *In* "Synaptic Function" (G. M. Edelman, W. E. Gall, and W. M. Cowan, eds.), pp. 549–601. Wiley, New York.

Crick, F. (1982). *Trends NeuroSci.* **5,** 44–46.

Dupont, J.-L., Gardette, R., and Crepel, F. (1987). *Dev. Brain Res.* **34,** 59–68.

Ekerot, C.-F., and Kano, M. (1985). *Brain Res.* **342,** 357–360.

Flanagan, S. D., Yost, B., and Crawford, G. (1982). *J. Cell Biol.* **94,** 743–748.

Fujita, M. (1982a). *Biol. Cybernet.* **45,** 195–206.

Fujita, M. (1982b). *Biol. Cybernet.* **45,** 207–214.

Gilbert, P. F. C., and Thach, W. T. (1977). *Brain Res.* **128,** 309–328.

Gonshor, A., and Melvill-Jones, G. (1976). *J. Physiol. (London)* **256,** 381–414.

Goodman, R. R., Kuhar, M. J., Hester, L., and Snyder, S. H. (1983). *Science* **220,** 967–969.

Grossberg, S. (1969). *Stud. Appl. Math.* **48,** 105–132.

Hackett, J. T. (1974). *Brain Res.* **80,** 527–531.

Ito, M. (1984). "The Cerebellum and Neural Control." Raven Press, New York.

Ito, M. (1986). *Neurosci. Res.* **3,** 531–539.

Ito, M., and Kano, M. (1982). *Neurosci. Lett.* **33,** 253–258.

Ito, M., Sakurai, M., and Tongroach, P. (1982). *J. Physiol. (London)* **324,** 113–134.

Kano, M., and Kato, M. (1987). *Nature (London)* **325,** 276–279.

Kano, M., Kato, M., and Chang, H. S. (1988). *Neurosci. Res.* **5,** 325–337.

Kano, M., and Kato, M. (1988). *Neurosci. Res.* **5,** 544–556.

Kawato, M., Kawaguchi, T., Murakami, F., and Tsukahara, N. (1984). *Biol. Cybernet.* **50,** 447–454.

Klein, M., and Kandel, E. R. (1980). *Proc. Natl. Acad. Sci. U.S.A.* **77,** 6912–6916.

Koch, C., and Poggio, T. (1983). *Proc. R. Soc. London, Ser. B* **218,** 445–447.

Kocsis, J. D., Eng, D. L., and Bhisitkul, R. B. (1984). *Proc. Natl. Acad. Sci. U.S.A.* **81,** 6531–6584.

Lee, M., Strahlendorf, J. C., and Strahlendorf, H. K. (1986). *Brain Res.* **361,** 107–113.

Lisberger, S. G. (1988). *Trends Neurosci.* **11,** 147–152.

Lohmann, S. M., Walter, U., Miller, P. E., Greengard, P., and Camilli, P. D. (1981). *Proc. Natl. Acad. Sci. U.S.A.* **78,** 653–657.

Lynch, G., and Baudry, M. (1985). *Science* **224,** 1057–1063.

Marr, D. (1969). *J. Physiol. (London)* **202,** 437–470.

Miles, F. A., and Lisberger, S. G. (1981). *Ann. Rev. Neurosci.* **4,** 273–299.

Ohga, Y., and Daly, J. W. (1977). *Biochim. Biophys. Acta* **498,** 61–75.

Sakurai, M. (1987). *J. Physiol. (London)* **394,** 463–480.

Sharif, N. A., and Roberts, P. J. (1980). *Eur. J. Pharmacol.* **61,** 213–214.

Steinbach, J. H., and Zempel, J. (1987). *Trends NeuroSci. (Pers. Ed.)* **10,** 61–64.

Thompson, R. F. (1986). *Science* **233,** 941–947.

Watanabe, E. (1984). *Brain Res.* **297,** 169–174.

Watanabe, E. (1985). *Neurosci. Res.* **3,** 20–38.

Wilkin, G. P., Hudson, A. L., Hill, D. R., and Bowery, N. G. (1981). *Nature (London)* **294,** 584–587.

Woodward, D. J., Moise, H. C., Waterhouse, B. D., Hoffer, B. J., and Freeman, R. (1979). *Fed. Proc., Fed. Am. Soc. Exp. Biol.* **38,** 2109–2116.

11

Simulation of a Classically Conditioned Response: A Cerebellar Neural Network Implementation of the Sutton–Barto–Desmond Model

John W. Moore and Diana E. J. Blazis

I. Introduction

Computational approaches to learning confront the problem of extending general mathematical models to specific instances such as classical conditioning of a particular response. We have recently shown how a *template* of the classically conditioned nictitating membrane response (NMR) of the rabbit can be incorporated into the neurally inspired model of connectionist learning proposed by Sutton and Barto (1981; Barto and Sutton, 1982). Our approach resulted in an implementation of the Sutton–Barto (SB) model that goes beyond the description of cumulative effects of training to address within-trial aspects of this conditioned response (CR) (Blazis *et al.*, 1986; Moore *et al.*, 1986).

The original SB model was presented in the context of the extensive behavioral literature on NMR conditioning (see Gormezano *et al.*, 1983). Our strategy for modeling the NMR was to constrain the SB model to predict response topography in a simple conditioning situation. Constraints were derived partly from electrophysiological experiments conducted in awake, behaving rabbits. We have shown that the physiologically constrained SB model retains the ability of the original implementation to describe multiple-CS (conditioned stimulus) phenomena such as blocking, conditioned inhibition, and higher-order conditioning. These more complex learning situations are predicted without further modification of the parameters of the model (Blazis *et al.*, 1986; Moore *et al.*, 1986). We refer to this variant of the SB model as the Sutton–Barto–Desmond (SBD) model.

NEURAL MODELS OF PLASTICITY

_____ **II. The Model** _____

The SB model can be viewed as a neuron-like device (adaptive or learning element) capable of receiving input from many potential CSs. In Fig. 1 these are designated as CS_i, $i = 1, \ldots, n$. Each CS_i gives rise to a representation that provides a synaptic input, designated x_i, to the element and has a variable synaptic weight or efficacy, designated V_i. The unconditioned stimulus (US) is signaled by a pathway of fixed efficacy, designated λ. The output of the element, s, is the weighted sum of its inputs.

A. Input

Our approach to extending the SB model to CR topography is to treat the input of the ith CS to the element, x_i, as a rectangular pulse defined by the onset and offset of the CS. With no further processing, such an input produces a square-wave output and with zero latency. In contrast, a real conditioned NMR begins well after CS onset and rises gradually in a ramped or S-shaped fashion within the CS–US or interstimulus interval (ISI). The CR attains a maximum at or near the temporal locus of the US, and then decays rapidly during the post-US period. This pattern of response topography is also reflected in the activity of some types of neurons that have been identified in single-unit recording studies as being linked to the generation of CRs. For example, Desmond (1985; see also Desmond and Moore, 1986) described the activity of brain stem neurons recorded during classical conditioning of the rabbit NMR with a 350-msec tone CS (ISI of 350 msec). In a typical cell, spikes began to be

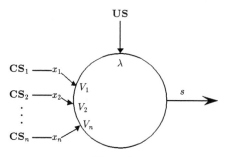

Figure 1.
The Sutton and Barto neuron-like adaptive element. The unconditioned stimulus (US) is signaled by a pathway of fixed efficacy, denoted λ. Inputs for each conditioned stimulus (CS) are denoted x_i, $i = 1, \ldots, n$, and vary in transmission efficacy according to the strength of a learned connection for each CS, the synaptic weight V_i. The output of the element, s, is computed as the weighted sum of all inputs.

recruited about 70 msec after CS onset. About 150 msec after CS onset, spike recruitment increased sharply and continued to increase throughout the remainder of the ISI. The momentary rate of firing prior to the US rarely exceeded 200 Hz. After US offset, firing initiated by the US declined toward a baseline rate of about 10 Hz.

We were able to fashion a suitable CR template by using an expression for CS input to the learning element that allows for variation in the recruitment and amplitude of the CR within the ISI. The input to the learning element at time t is given by $x_i(t)$. Each t corresponds to 10 msec. At CS_i onset, $t = 0$. For time steps $t = 1, \ldots, 7$, $x_i = 0$. For $t > 7$ and until CS_i offset, x_i is defined as follows:

(1) $x_i(t) = [\arctan(mt - 5.5) + 90]/180h$

The parameter m, $m > 0$, controls the rate of rise of x_i, and the parameter h, $h > 0$, controls CR amplitude. The simulation experiments reported by Moore et al. (1986) and illustrated in Fig. 2 used $m = 0.35$ and $h = 1.0$.

Holding $x_i = 0$ for the first seven time steps precludes any changes in V_i during this period and aligns the model with reports indicating a

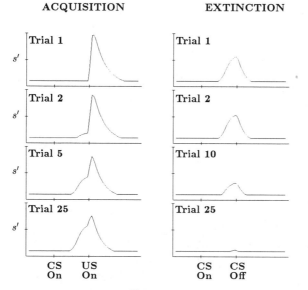

Figure 2.
Simulated response topographies, s' obtained with a 250-msec ISI during acquisition and extinction in a forward-delay paradigm. US duration = 30 msec. The data were generated with the following parameter values: $m = 0.35$, $h = 1.0$, $k = 0.85$, $\lambda = 0.9$; $c = 0.15$, and $\beta = 0.6$. The term s' is a sliding mean of the element's output s over three time steps, the current one and the two preceding, bounded between 0.1 and 1.0.

minimal conditionable ISI of 70 msec (Salafia *et al.*, 1980). It also precludes detectable CRs with latencies less than 70 msec.

A second function returns the CR generated by x_i to its pretrial baseline. It is implemented at CS_i offset, decays geometrically, and is computed as follows:

(2) $x_i(t + 1) = kx_i(t)$

where $0 < k < 1$. In Fig. 2, $k = 0.85$.

The variable x_i serves as a representation of CS_i as well as a template for the CR. As a CS representation, the parameters that govern the rise and decline of x_i determine such things as rate of increase of V_i over trials, the shape of learning curves, and ISI functions (Blazis *et al.*, 1986; Moore *et al.*, 1986). As a template, x_i determines the topography of the CR.

B. Learning Rule

Learning in the SBD model occurs according to a modified Hebbian rule (Sutton and Barto, 1981), which states that changes in synaptic weight, denoted ΔV_i, are proportional to the product of the eligibility of CS_i's input to the learning element $\bar{x}_i$ (defined below), and the difference between the current output $s(t)$ and the trace of preceding outputs $\bar{s}(t)$ (defined below). At time t, ΔV_i is computed as follows:

(3) $\Delta V_i(t) = c[s(t) - \bar{s}(t)]\bar{x}_i(t)$,

where c is a learning-rate parameter, $0 < c \leq 1$.

C. Output

The output of the learning element at time t, denoted $s(t)$, is defined as

(4) $$s(t) = \sum_{j=i}^{n} V_i(t)x_i(t) + \lambda'(t)$$

where $\lambda'(t)$ is defined below. While s can take on any real value in the SB model, in the SBD model it is confined to the closed unit interval and is linear within that range. This limitation on permissible values of s is imposed because of physiological constraints of the NMR: negative values of s are inappropriate in modeling NMR topography because they imply NM retraction and exopthalmus, CR-opposing responses that are not typically observed in the rabbit. The upper bound of 1.0 reflects the fact that, although the amplitude of the NMR is directly related to the intensity of the eliciting stimulus, there are limits on the number of involved motoneurons and their rate of firing (Berthier, 1984; Berthier and Moore, 1980; Moore and Desmond, 1982).

The variable $\lambda'(t)$ in Eq. (4) equals zero prior to the occurrence of the US. During US presentation λ' is calculated as the difference between λ, the weight of the US, and the largest positive starting weight among all CSs present on a given trial. (Starting weight refers to the weight of a given CS at $t = 0$.) Thus, if V_i is the largest starting weight among the CSs present on the trial, while the US is present,

$$
(5) \qquad \lambda' = \begin{cases} \lambda - V_i & \text{if } 0 \leq V_i \leq \lambda \\ 0 & \text{if } V_i > \lambda \\ \lambda & \text{if } V_i \leq 0 \end{cases}
$$

At US offset, λ' decreases as follows:

$$
(6) \quad \lambda'(t + 1) = 0.9\lambda'(t)
$$

Although λ in the model is a constant directly related to US intensity, λ' functions as a heuristic that implements the idea that US effectiveness can diminish progressively with training (e.g., Donegan and Wagner, 1987; Mackintosh, 1983). Thus, in the SBD model the effectiveness of a US on a given trial is the difference between the amount of learning that can be supported in the limit by the US and the amount of learning accumulated up to that point in training. Because V_i generally increases during training, λ' progressively decreases, and this can induce a corresponding decrease in response amplitude at the time the US is presented. Were $\lambda'(t)$ to be replaced in Eq. (4) by λ, post-US computations would cancel increments in V_i during time steps preceding US offset, and as a result there would be no net learning (see Moore *et al.*, 1986). In addition, response topography would be compromised.

D. Predicted Output

The trace of s, denoted $\bar{s}$, is computed by

$$
(7) \quad \bar{s}(t + 1) = \beta\bar{s}(t) + (1 - \beta)s(t)
$$

where $0 \leq \beta < 1$. The term $\bar{s}$ can be interpreted as the element's prediction or expectation of its output during the current time step.

The parameter β determines the rate of decay of $\bar{s}$. Ideally, β should range from 0.5 to 0.6. If it exceeds 0.6, the ability of the model to reach stable weights is disrupted and a "blow up" of weights can occur. The large weights result in unrealistic rectangular-shaped response profiles. Values of β less than 0.5 result in low-amplitude CRs that do not blend with unconditioned responses (URs) and inappropriate negative weights at less-than-optimal ISIs. Given the 10-msec time step assumed by the model, this narrow range of acceptable β values implies that the relationship between $\bar{s}$ and s can be described in continuous time by an exponential function with a time constant on the order of 30 msec. Hence, for any change in s on a given time step, $\bar{s}$ closes to within 1% of s within the ensuing 10 time steps, or 100 msec. This relationship imposes a key constraint on circuit models that would describe where $s - \bar{s}$ is computed and how this term interacts with CS_i input x_i at sites of synaptic modification.

E. Learning Eligibility

Variable $\bar{x}_i(t)$ in Eq. (3) is a duration-dependent stimulus trace that defines the period and extent to which the ith synapse or connection is eligible for modification. For a given time step t, this *eligibility trace* is defined as

(8) $\bar{x}_i(t) = x_i(t - 4)$

during time steps t that CS_i is on. Then $\bar{x}_i$ begins its decline four time steps after CS_i offset:

(9) $\bar{x}_i(t + 1) = \delta \bar{x}_i(t),$

where $\delta = e^{-3/d}$, $d = \max\{25,\ CS_i$ duration in units of 10 msec$\}$. The computations shown define a period of eligibility that begins some time after CS_i onset and persists beyond CS_i offset.

Equations (1) and (2) allow the SBD model to simulate features of the conditioned NMR: increasing amplitude and decreasing latency of the CR over training, decreasing amplitude and increasing latency of the response during extinction, and attainment of peak CR amplitude at the temporal locus of the US. These features are depicted in Fig. 2. Figure 2 also illustrates the progressive diminution of the UR over acquisition due to the progressively smaller contribution of λ' to s during the US.

_____ III. Neural Implementation _____
in Cerebellum

Several laboratories have demonstrated that the cerebellum plays an essential role in the acquisition and generation of conditioned NMRs (Thompson *et al.*, 1987; Yeo *et al.*, 1984, 1985a,b,c, 1986; see Chapter 9 in this volume). In this section we consider two frameworks for implementing the SBD model in cerebellar cortex. We begin by briefly discussing the hypothesis that changes of V occur through modification of parallel-fiber (PF)/Purkinje cell (PC) synapses. (Subscripts denoting different CSs are suppressed in ensuing discussion of variables V_i, x_i, and $\bar{x}_i$.) Although this viewpoint has its detractors (e.g., Llinas, 1985) as well as proponents (e.g., Ito, 1984; Thompson, 1986), there can be no denying the similarities between the SB adaptive element as depicted in Fig. 1 and the morphology and synaptic organization of cerebellar PCs. Like the SB adaptive element, a cerebellar PC can in principle receive many inputs from parallel fibers arising from many different CSs, the climbing-fiber input seems a natural means for providing input from the US, and the cell has basically a single output channel with only limited axon collateralization. Furthermore, cerebellar PCs have been shown to respond to CSs in a CR-related manner (e.g., Berthier and Moore, 1986). We next discuss the possibility that changes of V occur at mossy-fiber (MF)/granule cell synapses. This hypothesis represents a novel approach to cerebellar involvement in classical conditioning.

Figures 3 and 4 lay the groundwork for discussing schemes for implementing the SBD model and NMR conditioning in the cerebellum. In Fig. 3, the numbers 1–3 along the top and letters A–D along the left-hand edge provide a set of coordinates that will facilitate discussion. Figure 3 omits some of details included in most textbook renderings of the cerebellum. For example, climbing-fiber synapses onto PCs are not shown. The figure includes only those features needed later for integrating physiological evidence into a plausible circuit diagram for NMR conditioning under the constraints of the SBD model.

Figure 4 summarizes cerebellar and brain stem structures and pathways involved in NMR conditioning (see, e.g., Berthier *et al.*, 1987; Thompson, 1986). As noted above, it has been suggested that learning and generation of conditioned NMRs involves cerebellar PCs located in hemispheral lobule VI (HVI). The HVI receives acoustic, visual, and somesthetic inputs via the pontine nuclei (see Buchtel *et al.*, 1972; Shofer and Navhi, 1969; Thach, 1967). Lesions of HVI have been reported to dramatically attenuate NMRs (Yeo *et al.*, 1985b), and single-unit recording studies report CR-related patterns of activity by HVI PCs that are consistent with a causal role in this behavior (Berthier and Moore, 1986). Figure 4 shows that the route taken by neural commands initiated in HVI for generation of a conditioned NMR includes several synaptic links. The output of PCs in HVI goes to cerebellar nucleus interpositus (IP); it is then transmitted to contralateral red nucleus (RN). Efferent commands from RN are carried in the rubrobulbar tract as it crosses the midline ventral to the decussation of the brachium conjunctivum. Recent fiber-tracing studies (Robinson *et al.*, 1987; Rosenfield *et al.*, 1985) suggest that the pathway from RN bifurcates at the level of the seventh nerve. One branch terminates near the accessory abducens nucleus (AAN), where motoneurons chiefly responsible for the NMR are located (Grant and Horcholle-Bossavit, 1986); the other terminates within caudal portions of the principal sensory trigeminal nucleus and spinal trigeminal nucleus pars oralis (SpoV). This second branch from RN participates in the generation of NMRs because SpoV neurons synapse onto AAN motoneurons (Durand *et al.*, 1983). In addition to relaying efferent commands to motoneurons, these neurons could convey feedback about the incipient NMR back to cerebellar cortex via mossy fibers (Ikeda, 1979; Yeo *et al.*, 1985c).

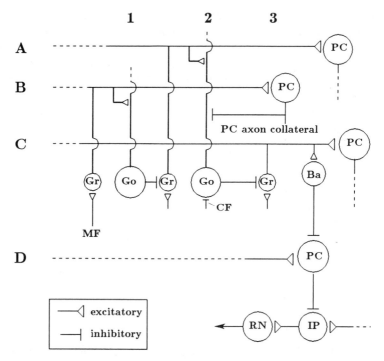

Figure 3.
Summary of cerebellar neural circuitry. Letters A–D represent beams of
parallel fibers (PF) in the molecular layer. These synapse onto Purkinje
cells (PC) and basket cells (Ba), one of which is indicated on the C beam.
Basket cells inhibit off-beam PCs, as exemplified by the basket cell on the
C beam and the PC on the D beam. The latter is shown as inhibiting a
projection neuron in cerebellar nucleus interpositus (IP), which, in turn,
excites a projection neuron in contralateral red nucleus (RN), leading to
some here-unspecified response. Mossy-fiber (MF) terminals and granule
cells (Gr) occupy the granular layer. Three granule cells are shown, and
two receive inhibitory input from Golgi cells (Go). Both Golgi cells are
excited by PF beams. The Golgi cell under 2 is shown receiving two
inhibitory inputs, one via a climbing fiber (CF) and another via a PC axon
collateral.

The circuit models discussed below argue for the possibility that
the output of cerebellar PCs, s in the model, is fed back to cerebellar
cortex for implementation of the learning rule. Based on the information
flow described in Fig. 3, a likely source for this feedback is brain stem
nucleus SpoV. This hypothesis raises questions of timing. Specifically,
does CR-related PC activity that initiates the conditioned NMR occur
with a sufficiently long lead time so that feedback from SpoV is not ob-
scured by other events such as the occurrence of the US? Berthier and
Moore (1986) observed CR-related firing patterns by PCs in HVI that

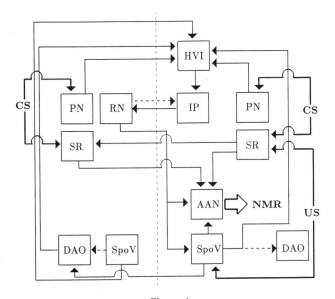

Figure 4.

Summary of cerebellar and brain stem circuitry and information flow
mediating NMRs. Solid lines indicate strong projections; dashed lines are
used to indicate projections that are comparatively weak or not universally
agreed upon. The vertical dashed line represents the medial axis of the
brain stem. The CS information (represented bilaterally) gains access to
hemispheral lobule VI (HVI) via mossy fibers arising from pontine nuclei
(PN). This information, as well as information about the US, also goes to
supratrigeminal reticular formation (SR), which is represented bilaterally.
The SR has been implicated in NMR conditioning as an independent
parallel system that appears to be essential for expression of CRs (see
Desmond and Moore, 1982, 1986). The US information gains access to
both SR and HVI via sensory trigeminal neurons. Spinal trigeminal
nucleus pars oralis (SpoV) provides synaptic drive to motoneurons in the
accessory abducens nucleus (AAN). SpoV also projects to HVI. There is a
direct mossy-fiber projection and an indirect climbing fiber projection via
the dorsal accessory olivary nucleus (DAO). Both sets of projections are
bilateral. The output of HVI is relayed to cerebellar nucleus interpositus
(IP) and from there to contralateral red nucleus (RN). The RN projection
neurons terminate in AAN and SpoV to complete the circuit and initiate a
conditioned NMR.

preceded CRs by as much as 200 msec. This is ample time in which to
initiate a CR (Moore and Desmond, 1982). Figures 3 and 4 show that
there are at least five synapses between PC output and any feedback
carried by parallel fibers, and the total conduction distance in the loop
could exceed 50 mm. Even allowing 1 msec for each synaptic relay and
a relatively slow conduction velocity for myelinated fibers of 20 m/sec,
circuit time for feedback would require no more than 10 msec, or one

time step in the model. As a cautionary note, the conjecture that PCs receive feedback about their output assumes that this information is transmitted with high fidelity through each link of the chain. That is, the output of neurons in IP, RN, AAN, and SpoV involved in the NMR must match or mirror the output of the PCs. Although evidence is sparse, recording studies indicate that this is probably the case (e.g., Thompson *et al.*, 1987).

A. Site of Plasticity: Purkinje Cells

Assuming that changes in V occur at PF/PC synapses, where is $s - \bar{s}$ computed and how does this information reach an involved PC? One option is that $s - \bar{s}$ is computed within the postsynaptic cell itself and is therefore readily available to modify eligible synapses. Another possibility is that $s - \bar{s}$ is computed outside the PC and fed back by other circuit elements. This could occur in a number of ways. For example, the PC might send an axon collateral to local circuit elements that provide feedback for computing $s - \bar{s}$. The PC axon collaterals have been reported as terminating on Golgi cells, basket cells, granule cells, and other PCs. Were we to rule out feedback from PC axon collaterals, the two remaining sources of feedback are climbing fibers and mossy fibers. For example, feedback information could arise as *efference* from collateral output from SpoV in the course of driving AAN motoneurons. As Fig. 4 indicates, in addition to its role as the locus of interneurons mediating unconditioned reflexive extension of the NM to direct stimulation of the eye, SpoV projects to HVI of cerebellar cortex. The projection is either a direct one via mossy fibers, or indirect via climbing fibers originating in the dorsal accessory olive (DAO), the source of climbing fibers to HVI. Both projections could be involved in computing $s - \bar{s}$.

B. Site of Plasticity: Granule Cells

Because of doubts expressed by a number of investigators about learning mediated by modification of PF/PC synapses (e.g., Bloedel and Ebner, 1985; Lisberger *et al.*, 1987; Llinas, 1985), we considered the possibility that learning occurs at MF/granule cell synapses. We propose that granule cells compute changes in V via convergence of $s - \bar{s}$ from Golgi cells and x conveyed by mossy fibers. This convergence of $s - \bar{s}$ and x implements the Hebbian mechanism assumed by the model.

Golgi cells appear to be particularly suitable for computing $s - \bar{s}$ for several reasons:

1. They receive input from a variety of sources, the principal ones being parallel fibers and mossy fibers. They also receive collateral inputs from PCs and climbing fibers. Hence, in principle they

could provide sites of convergence of information about s and $\bar{s}$ for computation of $s - \bar{s}$.

2. The output of Golgi cells varies smoothly as a function of input. Their tonic rate of discharge is regular with little moment-to-moment fluctuation in interspike intervals that could degrade information flow through the granular layer. Hence, they are capable of modulating their output to reflect their input with little noise or signal distortion (Miles *et al.*, 1980; Schulman and Bloom, 1981). This is a desirable feature of any circuit element that would transfer feedback about NMR topography with high fidelity.

3. In addition to Golgi cell/granule cell interactions within the granular layer, rabbits possess an extra, midmolecular sheet of "ectopic" Golgi cells and associated glomeruli that may coordinate interactions among mossy fibers and granule cells (Spacek *et al.*, 1973). The synaptic organization among elements in this midmolecular sheet appears to be no different from that of the granular layer. Though purely speculative, this extra sheet of Golgi cells may enhance information processing related to learning.

4. According to a study by Eccles *et al.* (1967), the temporal course of Golgi cell inhibition of information flow through the granular layer resembles the relationship between $\bar{s}$ and s in the SBD model. We suggest that Golgi cells compute $\bar{s}$ by acting on granule cells that receive s information simultaneously from mossy fibers. Possible circuits by which s and $\bar{s}$ converge onto other Golgi cells for computation of $s - \bar{s}$ will be considered later.

Figure 5 summarizes how mossy-fiber input carrying s information might be used to compute $\bar{s}$ in the way suggested by the Eccles *et al.* (1967) study: s information carried by mossy fibers is converted to $\bar{s}$ by the action of Golgi cells. The model assumes that Golgi cells that convert s to $\bar{s}$ are activated by parallel fibers. A group of granule cells (Gr), represented in the lower left-hand portion of the figure, receives mossy-fiber input carrying s information as feedback from SpoV (coordinate C1). The output of these granule cells passes s information through the granular layer with no distortion to form parallel-fiber beam B. Beam B excites Golgi cells (Go) that impinge on members of a second class of granule cells that also receive s via mossy fibers from SpoV. We emphasize that these Golgi cells and the second class of granule cells receive s simultaneously, that is, within the same 10-msec time step. The action of the Golgi cells on the second group of granule cells converts s to $\bar{s}$. The output of the second group of granule cells forms the parallel-fiber beam labeled A, which transmits $\bar{s}$ to other circuit elements.

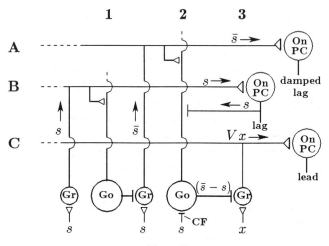

Figure 5.
Implementation of SBD model at mossy-fiber/granule cell synapses. Letters
A–C are parallel-fiber beams as in Fig. 4. From right to left: the variable s
is fed back to cerebellar cortex by mossy fibers arising in brain stem spinal
trigeminal nucleus pars oralis (SpoV in Fig. 4) in two streams. One stream
gives rise to parallel fibers that drive PCs with a firing pattern that lags the
CR. This beam (B) excites Golgi cells (Go) that impinge on granule cells
(Gr) excited by the other stream carrying s and thereby convert it into a
beam of parallel fibers (A) carrying $\bar{s}$ information. This beam drives PCs
with a firing pattern that lags the CR and is damped relative to the firing
patterns of PCs on beams B and C. Beam A contributes $\bar{s}$ to Golgi cells
that compute $s - \bar{s}$. The other term for this computation, s, is provided
either by axon collaterals from lag PCs on the B beam or by climbing
fibers. These Golgi cells pass $s - \bar{s}$ to granule cells that receive CS
information x and thereby mediate weight changes at these mossy-fiber/
granule cell synapses to the extent that they are eligible for modification.
These granule cells give rise to a beam of PFs (C) that drive PCs
proportionally to Vx and with a firing pattern that leads the CR.

The circuit model assumes that learning occurs at synapses of
granule cells that receive mossy-fiber input labeled x (coordinate C3).
Mechanisms that implement the eligibility of these synapses for modification, $\bar{x}$, presumably reside within these granule cells. The factor $s -$
$\bar{s}$ is contributed by Golgi cells that function as differential amplifiers.
These Golgi cells receive $\bar{s}$ as excitatory input from beam A (coordinate
A2), as described above. In Fig. 5, they receive s as an inhibitory input
(direct or indirect) from climbing fibers (coordinate C2). Later on, we
suggest that this climbing-fiber input for the variable s might be replaced
by input from a PC axon collateral such as the one indicated at coordinate
B3. The climbing-fiber input is omitted in a subsequent, more complete
version of the model described later on. Notice that the Golgi cell under
2 in the figure is actually computing $\bar{s} - s$. We have referred to the

computation as being $s - \bar{s}$ in interests of clarity. Because Golgi cells are inhibitory, the computation is *effectively* one of $s - \bar{s}$ with respect to the granule cells receiving x.

Because Golgi cells are inhibitory interneurons, when $s - \bar{s}$ is positive the tonic output of the Golgi cells is modulated downward, thereby disinhibiting granule cells that receive x. This disinhibition causes an increase in the weight of MF/granule cell synapses to the extent that they are eligible for change. Similarly, when $s - \bar{s}$ is negative the tonic output of these Golgi cells is modulated upward. This increases granule-cell inhibition and decreases the weight of eligible MF/granule cell synapses. Possible mechanisms for bidirectional weight changes in Hebbian synapses are suggested by experimental work on associative long-term potentiation in hippocampal slices (Kelso *et al.*, 1986) and by theoretical analyses of calcium dynamics in dendritic spines (Gamble and Koch, 1987).

C. CR-Related PC Activity: Lead, Lag, and Damped Lag

The circuit model in Fig. 5 (and subsequently Fig. 6) implies the existence of various types of CR-related firing patterns by PCs. For example, the PC on the $\bar{s}$ beam (A) is labeled "damped lag" because its firing pattern during a CS presentation would lag behind a CR and would also reflect the slow rise and decay of spike recruitment implied by the relationship between s and $\bar{s}$ in the model. The PC on the s beam (B) is labeled "lag" because its firing rate during a CS presentation would mirror response topography but with a lag by virtue of the fact that s represents efference from the brain stem. The CR-related "lead" PCs such as the one on the x beam (C) are also implied by the circuit. Berthier and Moore (1986) observed both lead and lag CR-related PCs in HVI during NMR conditioning. They also observed PCs that decreased their firing before the occurrence of CRs. These CR-related "off-cells" of the lead type are discussed below in connection with Figs. 6 and 7.

D. Role of Climbing Fibers

Some investigators have expressed strong reservations regarding climbing-fiber participation in classical conditioning (see, e.g., Llinas, 1985). Particularly contentious has been the idea that climbing fibers carry US information that reinforces learning in cerebellar cortex (e.g., Thompson, 1986). In the circuit model shown in Fig. 5, climbing fibers contribute to learning only insofar as they might provide feedback about s to Golgi cells that compute $s - \bar{s}$. A way this might be achieved without climbing fibers is also illustrated in Fig. 5. Instead of using climbing fibers, s might be transmitted to the Golgi cells by axon collaterals from lag PCs on the

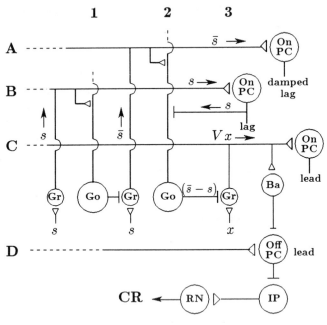

Figure 6.
Summary of cerebellar neural circuitry summarizing how basket cells (Ba) added to the parallel fiber beam (C) of Fig. 5 can account for off-type lead CRs observed by Berthier and Moore (1986). The CS onset excites beam C parallel fibers, thereby driving basket cells that inhibit tonic firing of PCs on the D beam. These off-PCs of the lead type disinhibit IP neurons and thereby initiate the sequence of motor commands that result in a CR.

parallel-fiber beam labeled B (coordinates B3). A circuit based on PC collaterals circumvents the computational difficulties implied by the low frequency of climbing-fiber firing while at the same time retaining the desirable inhibitory effect on the Golgi cells. Figure 5 shows these collaterals arising from lag PCs instead of lead PCs on beam C, which might serve as well from a computational standpoint. This is because PC collaterals are not generally oriented along the longitudinal axis of a parallel-fiber beam, as would be the case if they arose from PCs on the C beam. Instead, PC collaterals are oriented perpendicularly to the longitudinal axis (Ito, 1984), as would be the case if they came from PCs on an adjacent beam of parallel fibers such as B.

What role if any might we assign to climbing fibers if they do not contribute to computation of $s - \bar{s}$? Experimental evidence on the contribution of climbing fibers in NMR conditioning is controversial and open to interpretation. Thompson (1986) cites evidence that stimulation of DAO, the source of climbing fibers to HVI, reinforces conditioning. Consistent with this idea, he also reports that lesions of this structure

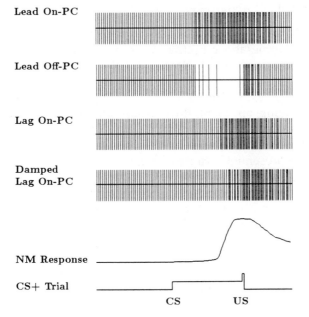

Figure 7.
Renderings of CR-related simple spike firing patterns predicted by the circuit model in Fig. 6. The baseline firing frequency for all four types of PCs is 100 Hz, and the CS–US interval on reinforced trials (CS+) is 350 msec.

cause a gradual extinction of the CR following training with an airpuff US. The stimulation results might reflect unintended antidromic activation of SpoV neurons and concommitant invasion of collaterals of mossy fibers that project to HVI (see Fig. 3). As for the lesion data, Yeo *et al.* (1986) report that DAO lesions cause an immediate disruption of NMR conditioning, not a gradual loss of CRs that would be expected if climbing fibers carry information that reinforces conditioning. A sudden and persistent loss of CRs such as that reported by Yeo *et al.* (1986) would be expected if climbing fibers perform some trophic function such as regulating PC excitability, as has been suggested by numerous investigators (e.g., Bloedel and Ebner, 1985; Strata, 1985).

Berthier and Moore (1986) found little support for the idea that climbing fibers carry US information related to reinforcing learning. They observed only a few cases of complex spikes elicited by the US employed in their study. However, these data were obtained after sufficient training to ensure that CRs occurred on a high proportion of trials. The likelihood of observing climbing fiber responses to the US might be greater during earlier stages of CR acquisition, that is, when $s - \bar{s}$ at US onset would be consistently large.

E. CR-Related PC Activity: On and Off

As noted, Berthier and Moore (1986) observed PCs that increased their simple spike firing above pretrial rates on trials with CRs. These cells were designated "on-cells." However, CR-related "off-cells," PCs that decreased their firing rate below pretrial rates, were also observed. Although off-PCs might arise from long-term depression of PF/PC synapses (Ito, 1984; Thompson, 1986), the circuit model shown in Fig. 6 provides an alternative explanation of off-PCs. These PCs are associated with the beam of parallel fibers labeled D. They become off-cells of the lead type when a CS is presented because of increased inhibition from basket cells (Ba) on the C beam (coordinate D3). (Like PC axon collaterals, basket-cell axons tend to project perpendicularly to the longitudinal axis of the parallel-fiber beam by which they are activated).

A CR is initiated when basket-cell inhibition of PCs on beam D becomes sufficiently great to *disinhibit* nucleus interpositus (IP) neurons to which they project. These IP cells project in turn to red nucleus (RN) neurons that excite the reflex pathways mediating the CR (Fig. 3). Because mossy fibers from pontine nuclei do not send collaterals to deep cerebellar nuclei (Brodal *et al.*, 1986), the model does not assume that CSs activate IP neurons. They are assumed to be tonically activated by neural traffic unrelated to a particular stimulus, but this activation is normally suppressed by inhibition imposed by PCs. Hence, a CS releases this inhibition and the level of activation of IP neurons increases sufficiently to drive the RN neurons in the next stage of the efferent pathway of the CR.

Figure 7 summarizes the four types of firing patterns discussed in connection with Fig. 6. As in the Berthier and Moore (1986) study, the interval between CS onset and US onset represents 350 msec. The CR in the figure begins 200 msec after the CS. Renderings of PC simple-spike firing were hand-crafted to resemble typical CR-related PC responses; they all assume baseline firing rates of 100 Hz, which is typical of that observed in our recording experiments. The firing patterns are labeled to correspond with the types of PCs indicated in the circuit model shown in Fig. 6. Hence, the increase in firing rate of the lag on-PC begins within a few milliseconds after CR initiation. The increase in firing of the damped lag on-PC begins slightly later and persists slightly longer. The increase in firing rate of the lead on-PC precedes the CR by more than 100 msec, and the lead off-PC begins to cease firing at this time, both profiles being typical of CR-elicited firing patterns observed by Berthier and Moore (1986).

Of the approximately 40 CR-related PCs reported by Berthier and Moore (1986), on-cells exceeded off-cells by 3 : 1, and lead and lag cells were equally distributed (ratio of 1 : 1). Although possibly a coincidence, it is nevertheless interesting that these ratios are implied by the circuit model, provided of course that parallel-fiber beams A–C are comparable in terms of number of fibers and levels of activation evoked by the variables $\bar{s}$, s, and x, respectively. The correspondence between the model's predictions regarding the statistical distribution of CR-related PC types encourages further experimental tests of the model. Such experiments might provide (a) reliable separation of damped-lag PCs from the lag PCs; (b) evidence of Golgi cell activity related to the variables s or $\bar{s}$, that is, the implied but as-yet-unsubstantiated CR-related firing of the lag and damped-lag variety among Golgi cells; and (c) evidence of CR-related neural traffic among parallel fibers (beams A–D in Fig. 6).

F. Cerebellar Implementation of Multiple-CS Phenomena

In this section we discuss the implications of a cerebellar circuit implementation of the SBD model for multiple-CS phenomena. Our effort to implement the SBD model in cerebellar cortex was guided by experimental evidence suggesting that this region of the brain not only is essential for robust CRs, but may be a site of learning as well. We have argued that a circuit implementation along the lines of Fig. 6 is a promising candidate for implementing the model, but our discussion has been limited to conditioning with a single CS. How adequate is this implementation for conditioning protocols involving more than one CS?

The principal multiple-CS phenomena of interest are higher-order conditioning, blocking, and conditioned inhibition. Like virtually all contemporary learning theories, including the original SB model (Barto and Sutton, 1982), the SBD model predicts appropriate outcomes in simulations of these multiple-CS protocols (Blazis *et al.*, 1986; Moore *et al.*, 1986). The model predicts higher-order conditioning because it is basically an S–R (stimulus–response) contiguity theory of learning, albeit one with an informational structure: A second-order CR can be established provided the temporal relationship between the primary and secondary CSs is appropriate and provided the primary, initially trained CS is capable of evoking a CR. Should the primary CS lose its capacity to evoke a CR (e.g., through extinction), the secondary CS would eventually follow suit. The model predicts blocking because of its perceptron-like architecture as depicted in Fig. 1 and the fact that the learning rule in Eq. (3) is basically a variant of the Widrow–Hoff rule (see Sutton and Barto, 1981). Conditioned inhibition also follows from Eq. (3) because the synaptic weight V of a CS that is never reinforced can take on negative value when it is presented in combination with another CS that possesses a consistently positive weight.

The circuit model in Figs. 5 and 6 could readily be extended to encompass higher-order conditioning and blocking. All that would be required is a global broadcast of the variables s and $\bar{s}$ over a sufficiently large region of HVI to encompass inputs from many potential CSs. This would permit local computation of $s - \bar{s}$ by Golgi cells. In the case of higher-order conditioning, synaptic weights at granule cells that receive input from the second-order CS would increase to the extent that they remain eligible for change at the time their associated Golgi cells compute the large negative value of $\bar{s} - s$ that results from evocation of a CR by the primary CS. Should the primary CS lose weight, the weight of the secondary CS would decline as well. In blocking, the CS combined with the originally trained CS would not accumulate weight gains over reinforced trials as long as the original CS retained the capacity to evoke a CR; a CR sufficiently robust to preclude large values of $s - \bar{s}$ at the time of US onset. However, extending the circuit model in the manner suggested here would not be appropriate because of experimental evidence indicating that blocking, higher-order conditioning, and certain other complex conditioning phenomena involve the participation of other brain regions besides the cerebellum, particularly the hippocampal formation (Berger *et al.*, 1986).

The idea of global broadcasting of s and $\bar{s}$ would also allow for the creation of negative weights in granule cells that receive input from a CS assigned the role of conditioned inhibitor. However, in addition to being resistant to subsequent acquisition procedures, a conditioned inhibitor must be capable of opposing the evocation of a CR by a conditioned exciter when the two stimuli are presented together. It is not obvious how this would be accomplished in the cerebellar circuit model. It may be inappropriate to alter the present circuit model so as to produce such CR suppression, in any case, because there is no evidence that the cerebellum is involved in conditioned inhibition. For example, Berthier and Moore (1986) used a differential conditioning procedure in order to assess the CR-relatedness of cerebellar units. Differential conditioning is closely related to conditioned inhibition in that both procedures include reinforced and nonreinforced trials. Although CRs were suppressed on a high proportion of trials to the nonreinforced CS, there were no instances of unit activity related to CR suppression. Furthermore, lesion studies by Mis (1977) and others suggest that conditioned inhibition involves the participation of brain regions outside the cerebellum (see Yeo *et al.*, 1983). If conditioned inhibition involves processes extrinsic to the cerebellum, as seems likely, there may be no need to assume a bidirectional Hebbian mechanism in the model. Learning theorists have long recognized that bidirectional modifiability is not necessary to account for conditioned inhibition (e.g., Moore and Stickney, 1985).

In sum, the SBD model is a mathematical description of a device capable of simulating an impressive array of facts about NMR conditioning at the behavioral and neurophysiological levels. Despite its potential ability to encompass multiple-CS effects within the framework of either a single neuron resembling Fig. 1 or a somewhat more elaborate circuit (e.g., Figs. 5 and 6), an implementation of the model confined to the cerebellum is not entirely appropriate for multiple-CS phenomena. This caveat aside, our investigations of the SBD model have nevertheless suggested a novel theory about the locus of synaptic changes for a real instance of conditioning and in a real nervous system. Further theoretical work should move toward a systems level of analysis that might point the way toward to a neural network architecture that not only accounts for phenomenology, but does so in a neurobiologically realistic manner. Further research on the circuit model could be conducted on a time scale compatible with the modeling of neural events such as action potentials, that is, in the domain of microseconds.

Acknowledgments

This research was supported by Air Force Office of Scientific Research grants 83-0125 and 86-01825, and National Science Foundation grant BNS 83-17920. The original simulation program was written by N. E. Berthier. The authors wish to thank A. G. Barto, N. E. Berthier, J. E. Desmond, W. Richards, and N. A. Schmajuk for helpful comments and discussions.

References

Barto, A. G., and Sutton, R. S. (1982). Simulation of anticipatory responses in classical conditioning by a neuron-like adaptive element. *Behav. Brain Res.* **4**, 221–235.

Berger, T. W., Weikart, C. L., Bassett, J. L., and Orr, W. B. (1986). Lesions of the retrosplenial cortex produce deficits in reversal learning of the rabbit nictitating membrane response: Implications for potential interactions between hippocampal and cerebellar brain systems. *Behav. Neurosci.* **100**, 802–809.

Berthier, N. E. (1984). The role of the extraocular muscles in the rabbit nictitating membrane response: A reexamination. *Behav. Brain Res.* **14**, 81–84.

Berthier, N. E., and Moore, J. W. (1980). Role of extraocular muscles in the rabbit (*Oryctolagus cuniculus*) nictitating membrane response. *Physiol. Behav.* **24**, 931–937.

Berthier, N. E., and Moore, J. W. (1986). Cerebellar Purkinje cell activity related to the classically conditioned nictitating membrane response. *Exp. Brain Res.* **63**, 341–350.

Berthier, N. E., Desmond, J. E., and Moore, J. W. (1987). Brain stem control of the nictitating membrane response. *In* "Classical Conditioning" (I. Gormezano, W. F. Prokasy, and R. F. Thompson, eds.), 3rd ed., pp. 275–286. Erlbaum, Hillsdale, New Jersey.

Blazis, D. E. J., Desmond, J. E., Moore, J. W., and Berthier, N. E. (1986). Simulation of the classically conditioned response by a neuron-like adaptive element: A real-time variant of the Sutton–Barto model. *In*: "The Eighth Annual Conference of the Cognitive Science Society," pp. 176–186. Erlbaum, Hillsdale, New Jersey.

Bloedel, J. R., and Ebner, T. J. (1985). Climbing fiber function: Regulation of Purkinje cell responsiveness. *In* "Cerebellar Functions" (J. R. Bloedel, J. Dichgans, and W. Precht, eds.), pp. 247–260. Springer-Verlag, Berlin and New York.

Brodal, P., Dietrichs, E., and Walberg, F. (1986). Do pontocerebellar mossy fibres give off collaterals to the cerebellar nuclei? An experimental study in the cat with implantation of crystalline HRP-WGA. *Neurosci. Res.* **4**, 12–24.

Buchtel, H. A., Iosif, G., Marchesi, G. F., Provini, L., and Strata, P. (1972). Analysis of the activity evoked in the cerebellar cortex by stimulation of the visual pathways. *Exp. Brain Res.* **15**, 278–288.

Desmond, J. E. (1985). The classically conditioned nictitating membrane response: Analysis of learning-related single neurons of the brain stem. Ph.D. Dissertation, University of Massachusetts. Amherst.

Desmond, J. E., and Moore, J. W. (1982). A brain stem region essential for the classically conditioned but not unconditioned nictitating membrane response. *Physiol. Behav.* **28**, 1029–1033.

Desmond, J. E., and Moore, J. W. (1986). Dorsolateral pontine tegmentum and the classically conditioned nictitating membrane response: Analysis of CR-related single-unit activity. *Exp. Brain Res.* **65**, 59–74.

Donegan, N. H., and Wagner, A. R. (1987). Conditioned diminution and facilitation of the UR: A sometimes opponent-process interpretation. *In* "Classical Conditioning" (I. Gormezano, W. F. Prokasy, and R. F. Thompson, eds.), 3rd ed., pp. 339–369. Erlbaum, Hillsdale, New Jersey.

Durand, J., Gogan, P., Gueritaud, J. P., Horcholle-Bossavit, G., and Tyc-Dumont, S. (1983). Morphological and electrophysiological properties of trigeminal neurones projecting to the accessory abducens nucleus of the cat. *Exp. Brain Res.* **53**, 118–126.

Eccles, J. C., Sasaki, K., and Strata, P. (1967). A comparison of the inhibitory action of Golgi and basket cells. *Exp. Brain Res.* **3**, 81–94.

Gamble, E., and Koch, C. (1987). The dynamics of free calcium in dendritic spines in response to repetitive synaptic input. *Science* **236**, 1311–1315.

Gormezano, I., Kehoe, E. J., and Marshall, B. S. (1983). Twenty years of classical conditioning with the rabbit. *Prog. Psychobiol. Physiol. Psychol.* **10**, 197–275.

Grant, K., and Horcholle-Bossavit, G. (1986). Red nucleus inputs to retractor bulbi motoneurons in the cat. *J. Physiol. (London)* **371**, 317–327.

Ikeda, M. (1979). Projections from the spinal and principal sensory nuclei of the trigeminal nerve to the cerebellar cortex in the cat, as studied by retrograde transport of horseradish peroxidase. *J. Comp. Neurol.* **184**, 567–586.

Ito, M. (1984). "The Cerebellum and Neural Control." Raven Press, New York.

Kelso, S. R., Ganong, A. H., and Brown, T. R. (1986). Hebbian synapses in hippocampus. *Proc. Natl. Acad. Sci. U.S.A.* **83**, 5326–5330.

Lisberger, S. G., Morris, E. J., and Tychsen, L. (1987). Visual motion processing and sensory-motor integration for smooth pursuit eye movements. *Annu. Rev. Neurosci.* **10**, 97–129.

Llinas, R. (1985). Functional significance of the basic cerebellar circuit in motor coordination. *In* "Cerebellar Functions" (J. R. Bloedel, J. Dichgans, and W. Precht, eds.), pp. 230–247. Springer-Verlag, Berlin and New York.

Mackintosh, N. J. (1983). "Conditioning and Associative Learning." Oxford Univ. Press, London and New York.

Miles, F. A., Fuller, J. H., Braitman, D. J., and Dow, B. M. (1980). Long-term adaptive changes in primate vestibuloocular reflex. III. Electrophysiological observations in flocculus of normal monkeys. *J. Neurophysiol.* **43**, 1437–1476.

Mis, F. W. (1977). A midbrain-brain stem circuit for conditioned inhibition of the nictitating membrane response in the rabbit (*Oryctolagus cuniculus*). *J. Comp. Physiol. Psychol.* **91**, 975–988.

Moore, J. W., and Desmond, J. E. (1982). Latency of the nictitating membrane response to periocular electrostimulation in unanesthetized rabbits. *Physiol. Behav.* **28**, 1041–1046.

Moore, J. W., and Stickney, K. J. (1985). Antiassociations: Conditioned inhibition in attentional-associative networks. *In* "Information Processes in Animals: Conditioned Inhibition" (R. R. Miller and N. E. Spear, eds.), pp. 209–222. Erlbaum, Hillsdale, New Jersey.

Moore, J. W., Desmond, J. E., Berthier, N. E., Blazis, D. E. J., Sutton, R. S., and Barto, A. G. (1986). Simulation of the classically-conditioned nictitating membrane response by a neuron-like adaptive element: Response topography, neuronal firing, and inter-stimulus intervals. *Behav. Brain Res.* **12**, 143–154.

Robinson, F. R., Houk, J. C., and Gibson, A. R. (1987). Limb specific connections of the cat magnocellular red nucleus. *J. Comp. Neurol.* **257**, 553–577.

Rosenfield, M. E., Dovydaitis, A., and Moore, J. W. (1985). Brachium conjunctivum and rubrobulbar tract: Brain stem projections of red nucleus essential for the conditioned nictitating membrane response. *Physiol. Behav.* **34**, 751–749.

Salafia, W. R., Lambert, R. W., Host, K. C., Chiaia, N. L., and Ramirez, J. J. (1980). Rabbit nictitating membrane conditioning: Lower limit of effective interstimulus interval. *Anim. Learn. Behav.* **8**, 85–91.

Schulman, J. A., and Bloom, F. E. (1981). Golgi cells of the cerebellum are inhibited by inferior olive activity. *Brain Res.* **210**, 350–355.

Shofer, R. J., and Nahvi, M. J. (1969). Firing patterns induced by sound in single units of cerebellar cortex. *Exp. Brain Res.* **8**, 327–345.

Spacek, J., Parizek, J., and Lieberman, A. R. (1973). Golgi cells, granule cells, and synaptic glomeruli in the molecular layer of the rabbit cerebellar cortex. *J. Neurocytol.* **2**, 401–428.

Strata, P. (1985). Inferior olive: Functional aspects. *In* "Cerebellar Functions" (J. R. Bloedel, J. Dichgans, and W. Precht, eds.), pp. 230–246. Springer-Verlag, Berlin and New York.

Sutton, R. S., and Barto, A. G. (1981). Toward a modern theory of adaptive networks: Expectation and prediction. *Psychol. Rev.* **88**, 135–170.

Thach, W. T. (1967). Somatosensory fields of single units in cat cerebellar cortex. *J. Neurophysiol.* **30**, 675–696.

Thompson, R. F. (1986). The neurobiology of learning and memory. *Science* **233**, 941–947.

Thompson, R. F., Donegan, N. H., Clark, G. A., Lavond, D. G., Lincoln, J. S., Madden, J., Mamounas, L. A., Mauk, M. D., and McCormick, D. A. (1987). Neuronal substrates of discrete, defensive conditioned reflexes, conditioned fear states, and their interactions in the rabbit. *In* "Classical Conditioning" (I. Gormezano, W. F. Prokasy, and R. F. Thompson, eds.), 3rd ed., pp. 371–400. Erlbaum, Hillsdale, New Jersey.

Yeo, C. H., Hardiman, M. J., Moore, J. W., and Steele-Russell, I. (1983). Retention of conditioned inhibition of the nictitating membrane response in decorticate rabbits. *Behav. Brain Res.* **10**, 383–392.

Yeo, C. H., Hardiman, M. J., and Glickstein, M. (1984). Discrete lesions of the cerebellar cortex abolish the classically conditioned nictitating membrane response. *Behav. Brain Res.* **13**, 261–266.

Yeo, C. H., Hardiman, M. J., and Glickstein, M. (1985a). Classical conditioning of the nictitating membrane response of the rabbit. I. Lesions of the cerebellar nuclei. *Exp. Brain Res.* **60**, 87–98.

Yeo, C. H., Hardiman, M. J., and Glickstein, M. (1985b). Classical conditioning of the nictitating membrane response of the rabbit. II. Lesions of the cerebellar cortex. *Exp. Brain Res.* **60**, 99–113.

Yeo, C. H., Hardiman, M. J., and Glickstein, M. (1985c). Classical conditioning of the nictitating membrane response of the rabbit. III. Connections of cerebellar lobule HVI. *Exp. Brain Res.* **60**, 114–126.

Yeo, C. H., Hardiman, M. J., and Glickstein, M. (1986). Classical conditioning of the nictitating membrane response of the rabbit. IV. Lesions of the inferior olive. *Exp. Brain Res.* **63**, 81–92.

12

Memory and the Hippocampus

Larry R. Squire, Arthur P. Shimamura, and David G. Amaral

I. Introduction

As this volume illustrates, questions about the organization and neural foundations of learning and memory are benefitting from many kinds of inquiry, including the study of neurons, neural systems, cognition, and quantitative computational models. Our focus here is on the neural systems level of analysis. In particular, we consider human amnesia and the structures that when damaged produce amnesia. The work to be discussed is based on the idea that detailed neuropsychological and neuropathological data can inform us about the functions of brain systems involved in memory processing and representation. Two recent developments have been particularly helpful: the achievement of an animal model of human amnesia in the monkey (Mahut and Moss, 1984; Mishkin et al., 1982; Squire and Zola-Morgan, 1983), and new findings from a case of human amnesia, where selective damage was found within the hippocampus (Zola-Morgan et al., 1986).

This chapter addresses questions about the neural substrates of memory, focusing especially on the role of the hippocampus. We begin by summarizing briefly the characteristics of amnesia. Next, we describe the just-mentioned case of human amnesia, which establishes the hippocampus as an essential component of the damaged memory system. We then consider the function of the hippocampus in the light of the neurobehavioral data. Finally, after a brief review of relevant neurophysiological data, we consider the anatomical organization of sensory inputs to the hippocampus, as well as its intrinsic connections, in order to develop more specific hypotheses about the contribution of the hippocampus to learning and memory.

208

_____ **II. Human Amnesia** _____

Amnesia involves most prominently a loss of new learning ability for both verbal and nonverbal material (i.e., anterograde amnesia). Usually, information acquired before the onset of amnesia is also affected (i.e., retrograde amnesia). These impairments occur without regard to the sensory modality in which information is presented. Nevertheless, the memory defect can be quite isolated. That is, memory can be affected without any noticeable impairment of general intelligence, personality, or social skills. In addition, certain aspects of memory are preserved in amnesia, including immediate (or short-term) memory (Baddeley and Warrington, 1970; Drachman and Arbit, 1966), memory for the very remote past (Cohen and Squire, 1981; Squire et al., 1975), and memory for skills (Brooks and Baddeley, 1976; Cohen and Squire, 1980; Corkin, 1968; Milner, 1962).

Several kinds of patients have been studied. These include surgical cases, the best known of which is patient H. M., who sustained a bilateral medial temporal resection for the relief of severe epilepsy (Scoville and Milner, 1957), patients with alcoholic Korsakoff's syndrome (Talland, 1965; Butters and Cermak, 1980), patients who have survived encephalitis (Cermak and O'Connor, 1983; Damasio et al., 1985; Rose and Symonds, 1960), patients with amnesia due to anoxia or ischemia (Volpe and Hirst, 1983; Zola-Morgan et al., 1986), patients with transient global amnesia (Kritchevsky et al., 1988), and patients who are transiently amnesic as the result of a prescribed course of electroconvulsive therapy (Squire, 1984). Certain other individual cases have also been useful, such as patient N. A., who has amnesia for verbal material as the result of a penetrating brain injury (Teuber et al., 1968).

Amnesia can vary considerably in terms of its severity and in the extent to which it is complicated by potentially dissociable cognitive impairment other than memory dysfunction. Indeed, the etiologies listed above by no means exhaust the types of patients with memory disorders. For example, patients recovering from severe closed head injury and patients with Alzheimer's disease typically have memory problems, but these tend to occur against a background of broadly impaired intellectual function. The patients best suited for neuropsychological investigations of memory functions are those with well-circumscribed, well-characterized memory impairment. Standardized tests are available for carefully describing study patients (Squire and Shimamura, 1986).

A. New Learning Ability

The deficit of new learning, which is the hallmark of amnesia, is easily demonstrated with tests of delayed recall or with tests of paired-associate

learning. To test delayed recall, patients are read a small amount of connected prose material. Recall is then requested immediately and again
after a delay of several minutes (Fig. 1). If the amount of presented information is not too large, amnesic patients can perform well on the
immediate recall test, but they invariably fail after the delay. The usual
interpretation of this finding has been that immediate (short-term) memory is intact in amnesia and independent of the neural system damaged
in amnesia.

If the amount of presented information is too large to be held in
immediate memory, as in tests of paired-associate learning, then amnesic
patients fail even an immediate recall test. To test paired-associate learning, patients are asked to learn 10 pairs of unrelated words (e.g., army–
table). The number of word pairs presented for study must be greater
than what could be simply rehearsed and maintained in immediate
memory. After presentation of the pairs for study, the first word of each
pair is presented and patients are invited to produce the second word.
Amnesic patients find this task extraordinarily difficult, usually producing
no more than one or two correct responses even after several repetitions
of the same word pairs.

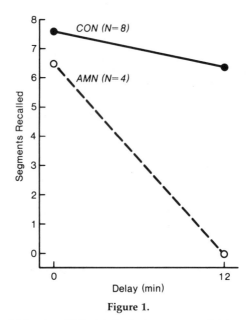

Figure 1.

Immediate and delayed recall (12 min) of a short prose passage (total segments =
21) by eight control subjects (CON) and four patients (AMN) who became amnesic
following either an anoxic or ischemic episode (N=3) or a bilateral thalamic infarction
(N=1). Although amnesic patients can exhibit good performance when tested
immediately after learning, performance is severely impaired after a short delay.

B. Retrograde Amnesia

Studies of retrograde amnesia following electroconvulsive therapy showed that amnesia for premorbid events can be temporally limited, affecting recent memories more than remote memories (Squire *et al.*, 1975). The same phenomenon has been observed in patients with amnesia resulting from brain injury. We recently assessed the retrograde

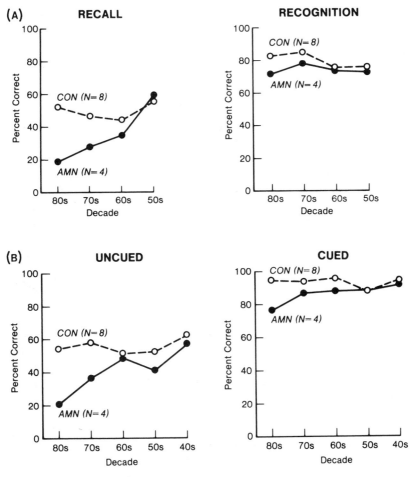

Figure 2.

Remote memory performance by eight control subjects (CON) and four patients who become amnesic (AMN) either following an anoxic or ischemic episode (N=3) or a bilateral thalamic infarction (N=1). The amnesia began between 1976 and 1986. Testing occurred in 1986 and 1987 when these patients averaged 50 years of age. (A) Recall and recognition memory of public events that occurred between 1950 and 1985. (B) Uncued and cued (recognition) memory for names of famous faces that became prominent between 1940 and 1985.

amnesia of four amnesic patients, all of whom became amnesic on a known date between 1976 and 1986. Figure 2 shows the performance of these patients on a test of past public events (1940–1985) and on a test of famous faces that had come into the news of 1930–1985. Each test was given first in a free-recall format and then as a test of recognition memory. Memory for the more recent events and faces was poor. Results for the recall tests suggested that retrograde amnesia affected memories that were formed in the 1970s and 1980s, that is, up to about 15 years prior to the onset of amnesia. On all the tests, very remote events were remembered equally well by both the amnesic patients and normal subjects. These results support the idea that old memories, but not recent memories, can survive the effects of amnesia.

C. Amnesia Affects Only One Type of Memory

The structures damaged in amnesia are not required for all kinds of learning and memory. Despite their severe impairment on many kinds of memory tasks, amnesic patients can acquire skills, often at a normal rate. In the case of skill-based tasks like mirror reading (Cohen and Squire, 1980; Squire *et al.*, 1984), in which subjects learn gradually the difficult task of reading mirror-reversed words, amnesic patients acquire the skill at a normal rate but then fail to recollect the learning episodes or the particular words that were presented. Amnesic patients also exhibit intact priming effects (for review, see Shimamura, 1986). For example, words such as MOTEL and ABSENT can be presented, followed by the word stems (MOT _____ and ABS _____). When amnesic patients are instructed to complete the stems to form "the first words that come to mind," they show the normal bias toward production of the target words. Whereas the baseline probability is about 10% that a target word will be selected when it has not been presented recently, the presentation of target words results in their being generated about 50% of the time. This priming effect is transient, declining to baseline levels in about 2 hr (Graf *et al.*, 1984; Squire *et al.*, 1987).

All of the examples of intact learning and memory performance so far identified in amnesic patients share common features. The knowledge acquired is implicit, inaccessible to conscious recollection. It is available only in performance. The term "procedural" may be applied to some of these cases (e.g., to skill learning), to capture the idea that the information seems to be acquired as procedures for performance, or as changes in the facility with which particular cognitive operations are carried out. Because so little is known about the similarities and differences between the spared abilities, it is not clear whether the term procedural aptly describes them all.

In contrast, the kind of memory that is impaired in amnesia is cognitive, representational, and affords the capacity for explicit recollections of previous encounters and previously acquired facts. The term "declarative" may be applied to this kind of memory, to capture the idea that this kind of information can be declared. That is, it can be brought to mind explicitly, either verbally as a proposition or nonverbally as an image. Declarative memory and nondeclarative memory refer to two kinds of memory processes or systems. The former stores facts and episodes; the latter refers to a collection of abilities: skills, procedures, biases, and activations, where what is learned is expressed without conscious recollection of previously acquired information.

III. Amnesia Can Result from Hippocampal Damage

The possibility of relating the functions damaged in amnesia to the hippocampus, and to particular neural circuitry within the hippocampus, came from a recently studied case. Patient R. B. became amnesic in 1978 at the age of 52, as the result of an ischemic event that occurred as a complication of open-heart surgery (Zola-Morgan et al., 1986). He survived for 5 years, during which time his memory impairment was repeatedly evaluated and documented. In 1983 R. B. died of congestive heart failure. At that time, with the consent and encouragement of his family, we were able to obtain the brain within a few hours after death and to examine it in some detail.

Figure 3 compares R. B. to other amnesic study patients on three tests of new learning ability. His performance on one of these tests (the nonverbal test) is illustrated in Fig. 4. The memory impairment was moderately severe and readily apparent during informal contacts with him and his family. He exhibited no retrograde amnesia for events that occurred during the several decades preceding the onset of his amnesia (Fig. 5). [He may have had a retrograde amnesia limited to the few months or 1–2 years preceding his injury (Zola-Morgan et al., 1986). If so, it would not have been detectable by these particular tests, which assessed past memory decade by decade.] His IQ (Wechsler Adult Intelligence Scale) score was 111, his MQ (Wechsler Memory Scale) score was 91, and during the several years that we studied him, we were unable to detect any cognitive impairment other than amnesia.

A continuous series of histological sections, taken through virtually the entire brain, were prepared and studied for signs of pathological change. The main finding, shown in Fig. 6, was a complete loss of neurons from the CA1 field of the hippocampus. The area of depletion was bilateral and extended the full rostrocaudal extent of the hippocampus. There was some other pathology—a unilateral lesion in left globus pallidus, a unilateral lesion in the right postcentral gyrus, scattered loss of

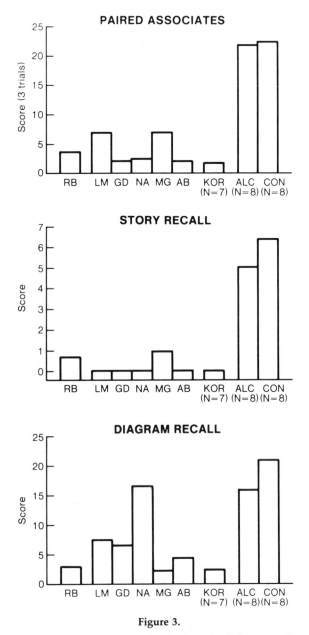

Figure 3.

Performance on three tests of new learning ability by patient R. B.; seven patients with
with Korsakoff's syndrome (KOR); five other amnesic patients— the four from Figures
1 and 2 (L. M., G. D., M. G., A. B.) and case N. A.; eight alcoholic control subjects (ALC);
and eight healthy control subjects (CON). For the six individual patients, scores were
based on the average of three separate test administrations (except for N. A.'s
diagram recall score, which was based on one test). The other subjects were tested once.
For descriptions of the tests, see Squire and Shimamura (1986).

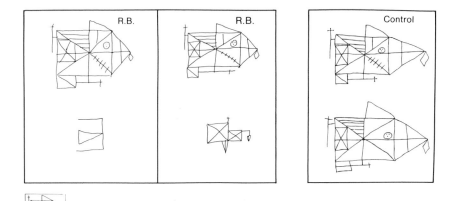

Figure 4.
Diagram recall performance by patient R. B. on two administrations of the
Rey–Osterreith complex figure test. R. B. was first asked to copy the
figure illustrated in the small box to the left. Then 10–20 min later,
without forewarning, he was asked to reproduce it from memory. Left
panel, R. B.'s copy (top) and reproduction (bottom) 6 months after the
onset of his amnesia. Middle panel, R. B.'s copy and reproduction 23
months after the onset of amnesia. Right panel, copy and reproduction by
a healthy control subject matched to R. B. for age and education. [From
Zola-Morgan *et al.* (1986).]

cerebellar Purkinje cells, and scattered acellular foci in neocortex. However, the only finding that we could reasonably associate with the memory impairment was the hippocampal damage. In particular, other mem-
ory-related structures such as the amygdala, mammillary nuclei, and the
mediodorsal nucleus of the thalamus showed no detectable pathology.
A plausible mechanism whereby a restricted CA1 lesion results from a
global ischemic event involves the supposed toxic effects of an excitatory,
glutamate-like neurotransmitter. Global ischemia in the rat also produces
neuronal loss in the CA1 field, as well as memory impairment (Davis *et
al.*, 1986; Volpe *et al.*, 1984).

It is important to emphasize that memory impairment can be more
severe than it was in R. B. The noted patient H. M., for example, is
more severely amnesic than R. B. (see discussion in Zola-Morgan *et al.*,
1986). In correspondence with the behavioral data, the area damaged in
H. M. is more extensive than in R. B. and reportedly involves the entire
anterior medial surface of both temporal lobes. H. M.'s lesion presumably
involves not only the CA1 field of the hippocampus, but also the rest
of the hippocampal formation, the adjacent parahippocampal gyrus,
perirhinal cortex, and the amygdala. Similarly, animal models of human
amnesia indicate that the severity of memory impairment depends on
the extent of medial temporal lobe damage. The memory impairment
associated with bilateral hippocampal removal is exacerbated by addi-

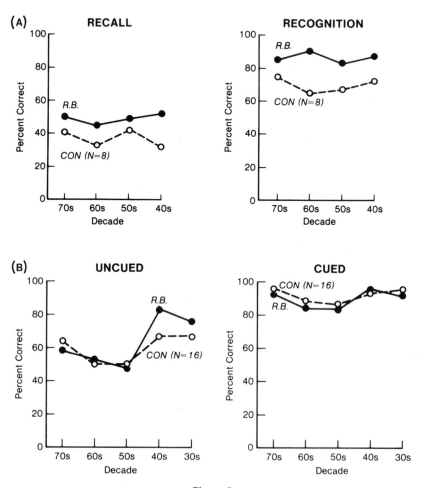

Figure 5.
Remote memory performance by R. B. and control subjects (CON).
Testing occurred in 1979. (A) Recall and recognition memory of public
events that occurred between 1940 and 1979. Data from Zola-Morgan *et al.*
(1986), except that the test was modified by removing seven questions
pertaining to public events from 1970 to 1979. This modified test was the
same one used to obtain the data shown in Fig. 2. (B) Uncued and cued
(recognition) memory for names of famous faces that became prominent
between 1930 and 1979.

tionally removing amygdala, anterior entorhinal cortex, and perirhinal
cortex (Mishkin, 1978; Squire and Zola-Morgan, 1985).

These issues notwithstanding, significant memory impairment can
occur following damage limited to the CA1 field of hippocampus. Figure
7 shows that such a lesion, although spatially limited and involving an
estimated 4.63 million pyramidal cells on each side of the brain (Brown
and Cassell, 1980), would significantly disrupt the flow of information

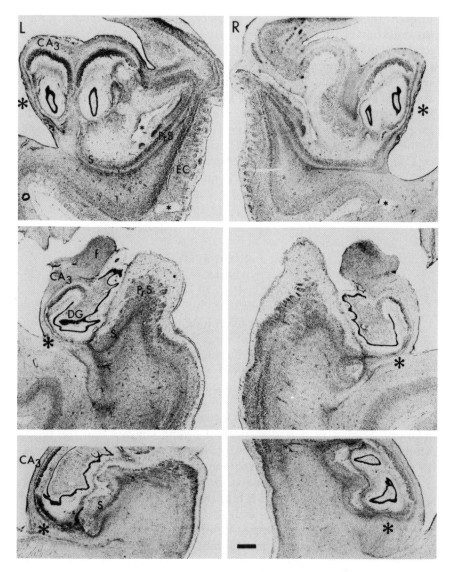

Figure 6.
Photomicrographs of thionin-stained coronal sections through the
hippocampal formation of R. B.'s brain. Sections are from the left (L) and
right (R) sides of the rostral extreme (top), the midportion (middle), and
the caudal extreme (bottom) of the hippocampal formation. The only
pathology evident in these sections is the complete loss of pyramidal cells
confined to the CA1 field of the hippocampus (asterisks). CA3, Field CA3
of the hippocampus; DG, dentate gyrus; EC, entorhinal cortex; PrS,
presubiculum; S, subiculum. Holes in tissue in top panels (small stars) are
artifactual. Calibration bar, 2 mm. [From Zola-Morgan *et al.* (1986).]

through the hippocampus. The primary hippocampal circuit begins in the entorhinal cortex, which originates the major input (perforant path) to the dentate gyrus granule cells. These cells give rise to the mossy fibers, which terminate in the CA3 field of the hippocampus. Neurons of CA3 send projections to the CA1 pyramidal cells by way of the Schaffer collateral system. The CA1 cells complete the circuit with projections to the subiculum and the entorhinal cortex. This trisynaptic circuit provides for an essentially unidirectional flow of information through the cell fields of the hippocampal formation and back to the entorhinal cortex. A lesion of CA1 would open this circuit, thereby disrupting processing within this circuitry that seems to be critical for learning and memory. The next section considers what the normal operation of the hippocampus might contribute to memory functions.

IV. The Neuropsychological Data

The data reviewed here[1] suggest that the hippocampus is needed to establish declarative representations in long-term memory and to permit access to them during a period of consolidation. The findings with skill learning and priming show that the hippocampus is required for establishing only a certain kind of memory, that is, declarative memory, which is explicitly available to conscious recollection as facts, events, or specific stimuli. Studies of delayed recall show that if recall is to succeed, the hippocampus is needed as soon as information is no longer in immediate memory. Studies of paired-associate learning suggest that the hippocampus is especially important for fast, one-trial learning, and for associating arbitrary stimuli that evolution never prepared us to encounter.

Studies of retrograde amnesia show that, because remote memories are preserved in patients with hippocampal damage, the site of permanent representations cannot be the hippocampus itself. While the contribution of the hippocampus to memory cannot yet be stated very precisely, the hippocampus must establish at the time of learning some kind of relationship with representations elsewhere, probably in neo-

---

[1]Our discussion emphasizes data from R. B., because R. B. 's amnesia resulted from damage limited to the hippocampus. The pathology is not known in the case of our other three patient with amnesia resulting from an anoxic or ischemic event. However, because the hippocampal formation is particularly vulnerable to damage by anoxia or ischemia, and was damaged in patient R. B., it seems likely that the pathology in our other patients will at least include the hippocampus. The neuropsychological findings for these three patients were similar to the findings for R. B. (Figs. 1, 2, and 3 [cases LM, GD, AB]). These patients on average may have somewhat more severe anterograde amnesia than R. B. did (IQ-MQ difference score for these patients = 24 versus 20 for R. B.), and they have more extensive retrograde amnesia than R. B. (compare Figs. 2 and 5).

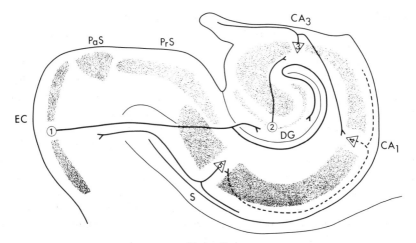

Figure 7.
Schematic drawing of the primate hippocampal formation. The numbers and the solid lines connecting them show the unidirectional flow of information (from entorhinal cortex 1, to dentate gyrus 2, to CA3 3 to CA1 4, to the subiculus 5). In case R. B., a lesion of the CA1 field (represented by cell 4 and the dashed lines) disrupted the sequence of information flow in the hippocampus. EC, Entorhinal cortex; PaS, parasubiculum; PrS, presubiculum; S, subiculum; DG, dentate gyrus; CA1 and CA3, fields of the hippocampus. [From Zola-Morgan *et al.* (1986).]

cortex. This interaction allows perceptions established in the neocortex to be transformed into permanent memories. As time passes after initial learning, representations in memory eventually become independent of the hippocampus.

It is not known what actually happens, in the absence of the hippocampus, to information that becomes successfully established in short-term memory. If the hippocampus is unable to participate in establishing long-term memory, then representations that had been established in short-term memory might literally be lost, or they might achieve an unorganized state. In the case of transient amnesic episodes (transient global amnesia; amnesia associated with electroconvulsive therapy), the events that occur during the period of anterograde amnesia are not subsequently remembered after recovery from amnesia. New learning again becomes possible, but events from the amnesic episode do not return to memory. In other words, if the hippocampus cannot do its job at the time of learning, memory is not established in a usable way and is not available thereafter. One would therefore think that in the absence of the hippocampus, representations in memory must achieve some abnormal fate. Memories do not become retrievable at a later time when normal hippocampal function recovers. These ideas suggest that the hippocampus is needed to establish an effective memory store rather than to retrieve from memory. Direct neurobiological data concerning the effect of hippocampal damage on those ensembles of synaptic changes, which together constitute stored information, will be needed to answer these questions definitively.

It is possible that the hippocampus, and perhaps also structures with a close anatomical relationship to hippocampus, such as entorhinal cortex or parahippocampal gyrus, are themselves sites of plasticity related to long-term memory. These sites could be established at the time of learning in addition to, and in conjunction with, sites of plasticity in neocortex that are the enduring substrates of permanent memory. They might serve as addresses, or provide some other kind of support, for the neocortical representations—until such time as these representations become unified (consolidated) and can function independently of the hippocampus (see Rolls, this volume; Teyler and DiScenna, 1986; Squire, 1987). By this account, when the hippocampus is damaged, these additional sites of plasticity would not be established.

_____ V. The Neurophysiological Data _____

Long-term potentiation (LTP) is a form of synaptic plasticity that occurs prominently in the hippocampus. It has several properties that make it a promising memory mechanism (Lynch, 1986; Barnes and McNaughton, 1985; McNaughton *et al.*, 1978; Swanson *et al.*, 1982; Teyler and DiScenna, 1986; see also chapters by Lynch, Bliss, and Brown, this volume). First, LTP is established quickly and lasts for a long time. Second, LTP is cooperative; that is, it depends on convergent inputs that occur simultaneously or nearly simultaneously. One input depolarizes the postsynaptic cell to enable a second input or a second stimulation of the same input to induce LTP. LTP appears to depend on a glutamate-like amino acid that induces an influx of calcium into the postsynaptic cell (Collingridge, Kehl, & McLennan, 1983; Jahr and Stevens, 1987; Smith, 1987). At some hippocampal synapses, the receptors that activate calcium influx have a strong affinity for N-methyl-D-aspartate (NMDA) binding, and they accordingly have been termed NMDA receptors (see Foster and Fagg, 1984, for review). Interestingly, there are more NMDA receptors in the hippocampus than in any other cortical or subcortical structure (Olverman *et al.*, 1984). Within the hippocampus these are most heavily concentrated in the CA1 field (Monaghan *et al.*, 1983). When NMDA receptors are blocked by an antagonist, such as D-2-amino-5-phosphonovalerate (APV), the formation of LTP is prevented but normal synaptic responses to single stimulation of afferent fibers is not affected (Harris *et al.*, 1984). Further, rats given infusions of APV sufficient to block LTP performed poorly on a spatial memory task (McNaughton and Morris, 1987; Morris *et al.*, 1986).

What function might LTP be supporting? An important clue comes from the findings of retrograde amnesia (see Section IV), which suggest that very remote, premorbid memories are preserved following hippo-campal damage. Accordingly, the hippocampus cannot be the permanent repository of all memories. It follows from this line of reasoning that LTP in the hippocampus cannot be a mechanism for permanently representing all memories. The data do not rule out the possibility that complex experiences are initially recorded in the hippocampus and later moved to neocortex. Nor do the data rule out the idea that there are two identical records of experience, a potentially permanent one recorded in neocortex and a temporary one in hippocampus. While these are possibilities, it seems more likely that the hippocampus performs a specific, time-limited function in the service of memories stored in neocortex. Thus, LTP could provide a mechanism whereby, as the result of a learning experience, the hippocampus establishes a relationship with memory storage processes in the neocortex.

One possibility is that LTP acts as a mechanism for forming and storing conjunctions between two distinct inputs, and that the output of the hippocampal circuitry back to entorhinal cortex signals the forming of this conjunction. In this way the plasticity that occurs within the hippocampal circuitry may function as a device that forms or strengthens associations between ordinarily unrelated events. In psychological terms, the hippocampus may contribute to the formation of new relationships in long-term memory, such as those formed when associating a stimulus and its spatial/temporal context (thus representing a new event or episode), or when associating facts and the semantic context to which they belong (thus representing a new concept). These ideas will be developed further after considering the anatomy of the hippocampus.

VI. The Neuroanatomical Data: Topography of Sensory Inputs to Hippocampus and Intrinsic Hippocampal Connections

As ideas are developed about how the hippocampal formation[2] contributes to learning and memory, and about synaptic mechanisms for plastic change, it becomes increasingly important to establish a precise description of hippocampal connections. Anatomical studies are beginning to

---

[2]The hippocampal formation comprises a number of distinct cytoarchitectonic fields, including the dentate gyrus, the hippocampus proper (which can be subdivided into fields CA3, CA2, and CA1 on cytoarchitectonic and connectional grounds), the subicular complex (which can be divided into three fields, the subiculum proper, the presubiculum, and the parasubiculum), and the entorhinal cortex. These fields are connected by a series of powerful and largely unidirectional projections, which, taken together, appear to unite them into a functional entity.

address a number of relevant questions. From which regions does the hippocampus receive its principal sensory innervation? Does the hippocampus receive elemental, "low-level" information (such as edge, motion, or color information from the visual system), or does it receive "higher-level" polysensory information (that might be involved, for example, in complex object or facial recognition)? What kind of information is sent out of the hippocampus? How much fidelity is maintained between the information that enters and leaves the hippocampus? Is there ultimately overlap and mixing among the original inputs, or might the information carried by separate inputs remain segregated as it moves through the hippocampal formation? Do the same regions of neocortex that originate input to the hippocampal formation also receive projections from the hippocampal formation? If so, for any given learning event, is the hippocampus able to send information back, selectively and precisely, to the same regions of neocortex that originated input to the hippocampus, or does the connectivity indicate that signals emerging from the hippocampus would not likely retain information about the original source of the input? These and other questions will be discussed in the light of current neuroanatomical knowledge.

A. Levels of Anatomical Analysis

It is important to keep in mind certain technical limitations that restrict the precision with which anatomical connectivity is described. While it is well within the means of modern neuroanatomy to demonstrate neural projections from one region to another, or to show that projections from two regions (A and B) project to a third region (C), it is more difficult to determine whether the projections from regions A and B terminate in different parts of region C (Fig. 8, panel 1, top) or whether the projections from regions A and B are coextensive in region C (Fig. 8, panel 1, bottom). Resolving this issue would require using two distinct anterograde tracers in the same experimental animal. While technically feasible, this procedure is rarely used. Moreover, it is even rarer (because of the technical difficulties involved) that information is generated concerning whether two projections terminate on the same or different neurons within the target region (Fig. 8, panel 2). Similarly, although it is often the case that multiple, divergent projections are found to originate from one brain region, it is generally not determined whether the same (Fig. 8, panel 3, left) or different (Fig. 8, panel 3, right) neurons originate the divergent projections.

The issues of pathway origination, topography, and convergence or divergence all concern what might be termed the *regional* level of anatomical organization. This level of detail is typically used to describe the connections between different neural structures or cortical areas. There is also a more refined level of anatomical description that might

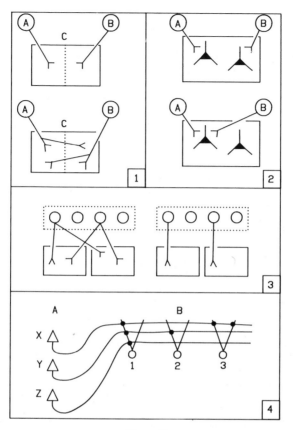

Figure 8.
Various technical limitations affect the precision with which anatomical organization can be described. Panel 1: While it is straightforward to demonstrate projections from two regions (A and B) to a third region (C), it is often not determined whether the two afferents terminate in different (top) or the same (bottom) parts of the innervated field. Panel 2: Even if it is known that two afferents terminate in the same general part of an innervated field, it is generally not known whether the terminations are on different (top) or on the same (bottom) cells in the field. Panel 3: Many cortical regions originate divergent projections to various other cortical areas. Until recent studies simultaneously employed two or more differentially detectable retrograde tracers, however, it was not clear whether the same (left) or different (right) cells give rise to the components of the projections. Panel 4: Computer models of hippocampal function will rely on precise, quantitative description of hippocampal anatomy, much of which is not available in the current literature. Many questions remain, for example, about the organization of the entorhinal projection (neurons X, Y, and Z) to the dendritic trees of the dentate granule cells (neurons 1, 2, and 3). Several questions about this projection are raised in the text.

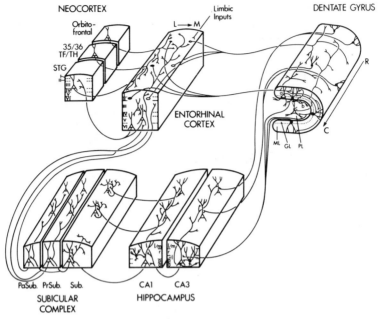

Figure 9.

Diagrammatic representation of the major intrinsic connections of the
hippocampal formation. Much of the sensory input to the hippocampal
formation arises in polysensory associational regions of the neocortex such
as the orbitofrontal cortex, the perirhinal and parahippocampal cortices
(35/36, TF/TH), and the dorsal bank of the superior temporal gyrus (STG).
Layer III pyramidal cells in these areas project principally, though not
exclusively, to the lateral aspect of the entorhinal cortex. Projection fields
from different associational cortices do not have sharp boundries in the
entorhinal cortex and there is substantial overlap. The entorhinal cortex
gives rise to the major input to the dentate gyrus, the so-called perforant
path, which terminates on the unipolar dendritic trees (located in the
molecular layer, ML) of the granule cells. This projection is organized such
that cells located laterally in the entorhinal cortex (close to the rhinal
sulcus) project preferentially to caudal levels of the dentate gyrus, and
progressively more medial bands of entorhinal cells project to more rostral
levels of the dentate gyrus. Within the dentate gyrus there are a variety of
neurons other than the granule cells. Some of these (a, b) are interneurons
that give rise to local, inhibitory projections. Other cells (c) located in the
polymorphic layer (PL), subjacent to the dentate gyrus, give rise to an
extensive associational system of fibers that terminate on dendrites in the
inner third of the molecular layer. Associational fibers that arise at any
particular level in the dentate gyrus terminate throughout much of the
remainder of the structure. The dentate granule cells give rise to a
nonreciprocated projection (the mossy fibers) to the CA3 field of the
hippocampus. Pyramidal cells in the CA3 field, in turn, originate several
intrinsic and extrinsic connections. Within the hippocampal formation CA3
neurons give rise to a widespread associational projection to other levels
of CA3. Other collaterals (the Schaffer collaterals) provide the major input
to the CA1 field of the hippocampus. Within field CA1 and CA3 there are

be termed the *local* or *intrinsic* level of anatomical organization. This level of description is concerned principally with the anatomy within a neural structure or cortical area, and it is especially reliant on point-to-point mapping of projections and on quantitative analyses. As shown in Fig. 8, panel 4, some examples of questions at the local or intrinsic level would include: Do axons from area A converge on the same neurons in B or on different neurons? If there is convergence, how many of the axons from region A terminate on a single cell in region B? How many synapses does each axon make on a single dendritic tree? Also, how many neurons in area B are contacted by single axons from area A? While data of this kind will undoubtedly be useful in providing boundary conditions for computational modeling of hippocampal function, little published information concerning the anatomical organization of the hippocampal formation is currently available at this level of precision. This level of precision requires methods that approach the limits of or even surpass the technical capabilities of modern neuroanatomy. To determine, for example, the total number of cells that one axon contacts, it would be necessary first to label selectively a single axon from an identified cell type and then to determine, by serial-section electron microscopy, the number of neurons with which the axon forms synaptic contacts. Even in the most favorable of systems this would be a formidable task.

While it is likely to be some time before the level of anatomical detail is sufficient to provide a complete picture of hippocampal circuitry, a substantial literature on hippocampal connectivity is available. In the following pages, we briefly survey the anatomical organization of the hippocampal formation by following the course of sensory information as it enters from the neocortex and traverses the various hippocampal fields. The major features of the hippocampal circuit are shown in Fig. 9. While this scheme is intended to convey the organization found in the primate brain, much of the information on which it is based is derived from the literature for the rat and cat.

---

also a variety of interneurons that originate local inhibitory projections. Unlike the CA3 field, CA1 pyramidal cells do not project to other levels of CA1. Rather, they give rise to a relatively dense and spatially restricted projection to the subiculum. The subiculum, in turn, projects both to the pre- and parasubiculum and to the entorhinal cortex. The pre- and parasubiculum provide a major input to the entorhinal cortex, which terminates principally in layers III and II. While not yet well studied, there is evidence that cells located deep in the entorhinal cortex project back to many of the cortical fields from which it receives input. Additional abbreviations: L, lateral; M, medial; R, rostral; C, caudal; GL, granule-cell layer; l/m, stratum lacunosum moleculare; r, stratum radiatum, l, stratum lucidum; p, pyramidal cell layer; o, stratum oriens.

B. The Entorhinal Cortex

Of the several fields that constitute the primate hippocampal formation, the entorhinal cortex appears to be the principal recipient of direct neocortical inputs (Van Hoesen and Pandya, 1975b; Van Hoesen *et al.*, 1975; Insausti *et al.*, 1987).[3] The major neocortical inputs to the entorhinal cortex arise from a band of adjacent cortex that includes the perirhinal cortices rostrally (areas 35 and 36 of Brodmann) and the parahippocampal cortex (areas TF and TH of Bonin and Bailey) caudally. In one study, for example (Insausti *et al.*, 1987), cells in the perirhinal and parahippocampal cortices accounted for an average of 62% of the labeled cortical cells resulting from injections of retrograde tracers into the entorhinal cortex. The perirhinal and parahippocampal cortices in turn receive inputs from a variety of unimodal and polymodal associational cortices (Fig. 10).[4] Thus, these regions have been likened to funnels which relay information from widespread areas of neocortex into the hippocampal formation.

The perirhinal and parahippocampal cortices are not the only cortical regions that project to the entorhinal cortex. It also receives prominent projections from the superior temporal gyrus, the insular cortex, the orbitofrontal cortex, and the cingulate cortex, especially its retrosplenial region (Fig. 10) (Insausti *et al.*, 1987). As with the perirhinal and parahippocampal cortices, each of these cortical regions receives rather diverse neocortical and limbic inputs, and each of these cortical regions can be classified as "polysensory associational cortices" (Pandya and Yeterian, 1986). For example, the anterior cingulate cortex (area 24) is reciprocally connected with areas 6, 8, and 9 of the dorsolateral frontal lobe, area 12 of the orbitofrontal cortex, the insula, area 7 of the posterior parietal cortex, and the amygdaloid complex (Pandya and Yeterian, 1986). Similarly, the insular cortex receives fairly extensive projections from unimodal associational areas related to somatosensory, auditory, visual, and gustatory function, as well as from polysensory cortical areas in the frontal lobe (areas 46 and 11), temporal lobe (anterior superior temporal gyrus), and amygdala (Mesulam and Mufson, 1986). Thus, while the hippocampal formation appears to receive direct inputs from a relatively limited number of neocortical regions, each of these regions likely provides information from a much broader extent of cortex. In this way, the hippocampal formation is ultimately privy to much of the processing that takes place within the cortical mantle.

---

[3]The subicular complex receives additional direct cortical inputs (Van Hoesen *et al.*, 1979; Seltzer and Pandya, 1976; Amaral *et al.*, 1983). Most of these appear to be from the same cortical regions that project to the entorhinal cortex. However, some cortical areas, such as the posterior parietal cortex, have been reported to project to the presubiculum but not to the entorhinal cortex (Seltzer and Pandya, 1976).

[4]This group of afferent regions is likely to be incomplete since the inputs to the perirhinal and parahippocampal cortices have not yet been adequately studied with retrograde methods.

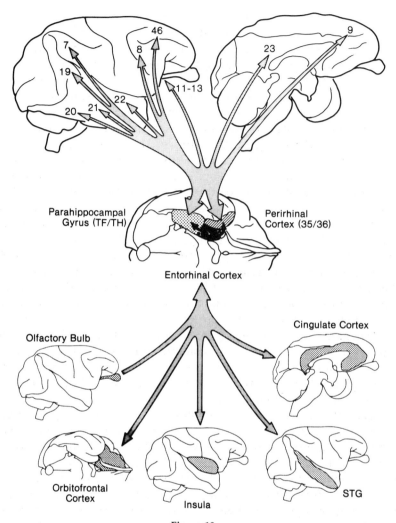

Figure 10.
The hippocampal formation receives much of its sensory innervation from polysensory associational cortices that project primarily to the entorhinal cortex. Most of these regions appear to receive a return projection from the entorhinal cortex. The major cortical input originates in a band of cortex adjacent to the entorhinal cortex that includes the perirhinal cortex (areas 35 and 36) rostrally, and the parahippocampal cortex (areas TF and TH) caudally. These regions, in turn, receive both unimodal and polymodal inputs from several regions in the frontal, temporal, and parietal lobes. The entorhinal cortex also receives cortical inputs from presumed polysensory regions in the cingulate cortex, the superior temporal gyrus (STG) of the temporal lobe, the insular cortex, and from several fields of the orbitofrontal cortex. The only obvious unimodal input to the entorhinal cortex arises in the olfactory bulb. This projection is much reduced in the primate relative to that in the rodent.

The entorhinal cortex is not a homogeneous region. In the monkey it has been divided into seven distinct cytoarchitectonic subdivisions (Amaral *et al.*, 1987). As many as 27 subdivisions have been suggested for the human entorhinal cortex (Rose, 1926). Studies carried out in the monkey (Insausti *et al.*, 1987) and cat (Room and Groenewegen, 1986) indicate that neocortical inputs to the entorhinal cortex terminate most heavily in its lateral aspect (near the rhinal sulcus) in what has been called the lateral division of the monkey entorhinal cortex (Amaral *et al.*, 1987) or the prorhinal region (Van Hoesen and Pandya, 1975a).

The distribution of fibers and terminals from each of the cortical afferents to the various subdivisions of the entorhinal cortex has not yet been adequately analyzed. In particular, double-labeling techniques have not been used to determine the amount of overlap of these projections. Preliminary studies, however, suggest that fibers and terminals arising from each of the afferent cortical regions are partially segregated in the entorhinal cortex. The insular and orbitofrontal cortices, for example, tend to project more heavily to rostral levels of the entorhinal cortex, whereas projections arising from the cingulate cortex and the superior temporal gyrus project more caudally. At the same time, there are no sharp boundaries between any of these cortical projections, and there appears to be extensive overlap. Certainly, the terminations of these projections give no indication of columnar organization or of laminar specificity. Moreover, because the zones of termination comprise rather broad regions of entorhinal cortex, they do not respect the boundaries of cytoarchitectonic subdivisions.

The information sent to the entorhinal cortex from "polysensory neocortical regions" may or may not preserve the unimodal characteristics of the information originally received by these polysensory regions. Moreover, mixing of sensory information is presumably increased within the entorhinal cortex by the overlap of projections arising from the different polysensory cortical regions. It is therefore difficult to draw conclusions regarding the possibility of sensory segregation within the entorhinal cortex. It is conceivable that certain subsets of entorhinal neurons are influenced only by inputs subserving one modality, though at present this seems unlikely. It seems more likely that the information sent to entorhinal cortex is already polymodal, and that some further mixing of inputs occurs within the entorhinal cortex. The next section suggests, furthermore, that the organization of the entorhinal projection to the dentate gyrus (the perforant path) in the cat (Witter and Groenewegen, 1984) and monkey (Witter *et al.*, 1988b) tends to obscure whatever segregation of cortical inputs might exist in the entorhinal cortex.

C. The Dentate Gyrus

It has been known for some time that cells located primarily in layer II of the entorhinal cortex project to the dentate gyrus. The entorhinal cortex also sends direct projections to the subiculum and to the CA fields of the hippocampus. While these projections have been largely neglected, they are likely to be important for normal functioning of the hippocampal formation (Witter *et al.*, 1988a). Witter and Groenewegen (1984) showed that rostrocaudally oriented, band-like zones of layer II cells project to different septotemporal levels of the dentate gyrus. In the monkey, cells located laterally in the entorhinal cortex (and extending the full rostro-caudal extent of the entorhinal cortex) project to caudal levels of the dentate gyrus, whereas bands of layer II cells that are situated progressively more medially in the entorhinal cortex project to progressively more rostral levels of the dentate gyrus. Within these bands, virtually all of the layer II neurons contribute to the projection.

The fact that cortical inputs terminate preferentially in the lateral aspect of the entorhinal cortex, and that this part of the entorhinal cortex projects to the caudal dentate gyrus, suggests that more caudal levels of the dentate gyrus are preferentially influenced by cortical inputs. Interestingly, in correspondence with these anatomical data, the majority of sensory responses in single-unit recordings from the human hippocampus are observed in the posterior third of the structure (Wilson *et al.*, 1987). In the cat, Witter and Groenewegen (1984) demonstrated that the lateral portion of the entorhinal cortex receives heavy neocortical innervation, while the medial parts are preferentially innervated by limbic inputs, such as those from the amygdaloid complex. They concluded that different levels of the cat hippocampus are therefore receiving qualitatively different information through the perforant path projection and are therefore likely to be carrying out different functions.

In the dentate gyrus, the entorhinal fibers terminate in the molecular layer on the unipolar dendritic trees of the principal cell type, the granule cell.[5] Each perforant path fiber extends for a considerable distance in the molecular layer and is therefore presumed to make *en passant* contacts with the dendrites of many granule cells. There are many unresolved issues about the local organization of this projection. It is not currently known, for example, how many entorhinal neurons contribute to the perforant path projection, or how many granule cells each perforant path fiber terminates on, or how many contacts each perforant path fiber makes on the dendritic tree of a single granule cell. Nevertheless, approximate answers to some of these questions can be deduced from available data.

It is known, for example, that there are approximately 6×10^5 to 1×10^6 granule cells in the rat dentate gyrus (Boss *et al.*, 1985; Seress and Pokorny, 1981; Seress, 1988) (approximately 5×10^6 granule cells in the monkey and about 9×10^6 in the human). Based on the spine density estimates of Desmond and Levy (1985), a rat granule cell contains

---

[5]A smaller component of entorhinal fibers also terminates in the CA3 and CA1 fields of the hippocampus.

about 5000 dendritic spines, distributed across a total average dendritic length of 3200 μm (Desmond and Levy, 1982; Claiborne *et al.*, 1988). Because the perforant path accounts for virtually all of the synapses in the outer three-fourths of the granule-cell dendritic tree, perforant path fibers would be expected to contact about 3700 of the spines on each granule cell. Based on our estimate that on the order of 2×10^5 layer II entorhinal cells project to the dentate gyrus, then each entorhinal cell would be expected to make about 18,500 synapses in the molecular layer of the dentate gyrus [(3700 synapses $\times 10^6$ granule cells) $(2 \times 10^5$ layer II cells)]. These 18,500 synapses could be made on 18,500 different granule cells, if each perforant path axon made only one synapse per granule-cell dendritic tree. In that case, the probability of a particular granule cell being contacted by an individual perforant path fiber would be about 0.02 (18,500 synapses/10^6 granule cells).

Viewed in a different way, each granule cell could receive input from as many as 3700 different entorhinal cells, if each entorhinal cell made only one contact on the dendritic tree; or from as few as 370 different cells, for example, if each perforant path fiber made 10 contacts on each dendritic tree. Regardless of the exact numbers, it appears that there is substantial convergence of entorhinal cells on the dendritic tree of individual granule cells. At the same time, the large number of granule cells allows for each perforant path fiber to contact at most only a relatively small proportion (about 2%) of the total number of granule cells.

The dentate granule cells give rise to distinctive axons, the so-called mossy fibers, which terminate both on neurons in the polymorphic region of the dentate gyrus and on the proximal dendrites of the CA3 pyramidal cells. In the rat, there are approximately 160,000 CA3 pyramidals (or a ratio of 1 pyramidal cell for every 3.75–6.25 granule cells; this ratio is about the same for the monkey and human). Because each mossy fiber in the rat terminates on about 14 CA3 pyramidal cells (Claiborne *et al.*, 1986), each CA3 pyramidal cell is therefore innervated by approximately 52–87 granule cells. Of all the intrahippocampal connections, the mossy-fiber projection maintains the most "lamellar" organization. By this is meant that any particular level of the dentate gyrus projects to a relatively restricted longitudinal spread of the CA3 field of the hippocampus. Not only is this projection topographically restricted, there is little convergence or divergence between the two cell populations.

The mossy fibers also give rise to numerous collaterals, which terminate on several types of neurons located either in the granule cell layer or in the subjacent polymorphic layer.[6] These neurons in turn give

---

[6]The area deep to the granule-cell layer is often given the term CA4, which conveys the mistaken notion that it is a portion of the hippocampus proper. We have argued previously (Amaral, 1978), in agreement with Blackstad (1956), that based on connectional criteria, this area is more reasonably considered a portion of the dentate gyrus. It does not, for example, as incorrectly asserted by Lorente de No, give rise to Schaffer collaterals to the CA1 field of the hippocampus. Nor do cells in this region project to the CA3 field.

rise to at least three intrinsic "feedback" projections. First, the well-known GABAergic, pyramidal basket cells reside in the deep aspect of the granule-cell layer, and their axons project around the cell bodies of the granule cells. The total number of basket cells in the rat dentate gyrus is on the order of 3500, yielding a basket cell/granule cell ratio of approximately 1/170 (Seress and Pokorny, 1981). Second, there is an ipsilateral associational projection that arises from large "mossy" cells and terminates on the proximal dendrites of the granule cells. This is a highly divergent projection; cells located at any particular level of the dentate gyrus project to much of its rostrocaudal extent. Seress (1988) has estimated that there are approximately 32,000 cells in the polymorphic layer of the rat dentate gyrus. Of these, at least 30%, or 9,600 are GABA- and somatostatin-immunoreactive, and these project to the distal dendrites of the granule cells (Amaral, unpublished observations). Since the polymorphic region contains cells other than the GABA/somatostatin and mossy cells, it would appear that the associational projection arises from fewer than 20,000 mossy cells. Interestingly, while the GABA/somatostatin projection terminates locally in the molecular layer, the classical associational projection projects instead to distant levels of the dentate gyrus.

D. The CA3 and CA1 Fields

The pyramidal cells of CA3 give rise to very extensive subcortical and intrinsic connections,[7] including a prominent projection through the fornix to the lateral septal nucleus. Within CA3, these cells originate an extensive associational projection, which, from virtually any starting point, terminates throughout much of the rostrocaudal extent of the entire CA3 field. Calculations suggest that, although the associational fiber system does exhibit widespread divergence, any particular CA3 pyramidal cell is probably innervated by fewer than 5% of the total CA3 pyramidal cell population.

CA3 pyramidal cells also originate the Schaffer collaterals, which provide the major input to the CA1 field of the hippocampus. There is a slightly greater number of cells in the rat CA1 field (approximately 250,000) than in the CA3 field (160,000). Interestingly, in the primate brain, field CA1 has undergone an enhanced development. In the human hippocampus, for example, there are about two times as many CA1 pyramidal cells (4.6×10^6) as CA3 pyramidal cells (2.3×10^6) (Seress, 1988).

These CA3 collateral axons terminate on both the apical dendrites of the CA1 pyramidal cells (in stratum radiatum) and also on their basal dendrites (in stratum oriens). Glutamate is the likely neurotransmitter

---

[7]But the CA3 field does not project back to the dentate gyrus. It is a hallmark of the hippocampal circuit that the projections are largely unidirectional. Thus, the perforant path projection from the entorhinal cortex to the dentate gyrus is not reciprocated by fibers arising in the dentate gyrus. Similarly, the CA3 field of the hippocampus does not project back to the dentate gyrus, nor does CA1 project back to CA3.

(Storm-Mathisen, 1981, 1984; Wolf *et al.*, 1984). The Schaffer collateral projection arising from any particular level of CA3 is strikingly divergent, terminating throughout much of the rostrocaudal extent of CA1. While the CA3 to CA1 projection is markedly divergent in the longitudinal plane, it nonetheless exhibits an elegant topographic organization in the transverse plane (Ishizuka *et al.*, 1986). Specifically, CA3 cells located in different transverse positions of the CA3 layer give rise to markedly different projections both within CA3 and to CA1. For example, cells located closest to the dentate gyrus have very limited associational projections within CA3 and project to the most distal transverse extent of CA1 (near the subicular border). The CA3 pyramidal cells located further away from the dentate gyrus give rise to the major CA3 associational projections, and they project to more proximal parts of CA1. Near the CA3/CA1 border, the pyramidal cells give rise to virtually no typical Schaffer collaterals but instead originate fibers that terminate close to the CA3/CA1 border, mainly in stratum oriens. The implication of this organization is that, despite the widespread distribution of projections from CA3 pyramidal cells to CA1, different subsets of CA1 cells will be activated by CA3 cells located in different transverse positions along the rostrocaudal extent of the CA3 field.

E. The Subicular Complex

Unlike CA3, field CA1 does not give rise to a major associational projection. Few if any collaterals of CA1 pyramidal cells terminate within the CA1 field. Rather, the CA1 field projects primarily into the subiculum. Although the organization of this projection is incompletely understood, CA1 axons terminate densely in restricted, columnar zones within the subiculum. Thus, there appears to be relatively less divergence of this projection than of the CA3 projection to CA1 (Tamamaki *et al.*, 1987). CA1 also contributes a projection directly to the entorhinal cortex, but this projection has not been well studied.

The subicular complex originates the well-known projection through the fornix to the anterior thalamus and mammillary nuclei. Subicular pyramidal cells also project to both the pre- and parasubiculum (Kohler, 1985), and the projection from any point in the subiculum appears to terminate widely in these fields. All three divisions of the subicular complex (presubiculum, parasubiculum, and subiculum) project to the entorhinal cortex. These projections are rather divergent, but restricted to caudal levels of the monkey entorhinal cortex (which is roughly homologous with the medial entorhinal cortex of the rat). For example, retrograde studies in the monkey indicate that large numbers of layer II presubicular pyramidal cells, distributed throughout virtually the entire rostrocaudal extent of the field, focus a projection to the caudal two-thirds of the entorhinal cortex. Accordingly, it appears that the presubiculum, which receives information from all rostro-caudal levels of the hippocampal formation, provides that information to primarily the caudal levels of the entorhinal cortex.

F. Entorhinal–Neocortex Projections

We thus return to the entorhinal cortex, from which the majority of sensory inputs to the hippocampus originated, and to which, through the subicular projections, the fully processed input is returned. The efferent projections of the entorhinal cortex, which carry this information away from the hippocampus, are still incompletely understood. It is clear, however, that cells located in layers V and VI of entorhinal cortex (i.e., not those that project to the dentate gyrus) give rise to several subcortical and cortical projections. In particular, a heavy projection arises from the entorhinal cortex to the parahippocampal gyrus (Kosel et al., 1982). Recent observations (D. G. Amaral and R. Insausti, unpublished observations) have confirmed this projection and in addition indicate that the entorhinal cortex projects to the orbitofrontal cortex and the insula. As these are all areas that project to entorhinal cortex, it is possible that the hippocampal formation influences cortical processing primarily through the relatively widespread efferent projections of the same polysensory association areas that originate input to the entorhinal cortex (see Fig. 10). In particular, there is so far no indication in the monkey brain that the entorhinal cortex projects directly to primary sensory and unimodal associational cortical regions, as has been indicated for the rat (Swanson and Kohler, 1986). Whereas it does seem likely that the entorhinal cortex is reciprocally connected with a number of polysensory association areas, the nature of this reciprocal relationship is not well understood. It is not known, for example, whether the projections are strictly reciprocal— that is, whether the same regions of the entorhinal cortex that receive projections from a particular neocortical region also originate the return projection to that region.

G. Summary of Neuroanatomical Data

While our understanding of the topography of hippocampal projections is obviously incomplete, a number of tentative conclusions can be drawn. First, it is clearly unreasonable to consider all rostrocaudal (or septotemporal) levels of the hippocampal formation to be processing the same types of information; different levels receive different complements of inputs. It is similarly unreasonable to think of the hippocampal formation as a series of isolated lamellae. The dentate gyrus and the CA3 field, for example, both have prominent associational connections that link all rostrocaudal levels. These extensive associational projections make it possible for inputs at one rostrocaudal level to influence processing throughout much of the hippocampus. Finally, it does not seem likely that the hippocampal formation can maintain a point-to-point correspondence between input and output information. There is extensive convergence of inputs from the entorhinal cortex to dentate gyrus, and there is considerable divergence of outputs both from field CA3 to field CA1 of the hippocampus and from the subicular complex to the entorhinal cortex.

These features of the anatomy suggest that there may be little fidelity in the hippocampal system. This conclusion cannot be a strong one, however, until neuroanatomical analysis is carried out at the cellular level, and it is shown directly that individual hippocampal neurons at one or more stages of processing do in fact mix information arriving from a previous stage. Nevertheless, available data make it difficult to see how the fidelity of inputs and outputs is preserved. In particular, it seems unlikely that information sent out of the hippocampal circuitry could be returned selectively to precisely the same cortical regions that originated it. It is possible that the hippocampal formation is performing very specific computations on the information it receives, and is ultimately computing a specific output. However, the output would likely be broadcast to widespread regions of the neocortex in a relatively nonspecific way.

VII. Memory and the Hippocampus: Conclusions

We have reviewed briefly certain neuropsychological, physiological, and anatomical findings relevant to memory and hippocampal function. Whereas many important facts have been uncovered, there is still much to learn about how the hippocampus contributes to memory functions. In this final section, we summarize the important points that mark our present understanding and raise some questions for future work.

Neuropsychological evidence from human amnesia suggests that the hippocampus is critically involved in the acquisition of new information. One of the most difficult tasks for an amnesic patient is to associate two unrelated pieces of information (such as remembering two unrelated words in a paired-associate learning test). At the same time, some kinds of new learning, such as skill learning and priming, can be accomplished normally. Skill learning and priming do not apparently require the integrity of the hippocampus. What does depend on the hippocampus is the ability to acquire new facts and episodes. Facts and episodes can be acquired explicitly and are then available in memory as conscious recollections, as what has been termed declarative knowledge.

Declarative knowledge continues to depend on the integrity of the hippocampus beyond the moment of initial learning. However, just how long after learning the hippocampus remains essential is not known. Based on findings for our three patients with amnesia resulting from anoxia or ischemia, one could conclude that information remains vulnerable for as long as 15 years after initial learning (see Fig. 2). Yet the extent of damage in these patients is unknown, and more than the hippocampus could be involved. R. B. is the only amnesic patient known to us where damage was limited to the hippocampus, and where data on retrograde amnesia are available. The retrograde amnesia tests given to R. B. were for the most part constructed to assess memory decade by decade, not in finer time divisions, and these tests did not detect retrograde amnesia (Fig. 5). At the same time, his performance on two other remote memory tests (Zola-Morgan *et al.*, 1986) raised the possibility that he had some retrograde amnesia covering the period just prior to the onset of his amnesia in 1978. Thus, the hippocampus may be essential to newly formed memories for a relatively short period after learning, perhaps for several months or a few years at the most. More data are needed concerning the temporal characteristics of retrograde amnesia associated with hippocampal lesions. Although additional patients with demonstrated lesions limited to the hippocampus are not readily available, valuable information about retrograde amnesia could be obtained from animal models of human amnesia (for this approach, see Salmon *et al.*, 1987).

Findings from studies of LTP suggest that the hippocampus may play a special role in associating inputs that occur simultaneously or in near succession. For example, the hippocampus may act to store conjunctions between neural events occurring in two distinct cortical locations. The NMDA receptors have been implicated in the establishment of LTP, and LTP may be maintained by morphological change at potentiated synapses. Because the hippocampus has a high concentration of NMDA receptors, information about the biochemical and biophysical properties of NMDA receptors will certainly contribute to our understanding of hippocampal function. Moreover, if LTP is an important mechanism by which the hippocampus contributes to memory function, then a number of other questions need to be asked. Exactly how long does LTP last? Does LTP occur in an animal when a task is acquired that is known to depend on the hippocampus? How does the time course of LTP compare to the time course of forgetting for such a task, and to the time course of retrograde amnesia produced by a hippocampal lesion? Once LTP is established, is the strength of LTP affected by subsequent behavioral events, such as a reminder (rehearsal) trial, a partial cue, or retrieval from memory of what was learned?

The hippocampal formation receives much, if not all, of its sensory information (other than from the olfactory system) from supramodal association cortices (see Fig. 10), and these supramodal regions project primarily to the entorhinal cortex. The information then undergoes further processing in each of the other three major divisions (the dentate gyrus, hippocampus and subicular complex) of the hippocampal formation. Ultimately, the processed information is returned to the entorhinal cortex, which originates corticofugal projections to the same polysensory regions from which it is innervated. This cascade of projections provides a means for the hippocampal formation to interact with neocortical memory storage sites. Yet, because of the extensive convergence and divergence at several stages in the hippocampal circuitry, it seems unlikely that specific point-to-point mapping of the source of information in neocortex is maintained as information traverses the hippocampal circuit. Thus, our current understanding of the anatomy of the hippocampal formation would argue against a role for the hippocampal formation in "indexing" the specific sites of cortical memory storage (e.g., Teyler and DiScenna, 1986).

The hippocampus is in a unique position to receive multimodal and highly integrated information from neocortex, to compare and combine this information, and then to influence neocortex. If the hippocampus cannot maintain specific indexing of cortical sites, then it may register relevant events and send information back to neocortex in a more diffuse manner. Even if the hippocampus acts in such a manner, it could contribute to the establishment of specific cortical representations. When an event occurs, multiple areas of neocortex may be involved in perceiving the event and representing it in short-term memory. One possible scenario is that converging projections from these cortical areas might interact in the hippocampal formation to establish LTP in a particular subset of neurons. The potentiated subset of hippocampal neurons might then generate a signal that emanates widely to neocortex. This signal from hippocampus would reach representations in neocortex through a series of stages, involving, for example, entorhinal cortex, parahippocampal gyrus, and neocortical polymodal association areas. In this way, the neuronal assemblies that had been cotemporaneously activated at specific, disparate cortical sites may be facilitated by hippocampal activity. Synaptic change related to learning might also occur at each of the stages between hippocampus and neocortex; and these changes might also be facilitated by signals from hippocampus.

During the period that LTP persists, it provides a mechanism whereby rehearsal, new learning events, or perhaps even quasi-random activity across time could serve to maintain or strengthen the set of connections in disparate cortical sites. While forgetting occurs, some aspects of the original representation, including the connections among its disparate parts, become stronger. If the hippocampus is damaged before LTP has dissipated, memory for the event will be lost to some degree— that is, retrograde amnesia will occur. If the area of damage includes entorhinal cortex or parahippocampal gyrus in addition to hippocampus, then the retrograde amnesia may well be more severe. However, after sufficient time has passed, representations in neocortex become independent of the hippocampus.

The hippocampal formation is often described as a relatively simple cortical structure. While this may be true in a general sense, recent anatomical studies have uncovered a wealth and subtlety of anatomical detail. Indeed, this intricacy of the hippocampal circuitry gives support to the notion that it can contribute in a sophisticated way to memory functions. Computer modeling of hippocampal function (see Chapter 13 of this volume) may provide the only feasible means to obtaining a detailed, accurate understanding of its contribution to memory. Realistic models will rely on quantitative information about hippocampal anatomy. In particular, indications of the specific processing function in each field of the hippocampal formation are likely to depend on determining the parameters of the neural networks that are formed by each of the cytoarchitectonic fields.

We are beginning to understand how memory is organized, what structures and connections are involved, and how they are involved. Although the ideas can still be stated in only rather general and descriptive terms, there are several reasons for optimism. First, we have seen that the information now available leads to a number of specific questions that can be addressed experimentally by cellular neurobiological and neuroanatomical studies. Second, facts and ideas developed at the level of neural systems can guide quantitative, computational approaches, which could then result in neural models and tests of specific mechanisms. It is precisely through these contacts across levels of analysis and among different approaches that the most complete and satisfying explanations are likely to emerge.

References

Amaral, D. G. (1978). *J. Comp. Neurol.* **182** (4), 851–914.

Amaral, D. G., Insausti, R., and Cowan, W. M. (1983). *Brain Res.* **275**, 263–277.

Amaral, D. G., Insausti, R., and Cowan, W. M. (1987). *J. Comp. Neurol.* **264**, 326–355.

Baddeley, A. D., and Warrington, E. K. (1970). *J. Verb. Learn. Verb. Behav.* **9**, 176–189.

Barnes, C. A., and McNaughton, B. L. (1985). *In* "Memory Systems of the Brain" (N. Weinberger, J. McGaugh, and G. Lynch, eds.), pp. 49–61. Guilford Press, New York.

Blackstad, T. W. (1956). *J. Comp. Neurol.* **105**, 417–538.

Boss, B. D., Peterson, G. M., and Cowan, W. M. (1985). *Brain Res.* **338**, 144–150.

Brooks, D. N., and Baddeley, A. D. (1976). *Neuropsychologia* **14**, 111–122.

Brown, M. W., and Cassell, M. D. (1980). *J. Physiol. (London)* **301**, 58P–59P.

Butters, N., and Cermak, L. S. (1980). "Alcoholic Korsakoff's Syndrome: An Information Processing Approach to Amnesia." Academic Press, New York.

Cermak, L. S., and O'Connor, M. (1983). *Neuropsychologia* **21**, 213–234.

Claiborne, B. J., Amaral, D. G., and Cowan, W. M. (1986). *J. Comp. Neurol.* **246**, 435–458.

Claiborne, B. J., Amaral, D. G., and Cowan, W. M. (1988). *J. Comp. Neurol.* (in press).

Cohen, N. J., and Squire, L. R. (1980). *Science* **210**, 207–209.

Cohen, N. J., and Squire, L. R. (1981). *Neuropsychologia* **19**, 337–356.

Collingridge, G. L., Kehl, S. J., and McLennan, H. (1983). *J. Physiol. (London)* **334**, 33–46.
Corkin, S. (1968). *Neuropsychologia* **6**, 225–265.
Damasio, A. R., Eslinger, P. J., Damasio, H., Van Hoesen, G. W., and Cornell, S. (1985). *Arch. Neurol. (Chicago)* **42**, 252–259.
Davis, H. P., Tribuna, J., Pulsinelli, W. A., and Volpe, B. T. (1986). *Physiol. Behav.* **37**, 387–392.
Desmond, N. L., and Levy, W. B. (1982). *J. Comp. Neurol.* **212**, 131–145.
Desmond, N. L., and Levy, W. B. (1985). *Neurosci. Lett.* **54**, 219–224.
Drachman, D. A., and Arbit, J. (1966). *Arch. Neurol. (Chicago)* **15**, 52–61.
Foster, A. C., and Fagg, G. E. (1984). *Brain Res. Rev.* **7**, 103–164.
Graf, P., Squire, L. R., and Mandler, G. (1984). *J. Exp. Psychol.: Learn., Memory, Cognit.* **10**, 164–178.
Harris, E. W., Ganong, A. H., and Cotman, C. W. (1984). *Brain Res.* **323**, 132–137.
Insausti, R., Amaral, D. G., and Cowan, W. M. (1987) (in press). *J. Comp. Neurol.* **264**, 356–395.
Ishizuka, N., Krzemieniewska, K., and Amaral, D. G. (1986). *Soc. Neurosci. Abstr.* **12** (Part 2), 1254.
Jahr, C. E., and Stevens, C. F. (1987). *Nature (London)* **325**, 522–525.
Kohler, C. (1985). *J. Comp. Neurol.* **236**, 504–522.
Kosel, K. C., Van Hoesen, G. W., and Rosene, D. L. (1982). *Brain Res.* **244**, 201–213.
Kritchevsky, M., Squire, L. R., and Zouzounis, J. (1988). *Neurology* **38**, 213–219.
Lynch, G. (1986). "Synapses, Circuits, and the Beginnings of Memory." MIT Press, Cambridge, Massachusetts.
Mahut, H., and Moss, M. (1984). *In* "Neuropsychology of Memory" (L. R. Squire and N. Butters, eds.), pp. 297–315. Guilford Press, New York.
McNaughton, B., and Morris, R. G. M. (1987). *Trends Neurosci* **10**, 408–415.
McNaughton, B., Douglas, R. M., and Goddard, G. (1978). *Brain Res.* **157**, 277–293.
Mesulam, M.-M., and Mufson, E. J. (1986). *In* "Cerebral Cortex" (A. Peters and E. G. Jones, eds.), Vol. 4, pp. 179–226. Plenum, New York.
Milner, B. (1962). *In* "Physiologie de l'hippocampe," pp. 257–272. CNRS, Paris.
Mishkin, M. A. (1978). *Nature (London)* **273**, 297–298.
Mishkin, M. A., Spiegler, B. J., Saunders, R. C., and Malamut, B. (1982). *In* "Alzheimer's Disease: A Report of Progress" (S. Corkin, K. L. Davis, J. H. Growden, and E. Usdia, eds.), pp. 235–247. Raven Press, New York.
Monaghan, D. T., Holets, V. R., Toy, D. W., and Cotman, C. W. (1983). *Nature (London)* **306**, 176–179.
Morris, R. G. M., Anderson, E., Lynch, G. S., and Baudry, M. (1986). *Nature (London)* **319**, 774–776.
Olverman, H. J., Jones, A. W., and Watkins, J. C. (1984). *Nature (London)* **307**, 460–465.
Pandya, D. N., and Yeterian, E. H. (1986). *In* "Cerebral Cortex" (A. Peters and E. G. Jones, eds.), Vol. 4, pp. 3–61. Plenum, New York.
Room, P., and Groenewegen, H. J. (1986). *J. Comp. Neurol.* **251**, 415–450.
Rose, F. C., and Symonds, C. P. (1960). *Brain* **83**, 195–212.
Rose, M. (1926). *J. Psychol. Neurol.* **34**, 1–99.
Salmon, D. P., Zola-Morgan, S., and Squire, L. R. (1987). *Psychobiology* **15**, 37–47.
Scoville, W. B., and Milner, B. (1957). *J. Neurol. Neurosurg. Psychiatry* **201**, 11–21.
Seltzer, B., and Pandya, D. N. (1976). *Exp. Neurol.* **50**, 146–160.
Seress, L. (1988). *J. Hirnforsch.* (in press).
Seress, L., and Pokorny, J. (1981). *J. Anat.* **133** (2), 181–195.
Shimamura, A. P. (1986). *Q. J. Exp. Psychol.* **38A**, 619–644.
Smith, S. J. (1987). *Trends NeuroSci. (Pers. Ed.)* **4**, 142–144.
Squire, L. R. (1984). *In* "ECT: Basic Mechanisms" (B. Lerer, R. D. Weiner, and R. H. Belmaker, eds.), pp. 156–163. John Libbey, London.
Squire, L. R. (1987). "Memory and Brain." Oxford Univ. Press, London and New York.

Squire, L. R., and Shimamura, A. P. (1986). *Behav. Neurosci.* **100**, 866–877.

Squire, L. R., and Zola-Morgan, S. (1983). *In* "The Physiological Basis of Memory" (J. A. Deutsch, ed.), 2nd ed., pp. 199–268. Academic Press, New York.

Squire, L. R., and Zola-Morgan, S. (1985). *In* "Memory Dysfunctions: An Integration of Animal and Human Research from Preclinical and Clinical Perspectives" (D. Olton, S. Corkin, and E. Gamzu, eds.), pp. 137–149. N.Y. Acad. Sci., New York.

Squire, L. R., Slater, P. C., and Chace, P. M. (1975). *Science* **187**, 77–79.

Squire, L. R., Cohen, N. J., and Zouzounis, J. A. (1984). *Neuropsychologia* **22**, 145–152.

Squire, L. R., and Shimamura, A. P. (1986). *Behav. Neurosci.* **100**, 866–877.

Squire, L. R., Shimamura, A. P., and Graf, P. (1987). *Neuropsychologia* **25**, 195–210.

Storm-Mathisen, J. (1981). *Adv. Biochem. Psychopharmacol.* **27**, 43–55.

Storm-Mathisen, J. (1984). *Neuroscience* **111**, 79–100.

Swanson, L. W., and Kohler, C. (1986). *J. Neurosci.* **6** (10), 3010–3023.

Swanson, L. W., Teyler, T. J., and Thompson, R. F. (1982). *Neurosci. Res. Program Bull.* **20**, 613–769.

Talland, G. A. (1965). "Deranged Memory." Academic Press, New York.

Tamamaki, N., Abe, K., and Nojyo, Y. (1987). *Brain Res.* **412**, 156–160.

Teuber, H.-L., Milner, B., and Vaughan, H. G. (1968). *Neuropsychologia* **6**, 267–282.

Teyler, T. J., and DiScenna, P. (1986). *Behav. Neurosci.* **100**, 147–154.

Van Hoesen, G. W., and Pandya, D. N. (1975a). *Brain Res.* **95**, 1–24.

Van Hoesen, G. W., and Pandya, D. N. (1975b). *Brain Res.* **95**, 39–59.

Van Hoesen, G. W., Pandya, D. N., and Butters, N. (1975). *Brain Res.* **95**, 25–38.

Van Hoesen, G. W., Rosene, D. L., and Mesulam, M. M. (1979). *Science* **205**, 608–610.

Volpe, B. T., and Hirst, W. (1983). *Arch. Neurol. (Chicago)* **40**, 436–445.

Volpe, B. T., Pulsinelli, W. A., Tribuna, J., and Davis, H. A. (1984). *Stroke* **15**, 558–562.

Wilson, C. O., Isokawa-Akesson, M., Babb, T. L., Engel, J., Jr., Cahan, L. D., and Crandall, P. H. (1987). *In* "Fundamental Mechanisms of Human Brain Function" (J. Engel, Jr. *et al.*, eds.), pp. 23–34. Raven Press, New York.

Witter, M. P., and Groenewegen, H. J. (1984). *J. Comp. Neurol.* **224**, 371–385.

Witter, M. P., Griffioen, A. W., Jorritsma-Byham, B., and Krijnen, J. L. M. (1988a). *Neurosci. Letters* **85**, 193–198.

Witter, M. P., Van Hoesen, G., and Amaral, D. G. (1988b). *J. Neurosci.* (in press).

Wolf, G., Schunzel, G., and Storm-Mathisen, J. (1984). *J. Hirnforsch.* **25**, 249–253.

Zola-Morgan, S., Squire, L. R., and Amaral, D. G. (1986). *J. Neurosci.* **6**, 2950–2966.

13

Functions of Neuronal Networks in the Hippocampus and Neocortex in Memory

Edmund T. Rolls

I. Functions of the Primate Hippocampus in Memory

It is known that damage to certain regions of the temporal lobe in humans produces anterograde amnesia evident as a major deficit following the damage in learning to recognize new stimuli (Scoville and Milner, 1957; Milner, 1972; Squire, 1986; this volume, Chapter 12). The anterograde amnesia has been attributed to damage to the hippocampus, which is within the temporal lobe, and to its associated pathways such as the fornix (Scoville and Milner, 1957; Milner, 1972; Gaffan, 1974, 1977), but this has been questioned, and instead it has been suggested that damage to both the hippocampus and the amygdala is crucial in producing anterograde amnesia, in that combined but not separate damage to the hippocampus and amygdala produced severe difficulty with visual and tactual recognition tasks in the monkey (Mishkin, 1978, 1989, 1982; Murray and Mishkin, 1984, 1985). In investigations of the particular aspects of memory for which the hippocampus may be essential, it has been shown that monkeys with damage to the hippocampo–fornical system have a learning deficit on memory tasks that require them to make associations between a stimulus—for example, a picture—and a spatial motor response such as touching one part of a screen (Gaffan, 1985; Rupniak and Gaffan, 1987), and are also impaired on memory tasks that require combinations of stimulus attributes with their locations in space to be processed together, such as memory not only for which object was shown but where it was shown (Gaffan and Saunders, 1985). Further, humans with right temporal-lobe damage are also impaired in conditional spatial response and object–place memory tasks (Petrides, 1985; Smith and Milner, 1981).

In order to analyze the functions being performed by the hippo-

240

campus in memory, the activity of 1510 single hippocampal neurons was recorded in rhesus monkeys learning and performing these memory tasks known to be impaired by damage to the hippocampus or fornix (Rolls *et al.*, 1989; Miyashita *et al.*, 1989; Cahusac *et al.*, 1989).

In an object–place memory task in which the monkey had to remember not only which object had been seen in the previous 7–15 trials but also the position in which it had appeared on a video monitor, neurons were found that responded differentially depending on which place on the monitor screen objects were shown (Rolls *et al.*, 1989). These neurons comprised 9.4% of the population recorded. It is notable that these neurons responded to particular positions in space (whereas "place" cells in the rat respond when the rat is in a particular place; O'Keefe, 1983). In addition, 2.4% of neurons responded more to a stimulus the first time it was shown in a particular position than the second time. These neurons thus responded to a combination of information about the stimulus being shown and about position in space, for only by responding to a combination of this information could the neurons respond only when a stimulus was shown for the first time in a certain position in space.

In tasks in which the monkeys had to acquire associations between visual stimuli and spatial responses, 14.2% of the neurons responded to particular combinations of stimuli and responses (Miyashita *et al.*, 1989). For example, in a task in which the monkey had to perform one response (touching a screen three times) when one visual stimulus was shown, but had to perform a withholding response for 3 sec to obtain reward when a different stimulus was shown (Gaffan, 1985), 9.2% of the neurons responded to one of the stimuli if it was linked to one of the responses in this task. The same neurons typically did not respond if the same stimuli or the same responses were used in different tasks, or if other stimuli were associated with the same responses in this task. Thus these neurons responded to a combination of a particular stimulus with a particular spatial motor response (Miyashita *et al.*, 1988).

It was possible to study the activity of 41 hippocampal neurons while the monkeys learned new associations between visual stimuli and spatial responses. In some cases it was possible to show that the activity of these neurons became modified during this learning (Cahusac *et al.*, 1986, 1989). Interestingly, 33% of the neurons that altered their responses during this learning showed a sustained differential response, but 67% of the neurons differentiated between the stimuli only at or just before the monkey learned the task, and stopped differentiating after 5–10 more trials. This is consistent with the possibility discussed below that the neurons that show large sustained differential responses inhibit the other neurons that show transient modification, so that as a result of competition not all neurons are allocated to one stimulus–spatial response association.

These results show that hippocampal neurons in the primate have

responses related to certain types of memory. One type of memory involves complex conjunctions of environmental information—for example,
when information about position in space (perhaps reflecting information
from the parietal cortex) must be memorized in conjunction with what
that object is (perhaps reflecting information from the temporal lobe visual areas), so that where a particular object was seen in space can be
remembered. The hippocampus is ideally placed anatomically for detecting such conjunctions, in that it receives highly processed information
from association areas such as the parietal cortex (conveying information
about position in space), the inferior temporal visual cortex (conveying
a visual specification of an object), and the superior temporal cortex
(conveying an auditory specification of a stimulus) (Van Hoesen, 1982)
(see Fig. 5). The positions of stimuli in space may be represented by the
firing of hippocampal neurons as described above so that conjunctions
of, for example, objects and their position can be formed. It is also suggested that one neurophysiological mechanism by which "place" cells
in the rat (see O'Keefe, 1983) may be formed is by conjunction learning
of sets of simultaneously occurring stimuli in different parts of space,
each set of which defines a place.

II. Computational Theory of
the Hippocampus

A possible theoretical basis for these results, and in particular how the
hippocampus may perform the conjunction or combination learning just
described, is now considered.

A schematic diagram of the connections of the hippocampus is
shown in Fig. 1. One feature is that there is a sequence of stages, in
each of which there is a major set of input axons that connect via a form
of matrix with the output neurons of that stage. The type of computation
that could be performed by one of these stages is considered first.

The perforant path connections with the dentate granule cells may
be taken as an example. A version of this represented as a simplified
matrix is shown in Fig. 2. Although the perforant path makes one set
of synapses with the output neurons in a form of matrix, the matrix is
clearly very different from an association matrix memory, in that in the
hippocampal system there is no unconditioned stimulus that forces the
output neurons to fire (see Rolls, 1987). Nor is there for each output cell
a climbing fiber that acts as a teacher as in the cerebellum (see Ito, 1984;
see Chapters 9 and 10 in this volume). In the hippocampal circuit there
is apparently no teacher—that is, this appears to be an example of an
unsupervised learning system. The following describes one mode of operation for such a network. Later, properties of the hippocampus that
suggest that it may operate in this way are discussed.

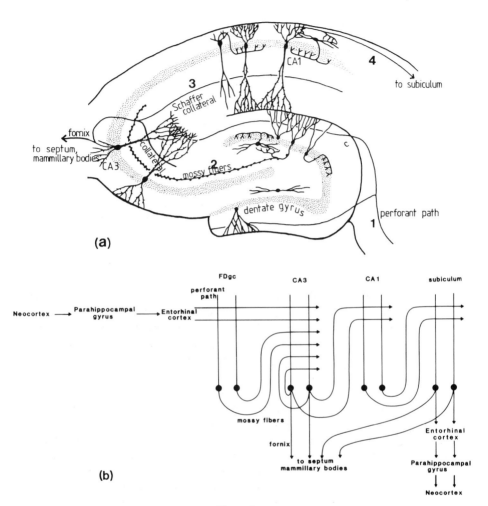

Figure 1.
(a) Representation of connections within the hippocampus. Inputs reach
the hippocampus through the perforant path (1), which makes synapses
with the dendrites of the dentate granule cells and also with the apical
dendrites of the CA3 pyramidal cells. The dentate granule cells project via
the mossy fibers (2) to the CA3 pyramidal cells. The well-developed
recurrent collateral system of the CA3 cells is indicated. The CA3
pyramidal cells project via the Schaffer collaterals (3) to the CA1 pyramidal
cells, which in turn have connections (4) to the subiculum. (b) Schematic
representation of the connections of the hippocampus, showing also that
the cerebral cortex (neocortex) is connected to the hippocampus via the
parahippocampal gyrus and entorhinal cortex, and that the hippocampus
projects back to the neocortex via the subiculum, entorhinal cortex, and
parahippocampal gyrus.

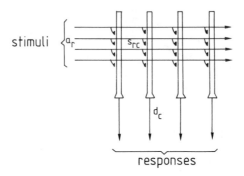

Figure 2.

A matrix for competitive learning in which the input stimuli are presented along the rows of the input axons (a_r), which make modifiable synapses (s_{rc}) with the dendrites of the output neurons, which form the columns (d_c) of the matrix.

Consider a matrix memory of the form shown in Fig. 2 in which the strengths of the synapses between horizontal axons and the vertical dendrites are initially random *(postulate 1)*. Because of these random initial synaptic weights, different input patterns on the horizontal axons will tend to activate different output neurons (in this case, granule cells). The tendency for each pattern to select or activate different neurons can then be enhanced by providing mutual inhibition between the output neurons, to prevent too many neurons responding to that stimulus *(postulate 2)*. This competitive interaction can be viewed as enhancing the differences in the firing rates of the output cells [cf. the contrast enhancement described by Grossberg (1982)]. Synaptic modification then occurs according to the rules of long-term potentiation in the hippocampus, namely, that synapses between active afferent axons and strongly activated postsynaptic neurons increase in strength (see McNaughton, 1983; Levy, 1985; Kelso *et al.*, 1986; Wigstrom *et al.*, 1986; see Chapter 14 of this volume) *(postulate 3)*. The effect of this modification is that the next time the same stimulus is repeated, the neuron responds more (because of the strengthened synapses), more inhibition of other neurons occurs, and then further modification to produce even greater selectivity is produced. The response of the system thus climbs over repeated iterations. One effect of this observed in simulations is that a few neurons then obtain such strong synaptic weights that almost any stimulus that has any input to that neuron will succeed in activating it. The solution to this is to limit the total synaptic weight that each output (postsynaptic) neuron can receive. In simulations this is performed by normalizing the sum of the synaptic weights on each neuron to a constant (e.g., 1.0) (cf. von der Malsburg, 1973; Rumelhart and Zipser, 1986). This has the effect of distributing the output neurons evenly between the different input patterns received by the network.

A simulation of the operation of such a matrix is shown in Fig. 3. It is shown that the network effectively selects different output neurons to respond to different combinations of active input horizontal lines. It thus performs a type of classification in which different complex input patterns are encoded economically onto a few output lines. It should be noted that this classification finds natural clusters in the input events; orthogonalizes the classes in that overlap in input events can become coded onto output neurons with less overlap, and in that many active input lines may be coded onto few active output lines; and does not allocate neurons to events that never occur (cf. Marr, 1970, 1971; Rumelhart and Zipser, 1986; Grossberg, 1982). It may be noted that there is no special correspondence between the input pattern and which output lines are selected. It is thus not useful for any associative mapping between an input and an output event, and is thus different from linear associative matrix memories (Rolls, 1987). Instead, this type of matrix finds associations or correlations between input events (which are expressed as sets of simultaneously active horizontal input lines or axons), allocates output neurons to reflect the complex event, and stores the required association between the input lines onto the few output neurons activated by each complex input event.

There is some evidence that in the hippocampus the synapses between inactive axons and active output neurons become weaker (see McNaughton, 1983; Levy, 1985). The effect of this in the learning system described would be to facilitate accurate and rapid classification, in that weakening synapses onto a postsynaptic neuron from axons that are not active when it is strongly activated would reduce the probability that it will respond to a stimulus that must be placed into a different class. It is also of interest that (postulate 4) it is not physiologically unreasonable that the total synaptic strength onto a postsynaptic neuron is somewhat fixed (Levy and Desmond, 1985).

Another feature of hippocampal circuitry is the mossy-fiber system, which connects the granule cells of the dentate gyrus to the CA3 pyramidal cells of the hippocampus. Each mossy fiber forms approximately 10 "mosses," in which there are dendrites of perhaps five different CA3 pyramidal cells. Thus each dentate granule cell may contact approximately 50 CA3 pyramidal cells (in the mouse; see Braitenberg and Schuz, 1983). In the rat, each mossy fiber forms approximately 14 "mosses" or contacts with CA3 cells, there are 1×10^6 dentate granule cells and thus 14×10^6 mosses onto 0.18×10^6 CA3 cells (D. Amaral, personal communication), and thus each CA3 pyramidal cell may be contacted by approximately 78 dentate granule cells. This means that (in the rat) the probability that a CA3 cell is contacted by a given dentate granule cell is 78 synapses/10^6 granule cells = 0.000078. These mossy-fiber synapses are very large, presumably because with such a relatively small number on each CA3 cell dendrite (and a much smaller number active at any one time), each synapse must be relatively strong.

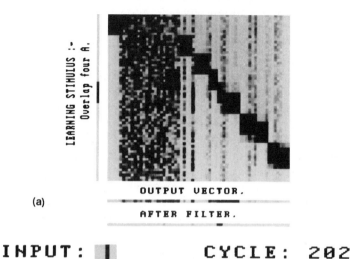

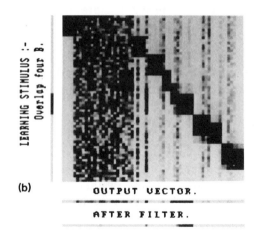

Figure 3.

Simulation of learning in a competitive matrix memory. The architecture is
as shown in Fig. 2, except that there are 64 horizontal axons and 64
vertical dendrites, which form the row and columns, respectively, of the
64 × 64 matrix of synapses. The strength of each synapse, which was
initially random, is indicated by the darkness of each pixel. The activity of
each of the 64 input axons is represented in the 64-element vector at the
left of the diagram by the darkness of each pixel. The output firing of the

One effect that can be achieved by this low probability of contact of a particular dentate granule cell with a particular pyramidal cell is pattern separation. This is achieved in the following way. Consider a pattern of firing present over a set of dentate granule cells. The probability that any two CA3 pyramidal cells receive synapses from a similar subset of the dentate granule cells is very low (because of the low probability of contact of any one dentate granule cell with a pyramidal cell), so that each CA3 pyramidal cell is influenced by a very different subset of the active dentate granule cells. Thus each pyramidal cell effectively samples a very small subset of the active granule cells, and it is therefore likely that each CA3 pyramidal cell will respond differently to the others, so that in this way pattern separation is achieved. [The effect is similar to codon formation described in other contexts by Marr (1970).] With mod-ifiability of the mossy-fiber synapses, CA3 neurons learn to respond to just those subsets of activity that do occur in dentate granule cells. More-over, because of the low probability of contact, and because of the com-petition between the CA3 neurons, the patterns that occur are evenly distributed over different ensembles of CA3 neurons. This pattern sep-aration effect can be seen in Fig. 4. (It may be noted that even if com-petition does not operate in this system to increase orthogonality, then the low probability of connections just described would nevertheless mean that the hippocampus could operate to produce relatively orthog-onal representations.)

It is notable that in addition to the mossy fiber inputs, the CA3 pyramidal cells also receive inputs directly from perforant path fibers

---

vertical neurons is represented in the same way by the output vectors at the bottom of the diagram. The upper output vector is the result of multiplying the input stimulus through the matrix of synaptic weights. The vector resulting from the application of competition between the output neurons (which produces contrast enhancement between the elements or neurons of the vector) is shown below by the vector labeled "after filter." The state of the matrix is shown after 203 cycles, in each of which stimuli with 8 of 64 active axons was presented and the matrix allowed to learn as described in the text. The stimuli were presented in random sequence, and consisted of a set of vectors that overlapped in 0, 1, 2, 3, 4, 5, or 6 positions with the next vector in the set. The columns of the matrix were sorted after the learning to bring similar columns together, so that the types of neuron formed, and the pattern of synapses formed on their dendrites, can be seen easily. The dendrites with random patterns of synapses have not been allocated to any of the input stimuli. It is shown that application of one of the input stimuli (overlap four A) produced one pattern of firing of the output neurons, and that application of input stimulus overlap four B produced a different pattern of firing of the output neurons. Thus the stimuli were correctly classified by the matrix as being different.

248   E. T. Rolls

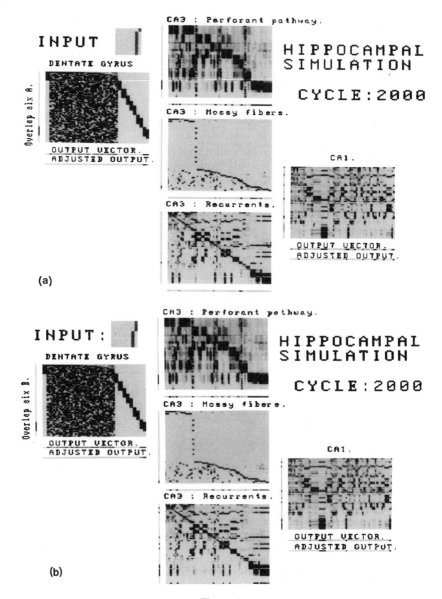

Figure 4.
Hippocampal stimulation. Conventions as in Fig. 3. The dentate gyrus is
shown as a competition matrix at the left, receiving input stimuli from the
perforant path. The vertical dendrites of the CA3 pyramidal cells extend
throughout the three submatrices shown in the middle. The middle
submatrix receives the output of the dentate granule cells via the mossy
fibers with potentially powerful synapses and a low contact probability,
and operates as a competition matrix. Pattern separation can be seen to
operate in that input vectors are converted into output vectors with many
elements activated by the inputs about which the submatrix has learned,

(see Figs. 1 and 2). This is not a sparse projection, in that each pyramidal cell may receive on the order of 2300 such synapses. [This is calculated using the evidence that of 15 mm of total dendritic length with 10,000 spines, approximately 3.5 mm (range 2.5–4.5 mm) is in the lacunosum moleculare and thus receives inputs from the perforant path (D. G. Amaral, personal communication).] What would be the effect of this input together with the very sparse, but strong, synapses from the mossy fibers? One effect is that the mossy-fiber input would cause the pattern of synapses (considered as a vector) on each pyramidal cell to point in a different direction in a multidimensional space. However, the precise direction in that multidimensional space could not be well specified by the relatively small number of mossy-fiber synapses onto each CA3 pyramidal cell. However, once pointed to that part of space by the mossy fibers, a particular cell would show cooperative Hebbian learning between its activation by the mossy input and the direct perforant path input, allowing the direct input to come by learning to specify the exact direction of that cell in multidimensional space much more effectively than by the coarse mossy-fiber input alone. This effect can be seen in Fig. 4. The relative weighting in this simulation was that the mossy-fiber input had an effect on each neuron that was five times greater than that of the direct perforant path input. Thus it is suggested that the combination of the sparse mossy-fiber input and the direct perforant path input is to achieve pattern separation, and at the same time to allow the response of the neuron to be determined not just by the sparse mossy-fiber input, but much more finely by making use in addition of the direct perforant path input.

An additional feature of the hippocampus, which is developed in the CA3 pyramidal cells in particular, is the presence of strong recurrent collaterals, which return from the output of the matrix to cross over the neurons of the matrix, as shown in Figs. 1 and 2. This anatomy immediately suggests that this is an autoassociation matrix. The effect of such recurrent collaterals is to make that part of the matrix into an autoassociation (or autocorrelation) matrix. The autoassociation arises because the output of the matrix, expressed as the firing rate of the CA3

---

and in that different output vectors are produced for even quite similar input vectors. The upper CA3 submatrix operates as a competition matrix with a direct perforant path input. The lower CA3 submatrix operates as an autoassociation matrix (formed by the recurrent collaterals). The output of the CA3 cells (summed vertically up and down the dendrite) is then used as the input (via the Schaffer collaterals) to the CA1 cells, which operate as a competition matrix. The states of the matrices after 2000 presentations of the same set of stimuli used for Fig. 3 are shown. One point demonstrated is that two very similar stimuli, overlap six A in Fig. 4a, and overlap six B in Fig. 4b, produce output vectors at CA1 that are relatively orthogonal to each other.

pyramidal cells, is fed back along the horizontally running axons so that the pattern of activity in this part of the matrix (the CA3 pyramidal cells) is associated with itself (see, e.g., Kohonen et al., 1981; Rolls, 1987a). It can be noted here that for this suggestion to be the case, the synapses of the recurrent collaterals would have to be modifiable, and the modification rule would require alteration of synaptic strength when both the presynaptic fiber and the postsynaptic dendrite were strongly activated. Further, the probability of contact of the neurons in the autoassociation matrix must not be very low if it is to operate usefully (see Marr, 1971). Given that the region of the CA3 cell dendrites on which the recurrent collaterals synapse is long (approximately 11.5 mm), and that the total dendritic length is approximately 15 mm and has approximately 10,000 spines (D. G. Amaral, personal communication), approximately 7700 synapses per CA3 pyramidal cell could be devoted to recurrent collaterals, which with 180,000 CA3 neurons in the rat makes the probability of contact between the CA3 neurons 0.043. This is high enough for the system to operate usefully as an autoassociation memory (see Marr, 1971). It is remarkable that the contact probability is so high, and also that the CA3 recurrent collateral axons travel so widely in all directions that they can potentially come close to almost all other CA3 neurons (D. G. Amaral, personal communication).

The importance of the autoassociation performed by this part of the matrix is that it forms a recognition memory, with all the advantageous emergent properties of a matrix memory, such as completion, generalization, and graceful degradation (see Kohonen et al., 1977, 1981; Kohonen, 1984; Rolls, 1987). One property that is particularly relevant here is completion, in that if part of a stimulus (or event) occurs, then the autoassociation part of the matrix completes that event. Completion may operate particularly effectively here, because it operates after the granule-cell stage, which will reduce the proportion of neurons firing to represent an input event to a low number partly because of the low probability of contact of the granule cells with the CA3 pyramidal cells. It is under these conditions that the simple autocorrelation effect can reconstruct the whole of one pattern without interference, which would arise if too high a proportion of the input neurons was active. It is of interest that a scheme of this type, although expressed in a different way to the autoassociation matrix formulation, was proposed by Marr in 1971. Another effect of the autoassociation matrix is that patterns of activity that are not similar to those already learned by this type of recognition memory are lost, so that noisy patterns can be cleaned up by the autoassociation matrix. It is further notable that these completion and cleaning-up processes benefit from several iterations (repeated cycles) of the autoassociation feedback effect. It has been suggested by B. McNaughton (personal communication, 1987) that one function of hippocampal theta activity may be to allow this autoassociation effect produced by the recurrent collaterals to cycle for several iterations (in a period of approximately 50 msec), and then to stop, so that the system can operate again with maximal sensitivity to new inputs received on the mossy fiber and perforant path systems by the CA3 cells.

The CA1 pyramidal cells that receive from the CA3 cells are considered to form a further stage of competitive learning, which has the effect of further classification of signals received, perhaps enabled by the pattern of connections within the hippocampus to form these classifications over inputs received from any part of the association neocortex. The firing of the CA1 cells would thus achieve a much more economical and orthogonal classification of signals than that present in the perforant path input to the hippocampus. These signals are then returned to the association neocortex via the subiculum, entorhinal cortex, and parahippocampal gyrus, as indicated in Figs. 1 and 2. It is suggested below that one role that these economical (in terms of the number of activated fibers) and relatively orthogonal signals play in neocortical function is to guide information storage or consolidation in the neocortex.

It may be noted that multilayer networks (such as the hippocampus) can potentially solve classes of problems that cannot be solved in principle by single-layer nets (Rumelhart and Zipser, 1986). This is because subcategories formed in an early stage of processing can enable a later stage to find solutions or categories that are not linearly separable in the input information space.

Having considered the computational theory of how the hippocampal circuitry may function, we can now turn to a systems-level analysis, in which the inputs and outputs of the hippocampus are considered, and the function performed by the hippocampus in relation to overall brain function can be formulated.

III. Systems-Level Theory of Hippocampal Function

First the anatomical connections of the primate hippocampus with the rest of the brain will be considered, in order to provide a basis for considering how the computational ability of the hippocampus could be used by the rest of the brain.

The hippocampus receives inputs by two main routes, the entorhinal cortex and the fimbria/fornix. The entorhinal cortex (area 28) provides it with extensive inputs from the neocortex (see Fig. 5). Thus all temporal neocortical areas project to area 35, the perirhinal cortex, or to area TF–TH, in the parahippocampal gyrus, which in turn projects to the entorhinal cortex (Van Hoesen and Pandya, 1975a,b; Van Hoesen, 1982; Amaral, 1987). The parietal cortex (area 7) projects to area TF–TH, and thus can potentially influence the hippocampus. The orbitofrontal

AFFERENT CONNECTIONS   EFFERENT CONNECTIONS

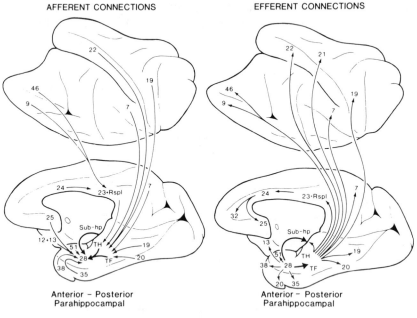

Anterior – Posterior   Anterior – Posterior
Parahippocampal   Parahippocampal

Figure 5.

Connections of the primate hippocampus with the neocortex (from Van
Hoesen, 1982). A medial view of the macaque brain is shown below, and a
lateral view is shown inverted above. The hippocampus receives its inputs
via the parahippocampal gyrus, areas TF and TH, and the entorhinal
cortex, area 28. The return projections to the neocortex (shown on the
right) pass through the same areas. Cortical areas 19, 20, and 21 are visual
association areas, 22 is auditory association cortex, 7 is parietal association
cortex, and 9, 46, 12, and 13 are frontal cortical association areas.

cortex, areas 12 and 13, projects directly to the entorhinal cortex (Van
Hoesen et al., 1975). In addition, the entorhinal cortex receives inputs
from the amygdala. The entorhinal cortex itself projects via the perforant
path to reach primarily the dentate granule cells of the hippocampus
proper. Thus by these routes the hippocampus receives information after
it has been highly processed through the temporal, parietal, and frontal
cortices. It must thus be of great importance for hippocampal function
in the primate that by its main input, the perforant path, it receives
information from the highest parts of the neocortex. There are also inputs
to the hippocampus via the fimbria/fornix from the cholinergic cells of
the medial septum and the adjoining limb of the diagonal band of Broca.
The hippocampus also receives a noradrenergic input from the locus
coeruleus, and a 5-hydroxytryptamine (5-HT) input from the median
raphe nucleus.

A major output of the hippocampus arises from the hippocampal
pyramidal cells, and projects back via the subiculum to the entorhinal

cortex, which in turn has connections back to area TF–TH, which in turn projects back to the neocortical areas from which it receives inputs (Van Hoesen, 1982) (see Figs. 5 and 1). Thus the hippocampus can potentially influence the neocortical regions from which it receives inputs. This is the pathway suggested as being involved in guiding memory storage in the neocortex. A second efferent projection of the hippocampal system reaches the subiculum from the CA1 pyramidal cells, and travels via the fimbria and (postcommissural) fornix to the anterior thalamus, and to the mammillary bodies, which in turn project to the anterior thalamus. The anterior thalamus in turn projects into the cingulate cortex, which itself has connections to the supplementary motor cortex, providing a potential route for the hippocampus to influence motor output (Van Hoesen, 1982). It is suggested that functions of the hippocampus in, for example, conditional spatial response learning utilize this output path to the motor system.

The connections of the hippocampus with other parts of the brain, and the internal connections and synaptic modifiability described above, suggest that the hippocampus should be able to detect, and classify onto a few specifically responding neurons, specific conjunctions of complex (cortically processed) events, such as that a particular object (presumably reflecting temporal lobe visual processing) has appeared in a particular position in space (presumably reflecting parietal input). Another example might be that a particular stimulus should be associated with a particular spatial motor response. It has been shown above that this is the type of quite specific information that comes to activate different hippocampal neurons while monkeys are performing object–place memory and conditional spatial response learning tasks. Indeed, the neurophysiological findings described above provide evidence that supports the model of hippocampal function just described. The model is also supported by the evidence that during learning of conditional spatial responses some hippocampal neurons start, but then stop, showing differential responses to the different stimuli, consistent with competitive interactions between hippocampal neurons during learning, so that only some hippocampal neurons become allocated to any one learned event or contingency (see above).

The analyses above have shown that the hippocampus receives from high-order areas of association cortex; is able by virtue of the large number of synapses on its dendrites to detect conjunctions of events even when these are widely separated in information space, with their origin from quite different cortical areas; allocates neurons to code efficiently for these conjunctions probably using a competitive learning mechanism; and has connections back to the neocortical areas from which it receives, as well as to subcortical structures via the fimbria/fornix system. What could be achieved by this system? It appears that the long-term storage of information is not in the hippocampus, at least in humans, in that damage to the hippocampus in humans does not necessarily result in major retrograde amnesia (Squire, 1986; this volume, chapter 12). On the other hand, the hippocampus does appear to be necessary for the storage of certain types of information (characterized by the description declarative, or knowing that, as contrasted with procedural, or knowing how). How could the hippocampus then be involved in the storage of information?

The suggestion that is made on the basis of these and the other findings described above is that the hippocampus is specialized to detect the best way in which to store information, and then by the return paths to the neocortex directs memory storage there. Clearly the hippocampus, with its large number of synapses on each neuron and its potentiation type of learning, is able to detect when there is coherence (i.e., conjunctive activation of arbitrary sets of its input fibers), and is able, as indicated both theoretically and by recordings made in the behaving monkey, to allocate neurons to economically (i.e., with relatively few neurons active) code for each complex input event. Such neurons could then represent an efficient way in which to store information, in that redundancy would effectively have been removed from the input signal. In a sense, the optimal way in which to build high-level feature analyzers could be determined by the hippocampus. It should be noted that this theory is not inconsistent with the possibility that the hippocampus provides a working memory, in that in the present theory the hippocampus sets up a representation using Hebbian learning, which is useful in determining how information can best be stored in the neocortex. [The representation found by the hippocampus could provide a useful working memory (see Olton, 1983), and indeed in the object–place memory task described above the object and place combinations formed onto single hippocampal neurons would provide a useful working memory. It may be that by understanding the operations performed by the hippocampus at the neuronal network level, it can be seen how the hippocampus could contribute to several functions that are not necessarily inconsistent.]

The question then arises of where the long-term storage occurs, and how it may be directed by the hippocampus. Now the hippocampus is reciprocally connected via the subiculum and entorhinal cortex with the parahippocampal gyrus, which in turn is reciprocally connected with many high-order areas of association neocortex (see Fig. 5). It is therefore possible that the actual storage takes place in the parahippocampal gyrus, and that this might be particularly appropriate for multimodal memories. However, having detected that, for example, a visual stimulus is regularly associated with an event in another modality such as a response, it might be useful to direct the unimodal representation of that visual image, so that it is stored efficiently and can provide a useful input to the multimodal conjunction store. Thus it is suggested that return pathways (for example, via the parahippocampal gyrus) to unimodal cortex (for example, inferior temporal cortex, area TE) might be used to direct uni-modal storage, too, by contributing to detection of the most economical way in which to store representations of stimuli.

The question of how the hippocampal output is used by the neocortex will be considered next. Given that the hippocampal output returns to the neocortex, a theory of backprojections in the neocortex will be needed. This is developed next. By way of introduction to this, it may be noted that which particular hippocampal neurons happen to represent a complex input event is not determined by any teacher or forcing (unconditioned) stimulus. Thus the neocortex must be able to utilize the signal rather cleverly. One possibility is that any neocortical neuron with a number of afferents active at the same time that hippocampal return fibers in its vicinity are active modifies its responses, so that it comes to respond better to those afferents the next time they occur. This learning by the cortex would involve a Hebb-like learning mechanism. It may be noted that one function served by what are thus in effect backprojections from the hippocampus is some guidance for or supervision of neocortical learning. It is a problem of unsupervised learning systems that they can detect local conjunctions efficiently, but that these are not necessarily those of most use to the whole system. It is proposed that it is exactly this problem that the hippocampus helps to solve, by detecting useful conjunctions globally (i.e., over the whole of information space), and then directing storage locally at earlier stages of processing so that filters are built locally that provide representations of input stimuli that are useful for later processing.

IV. Theoretical Significance of Backprojections in the Neocortex

The forward and backward projections that will be considered are shown in Fig. 6 [for further anatomical information see Peters and Jones (1984)]. In primary sensory cortical areas, the main extrinsic "forward" input is from the thalamus and ends in layer 4, where synapses are formed onto spiny stellate cells. These in turn project heavily onto pyramidal cells in layers 3 and 2, which in turn send projections forward to terminate strongly in layer 4 of the next cortical layer [on small pyramidal cells in layer 4 or on the basal dendrites of the layer-2 and -3 (superficial) pyramidal cells]. (Although the forward afferents end strongly in layer 4, the forward afferents have some synapses also onto the basal dendrites of the layer-2 pyramidal cells, as well as onto layer-6 pyramidal cells and inhibitory interneurons). Inputs reach the layer-5 (deep) pyramidal cells from the pyramidal cells in layers 2 and 3 (Martin, 1984), and it is the deep pyramidal cells that send backprojections to end in layer 1 of the

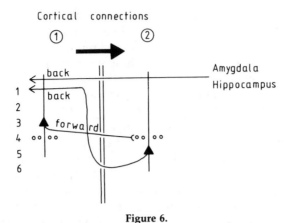

Figure 6.
Schematic diagram of forward and backward projections in the neocortex.
The superficial pyramidal cells (triangles) in layers 2 and 3 project forward
to terminate in layer 4 of the next cortical area. The deep pyramidal cells
in the next area project back (mainly) to layer 1 of the preceding cortical
area, in which there are apical dendrites of pyramidal cells. The
hippocampus and amygdala also are the source of backprojections that
end (mainly) in layer 1. Spiny stellate cells are represented by small circles
in layer 4. See text for further details.

preceding cortical area (see Fig. 6), where there are apical dendrites of
pyramidal cells. There are few current theories about the functions sub-
served by the cortico–cortical backprojections, even though there are
almost as many backprojecting as forward-projecting axons. It is important to note that in addition to the axons and their terminals in layer
1 from the succeeding cortical stage, there are also axons and terminals
in layer 1 in many stages of the cortical hierarchy from the amygdala
and (via the subiculum, entorhinal cortex, and parahippocampal cortex)
from the hippocampal formation (see Fig. 6) (Van Hoesen, 1981; Turner,
1981; Amaral and Price, 1984; Amaral, 1986, 1987). The amygdala and
hippocampus are stages of information processing at which the different
sensory modalities (such as vision, hearing, touch, and taste for the
amygdala) are brought together, so that correlations between inputs in
different modalities can be detected in these regions, but not at prior
cortical processing stages in each modality, as these cortical processing
stages are unimodal. As a result of bringing together the two modalities,
significant correspondences between the two modalities can be detected.
One example might be that a particular visual stimulus is associated with
the taste of food. Another example might be that another visual stimulus
is associated with painful touch. Thus at these stages of processing, but
not before, the significance of, for example, visual and auditory stimuli
can be detected and signalled, and sending this information back to the
neocortex thus can provide a signal that indicates to the cortex that in-

formation should be stored, but even more than this, provides an orthogonal signal that could help the neocortex to store the information
efficiently.

The way in which backprojections could assist learning in the cortex
can be considered using the architecture shown in Fig. 7. The (forward)
input stimulus occurs as a vector applied to (layer-3) cortical pyramidal
cells through modifiable synapses in the standard way for a competitive
net. (If it is a primary cortical area, the input stimulus is at least partly
relayed through spiny stellate cells, which may help to normalize and
orthogonalize the input patterns in a preliminary way before the patterns
are applied to the layer-3 pyramidal cells. If it is a nonprimary cortical
area, the cortico–cortical forward axons may end more strongly on the
basal dendrites of neurons in the superficial cortical layers.) The lower
set of synapses on the pyramidal cells would then start by competitive
learning to set up representations on the lower parts of these neurons,
which would represent correlations in the input information space and
could be said to correspond to features in the input information space,
where a feature is defined simply as the representation of a correlation
in the input information space.

Consider now the application of one of the (forward) input stimulus
vectors with the conjunctive application of a pattern vector via the backprojection axons with terminals in layer 1. Given that all the synapses
in the matrix start with random weights, some of the pyramidal cells
will by chance be strongly influenced both by the (forward) input stim-

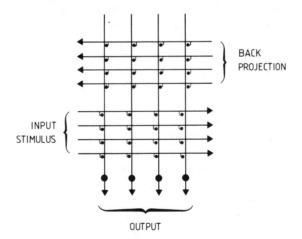

Figure 7.
The architecture used to simulate the properties of backprojections. The
forward-projected ("input stimulus") and backprojected axons make Hebb
modifiable synapses onto the same set of vertical dendrites, which
represent cortical pyramidal cells.

ulus and by the backprojecting vector. These strongly activated neurons will then compete with each other as in a standard competitive net, to produce contrast enhancement of their firing patterns. [The relatively short-range (50 μm) excitatory operations produced by bipolar and double bouquet cells, together with more widespread (300–500 μm) recurrent lateral inhibition produced by the smooth nonpyramidal cells and perhaps the basket cells, may be part of the mechanism of this competitive interaction.] Next, Hebbian learning takes place as in a competitive net, with the addition that not only are the synapses between forward-projecting axons and active postsynaptic neurons modified, but also the synapses in layer 1 between the backward projecting axons and the (same) active postsynaptic neurons are modified.

This functional architecture has the following properties. First, the backprojections, which are assumed to be relatively information-rich and orthogonal to each other as a result of the conjunctions formed by the hippocampus, amygdala, or next cortical stage, help the neurons to learn to respond differently to (and thus to separate) input stimuli (on the forward projection lines) even when the stimuli are very similar. This is illustrated in the simulation shown in Fig. 8, in which it is shown that input stimuli that overlap even in six positions out of eight can be easily learned as separate if presented conjunctively with different orthogonal backprojecting "tutors." [For a similar idea on the guidance of a competitive learning system see Rumelhart and Zipser (1986).]

In the neocortex, the backprojecting tutors can be of two types. One originates from the amygdala and hippocampus, and, by benefiting from cross-modal comparison, can provide an orthogonal backprojected vector. Moreover, this backprojection may only be activated if the multimodal areas detect that the visual stimulus is significant, because (for example) it is associated with a pleasant taste. This provides one way in which guidance can be provided for a competitive learning system as to what it should learn, so that it does not attempt to lay down representations of all incoming sensory information. Another way for this important function to be achieved is by activation of neurons that "strobe" the cortex when new or significant stimuli are shown. The cholinergic system originating in the basal forebrain (which itself receives information from the amygdala), and the noradrenergic input to layer 1 of the cortex from the locus coereleus may also contribute to this function (see Rolls, 1987; Bear and Singer, 1986). However, in that there are relatively few neurons in these systems, it is suggested that these projections only provide a simple "strobe," rather than carrying pattern-specific information to guide how information is consolidated (Rolls, 1987). The second type of backprojection is that from the next cortical area in the hierarchy. This operates in the same manner, and because it is a competitive system, is able to further categorize or orthogonalize the stimuli it receives. This next cortical stage then projects back these more orthogonal representations as tutors to the preceding stage, to effectively build at the preceding stage better filters for the diagnosis of the categories being found at the next stage.

A second property of this architecture is that if only the tutor is presented, then the neurons originally activated by the forward projecting input stimuli are activated. This occurs because the synapses from the backprojecting axons onto the pyramidal cells have been modified only where there was conjunctive forward and backprojected activity during learning. This thus provides a mechanism for recall. A simulation of this is shown in Fig. 8. Consider the situation when in the visual system the sight of food is forward-projected onto pyramidal cells, and conjunctively there is a backprojected representation of the taste of the food. Neurons that have conjunctive inputs from these two stimuli set up representations of both, so that later if only the taste representation is backprojected, then the visual neurons originally activated by the sight of that food will be activated. In this way many of the low-level details of the original visual stimulus can be recalled. Evidence that during recall relatively early cortical processing stages are activated comes from cortical blood flow studies in humans, in which it has been found, for example, that quite early visual cortical association areas are activated during recall of visual (but not auditory) information (Roland and Friberg, 1985; Roland et al., 1980).

A third property of this architecture is that attention could operate from higher to lower levels to selectively facilitate only certain pyramidal cells by using the backprojections. Indeed, the backprojections described could produce many of the "top-down" influences that are common in perception. A fourth property is that semantic priming could operate by using the backprojecting neurons to provide a small activation of just those neurons in earlier stages that are appropriate for responding to that semantic category of input stimulus.

A fifth property of such a return mechanism, which on detecting a conjunction (perhaps across modalities) improved unimodal representations of the input stimuli, would be a form of positive feedback, which would result in gradually improving storage as a result of the reciprocal interactions, as the feedback effect produced a better representation at the preceding level to be fed forward, with this occurring repeatedly. This might provide a neurophysiological and computational basis for any gradient of retrograde amnesia that may occur for the period just before disruption of temporal-lobe function (Squire, 1986; this volume, chapter 12). A sixth property of the backprojections is that they would assist the stability of the preceding competitive networks by providing a relatively constant guiding signal as a result of associations made at a higher stage, for example to an unconditioned taste or somatosensory input.

This theory of the functions of backprojections in the neocortex

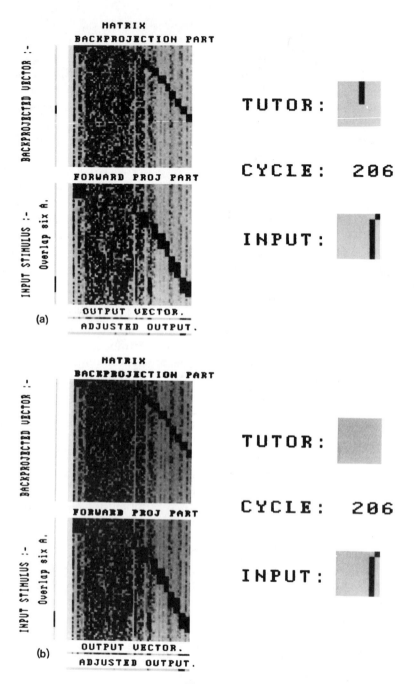

Figure 8.
Simulation of neocortical backprojection learning matrix. Conventions as in
Fig. 3. (a) During learning, both a forward input (chosen from the same
set as used in Fig. 3) and a backprojected vector that was orthogonal to
the other backprojected vectors were presented simultaneously. After 206
cycles with input stimulus + backprojected tutor pairs chosen in random
sequence, the synapses had modified as shown. Two quite similar input

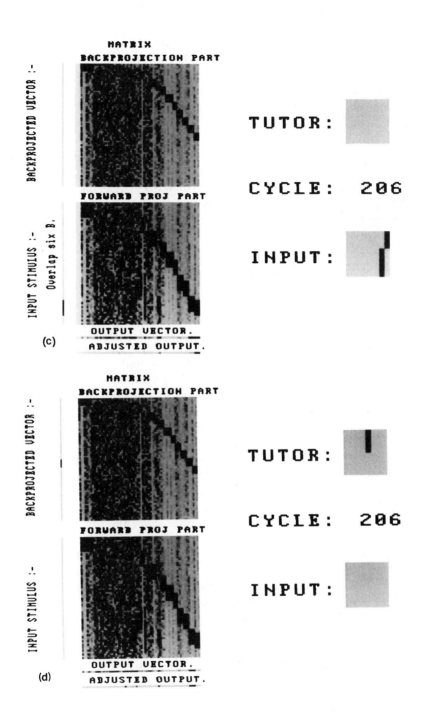

stimuli (overlap six A and six B) produce different outputs (b and c). The learning has been guided by the backprojected tutors presented during learning. If only the tutor originally paired with input stimulus overlap six A is presented, then recall of the output vector normally recognized by input stimulus overlap six A occurs (d).

requires a large number of backprojecting axons, as pattern-specific information (used to guide learning by providing a set of mutually orthogonal guidance signals, or to produce recall) must be provided by the backprojections. It also solves the de-addressing problem, for the hippocampus does not need to know exactly where in the cortex information should be stored. Instead, the backprojection signal spreads widely in layer 1, and the storage site is simply on those neurons that happen to receive strong (and precise) forward activity as well as backprojected activity. This scheme is consistent with neocortical anatomy, in that it requires the same pyramidal cell to receive both forward and (more diffuse) backprojected activity, which the arrangement of pyramidal cells with apical dendrites that extend all the way up into layer 1 achieves (see Peters and Jones, 1984). Indeed, in contrast to the relatively localized terminal distributions of forward cortico–cortical and thalamo–cortical afferents, the cortico–cortical backward projections that end in layer 1 have a much wider horizontal distribution, of up to several millimeters (Amaral, 1986). The suggestion is thus that this enables the backward projecting neurons to search over a larger number of pyramidal cells in the preceding cortical area for activity that is conjunctive with their own. It is also of interest that the theory utilizes a Hebbian learning scheme that provides for learning to occur when conjointly there is forward and backprojected input to a pyramidal cell resulting in sufficient postsynaptic activation to provide for modification of synapses that happen to be active. This provides the opportunity to make it clear that the theoretical ideas introduced here make clear predictions that can be empirically tested. For example, the theory of backprojections just proposed predicts that the backprojections in the cerebral cortex have modifiable synapses on pyramidal cells in the previous cortical area. If this were found not to be the case in empirical tests, then the theory would be rejected.

The ideas introduced here also have many theoretical implications. One is that if the backprojections are used for recall, as seems likely as discussed above (see also Roland and Friberg, 1985), then this would place severe constraints on their use for functions such as error backpropagation. Error backpropagation is an interesting and powerful algorithm in parallel distributed processing networks for setting the weights in hidden units (i.e., nodes in layers that are not input and output layers) to allow networks to learn useful mappings between input and output layers (Rumelhart et al., 1986). However, the backprojections in the architecture in which this algorithm is implemented have very precise functions in conveying error from the output layer back to the earlier, hidden, layers. It would be difficult to use the weights (synaptic strengths) from the backprojecting neurons to neurons in earlier layers both to convey the error correctly and to have the appropriate strengths for recall.

In conclusion, in this chapter experimental evidence on and theoretical approaches to the function of the hippocampus and of backprojections in the neocortex have been considered. Theories of how the hippocampus functions and of the functions of backprojections in the neocortex have been proposed. The theories are at the level of neuronal networks, and are based partly on evidence on the fine architecture of the networks, on the rules of synaptic modifiability incorporated, and on the systems-level connections. It is suggested that this approach will be useful in the future in linking anatomical evidence on structure to physiological evidence on modifiability, understanding the global properties of the networks, and thus understanding the role of the networks in brain function and behavior.

Acknowledgments

The author has worked on some of the experiments and neuronal network modeling described here with P. Cahusac, D. Cohen, J. Feigenbaum, R. Kesner, Y. Miyashita, and H. Niki, and their collaboration is sincerely acknowledged. Discussions with David G. Amaral of the Salk Institute, La Jolla, California, were also much appreciated. This research was supported by the Medical Research Council.

References

Amaral, D. G. (1986). Amygdalohippocampal and amygdalocortical projections in the primate brain. *In* "Excitatory Amino Acids and Epilepsy" (R. Schwarz and Y. Ben-Ari, eds.), pp. 3–17. Plenum, New York.

Amaral, D. G. (1987). Memory: Anatomical organization of candidate brain regions. *In* "Handbook of Neurophysiology—The Nervous System. Am. Physiol. Soc., Washington, D.C.

Amaral, D. G., and Price, J. L. (1984). Amygdalo-cortical projections in the monkey (*Macaca fascicularis*). *J. Comp. Neurol.* **230,** 465–496.

Bear, M. F., and Singer, W. (1986). Modulation of visual cortical plasticity by acetylcholine and noradrenaline. *Nature (London)* **320,** 172–176.

Braitenberg, V., and Schuz, A. (1983). Some anatomical comments on the hippocampus. *In* "Neurobiology of the Hippocampus" (W. Seifert, ed.), Chapter 2, pp. 21–37. Academic Press, London.

Cahusac, P. M. B., Feigenbaum, J., Rolls, E. T., Miyashita, Y., and Niki, H. (1986). Modifications of neuronal activity during learning in the primate hippocampus. *Neurosci. Lett.* **S24,** S29.

Cahusac, P. M. B., Miyashita, Y., and Rolls, E. T. (1989). Responses of hippocampal neurons in the monkey related to delayed response and object-place memory tasks. *Behav. Brain Res.,* in press.

Cahusac, P. M. B., Rolls, E. T., Miyashita, Y., and Niki, H. (1989). Modification of hippocampal neuronal responses during the learning of a conditional response task in the monkey. In preparation.

Gaffan, D. (1974). Recognition impaired and association intact in the memory of monkeys after transection of the fornix. *J. Comp. Physiol. Psychol.* **86,** 1100–1109.

Gaffan, D. (1977). Monkey's recognition memory for complex pictures and the effects of fornix transection. *Q. J. Exp. Psychol.* **29,** 505–514.

Gaffan, D. (1985). Hippocampus: Memory, habit and voluntary movement. *Philos. Trans. R. Soc. London, Ser. B* **308,** 87–99.

Gaffan, D., and Saunders, R. C. (1985). Running recognition of configural stimuli by fornix transected monkeys. *Q. J. Exp. Psychol.* **37B**, 61–71.

Grossberg, S. (1982). "Studies of Mind and Brain." Reidel, New York.

Ito, M. (1984). "The Cerebellum and Neural Control." Raven Press, New York.

Jones, E. G., and Peters, A., eds. (1984). "Cerebral Cortex," Vol. 2. Plenum, New York.

Kelso, S. R., Ganong, A. H., and Brown, T. H. (1986). Hebbian synapses in the hippocampus. *Proc. Natl. Acad. Sci. U.S.A.* **83**, 5326–5330.

Kohonen, T. (1984). "Self-Organization and Associative Memory." Springer-Verlag, Berlin and New York.

Kohonen, T., Lehtio, P., Rovamo, J., Hyvarinen, J., Bry, K., and Vainio, L. (1977). A principle of neural associative memory. *Neuroscience* **2**, 1065–1076.

Kohonen, T., Oja, E., and Lehtio, P. (1981). Storage and processing of information in distributed associative memory systems. *In* "Parallel Models of Associative Memory" (G. E. Hinton and J. A. Anderson, eds.), Chapter 4, pp. 105–143. Erlbaum, Hillsdale, New Jersey.

Levy, W. B. (1985). Associative changes in the synapse: LTP in the hippocampus. *In* "Synaptic Modification, Neuron Selectivity, and Nervous System Organization" (W. B. Levy, J. A. Anderson, and S. Lehmkuhle, eds.), Chapter 1, pp. 5–33. Erlbaum, Hillsdale, New Jersey.

Levy, W. B., and Desmond, N. L. (1985). The rules of elemental synaptic plasticity. *In* "Synaptic Modification, Neuron Selectivity, and Nervous System Organization" (W. B. Levy, J. A. Anderson, and S. Lehmkuhle, eds.), Chapter 6, pp. 105–121. Erlbaum, Hillsdale, New Jersey.

Marr, D. (1970). A theory for cerebral cortex. *Proc. R. Soc. London, Ser. B* **176**, 161–234.

Marr, D. (1971). Simple memory: A theory for archicortex. *Philos. Trans. R. Soc. London, Ser. B* **262**, 23–81.

Martin, K. A. C. (1984). Neuronal circuits in cat striate cortex. *In* "Cerebral Cortex" (E. G. Jones and A. Peters, eds.), Vol. 2, Chapter 9, pp. 241–285. Plenum, New York.

McNaughton, B. L. (1983). Activity dependent modulation of hippocampal synaptic efficacy: Some implications for memory processes. *In* "Neurobiology of the Hippocampus" (W. Seifert, ed.), Chapter 13, pp. 233–252. Academic Press, London.

Milner, B. (1972). Disorders of learning and memory after temporal lobe lesions in man. *Clin. Neurosurg.* **19**, 421–446.

Mishkin, M. (1978). Memory severely impaired by combined but not separate removal of amygdala and hippocampus. *Nature (London)* **273**, 297–298.

Mishkin, M. (1982). A memory system in the monkey. *Philos. Trans. R. Soc. London, Ser. B* **298**, 85–95.

Mishkin, M. (1989). Neural circuitry and mechanisms for visual recognition and memory. *In* "Neural Models of Plasticity: Theoretical and Empirical Approaches" (J. Byrne and W. O. Berry, eds.). Academic Press, New York.

Miyashita, Y., Rolls, E. T., Cahusac, P. M. B., and Niki, H. (1989). Activity of hippocampal neurons in the monkey related to a conditional response task. *J. Neurophysiol.*, in press.

Murray, E. A., and Mishkin, M. (1984). Severe tactual as well as visual memory deficits follow combined removal of the amygdala and hippocampus in monkeys. *J. Neurosci.* **4**, 2565–2580.

Murray, E. A., and Mishkin, M. (1985). Amygdalectomy impairs crossmodal association in monkeys. *Science* **228**, 604–606.

O'Keefe, J. (1983). Spatial memory within and without the hippocampal system. *In* "Neurobiology of the Hippocampus" (W. Seifert, ed.), Chapter 20, pp. 375–403. Academic Press, London.

Olton, D. S. (1983). Memory functions and the hippocampus. *In* "Neurobiology of the Hippocampus" (W. Seifert, ed.), Chapter 19, pp. 335–373. Academic Press, London.

Peters, A., and Jones, E. G., eds. (1984). "The Cerebral Cortex," Vol. 1. Plenum, New York.

Petrides, M. (1985). Deficits on conditional associative-learning tasks after frontal- and temporal-lobe lesions in man. *Neuropsychologia* **23**, 601–614.

Roland, P. E., and Friberg, L. (1985). Localization of cortical areas activated by thinking. *J. Neurophysiol.* **53**, 1219–1243.

Roland, P. E., Vaernet, K., and Lassen, N. A. (1980). Cortical activations in man during verbal report from visual memory. *Neurosci. Lett., Suppl.* **5**, S478.

Rolls, E. T. (1987). Information representation, processing and storage in the brain: analysis at the single neuron level. *In* "The Neural and Molecular Bases of Learning" (J.-P. Changeux and M. Konishi, eds.), pp. 503–540. Wiley, New York.

Rolls, E. T. (1989). Visual information processing in the primate temporal lobe. *In* "Models of Visual Perception: From Natural to Artificial" (M. Imbert, ed.). Oxford Univ. Press, London and New York.

Rolls, E. T., Miyashita, Y., Cahusac, P. M. B., Kesner, R. P., Niki, H., Feigenbaum, J., and Bach, L. (1989). Hippocampal neurons in the monkey with activity related to the place in which a stimulus is shown. *J. Neurosci.*, in press.

Rumelhart, D. E., and Zipser, D. (1986). Feature discovery by competitive learning. *In* "Parallel Distributed Processing" (D. E. Rumelhart and J. L. McClelland, eds.), Vol. 1, Chapter 5, pp. 151–193. MIT Press, Cambridge, Massachusetts.

Rumelhart, D. E., Hinton, G. E., and Williams, R. J. (1986). Learning internal representations by error propagation. *In* "Parallel Distributed Processing" (D. E. Rumelhart and J. L. McClelland, eds.), Vol. 1, Chapter 8, pp. 318–362. MIT Press, Cambridge, Massachusetts.

Rupniak, N. M. J., and Gaffan, D. (1988). Monkey hippocampus and learning about spatially directed movements. *J. Neurosci.* **7**, 2331–2337.

Scoville, W. B., and Milner, B. (1957). Loss of recent memory after bilateral hippocampal lesions. *J. Neurol., Neurosurg. Psychiatry* **20**, 11–21.

Smith, M. L., and Milner, B. (1981). The role of the right hippocampus in the recall of spatial location. *Neuropsychologia* **19**, 781–793.

Squire, L. (1986). Mechanisms of memory. *Science* **232**, 1612–1619.

Squire, L. (1989). Complex connections involved in memory functions. *In* "Neural Models of Plasticity: Theoretical and Empirical Approaches" (J. Byrne and W. O. Berry, eds.). Academic Press, New York.

Turner, B. H. (1981). The cortical sequence and terminal distribution of sensory related afferents to the amygdaloid complex of the rat and monkey. *In* "The Amygdaloid Complex" (Y. Ben-Ari, ed.), pp. 51–62. Elsevier, Amsterdam.

Van Hoesen, G. W. (1981). The differential distribution, diversity and sprouting of cortical projections to the amygdala in the rhesus monkey. *In* "The Amygdaloid Complex" (Y. Ben-Ari, ed.), pp. 79–90. Elsevier, Amsterdam.

Van Hoesen, G. W. (1982). The parahippocampal gyrus. New observations regarding its cortical connections in the monkey. *Trends NeuroSci.* **5**, 345–350.

Van Hoesen, G. W., and Pandya, D. N. (1975a). Some connections of the entorhinal (area 28) and perirhinal (area 35) cortices in the monkey. I. Temporal lobe afferents. *Brain Res.* **95**, 1–24.

Van Hoesen, G. W., and Pandya, D. N. (1975b). Some connections of the entorhinal (area 28) and perirhinal (area 35) cortices in the monkey. III. Efferent connections. *Brain Res.* **95**, 39–59.

Van Hoesen, G. W., Pandya, D. N., and Butters, N. (1975). Some connections of the entorhinal (area 28) and perirhinal (area 35) cortices in the monkey. II. Frontal lobe afferents. *Brain Res.* **95**, 25–38.

von der Malsburg, C. (1973). Self-organization of orientation-sensitive columns in the striate cortex. *Kybernetik* **14**, 85–100.

Wigstrom, H., Gustaffson, B., Huang, Y.-Y., and Abraham, W. C. (1986). Hippocampal long-term potentiation is induced by pairing single afferent volleys with intracellularly injected depolarizing currents. *Acta Physiol. Scand.* **126**, 317–319.

14

Long-Term Potentiation in Two Synaptic Systems of the Hippocampal Brain Slice

Thomas H. Brown, Alan H. Ganong, Edward W. Kairiss, Claude L. Keenan, and Stephen R. Kelso

I. Introduction

A particular focus of this laboratory has been on synaptic plasticity in brain regions that have been implicated in aspects of rapid information storage. Accordingly, a major effort has been placed on developing cellular neurophysiological and optical techniques that can enable a detailed understanding of synaptic activity-modification relationships in the hippocampus and amygdala. Here we summarize some developments of the past year that bear on our present and projected understanding of a rapid and persistent synaptic modification called *long-term synaptic potentiation* (LTP).

LTP is a use-dependent synaptic strengthening that can be induced by seconds or less of the appropriate activity. The synaptic enhancement has been reported to last for hours, days, or longer (for general review, see Bliss and Lynch, 1988). Some of the features of LTP have caused it to become a leading candidate synaptic substrate for certain of the suspected adaptive functions of hippocampal and other neural networks (Eccles, 1983; Teyler and DiScenna, 1984, 1987; Morris and Baker, 1984; McNaughton, 1983; Buzsaki, 1985; Brown *et al.*, 1988; Swanson *et al.*, 1982; Racine and Kairiss, 1987).

Most of what is known about the cellular neurophysiology of hippocampal LTP is based on studies of two synaptic systems in the hippocampal brain slice preparation. Here we summarize some recent developments that bear on our current and projected understanding of LTP in these two synaptic systems. We explore some testable models of LTP and suggest that the underlying mechanisms and activity-modification relationships may not be identical in different regions of the hippocampus.

266

II. Hippocampal Circuitry and the Brain Slice

To appreciate the subsequent *in vitro* experiments, we need to consider the synaptic organization in a thin slice of hippocampal tissue taken transversely to its long axis. Living slices in this orientation that are no more than a few tenths of a millimeter thick preserve much of the intrinsic connectivity and allow the use of optical and neurophysiological techniques, some examples of which are illustrated below, that would be impracticable *in vivo*. Figure 1 illustrates three synaptic systems that are commonly preserved in the slice.

This diagram shows the so-called "trisynaptic circuit," to which neurophysiologists often refer. The actual circuitry—even within the confines of a transverse rat hippocampal slice—contains several additional circuit elements, but this simplification is sufficient for understanding the experiments discussed here. The first synapse is from the fibers of the perforant pathway (pp) onto the granule cells (G) of the dentate gyrus (DG). The second synapse is from the mossy-fiber (mf) axons onto the pyramidal neurons (P) of the CA3 region of the hippocampus. The third synapse is from the Schaffer collaterals (Sch) onto the pyramidal (P) neurons of the CA1 region. The latter neurons also

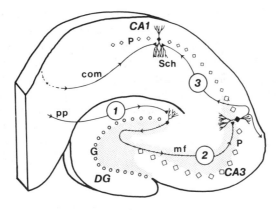

Figure 1.
Schematic representation of the "trisynaptic circuit" elements within a transverse hippocampal slice (drawn from Fig. 2B). Neurons include granule cells (G) in the dentate gyrus (DG) and pyramidal cells (P) in the CA1 and CA3 regions of the hippocampus. Synapses include the perforant-pathway (pp) inputs to the DG, the mossy-fiber (mf) inputs to CA3, and the Schaeffer collateral (Sch) and commissural (com) inputs to CA1. The stippled area shows the distribution of granule cell synaptic projections as the mossy-fiber axons and the axon collaterals course through the infragranular layer of the DG and terminate in the stratum lucidum of CA3.

receive an excitatory synaptic input from the commissural fibers (com), which arise from the contralateral hippocampus. Circuit elements not illustrated include the extensive network of recurrent excitation in the CA3 region (see Johnston and Brown, 1986), as well as the inhibitory synapses (cf. Brown and Johnston, 1983; Griffith *et al.*, 1986; Taube and Schwartzkroin, 1987). Also not shown are neuromodulatory systems, such as the noradrenergic input to the CA3 region and dentate gyrus (Johnston, see Chapter 15, this volume).

The appearance of a living hippocampal brain slice (200 μm thick) from a 28-day-old Sprague-Dawley rat—viewed in the conventional manner through a dissecting microscope using reflected light—is illustrated in Fig. 2A. The barely discernable gray line that curves across the CA1 region of the slice (compare with Fig. 1, which was drawn from a photograph of a videomicroscopic image of this slice) is the layer that contains the cell bodies of the CA1 pyramidal neurons (the stratum pyramidale of regio superior). The extension of this line that bends downward on the right and then loops back to the left at the bottom of the slice is the layer that contains the somata of the pyramidal neurons of the CA3 region (the stratum pyramidale of regio inferior). The C-shaped line on the lower left is the region of the dentate gyrus containing the cell bodies of the granule cells (the stratum granulosum). Only these types of gross landmarks can be visualized using this conventional optical method.

To enable visualization of much more of the cellular and subcellular detail, we have been applying video-enhanced contrast, differential-interference contrast (VEC-DIC) microscopic techniques to the slices (Brown and Keenan, 1987; Brown *et al.*, 1988; Keenan *et al.*, 1988). The hippocampal slices are placed on the stage of an inverted compound microscope (equipped for differential interference contrast as well as epifluorescence microscopy) that contains a port for a video camera. Even with a low-power objective, the stratum pyramidale and stratum granulosum are much more sharply defined (Fig. 2B). The area in which the mossy-fiber synapses are distributed within the CA3 region (the stratum

---

Figure 2.
Visualization of hippocampal brain slices at low magnification. (A) Hippocampal slice (200 μm thick) prepared for electrophysiology in a conventional recording chamber and viewed through a dissecting microscope. The cell body layers are faintly visible as grey lines. (B) Same slice photographed from a TV monitor after analog video enhancement of the image. The slice was placed in a special recording chamber on the stage of an inverted compound microscope and viewed using a differential interference contrast (DIC) condenser (NA = 0.55) and a 3.2× objective. The arrows mark what we believe is the distal projection of the mossy-fiber synaptic system. Calibration bar: 500 μm. [From Keenan *et al.* (1988).]

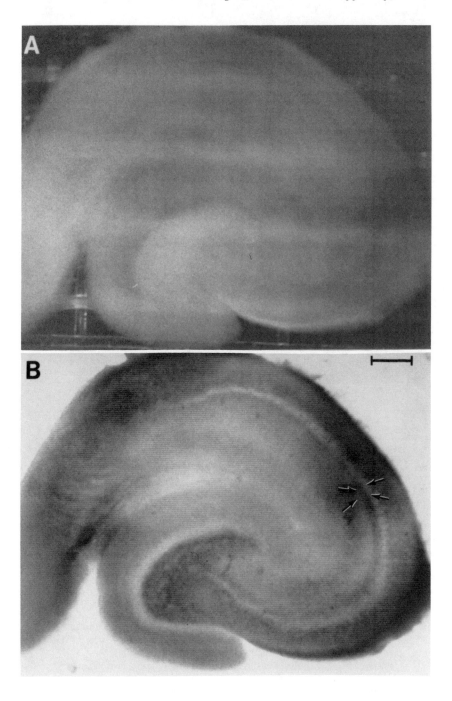

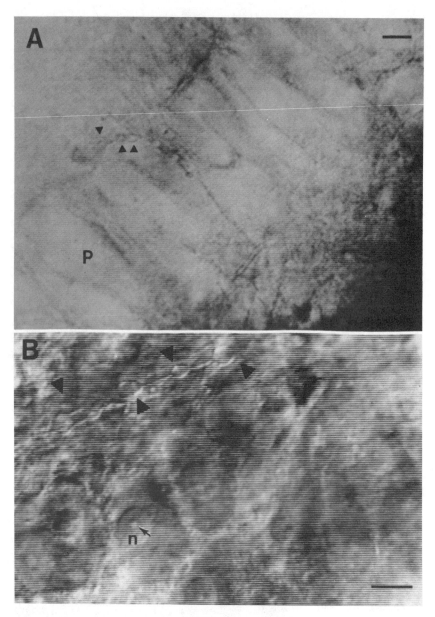

Figure 3.
Enhanced video micrographs of the pyramidal cell body (stratum
pyramidale) layer of the CA3 region. The hippocampal slice (300 μm thick)
was imaged using a long-working-distance DIC condenser (NA = 0.55)
with (A) a 40× dry (NA = 0.6) or (B) a 60× oil-immersion (NA = 1.4)
objective. (A) The outlines of the cell bodies (P) are fairly distinct and
possible mossy-fiber synaptic expansions can be discerned (black
triangles). (B) Better resolution enables visualization of the nucleus (n) and
nucleolus (arrow) as well as several profiles suspected to be mossy-fiber
synaptic expansions (black triangles). Calibration bars: 10 μm. [Modified
from Keenan *et al.* (1988).]

lucidum—see stippled area in Fig. 1) has a distinctly coarse texture. A somewhat similar texture is evident in the infragranular region of the dentate gyrus (see stippled area in Fig. 1), which contains synaptic varicosities and expansions formed by granule-cell collaterals (see Amaral and Dent, 1981; Johnston and Brown, 1983; Brown and Johnston, 1983; Claiborne *et al.*, 1986).

With a medium-power objective, some of the cellular and subcellular details are evident, including the somata of the pyramidal neurons (P) and even the nuclei (Fig. 3A). By using microelectrodes filled with a fluorescent compound (such as lucifer yellow or carboxyfluorescein), it is possible to demonstrate that a particular target cell under visualization can be penetrated with the recording microelectrode. The area of the slice in which the mossy-fiber and collateral synaptic expansions are known to be distributed (the stratum lucidum and the infragranular region of the dentate) appears to be filled with particle-like structures (Fig. 3A).

With a higher-power objective, more of the subcellular details can be discerned (Fig. 3B). The nuclei (n) and nucleoli of the pyramidal neurons are clearly visualizable (the edges of the cell bodies are not in the plane of focus). In the stratum lucidum one can see ovoid structures connected to very fine processes (Fig. 3B). Similar structures are evident in the infragranular region. Our preliminary evidence (Brown and Keenan, 1987; Keenan *et al.*, 1988) suggests that the size, distribution, and developmental time of appearance of these structures parallels that described for the mossy-fiber synapses in CA3 (cf. Amaral and Dent, 1981; see also Claiborne *et al.*, 1986).

III. LTP Induction and Expression in Hippocampal Brain Slices

The problem of understanding the mechanisms responsible for LTP can be usefully divided into three parts, which we term the *induction* of LTP, the *expression* of LTP, and the *coupling* of the early induction events to the final expression of the synaptic enhancement (further explained in Brown *et al.*, 1988). The induction of LTP refers to the initial sequence of events that triggers or sets into motion the process of synaptic modification. The expression of LTP refers to those neurophysiological and biophysical changes that represent the ultimate consequence of this modification process, and that constitute the proximal cause of the observed synaptic enhancement.

In some synaptic systems, the expression of LTP appears to result, at least in part, from a *presynaptic* modification that increases transmitter release (Baxter *et al.*, 1985; Briggs *et al.*, 1985a,b; Bliss and Lynch, 1988).

However, most investigators would agree that the issue of whether the expression of LTP in the mossy-fiber and Sch/com synapses of the hippocampus results from a presynaptic and/or a postsynaptic modification is still unsettled (see Bliss and Lynch, 1988; Brown *et al.*, 1988). There is in fact evidence (described below) that some of the key molecular events leading to the induction of LTP in the Sch/com synapses are associated with the *postsynaptic* side of the cleft. If the process of inducing the change is initiated on the postsynaptic side of the cleft, but the expression of the enhancement reflects a presynaptic modification, then there may be an interesting form of *retrograde* synaptic control mechanism (further discussed in Brown *et al.*, 1988; Errington et al., 1987).

When more is known about the early (induction) and late (expression) events in the modification process, it will be easier to narrow the range of viable mechanisms for the intermediate events (induction-expression coupling), Some of the intermediate events that others have proposed are discussed in Brown *et al.*, (1988). From what follows it will be apparent that the mossy-fiber and Sch/com synaptic systems differ at least in regard to some of the molecular/biophysical mechanisms responsible for LTP induction. Whether there are also differences with respect to the expression of LTP remains to be determined.

IV. LTP in the Mossy-Fiber Synapses of the Hippocampus

The first voltage-clamp studies of synaptic transmission in the brain were performed on the mossy-fiber synapses (Brown and Johnston, 1983) because they offer several advantages for exploring structure–function relationships in a system that displays LTP (Johnston and Brown, 1984). One advantage is that these synapses are located, on the average, at only about 3% of a space constant from the cell soma (Johnston and Brown, 1983). The electrotonic proximity of this input to the soma is important because it reduces errors associated with imperfect space-clamp conditions. Another advantage is that single quantal events can be easily resolved in both current-clamp (Brown *et al.*, 1979; Johnston and Brown, 1983) and voltage-clamp (Johnston and Brown, 1984; Rong *et al.*, 1987) recordings, which is important for evaluating several major hypotheses regarding LTP mechanisms (see Figs. 7 & 8, Table I, and associated text). A final advantage is that the large size of the mossy-fiber synapses (see Amaral and Dent, 1981; Johnston and Brown, 1983) raises the possibility of visualizing them clearly in the living state (Fig. 3B) (Keenan *et al.*, 1988).

The postsynaptic response that is normally produced in CA3 pyramidal neurons by stimulating the granule cells consists of an excitatory/inhibitory conductance sequence (Fig. 4) (Brown and Johnston, 1983;

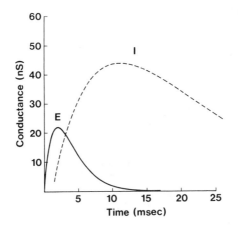

Figure 4.
Schematic representation of the normal conductance sequence observed in
CA3 pyramidal neurons of the guinea pig hippocampus in response to
stimulating granule cells in the dentate gyrus. The solid curve (E)
illustrates the time course of the monosynaptic mossy fiber excitatory
synaptic response. The broken curve (I) illustrates the conductance
thought to arise from recurrent or feedforward inhibition. [From
Barrionuevo *et al.* (1986).

Griffith *et al.*, 1986). In addition to the monosynaptic response generated
by the mossy-fiber input, there is an inhibitory response produced by
recurrent or feed-forward circuitry. The onset of the inhibitory conductance begins before the excitatory conductance has reached its peak
amplitude. The presence of these temporally overlapping conductance
increases means that changes in either could in principle contribute to
the enhanced synaptic efficacy observed during LTP (Barrionuevo *et al.*,
1986). To avoid this ambiguity, the inhibitory component was pharmacologically blocked (by adding picrotoxin to the bathing medium) in
all the experiments illustrated here.

An example of LTP in the mossy-fiber synapses, recorded from a
pharmacologically disinhibited hippocampal slice, is shown in Fig. 5.
The traces on the left are the postsynaptic voltage response recorded
under current-clamp conditions (Fig. 5A), while those on the right indicate the corresponding postsynaptic currents recorded under voltage-
clamp conditions (Fig. 5B; current is on the lower trace, and voltage is
on the upper trace). Both sets of recordings were done using a single-
electrode clamp (SEC). The SEC is a time-share (asynchronous) current-
and voltage-clamp system that uses one electrode to do the job of two
(Johnston and Brown, 1983, 1984). The device switches (usually at 3–8
kHz) between measuring voltage and passing current via a single microelectrode.

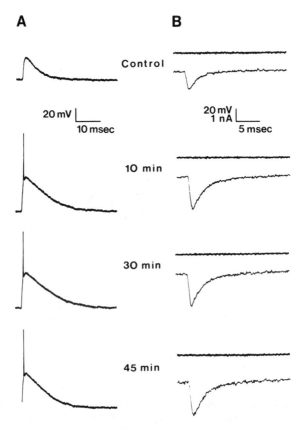

Figure 5.
LTP in the mossy-fiber synaptic input to a CA3 pyramidal neuron of the
rat hippocampal slice. The membrane potential was maintained at −90
mV in both current-clamp (A) and voltage-clamp modes (B). (A) Current-
clamp records of EPSPs obtained during the control period and at
indicated times after tetanic stimulation of the mossy fiber synaptic inputs.
Illustrated action potential amplitudes are attenuated due to filtering and
the switching rate of the SEC. (B) Voltage-clamp recordings of EPSCs
obtained from the same neuron at the indicated times. Top traces show
the voltage control; bottom traces are individually recorded EPSCs. [From
Barrionuevo *et al.* (1986).]

During the control period, the excitatory postsynaptic potential
(EPSP) was subthreshold for generating an action potential in the postsynaptic neuron (Fig. 5A). Following brief, high-frequency (tetanic),
synaptic stimulation (100 Hz for 1 sec), there was a large and persistent
increase in the synaptic efficacy that lasted for the duration of the experiment. After the tetanic stimulation, the synapses generated a su-

prathreshold postsynaptic response (Fig. 5A) and there was an increase in the excitatory postsynaptic currents (EPSCs) (Fig. 5B).

This experiment illustrates the defining features of LTP—namely, that it is a rapid and persistent, use-dependent form of synaptic enhancement. By "persistent" we mean only that it clearly outlasts another form of use-dependent synaptic enhancement called *posttetanic potentiation* (PTP), examples of which are illustrated in Figs. 6, 11, and 13. By "rapid" we mean that it can be induced by seconds or less of the appropriate synaptic activity. The dynamics of the posttetanic synaptic enhancement can often be seen most clearly in voltage-clamp recordings of the EPSCs, which typically decay rapidly during the first few minutes (PTP) before stabilizing at a new level (LTP) (Fig. 6). The use of the voltage clamp improves analysis of the time course of the synaptic modification by removing some secondary nonlinear components of the postsynaptic response.

What is the proximal cause of this synaptic enhancement? The major possibilities that have guided the research in this laboratory are illustrated in Fig. 7. The plan has been to develop those techniques that would allow critical tests at all of the key choice points on the logic tree. The expression of LTP was found (Barrionuevo *et al.*, 1986) not to be accompanied by significant postsynaptic changes in (1) the input resistance

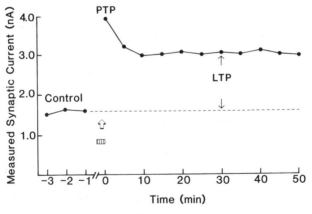

Figure 6.
Mossy-fiber EPSC amplitudes plotted over time, before and after the induction of LTP (from the same cell illustrated in Fig. 5). Brief tetanic stimulation was applied at the time indicated (striped bar and arrow). Note the change in the time scale at the time of stimulation. Each data point is the average of five EPSCs obtained from a holding potential of −90 mV. The tetanic stimulation induced posttetanic potentiation (PTP) and long-term potentiation (LTP). [From Barrionuevo *et al. (1986).]*

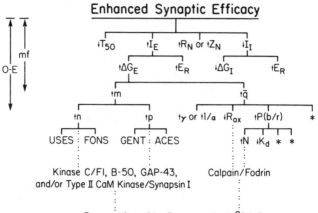

Figure 7.
Logic tree used to direct experimental analysis of LTP expression. Symbols at each of the choice points are explained in the text. Possible molecular mechanisms that others have proposed are indicated at the bottom. The arrows indicate the experimental level that has been reached in studies of LTP expression in the crayfish opener–excitor synapse (O-E) and the hippocampal mossy-fiber (mf) synapses. Asterisks indicate other possibilities that are beyond the scope of this chapter. The predictions and implications of the remaining three most promising hypotheses are illustrated in Fig. 8.

R_N, measured from the steady-state voltage response produced by a current step injected into the soma; (2) an approximation of the "effective synaptic input resistance" Z_N, assessed from the peak voltage response produced by a transient current (with a waveform that closely resembles that of the measured synaptic currents) injected into the soma; (3) the spike threshold T_{50}, measured using the same transient waveform (an alpha function—see Brown *et al.*, 1988); or (4) the reversal potential for the excitatory synaptic currents E_R, determined directly or by extrapolation. Because the experiments were done in disinhibited slices, a decrease in the inhibitory synaptic currents I_I could also be ruled out in these experiments (Barrionuevo *et al.*, 1986). The only detected changes were (1) an increase in the peak excitatory postsynaptic currents I_E and (2) a corresponding increase in the measured peak of the excitatory synaptic conductance ΔG_E (Barrionuevo *et al.*, 1986).

The primary interest has therefore been on explanations for the increase in ΔG_E (Fig. 7). There are three interesting possibilities, which we termed (Brown *et al.*, 1988) (1) the release hypothesis (an increase in the amount of transmitter release); (2) the spine series-resistance hypothesis (a dendritic spine change that decreases its axial resistance); and (3) the occult-receptor hypothesis (an increase in the number of postsynaptic receptors for the neurotransmitter). Efforts to simulate quantitative models of all three have already begun.

A. The Release Hypothesis

Most forms of synaptic enhancement that have been carefully studied in mammals—facilitation, augmentation, and PTP—result from a presynaptic modification that increases transmitter release and therefore increases ΔG_E (Brown *et al.*, 1988). Under certain conditions (see Johnston and Brown, 1984a; Baxter *et al.*, 1985), the mean value of ΔG is the product of two *quantal parameters*

$$(1) \quad \overline{\Delta G} = m\,\overline{\Delta g}$$

where $\overline{\Delta g}$ is the mean single quantal conductance increase and m is the average number of quantal packets of neurotransmitter released per nerve impulse. The experimental goal is therefore to determine which of these quantal parameters changes during the expression of LTP. Only the release hypothesis can easily account for an increase in m.

The release model is illustrated in Fig. 8A. In our simulations, we commonly assume that the number of quantal discharges produced by each presynaptic action potential can be modeled adequately by a simple binomial probability function—the shape of which is specified by two parameters, n and p, whose product m [the "mean quantal content"; see Eq. (1) and Fig. 7] we wish to estimate (cf. Brown *et al.*, 1976). The "quantal size" probability density is represented by a gamma function that can have two or three parameters. It is the mean value of this density function (the "mean quantal size") that we wish to estimate accurately. By convention, the mean quantal size $\bar{q}$ refers to the average postsynaptic response [measured as a conductance increase as in Eq. (1), a peak current, a net charge transfer, or a voltage response] produced by the release of individual quanta. Finally, the model contains an additive noise function, which is represented by a gaussian probability density, the two parameters of which can be measured from the data or estimated. The parameters are estimated using a maximum-likelihood method.

B. The Occult-Receptor Hypothesis

The occult-receptor hypothesis proposes that the increase in ΔG_E observed during LTP results from an increase in the sensitivity of the postsynaptic membrane to neurotransmitter release due to the "unmasking" of "occult receptors" (Lynch and Baudry, 1984). Thus the increase in the mean value of ΔG_E results from an increase in the number N of postsynaptic receptors (see Figs. 7 and 8B). One testable prediction (Barrionuevo *et al.*, 1986; Brown *et al.*, 1988) of this hypothesis is that LTP is accompanied by an increase in the mean quantal size $\bar{q}$. Perkel (1986)

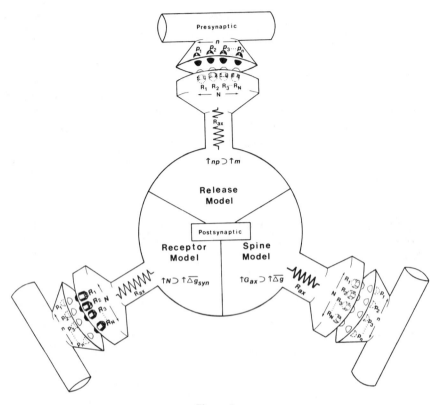

Figure 8.
Three models for LTP expression. Modification sites are emphasized by
bolded lines and theoretical implications are shown by alphanumeric
symbols (see key). (A) The release model assumes a presynaptic
modification that increases m, due to an increase in the product of the
binomial parameters n and p. (B) The occult-receptor hypothesis assumes a
postsynaptic modification that increases N, the number of transmitter
receptors (R). This change is assumed to increase the mean size of the true
single quantal conductance (Δg_{syn}). Obviously $N \gg n$ and its value must
be assumed to limit the conductance. (C) The spine (series-resistance)
hypothesis assumes a postsynaptic modification that decreases the spine
axial resistance (R_{ax}). This would be expressed as an increase in the mean
size of the apparent (measured) quantal conductance ($\overline{\Delta g}$). See text and
Table I for details.

has begun to construct a formal model that incorporates this idea. His
preliminary simulations suggest that under a wide range of conditions
an increase in N can increase $\overline{\Delta g}$.

C. The Spine (Series-Resistance) Hypothesis

According to this hypothesis (see Rall, 1974, 1978), the spine stem offers
a substantial series resistance that reduces the amplitude of the voltage

response in the shaft of the parent dendrite (explained in Brown *et al.*, 1988). Under voltage clamp conditions, the presence of this series resistance, which is outside the positive feedback loop of the voltage-clamp circuit, will reduce the apparent synaptic conductance increase ΔG_E relative to its true value ΔG_{syn} according to the relation (derived in Brown *et al.*, 1988)

$$(2) \qquad \Delta G_E = \frac{G_{ax} \, \Delta G_{syn}}{G_{ax} + \Delta G_{syn}}$$

where G_{ax} is the spine axial conductance (reciprocal of the spine series resistance).

Under appropriate conditions (discussed in detail in Brown *et al.*, 1988), a spine shape change (shortening or thickening) that increased G_{ax} could manifest itself as an increase in the apparent (measured) synaptic conductance ΔG_E in the absence of a change in the true synaptic conductance ΔG_{syn}. Simulations of the type of model suggested by Fig. 8C are presented in Brown *et al.* (1988). Like the preceding model, this one also predicts an increase in the mean quantal size $\bar{q}$. If spines do in fact "twitch" (Crick, 1982), or otherwise change their shape or internal structure by an amount that could have an appreciable effect on G_{ax}, it might be possible to see such movements directly in living neurons using some of the newer optical techniques.

D. Predicted Changes in Quantal Parameters

The three models sketched in Fig. 8 make different predictions in regard to changes in the various parameters that we use to characterize the synaptic strength (Table I). Both postsynaptic models require that LTP be accompanied by an increase in the mean quantal size $\bar{q}$, however it is measured. Only the presynaptic model can easily account for an in-

Table I

Predictions of the Three Hypotheses for LTP Expression[a]

Proposed explanation for LTP	Modified conductance or quantal parameter					
	ΔG_E	G_{ax}	ΔG_{syn}	$\overline{\Delta g}$	$\overline{\Delta g}_{syn}$	m
Spine hypothesis	↑	↑	NC	↑	NC	NC
Receptor hypothesis	↑	NC	↑	↑	↑	NC
Release hypothesis	↑	NC	↑	NC?	NC?	↑?

[a] Symbols refer to the following: ΔG_E, measured synaptic conductance increase; G_{ax}, spine axial conductance; ΔG_{syn}, true synaptic conductance increase; $\overline{\Delta g}$, measured single quantal conductance increase; $\overline{\Delta g}_{syn}$, true single quantal conductance; and m, mean quantal content. The question marks reflect the possibility that more release could also occur if each quantal packet contained a greater amount of neurotransmitter, in which case $\overline{\Delta g}$ and $\overline{\Delta g}_{syn}$ would increase instead of m (see Brown *et al.*, 1988a).

crease in the mean quantal content m. It is therefore important that we know the quantal basis of LTP expression.

The quantal basis of LTP expression has been studied in the opener–excitor neuromuscular synapses of the crayfish (Baxter *et al.*, 1985). In these synapses, three different classical methods of quantal analysis all

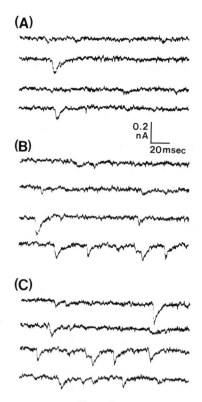

(A)

(B)

(C)

0.2 nA

20 msec

Figure 9.
Voltage-clamp recordings of spontaneous miniature synaptic currents (mEPSCs) in a rat CA3 hippocampal neuron. Each set of four successive traces (A–C) were recorded at three different times from the same cell at the same holding potential (-120 mV). The sampling rate was 5.1 KHz; the electrode resistance was 22 MΩ; and the output band width was 300 Hz. To prevent evoked release, the slice was bathed in modified saline. The divalent cation concentration was altered (1 mM Ca^{2+} and 2 mM Mn^{2+}) and tetrodotoxin (TTX) was added (1 μM). Spontaneous miniature inhibitory currents (mIPSCs) were blocked by adding 10 μM picrotoxin to the bath. To reduce the holding current required to clamp the membrane potential at very negative potentials, 2 mM Cs^+ was also added to the bath. Assuming a reversal potential of about 0 mV (Johnston and Brown, 1984; unpublished observations), the larger events shown correspond to a measured single quantal conductance ($\overline{\Delta g}$) of about 2–3 nS. We are currently attempting to improve the signal-to-noise ratio. [From Brown *et al.* (1988).

indicated that LTP results entirely from an increase in m, suggesting a presynaptic modification that increases neurotransmitter release. However, it is possible that the mechanism responsible for LTP expression in some of the synaptic systems of the hippocampus is different from that in the opener–excitor synapses of the crayfish. For this reason, we are currently attempting to determine the quantal basis of LTP expression in the mossy-fiber synapses.

For such an analysis to be meaningful and reliable, we felt that three developments were necessary. First, for reasons discussed elsewhere (Johnston and Brown, 1984; Brown et al., 1988), the analysis is best done on the EPSCs measured under voltage-clamp conditions in disinhibited slices. This is now possible (see Figs. 5B and 6). Second, it was necessary to develop a new method of quantal analysis, because the three classical methods that were used on the opener–excitor synapses are not well suited for studies of LTP in hippocampal brain slices. We have just completed preliminary tests of a maximum-likelihood method of quantal parameter estimation that appears to be appropriate for the mossy-fiber synapses. Third, it was important to improve the quantal signal-to-noise ratio, because no method can furnish reliable quantal parameter estimates if the noise fluctuations are large relative to the quantal fluctuations. The quantal signal-to-noise ratio has been improved to a level that should be acceptable (Fig. 9).

We believe that it should now be possible to furnish reasonable estimates of the quantal parameters before and after LTP induction in the mossy-fiber synapses. The results should be pertinent to all three of the models reviewed above (Fig. 8 and Table I). Further developments will be necessary before equally convincing quantal parameter determinations can be obtained from the other two excitatory synaptic systems depicted in Fig. 1. It will be important to compare these three, because there is evidence (described below) for more than one form of LTP in the hippocampus.

V. LTP in the Schaffer Collateral/Commissural Synapses of the Hippocampus

We were originally attracted to the mossy-fiber synapses for studies of LTP because of the obvious experimental advantages already mentioned. However, we also began studies of the Sch/com synapses of the CA1 region, partly to examine the possibility that there might be more than one form of LTP in the hippocampus. The Sch/com synapses are especially convenient for exploring interactions among separate sets of excitatory inputs to pyramidal neurons in disinhibited slices. With proper positioning of the stimulating electrodes in the stratum radiatum of the

CA1 region, it is possible to activate two (Barrionuevo and Brown, 1983) or even three (Kelso and Brown, 1985, 1986) separate sets of Sch/com synaptic inputs (Fig. 10A).

The strength of the postsynaptic responses can be controlled by adjusting the current delivered to the stimulating electrodes, which determines the number of stimulated afferent fibers. For reasons that will become clear, we were especially interested in the manner in which weak (W) and strong (S) synaptic inputs interact in the induction of LTP. Il-

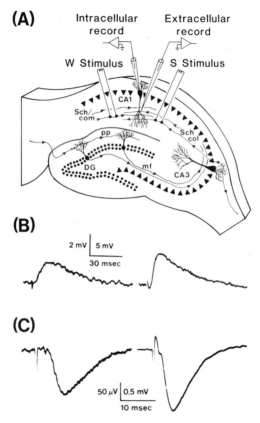

Figure 10.

Typical recordings from electrode arrangements used to study interactions between weak (W) and strong (S) afferent inputs in the CA1 region of the slice. (A) Stimulating and extracellular recording electrodes are placed in the Schaffer collateral/commissural (Sch/com) fiber trajectories. (B) Typical intracellular EPSPs recorded from the soma and produced by single stimulations of the weak (left traces) and strong (right traces) inputs (note difference in voltage scale). (C) Typical extracellular (population) EPSPs recorded in the stratum radiatum and produced by these same inputs (note difference in voltage scale). [Modified from Barrionuevo and Brown (1983).]

lustrated below are examples of what we term W and S postsynaptic responses, which can be recorded intracellularly as an excitatory postsynaptic potential (EPSP) (Fig. 10B) or extracellularly as a population EPSP (Fig. 10C). Both inputs were subthreshold for discharging the postsynaptic neurons in response to a single afferent volley. The W inputs, but not the S inputs, were also subthreshold for firing the postsynaptic neurons in response to a high-frequency train (100 Hz) of afferent volleys.

A. Interactions among Separate Afferents

The magnitude of LTP or the probability of its occurrence following tetanic synaptic stimulation of the Sch/com inputs is a monotonic increasing function of the total number of synapses that are stimulated. Thus tetanic stimulation of a W input fails to induce LTP, whereas the identical stimulation pattern applied to an S input does result in LTP induction [a quantitative interpretation of W and S is given in Brown *et al.* (1988)]. This phenomenon has been discussed in terms of a "cooperativity" requirement for LTP (McNaughton *et al.*, 1978; Lee, 1983).

Cooperativity has been reported at two of the three most commonly studied synaptic systems of the hippocampus (see Fig. 1)—the perforant-pathway inputs to the dentate gyrus (McNaughton *et al.*, 1978) and the Sch/com inputs to CA1 pyramidal neurons (Lee, 1983). It has not yet been reported to be a feature of the mossy-fiber inputs to the CA3 pyramidal neurons. An early but generally unspoken concern was that cooperativity could reflect an unnatural condition—associated with changes at the interface between the metal stimulating electrode and the neural tissue—that results from the passage of large amounts of current.

This possibility of an experimental artifact was eventually eliminated by the results of experiments that explored interactions among two or more separately stimulated sets of W and S synaptic inputs, an example of which is illustrated in Fig. 11. In this graph, each data point is the mean amplitude of the population EPSP (average of five consecutive responses) produced by the W input. After establishing a stable baseline, the W input was tetanically stimulated (100 Hz for 600 msec) at the time indicated (stippled bar). This repetitive stimulation produced PTP but not LTP. Next, the S input was tetanically stimulated (100 Hz for 400 msec) at the time indicated (striped bar). Heterosynaptic enhancement (potentiation of the W input) did not occur. Thus tetanic stimulation of either pathway *alone* failed to induce LTP in the W input. However when both pathways were stimulated at about the same time (stippled and striped bars), using these same parameters, both PTP and LTP were induced in the W input. Results such as these (and those described below) cannot be easily explained in terms of a change in the interface between the stimulating electrode and the tissue.

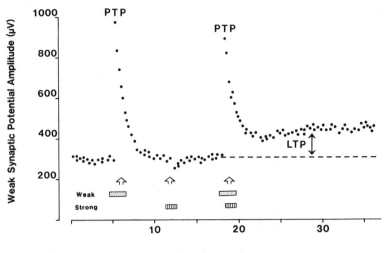

Figure 11.

Associative LTP in the CA1 region of hippocampus. Each data point is the mean amplitude of the population EPSP (five consecutive responses) produced by a weak (W) stimulus. Brief tetanic stimulation of the W input (100 Hz for 600 msec) alone (stippled bar) produced posttetanic potentiation (PTP) but did induce LTP. Similarly, tetanic stimulation of the strong (S) input (100 Hz for 400 msec) alone (striped bar) did not cause LTP in the W input. However, when both the W and S were stimulated (same parameters) at about the same time, PTP and LTP were induced in the W input. (From S. R. Kelso and T. H. Brown, unpublished observations.)

B. Spatiotemporal Specificity of the Interactions

The fact that stimulation of W inputs alone fails to induce LTP in the Sch/com system was used to explore the spatiotemporal specificity of the activity-enhancement relationships that govern LTP in the CA1 region of the hippocampus (Barrionuevo and Brown, 1983; Kelso and Brown, 1984, 1985, 1986; Kelso *et al.*, 1986). The *spatial specificity* was evaluated (Kelso and Brown, 1985, 1986) using three sets of separate pathways— an S input and two W inputs (W1 and W2). LTP could be selectively induced in either W1 or W2 by pairing (as in Fig. 11) tetanic stimulation of one of them with tetanic stimulation of the S input. Temporally overlapping W–S pairings but not temporally separate pairings caused this enhancement, which was specific to the appropriately paired input.

The averaged results from such experiments done on 14 slices reveal the extreme spatial specificity of associative LTP in this system (Fig. 12). In half the experiments, W1 and S were stimulated at the same time (as in Fig. 11) and W2 was stimulated shortly afterward (see Fig. 13 for tim-

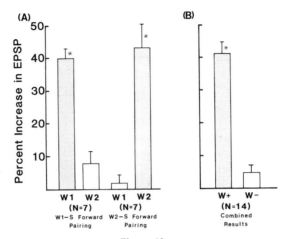

Figure 12.
Approach used to explore spatial specificity of associative LTP in the CA1
region of hippocampus. The experimental paradigm was like that
illustrated in Figs. 10 and 11 except that there were two weak inputs (W1
and W2) and one strong input (S). One W input was stimulated at the
same time as the S input (a forward and temporally overlapping W–S
pairing) and the other was stimulated with a delay (a backward and
temporally separate W–S). The timing relationships are illustrated in Fig.
13. (A) Only the forward and temporally overlapping W–S pairings (the
stippled bars) caused significant enhancement (asterisks) of the population
EPSP amplitude. (B) Pooled summary of the same data, where W$^+$ and
W$^-$ represent, respectively, results from the forward-paired (temporally
overlapping) and backward-paired (temporally separate) cases. Only the
forward-paired group (stippled bar) showed significant enhancement
(asterisk). [Data from Kelso and Brown (1986).]

ing). The temporal relationships were reversed in the other half of the
experiments. LTP was only induced in the W input that was stimulated
at the same time as the S input (Fig. 12A). The pooled results are shown
in Fig. 12B, where W + is the input (W1 or W2) that was stimulated at
the same time as the S input, and W − is the input that was stimulated
shortly afterward.

This persistent synaptic enhancement was called *associative* rather
than *heterosynaptic* LTP (Levy and Steward, 1979, 1983; Barrionuevo and
Brown, 1983; Levy *et al.*, 1983) because stimulating the S input alone
failed to induce LTP in the W input when the latter was unstimulated.
True heterosynaptic LTP apparently does not occur or is difficult to demonstrate experimentally among Sch/com inputs to CA1 (Barrionuevo and
Brown, 1983; Kelso and Brown, 1984, 1985, 1986). By "true heterosynaptic
LTP" we mean to exclude any changes in the neural circuitry other than
the direct, monosynaptic inputs to the neuron. Elimination of hetero-

synaptic LTP as an explanation for the enhancement in the W input was in fact part of the original definition of associative LTP (Barrionuevo and Brown, 1983). The absence of heterosynaptic LTP in this synaptic system is an important consideration in some of the molecular/biophysical models that we shall explore below.

The *temporal specificity* was examined by varying the interstimulus intervals (ISIs) between the tetanic stimulations. The ISI is defined as the time from the onset of the W to the onset of the S stimulation. An ISI > 0 means that the onset of high-frequency activity in the W input precedes the onset of activity in the S input, although the tetanic stimulation trains may overlap. This is sometimes called a "forward" pairing

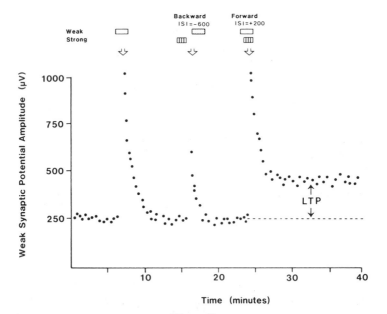

Figure 13.
Approach used to explore temporal specificity of associative LTP in the CA1 region of the hippocampus. The stimulation parameters are the same as in Figs. 11 and 12. Stippled bars denote the tetanus delivered to the W input (100 Hz for 600 msec); striped bars indicate the tetanus delivered to the S input (100 Hz for 400 msec). The stimulus trains were presented five times at 12-sec intervals. A backward (temporally separate) pairing failed to induce LTP, whereas a subsequent forward (temporally overlapping) pairing did cause LTP (a 77% increase in the EPSP amplitude). The interstimulus interval (ISI) was +200 msec for the forward pairing (there was 400 msec of overlap) and −600 msec for the backward pairing (there was a 200-msec gap separating the two stimulus trains). In different slices the ISIs were varied to construct an ISI-synaptic enhancement function, illustrated in Fig. 14. (From S. R. Kelso and T. H. Brown, unpublished observations.)

relationship. An ISI < 0 implies the reverse temporal relationship, and is sometimes called a "backward" pairing. An example of a backward (ISI = −600 msec) followed by a forward (ISI = +200) pairing is illustrated in Fig. 13 (the stimulation parameters were the same as in Fig. 11). PTP was evident in both cases, but only the forward (and temporally overlapping) pairing induced LTP.

We were interested in knowing the shape of the relationship between the ISI and the average amount of synaptic enhancement. An example of an ISI-synaptic enhancement function is illustrated in Fig. 14. The vertical bars show the average magnitude of LTP (expressed as a percentage increase above the control level) at each ISI that was tested. These experiments used a design similar to that shown in Fig. 11. The stimulation current carried by two separate stimulating electrodes positioned in the stratum radiatum of CA1 was adjusted to give a W and S extracellular synaptic response. First, tetanic stimulation of either input alone was shown not to produce LTP in the W pathway. Next, both pathways were tetanically stimulated at one of several ISIs. There was a narrow temporal window within which the W–S pairings were effective in inducing LTP of the W pathway. Associative LTP only occurred when the stimulus trains overlapped. In these experiments, temporal overlap only occurred for an ISI greater than −400 msec and less than +600 msec.

The ISI-enhancement function is not symmetrical about ISI = 0, but instead is displaced to the right. This could suggest a preference for forward W–S pairing relationships (see below). An alternative explanation is that the amount of LTP is linearly related to the duration of temporal overlap. The broken line in Fig. 14 gives the expected shape of the ISI-enhancement function assuming such a linear temporal overlap rule. This simple rule accounted for almost all of the variance in the histogram ($r^2 = 0.94$). According to this interpretation, the rightward shift in the ISI-enhancement function results simply from the fact that unequal stimulus durations were used. Using these stimulation parameters, the induction of associative LTP appears to require simultaneous activation of the two inputs.

The stimulation durations used in these experiments (600 and 400 msec, respectively, for the W and S inputs) were chosen to resemble those commonly used in pavlovian conditioning studies and to optimize LTP induction. However, these long stimulus trains are not ideal for resolving the temporal contiguity requirements on a millisecond time scale. One reason is that synaptic depression and other changes could cause the late part of the stimulus train to be less effective in inducing LTP than the early part of the train. In fact, others have reported that— when very short tetanic stimulations are used—associative LTP can be induced even if there is no temporal overlap between the W and S stimulus trains.

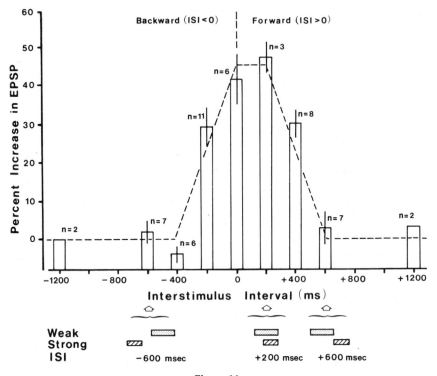

Figure 14.

ISI-synaptic enhancement function. The ISI is the time between *onset* of the W tetanic stimulation and the *onset* of the S tetanic stimulation. Negative ISI values (backward pairings) and positive values (forward pairings) indicate the temporal relationship between the W and S stimulations, as shown by the three examples in the bottom display. A range of ISIs was explored in different slices as described in Fig. 13 and text. The number (*n*) of W–S pathway pairs (slices) studied at each ISI is indicated. The vertical bars show the amount of synaptic enhancement at each ISI. The dashed line is proportional to the duration of temporal overlap between the W and S stimulations. Using the present stimulus durations (see Fig. 13), there is no temporal overlap when ISI < −400 msec or ISI > +600 msec. The horizontal stripped and stippled bars are drawn to approximately to scale. The mean percent increase in the population ESPS amplitudes at each ISI is based on the number (*n*) of W inputs shown adjacent to each vertical bar. (From S. R. Kelso and T. H. Brown, unpublished observations.)

Levy and Steward (1983) reported that LTP could occur using forward W–S pairings having temporal gaps (between the offset of the W stimulation and the onset of the S stimulation) as large as 20 msec. Their results (done *in vivo* on perforant path inputs to the dentate gyrus) raise the possibility of a small forward-pairing bias. Similarly, Gustafsson and Wigström (1986) have reported instances of LTP in the Sch/com synapses using forward W–S pairings with gaps of up to 40 msec. These reports suggest that following stimulation of a W input there remains a "trace" of previous activity, which can last for tens of milliseconds, during which the synapses continue to be eligible for associative LTP. We did not find evidence for such a trace period—either because of a detection problem associated with small sample sizes or because the duration of this post-tetanic trace period is much briefer for longer tetanic stimulations.

These and other experiments on associative LTP in the CA1 region of the hippocampus have revealed several features of this activity-dependent form of neuroplasticity that are potentially relevant to its role as a synaptic substrate for aspects of learning (Kelso and Brown, 1986; Brown et al., 1988). Specifically, (1) the induction of the functional modulation is rapid; (2) the expression of the enhanced synaptic strength is persistent; (3) modification of one synaptic input can be conditionally controlled by temporal contiguity with activity in another synaptic input to the same region; and (4) the associative enhancement appears to be specific to just those synapses whose activity conforms to the temporal requirement. These are also features of the synaptic interactions in certain identified circuits of *Aplysia* that have been demonstrated to mediate differential Pavlovian conditioning (Hawkins et al., 1983; Walters and Byrne, 1983; Clark and Kandel, 1984; Carew and Sahley, 1986). Understanding the spatiotemporal features of the activity-enhancement relationships has led to the development of testable hypotheses concerning the molecular and biophysical mechanisms underlying associative LTP (see below), which helps us to envision more concretely and then explore experimentally the conditions under which this form of synaptic plasticity can be expected to be induced and expressed endogenously.

C. Conjunctive Mechanism Controlling LTP Induction

The spatiotemporal features of the activity-enhancement relationships that describe the induction and expression of associative LTP clearly place severe constraints on the range of plausible underlying mechanisms. In principle, these features can easily be explained by a "Hebb-like" mechanism (discussed below; Brown et al., 1989). According to this interpretation (Kelso et al., 1986; Brown et al., 1988), the postsynaptic currents produced by stimulating the S input allow the required coincidence between activity in the W input and the postsynaptic cell. An alternative possibility is that the essential contribution of activity in the S input is unrelated to consequences of postsynaptic depolarization, but instead involves the concomitant release of a critical amount of a necessary "LTP factor" (Goddard, 1982).

To evaluate these possibilities, Kelso et al. (1986) substituted for the usual S input a combination of current- and voltage-clamp procedures that either *forced* or *prevented* postsynaptic spiking during stimulation of a W input (Fig. 15). Application of a strong, outward (depolarizing) current step (1.5 nA for 200 msec) alone, which forced the postsynaptic cell to fire action potentials in the absence of presynaptic activity, failed to induce LTP. Tetanic synaptic stimulation (100 Hz for 200 msec) delivered while applying a voltage clamp that maintained the soma at a negative potential (-80 mV)—which prevented postsynaptic spiking (Fig. 15)—also failed to induce LTP. However the same synaptic stimulation delivered during the outward current step (Fig. 15) did induce LTP in the stimulated input. Thus LTP was induced only following conjoint pre- and postsynaptic activity, an outcome that satisfies some interpretations (Kelso *et al.*, 1986; Brown *et al.*, 1989) of a Hebb-like mechanism (elaborated below).

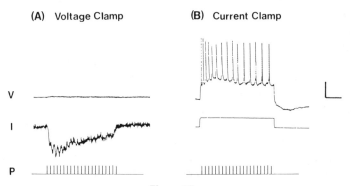

Figure 15.
Voltage- and current-clamp manipulations used to demonstrate the conjunctive mechanism underlying associative LTP in the Sch/com synapses of the CA1 region. Top traces are the membrane potential (V); middle traces are the current passed by the single-electrode clamp (I); and the bottom traces indicate the time of presynaptic stimulation. Under both voltage-clamp (A) and current-clamp (B) conditions the steady-state membrane potential at the cell soma was maintained at -80 mV. (A) Repetitive presynaptic stimulation (100 Hz for 200 msec) of a W input during application of a voltage clamp to the soma to prevent the postsynaptic cell from spiking. LTP was not induced under these conditions (Kelso *et al.*, 1986). (B) The same presynaptic stimulation of the W input delivered during a simultaneous outward (depolarizing) current step (1.5 nA for 200 msec) applied through the intracellular electrode. The current step (with or without synaptic stimulation) forced spiking in the postsynaptic cell. LTP was induced under these conditions (Kelso *et al.*, 1986). However the current step alone (in the absence of presynaptic stimulation) did not induce LTP. Calibration bars: vertical, 20 mV (A, B) and 0.5 nA (A), 2.0 nA (B); horizontal, 40 msec (A, B). [Modified from Kelso *et al.* (1986).]

D. Role of Sodium Spikes in the Conjunctive Mechanism

Some consequence of postsynaptic depolarization evidently is critical for enabling LTP induction at just those synapses that are eligible to change by virtue of being active at about the same time. Hebb (1949) considered "firing" the postsynaptic cell to be critical:

> When an axon of cell A is near enough to excite cell B or repeatedly or consistently takes part in firing it, some growth process or metabolic change takes place in one or both cells such that A's efficiency, as one of the cells firing B, is increased (p. 62).

This suggestion has been termed (Stent, 1973) "Hebb's postulate" for learning. The idea was that such a process could serve as the basis for a memory formation and storage process that would cause enduring modifications in the elicited activity patterns of spatially distributed "nerve cell assemblies." The modern view of a "Hebbian synapse" (Brown et al., 1989) includes the notion that *coincident or correlated* pre- and postsynaptic activity produces a persistent increase in synaptic strength. One interpretation is that sodium action potentials must be generated in the soma for the LTP mechanism to operate.

Both for historical reasons and to learn more about the underlying LTP mechanism, it was of interest to find out whether the elicitation of postsynaptic sodium spikes was in fact necessary. Two groups (Kelso et al., 1986; Gustafsson et al., 1987) examined the role of sodium spikes by repeating the preceding type experiment under conditions in which postsynaptic sodium spikes were pharmacologically blocked by ionto-phoretically injecting the postsynaptic neurons with a local anesthetic (QX222 or QX314, lidocaine derivatives that block the channels responsible for sodium action potentials). Both groups found that blocking sodium spikes did not interfere with the LTP mechanism. Thus a critical amount of postsynaptic depolarization is normally required to induce LTP in active Sch/com synapses, but sodium spikes do not play an essential role in the LTP mechanism.

E. Role of Glutamate Receptors in the Conjunctive Mechanism

Several investigators have speculated that the essential consequence of postsynaptic depolarization might involve Ca^{2+} influx, a popular notion for which experimental evidence has been mounting (Dunwiddie et al., 1978; Eccles, 1983; Izumi et al., 1987; Kuhnt et al., 1985; Lynch et al., Bliss and Lynch, 1988). The possibility that Ca^{2+} influx triggers the modification process immediately raises several related questions. What type of ionic channel(s) might be responsible? Are there Ca^{2+}-permeable channels that have the required properties to account for the spatiotemporal specificity of the activity-enhancement relationships? Or does this specificity emerge as a consequence of complex subcellular interactions? Where on the cell might such channels be located? Recent evidence points to the involvement of a Ca^{2+}-permeable ionic channel that is gated by a type of glutamate receptor.

Glutamate is thought to be the major excitatory transmitter at many mammalian central nervous system (CNS) synapses (Fonnum, 1984; Fagg and Foster, 1983). There are two major two classes of postsynaptic glutamate receptors, termed kainate–quisqualate (K-Q) and N-methyl-D-aspartate (NMDA) (Fagg *et al.*, 1986; Mayer and Westbrook, 1987; Watkins and Evans, 1981; Cotman *et al.*, 1988). The first evidence linking a particular glutamate receptor to LTP induction came from reports (Collingridge *et al.*, 1983; Harris *et al.*, 1984, 1986; Wigstrom and Gustafsson, 1984) that selective NMDA receptor antagonists prevent LTP induction without blocking synaptic transmission or preventing the expression of LTP that has already been induced. One such NMDA receptor antagonist is DL-2-amino-5-phosphonopentanoic acid (AP5; see Fagg *et al.*, 1986), the action of which is illustrated in Fig. 16.

The effects of AP5 support the idea that postsynaptic calcium influx is involved in triggering LTP induction. This conclusion is based on voltage-clamp experiments that have recently elucidated the nature of the conductances that are controlled by glutamate binding to K-Q and NMDA receptors (Mayer and Westbrook, 1987; Jahr and Stevens, 1987; Mac-Dermott *et al.*, 1986). The K-Q receptors are associated with a conventional (voltage-independent or minimally voltage-dependent) conductance increase to Na^+ and K^+, analogous to the cholinergic response that underlies synaptic transmission at the vertebrate motor endplate (cf. Steinbach and Stevens, 1976). By contrast, the NMDA receptors are associated with a conductance increase to Ca^{2+} (and, to a lesser extent, Na^+ and K^+) (Mayer and Westbrook, 1987; Jahr and Stevens, 1987; MacDermott *et al.*, 1986). This Ca^{2+} conductance increase is strongly voltage-dependent, due to a block of the channel by Mg^{2+} at negative membrane potentials (Jahr and Stevens, 1987; Nowak *et al.*, 1984; Mayer *et al.*, 1984). The Mg^{2+} block becomes progressively relieved as the membrane containing the channel becomes more depolarized than the normal resting values (-70 to -80 mV).

For purposes of simulating the macroscopic synaptic currents in the spine model illustrated in Fig. 18A, we need a kinetic model of the glutamate-gated channels. The gating is complicated and still poorly understood (Cull-Candy and Usowicz, 1987b). Pending a more suitable kinetic model for such macroscopic current simulations, it may be useful initially to make the following simplifying assumptions. First, there are two types of glutamate-activated channels: one is associated with K-Q

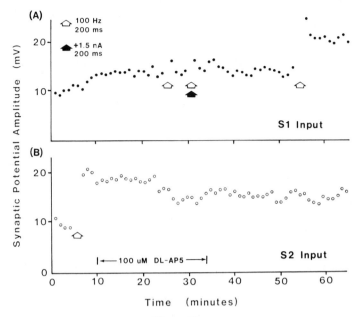

Figure 16.
Demonstration that DL-2-amino-5-phosphonopentanoate (AP5) prevents
induction of LTP in the Sch/com pathway but does not block synaptic
transmission or LTP expression. Two strong inputs (S1 and S2) of the Sch/
com pathway were alternately tested in a rat CA1 pyramidal cell
(maintained at −80 mV under current-clamp conditions). (A) Bath
application of 100 μ*M* DL-AP5 does not attenuate the S1-produced EPSPs.
However, neither tetanic stimulation (three trains 12 sec apart, 100 Hz for
200 msec each) alone (open arrow) nor when paired (open and solid
arrows) with simultaneous outward current steps (1.5 nA, 200 msec)
induced LTP in the S1 pathway in the presence of the AP5. Upon washout
of the AP5, the same brief tetanic stimulation induced LTP in this
pathway. (B) Prior to the bath application of AP5, LTP was induced in the
S2 following a brief tetanic stimulation (same parameters used on S1).
Subsequent bath application of AP5 did not block LTP expression in this
pathway. (From A. H. Ganong and T. H. Brown, unpublished
observations).

receptors and the other with NMDA receptors. Thus, we ignore the fact
that a given agonist is only probabilistically connected to any of several
different channel subconductance levels (Jahr and Stevens, 1987; Cull-
Candy and Usowicz, 1987a). Second, the K-Q receptor-gated channels
operate in a voltage-independent fashion to produce a conductance increase only to Na^+ and K^+, whereas (in the presence of normal $[Mg^{2+}]$)
the NMDA receptor-gated channels produce a voltage-dependent conductance increase only to Ca^{2+}.

For purposes of the present discussion, we shall also ignore multiple glutamate-binding steps, asymmetric transition probabilities among particular subconductance levels, desensitization, and several other issues that need to be understood (Cull-Candy and Usowicz, 1987b; Johnson and Ascher, 1987). For the initial simulations, we want the simplest possible model of the macroscopic currents—especially those associated with the AP5 binding site. The four-state kinetic scheme illustrated in Fig. 17 is possibly a reasonable first-approximation for modeling the AP5-sensitive Ca^{2+} influx into the spine head. The four channel states include two that are not Mg^{2+}-bound (C, closed, and O, open) and two that are Mg^{2+}-bound (C-Mg^{2+} and O-Mg^{2+}). Only the O state has a high Ca^{2+} conductance. The transition from the C and C-Mg^{2+} states to the O and O-Mg^{2+} states is assumed to be dependent on glutamate (Glu) binding and unbinding to the NMDA receptor. The transition from the O and C states to the O-Mg^{2+} and C-Mg^{2+} states is assumed to be controlled by the [Mg^{2+}] and the potential across the channel V_m. The dependence of this transition on V_m becomes negligible for low [Mg^{2+}].

This model assumes that the binding and unbinding of Mg^{2+} and the binding and unbinding of Glu are independent events. When glutamate is bound to the NMDA receptor, the Ca^{2+}-permeable O state becomes relatively more probable during depolarization or in media

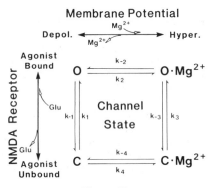

Figure 17.
Four-state kinetic model for NMDA receptor-activated channels. The state of the channel is dependent on whether the receptor is bound by a glutamate (Glu) agonist and by Mg^{2+}; the latter is dependent on the transmembrane potential (V_m). Transmitter binding to the NMDA receptor increases the probability that the channel undergoes a transition from the closed (C) or Mg^{2+}-bound closed (C-Mg^{2+}) states to either the open (O) or Mg^{2+}-bound open (O-Mg^{2+}) states. The relative probabilities of the latter two states depend on the membrane potential V_m and the [Mg^{2+}]. Depolarization (Depol.) increases the rate of Mg^{2+} unbinding ($k_{-2} + k_{-4}$; hyperpolarization (Hyper.) decreases rate of Mg^{2+} unbinding ($k_2 + k_4$). The Mg^{2+} and Glu binding and unbinding are assumed to be independent. Only the O state is permeable to Ca^{2+}. (See text for discussion.)

containing low $[Mg^{2+}]$. In medium containing a normal $[Mg^{2+}]$, there is a crude sense in which the early steps that cause LTP induction can be compared to a logical AND-gate (Brown *et al.*, 1988). The two conditions that are normally necessary for producing a conductance increase to Ca^{2+} (the O state) are binding of the postsynaptic NMDA receptor by presynaptically released glutamate *and* sufficient depolarization of the postsynaptic cell to relieve the voltage-dependent Mg^{2+} block.

Thus synaptic stimulation will cause Ca^{2+} influx only if glutamate release is accompanied by sufficient depolarization. If the membrane containing the glutamate receptor-gated channels is not sufficiently depolarized, or if the NMDA receptors are blocked by an antagonist, then glutamate release will only cause the conductance increase to Na^+ and K^+ that is associated with the K-Q receptors. In some hippocampal synapses, the latter conductance increase is thought to be sufficient to account for the fast EPSPs that are observed *in vitro* (under normal ionic conditions) in response to single afferent volleys, provided the resting potential is sufficiently negative relative to the strength of the synaptic input (Mayer and Westbrook, 1987; Coan and Collingridge, 1987; Herron *et al.*, 1986; Dingledine *et al.*, 1986).

Our spine model for LTP induction in the Sch/com synapses (Brown *et al.*, 1988) can be briefly stated as follows: *Ca^{2+} influx through the ionic channels associated with NMDA receptors on postsynaptic spine heads results in a spatially restricted transient increase in $[Ca^{2+}]_i$ that triggers Ca^{2+}-dependent reactions responsible for the synaptic enhancement* (For discussion of Ca^{2+} regulation, see Chapter 19, this volume) Our model has six key features (see Fig. 18A):

1. The induction of LTP is triggered, at least in part, by a postsynaptic $[Ca^{2+}]$ increase in the dendritic spine.

2. Postsynaptic Ca^{2+} entry into the spine is controlled by the NMDA receptor-gated channel, which is located on the subsynaptic membrane.

3. The subsynaptic membrane also contains K-Q receptor-gated channels, which permit synaptic transmission at negative membrane potentials and in the presence of NMDA receptor antagonists.

4. The physical geometry of the spine, combined with intracellular Ca^{2+} sequestration mechanisms, amplifies and restricts the peak $[Ca^{2+}]$ transient to the spine region, near the site of entry.

5. The Ca^{2+} binding sites that trigger LTP induction are located near the NMDA receptor-gated channel.

6. The postsynaptic conductance increase produced on individual dendritic spines by single quantal releases is suitably matched

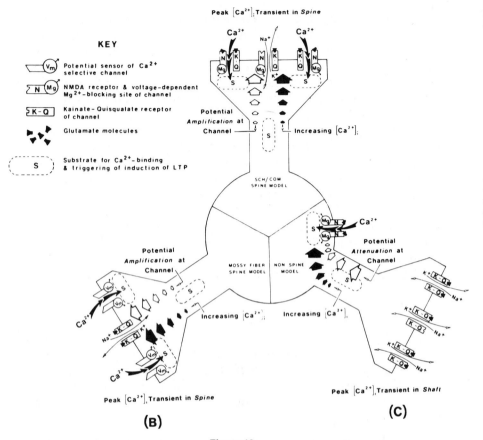

Figure 18.
Three models for LTP induction (see Brown *et al.*, 1988). The perspective is
orthogonal to the cross section of the dendritic shaft (central region). The
three radially oriented spines illustrate the main features of each model
(see key for symbols). Expected gradients for peak voltage (open arrows)
and peak $[Ca^{2+}]i$ transients (solid arrows) are shown in relationship to the
presumed locations of substrates (S) for Ca^{2+}. (A) Spine model proposed
(Brown *et al.*, 1988) for LTP induction in the Sch/com synapses. Both
NMDA and K-Q receptor-gated channels are present on the subsynaptic
membrane (spine head). They may *additionally* be present on other parts of
the neuron. For simplicity, the receptors are shown here coupled to a
single channel (cf. Jahr and Stevens, 1987), although this is not an
essential feature of the model (see text). (B) An alternative model
suggested (Gamble and Koch, 1987) for certain synapses of the CA3
region. It differs qualitatively from the first model (A) only in regard to the
type of channel that is proposed to mediate Ca^{2+} influx. Ca^{2+} entry into
the spine is through voltage-dependent calcium channels, which are
substituted for the NMDA receptor-gated channels. (C) A non-spine
model (cf. Bliss and Lynch, 1988; Dingledine, 1986) in which the NMDA
receptor-gated channels are located *only* on the dendritic shaft. It is not
certain whether there are differences between subsynaptic and extrasynaptic NMDA receptor-gated channels.

to the local input admittance (reciprocal of the input impedance) to enable conditional control of the NMDA receptor-gated channel. This last point is elaborated below in conjunction with the non-spine model (Fig. 18C).

Although we have not yet simulated this model (Fig. 18A), one can see qualitatively that with suitable parameter selections it should be able to reproduce (1) the cooperativity requirement, (2) the high spatiotemporal specificity of the conjunctive mechanism, (3) the blockade of LTP induction (but not synaptic transmission or LTP expression) by NMDA receptor antagonists, and (4) the fact that it is difficult or impossible to induce LTP in media containing greatly reduced $[Ca^{2+}]$ (Dunwiddie et al., 1978; Wigstrom et al., 1979) or in cells injected with a Ca^{2+} chelator (Lynch et al., 1983). Cooperativity results from the requirement for transmitter release and binding to be accompanied by a critical amount of postsynaptic depolarization. Otherwise the Mg^{2+} channel block is not relieved and Ca^{2+} influx into the spine does not occur (Figs. 17 and 18). In the absence of other sources of depolarization, LTP induction therefore occurs following stimulation of S but not W inputs. The channel location and gating properties, combined with the spine microphysiology, give rise to the required spatiotemporal specificity for the Hebb-like mechanism (see Brown et al., 1988) underlying associative LTP. The model is specifically designed to reduce the likelihood of heterosynaptic LTP occurring among Sch/com synapses.

Can the model (Figs. 17 and 18) accommodate a 10- to 30-msec forward-pairing trace period? Quantitative questions at this level are difficult to intuit without actually performing the simulations with all of the rate constants selected. It is not certain whether the channel kinetics (of the subsynaptic NMDA receptor–iontophore complex) alone can account for a 10- to 30-msec trace period. There is evidence that the channel open times can sometimes last tens of milliseconds (Nowak et al., 1984; Jahr and Stevens, 1987; Cull-Candy and Usowicz, 1987a), suggesting that glutamate unbinding can be slow. If glutamate unbinding (from the subsynaptic NMDA receptor) in the presence of a normal $[Mg^{2+}]$ is sufficiently slow, then a forward-pairing trace period could, in principle, result from a transition from the $O-Mg^{2+}$ to the O states (Fig. 17), as illustrated in Fig. 19. To evaluate this type of explanation, we need to know more about the voltage dependence of synaptically controlled macroscopic currents during the trace period. Depending on precise estimates of some of the key rate constants and the macroscopic currents, we may be forced to consider more complex models—possibly including additional channel states, slow removal of glutamate from the synaptic cleft, slow channel block, or other sources of Ca^{2+} influx (or other activity-dependent steps) that can summate temporally (or interact) with the trace left by the W input.

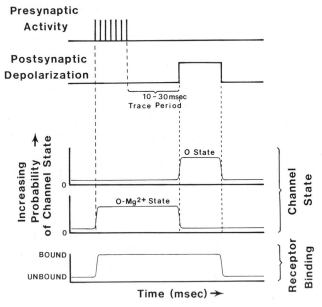

Figure 19.
One possible interpretation of a forward-pairing trace period based on the
kinetic models in Fig. 17 (see associated text). If postsynaptic
depolarization (due to current injection or to an S synaptic input) occurs
within 10–30 msec following a single presynaptic volley in another W
input, and if glutamate (Glu) remains bound for this duration, then the
channels could remain in the O-Mg^{2+} state during the trace period and
undergo a transition to the O state during subsequent depolarization.
Additional studies will be needed to appreciate the actual relationship
between channel kinetics and the trace period. Is Glu unbinding (Figs. 17
and 19) from the subsynaptic NMDA receptor normally slow enough *in
situ* to account for a 30-msec trace period? To evaluate the adequacy of
various kinetic models derived from studies of channel openings in
synaptic or extrasynaptic membrane patches, we need to know more at
the macroscopic level about the synaptic control of voltage-dependent and
AP5-sensitive postsynaptic Ca^{2+} currents during the trace period.

Bliss and Lynch (1988) have suggested an alternative model of LTP
induction in which the subsynaptic membrane contains only K-Q receptor-gated channels. In this model, illustrated in Fig. 18C, the NMDA
receptor-gated channels are located only on the dendritic shaft and are
activated by glutamate that diffuses out of the synaptic cleft (Bliss and
Lynch, 1988; Dingledine, 1986). Bliss and Lynch (1988) suggested this
type of model because, as explained below, they doubted that the synaptic conductance is in fact suitably matched to the input admittance at

the spine head to enable conditional control of the NMDA receptor-gated channel. They noted that if the release of a single quantum of glutamate (the smallest amount that can be evoked by a presynaptic nerve impulse) produces a conductance increase similar to that reported at the vertebrate motor endplate, then the voltage at the spine head would be driven to values approaching the synaptic reversal potential, which is near 0 mV in the hippocampus (Brown and Johnston, 1983; Barrionuevo et al., 1986). If the weakest possible synaptic input produced such a strong depolarization, then it would indeed be difficult to explain the cooperativity requirement and the Hebb-like mechanism underlying associative LTP. Such a large depolarization would eliminate conditional control of LTP induction in a W input, which would undergo enhancement regardless of coactivity in other inputs.

However, this model does not address the problem of input specificity. How does a rise in $[Ca^{2+}]$ in the dendritic shaft trigger a change in just those synapses whose activity caused the Ca^{2+} influx? Although this problem is not insurmountable, we suggest as a simple and testable alternative that the single quantal conductance in hippocampus is not so large as to eliminate conditional control of local calcium influx at the spine head. Our preliminary estimates (Brown et al., 1988; Rong et al., 1987) suggest that the single quantal conductance may be of the order of 10^{-9} S, and our simulations indicate that this value is not so large that it would drive the subsynaptic membrane potential into a voltage range that would preclude conditional control (Brown et al., 1988).

VI. Two Forms of Hippocampal LTP Based on Receptor-Mediated Controls

How general are these models of LTP induction that are based on NMDA receptor-gated channels (Figs. 18A and 18C)? Autoradiographic studies using radiolabeled glutamate or specific NMDA antagonists indicate that NMDA binding sites are present in relatively high levels throughout many regions of the brain, including neocortical regions, the basal ganglia, and sensory systems (Monaghan and Cotman, 1985; Cotman et al., 1988). The termination zone of the Sch/com projection to CA1 pyramidal neurons of the hippocampus has one of the highest levels of binding in the central nervous system (Monaghan and Cotman, 1985). However, the regions of the hippocampus to which the granule cell mossy-fiber and collateral axons are known to project (Fig. 20A, stippled area) have a much lower NMDA receptor binding density (Fig. 20B) (Monaghan and Cotman,1985).

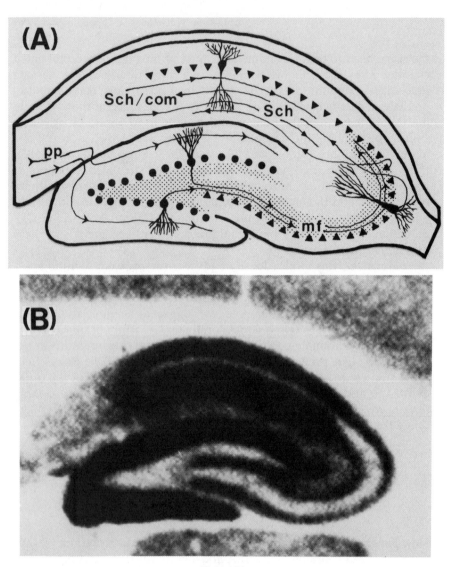

Figure 20.
Distribution of NMDA receptor binding sites in a transverse section of the
rat hippocampus as determined by autoradiography of NMDA-sensitive
[^{3}H]-glutamate binding (Monaghan and Cotman, 1985). (A) Schematic
tracing of the photograph in (B) showing the major hippocampal synaptic
pathways and cell body layers. The granule cell projection zone, where
the least amount of NMDA-sensitive binding occurs, is stippled. (B)
Increasing binding density is coded by the increasing darkness of the
halftones. The highest levels of binding occur in the termination zone of
the Sch/com synapses (stratum oriens and stratum radiatum) in CA1
region and the inner molecular layer (proximal dendrites) of granule cells
in the dentate gyrus. One of the lowest levels is in the terminal field of
the mossy-fiber projections to the CA3 region (the stratum lucidum). The
relative density of subsynaptic and extrasynaptic NMDA receptors is
unknown. (Photograph supplied courtesy of Dr. D. T. Monaghan and
Dr. C. W. Cotman.)

A. Differences in Receptor-Mediated Control of LTP Induction

The low levels of NMDA binding sites of the mossy-fiber projection zone present an opportunity to test the generality of the model that we have suggested for the Sch/com synapses (Fig. 18A). Despite the low levels of NMDA binding sites, robust LTP can be obtained in this pathway (see Figs. 5 and 6) (Barrionuevo *et al.*, 1986; Griffith *et al.*, 1986). Interestingly, NMDA receptor antagonists do not block LTP induction at these synapses (Harris and Cotman, 1986). On the other hand, antagonists for the β-noradrenergic receptor do interfere with LTP in the mossy-fiber synapses, in contrast to their apparent lack of effect in the Sch/com synapses (see Chapter 15, this volume). The above observations imply that, in regard to receptor-mediated control of the induction step, there appear to be at least two forms of LTP within the hippocampus.

For the mossy-fiber pathway we are therefore forced to consider an alternative mechanism for LTP induction, one that does not involve NMDA receptors. Gamble and Koch (1987) have proposed such a model (Fig. 18B) for LTP. The Gamble-Koch (G-K) model shares five features with the spine model that we favor (Fig. 18A) for the Sch/com synapses. It differs with respect to the type of calcium-permeable channel on the subsynaptic membrane. The G-K model can be summarized as follows: Ca^{2+} *influx through voltage-dependent* Ca^{2+} *channels on postsynaptic spine heads results in a spatially restricted increase in* $[Ca^{2+}]_i$ *that triggers* Ca^{2+} *-dependent reactions responsible for the synaptic enhancement.* The G-K model does not address the role of β-adrenergic receptors (Brown *et al.*, 1988a; see Chapter 15, this volume), the possible actions of released Zn^{2+} (Peters *et al.*, 1987; Westbrook and Mayer, 1987), or the role of opiates (Gall *et al.*, 1981; McGinty *et al.*, 1983; Moises and Walker, 1985)—none of which are clearly understood in relationship to LTP in the mossy-fiber synapses. The simulations of Gamble and Koch (1987) were useful in illustrating conditions under which tetanic stimulation of a synaptic input can result in a highly localized, transient increase in the $[Ca^{2+}]$ in the spine. The high degree of *compartmentalization* and *local amplification* of the Ca^{2+} signal revealed by these simulations is also required in the Sch/com spine model (Fig. 18A).

B. Comparison of the Three Models for LTP Induction

In all three of the models, cooperativity emerges naturally from the relationship between synaptic strength, Ca^{2+} influx, and LTP induction. However, cooperativity has not yet been demonstrated to be a feature of LTP induction at the mossy-fiber synapses. If cooperativity cannot be demonstrated in these synapses, then the G-K model for the mossy-fiber synapses will have to be rejected or substantially revised. A related prediction of the G-K model is that the induction of LTP in the mossy-fiber synapses should be controllable by manipulations of the postsynaptic membrane potential. Specifically, LTP induction should be prevented if the postsynaptic membrane potential is maintained under voltage-clamp conditions at a relatively negative potential during tetanic stimulation of the mossy-fiber synaptic inputs (Brown *et al.*, 1988). Furthermore, LTP should be induced simply by strong depolarization of the postsynaptic neuron—in the absence of synaptic stimulation (Brown *et al.*, 1988). Ca^{2+} influx into the spines is not dependent on transmitter release, but only on the potential at the spine head—which should be controllable from the soma (Brown *et al.*, 1988). Neither prediction has been adequately assessed in the mossy-fiber synapses.

The models also differ in regard to the occurrence of associative versus heterosynaptic LTP. Only the Sch/com spine model (Fig. 18A) contains strong constraints against true heterosynaptic LTP. The G-K model predicts that heterosynaptic LTP should occur among mossy-fiber synapses. Because the mossy-fiber synapses are electrotonically near each other (Brown *et al.*, 1988), tetanic stimulation of an S input should cause sufficient depolarization in spines associated with unstimulated synapses inputs to induce LTP in them. Testing this prediction of the model is complicated by the extensive recurrent circuitry in the CA3 region (Johnston and Brown, 1986; Miles and Wong, 1987). In the absence of further constraints, the non-spine model (Fig. 18C) might also predict heterosynaptic LTP among closely adjacent synapses. Other differential and testable predictions among the models are considered elsewhere (Brown *et al.*, 1988).

VII. Summary and Conclusions

In this review we (1) summarized what is known and unknown about the activity-enhancement relationships that govern LTP in two synaptic systems of the hippocampus, (2) described the evidence and rationale underlying several models for the expression and induction of LTP in these two systems, and (3) explored ways in which certain aspects of these models can be tested experimentally using a combination of optical and neurophysiological techniques.

The evidence indicates that there is more than one form of LTP in the hippocampus, at least in terms of receptor-mediated control of the induction step. The models that have been proposed for hippocampal LTP induction predict some interesting differences in the activity-modification relationships. One of these models, which we proposed for the Sch/com synapses, is consistent with a Hebb-like mechanism. It can account for cooperativity, the known properties of associative LTP, and pharmacological studies that implicate the NMDA receptor. It was specifically designed to preclude the occurrence of heterosynaptic LTP. In this model, Ca^{2+} influx through NMDA receptor-gated channels located on the spine head plays an essential role in LTP induction.

An alternative model, suggested by Gamble and Koch (1987), is consistent with a cooperative but non-Hebbian activity-enhancement relationship. Originally proposed for synapses in the CA3 region, this model cannot support associative LTP of the type known to occur in the Sch/com synapses. It predicts that heterosynaptic LTP should occur among nearby synapses. In this model, Ca^{2+} influx through voltage-dependent calcium channels located in the spine head triggers LTP induction.

Both models are useful because they can be simulated, they lead to different and testable predictions, and they emphasize the fact that seemingly small differences at the molecular/biophysical level can produce activity-modification relationships that could yield radically different behavior in an adaptive neural network. They also illustrate concretely that the formal requirements for generating cooperativity are less stringent than those for producing associativity—terms that have sometimes been incorrectly used interchangeably. Such seemingly small differences may be important when considering the manner in which the circuitry of the hippocampus carries out its suspected mnemonic functions. We may have only just begun to appreciate the varieties of synaptic plasticity that can occur even within the delimited confines of a hippocampal brain slice.

Whether the quantal basis of LTP expression is the same at different synapses in the hippocampus is unknown, but the key experiments can now be done. A quantal analysis of LTP, which is now underway, will test predictions of the three models for LTP expression that were discussed. If the results show that the expression of LTP involves a presynaptic modification, then there may be a novel form of retrograde synaptic control mechanism.

The experiments and models reviewed here may suggest a more general lesson for computational neuroscience. Theoretical studies of adaptive networks commonly assume or search for a single activity-modification relationship as the basis for learning (see Chapter 7, this volume). It is possible, however, that certain mnemonic functions in mammals emerge from concatenations of several different forms of use-dependent synaptic plasticity. The adaptive power of the mammalian nervous system may emerge from various combinations of different activity-modification relationships embedded into different types of local circuits. This is known to be the case for simple forms of nonassociative and associative learning in *Aplysia* (see Chapters 1, 2, 3, and 4, this volume; Carew and Sahley, 1986), and there is no reason to believe that the adaptive variability of synapses in mammals is less than that known to exist in higher mollusks.

Acknowledgments

This work has been supported by grant F49620-86-C-0099 from the Air Force Office of Scientific Research, and a Neuroscience, Development Award from the McKnight Foundation. We thank Dr. Richard Aldrich, Dr. Craig Jahr, and Dr. Charles Stevens for useful discussion regarding the kinetics of the NMDA receptor-gated channel and Dr. Brenda Claiborne for enlightenment regarding the topography of the granule cell projection system.

References

Amaral, D. G., and Dent, J. A. (1981). *J. Comp. Neurol.* **195,** 51–86.
Barrionuevo, G., and Brown, T. H. (1983). *Proc. Natl. Acad. Sci. U.S.A.* **80,** 7347–7351.
Barrionuevo, G., Kelso, S. R., Johnston, D., and Brown, T. H. (1986). *J. Neurophysiol.* **55,** 540–550.
Baxter, D. A., Bittner, G. D., and Brown, T. H. (1985). *Proc. Natl. Acad. Sci. U.S.A.* **82,** 5978–5982.
Bliss, T. V. P., and Lynch, M. A. (1988). *In* "Long-Term Potentiation: From Biophysics to Behavior" (P. W. Landfield and S. Deadwyler, eds.), pp. 3–72. Alan R. Liss, New York.
Briggs, C. A., Brown, T. H., and McAfee, D. A. (1985a). *J. Physiol. (London)* **359,** 503–521.
Briggs, C. A., McAfee, D. A., and McCaman, R. E. (1985b). *J. Physiol. (London)* **363,** 181–190.
Brown, T. H., and Johnston, D. (1983). *J. Neurophysiol.* **50,** 487–507.
Brown T. H., and Keenan, C. L. (1987). *Soc. Neurosci. Abstr.* **13,** 1516.
Brown, T. H., Perkel, D. H., and Feldman, M. W. (1976). *Proc. Natl. Acad. Sci. U.S.A.* **73,** 2913–2917.
Brown, T. H., Wong, R. K. S., and Prince, D. A. (1979). *Brain Res.* **177,** 194–199.
Brown, T. H., Chang, V. C., Ganong, A. H., Keenan, C. L., and Kelso, S. R. (1988). *In* "Long-Term Potentiation: From Biophysics to Behavior" (P. W. Landfield and S. Deadwyler, eds.), pp. 201–264. Alan R. Liss, New York.
Brown, T. H., Ganong, A. H., Kairiss, E. W., and Keenan, C. L. (1989). *Annu. Rev. Neurosci.* (in press).
Buzsaki, G. (1985). *In* "Brain Plasticity, Learning, and Memory" (B. E. Will, P. Schmitt, and J. C. Dalrymple-Alford, eds.), pp. 157–166. Plenum, New York.
Carew, T. J., and Sahley, C. L. (1986). *Annu. Rev. Neurosci.* **9,** 435–487.
Claiborne, B. J., Amaral, D. G., and Cowan, W. M. (1986). *J. Comp. Neurol.* **246,** 435–458.
Clark, G. A., and Kandel, E. R. (1984). *Proc. Natl. Acad. Sci. U.S.A.* **81,** 2577–2581.
Coan, E. J., and Collingridge, G. L. (1987). *Neuroscience* **22,** 1–8.
Collingridge, G. L., Kehl, S. J., and McLennan, H. (1983). *J. Physiol. (London)* **334,** 33–46.
Cotman, C. W., Monaghan, D. T., and Ganong, A. H. (1988). *Annu. Rev. Neurosci.* **11,** 61–80.
Crick, F. (1982). *Trends NeuroSci. (Pers. Ed.)* **5,** 44–46.
Cull-Candy, S. G., and Usowicz, M. M. (1987a). *Nature (London)* **325,** 525–528.
Cull-Candy, S. G., and Usowicz, M. M. (1987b). *Trends Pharmacol. Sci.* **8,** 218–224.
Dingledine, R. (1986). *Trends NeuroSci. (Pers. Ed.)* **9,** 47–49.
Dingledine, R., Hynes, M. A., and King, G. L. (1986). *J. Physiol. (London)* **380,** 175–189.
Dunwiddie, T., Madison, D., and Lynch, G. (1978). *Brain Res.* **150,** 413–417.
Eccles, J. C. (1983). *Neuroscience* **10,** 1071–1081.
Errington, M. L., Lynch, M. A., and Bliss, T. V. P. (1987). *Neuroscience* **20,** 279–284.
Fagg, G. E., and Foster, A. C. (1983). *Neuroscience* **9,** 701–719.
Fagg, G. E., Foster, A. C., and Ganong, A. H. (1986). *Trends Pharmacol. Sci.* **7,** 357–363.
Fonnum, F. (1984). *J. Neurochem.* **42,** 1–11.

Gall, C., Brecha, N., Karten, H. J., and Chang, K. J. (1981). *J. Comp. Neurol.* **198**, 335–350.
Gamble, E., and Koch, C. (1987). *Science* **236**, 1311–1315.
Goddard, G. (1982). *Neurosci. Res. Program. Bull.* **20**, 676–680.
Griffith, W. H., Brown, T. H., and Johnston, D. (1986). *J. Neurophysiol.* **55**, 767–775.
Gustaffson, B., and Wigstrom, H. (1986). *J. Neurosci.* **6**, 1575–1582.
Gustaffson, B., Wigstrom, H., Abraham, W. C., and Huang, Y.-Y. (1987). *J. Neurosci.* **7**, 774–780.
Harris, E. W., and Cotman, C. W. (1986). *Neurosci. Lett.* **70**, 132–137.
Harris, E. W., Ganong, A. H., and Cotman, C. W. (1984). *Brain Res.* **323**, 132–137.
Harris, E. W., Ganong, A. H., Monaghan, D. T., Watkins, J. C., and Cotman, C. W. (1986). *Brain Res.* **382**, 174–177.
Hawkins, R. D., Abrams, T. W., Carew, T. J., and Kandel, E. R. (1983). *Science* **219**, 400–405.
Hebb, D. O. (1949). "The Organization of Behavior." Wiley, New York.
Herron, C. E., Lester, R. A. J., Coan, E. J., and Collingridge, G. L. (1986). *Nature (London)* **322**, 265–268.
Izumi, Y., Ito, K., Miyakawa, H., and Kato, H. (1987). *Neurosci. Lett.* **77**, 176–180.
Jahr, C. E., and Stevens, C. F. (1987). *Nature (London)* **325**, 522–525.
Johnson, G. W., and Ascher, P. (1987). *Nature (London)* **325**, 529–531.
Johnston, D., and Brown, T. H. (1983). *J. Neurophysiol.* **50**, 464–486.
Johnston, D., and Brown, T. H. (1984). *In* "Brain Slices" (R. Dingledine, ed.), pp. 51–86. Plenum, New York.
Johnston, D., and Brown, T. H. (1986). *In* "Basic Mechanisms of the Epilepsies: Molecular and Cellular Approaches" (A. V. Delgado-Escueta, A. A. Ward, Jr., D. M. Woodbury, and R. J. Porter, eds.), pp. 263–274. Raven Press, New York.
Keenan, C. L., Chapman, P. F., Chang, V. C., and Brown, T. H. (1988). *Brain Res. Bull.*, in press.
Kelso, S. R., and Brown, T. H. (1984). *Soc. Neurosci. Abstr.* **10**, 78.
Kelso, S. R., and Brown, T. H. (1985). *Soc. Neurosci. Abstr.* **11**, 780.
Kelso, S. R., and Brown, T. H. (1986). *Science* **232**, 85–87.
Kelso, S. R., Ganong, A. H., and Brown, T. H. (1986). *Proc. Natl. Acad. Sci. U.S.A.* **83**, 5326–5330.
Kuhnt, U., Mihaly, A., and Joo, F. (1985). *Neurosci. Lett.* **53**, 149–154.
Lee, K. S. (1983). *J. Neurosci.* **3**, 1369–1372.
Levy, W. B., and Steward, O. (1979). *Brain Res.* **175**, 233–245.
Levy, W. B., and Steward, O. (1983). *Neuroscience* **8**, 791–797.
Levy, W. B., Brassel, S. E., and Moore, S. D. (1983). *Neuroscience* **8**, 799–808.
Lynch, G., and Baudry, M. (1984). *Science* **224**, 1057–1063.
Lynch, G., Larsen, J., Kelso, S., Barrionuevo, G., and Schottler, F. (1983). *Nature (London)* **305**, 719–721.
MacDermott, A. B., Mayer, M. L., Westbrook, G. L., Smith, S. J., and Barker, J. L. (1986). *Nature (London)* **321**, 519–522.
Mayer, M. L., and Westbrook, G. L. (1987). *Prog. Neurobiol.* **28**, 197–276.
Mayer, M. L., Westbrook, G. L., and Guthrie, P. B. (1984). *Nature (London)* **309**, 261–263.
McGinty, J. F., Hendriksen, S. J., Goldstein, A., Terennis, L., and Bloom, F. E. (1983). *Proc. Natl. Acad. Sci. U.S.A.* **80**, 589–593.
McNaughton, B. L. (1983). *In* "The Neurobiology of the Hippocampus" (W. Seifert, ed.), pp. 233–251. Academic Press, London.
McNaughton, B. L., Douglas, R. M., and Goddard, G. V. (1978). *Brain Res.* **157**, 277–293.
Miles, R., and Wong, R. K. S. (1987). *J. Physiol. (London)* **388**, 611–629.
Moises, H. C., and Walker, J. M. (1985). *Eur. J. Pharmacol.* **108**, 85–98.
Monaghan, D. T., and Cotman, C. W. (1985). *J. Neurosci.* **5**, 2909–2919.
Morris, R. and Baker, M. (1984). *In* "Neuropsychology of Memory" (L. R. Squire and N. Butters, eds.), pp. 521–535. Guilford Press, New York.

Nowak, L., Bregestovski, P., Ascher, P., Herbet, A., and Prochiantz, A. (1984). *Nature (London)* **307**, 462–465.

Perkel, D. H. (1986). *Soc. Neurosci. Abstr.* **12**, 1167.

Peters, S., Koh, J., and Choi, D. W. (1987). *Science* **236**, 589–593.

Racine, R. J., and Kairiss, E. W. (1987). *In* "Neuroplasticity, Learning, and Memory" (N. W. Milgram, C. M. MacLeod, and T. L. Petit, eds.), pp. 173–197. Alan R. Liss, New York.

Rall, W. (1974). *In* "Cellular Mechanisms Subserving Changes in Neuronal Activity" (C. D. Woody, K. A. Brown, T. J. Crow, and J. D. Knispel, eds.), pp. 13–21. Brain Inf. Serv., Los Angeles, California.

Rall, W. (1978). *In* "Studies of Neurophysiology" (R. Porter, ed.), pp. 203–209. Cambridge Univ. Press, London and New York.

Rong, X.-W., Keenan, C. L., and Brown, T. H. (1987). *Soc. Neurosci. Abstr.* **13**, 975.

Steinbach, J. H., and Stevens, C. F. (1976). *In* "Frog Neurobiology: A Handbook" (R. Llinas and W. Precht, eds.), pp 33–92. Springer-Verlag, Berlin and New York.

Stent, G. S. (1973). *Proc. Natl. Acad. Sci. U.S.A.* **70**, 997–1001.

Swanson, L. W., Teyler, T. J., and Thompson, R. F. (1982). *Neurosci. Res. Program, Bull.* **20**, 613–769.

Taube, J. S., and Schwartzkroin, P. A. (1987). *Brain Res.* **419**, 32–38.

Teyler, T. J., and DiScenna, P. (1984). *Brain Res. Rev.* **7**, 15–28.

Teyler, T. J., and DiScenna, P. (1987). *Annu. Rev. Neurosci.* **10**, 131–161.

Walters, E. T., and Byrne, J. H. (1983). *Science* **219**, 405–408.

Watkins, J. C., and Evans, R. H. (1981). *Annu. Rev. Pharmacol. Toxicol.* **21**, 165–204.

Westbrook, G. L., and Mayer, M. L. (1987). *Nature (London)* **328**, 640–643.

Wigström, H., and Gustafsson, B. (1984). *Neurosci. Lett.* **44**, 327–332.

Wigström, H., Swann, J. W., and Anderson, P. (1979). *Acta Physiol. Scand.* **105**, 126–128.

15

The Role of Norepinephrine in Long-Term Potentiation at Mossy-Fiber Synapses in the Hippocampus

Daniel Johnston, William F. Hopkins, and Richard Gray

―――――――――― I. Introduction ――――――――――

Our lab has been investigating the biophysical properties of neurons and synapses in the hippocampus (Brown and Johnston, 1983; Johnston and Brown, 1983, 1984a; Gray and Johnston, 1987; Johnston et al., 1980). In particular, we have been interested in the cellular and membrane mechanisms associated with epileptogenesis and long-term synaptic plasticity (Johnston and Brown, 1984b, 1986; Barrionuevo et al., 1986; Griffith et al., 1986). For a variety of reasons, which will be described below, we focused our attention on neurons in the regio inferior of the hippocampus and on the mossy fiber synapses that arise from dentate granule cells and terminate on the CA3 pyramidal neurons. In this chapter, we will briefly review the results of experiments that have demonstrated that norepinephrine (NE) can enhance the magnitude, duration, and probability of induction of long-term potentiation (LTP) at the mossy fiber synapses (Hopkins and Johnston, 1984, 1988; Hopkins, 1986). These experiments also suggest that under normal conditions (see Hopkins and Johnston, 1988), the release of NE may play a required role in the induction of LTP at these synapses.

―――――――――― II. Characteristics of Mossy ――――――――――
Fiber Synapses

The now-familiar schematic of a hippocampal slice is illustrated in Fig. 1. Depicted in the diagram are several important features of the hippocampus that we would like to focus attention on.

First, in our experiments we have used both intracellular and extracellular recordings from CA3 pyramidal neurons to measure the synaptic responses to stimulation of the dentate granule cells.

307

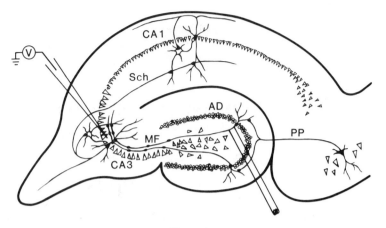

Figure 1.
Schematic diagram of the hippocampal slice preparation illustrating the
typical placement of stimulating and recording electrodes. MF, mossy
fibers; AD, area dentata; PP, perforant path; Sch, Schaffer collaterals.
[Adapted from Hopkins (1986).]

Second, the mossy fiber synapses are relatively unique. They are
large (4–8 μm), they contain zinc and dynorphin, and they are ultra-
structurally identifiable with both light and electron microscopes (Claiborne *et al.*, 1986; McGinty *et al.*, 1983; Amaral, 1979; Frotscher *et al.*,
1981; Hamlyn, 1961, 1962). In early anatomical studies using Timm stain
(Blackstad and Kjaerheim, 1961; Haug, 1967), the mossy fiber synapses
were shown to terminate on the proximal portion of the apical dendrites.
We performed an extensive anatomic, physiologic, and electrotonic
analysis of this synaptic input and found that the maximum electrotonic
distance of the mossy fiber synapses from the cell bodies of the CA3
pyramidal neurons was approximately 0.06, or 6% of a length constant
(Johnston and Brown, 1983). This relatively short electrotonic distance
allowed us to evaluate the errors associated with voltage clamping this
synaptic input via a point clamp applied at the soma and then to determine reasonable values for the conductance increase, reversal potential, and kinetics of the synaptic response (Brown and Johnston, 1983).

Third, activation of the mossy fiber pathway results in not only
excitation to pyramidal neurons but also a very powerful inhibition mediated through interneurons (Brown and Johnston, 1983; Griffith *et al.*,
1986). These interneurons are excited directly by mossy fiber synapses
and indirectly by recurrent collaterals from the CA3 pyramids, producing
feedforward and recurrent inhibition, respectively. This inhibition, which
is presumably mediated by γ-aminobutyric acid (GABA) (Storm-Mathisen, 1977), exerts a very powerful influence on the neurons in this region
of the hippocampus. The collaterals from the CA3 pyramidal neurons

also synapse directly onto other pyramidal neurons, forming a recurrent excitatory network, which is believed to play a prominent role in epileptogenesis (Johnston and Brown, 1986) and perhaps in information storage mechanisms (Miles and Wong, 1987).

The mossy fiber synapses are the only synapses in the hippocampus for which changes in their biophysical properties, and in the biophysical properties of their postsynaptic neurons, have been investigated before and during LTP. For example, the induction of mossy fiber LTP is not associated with changes in membrane time constant, input resistance, spike threshold, or synaptic reversal potential in CA3 pyramidal neurons (Barrionuevo *et al.*, 1986). Furthermore, there is no long-term decrease in recurrent or feedforward inhibition that could produce an "apparent" LTP of the excitatory response (Griffith *et al.*, 1986). LTP of the mossy fiber input is accompanied by about a 50% increase in the measured excitatory synaptic conductance increase (Barrionuevo *et al.*, 1986; Brown *et al.*, Chapter 14, this volume).

In general, however, much less is known about LTP at mossy fiber synapses than, for example, the Schaffer collateral synapses in the hippocampus (cf. Swanson *et al.*, 1982; Teyler, 1987). This is particularly important since it appears that certain features of LTP at mossy fiber synapses are different (cf. Brown *et al.*, Chapter 14, this volume). Although we will continue to utilize the term LTP to describe the long-term enhancement of synaptic efficacy observed at mossy fiber synapses, it is important to note that one should not necessarily generalize mechanisms from one class of synapse to another.

III. Norepinephrine in Hippocampus

Norepinephrine-containing fibers from the locus coeruleus (LC) are diffusely distributed throughout the central nervous system (Swanson and Hartman, 1975; Descarries *et al.*, 1977). The innervation of the hippocampus from LC is particularly prominent (Loy *et al.*, 1980; Moore and Bloom, 1979). The NE inputs are dense in the hilus of the dentate gyrus and in the stratum lucidum of the CA3 subfield but are much less dense in stratum radiatum of CA1. The density of the innervation is thus quite heterogeneous in the hippocampus.

The NE pathways have been suggested to play a role as a so-called "plasticizing pathway"—that is, a pathway that would be active during periods of arousal or other states in which it would be of significance for an organism to remember associated stimuli (Young, 1963; Konorski, 1967). Because NE was shown to be released during periods of arousal (Maynert and Levi, 1964), it was suggested that NE might act as such a plasticizing agent in developmental plasticity, control of behavioral states, and learning and memory (Crow, 1968; Kety, 1970; Pettigrew and Ka-samatsu, 1978; Woodward *et al.*, 1979; Ogren *et al.*, 1980; Aston-Jones and Bloom, 1981a,b; Mason, 1981; Foote *et al.*, 1983; Bear and Singer, 1986). Whether NE plays a role as a plasticizing agent or modulator of learning and memory, however, is controversial.

Previous studies have addressed the question of whether NE has a role in LTP in the hippocampal formation. NE and several α- and β-adrenoceptor agonists and antagonists were shown to have no effects on LTP at Schaffer collateral synapses in the CA1 region (Dunwiddie *et al.*, 1982). Other studies have reported a variety of effects of NE on LTP in the dentate gyrus. The depletion of NE was shown to have either adverse effects on certain features of LTP (Bliss *et al.*, 1983; Stanton and Sarvey, 1985) or little or no effect (Krug *et al.*, 1983; Robinson and Racine, 1985). One consistent finding is that responses to perforant path stim-ulation can be augmented by brief bath application of NE in the absence of tetanic stimulation (Lacaille and Harley, 1985; Neuman and Harley, 1983). Whether this NE-inducted LTP is mechanistically similar to tetanic stimulation-induced LTP is not known.

With the assumption that LTP is somehow involved in learning and memory (Teyler and DiScenna, 1984), our experiments were de-signed as a test of the hypothesis that NE modulates LTP at mossy fiber synapses. We found that, unlike in the dentate gyrus, there is no effect on mossy fiber evoked synaptic responses during brief bath applications of NE in the absence of tetanic stimulation. In the presence of tetanic stimulation, however, bath application of NE-augmented features of LTP (Hopkins, 1986; Hopkins and Johnston, 1984, 1988).

--------------- IV. Norepinephrine and Mossy ---------------
Fiber LTP

Figure 2 illustrates a typical LTP experiment. An intracellular electrode is recording the synaptic events in a CA3 neuron in response to stim-ulation of the mossy fibers. The mossy fibers were stimulated at a fre-quency of 0.2 Hz, and three superimposed traces are shown in each panel. Several years ago, we showed that in normal saline, the synaptic input from mossy fiber stimulation is biphasic, consisting of a small, early depolarizing phase followed by a longer-lasting hyperpolarizing phase (Brown and Johnston, 1983). This biphasic response results from an overlap in time of the mossy fiber excitatory postsynaptic potential (EPSP) and the feedforward or recurrent inhibitory postsynaptic potential (IPSP). Even the early depolarizing phase is actually a mixture of the EPSP and the IPSP, because the two events almost completely overlap in time (Griffith *et al.*, 1986).

Figure 2B illustrates the synaptic responses 1 min following three

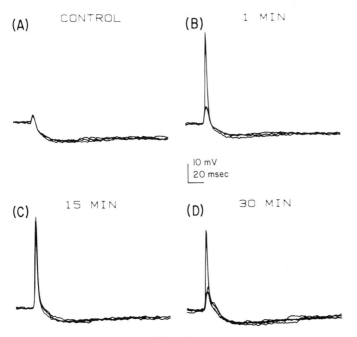

Figure 2.

Mossy fiber evoked synaptic responses recorded intracellularly before and
during LTP. The mossy fibers were stimulated at 0.2 Hz with the cell at
the resting membrane potential (-60 mV). Three superimposed traces are
shown for each time period. (A) The control mossy fiber evoked synaptic
responses are illustrated. The synaptic responses consist of an early
depolarizing phase followed by a longer-lasting and slower-
hyperpolarizing phase. (B) The responses to mossy fiber stimulation are
illustrated at 1 min following three 100-Hz, 1-sec stimulus trains to the
mossy fibers. An action potential was triggered by one of the synaptic
responses. When an action potential was not generated, the depolarizing
phase of the response appears bigger than control. (C) At 15 min after the
high-frequency stimulation of the mossy fibers, each synaptic response
triggered an action potential. At this 15-min criterion point for the
measurement of LTP, an enhancement in synaptic efficacy is evident. (D)
At 30 min after high-frequency stimulation the synaptic response was still
of sufficient amplitude to trigger an action potential. The amplitude of the
depolarizing phase of the underlying synaptic component appears bigger
than control when an action potential was not generated. The input
resistance of this cell was about 100 MΩ. [From Griffith *et al.* (1986).]

100-Hz, 1-sec stimulus trains to the mossy fibers. It appears from these
recordings that the depolarizing phase has increased and an action potential has been triggered in one of the three trials. In Fig. 2C, 15 min
following the train, each shock to the mossy fibers now elicits an action
potential; 30 min later (Fig. 2D) the depolarizing phase continues to appear larger, and action potentials are triggered on some of the trials.

Clearly, an increase in synaptic efficacy has occurred in this pathway following the high-frequency stimulus trains to the mossy fibers. This increase in efficacy lasted at least 30 min and is what has commonly been referred to as LTP. In this and most of our experiments, the magnitude of LTP was measured 15 min after tetanic stimulation, because shorter forms of plasticity, such as facilitation and posttetanic potentiation, are decayed within about 10 min (Hopkins and Johnston, 1984, 1988).

LTP at the mossy fibers appears to have at least two time courses (Hopkins and Johnston, 1984). In some experiments, we found that LTP decayed within approximately 1 hr, and we have called this decremental LTP. In other experiments, LTP shows very little decay during the course of an *in vitro* slice experiment (several hours), and we have called this nondecremental LTP. Whether these two decay modes represent different forms of LTP and how they compare to LTP described at other hippocampal synapses is not clear. Decremental LTP is observed in about 20% of the experiments using normal saline in the bath, but if one uses picrotoxin (PTX) to block GABAergic inhibition, one almost never observes decremental LTP (Hopkins and Johnston, 1988). We have found similar effects of NE on both forms of LTP (Hopkins and Johnston, 1984, 1988).

The first type of experiment used to test for effects of NE on mossy fiber synaptic responses is illustrated in Fig. 3. Mossy fibers were stimulated at 0.2 Hz with slices bathed in normal saline. A simple input–output curve is plotted for the mossy fiber population (p) EPSP before, during, and after perfusing 10 μM NE into the bath. We found that NE did not increase the pEPSP when the mossy fibers were stimulated at these relatively low frequencies. If this low-frequency stimulation was continued, we found that in a few experiments NE actually increased a low frequency depression that is commonly observed at these synapses. We never observed any increase in the synaptic response due to the addition of NE to the bath. This lack of effect of NE on mossy fiber responses is in contrast to that seen at perforant path synapses (see above), suggesting again that the action of NE is regionally heterogeneous in the hippocampus.

In contrast to the lack of effect of NE on mossy fiber responses obtained with low-frequency stimulation, we found that NE had pronounced effects on LTP. One type of experiment we used to investigate LTP is shown in Fig. 4. (In this experiment, we investigated the effects of NE on decremental LTP, because we wished to elicit repeated episodes of LTP in the same slice before, during, and after the application of NE. This obviously would not be possible with the nondecremental form of LTP.) The arrows in Fig. 4 illustrate the time at which the high frequency stimulus train was given to the mossy fibers. During the first episode of LTP, there was approximately a 50% increase in the pEPSP, which

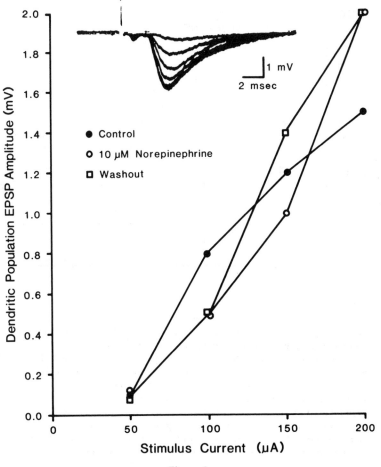

Figure 3.
Input–output curves for the pEPSP versus stimulus current intensity
before, during, and after bath application of 10 μM NE. The inset depicts
examples of pEPSPs evoked by a series of different stimulus current
intensities. [Adapted from Hopkins and Johnston (1988).]

decayed to baseline within 1 hr. The 15-min time point for measuring
the magnitude of LTP is noted by the "X" in the figure. Each symbol
represents an average of 10 responses obtained at 0.2 Hz. After the control episode of LTP, 10 μM NE was added to the bath, and then a second
high-frequency stimulus train was given to the mossy fibers. NE was
washed from the bath immediately following the train. With NE present
during the high-frequency train, there was a pronounced increase in
both the magnitude and the duration of LTP. The third high-frequency
stimulus train elicited a near control level of LTP, showing that the effect
of NE was reversible. In other experiments (not shown), we found that

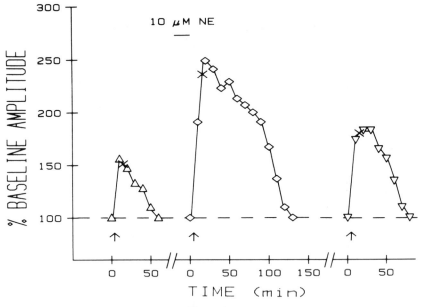

Figure 4.
Effects of brief bath application of NE (10 μ*M*) on LTP. NE was present 20
min before and during tetanic stimulation but was washed out
immediately after the high-frequency train. The arrows in this and all
figures indicate high-frequency trains used to induce LTP (100 Hz, 2 sec).
The stimulus intensity for the train was 50 μA. Symbols represent 10-
sweep (0.2 Hz) averages of pEPSP amplitudes normalized to the
pretetanus average amplitude. The crosses represent the 15 min
posttetanus time points at which LTP magnitude was quantified. In this
and all figures, the standard errors of the mean for each time point are
smaller than the symbols. [From Hopkins and Johnston (1988).]

the β-adrenoceptor agonist isoproterenol would mimic this action of NE,
suggesting the involvement of a β-adrenoceptor (see Hopkins and Johnston, 1984, 1988).

It is well known that with slices in normal saline, there is a stimulus
intensity threshold for eliciting LTP. If the stimulus intensity is below a
certain value, a high-frequency stimulus train will not elicit LTP (Hopkins
and Johnston, 1984). We wondered whether NE might decrease this intensity threshold, so we designed the experiment shown in Fig. 5. Each
arrow in Fig. 5 represents a low-intensity, 100-Hz, 2-sec stimulus train
to the mossy fibers. The first stimulus train elicits a brief period of posttetanic potentiation but no LTP. We gave a second stimulus train at the
same intensity to ensure that we were still below threshold for eliciting
LTP. Before the third stimulus train, we added 10 μ*M* NE to the bath.

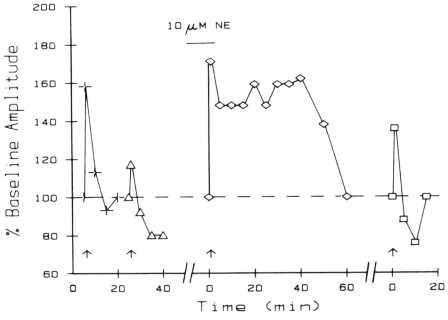

Figure 5.
Effect of bath-applied NE on the induction of LTP. In the first two
episodes, repetitive stimulation (100 Hz, 2 sec, 30 μA) resulted in brief
PTP, followed by a somewhat longer-lasting response depression, but no
LTP. When NE was present during the conditioning train in the third
episode, LTP was induced. Data from episode 4 demonstrate that the
effect was reversible. [From Hopkins and Johnston (1984). Copyright 1984
by the AAAS.]

This third train, at the same stimulus intensity but with NE in the bath,
elicited LTP.

From these experiments, we concluded that NE, possibly through
β-adrenoceptors, enhances the magnitude, duration, and probability of
induction of LTP at mossy fiber synapses. To test further the involvement
of β-adrenoceptors, we used antagonists such as propranolol and timolol.
We found that the β-antagonists blocked the enhancement of LTP by
NE, strengthening our conclusion for the involvement of a β-adrenoceptor (see Fig. 6). We also found, however, that propranolol and timolol
blocked LTP in the absence of exogenously applied NE. These experiments suggested that the release of NE from surviving fibers may be
involved in the normal expression of LTP and may actually be required
for LTP in normal saline. Figure 7 summarizes the results from a number
of such experiments. Timolol and propranolol profoundly reduce the
probability of induction of LTP at mossy fiber synapses.

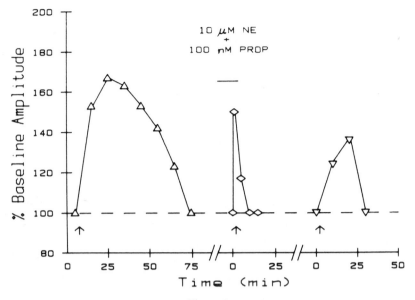

Figure 6.
Effect of 10 µM NE plus 100 nM propranolol, a β-receptor antagonist, on
the induction of LTP. Data sampled at 1, 5, 10, and 15 min after
conditioning are shown for the second episode to illustrate PTP. The
enhancement of LTP by NE was blocked by propranolol. Conditioning
parameters were 100 Hz, 2 sec, 75 µA. [From Hopkins and Johnston
(1984). Copyright 1984 by the AAAS.]

Because of the overlap in the EPSP and IPSP, which was illustrated
in Fig. 2, one possible mechanism for the enhancement of LTP by NE
is through a decrease in GABA-mediated inhibition (Madison and Nicoll,
1984). Such a disinhibition has been demonstrated elsewhere in the hippocampus to increase the probability of induction of LTP (Wigstrom and
Gustafsson, 1983a,b). To test this hypothesis, we first blocked GABAergic
inhibition by perfusing slices with 10 µM PTX and then tested for effects
of isoproterenol on LTP. Figure 8 summarizes the results from several
experiments. We found that in the presence of PTX, isoproterenol still
increased the magnitude and probability of induction of LTP, suggesting
that disinhibition is not required for the enhancement of LTP by NE.

The activation of β-adrenoceptors in hippocampus and elsewhere
has been shown to stimulate the synthesis of cyclic adenosine mono-
phosphate (cAMP) (Bloom, 1975; Dolphin *et al.*, 1979; Segal *et al.*, 1981;
Lefkowitz *et al.*, 1983). A reasonable hypothesis is that cAMP mediates
the action of NE in enhancing LTP (Madison and Nicoll, 1986). We tested
this hypothesis by using forskolin, a compound shown to stimulate the

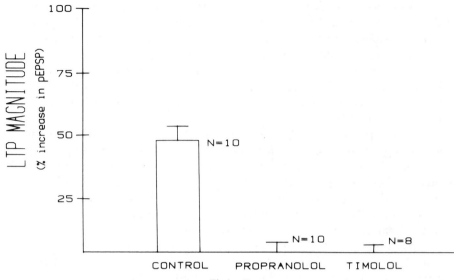

Figure 7.
Summary graph of the effect of propranolol and timolol on LTP (NE not
present). LTP magnitude was measured at 15 min posttetanus, and bars
represent the standard error of the mean (SEM) for each group. [From
Hopkins and Johnston (1988).]

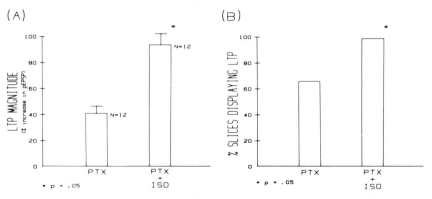

Figure 8.
The β-adrenoceptor agonist isoproterenol (1 μM) mimicked the frequency-
dependent effects of NE in disinhibited slices. (A) Summary graph
comparing LTP magnitude in control and isoproterenol-treated slices. (B)
The percentage of slices displaying LTP with or without isoproterenol in
the bath. Picrotoxin (10 μM) was present in all of the experiments
summarized here. [From Hopkins and Johnston (1988).]

synthesis of cAMP (Seamon and Daly, 1981), in a series of experiments similar to those with NE or isoproterenol. Figure 9 summarizes the results of those experiments. We found that forskolin indeed mimicked the action of NE and isoproterenol by increasing the magnitude and probability of induction of LTP. It should be noted that forskolin did not produce LTP; that is, forskolin in the absence of tetanic stimulation produced no long-lasting changes in the mossy fiber synaptic response (see Hopkins and Johnston, 1988).

An important question arising from these studies is whether the enhancing action of NE on LTP takes place pre- or postsynaptically. Given our previous results, which indicated (1) that the effect of NE could be mimicked by increasing cAMP and (2) that propranolol could significantly decrease the probability of induction of LTP, we designed the following experiment. The slices were bathed in 100 nM propranolol but otherwise normal saline. We obtained data from three groups of cells. In two groups, 8-bromo-cAMP was injected intracellularly into the postsynaptic cell. One of these groups also received tetanic stimulation to the mossy fibers to elicit LTP and one did not. In the third group of cells, we injected the inactive metabolite of cAMP, 5'-AMP, and also gave tetanic stimulation to the mossy fibers. Measurements of LTP were made under voltage clamp, and we compared the synaptic conductance before and after the high-frequency stimulus train (see Fig. 10). The results of these experiments are shown in Fig. 11. We found that only the group of cells

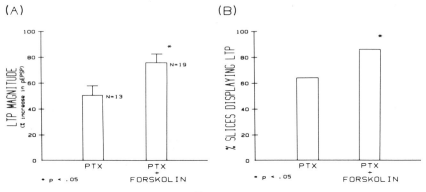

Figure 9.
Forskolin (50 μM), applied 20–50 min before tetanic stimulation, mimicked the effects of NE and isoproterenol on LTP in disinhibited slices. (A) Summary graph comparing LTP magnitude in control and forskolin-treated slices. (B) The percentage of slices displaying LTP with or without forskolin. Picrotoxin was present in all of the experiments summarized here. [From Hopkins and Johnston (1988).]

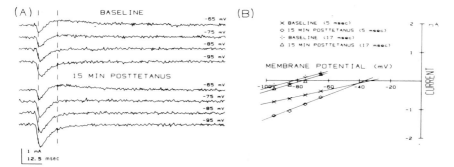

Figure 10.
The phenomenon of LTP measured under voltage-clamp conditions. (A) Mossy fiber synaptic currents (single sweeps) sampled at four different holding potentials before and 15 min after high-frequency stimulation. The dashed vertical lines correspond to the fixed latencies (5 and 17 msec following stimulus artifact) at which synaptic currents were measured. (B) Current–voltage plots for the cell shown in (A). Each data point is the mean of five sweeps. Before tetanic stimulation, the slope conductance for the early current measurement (5 msec) was 12 nS and the extrapolated reversal potential was −34 mV. At 15 min following the high-frequency train, the slope conductance for the early current measurement was 22 nS and the extrapolated reversal potential was −38mV. The baseline slope conductance for synaptic current measured at 17 msec was 16 nS, and was 17 nS at 15 minutes posttetanus. The apparent reversal potential for this current changed from −81 mV to −76 mV over this time period. This experiment was performed in normal saline, and the recording pipette contained 2 M potassium methylsulphate. This cell had an input resistance of 50 MΩ and a resting potential of −55 mV. [From Hopkins and Johnston (1988).]

injected with 8-bromo-cAMP and receiving tetanic stimulation to the mossy fibers displayed significant LTP. Neither the 5′-AMP group nor the nontetanized 8-bromo-cAMP group displayed significant LTP (Fig. 11). These results suggest that (1) the injection of 8-bromo-cAMP postsynaptically does not produce LTP and (2) postsynaptic 8-bromo-cAMP, in conjunction with tetanic stimulation, can overcome the block of LTP by propranolol.

A clue to the possible mechanism for the 8-bromo-cAMP enhancement of LTP was gleaned by comparing the membrane potential during tetanic stimulation between the 8-bromo-cAMP and the 5′-AMP groups of cells. Figure 12 illustrates the results from one experiment. We found that there was a greater and longer-lasting depolarization of the membrane potential in cells injected with 8-bromo-cAMP. Results from a number of similar experiments are summarized in Fig. 13.

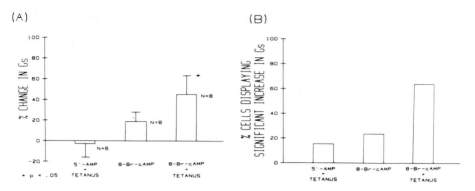

Figure 11.
Summary data from experiments in which LTP was measured under
voltage-clamp conditions with intact inhibition in the presence of
propranolol (100 nM). (A) Bar graph depicts the percent change in the
mossy fiber slope conductance for the three groups of cells (see text); G_s
refers to the mossy fiber slope conductance measured 5 msec after the
stimulus artifact. Only the cells injected with 8-bromo-cAMP and
tetanically stimulated demonstrated a significant increase in G_s as a group.
(B) Graph indicates the probability of observing a significant increase in G_s
for the three groups of cells. [From Hopkins and Johnston (1988).]

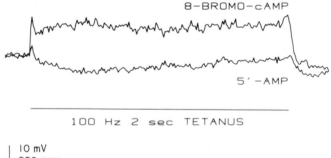

Figure 12.
(A) A comparison of the membrane potential during tetanic stimulation
(100 Hz, 2 sec) in a cell injected with 8-bromo-cAMP (10 mM, top trace)
with a cell injected with 5′-AMP (10 mM, bottom trace). Both cells were
kept at −65mV in current clamp during the train. The duration of the
high-frequency train is indicated by the bar under the traces. The cell
injected with 8-bromo-cAMP demonstrated LTP, while the cell injected
with 5′ AMP did not. Data were obtained with intact inhibition in the
presence of propranolol (100 nM). The cell injected with 8-bromo-cAMP
had an input resistance of 42 MΩ and a resting potential of −54 mV, and
the cell injected with 5′-AMP had an input resistance of 35 mΩ and a
resting potential of −52 mV. The membrane potential was sampled at 100
Hz to obtain the traces for this figure. [From Hopkins and Johnston
(1988).]

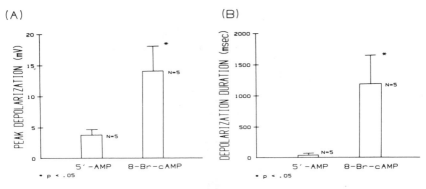

Figure 13.
A comparison of parameters of the depolarization during tetanic
stimulation in the 8-bromo-cAMP-injected cells that displayed LTP with
the 5'-AMP-injected cells that did not. (A) The peak amplitude of the
depolarization during the high-frequency train was significantly greater in
the 8-bromo-cAMP-injected group. (B) The duration of the depolarization
during the train was also significantly greater in the 8-bromo-cAMP-
injected group. [From Hopkins and Johnston (1988).]

V. Membrane Mechanisms of Norepinephrine

To investigate the membrane mechanisms of NE on hippocampal neurons, we felt it necessary to develop a new preparation that would allow
the use of patch clamp techniques (Hamill *et al.*, 1981) with adult neurons.
The preparation is diagrammed in Fig. 14 and entails treating hippocampal slices from adult guinea pigs with proteolytic enzymes and gentle
agitation until the slices split apart along the boundaries of the cell body
layers (see Gray and Johnston, 1985). Cell bodies are found to protrude
from one edge of the slice and are accessible with patch electrodes. Major
apical dendrites are intact, and synaptic inputs are functional (Griffith
et al., 1983). This preparation results in acutely exposed pyramidal neurons, either CA1 or CA3 (Gray and Johnston, 1985), and dentate granule
cells (Gray and Johnston, 1987).

For the experiments presented here, we recorded in the cell-attached patch configuration. Isotonic potassium aspartate was used in
the bath to zero the membrane potential, and isotonic barium chloride
with tetrodotoxin (TTX), tetraethylammonium (TEA), and 3,4-diami-
nopyridine was used in the pipette (see Gray and Johnston, 1987). Drugs
were applied to the surface membrane of the cell with a single- or double-
barrel puffer pipette. We recorded current flow through voltage-dependent calcium channels with barium as the permeant ion. A series of

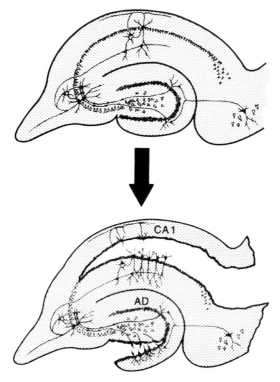

Figure 14.
Schematic drawing of a hippocampal slice before (above) and after (below)
it was split along cell body regions to expose pyramidal neurons and
dentate granule cells. The slice was split along the major cell body layers
[pyramidal CA1 and area dentata (AD)], exposing the somata and
proximal processes. [Adapted from Gray and Johnston (1985).]

step commands was given from -100 to -10 before and after applying
NE, isoproterenol, or 8-bromo-cAMP via a brief, 500-msec pressure pulse
to the puffer pipette (Fig. 15). Norepinephrine, isoproterenol, and 8-
bromo-cAMP significantly increased the activity of voltage-dependent
calcium channels. We quantified the increase in activity by measuring
the fractional open time, which consisted of the fraction of time during
the command that the current exceeded -3 times the standard deviation
of the baseline noise.

The increase in the fractional open time could be due to an increase
in the single channel conductance, the probability of opening, or the
number of channels. We tested for possible changes in single channel
conductance by measuring calcium channel current levels at different

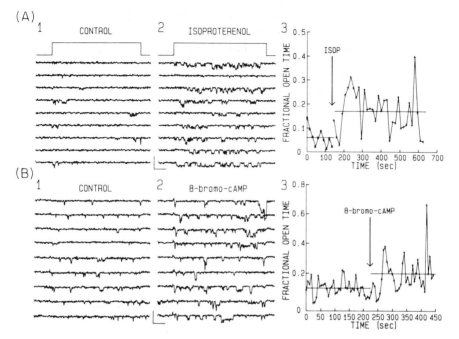

Figure 15.

(A) Application of isoproterenol increases the activity of Ca channels in a cell-attached patch from a granule cell. Patch pipettes contained 96 mM BaCl$_2$, 100 μM 3,4-DAP, 1 μM TTX, and 10 mM HEPES; the pH was adjusted to 7.35 with TEA-OH. The exposed cells were bathed in 140 mM potassium aspartate, 20 mM dextrose, 1 MgCl$_2$, 10 mM EGTA, 10 mM HEPES. The pH was adjusted to 7.4 with KOH. The potassium aspartate saline was used to zero the membrane potential across the whole cell (see Nowycky et al., 1985). Voltage jumps were applied to the membrane patch through the patch electrode, and potentials given refer to the patch membrane potential. 1, Consecutive traces of channel activity in control saline in response to step commands from −100 to −10 mV. 2, Channel activity in the same patch 95 sec after a 500-msec pressure pulse was applied to a puffer pipette that was located near the cell body and contained potassium aspartate saline plus 2 μM isoproterenol. 3, Plot of the fraction of time during the command when the current level was more negative than a threshold level (−0.3 pA) before and after application of isoproterenol. The threshold was set at −3 times the standard deviation of the baseline noise calculated from traces in which no channel activity was visible. Each plotted point is the average of three traces, and the horizontal lines indicate the means for all traces before and after drug application. Current traces shown were filtered at 2 kHz (−3 dB, Bessel response) and sampled at 10 kHz. Calibration bar: 2 pA × 10 msec. (B) Experiment in which 8-bromo-cAMP was applied in a manner similar to (A). [From Gray and Johnston (1987). Reprinted by permission from *Nature* **327,** 620–622. Copyright © 1987 Macmillan Magazines Limited.]

voltages before and after applying isoproterenol (see Fig. 16). We found
no evidence for any change in the single channel conductance under
conditions where there was a significant increase in the fractional open
time, suggesting that the increase in fractional open time is due to either
an increase in the probability of opening of individual channels or in
the number of channels in the patch.

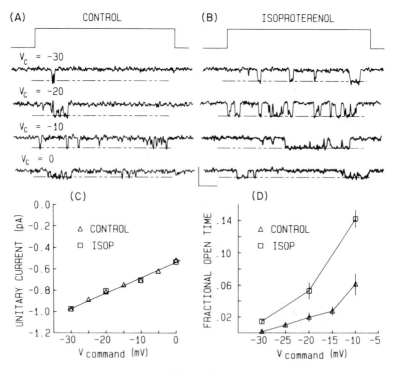

Figure 16.
Single-channel activity at different command voltages before and after
isoproterenol. The holding voltage was -100 mV. Patch voltages are
relative to the cell potential, which was near zero in potassium aspartate
saline. Data are from the same patch as that illustrated in Fig. 15A. (A)
Sample traces are shown for each of four different command voltages. The
major current level at each command voltage is indicated by the dashed
line. These data were filtered at 1 kHz. (B) Same as (A), but 400–800 sec
after a 500-msec pressure pulse was applied to a puffer pipette containing
potassium aspartate saline plus 2 μM isoproterenol. Calibration bar: 1 pA
$\times$ 10 msec. (C) Plot of major single-channel current levels versus patch
potential before and after applying isoproterenol. The slope conductance
was 14.5 pS (see Gray and Johnston, 1986) and did not change after
isoproterenol application. (D) Plot of fractional open time versus patch
potential before and after isoproterenol. [From Gray and Johnston (1987).
Reprinted by permission from *Nature* **327**, 620–622. Copyright © 1987
Macmillan Magazines Limited.]

_____ VI. Conclusions _____

Our experiments have shown that NE enhances the magnitude, duration, and probability of induction of LTP at mossy fiber synapses. Furthermore, this action of NE appears to be mediated through β-adrenoceptors, leading to an increase in cAMP. Because LTP could be blocked by β-adrenoceptor antagonists propranolol and timolol, this suggests that the release of NE from noradrenergic fibers may actually be required for the normal expression of LTP at these synapses (see Hopkins and Johnston, 1988). Using whole-cell and single-channel recordings, we found that NE, through activation of β-adrenoceptors, increases the activity of voltage-dependent calcium channels (see Gray and Johnston, 1987). One obvious hypothesis that can be drawn from these results is that the enhancement of LTP by NE results from enhanced calcium influx. The experiments with postsynaptic injection of cAMP suggest that the action of NE in modulating LTP takes place postsynaptically. We therefore suggest that the enhanced calcium influx is into the postsynaptic neuron. Figure 17 illustrates a model of this working hypothesis.

We propose that high-frequency stimulation of the mossy fiber results, either directly or indirectly, in the release of NE from LC fibers. The NE, in turn, causes greater calcium influx and greater depolarization in the postsynaptic neuron during the high-frequency train. This mechanism assumes, as proposed by others (Dunwiddie and Lynch, 1979; Lynch et al., 1983), that postsynaptic calcium influx leads to LTP. We are suggesting that in CA3 neurons, the calcium influx required for the expression of LTP occurs at least partly through the voltage-dependent calcium channels rather than the NMDA-activated channels demonstrated to be essential for LTP at perforant path and Schaffer collateral synapses (see Brown et al., chapter 14, this volume). It should be noted that Monaghan and Cotman (1985) have shown that there are no NMDA receptors in the region of the mossy fibers and APV, a specific antagonist for NMDA receptors, does not block LTP at mossy fibers as it does at other excitatory synapses in hippocampus (Harris and Cotman, 1986; see also Brown et al., chapter 14, this volume).

There are certainly other hypotheses that can account for our results. Furthermore, we cannot rule out that NE may also have presynaptic effects or that NE may inhibit inhibitory neurons, leading to disinhibition (Madison and Nicoll, 1984). However, our results with PTX suggest that NE can enhance LTP in the absence of GABA-mediated inhibition, and therefore, such a disinhibitory mechanism is not required to explain the action of NE on LTP.

Our model (Fig. 17) for the action of NE should not be generalized to other regions of the hippocampus. The effects of NE may be quite heterogeneous in the hippocampus and elsewhere in the brain. These

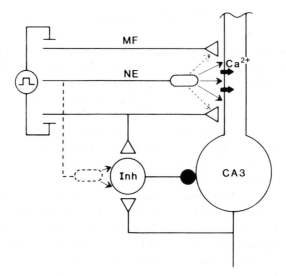

Figure 17.
Schematic diagram depicting a working hypothesis for the manner in
which NE could modulate LTP. Gross stimulation could activate both
mossy fibers (MF) and surviving NE-containing fibers in the hilus and
CA3 subfield. The effects of NE would be specifically expressed after high-
frequency activation of the mossy fibers through a number of possible
mechanisms, such as increasing the activity of voltage-dependent calcium
channels (Ca^{2+}) in the postsynaptic CA3 neurons. The dashed lines
suggest the possibilities that NE could exert effects on GABAergic
inhibitory interneurons as well as mossy fiber presynaptic terminals.
[Adapted from Hopkins (1986).]

studies leave many unanswered questions, including how such a mechanism leads to specificity of long-term plasticity. Could depolarization
alone, in the absence of synaptic stimulation, lead to LTP at mossy fiber
synapses? Or is there some other conjunctive mechanism requiring both
depolarization and activation of the mossy fibers, as has been shown in
the CA1 subfield? These questions and many others will provide the
impetus for further work on investigating the mechanisms of LTP at this
interesting excitatory synapse in the hippocampus.

References

Amaral, D. G. (1979). *Anat. Embryol.* **155,** 241–251.
Aston-Jones, G., and Bloom, F. E. (1981a). *J. Neurosci.* **1,** 876–886.
Aston-Jones, G., and Bloom, F. E. (1981b). *J. Neurosci.* **1,** 887–900.
Barrionuevo, G., Kelso, S. R., Johnston, D., and Brown, T. H. (1986). *J. Neurophysiol.* **55,**
    540–550.

Bear, M. F., and Singer, W. (1986). *Nature (London)* **320,** 172–176.

Blackstad, T. W., and Kjaerheim, A. (1961). *J. Comp. Neurol.* **117,** 133–159.

Bliss, T. V. P., Goddard, G. V., and Riives, M. (1983). *J. Physiol. (London)* **334,** 475–491.

Bloom, F. E. (1975). *Rev. Physiol. Biochem. Pharmacol.* **74,** 1–103.

Brown, T. H., and Johnston, D. (1983). *J. Neurophysiol.* **50,** 487–507.

Brown, T. H., Ganong, A. H., Kairiss, E. W., Keenan, C. L., and Kelso, S. R. (1989). *In* "Neural Models of Plasticity" (J. H. Byrne and W. O. Berry, eds.), pp. 266–306. Academic Press, New York.

Claiborne, B. J., Amaral, D. G., and Cowan, W. M. (1986). *J. Comp. Neurol.* **246,** 435–458.

Crow, T. J. (1968). *Nature (London)* **219,** 736–737.

Descarries, L., Watkins, K. C., and Lapierre, Y. (1977). *Brain Res.* **133,** 197–222.

Dolphin, A., Hamont, M., and Bockaert, J. (1979). *Brain Res.* **179,** 305–317.

Dunwiddie, T. V., and Lynch, G. (1979). *Brain Res.* **169,** 103–110.

Dunwiddie, T. V., Roberson, N. L., and Worth, T. (1982). *Pharmacol. Biochem. Behav.* **17,** 1257–1264.

Foote, S. L., Bloom, F. E., and Aston-Jones, G. (1983). *Physiol. Rev.* **63,** 844–914.

Frotscher, M., Misgeld, U., and Nitsch, C. (1981). *Exp. Brain Res.* **41,** 247–255.

Gray, R., and Johnston, D. (1985). *J. Neurophysiol.* **54,** 134–142.

Gray, R., and Johnston, D. (1986). *Biophys. J.* **49,** 432a.

Gray, R., and Johnston, D. (1987). *Nature (London)* **327,** 620–622.

Griffith, W. H., Gray, R., and Johnston, D. (1983). *Soc. Neurosci. Abstr.* **9,** 1190.

Griffith, W. H., Brown, T. H., and Johnston, D. (1986). *J. Neurophysiol.* **55,** 767–775.

Hamill, O. P., Marty, A., Neher, E., Sakmann, B., and Sigworth, F. J. (1981). *Pfluegers Arch.* **391,** 85–100.

Hamlyn, L. H. (1961). *Nature (London)* **190,** 645–648.

Hamlyn, L. H. (1962). *J. Anat.* **96,** 112–126.

Harris, E. W., and Cotman, C. W. (1986). *Neurosci. Lett.* **70,** 132–137.

Haug, F. -M. S. (1967). *Histochemie* **8,** 355–368.

Hopkins, W. F. (1986). Ph. D. Thesis, Baylor College of Medicine, Houston, Texas.

Hopkins, W. F., and Johnston, D. (1984). *Science* **226,** 350–352.

Hopkins, W. F., and Johnston, D. (1988). *J. Neurophysiol.* **59,** 667–687.

Johnston, D., and Brown, T. H. (1983). *J. Neurophysiol.* **50,** 464–486.

Johnston, D., and Brown, T. H. (1984a). *In* "Brain Slices" (R. Dingledine, ed.), pp. 51–86. Plenum, New York.

Johnston, D., and Brown, T. H. (1984b). *In* "Electophysiology of Epilepsy" (P. A. Schwartzkroin and H. V. Wheal, eds.), pp. 277–301. Academic Press, London.

Johnston, D., and Brown, T. H. (1986). *In* "Basic Mechanisms of the Epilepsies: Molecular and Cellular Approaches" (A. V. Delgado-Escueta, A. A. Ward, Jr., D. M. Woodbury, and R. J. Porter, eds.), pp. 263–274. Raven Press, New York.

Johnston, D., Hablitz, J. J., and Wilson, W. A. (1980). *Nature (London)* **286,** 391–393.

Kety, S. S. (1970). *In* "The Neurosciences: Second Study Program" (F. O. Schmitt, ed.), pp. 324–336. Rockefeller Univ. Press, New York.

Konorski, J. (1967). "Integrative Activity of the Brain." Univ. of Chicago Press, Chicago, Illinois.

Krug, M., Chepkova, A. N., Geyer, C., and Ott, T. (1983). *Brain Res. Bull.* **11,** 1–6.

Lacaille, J.-C., and Harley, C. W. (1985). *Brain Res.* **358,** 210–220.

Lefkowitz, R. J., Stadel, J. M., and Caron, M. G. (1983). *Annu. Rev. Biochem.* **52,** 159–186.

Loy, R., Koziell, D. A., Lindsey, J. D., and Moore, R. Y. (1980). *J. Comp. Neurol.* **189,** 699–710.

Lynch, G., Larson, J., Kelso, S., Barrionuevo, G., and Schottler, F. (1983). *Nature (London)* **305,** 719–721.

Madison, D. V., and Nicoll, R. A. (1984). *Soc. Neurosci. Abstr.* **10,** 660.

Madison, D. V., and Nicoll, R. A. (1986). *J. Physiol. (London)* **372,** 245–259.

Mason, S. T. (1981). *Prog. Neurobiol.* **16**, 263–303.

Maynert, E. W., and Levi, R. (1964). *J. Pharmacol. Exp. Ther.* **143**, 90–95.

McGinty, J. F., Henriksen, S. J., Goldstein, A., Terenius, L., and Bloom, F. E. (1983). *Proc. Natl. Acad. Sci. U.S.A.* **80**, 589–593.

Miles, R., and Wong, R. K. S. (1987). *Nature (London)* **329**, 724–726.

Monaghan, D. T., and Cotman, C. W. (1985). *J. Neurosci.* **5**, 2909–2919.

Moore, R. Y., and Bloom, F. E. (1979). *Annu. Rev. Neurosci.* **2**, 113–168.

Neuman, R. S., and Harley, C. W. (1983). *Brain Res.* **273**, 162–165.

Nowycky, M. C., Fox, A. P., and Tsien, R. W. (1985). *Nature (London)* **316**, 440–443.

Ogren, S. O., Archer, T., and Ross, S. B. (1980). *Neurosci. Lett.* **20**, 351–356.

Pettigrew, J. D., and Kasamatsu, T. (1978). *Nature (London)* **271**, 761–763.

Robinson, G. B., and Racine, R. J. (1985). *Brain Res.* **325**, 71–78.

Seamon, K. B., and Daly, J. W. (1981). *J. Cyclic Nucleotide Res.* **7**, 201–224.

Segal, M., Greenberger, V., and Hofstein, R. (1981). *Brain Res.* **213**, 351–364.

Stanton, P. K., and Sarvey, J. M. (1985). *J. Neurosci.* **5**, 2169–2176.

Storm-Mathisen, J. (1977). *Prog. Neurobiol.* **8**, 119–181.

Swanson, L. W., and Hartman, B. K. (1975). *J. Comp. Neurol.* **163**, 467–506.

Swanson, L. W., Teyler, T. J., and Thompson, R. F. (1982). *Neurosci. Res. Program Bull.* **20**, 613–769.

Teyler, T. J. (1987). *Annu. Rev. Neurosci.* **10**, 131–161.

Teyler, T. J., and DiScenna, P. (1984). *Brain Res. Rev.* **7**, 15–28.

Wigstrom, H., and Gustafsson, B. (1983a). *Nature (London)* **301**, 603–604.

Wigstrom, H., and Gustafsson, B. (1983b). *Brain Res.* **275**, 153–158.

Woodward, D. J., Moises, H. C., Waterhouse, B. D., Hoffer, B. J., and Freedman, R. (1979). *Fed. Proc., Fed. Am. Soc. Exp. Biol.* **38**, 2109–2116.

Young, J. Z. (1963). *Nature (London)* **198**, 626–630.

16

Some Possible Functions of Simple Cortical Networks Suggested by Computer Modeling

Gary Lynch, Richard Granger, and John Larson

I. Introduction

Neural network models provide a description of how collective interactions between independent processing units like brain cells might produce particular behaviors. The simulations are constrained to varying degrees both by behavioral data and by the amount of neurobiological data they incorporate. Thus, phenomena under study range from classical conditioning, for which there is a very rich behavioral literature with stringent criteria to be satisfied, to more abstract statements about behavior that are not directly linked to any particular instances; similarly, some models are of elements and circuitries that are only vaguely neurobiological in character while others are based on anatomical descriptions of specific networks (e.g., cerebellum, *Aplysia* ganglia, thalamo–cortical connections). These differences reflect variations on the goal of achieving unifying theories of how nervous systems generate behavior. Some workers are concerned with specific behaviors known to be produced by defined anatomical networks in brain or nervous system while others seek broader principles that operate across many behaviors and many brain architectures.

The work discussed in this review uses computer modeling for a somewhat different purpose. Developments in physiological techniques have led to a rapid increase in the body of knowledge about synaptic interactions between central neurons and the events that follow from them. At the same time, neuroanatomical research has produced increasingly precise descriptions of the organization of particular brain regions, including some of the simpler cortical structures of the forebrain (e.g., hippocampus). Using computer simulations, it is thus possible to ask what emerges when a variety of neurophysiological properties are integrated into networks based on specific cortical layers. The goal of this exercise differs from that of theoretically oriented modeling. It seeks to find functions residing in restricted portions of brain ("local properties") that are visible in behavior and to understand how these emerge from biological designs. This program has both pragmatic and theoretical aspects to it. Building simulations forces the modeler to ask anatomical and physiological questions, some of which are almost certain to have been overlooked by experimentalists. If successful in identifying properties that are local or fundamental to restricted brain networks, the simulations also should point to psychological "primitives," attributes that can be expected to be found in a very wide range of behavioral operations. We do not know what the fundamental psychologies are that give rise to particular performance characteristics during experimentally dictated tasks; presumably the psychologies are large and the observed task behaviors are simply special cases. Biological simulations may allow us not only to understand the biological correlates of known behaviors, but also to identify which of those behaviors are fundamental and which are less so, based on whatever turn out to be fundamental emergent properties found in restricted parts of brain (i.e., what is local versus what develops from interactions between localities).

II. Network Operating Rules Deduced from Physiological Experiments

Information about the operating rules governing brain networks can be obtained from biophysical studies of neurons, analyses of their synaptic interactions, and recordings of neuronal activity in the network during behavior. Additional insights can be gained from anatomical descriptions of the network, as these are often suggestive of rules (e.g., does the network have recursive feedback?). Here we will focus on the hippocampus and restrict ourselves to a few salient points that quite probably play major roles in generating and pacing physiological events. For purposes of brevity we will not include biophysical results, although these should properly be included, particularly in the rules describing how neurons sum their inputs.

A. EPSP–IPSP Sequences

Figure 1 is a schematic of what might be called a basic hippocampal circuit. The vast majority of cells are pyramidal neurons with extended dendrites studded with small spines, but several types of interneurons are also present (Lorente de Nó, 1934). Physiological studies indicate that stimulation of Schaffer-commissural afferents produces a sequence of excitation and inhibition in CA1 pyramidal cells (see Fig. 2). The ex-

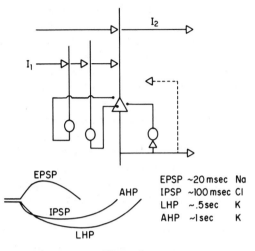

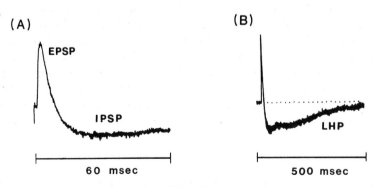

Figure 1.
Excitatory and inhibitory circuitry in hippocampus. Extrinsic input (I)
produces an EPSP in a pyramidal neuron and also excites two types of
feedforward interneuron. One of the interneurons produces a fast IPSP
and the other produces an LHP. Recurrent collaterals from the pyramidal
fast cell also produce a feedback IPSP via an interneuron. Dashed line
indicates excitatory feedback such as is present in field CA3 (but not CA1).

(A)   **(B)**

EPSP

IPSP

60 msec

LHP

500 msec

Figure 2.
Intracellular responses of a CA1 pyramidal neuron in a hippocampal slice
to stimulation of Schaffer-commissural afferents. (A) Recording at fast
sweep speed shows the sequence of excitation (EPSP) and inhibition
(IPSP). The EPSP peak amplitude in this case was 14 mV, IPSP amplitude
was 6 mV, and the resting membrane potential was −65 mV. (B)
Recording of the same response at slower speed illustrates the time course
of the LHP.

citatory postsynaptic potential (EPSP) is mediated by direct, monosynaptic connections between the afferents and the pyramidal cell (Andersen *et al.*, 1966); inhibitory postsynaptic potentials (IPSPs) are generated both by feed forward (Lynch *et al.*, 1981; Alger and Nicoll, 1982) and feedback (Andersen *et al.*, 1964) interneurons. The extent to which populations of feedforward and feedback interneurons overlap is not known.

Recent studies also indicate that afferent stimulation produces a delayed and longer-lasting inhibitory response—the late hyperpolarizing potential (LHP) (Alger, 1984; Newberry and Nicoll, 1984). It is not known if the IPSP and LHP are due to different interneurons, although this is a likely possibility. The fast IPSP is mediated by gamma-aminobutyric acid (GABA) receptors (Curtis *et al.*, 1970) and involves a large increase in chloride conductance (Eccles *et al.*, 1977) that presumably shunts excitatory currents; the receptor for the LHP is not known but it has been established that this potential involves a somewhat smaller increase in potassium conductance (Alger, 1984; Newberry and Nicoll, 1984; Hablitz and Thalmann, 1987). Because the fast IPSP both hyperpolarizes the cell and shunts excitatory currents, it is more effective in preventing cell firing in response to input than is the LHP. A greatly simplified but useful representation of these observations is that afferent input first excites cells and then raises their threshold, considerably at first, and then with much less efficiency. The above arrangements have also been identified in piriform cortex and indeed may be common features of cortex (see Haberly, 1985, for review).

A biophysical variable needs to be added at this juncture: namely, the number of spikes that a cell is likely to emit once its threshold has been crossed. Pyramidal cells in the intact hippocampus often, but by no means always, discharge in short (30 msec) bursts of three or four spikes (Ranck, 1973); other cells including interneurons fire less rapidly for longer periods (e.g., granule cells of the dentate gyrus) (Rose *et al.*, 1983; Fox and Ranck, 1981). The intensity of a cell's response will be directly related to the rate and degree to which it is depolarized by its inputs as well as by its biophysical properties. Events occurring once threshold has been passed need to be incorporated into simulations.

B. After-Potentials

In modeling neuronal properties, the possibility must be considered that excitatory inputs of sufficient strength set in motion voltage-dependent hyperpolarizing responses in addition to the interneuron mediated inhibition. A prominent example of this category of events is the after-hyperpolarization (AHP) that follows spiking of hippocampal pyramidal cells (Fig.3). The AHP is a calcium-triggered long-lasting potassium conductance that is readily observed when cells are depolarized by intra-

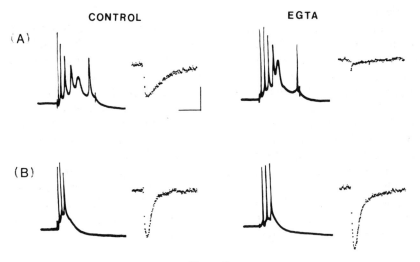

Figure 3.
Comparison of the LHP and AHP. Intracellular recordings from CA1
pyramidal cell impaled with an electrode containing potassium acetate
(control) and another cell impaled with electrode containing potassium
acetate and 0.5 M EGTA. Slices were bathed in 20 μM picrotoxin to block
GABA-mediated IPSPs. The left-hand record of each pair is the response
recorded at low gain and fast sweep speed (calibration bar: 25 mV and 25
mS); the right-hand record is the same response as a digitized record at
high gain and slow sweep speed (calibration bar: 5 mV and 1 sec). (A)
Depolarizing current injection produces a burst response, which is
followed by a slow AHP in the control cell. AHP is blocked in cell injected
with EGTA. (B) Stimulation of Schaffer-commissural fibers in presence of
picrotoxin induces repetitive firing followed by the LHP, which is not
blocked by EGTA injection. [From Lynch *et al.* (1983).]

cellular current injection to a level at which a train of action potentials
is produced (Hotson and Prince, 1980; Alger and Nicoll, 1980). A device
of this type would profoundly affect the performance of a neural network,
since it would reduce for hundreds of milliseconds the likelihood that
a cell would respond to inputs once that cell had been intensely active;
it would in effect tend to temporarily inactivate those cells most responsive to a given input signal. However, we cannot assume that the
AHP is a routine participant in network activity, since the effect requires
prolonged depolarization and the types of synaptic events that might
produce it have not been explored. To speculate, we can assume that
the fast IPSP and feedback IPSPs restrict cell firing to very short bursts
and prevent the development of large AHPs. Presumably then the most
likely way to activate a robust version of the response would be to time
the arrival of a large excitatory input with a momentary suppression of
the fast IPSPs. There are at least two routes through which this could

be achieved. First, anatomical studies strongly suggest that interneurons in hippocampus are innervated by diffuse ("nonspecific") afferents arising in the brainstem, diencephalon, and, most prominently, basal forebrain (Mosko *et al.*, 1973). This last group of inputs is cholinergic in nature and is part of a system that projects to all areas of cortex and influences rhythmic activity (Shute and Lewis, 1967; Stumpf, 1965). It is thus not unlikely that the activity of interneurons in hippocampus is to a degree regulated by extrinsic afferents. Suppression of interneurons would allow longer bursts to occur in response to strong inputs and therefore possibly for the AHP to emerge. Second, recent studies indicate that the fast IPSP system once activated enters a brief period during which it cannot be reactivated (McCarren and Alger, 1985). This point will be discussed below, but for the moment the refractoriness of the IPSP raises the possibility that a large input delivered at the right moment could elicit a supranormal response, intense firing, and the AHP.

C. Timing Rules

The excitatory and inhibitory events described above have quite different temporal parameters. EPSPs have a time course of ~10–20 msec, the fast IPSP lasts ~50–100 msec, the LHP can persist for several hundred milliseconds, and large AHPs can be measured for seconds. In a network operating synchronously, this means that the different events set in motion by an excitatory input will be operative over different numbers of time steps. Thus inputs arriving at 50 msec intervals will not be directly affected by earlier inputs but will interact with IPSPs from the previous time step, and the LHPs from two or more earlier time steps. Shaw and co-workers (1985) have noted that a system of this kind can be described by higher-order difference equations and thus is likely to exhibit complex harmonics. In essence, differences in the duration of events should promote the development of quasi-stable spatiotemporal patterns of activity. In their Trion model, Shaw and co-workers (1985) exploit these patterns to vastly increase the storage capacity of a cycling neural network; in a more limited sense, the different time frames can be employed in such a way as to cause different patterns of spatial activation to emerge over time in response to the same input administered repetitively (see below).

    Two other aspects of inhibitory processes will complicate their influence on network behavior. First, interneurons project locally but densely; that is, a given inhibitory cell has a reasonably high probability of contacting any principal cell within a short radius of that inhibitory cell. In general, excitatory axons as inputs or feedback appear to have much lower probabilities of making contacts (see Lynch, 1986). These arrangements suggest that intensely excited cells in a network are likely to be surrounded by inhibition, as well as being themselves inhibited, because of two factors: (1) the convergence of input required for excitation will activate feedforward interneurons, and (2) feedback inhibition will be triggered by the activated neurons. In some senses, the network may be converted into a patchwork of areas of high and low inhibition. Second, as mentioned, there is evidence that the feedforward inhibitory system has a refractory period lasting for a few hundred milliseconds (McCarren and Alger, 1985). When two stimulation pulses are given 200 msec apart, the inhibition present at the second response is somewhat less than that found in the first response. Inhibition reappears progressively after this interval, and normal effects are evident at 500–1000 msec after the first pulse. Since the IPSP normally truncates the EPSP, the refractory period results in a broadening of the second of two responses elicited by stimulation pulses separated by 200 msec (Larson and Lynch, 1986). If the second response occurs prior to 200 msec, then it falls in the range of the IPSP initiated by the first excitatory input; hence, maximal-duration EPSPs occur about 200 msec after an initial input. Although broadened, the delayed response is likely to be less effective than the first in terms of spiking the cell because it occurs while the LHP is still present. However, because they are longer, appropriately delayed EPSPs are capable of much greater temporal summation in response to short bursts of high frequency input (see below).

These factors emphasize the point that inhibition serves to favor certain patterns of input activity. As will be discussed in a later section, patterns that would be expected to be particularly effective do in fact occur in behaving animals.

While the available data on synaptic events point to descriptive hypotheses concerning timing rules, they leave unanswered several important questions raised by efforts to develop simulations. Quantitative data regarding the relationship between amount of input (number of active afferent fibers, frequency of firing) and degree of inhibition produced are badly needed for modeling work. Interneurons are known to have low thresholds and to follow input frequency more faithfully than pyramidal cells in hippocampus (Buzsaki, 1984). Presumably then they are reactive to smaller inputs. However, the inhibitory cells are found in much smaller numbers than the pyramidal cells and possess simpler dendritic trees; hence they are likely to receive a smaller fraction of the total input than the pyramidal cells in a given "patch." The extent to which these anatomical and physiological features balance each other cannot be realistically calculated. The behavior of pyramidal neurons in field CA1 suggests that inhibitory processes are effective in suppressing activity in cells surrounding active neurons. The dendrites of the pyramidal cells overlap extensively, and hence neighboring cells are likely to receive overlapping inputs; despite this, chronic recording studies suggest that the adjacent neurons are differentially coded to stimuli in the environment (e.g., O'Keefe and Nadel, 1978). This points to the conclusion that inhibitory cells produce "winner-take-all" relationships of a type found to be useful in some network models (Feldman, 1981).

It is also the case that the refractoriness of the IPSP has not yet been widely studied. Although it does appear to be related to the number of input fibers, how it responds to different frequencies of input activity is an important and unstudied question. Preliminary work indicates that the interneurons themselves do not enter a refractory period, suggesting that the transient suppression of IPSPs is due to changes at the inhibitory synapses or in the ionic gradients across the target cell membrane. A reasonable hypothesis is that the refractory period reflects a very transient modification initiated by the IPSP itself and hence will depend on the intensity of the inhibitory potentials set up by the first input.

III. Synaptic Modification Rules

A. Increasing Synaptic Strength (LTP)

As discussed elsewhere (see reviews in Landfield and Deadwyler, 1987), the hippocampal long-term potentiation (LTP) effect provides a model for synaptic modification processes of a type that are quite possibly involved in learning. LTP has been used to test the biological validity of theoretical synaptic modification rules; here it will be employed not to test rules but to construct them. That is, we will attempt to use empirical rules for LTP induction to derive algorithms that describe when connections in a network should be changed during a learning episode.

1. Mechanisms

While much has been learned in the past decade about the mechanisms involved in eliciting LTP, it is still not possible to develop from this level of analysis a general rule about when the effect will occur. Nonetheless, it will be useful to briefly review the physiology and chemistry of LTP so as to provide some explanation for the results of parametric studies that will be used to develop synaptic modification rules.

Two pharmacological treatments have been identified that selectively block LTP induction: (1) extracellular application of drugs that block an unusual class of excitatory amino acid receptors (N-methyl-D-aspartate or NMDA receptors) (Collingridge *et al.*, 1983; Harris *et al.*, 1984; Morris *et al.*, 1986; see also Chapter 14, this volume), and (2) injections of a calcium buffering compound into the postsynaptic target cell (Lynch *et al.*, 1983). The NMDA receptors appear to be transmitter receptors (glutamate or a near relative is thought to be a transmitter in pathways in hippocampus and cortex) that are coupled to a channel that is blocked at resting membrane potential but becomes functional when the cell is highly depolarized (Mayer *et al.*, 1984). Apparently then the NMDA receptor plays a minor role in normal synaptic transmission but operates when the synaptic zone has become sufficiently depolarized by stimulation of other classes of transmitter receptors. A second unusual property of the NMDA receptor is that it is coupled to an ionic channel that passes calcium into the target cell (MacDermott *et al.*, 1986). This fits nicely with the second pharmacological result noted above, namely, that intracellular buffering of calcium blocks the development of LTP. This occurs without any change in membrane potential or EPSP amplitude and thus strongly suggests that the trigger for LTP is a transient elevation in intracellular calcium levels.

Recently, a third pharmacological treatment that suppresses LTP with a reasonable degree of selectivity was described: chronic infusion of leupeptin, a thiol proteinase inhibitor, blocked LTP without detectably disturbing baseline responses (Staubli *et al.*, 1988b). This provides support for the hypothesis that a calcium-stimulated neutral protease (calpain) is an essential step in the chain leading to LTP. Calpain degrades structural proteins, including the predominant cytoskeletal protein (spectrin) found in postsynaptic densities (see Lynch *et al.*, 1987, for review). It is thus well suited for eliciting the morphological changes that constitute a further, and quite possibly causal, stage in the development of LTP (Lee *et al.*, 1980a,b; Chang and Greenough, 1984).

The above results suggest the following sequence for the origins of LTP:

1. NMDA receptor activation against a background of sufficient depolarization to unblock the receptor channels

2. Influx of calcium into spines

3. Calpain activation—cytoskeletal disassembly

4. Cytoskeletal reassembly—morphological changes

In support of this argument, recent work shows that NMDA receptor activation causes proteolysis of spectrin, with the production of breakdown products identical to those resulting from calpain's digestion of purified spectrin (Seubert *et al.*, 1988).

Useful as they might be, synaptic modification rules based on these neurobiological data, even with generous allowances for assumptions, would be premature. The sequence is hypothetical and incomplete, most crucially with regard to temporal factors. For example, the binding times of transmitters to the NMDA receptors can only be crudely approximated, and the necessary timing of depolarization to that binding (point 1 above) is unknown. Experimental results suggest that intense depolarization can follow the transmitter release event and yield LTP (Wigstrom *et al.*,

1986), which certainly suggests that receptor activation must persist for tens of milliseconds. The optimal pacing of afferent activity is presumably dictated by these factors as well as by the kinetics of calcium accumulation, and little can be said with certitude about this latter factor. Similarly, the structural reorganization process, something which is virtually a complete mystery, may set constraints on the patterning of activity. Research on these issues is in progress and should begin to suggest more about the relationship of activity patterns to the chemistries involved in LTP. For now, LTP-based synaptic modification rules will have to be developed from empirical work varying stimulation parameters.

2. Activity Patterns That Produce Change

Theta Rhythm.   Pyramidal cells in hippocampus of freely moving animals commonly fire in short bursts of three or four spikes (Ranck, 1973). This provides a reasonable starting point to search for patterns of naturally occurring activity that produce LTP. A study of this type (Larson *et al.*, 1986b) led to the discovery that stimulation trains designed to mimic the burst pattern of firing result in robust LTP when the bursts were separated by 200 msec; shorter or longer interburst intervals produced smaller degrees of synaptic change (Fig. 4). The intriguing aspect of this finding is that the 200-msec interval corresponds to the "theta" rhythm. Theta is a striking 5- to 7-Hz electroencephalograph (EEG) wave that appears when animals are engaged in movements or "voluntary" behavior (e.g., manipulating an object) (Vanderwolf, 1969). The rhythm is dependent on the cholinergic projections from septum to hippocampus (see Bland, 1986, for review). and there is reason to suspect that these fibers terminate, in part at least, on interneurons (Lynch *et al.*, 1978). Behaviorally, theta appears to be locked to the sniffing rate of rats and the suggestion has been made that it constitutes a stimulus sampling mode of hippocampal function (Komisaruk, 1970; Macrides *et al.*, 1982).

Studies in rats implanted with chronic stimulation and recording electrodes (Staubli and Lynch 1987) showed that the LTP induced by "theta burst" stimulation was stable for weeks (Fig. 5). Subsequent work described elsewhere linked the theta bursting pattern to certain basic aspects of synaptic physiology discussed above. When bursts were given to separate afferents in succession 200 msec apart, the postsynaptic response to the second burst was greatly enhanced. LTP was induced only at the synapses activated by the second burst (Larson and Lynch, 1986). Thus, the first burst produced a spatially diffuse "priming" effect that amplified the postsynaptic response to a subsequent burst. Priming is associated with a prolongation of EPSPs (Larson and Lynch, 1986) that is apparently due to the IPSP suppression effect observed by McCarrren and Alger (1985). Primed EPSPs exhibit enhanced temporal summation

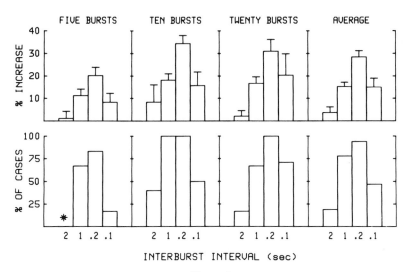

Figure 4.
Burst stimulation at the theta frequency induces optimal LTP. Population EPSPs were recorded in the apical dendritic field of CA1 in response to Schaffer–commissural stimulation before and after patterned burst stimulation. Five, 10, or 20 bursts were given at intervals of 0.1, 0.2, 1, or 2 sec to each slice (n = 71). LTP was assessed 20 min after the burst stimulation episode. Top: Average percent increase (mean ± sem, n = 5–7 slices per group) in population EPSP slope 20 min after burst stimulation. Bursts repeated at 5 Hz (200-msec intervals) induced maximal LTP. At right, the average LTP across different numbers of bursts is shown. Bottom: Incidence of LTP (at least 10% increase lasting 20 min). Asterisk marks a lack of LTP in all slices in that group. [From Larson et al. (1986b).]

during a high-frequency burst; application of an NMDA receptor antagonist both reduces this enhancement and prevents LTP induction (Larson and Lynch, 1988).

These results provide the beginnings of an LTP-based synaptic modification rule. Thus priming blocks the threshold shifting due to the fast IPSP and provides for a transient augmentation of burst-induced depolarization; these effects are maximal at 200 msec (Larson *et al.*, 1986a). If sufficient inputs are coactive on a given cell, then the NMDA receptor-channel threshold will be crossed and LTP will emerge. The performance (nonlearning) mode of the network might use more widely spaced bursts, or single-pulse activity, and hence avoid any synaptic changes. However, attempts to incorporate LTP into a simulation based on a defined cortical network (see below) quickly revealed that the rules were not adequate in that they did not cover many commonly arising situations.

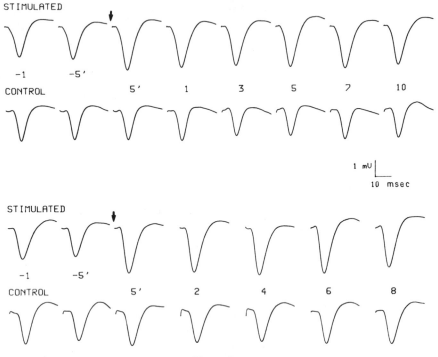

Figure 5.
LTP induced by "theta" stimulation remains stable for many days.
Animals were chronically implanted with a recording electrode in the
apical dendritic field of CA1 and a stimulation electrode in the ipsilateral
and contralateral hippocampus to activate Schaffer and commissural fibers.
One electrode was stimulated with two episodes of five bursts at 5 Hz,
and the other served as a control. Shown are data from two animals with
representative population EPSPs evoked at various times (in days with the
exception of 5 min pre and 5 min post) before and after theta stimulation
(arrow). In both cases the responses to the stimulated pathway were
potentiated without decrement, and the control pathway remained
unchanged. [From Staubli and Lynch (1987).]

(b) *Timing Rules.*   Theta bursting, with its consequences to the
EPSP–IPSP and temporal summation, is a timing rule for networks.
However, it is not sufficient for simulation work because it does not
predict what should happen when the inputs to a cell are stimulated
asynchronously, something that undoubtedly occurs *in situ* as well as
in any network model containing feedback. Experiments using the dentate gyrus show that weak inputs (few axons) would potentiate only if
they arrived 10 msec or less *in advance* of a larger input and did not
exhibit LTP if it followed the strong input (Burger and Levy, 1985). To
place these timing rules in the theta bursting paradigm, it was necessary

to use two or three converging afferents of equal size. One experiment of this type has been performed using three inputs with each input carrying a short (30 msec) four-pulse burst. The experiment was designed so that each of the inputs by itself was too small to elicit a measurable LTP effect. Each input was given a priming pulse; 200 msec later bursts were given in a staggered fashion such that input 2 began halfway through input 1 and input 3 began halfway through input 2. It was found that robust LTP occurred in input 1 while input 3 was only slightly modified (J. Larson and G. Lynch, unpublished data). It would appear then that for homogeneous afferents, the amount of synaptic modification induced during convergence is determined by the order in which the afferents arrive.

(c) *Frequency of Firing.* As discussed, firing frequency of cells is dependent on a variety of factors, prominent among which is the level of depolarization produced by converging inputs. For pyramidal neurons in hippocampus, the neurons tend to fire singly at threshold depolarization and in short bursts to larger drops in membrane potentials. Thus pyramidal cells might be expected to emit anywhere from one to four spikes in a brief interval (e.g., one peak of theta) to a given input, and this corresponds to what is observed *in situ* (Ranck, 1973). Firing over longer periods of time (seconds) seems to be more variable; that is, the neuron has a wider repertoire of response patterns when viewed over several seconds. If we accept the hypothesis that learning occurs while theta is present, a first question raised by simulations concerns the degree of LTP that emerges when bursts contain one to four spikes. Studies related to this question have been conducted using the granule cells of the dentate gyrus and a weak (few afferents) and strong (many axons) input paradigm. Briefly, the strong input was stimulated with high-frequency trains delivered in a manner that produced LTP. The weak input, which terminated in the same dendritic field, was stimulated at various frequencies and then tested for LTP. The results indicate that LTP is critically dependent on high-frequency stimulation (Levy *et al.*, 1983). Preliminary work in field CA1 has explored this question with a somewhat different paradigm in which two groups of Schaffer–commissural fibers were stimulated at the same time. One of these received four pulse bursts while the other had two pulses in each primed burst. The pathway receiving only two pulses exhibited considerably less LTP than its four pulse neighbor (J. Larson and G. Lynch, unpublished data).

It is important to note that intraburst frequency should affect the LTP process in two ways: via an effect (1) on cell-wide depolarization, and (2) on events occurring at specific synapses. The above experiments on frequency of afferent activity describe a situation in which the test input is not primarily responsible for the net depolarization of the cell; that is, other inputs are either larger than the test afferent or are stimulated at higher frequencies. The results thus pertain to the effects of frequency on synapses located on cells that are greatly depolarized. Very different effects might obtain if *all* inputs to the neuron are activated with bursts that contain less than four pulses. While formal studies have not been conducted, we have rarely elicited LTP when two collections of inputs are stimulated with two pulse bursts. Thus an LTP-based learning rule should incorporate terms that define the relationships between presynaptic activity and net depolarization of the cell as well as between presynaptic activity and changes at individual synapses. Further complexity is added by the fact that the second term (activity versus change at an individual contact) is certainly related to the first (level of depolarization in the dendritic tree). In the absence of appropriate experimental data, modeling studies necessarily must make assumptions about the relationships between these variables. Finally, it bears repeating that the system has a threshold (degree of local depolarization needed to unblock NMDA receptor channels).

3. Fractional LTP

Experiments discussed to this point typically used 10 bursts with individual bursts separated by 200 msec. Additional bursts do not produce greater LTP, so it appears that the maximal change is about 40–50% above the "naive" state (Larson *et al.*, 1986b). Moreover, chronic recording experiments reveal that the LTP produced in this manner is stable for weeks, indicating that the 10 bursts given in a theta pattern also elicit maximal stability (Staubli and Lynch, 1987). Network simulations under many circumstances give rise to far fewer repetitive bursts during a given learning episode. This raised a question about the nature of the function that defines the relationship between number of bursts and degree of LTP produced. Some experimental data are pertinent to this point. In one study it was shown that one primed burst was sufficient to produce a very small LTP effect (about 10% increase above baseline) (Larson and Lynch, 1986). In a second experiment, 10 primed bursts were given at 2-min intervals (Larson and Lynch, 1986). Under these conditions LTP increased in equal increments up to five pairs; that is, each pair added a 10% increase in strength above the baseline condition. It would appear then that within the constraints of these experimental paradigms, LTP increases linearly with number of bursts up to 40–50% after which further change does not occur (see Fig. 6).

Two points should be added here. First, there are no studies on the stability of fractional LTP—while the LTP produced by a suboptimal number of bursts persists unchanged for at least 30 min, longer testing intervals may reveal that declines set in over a period of days. Second, we cannot assume that a "unit" of LTP exists. That is, the 10% increments found in the Larson and Lynch (1986) study may be a reflection of four

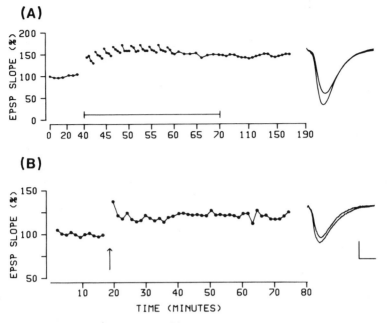

Figure 6.

Incremental LTP. (A) Slope of the dendritic population EPSP evoked by
Schaffer–commissural stimulation during an experiment in which 10
primed bursts were given at 2-min intervals. Each discontinuity in the
graph represents one burst presentation. Note that the potentiation
present 2 min after each burst increases for the first five bursts and then
saturates; the LTP present 2 min after the tenth burst did not decrease for
over 2 hr. Note the expanded time base indicated by the bar. (B)
Significant LTP is produced by only one primed burst (arrow) in another
experiment. The waveforms at right show control and potentiated
population EPSPs. Calibration bar: 1 mV, 5 msec. [From Larson and Lynch
(1986).]

pulse trains or the degree of convergence used; different values might
well occur if longer delays between the bursts or fewer pulses in a burst
were used. Thus while the available data do provide us with a simple
rule relating degree of synaptic modification to amount of stimulation,
it can be appreciated that the rule is still quite incomplete.

4. Interactions between Past and Present LTP Episodes

Experimental work described above indicated that two aspects of
hippocampal physiology act synergistically to produce a brief period in
which responses to bursts are greatly facilitated (the "priming" effect).
Simulations raise the question of how this transient facilitation interacts

with synapses that have already been potentiated. Maximal LTP is a 40–50% increase in the EPSPs elicited by single pulses of stimulation—the IPSP blocking occurring during theta burst stimulation results in a similar increase in the net depolarization occurring during a 30-msec burst of four pulses (i.e., 100 Hz for 30 msec). In network simulations it frequently occurs that previously potentiated synapses are activated in a theta burst pattern and it is necessary to specify a function that combines their stable synaptic strength value (+40%) with the increment due to transient facilitation. The simulations also indicate that the algorithms selected have great impact on the behavior of the network, a point that will be taken up in a later section. In any event, preliminary experiments have been conducted to provide guidelines for the model under construction. Comparisons were made of the net depolarization produced by four pulse bursts given in the theta pattern by "naive" synapses versus contacts in which LTP had already been established. Early results indicate that the LTP does not sum linearly with priming; that is, previously potentiated synapses are only slightly more effective in depolarizing target dendrites than are naive synapses during theta bursting stimulation (J. Larson and G. Lynch, unpublished data).

Much more work needs to be done on this issue, but if these findings are correct then we find here an instance in which an LTP-based learning rule will differ markedly from theoretically deduced rules. That is, the neurophysiology suggests that the changes in synaptic strength produced by past learning experiences will manifest themselves differently, in a quantitative sense, between performance (e.g., non-theta bursting) and learning (theta mode). This is not the case for network models.

B. Reducing Synaptic Strength

1. Synaptic Depression

Network models almost without exception use presynaptic–postsynaptic activity correlation algorithms to adjust synaptic strength during learning episodes (Little and Shaw, 1978; Shaw *et al.*, 1985; Kohonen, 1984; see also Chapters 6, 7, 9, 10, 13, and 14 of this volume). Taking high activity to be a plus state and low activity to be a minus state, there are two conditions that increase connection strength (+ + and − −) and two that reduce it (+ − and − +). It has been argued that LTP is an example of this rule in operation; that is, the presynaptic fibers forming synapses must be extremely active and the target cell must be extremely depolarized (+ +) (Kelso *et al.*, 1986). The (− −) case is difficult to interpret in neurobiological terms; certainly there is no evidence that inactive inputs to inactive cells become more potent. The disjunctive cases are interesting and point to testable predictions. We should expect to find that active synapses on hyperpolarized cells (+ −) would become weaker, as would inactive synapses on depolarized cells ($-$ $+$). Studies in field CA1 in slices of hippocampus do not support either of these ideas. Thus high-frequency bursts delivered to hyperpolarized pyramidal neurons ($+$ $-$) fail to produce synaptic depressions (Kelso *et al.*, 1986; see also Chapter 14, this volume), while induction of LTP in one group of contacts (and thus intense depolarization in the target cell) does not depress the strength of neighboring inactive synapses (Dunwiddie and Lynch, 1978; Andersen *et al.*, 1980; Larson and Lynch, 1986). This last effect has been confirmed in rats with chronically implanted electrodes (U. Staubli and G. Lynch, unpublished). However, there is evidence that *low-* frequency stimulation can depress synaptic strength in hippocampus. Lynch *et al.* (1977) found that 15-Hz stimulation for 15 sec produced a measurable degree of potentiation in activated contacts and in many cases a depression of responses to other inputs. Subsequent work using a fixed number of stimulation pulses showed that high-frequency stimulation was optimal for inducing LTP and did *not* affect other inputs while low-frequency stimulation (1–5 Hz) caused little LTP but did depress responses to all inputs. Heterosynaptic depression has also been found in the dentate gyrus (Levy and Steward, 1979; Abraham and Goddard, 1983). It is important to note that in none of the experiments discussed above is there evidence that depressive effects are selective to synapses and that it is possible that they reflect a global change in the target cell population.

Levy and co-workers (1983) have described effects in dentate gyrus that support the idea that one type of disjunction does result in depression. They used weak (few axons) and strong (many axons) inputs to the same cells and measured the consequences of inducing LTP in the latter on the size of responses to the former. When the weak input was stimulated at high frequency along with the strong input (conjunction), it became potentiated. However, when the weak input was stimulated at low frequency while LTP was being induced in the strong input (disjunction), the weak input's responses were reduced.

2. Reversing LTP

A crucial issue for any network simulation concerns the possibility that LTP can be reversed, a question not directly addressed in the studies described above. One study, however, suggests that something of this sort may be possible. In those experiments (see Fig. 7) low-frequency trains (1–5 Hz) were applied to the Schaffer–commissural projections to CA1 in anesthetized rats 15 min after LTP had been induced with high-frequency stimulation. In about 80% of the cases, the previously established potentiation was essentially abolished; interestingly enough, the same low-frequency trains applied to naive synapses caused depression in only about 10% of the animals (Barrionuevo *et al.*, 1979).

A major difficulty in interpreting these and the other results on

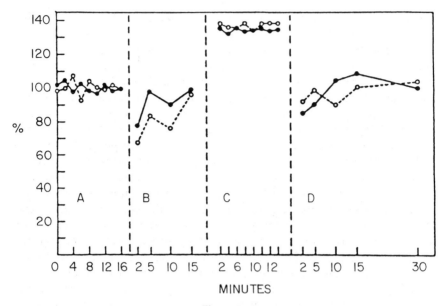

Figure 7.
Persistent depression of potentiated but not unpotentiated responses after low-frequency stimulation. Responses to Schaffer–commissural stimulation were recorded in the apical dendritic field of CA1 in the anesthetized rat. Slope (open circles) and amplitude (filled circles) are plotted for one experiment. (A) Responses during a 16-min control (baseline) period. (B) Transient depression after low-frequency (1 Hz for 100 sec) stimulation. (C) effect of high-frequency (100 Hz for 1 sec) stimulation (LTP). (D) A lasting depression of the potentiated response after low-frequency stimulation. All values are expressed as percent of baseline. [From Barrionuevo *et al.* (1979).]

depression is that recordings were made for short periods (< 1 hr). It cannot be said then the reductions in strength persist for anything like the time periods that characterize LTP. However, preliminary work with chronic rats has supported the observation that low-frequency stimulation reverses LTP in a significant percentage of cases and moreover that the potentiation does not reappear 24 hr later (U. Staubli and G. Lynch, unpublished data).

To summarize the work on reducing synaptic strength:

1. Induction of LTP in dentate gyrus *can* cause heterosynaptic depression.

2. LTP in CA1 is not correlated with heterosynaptic depression.

3. Generalized depression does occur in CA1 but only when long trains of low frequency are used.

4. In none of these cases is there evidence that the observed depressions are synaptic in nature or long lasting; the effects could be due to global, transient changes.

5. Low-frequency trains applied to the afferents of CA1 in the intact hippocampus may produce a reduction or even reversal of LTP. This result cannot be considered as definitive and awaits confirmation.

Neurophysiological studies thus do not provide a coherent picture concerning reductions of synaptic strength. It would be of interest to explore point 5 in network simulations. If confirmed, the homosynaptic reversal effect suggests a rule in which one type of disjunction between past and present input patterns can reduce synaptic strength.

C. Summary

1. Patterned Activity

Theta stimulation studies indicate that a window of opportunity for synaptic modification opens maximally in a small collection of cells 200 msec after that collection has received a reasonable sized input. During this period, EPSPs are prolonged because truncating IPSPs are inoperative, and hence exhibit far greater temporal summation during high-frequency bursts than is normally the case. Thus simulations must transiently change the relative potency of the synapses during the learning episode.

2. Convergence

Inputs arriving at the appropriate time must depolarize their target spines to a degree that the threshold for activating the NMDA receptor-channel threshold is crossed. The level of depolarization in the spine depends upon two factors: (1) that produced by the single input fiber to the spine of interest, and (2) the net depolarization produced in the dendritic tree by all active input fibers. The second factor will be dependent on the number of active input axons and the frequencies and number of pulses they carry while the depolarization at the spine will reflect net dendritic depolarization (the first factor) and the frequency and number of pulses in the single axon innervating that spine. The charging curves (i.e., dv/dt as a function of amount of presynaptic activity) for the spine and dendrite will be different because their biophysics are different. Accordingly, an accurate simulation must specify input/output curves for spines and for dendrites and then specify a parameter or function that describes their interaction. Experimentation suggests that the curve for spines is steeper than that for dendrites. Thus two pulses or even one pulse will produce a degree of LTP if administered to an input that is active at the same time or nearly the same time as other inputs receiving bursts of four pulses. However, when even a large number of axons are stimulated with two pulse bursts, LTP is not likely to occur.

3. Past Experience

The transient facilitation of synapses during a learning episode mentioned in point 1 need not interact linearly with existing long-term potentiation in synapses established by previous learning episodes, and indeed experimentation suggests that it does not. The simulation needs to specify the degree of interaction between very transient and more stable forms of potentiation.

4. Order Effects during Convergence

Experimentation indicates that the order in which converging inputs arrive at a primed dendrite has a strong impact on the degree of potentiation they produce, with early arrivals favored over later ones (J. Larson and G. Lynch, in preparation). (Facilitation is greater in a retrograde direction.)

IV. Simulations of a Cortical Layer

A. Advantages of Olfactory Cortex as a Model

1. Overview of the Olfactory Cortex

Layer II of piriform cortex has a number of advantages for simulation work. The anatomy of the cortex is relatively simple. It receives only two major sources of input—the lateral olfactory tract (LOT) carrying the output of the olfactory bulb and a massive feedback system originating from the ipsilateral and contralateral layer II. Less numerous afferents reach layer II from the deeper layers of the cortex and probably from the diffuse aminergic brainstem projections and ascending cholinergic projections originating in the basal forebrain (Haberly and Price, 1978). The anatomy of piriform layer II has been described in considerable detail, most notably in the exquisite studies of Price and his collaborators. The LOT projections are not organized with any evident degree of topography; small parts of the bulb project to all parts of the cortex, and even very small parts of the cortex are innervated by all regions of the bulb (Haberly and Price, 1977). The commissural–associational feedback system is also very loosely organized (Haberly and Price, 1978; Luskin and Price, 1983). Haberly (1985), Shepherd (1979), and others have described certain aspects of the physiology of the cortex. Not surprising, it is similar to that of hippocampus and in particular shows the EPSP–

IPSP sequence described earlier and IPSP blocking during repetitive stimulation (Satou et al., 1982).

The above points also apply to the hippocampus, and in fact the hippocampus has been more intensively studied than piriform cortex. Why not then simulate one of the subdivisions of hippocampus? The answer is that much more can be inferred from anatomical data about the functions of piriform than is the case for hippocampus. Layer II is only two synapses removed from nasal receptors for odors and therefore must play a role in olfactory perception and recognition. Something of the nature of the type of information processing accomplished by the cortex can also be inferred from the surprising anatomical organization of the olfactory system. Work from several laboratories indicates that single odorants activate one or perhaps two discrete patches on the bulb (Stewart et al., 1979; Jourdan et al., 1980; Lancet et al., 1982), a result that presumably reflects the loose topography existing between the nasal epithelium and the surface of the bulb. It thus appears that a crude spatial coding is involved at the earliest stages of olfactory processing. But, as noted, the mitral cell projections to layer II piriform–entorhinal cortex exhibit little evident topography and must be assumed to sacrifice spatial information, thereby raising questions about what is gained in return. One possibility (see Lynch, 1986) is that quasi-random organization insures that some set of layer II cells will exist that are innervated by any possible (sufficiently large) combination of mitral cells. This might be necessary in dealing with odors that are composites of several chemicals; according to this idea, the lack of point-to-point organization in the olfactory system reflects the combinatorial possibilities and lack of predictability inherent in the stimulus world it must process. In any event, anatomy suggests that cells coded to particular cues should be found dispersed virtually at random throughout layer II of the piriform-entorhinal cortex.

In summary, the piriform–entorhinal cortex is one of the earliest stages of the chain of connections beginning with nasal receptors, and we can assume therefore that physiological events occurring there will manifest themselves in even the simplest of olfactory behaviors. This should be a valuable property in the effort to predict behavior from simulations, something that would be exceedingly difficult to do using models of cortical regions further removed from the periphery.

2. "Electric" Odors

The signalling patterns used by the bulb to convey information to the cortex are not known. This constitutes a major stumbling block for simulation work. In an effort to define a simple pattern that would be recognized by the cortex, studies were carried out in which electrical stimulation of the LOT was used as a cue in an olfactory discrimination problem (Roman et al., 1987). It was found that theta bursting stimulation was effective in this regard. Thus rats were able to discriminate such stimulation from natural odors and showed excellent retention of the electric odor. They were also able to discriminate between two electric odors, thereby indicating that something more than a vague sensation was involved. That the animals were able to do this is perhaps not too surprising given the nontopographic organization of the LOT and the fact that the animals sniff at about 5 times per second.

An interesting feature of this experiment was that theta bursting led to long-term potentiation in layer II only when it was administered to animals in a learning situation. Thus, unlike the hippocampus, elicitation of LTP in piriform required a certain type of context in which the rats had already learned that odors were important cues.

B. Results from Simulations

Simulations were used in an effort to understand the collective behaviors that might appear when physiological rules of the form described earlier were incorporated into a network based on the design of the olfactory cortex. These first studies make no claim to reproduce the actual firing patterns of cells in layer II during olfactory behavior. To do this, it would be necessary to have data describing the output of the bulb and responses of piriform–entorhinal cells in behaving animals, two subjects that have not been extensively examined. Instead, the simulation used theta bursting inputs of the type employed in the "electric odor" experiments. The model *does* make predictions about the activity patterns of units in that paradigm and these are currently being tested.

Simulations necessarily emphasize certain biological variables and ignore or greatly simplify others. While this virtually insures that some body of physiological phenomena will not be reproduced by the model, it still is the case that prominent aspects or themes found in the cortical network can be predicted by the model. In the work described here, biophysics and biological time were greatly simplified. EPSPs and IPSPs were represented as simple voltage changes, and their onset and rise times were essentially ignored. However, the differences in time courses of the EPSP, IPSP, LHP, and after-hyperpolarization (AHP) were represented and indeed were crucial to the results to be described.

Computations were done using discrete time steps, and the model thus lacked the continuity of brain. In essence, the simulation began with LOT inputs, set in motion the inhibitory events discussed earlier, and added positive feedback. This constituted one sniff. Long-lasting events continued over successive sniffs. Among the features represented in the simulation were the following:

Fast IPSP

LHP

Refractoriness of the IPSP

Voltage threshold for long-term potentiation

Enhanced temporal summation in primed bursts

Nonlinear summation of LTP with priming

Order effects for LTP in the LOT (e.g., delayed feedback facilitated LTP to a greater degree than the converse)

Two modes of cell firing, bursts and pulses

The network itself consisted of 100 target neurons, 100 LOT input lines, and 100 feedback axons. Interneurons were assumed to be randomly scattered and activated by total activity (i.e., all active LOT and feedback lines).

Contacts were formed at random with $p = 0.2$ for both LOT and feedback; the resulting network was thus a sparse matrix.

Many of the most interesting experiments involved multicomponent odors. A component consisted of a group of contiguous LOT lines: that is, the output of a patch of the olfactory bulb. Dominant components (higher concentration of odorant) were represented by more lines rather than higher frequency of firing. The assumption was made that the olfactory bulb normalized its output to a total of 20% of all LOT lines.

The network operated in learning and performance modes; during the former, the input lines fired in short bursts at the theta frequency. Inhibition was the same in response to bursts or pulses, an assumption that is currently being tested.

When the network was in performance mode, only a very few cells (sometimes none) would respond to a novel odor; those that did fire would not fire regularly over successive sniffs because of the inhibition (LHP) remaining from one sniff to the next. The simulation would then switch to learning mode, resulting in an interaction between the input burst and the refractoriness of the IPSP (priming). LTP (a 40% increase in synaptic strength) would then occur. On subsequent presentations of the odor, about 7% of the cells would respond reliably to successive sniffs. Moreover, the network would produce essentially the same response when the cue had missing components (degradation) or when a component (noise) were added.

These behaviors were expected and are common to most network models (Anderson and Mozer, 1981; Kohonen, 1984; Rumelhart and Zipser, 1986; see Chapter 13, this volume). A more interesting effect appeared when the model was presented with a series of odors as part of an exploration of its fidelity and capacity. Initially the network acted as before, and it was noted that the representation of one odor was not disturbed by learning of several other odors including some that shared 70% of its components. After considerable sampling, the model in performance mode would, to certain novel cues, emit a robust signal on early sniffs that would disappear in later sniffs. On examining the data, it became evident that this occurred when the network had previously learned three to five other odors with components in common with the novel odor. Moreover, the early response was now found to be present in the responses to each of the odors in that group. Second and third sniffs for members of the group were quite different—the spatial pattern of cells responding did not greatly overlap. Thus with extensive training on different odors, the network responded to an odor with two patterns of output: an early response that was common to several odors, and a later response that was unique to a specific cue. In effect, it used time to both categorize and differentiate its inputs. In experiments using more than 20 odors, the network was observed to form five categories with reliable, differentiated responses to each individual odor.

More recent work has incorporated several additional features into the simulation, including the following:

Probabilistic "release"—Random variations are probably present in most neurophysiological variables but perhaps nowhere more prominently than in transmitter release. Accordingly, the simulation was modified to include probabilistic synapses.

Plasticity—It was noted in an earlier section that the LTP effect is correlated with structural changes; these include modification of dendritic spines and the apparent formation of new contacts. Viewed from the perspective of a single afferent axon, the growth of new synapses will affect the probabilistic nature of communication between it and its target cell since the axon will have additional release sites. This idea was also incorporated into the simulation.

Local interneurons—As discussed, interneurons innervate a restricted local group of neurons and thus in some sense will subdivide a broad collection of principal cells into a group of patches. Rather than assuming a universal and uniform inhibition, the modified simulation represented interneurons as acting upon small groups (~ 8) of principal cells. This effectively converted the network into a group of winner-take-all patches in which only one or two neurons (in each patch) would react to any given collection of inputs. This type of device has been used with good success in several network models (Cooper, 1984).

After-hyperpolarization—In the modified network, the assumption was made that cells that fired repeatedly in long bursts triggered a large after-hyperpolarizing potential (see above) that effectively prevented them from firing again for several sniffs (~ 1 sec). The AHP has been widely studied in experiments using intracellular recording but has not been systematically examined using synaptic inputs. Nonetheless, it is likely to occur after periods of high frequency activity.

"Tapered" anatomy—The first simulation ignored an important feature of the anatomy of the olfactory cortex: namely, that the number of LOT contacts per cell decreases in a rostro-caudal dimension while the number of feedback contacts increases (Schwob and Price, 1978). Thus the balance of LOT to feedback connections changes markedly along the long axis of the cortex. To represent this feature, the probability of contact for the LOT axons decreased along the axis of the network while feedback lines were allowed to accumulate.

The modified simulation exhibited the same behaviors as its predecessor with one major exception: it was far superior in differentiating cues. Responses to cues that overlapped by ~90% did not reliably produce very different output patterns in the first model, while experiments on the second version did (overlap in output ranged from 15–30%). Thus the modified network proved to be efficient in orthogonalizing input vectors. It is of interest that each of the features added to the second network could be found to contribute to this result. The accumulation of feedback lines, for example, produced a situation in which the size of the response of the "caudal" end of the network increased exponentially with increases in responses at the rostral end; local inhibition effectively controlled this problem. Probabilistic release resulted in a somewhat random addition of cells to the representation of a particular cue—combined with the AHP mechanism and asymmetrical matrices, this significantly facilitated the differentiation of similar stimuli (for further description, see Lynch and Granger, 1988).

C. Discussion

The simulation work generated hypotheses first about the functional contributions of various neurobiological features to network behavior and second about the types of properties (functions) that are inherent in one type of cortical organization. The different time constants of excitatory and inhibitory potentials, besides favoring certain rhythms and patterns of activity, serve to generate a system in which the network as a whole can extract different kinds of information from the same input signal. In the present case, the temporal parameters of the fast IPSP and LHP, coupled with an LTP-based learning rule, resulted in sequential outputs related to commonality and differences.

It will be noted that the pattern of input signals used in the network was built around the theta rhythm, which in turn is closely linked to the sampling frequency used by the olfactory system. It will be of interest to test the simulation using other input rhythms. Selectively augmenting or inhibiting certain of the inhibitory devices in the network should result in other preferred input patterns, something that might be of use in dealing with very weak or degraded signals (see below).

Other features identified by the simulation as being of great utility were local interneurons, probabilistic release, after-hyperpolarizations, and tapered anatomy. Together, these facilitated differentiation of cues, something that is of primary importance to any sensory modality. It is indeed intriguing that these features "cooperate" as effortlessly as they do. The addition of several neurobiological variables to those present in the first simulation enhanced performance despite the fact that no significant attempts were made to coordinate their effects. This encourages the idea that the network simulation captures something of the interaction that actually occurs in cortex. To the extent that this is the case, then the robust collective properties of the entire system are likely to be inherent to the simple cortex that was used as a guide in the construction of the simulation.

1. Categorization

The simulation results suggest that differentiation and categorization are local properties of cortical designs of the type found in the superficial layers of olfactory cortex. While the first of these operations might have been expected, categorization was not anticipated. Clustering is distinguishable from the simple detection of similarity as, for example, in stimulus generalization. The categorical response was not uniquely associated with any particular stimulus in the category; instead the response appeared only after learning several samples. Human sensory categories involve "prototypes" (see, e.g., Smith and Medin, 1981), representations that have no correspondence to a specific member of a group but instead reflect a composite of elements common to members of the group (consider, for example, the representation for tree or animal). Developing categories is by no means a simple task, at least not in computational terms, since the number of possible categorizing schemes grows exponentially as new elements are added to the stimulus set (Fisher, 1985). Other factors to be discussed shortly make the problem still more difficult.

Having said that categorization seems inherent in the network, we should emphasize that we do not know how efficient it is in this regard. A number of measures of the appropriateness of a particular categorizing scheme are available; for example, information theorists calculate the amount of information gained and lost by grouping stimuli (and show that humans are quite efficient in this regard) (Fisher, 1985; Gluck and Corter, 1985). In all cases, development of a useful collection of categories involves not simply a calculation of the similarity of a group of stimuli but also a measure of the variability or heterogeneity of the stimulus set.

In a world where things are very different, these categories should be very broad, and vice versa. At this time we do not know how flexible the layer II network is in setting category boundaries and the extent to which these boundaries reflect the variability of the stimulus world. It seems evident, however, that many problems could be devised that would not be appropriately treated by the network. However, the model as operated thus far is totally "naive" when confronted with its stimulus set. Animals have the advantage of a long developmental period in which they presumably learn about the heterogeneity of the sensory world. A question now under exploration is whether the network might also benefit from early learning sessions in which key parameters are determined by the variability of inputs. In other words it may be the case that early experience can be used to adjust cell-wide or network-wide parameters in such a way that subsequent learning, encoded by changing specific synaptic weights, is aligned with information about the cue world as a whole. It is interesting in this regard that some models use both type of changes (cell-wide and synapse-specific) to obtain optimal performance. Cooper (1984), for example, adjusts cell firing thresholds according to a complex function as well as changing synaptic weights in a model of visual cortical development.

It will be noted that our model deals only with long-term memory, and stimuli need not be presented in a single session. Experimental work on categorization in humans has not addressed this type of situation and instead has focused on learning in which all cues are presented repeatedly in rapid succession. Some of the dynamic behavior exhibited by humans under these conditions would not be reproduced by our current model. Categorization in the single-session paradigm is a nonmonotonic problem in which a new piece of information can radically change an organization scheme built up from a large number of prior inputs (e.g., splitting and merging of categories). Something of this sort might occur in the model if we were to add a synapse depression or LTP reversal rule. As discussed, the physiological data on these subjects is ambiguous and for this reason reversal rules have not been included to date. Beyond this, it is not clear that stable (long-term) categories are readily split and merged in humans, and we have no data on categorization in the olfactory modality. We have used multicomponent odors in behavioral studies with rats (Staubli et al., 1988a), and it may be possible to exploit this paradigm in exploring the dynamics associated with developing and modifying stable olfactory categories.

Studies of the type just mentioned, coupled with chronic unit recording, will also serve to test certain of the stronger predictions arising from the simulation work. Some of these are as follows:

Sparse coding by the olfactory cortex

Differences between rostral and caudal cortex in terms of categorization and individuation of cues

Suppression of firing after bursts

Sequential responses from individual cells, with responses to later sniffs being more differentiated

2. Implications for Behavioral Theories

The simulation work suggests that learning in layer II cortex not only forms highly differentiated representations of sensory cues but also imposes organization on the body of stored cues. Acquiring new information not only adds to memory but can also affect the organization of already stored memories. The network then uses time and successive sampling to access this information. It need not be emphasized that the category information allows the animal to deal with an enormous range of novel inputs based on the probabilities that similar inputs have occurred in the past (common occurrences have well developed categories). Note also that the temporal properties of the system result in hierarchical processing with categorical information being available prior to specific information. In terms of memory theories, categorization represents a peculiar type of association—elements are linked together that may not have been associated (either spatially or temporally) in the environment. Yet if our simulations are accurate reflections of neurobiology, clustering is a local property of one common type of cortical design and hence is likely to be present in virtually all memory operations.

It is interesting in this respect to consider the learning rules that have been adopted by most network modelers. That is, Hebb synapses are used first because they are mathematically attractive but also because they map nicely onto associative conditioning (Sutton and Barto, 1981; see Granger *et al.*, 1988, for a review). Olfactory cortex is an unlikely site for associative learning. It receives only one major extrinsic afferent and appears better suited for combining components of a signal into a unitary response rather than associating them. Introspection suggests that associations between odors are not commonplace. A priori, then, we might have expected the olfactory cortex to perform associations of a type not commonly discussed in the behavioral literature (i.e., categorization) and therefore to employ learning rules of an uncommon type.

This argument illustrates two general points about the relationship between simulation results and behavior. First, we cannot assume that behavioral phenomena reflect local properties common to many types of brain network. Animals do learn associations between odors and objects in the environment, but this fact cannot be used to deduce learning rules for olfactory cortex since associations of this form probably do not take place in the piriform. The use of behavioral results in the design and evaluation of networks must be done with extreme caution if we intend to understand how the brain produces behavior. Second, and to return to a point raised above, network simulations have the potential to illuminate the operation of brain networks but also to suggest new ideas about behavior. There has been considerable discussion recently of the idea that two memory systems are present in brain, one associated with the storage of facts and the second with forming procedural rules (Squire, 1986; see also Chapter 12, this volume). Facts can be recognition memories (a face) or an association between recognitions (face, name). The organization of fact memory has not been the subject of much concern in behavioral neuroscience (although there is considerable literature on it in cognitive sciences and artificial intelligence), and it is probably fair to say that it is generally thought of as a higher-order process. Our results suggest a different emphasis and point to associative organizations as being an integral part of the encoding process.

Questions now arise as to when categorical versus individuated representations are used in further processing of input signals at levels beyond the primary cortex. In this regard it is of interest that layer II of olfactory cortex gives rise to two large telencephalic pathways, one from piriform through deeper layers of piriform and then to thalamus, and a second, from the entorhinal cortex to the hippocampus (see Price, 1985, for review). The first of these appears to be highly convergent while the second is not (see Lynch, 1986). It has been suggested that the thalamic pathway serves to link odors with response sequences (e.g., approach, explore) while the hippocampal route associates specific odors with objects and environments (Lynch, 1986). It is tempting to speculate that the convergent path utilizes the abstracted categorical response, common to several odors, while the more massive connections to hippocampus exploit the highly differentiated output signals.

The simulation results point to this conclusion since the projection to thalamus arises from the rostral portions of the cortex, where categorical responses are most robust, while that to hippocampus originates in the caudal cortex where individuated responses are prevalent. Possibly the bottleneck imposed by convergence restricts the amount of information that can be sent from the larger brain region to the smaller, and clustering (categorization) provides a means for dealing with this difficulty. In this case, clustering would have to be a common property since many of the links between cortical regions are certain to be convergent if for no other reason than to prevent an explosive growth of interconnections with increasing brain size. These ideas, prompted by analyses of networks, have implications for behavioral studies of memory. If the dorso-medial nucleus of thalamus, which generates the major input to frontal cortex (Krettek and Price, 1977), were to sample categorical output of the type described by the simulation, then animals should have difficulty in attaching members of the same category to very different, complex sequences of responses (assuming that the dorsomedial nucleus (DMN)–frontal cortex system serves this function). In a broader sense, we would have to begin thinking about memory processes involving categorical information as distinct from those concerned with more differentiated signals.

3. Untested Behavioral Constraints

As has been emphasized, the network model incorporated a variety of seemingly fundamental neurobiological data without regard to their computational properties and then was tested for the types of behaviors that emerge. Once developed, however, it becomes of interest to expose the simulation to a variety of behavioral problems. To reiterate, we cannot know in advance which behavioral phenomena are due to local network properties as opposed to being the result of interactions between different types of networks. This problem cannot be long avoided, even by simulations intended to explicate a single layer, simply because the need for interactions presumably imposes constraints on the design and operating rules of that layer. Ultimately then the network model must evolve to incorporate some notion of realistic inputs and behavioral problems that it, by itself, cannot resolve. In the case of olfaction, effects that the present simulation do not address include the extraordinary range of stimulus intensities that must be processed by the olfactory system and its capacity to analyze, to some degree at least, complex odors. We have assumed that the olfactory bulb normalizes variations in input intensity and number of components by discharging a relatively constant number of output lines in the face of variations in the intensity of input. While the extensive inhibitory network in the bulb, coupled with feedback from the most anterior end of the olfactory cortex, appears well-suited for this function, the more complex problem of detecting the presence of one known odor when it is but a small component in a larger odor would seem to require interactions between bulb and cortex. Using a very simple probabilistic lateral inhibition rule for the input to the network, we noted in some experiments that the early model could detect the simultaneous presence of two odors belonging to known categories when the relevant odors were equal in strength. That is, one categorical signal and then the other would occur in an unpredictable sequence on different sniffs; a third, mixed, response also occurred on many sniffs. While the network might be able to solve problems of this sort, it cannot in its present form detect a weak, familiar odor that is masked by a more powerful signal. Solution of this problem might require a type of modification of bulbar activity so as to suppress output from (bulb) patches intensely responsive to the compound stimulus and to facilitate more weakly responding areas. The olfactory cortex projects back to the bulb via the anterior olfactory nucleus, while hippocampus does so via the diagonal bands. Possibly then these regions execute functions of this kind. This idea is reminiscent of Freeman's (1981) concept that spatial distribution of bulbar activity is a reflection of a "search" pattern imposed on it by the brain. Returning to the question of network properties, it is also possible that physiological properties of cortex might be exploited for detecting hidden odors. The excitation–inhibition sequences described earlier were assumed to predispose the cortex to respond preferentially to certain frequencies and patterns of activity. It will be of interest to manipulate the parameters of the simulation to see if other patterns or frequencies might be favored and if so to ask if these might be useful in discriminating between inputs from bulbar patches experiencing weak versus strong inputs.

References

Abraham, W. C., and Goddard, G. V. (1983). Asymmetric relationships between homosynaptic long-term potentiation and heterosynaptic long-term depression. *Nature (London)* **305**, 717–719.

Alger, B. E. (1984). Characteristics of a slow hyperpolarizing synaptic potential in rat hippocampal pyramidal cells in vitro. *J. Neurophysiol.*, **52**, 892–910.

Alger, B. E., and Nicoll, R. A. (1980). Epileptiform burst after-hyperpolarization: calcium-dependent potassium potential in hippocampal CA1 pyramidal cells. *Science* **210**, 1122–1124.

Alger, B. E., and Nicoll, R. (1982). Feed-forward dendritic inhibition in rat hippocampal pyramidal neurons studied *in vitro*. *J. Physiol. (London)* **328**, 105–123.

Andersen, P., Eccles, J. C., and Loyning, Y. (1964). Pathway of postsynaptic inhibition in the hippocampus. *J. Neurophysiol.* **27**, 608–619.

Andersen, P., Holmquist, B., and Voorhoeve, P. E. (1966). Excitatory synapses on hippocampal apical dendrites activated by entorhinal stimulation. *Acta Physiol. Scand.* **66**, 461–472.

Andersen, P., Sundberg, S. H., Sveen, O., Swann, J. W., and Wigstrom, H. (1980). Possible mechanisms for long-lasting potentiation of synaptic transmission in hippocampal slices from guinea pigs. *J. Physiol. (London)* **302**, 463–482.

Anderson, J. A., and Mozer, M. (1981). Categorization and selective neurons. *In* "Parallel Models of Associative Memory" (G. E. Hinton and J. A. Anderson, eds.), pp. 213–236. Erlbaum, Hillsdale, New Jersey.

Barrionuevo, G., Schottler, F., and Lynch, G. (1979). The effects of repetitive low frequency stimulation on control and "potentiated" synaptic responses in the hippocampus. *Life Sci* **27**, 2385–2391.

Bland, B. H. (1986). The physiology and pharmacology of hippocampal formation theta rhythms. *Prog. Neurobiol.* **26**, 1–54.

Burger, B., and Levy, W. B. (1985). Long-term associative potentiation/depression as an analogue of classical conditioning. *Soc. Neurosci. Abstr.* **11**, 834.

Buzsaki, G. (1984). Feed-forward inhibition in the hippocampal formation. *Prog. Brain Res.* **22**, 131–153.

Chang, F. L. F., and Greenough, W. T. (1984). Transient and enduring morphological correlates of synaptic activity and efficacy change in the rat hippocampal slice. *Brain Res.* **309**, 35–46.

Collingridge, G. L., Kehl, S. J., and McLennan, H. (1983). The antagonism of amino-acid-induced excitation of rat hippocampal CA1 neurones *in vitro*. *J. Physiol. (London)* **334**, 19–31.

Cooper, L. N. (1984). Neuron learning to network organization. *In* "J. C. Maxwell, the Sesquicentennial Symposium," pp. 41–90. Elsevier, Amsterdam.

Curtis, D. R., Felix, D., and McLennan, H. (1970). GABA and hippocampal inhibition. *Br. J. Pharmacol.* **40,** 881–883.

Dunwiddie, T., and Lynch, G. (1978). Long-term potentiation and depression of synaptic responses in the rat hippocampus: Localization and frequency dependency. *J. Physiol. (London)* **276,** 353–367.

Eccles, J. C., Nicoll, R. A., Oshima, T., and Rubia, F. J. (1977). The anionic permeability of the inhibitory postsynaptic membrane of hippocampal pyramidal cells. *Proc. R. Soc. London, Ser. B* **198,** 345–361.

Feldman, J. A. (1981). A connectionist model of visual memory. *In* "Parallel Models of Associative Memory" (G. E. Hinton and J. A. Anderson, eds.), pp. 49–81. Erlbaum, Hillsdale, New Jersey.

Fisher, D. (1985). "A Hierarchical Conceptual Clustering Algorithm," Tech. Rep. 85-21. ICS Dept., University of California, Irvine.

Fox, S. E., and Ranck, J. B., Jr. (1981). Electrophysiological characteristics of hippocampal complex-spike and theta cells. *Exp. Brain Res.* **41,** 399–410.

Freeman, W. J. (1981). A physiological hypothesis of perception. *Perspect. Biol. Med.* **24,** 561–592.

Gluck, M., and Corter, J. (1985). Information, uncertainty and the ability of categories. *Proc. 7th Ann. Conf. Cog. Sci.,* 283–287.

Granger, R., Baudry, M., and Lynch, G. (1988). Mapping Hebbian psychology onto Hebbian biology. *Trends NeuroSci. (Pers. Ed.)* (in press).

Haberly, L. B. (1985). Neuronal circuitry in olfactory cortex: Anatomy and functional implications. *Chem. Senses* **10,** 219–238.

Haberly, L. B., and Price, J. L. (1977). The axonal projection patterns of the mitral and tufted cells of the olfactory bulb in the rat. *Brain Res.* **129,** 152–157.

Haberly, L. B., and Price, J. L. (1978). Association and commissural fiber systems of the olfactory cortex of the rat. I. Systems originating in the piriform cortex and adjacent areas. *J. Comp. Neurol.* **178,** 711–740.

Hablitz, J. J., and Thalmann, R. H. (1987). Conductance changes underlying a late synaptic hyperpolarization in hippocampal CA3 neurons. *J. Neurophysiol.* **58,** 160–179.

Harris, E. W., Ganong, A. H., and Cotman, C. W. (1984). Long-term potentiation in the hippocampus involves activation of N-methyl-D-aspartate receptors. *Brain Res.* **323,** 132–137.

Hotson, J. R., and Prince, D. A. (1980). A calcium-activated hyperpolarization follows repetitive firing in hippocampal neurons. *J. Neurophysiol.* **43,** 409–419.

Jourdan, F., Dyvean, A., Astic, L., and Holley, A. (1980). Spatial distribution of ^{14}C-2-deoxyglucose uptake in the olfactory bulbs of rats stimulated with two different odors. *Brain Res.* **188,** 139–154.

Kelso, S. R., Ganong, A. H., and Brown, T. H. (1986). Hebbian synapses in hippocampus. *Proc. Natl. Acad. Sci. U.S.A.* **83,** 5326–5330.

Kohonen, T. (1984). "Self-Organization and Associative Memory." Springer-Verlag, Berlin and New York.

Komisaruk, B. R. (1970). Synchrony between limbic system theta activity and rhythmical behavior in rats. *J. Comp. Physiol. Psychol.* **70,** 482–492.

Krettek, J. E., and Price, J. L. (1977). The cortical projections of the mediodorsal nucleus and adjacent thalamic nuclei in the rat. *J. Comp. Neurol.* **171,** 157–192.

Lancet, D., Greer, C. A., Kaner, J. S., and Shepherd, G. M. (1982). Mapping of odor-related neuronal activity in the olfactory bulb by high resolution 2-deoxyglucose autoradiography. *Proc. Natl. Acad. Sci. U.S.A.* **79,** 670–674.

Landfield, P. W., and Deadwyler, S., eds. (1987). "Long-Term Potentiation: From Biophysics to Behavior." Alan R. Liss, New York.

Larson, J., and Lynch, G. (1986). Induction of synaptic potentiation in hippocampus by patterned stimulation involves two events. *Science* **232,** 985–988.

Larson, J., and Lynch, G. (1988). Role of N-methyl-D-aspartate receptors in the induction of synaptic potentiation by burst stimulation patterned after the hippocampal theta rhythm. *Brain Res* **441**, 111–118.

Larson, J., Passani, M. B., and Lynch, G. (1986a). Patterned stimulation reveals postsynaptic correlate of LTP induction. *Soc. Neurosci. Abstr.* **12**, 507.

Larson, J., Wong, D., and Lynch, G. (1986b). Patterned stimulation at the theta frequency is optimal for induction of hippocampal long-term potentiation. *Brain Res.* **368**, 347–350.

Lee, K., Schottler, F., Oliver, M., and Lynch, G. (1980a). Brief bursts of high-frequency stimulation produce two types of structural change in rat hippocampus. *J. Neurophysiol.* **44**, 247–258.

Lee, K., Oliver, M., Schottler, F., and Lynch, G. (1980b). Electron microscopic studies of brain slices: The effects of high frequency stimulation on dendritic ultrastructure. *In* "Electrophysiology of Isolated Mammalian CNS Preparations" (G. A. Kerkut and H. V. Wheal, eds.), pp. 189–212. Academic Press, New York.

Levy, W. B., and Steward, O. (1979). Synapses as associative memory elements in hippocampal formation. *Brain Res.* **175**, 233–245.

Levy, W. B., Brassel, S. E., and Moore, S. D. (1983). Partial quantification of the associative synaptic learning rule of the dentate gyrus. *Neuroscience* **8**, 799–808.

Little, W. A., and Shaw, G. L. (1978). Analytic study of the storage capacity of a neural network. *Math. Biosci.* **39**, 281–290.

Lorento de Nó, R. (1934). Studies on the structure of the cerebral cortex. II. Continuation of the study of the ammonic system. *J. Psychol. Neurol.* **19**, 113–117.

Luskin, M. B., and Price, J. L. (1983). The laminar distribution of intracortical fibers originating in the olfactory cortex of the rat. *J. Comp. Neurol.* **216**, 292–302.

Lynch, G. (1986). "Synapses, Circuits and the Beginnings of Memory." MIT Press, Cambridge, Massachusetts.

Lynch, G., and Granger, R. (1988). Simulation and analysis of a simple cortical network. *Psychol. Learning Motiv.*, in press.

Lynch, G., Rose, G., and Gall, C. (1978). Anatomical and functional aspects of the septohippocampal projections. *Ciba Found. Symp.* **58**.

Lynch, G., Larson, J., Kelso, S., Barrionuevo, G., and Schottler, F. (1983). Intracellular injections of EGTA block the induction of hippocampal long-term potentiation. *Nature (London)* **305**, 719–721.

Lynch, G., Larson, J., Staubli, U., and Baudry, M. (1987). New perspectives on the physiology, chemistry, and pharmacology of memory. *Drug Dev. Res.* **10**, 295–315.

Lynch, G. S., Dunwiddie, T. V., and Gribkoff, V. (1977). Heterosynaptic depression: A postsynaptic correlate of long-term potentiation. *Nature (London)* **266**, 737–739.

Lynch, G. S., Jensen, R. A., McGaugh, J. L., Davila, K., and Oliver, M. W. (1981). Effects of enkephalin, morphine, and naloxone on the electrical activity of the *in vitro* hippocampal slice preparation. *Exp. Neurol.* **71**, 527–540.

MacDermott, A. B., Mayer, M. L., Westbrook, G. L., Smith, S. J., and Barker, J. L. (1986). NMDA-receptor activation increases cytoplasmic calcium concentration in cultured spinal cord neurones. *Nature (London)* **321**, 519–522.

Macrides, F., Eichenbaum, H. B., and Forbes, W. B. (1982). Temporal relationship between sniffing and the limbic θ rhythm during odor discrimination reversal learning. *J. Neurosci.* **2**, 1705–1717.

Mayer, M. L., Westbrook, G. L., and Guthrie, P. B. (1984). Voltage-dependent block by Mg^{2+} of NMDA responses in spinal cord neurones. *Nature (London)* **309**, 261–267.

McCarren, M., and Alger, B. E. (1985). Use-dependent depression of IPSPs in rat hippocampal pyramidal cells *in vitro*. *J. Physiol. (London)* **53**, 557–571.

Morris, R. G. M., Anderson, E., Lynch, G., and Baudry, M. (1986). Selective impairment of learning and blockade of long-term potentiation by an N-methyl-D-aspartate receptor antagonist, AP-5. *Nature (London)* **319**, 774–776.

Mosko, S., Lynch, G., and Cotman, C. (1973). The distribution of the septal projections to the hippocampus of the rat. *J. Comp. Neurol.* **152,** 163–174.

Newberry, N. R., and Nicoll, R. A. (1984). A bicuculline-resistant inhibitory postsynaptic potential in rat hippocampal pyramidal cells *in vitro*. *J. Physiol. (London)* **345,** 239–254.

O'Keefe, J., and Nadel, L. (1978). "The Hippocampus as a Cognitive Map." Oxford Univ. Press, London and New York.

Price, J. L. (1985). Beyond the primary olfactory cortex: Olfactory-related areas in the neocortex, thalamus and hypothalamus. *Chem. Senses* **10,** 239–258.

Ranck, J. B., Jr. (1973). Studies on single neurons in dorsal hippocampal formation and septum in unrestrained rats. *Exp. Neurol.* **41,** 462–531.

Roman, F., Staubli, U., and Lynch, G. (1987). Evidence for synaptic potentiation in a cortical network during learning. *Brain. Res.* **418,** 221–226.

Rose, G., Diamond, D., and Lynch, G. (1983). Dentate granule cells in the rat hippocampal formation have the behavioral characteristics of theta neurons. *Brain Res.* **266,** 29–37.

Rumelhart, D., and Zipser, D. (1986). Feature discovery by competitive learning. *In* "Parallel Distributed Processing" (D. Rumelhart and J. McClelland, eds.). MIT Press, Cambridge, Massachusetts.

Satou, M., Mori, K., Tazawa, Y., and Takagi, S. (1982). Long-lasting disinhibition in pyriform cortex of the rabbit. *J. Neurophysiol.* **48,** 1157–1163.

Schwob, J. E., and Price, J. L. (1978). The cortical projection of the olfactory bulb: Development in fetal and neonatal rats correlated with quantitative variations in adult rats. *Brain Res.* **151,** 369–374.

Seubert, P., Larson, J., Oliver, M., Jung, M. W., Baudry, M., and Lynch, G. (1988). Stimulation of NMDA receptors induces proteolysis of spectrin in hippocampus. *Brain Res.* **460,** 189–194.

Shaw, G. L., Silverman, D. J., and Pearson, J. C. (1985). Model of cortical organization embodying a basis for a theory of information processing and memory recall. *Proc. Natl. Acad. Sci. U.S.A.* **82,** 2364–2366.

Shepherd, G. M. (1979). "The Synaptic Organization of the Brain," 2nd ed. Oxford Univ. Press, London and New York.

Shute, C. E. D., and Lewis, P. R. (1967). The ascending cholinergic reticular system: Neocortical, olfactory and subcortical projections. *Brain* **90,** 497–520.

Smith, E., and Medin, D. (1981). *In.* Categories and Concepts," Harvard Univ. Press, Cambridge, Massachusetts.

Squire, L. S. (1986). Mechanisms of memory. *Science* **232,** 1612–1619.

Staubli, U., and Lynch, G. (1987). Stable hippocampal long-term potentiation elicited by "theta" pattern stimulation. *Brain Res.* **435,** 227–234.

Staubli, U., Fraser, D., Faraday, R., and Lynch, G. (1988a). Olfaction and the "data" memory system in rats. *Behav. Neurosci.* (in press).

Staubli, U., Larson, J., Baudry, M., Thibault, O., and Lynch, G. (1988b). Chronic administration of a thiol-proteinase inhibitor blocks long-term potentiation of synaptic responses. *Brain Res.* **444,** 153–158.

Stewart, W. B., Kaner, J. S., and Shepherd, G. M. (1979). Functional organization of rat olfactory bulb analyzed by the 2-deoxyglucose method. *J. Comp. Neurol.* **185,** 715–734.

Stumpf, C. (1965). Drug action on the electrical activity of the hippocampus. *Int. Rev. Neurobiol.* **8,** 77–138.

Sutton, R. S., and Barto, A. G. (1981). Toward a modern theory of adaptive networks. Expectation and prediction. *Psychol. Rev.* **38,** 135–171.

Vanderwolf, C. H. (1969). Hippocampal electrical activity and voluntary movement in the rat. *Electroencephalogr. Clin. Neurophysiol.* **26,** 407–418.

Wigstrom, H., Gustafsson, B., Huang, Y. Y., and Abraham, W. C. (1986). Hippocampal long-term potentiation is induced by pairing single afferent volleys with intracellularly injected depolarizing current pulses. *Acta Physiol. Scand.* **126,** 317–319.

17

Neural Architecture and Biophysics for Sequence Recognition

J. J. Hopfield and D. W. Tank

I. Introduction

There are two conceptually separable ideas having to do with time sequences of events, positions, or actions. One concerns *generating* such sequences, as in the singing of bird song, or the walking of a millipede, or playing the piano rapidly. The other has to do with *recognizing* sequences generated in the external world or by another organism. Such recognition problems occur in vision, where for example one can recognize a friend at a great distance by her/his walk; in hearing, where a sequence of complex sounds is recognized as a spoken word; and in other sensory domains.

Fixed sequence generation is by far the easier problem. A given sequence can be described by an ordered set of states, A followed by B followed by C. . . . If one understands how to generate a doublet sequence, A followed by B, a long and complex sequence can be generated by iterating the doublet mechanism. Sequence recognition is much harder, since the idea is to be able to recognize sequences of great variability as being "the same" sequence. It is not then adequate to represent a sequence as slavishly requiring first one precise event and then another, when no individual element or step can be viewed as reliable. Instead, the sequence must be evaluated overall for its similarity to previously experienced sequences. The difference in difficulty can be illustrated in speech, where it has been possible to generate artificial continuous speech since the invention of the Edison phonograph, while recognizing spoken words in continuous speech is at present still a difficult technological problem.

To some extent, the ability to generate sequences can be used as a means of recognizing sequences (Kleinfeld, 1986), qualitatively like the way that an oscillator circuit can be synchronized by an external signal that is close to the natural frequency of the oscillator. The motor theory of speech perception (Liberman *et al.*, 1967) explicitly invokes this class of recognition mechanism. It is theoretically difficult, however, to generate holistic recognition in this manner. Furthermore, it is clear that neurobiology manages to recognize sequences that it cannot generate in a motor sense, as when a dog has a vocabulary of 50 English words. The mechanism we describe does not require any ability to generate the pattern being recognized, either as a motor activity or as an equivalent internal stimulation pattern.

II. The Recognition Problem

The problem of syllable or simple word recognition is a general problem of audition, and does not intrinsically involve linguistic ability. The most familiar words can be picked out without preattention in background sounds, as when you suddenly recognize your name spoken in an adjacent conversation in a crowded party. Because this task is preattentive for many words in parallel, it is presumably a low-level task (in analogy to low-level or "early" vision) done by a network of cooperating neurons as a complex form of feature detection. This feature detection necessarily involves information and comparisons over an interval of time. When a very familiar simple sound or word is recognized in this fashion, many neurons are involved in processing the incoming information. The electrophysiological correlate of *recognition* is presumably a strong activity of a few neurons, which (separately as "grandmother cells" or together as an ensemble) represents that recognition. That activity should take place for a short time when adequate information to make a reliable identification has been received, generally at or near the completion of the acoustic stimulus from that word. Our problem is to understand the twofold focusing of the stimulus signal, in time (signals due to different parts of the stimulus arriving at different times must all arrive together at the appropriate recognition instant) and in space (only appropriate cells must be stimulated).

An example of how a simple time-sequence can be decoded into a meaningful signal can be seen in FM (frequency modulated) sonar in some varieties of bats (Suga, 1984). The ideal sonar signal for range determination is a single strong, very short pulse. A small object will generate a weak echo, but the determination of a precise delay time (accurate sonar range) can be done effectively since the return pulse has a high peak power and a time duration short compared to the delay time. Unfortunately, generating short pulses of very high peak power is a difficult requirement on the "transmitter." In bats (and in human-made sonar and radar) a finite duration burst of a carrier frequency is generated. Although a simple pulse of this form (Fig. 1a) solves the transmitter power problems, considerable signal processing is necessary to use the entire signal energy and duration to determine the time of arrival of the front of the weak echo frequency burst.

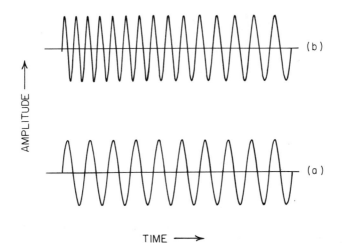

Figure 1.
(a) The waveform of a sonar pulse with a fixed carrier frequency. (b) The waveform of a down-chirp sonar pulse.

Chirping the pulse leads to a simple method of using the entire echo signal energy to obtain the delay time. The signal burst is sent with an instantaneous frequency which changes in time, as shown in Fig 1b. In this example, the frequency is swept from high to low, a down-chirp. The chirp pulse of an FM bat lasts a few milliseconds, and represents several decimeters in range.

The neural apparatus necessary to concentrate the appropriate information in time could have a simple structure. In early auditory nuclei, there is generally a spatial map of frequency (tonotopic map) available. Suppose that there is a down-sweep recognition cell in a second nucleus connected to the first one by axons with a graded set of propagation velocities, as sketched in Fig. 2. If the axons connecting the high frequencies to a cell in the second nucleus have small diameters and those connecting the low frequencies of larger diameter, then the high-frequency pathways are delayed with respect to the low-frequency pathways. When a chirped signal is received, the high-frequency cells in the first processing nucleus will be activated before the low frequency cells, since the first-arriving part of the reflected signal will be the high-frequency part. The difference of axon propagation time for different frequencies results in the arrival of the high-frequency part and the low-frequency part of the signal at the target cell at the same time. This neuron is strongly driven by a down-chirp, since the delays have been organized to "focus" a down-chirp signal. This same neuron would be insensitive to an up-chirp, for when the low frequencies arrive first the propagation delays would spread out the times of arrival of different parts of the up-chirp. The organization of appropriate time delays is essential to chirp

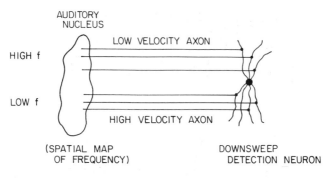

Figure 2.
The connections between neurons in a tonotopic map and a pulse
recognition neuron. When a down-chirp arrives, the high-frequency
neurons are activated earliest, and the activation of lower-frequency
neurons is successively later. The delayed signals arriving at the pulse
recognition neuron from the different frequency channels all arrive at the
same time.

detection. The mechanism of the time delay does not matter. In sound
location in the barn owl, a variation of axon length seems to be used for
a similar function (Sullivan and Konishi, 1986). The organization of the
time delays compresses all the signals of a particular form, essentially a
sequence of frequencies occurring over an appreciable time duration,
into a short recognition impulse at the end. We use organized time delays, on a rather longer time scale, to produce holistic recognition of
speech-like auditory sequences (Tank and Hopfield, 1987a), and illustrate
with applications to spoken syllables or simple words (Tank and Hopfield, 1987b).

Figure 3a shows the form of the actual acoustic signal for the spoken
phrase "six seven five." The dominant structure visible is due to voicing,
a characteristic low-frequency modulation present in sounds like "a"
and "en" and lacking in the consonants "v" and "s" (the consonant
sounds, not the letter names "vee" and "ess"). The frequency of the
fundamental voicing is speaker-specific. Voicing carries some information
about the words, but the fact that we also understand whispered words,
which lack voicing, make it an inappropriate focus for word recognition.
A short-time Fourier transform power spectrum of this speech signal as
a function of time is shown in Fig. 3b. This representation makes more
of the characteristic patterns of speech sounds visible. Speech is not a
random signal, with an arbitrary spectrum. The anatomy and physics
of its generation result in spectra of quite restricted forms. One useful
way to think about the nature of the speech signal is to consider its
spectra in "time bins" of ~10 msec duration. During such a time interval,
the spectrum tends to have a stereotype form, and the number of such

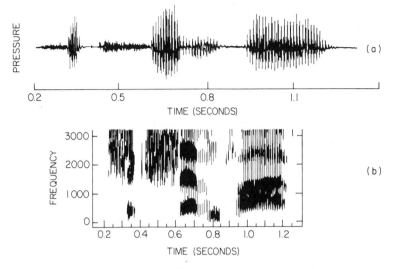

Figure 3.
(a) The electrical signal as a function of time recorded from a microphone responding to the spoken phrase "six seven five." (b) The power spectrum as a function of time for the acoustic signal above. The blackness of the recording indicates the level of acoustic power at the corresponding frequency and time. This calculation corresponds to measuring the power received by a bank of broadband (fast response) filters with varied center frequencies. The time interval between 0.50 and 0.55 sec is an overlap region belonging both to "six" and to "seven." There is no indication that "six" and "seven" are separate words.

forms is limited. For this discussion, ~100 such characteristic forms is adequate, and the speech in a particular time bin will be assigned to the characteristic form (symbol) that it most closely resembles. A short word, lasting 0.5 sec, can then be thought of as a sequence of 50 characteristic forms. In symbolic representation, a particular short vocal utterance can be described as a ~50-letter word, where each letter is taken from an alphabet of ~100 symbols.

The problem of word recognition can be precisely described in this representation. The model utterance for a given word is some particular list of symbols such as ACCHEUUUTUPELVVVVVKHGGGJQWWPPP. When this word is uttered by a speaker, however, this model sequence is not accurately reproduced. Different speakers, or a single speaker under varied circumstances, do not produce invariant sounds, so in this representation there will be symbol substitution errors in the data stream. A second problem is that speech can be produced at different rates, and idiosyncratic variations may even take place within a word. The differences that this "time warp" produces between the model utterance and an actual utterance involve symbol insertions and deletions. Time warp is a major problem, for it prevents comparing between an actual utterance and model words by a rigid template superposition. Finally, in continuous speech the location of the ends of words are often not indicated in the acoustic signal. For example, the phrase "six seven" is generally spoken together as "sixseven", and there is no indication in the signal or its spectrum of the end of "six" and the beginning of "seven". This word-break problem greatly increases the difficulty of understanding words in continuous speech (see Fig. 3). The neural network approach to word identification (Tank and Hopfield, 1987a) that we will describe deals with all three of these fundamental difficulties.

III. Model Circuitry Styled on Neurobiology

A simple model anatomy for doing phoneme, syllable, or word recognition tasks is shown in Fig. 4. The model is chosen in an attempt to meet two goals. First, the network must be a recognizable simplification of the kinds of electrophysiology and anatomy seen in mammalian brains. Second, a quantitative analysis of the electrophysiological response of the model must be possible to demonstrate that the network can solve the time series recognition problem. The model should also clearly indicate the kinds of signals and biophysics to be expected in a biological system that recognizes time sequences in the same generic fashion that the model network does. A review of modeling in this style and its relation to neurobiology has been recently published (Hopfield and Tank, 1986).

Area A in Fig. 4 begins the processing in the model network, and might correspond to a brainstem area of the auditory pathway in mammals, having a tonotopic map of the incident sound signal. The activity of a neuron reflects the intensity of the sound in the narrow frequency band to which the cell is primarily responsive. We will not describe the pathways by which this tonotopic representation is produced, but only use the output of such a known area as input to the sequence recognition system.

Area B contains two types of neurons. Its principal neurons are excitatory, and receive excitatory inputs in a tonotopic or direct map fashion from area A. These neurons also have axons projecting to area C. The other neurons in area B are inhibitory interneurons, which receive inputs from the excitatory cells in B and in turn inhibit these excitatory cells (local inhibitory feedback).

Area C is slightly more complex. It receives diffuse, nontonotopic inputs from area B. Area C has both excitatory principal neurons and inhibitory interneurons. Some of the interneurons receive direct inputs from area B, and provide prompt feedforward inhibition to the principal

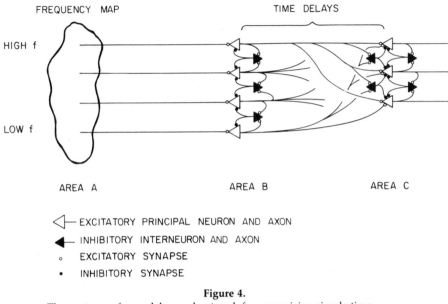

Figure 4.
The anatomy of a model neural network for recognizing simple time
sequences. Area A contains a tonotopic map, and is the source of signals
for the processing areas B and C.

neurons. Other inhibitory cells receive their inputs from the principal
neurons in C and produce feedback inhibition. There is also some particular biophysics that must be present in the B–C pathway to generate
time delays and that will be described later.

While these two areas are much simpler in architecture and connections than is real cortical anatomy, their structure has generic similarity to the kinds of structures that have been observed in neurobiology.
Stability (the absence of oscillations or large-amplitude spontaneous behaviors) is always a problem for neural circuits, whether model or real.
There are two simple systems that have no stability problem, feedforward
systems (in which there is no indirect return path from the axon of a
neuron back to its dendrites) and symmetrically connected networks
(Hopfield, 1982, 1984). Areas A and B are not literally symmetric, but if
the inhibition pathways are fast compared to the time response of the
principal neurons, they can be made equivalent to symmetric systems
(Tank and Hopfield, 1986). This architectural design with feedforward
connections between equivalently symmetrical areas has stability because
it is an elementary hierarchical composition of the two kinds of stable
structures.

We next describe the processing done in this system in terms of
hypothetical electrophysiological experiments performed on such a system. The most elementary experiment is to record from the principal

neurons in area A while the preparation is treated with a pharmacological agent that suppresses inhibition, using a pure tone as an input signal. Any particular principal neuron would be found to have a tuning curve centered on an optimal sound frequency, and the optimum frequency would change smoothly as a function of physical location. The response of the same cells to the auditory stimulus of the spoken word "one" could also be measured, and typical such peristimulus time histograms (PSTH) for neurons of several different center frequencies (in the absence of inhibition) are shown in Fig. 5a. Most monosyllables will have qualitatively similar PSTH, for all spoken words have very broad power spectra, and will drive neurons having a wide range of center frequencies. There is nothing in such patterns that easily distinguishes one spoken word from another.

When the inhibitory system is also functioning, the single-tone experiments would look qualitatively similar, but with quantitative differences. First, the observed tuning curves would be sharper, due to the (indirect) inhibitory effect of one principal neuron on another. Second, the maximum response would be generally less, due to the operation of the inhibitory system. More elaborate experiments would display qualitatively different effects. Two tone experiments at frequencies f_1, f_2 would demonstrate two-tone suppression, in which the response of a principal neuron of center frequency f_1 is suppressed by increasing the auditory signal at frequency f_2 (for this effect, f_1 and f_2 must not be too close together). The inhibitory pathway can produce two-tone suppression. (Two-tone suppression also occurs at the level of the hair cell from mechanical inhibition.) Such suppression is a well-known part of auditory psychophysics and electrophysiology, and is the auditory equivalent of the center-surround receptive fields of early visual processing.

With inhibition functioning, the response of this system to the spoken word "one" is much more dramatic. The PSTH in the presence of inhibition (Fig. 5b) is qualitatively different from that without inhibition. Instead of all neurons being generally active, at any particular time only one or two now tend to be active. Furthermore, the pattern of times in which a neuron is active during a word stimulus is rather characteristic of that word, differing markedly from word to word. The inhibition has a major effect on the information processing, and is responsible for the feature enhancement that will eventually allow the identification of individual words in area C. The fact that we can now see patterns that are identifiable in the PSTH indicates that area C has some reasonable information to work with. While the inhibition reduces the amount of signal that is transmitted from A to the output of B, it reduces the noise and useless information much more than the true signal, and overall makes the pattern easier to identify.

If the signals are appropriately delayed prior to arriving at area C so that all the information relevant to a particular word arrives at once,

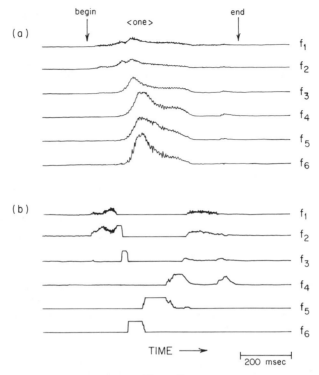

Figure 5.
(a) The peristimulus time histogram (PSTH) of the principal neurons of area B during the presentation of the spoken word "one" as a stimulus. Inhibition in area B has been suppressed. (b) Stimulus and recording as in (a), but in the presence of normal inhibition. An easily visible systematic organization of activity has been created.

word recognition can be carried out in that processing area on the basis of the total information relevant to the word. We have already seen how to do this for a frequency sweep, which is one of the readily visible features of Fig. 5b, indicated by the sequential activation of f_6, f_5, f_4, and f_3.

The architecture of the model network performs the recognition of words in three stages. Area A provides the basic signal decomposition into frequency bands. Area B does feature extraction. The connections between area B and area C use time delays in a systematic fashion to organize the signals arriving at C. For simple word or syllable recognition, the requisite time delays lie in the interval 0.05–0.5 sec. To recognize a word as a whole, it is necessary to store in one way or another the information about the earlier parts of the utterance until the latter parts of the utterance have arrived. A delay mechanism is an elementary physical method for information storage. (In earlier times, electronic computers used mercury delay lines—sound waves propagating in liquid mercury—for fast memory storage.)

We have developed and tested (Tank and Hopfield, 1987a) a model of how these time delays must be organized in order to recognize patterns as a whole in the presence of distortions. It was based on the idea that if some particular recognition neuron or neurons are to indicate recognition of a word by firing strongly for a short period of time immediately after the completion of the word, then the diverse signals that make up the word must all arrive coherently at that time. Looking at Fig. 5b, we see that if the neuron with optimal frequency f_2 is connected to a recognition cell by a pathway that delays the signal for 0.6 seconds, f_3 for 0.5 sec, f_4 for 0.4. sec, 0.3 sec, and 0.1 sec, and f_5 with 0.4 sec, then all these signals will arrive at the recognition neuron at the same time and drive that neuron strongly at that time, the termination of the utterance "one." These delays should not be precise. Because the word "one" might last anywhere from 0.6 to 0.75 sec, in order for the signals to add up coherently even in the presence of such time warp, a signal denoting the recognition of the feature (in f_2) that might indicate the beginning of the word "one" should be sent to the recognition neurons with a variety of delays spread over this range. The appropriate response of the delay pathways to signals of short duration is shown in Fig. 6. The increasing width of these responses as a function of the mean delay is what makes the system able to cope with the time distortions typical of spoken sounds or other sequential recognition problems.

The feedforward inhibition in area C serves the function of de-

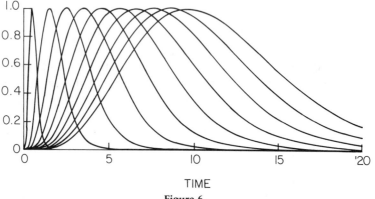

TIME

Figure 6.
The impulse response of the delayed signal propagation from the output of the principal neurons in B to the effect which these outputs have on the neurons in area C. Response curves for five different mean time delays are shown. The peak location indicates the mean delay. For a particular mean delay, a distribution of actual delays is needed, representing the fact that the time duration of a segment of a speech utterance has a probability distribution.

scribing negative evidence. For example, since the neuron f_2 is not active 0.4 sec before the end of the word "one," an inhibitory pathway with a delay of 0.4 sec from f_2 to a neuron that is to recognize "one" can be made. In computational terms, activation of f_2 0.4 sec earlier is evidence that a "one" recognition should not occur at the present time. The feedback inhibition in area C indirectly generates inhibitory pathways between neurons that are strongly activated by different words. Thus the activity of principal neurons in C will be dominated at any time by those neurons that are associated with a single word. The feedback inhibition is the physical representation of the logical idea that at any particular time, two different words cannot have been simultaneously completed.

The model network has been described in a neurobiological metaphor, and its processing specified. All the elements present in Fig. 4 can be implemented in simple analog electronic hardware, using only resistors, capacitors, and operational amplifiers. We have built such a network to recognize 10 short words (Tank and Hopfield, 1987b). With connections chosen on the basis of the previous discussion it is capable of recognizing its vocabulary of a few words in continuous speech. Figure 7 shows the acoustic signal $S(t)$ and output of several different recognition units (electronic model "neurons") in area C when the phrase "six network repeat six" was spoken. Each recognition neuron becomes strongly driven for a short time near the completion of its corresponding word, and is inactive at other times. The PSTH shown in Fig. 5 for the utterance "one" was actually obtained from the voltages in the corresponding

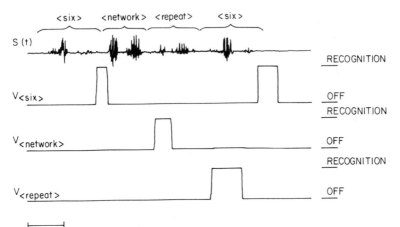

Figure 7.
Top trace: the waveform of the utterance "network six repeat network."
Second, third, and fourth traces: the activity of amplifiers playing the role
of principal neurons in area C. The first of these amplifiers is a recognizer
for the word "network," the second is for the word "repeat," and the
third for "six."

electronic circuit when the word "one" was presented. [In the analog electronic system, the output voltages of amplifiers correspond to the instantaneous firing rates of the biological neurons, and the output voltage as a function of time is equivalent to a PSTH (Hopfield and Tank, 1986)]

_____ IV. What the Model Implies for _____
Neurobiology

The computational problem of word recognition might be stated as follows. The recognizing system has information about a few words. For any short sequence of sound, and given an understanding of how words are likely to be distorted in ordinary speech, there exists a probability P_{six} that, if "six" were spoken, it would result in the observed sound segment. The recognition system should compute P_{six}, $P_{network}$, etc. for all the words it knows (based on the input and the distortion model), find the largest such probability, and if that probability is not too small, then produce an output signal signifying that a particular word has just been spoken (Levinson et al., 1983; Bahl et al., 1983). The feature extraction, time delay, and competitive recognition neurons are a dynamic system that carries out the essence of this computational procedure for continuous speech in the presence of time warp and symbol substitution errors.

Since we understand how this model network responds and functions, we can ask what might be learned about its processing from some of the classic ways of studying a neural system. Consider for example an "electric shock to a tract" applied to the entire pathway between the tonotopic nucleus A and area B. Area B will give a brief response, which need not resemble any response elicited by a natural stimulus. Responses will be recorded in area C for times from 0 to 0.8 sec after the shock stimulus. Since these time-delayed responses are the essential mechanism by which the information in the time-dependent signal is organized for recognition, the discovery of these time delays would be of considerable significance. But the computational meaning of these delays could not be deduced from shock stimuli, nor would it even be evident whether these delays had *any* meaning in terms of information processing.

In this network, the feature extraction done in area B requires the inhibitory interneurons. Eliminating this inhibition results in unfamiliar and unrecognizable information being sent to area C. The information processing aspects of inhibition are equally important within area C. In our model circuit, the inhibition does not simply "keep the total activity down." The specific form of the inhibition, the synaptic interconnection topology and time course, are essential physical components of the computational structure. While decreasing the level of inhibition—for example, by pharmacological agents—can be a useful way to study electroanatomy, it has disastrous consequences for information processing in such a circuit.

We turn finally to the relation between these ideas and synapses, synapse dynamics, and synapse plasticity. The time scale of delays required are so long that mechanisms other than a soma RC (resistance– capacitance) time constant or propagation delays would seem necessary. A variety of known mechanisms could produce such delays. Llinas and Yarom (1981) have studied posthyperpolarization rebound Ca^{2+} spikes, delayed by up to 0.3 sec after the release of hyperpolarization. Byrne (1980, 1982) has noted that an ordinary neuron with a fast potassium channel activation mechanism (A current) will have a delayed response to excitation, since depolarizing conductances will be masked by the K^+ conductance until the potassium channel inactivates. Indirect pathways (Kehoe and Marty, 1980) by which the binding of a transmitter molecule activates a chain of biochemistry that terminates in the phosphorylation of a channel protein and increasing the open time of the channel could have delays of seconds. Thus there are many known mechanisms by which an appropriate length of delay could be generated between the activation of a presynaptic neuron and its electrical effect on a postsynaptic neuron. Of course, short delays could also be concatenated into longer delays by multicellular pathways.

Delay mechanisms like axon propagation delays (due to different propagation velocities or different lengths) and slow synaptic potentials are directly observable with straightforward electrophysiological techniques. Their action results in a direct change in a current or membrane potential in a neuron in some section of the delay pathway and can be observed with a microelectrode.

A perhaps richer class of delay mechanisms is beginning to be characterized that can be distinguished from the above by the fact that the mechanisms are in a sense "hidden": a biochemical change can occur in ion channel proteins with a time course similar to one of our spreadout delays (Fig. 6) but that will cause no observable change in current or membrane potential unless "tested." For example, Johnson and Ascher (1987) observed an interaction of glycine with the N-methyl-D-aspartate (NMDA) receptor. Application of glycine dramatically potentiates the membrane current produced by NMDA. The potentiation has a delay that lasts several seconds (the unbinding rate appears to be slow; the glycine binding rate has not yet been reported). A mechanism such as this is an elementary form of memory, and any such mechanism in conjunction with other machinery could be used to form the kind of delay and organize sequential information in the general fashion we have discussed. But the temporary change in the nervous system that happens to the NMDA receptor upon glycine application is hidden to the investigator unless probed with an appropriate electrophysiological experiment. The simple circuit that we have described could be generalized to make use of such "hidden" delays in place of the more overt or direct delays.

Appropriate delayed connections would need to be made when an animal learns to recognize a particular sound or word. Such plasticity could be of two forms. In the simplest case, a distribution of intrinsic time delays would always be present and located before the modifiable synapses in the recognition network. To learn new sounds, ordinary synapses could be modified, and the necessary modification algorithm would be qualitatively similar to that described by Hebb (see Chapter 6, this volume). Alternatively, the synapse modification process could change the delay time of already existing connections. In either case, the modification paradigm would necessarily involve signals that arrive at the sensory system at different times, and then converge onto a synapse in such a fashion that together they alter its efficacy or the delay it produces.

The complex anatomy, biophysics, and biochemistry of the central nervous system contain a wealth of details that could be used as the basis for information and signal processing. Every experimenter finds immensely more facts and peculiarities than ever can be published, and selects for publication those that seem to be the most significant or interpretable. One function of this kind of modeling is to indicate how some of the unusual details of neurobiology may be used for processing information in unexpected ways. L. Kitzes (private comunication) has observed long delays (among other unpublished complex behaviors) in A_1 cortex of awake monkeys. T. M. McKenna and co-workers (1988) have shown that the majority of neurons in primary auditory cortex of alert cats show tuning effects due to prior tones of different frequency which arrive 0.3–1.6 sec earlier. We have shown in a detailed model stylized on neurobiology that such delays in signalling between cells can be a general and simple biological method to organize sequence information, and can be central to understanding aspects of audition.

References

Bahl, L. R., Jelinek, F., and Mercer, R. L. (1983). *IEEE Trans. Pattern. Anal. Mach. Int.* **PAMT-5**, 179–190.

Byrne, J. H. (1980). *J. Neurophysiol.* **43**, 630, 651–668.

Byrne, J. H. (1982). *Fed. Proc., Fed. Am. Soc. Exp. Biol.* **41**, 2147–2152.

Hopfield, J. J. (1982). *Proc. Natl. Acad. Sci. U.S.A.* **79**, 2554–2558.

Hopfield, J. J. (1984). *Proc. Natl. Acad. Sci. U.S.A.* **81**, 3088–3092.

Hopfield, J. J., and Tank, D. W. (1986). *Science* **233**, 626–633.

Johnson, J. W., and Ascher, P. (1987). *Nature (London)* **325**, 529.

Kehoe, J. S., and Marty, A. (1980). *Annu. Rev. Biophys. Bioeng.* **9**, 437.

Kleinfeld, D. (1986). *Proc. Natl. Acad. Sci. U.S.A.* **83**, 9469.

Levinson, S. E., Rabiner, L. R., and Sondhi, M. M. (1983). *Bell Syst. Tech. J.* **62**, 1035–1074.

Liberman, A. M., Cooper, F. S., Shankweiler, D. P., and Studdert-Kennedy, M. (1967). *Psychol. Rev.* **74,** 431.

Llinas, R., and Yarom, Y. (1981). *J. Physiol. (London)* **315,** 569.

Suga, N. (1984). *Trends NeuroSci.* **7,** 20 (1984).

Sullivan, W. E., and Konishi, M. (1986). *Proc. Natl. Acad. Sci. U.S.A.* **83,** 8400–8404.

Tank, D. W., and Hopfield, J. J. (1986). *IEEE Trans. Circuits and Systems* **33,** 533–541.

Tank, D. W., and Hopfield, J. J. (1987a). *Proc. Natl. Acad. Sci. U.S.A.* **84,** 1896–1900.

Tank, D. W., and Hopfield, J. J. (1987b). *Proc. Int. Conf. Neurol Networks, 1st* **IV,**, 455–468.

18

Local Synaptic and Electrical Interactions in Hippocampus: Experimental Data and Computer Simulations

F. Edward Dudek and Roger D. Traub

I. Introduction

An understanding of neuronal plasticity requires three types of information. First is a picture of how brain function proceeds at a given time and in the absence of external disturbances that modify the underlying physical substrate of the brain itself. Such a picture must integrate results on membrane biophysics and single-neuron electrophysiology with data on synaptic circuitry and other relevant interactions between neurons. Thus a single model must include experimental results ranging from the properties of membrane channels to the behavior of neuronal circuits. Second, we must have a picture of how experiences (i.e., inputs to the brain) are transformed into changes in specific physical parameters within the brain. How does experience excite particular cellular activities, and then how do these lead to long-lasting modifications in channels, synapses, and neuronal populations? Finally, given that certain parameters of the brain have indeed been altered, by whatever mechanisms, how is brain function now different than it was before? Thus, in what meaningful ways does the system as a whole alter its activities once particular neurons and their synapses have in fact been modified? In this chapter, we shall deal mainly with an example of the first type of problem. We present experiments and computer simulations aimed at elucidating the collective behavior of populations of hippocampal neurons, in the absence of so-called plastic changes.

Two dominant features of the evolutionary progression from invertebrates to lower mammals to humans have been the increase in the number of neurons in the brain and the enhancement of both the number and complexity of local neuronal interactions. Numerous model systems for the study of synaptic plasticity and learning in lower animals, such

378

as gastropod mollusks (e.g., *Aplysia*, *Limax*, and *Hermissenda*), have provided important information about how individual neurons and their biophysical properties operate within neural circuits to generate simple behaviors and behavioral modifications. Although these studies (many reviewed in this volume) have produced valuable information that will almost certainly apply to the mammalian brain, a distinct feature of the human brain that is not represented in simple "model" systems is the enormous integrative complexity via local neuronal interactions. These integrative local mechanisms include (1) recurrent inhibition and excitation mediated by chemical synapses, (2) electrotonic coupling via gap junctions, (3) electrical field effects (ephaptic transmission), which arise from current flow through the extracellular space, and finally (4) changes in the concentration of extracellular ions, such as K^+ and Ca^{2+}. Each of these mechanisms has been found to occur in "simple" systems, and information from these preparations has been extremely valuable in understanding biophysical principles. However, when operating *together* and involving large numbers of cells simultaneously, these neuronal interactions confer an enormous degree of complexity on a neuronal network. This is true even with relatively simple forms of experimental analysis such as input–output relations and the effects of previous activity. During the normal functions of the brain, it is likely that the tremendous number of neurons in each structure combined with their large array of integrative mechanisms leads to new physiological processes not found in "simple" systems. Even a rudimentary understanding of this complexity requires computer models of neural networks using neurons with realistic (if not precise) electrophysiological properties. The approach of electrophysiological experimentation involving membrane conductances, whole nerve cells, and neuronal populations *combined* with computer models of the appropriate magnitude and detail has the potential to reveal the collective or *emergent* properties that occur in large ensembles of neurons characteristic of the mammalian brain. Some of the collective properties may not be obvious (and may even be counterintuitive) from considerations simply of the properties of simple cells and of interactions between pairs of cells.

Many forms of neuronal plasticity, such as long-term potentiation (LTP), should lead to alterations in local neuronal interactions. The relative importance of each form of local interaction depends on the particular situation. Chemical synapses, whether from long-distance projections or local neuronal circuits, are considered the basis for neural integration under normal conditions. On the other hand, certain abnormal conditions, such as epileptiform activity, provide insights into a broader range of neuronal interactions—a range that includes, but is not limited to, chemical synapses. Epileptiform bursting is characterized by extreme synchrony and hyperactivity, and it represents a useful model for studying how such synchrony can arise in the first place and how increases in firing frequency can in turn influence local neuronal inter-actions. Although local chemical synapses are known to play a critical role in the spread and synchronization of epileptiform activity, electrical interactions are also likely to be important.

As background for this chapter, we will first briefly review elec-trophysiological data and computer simulations concerning the char-acteristics of single pyramidal cells and the network properties associated with a sparse system of local excitatory synapses. Our primary aim, however, will be to describe recent efforts to incorporate electrical in-teractions, particularly field effects (i.e., ephaptic transmission), into this network model so that it reproduces and predicts electrical behavior of complex neuronal populations from known properties of single cells and synaptic interactions between neuron pairs. Our starting point in the results section will be the rather surprising observation obtained by sev-eral groups that exposure of hippocampal slices to low-[Ca^{2+}] solutions, which completely block spike-dependent chemical synaptic transmission and also increase membrane excitability, leads to synchronous bursting. After briefly reviewing data that suggest an important role for electrical field effects in this synchronization process, we will describe simulations that reproduce this behavior and provide a quantitative, conceptual framework for understanding how this occurs. Next, we will review fur-ther data and modeling efforts to incorporate simultaneously both local excitatory synapses and electrical interactions into models of synchronous bursting by hippocampal neurons. The conclusions that derive from this combined approach, in turn, suggest new physiological processes that now appear difficult to analyze experimentally, but which may be studied further with an appropriate computer model. Conversely, computer models provide important insights into those experimental issues that are the most critical for further research.

A. The Hippocampus

The hippocampus has long been considered important for learning and memory (see Chapters 12 and 13, this volume), and it is also particularly sensitive to epileptic seizures. One important experimental advantage of this structure is that most of the projection neurons are of a single type, pyramidal cells. Although considerable information was and is available from research in intact animals, the use of slice preparations in the last decade or two has greatly expanded our knowledge of mem-brane conductances, whole-cell electrophysiology, local interactions, and projections to and from the hippocampus. These data have recently been supplemented by results from isolated dissociated neurons. This large body of information, at many levels and from numerous laboratories, has been instrumental in the development of a model of hippocampal network properties.

B. Electrophysiology of Single Pyramidal Cells

A wide range of intracellular studies in the late 1970s and throughout the 1980s have yielded a general picture of the ionic conductances of CA1 and CA3 pyramidal cells. Biophysical analyses of pyramidal cells have indicated that their electrotonic length corresponds to about one space constant (Johnston and Brown, 1982; Brown and Johnston, 1982). Intracellular recordings have shown that hippocampal pyramidal cells possess dendritic Ca^{2+} conductances (Wong et al., 1979), that their Ca^{2+}-mediated depolarizing afterpotentials lead to intrinsic bursts (Wong and Prince, 1981), and that spike bursts are followed by a Ca^{2+}-activated K^+ conductance (Brown and Griffith, 1983). Although the kinetics of the voltage-dependent conductances and the precise location and density of each channel type are still unknown (however, see Kay and Wong, 1987; Numann et al., 1987), enough information has been available to construct a single-cell computer model that reproduces many of the known properties of hippocampal cells. In the model, each neuron contains 19–28 compartments (depending on the presence or absence of apical dendritic branching), including one for the soma. Each compartment has a membrane capacitance and leakage conductance, and is connected to adjacent compartments through a resistance comparable to that of the intracellular medium. Dendrites are modeled as equivalent cylinders (Rall, 1962), with a single or branched apical dendrite and a single basilar dendrite. The apical and basilar dendrites are 1.0 and 0.8 space constants, respectively, in electrotonic length. The soma and occasionally one dendritic compartment have active conductances capable of burst generation (Traub, 1982). As a minimum, the model of a single neuron contains (1) a Na^+ current for action potential generation, (2) a Ca^{2+} current to produce spike depolarizing afterpotentials and slow action potentials, and to control a slow Ca^{2+}-dependent K^+ current, (3) a fast voltage-dependent K^+ current with voltage-dependent inactivation, which represents a hybrid of the delayed rectifier and A-currents, and (4) a Ca^{2+}-dependent K^+ current that produces a long hyperpolarization after a spike burst. In this form, the model reproduces faithfully a wide variety of spontaneous and current-evoked events characteristic of hippocampal pyramidal cells.

C. Local Neuronal Interactions

It has long been established that antidromic or synaptic activation of hippocampal pyramidal cells is followed by powerful gamma-aminobutyric acid (GABA) mediated recurrent inhibition, and that blockade of this system leads to synchronous bursting throughout the hippocampal population. Dual intracellular recordings have shown unequivocally that recurrent excitation is present among CA3 pyramidal cells, although the connectivity seems to be relatively sparse (MacVicar and Dudek, 1980; Miles and Wong, 1986). Several studies have provided evidence that recurrent excitation is the primary contributor to synchronization of epileptiform bursts in the CA3 area (Johnston and Brown, 1981; Traub and Wong, 1982). Several independent lines of evidence have suggested the presence of electrotonic junctions, but these also appear to be sparse (see Dudek *et al.*, 1983, 1986, for review) and their role in synchronization remains uncertain. Differential recordings of transmembrane potential have shown that electrical field effects (i.e., ephaptic transmission) occur during synchronous firing or so-called "population spikes" (see Dudek *et al.*, 1986, for review). Thus, hippocampal neurons can communicate with their neighbors through several possible mechanisms, although this chapter will focus primarily on electrical field effects.

D. Recurrent Excitation and Synchronous Bursting

Considerable evidence from research in the 1970s had suggested that local excitatory synapses play a critical role in synchronization when inhibitory synapses are blocked with penicillin or picrotoxin (Ayala *et al.*, 1973). Biophysical studies supported the hypothesis that a large synaptic conductance is responsible for the depolarization shift that occurrs in CA3 pyramidal cells when inhibition is pharmacologically blocked (Johnston and Brown, 1981). Nonetheless, the initial studies with dual intracellular recording suggested that only a few percent of the cell pairs, at most, were connected by excitatory synapses (MacVicar and Dudek, 1980). Traub and Wong (1982) used computer simulations with a 100-neuron network, which contained realistic single-cell electrical properties and excitatory synaptic interconnections, and were able to reproduce bursting behavior at the single-neuron and hippocampal-population levels. Conceptually, the model involved a cascade effect whereby a small group of excited neurons activated the entire population in progressive stages of synaptically induced bursting. Connectivity was too sparse for any small group of cells to excite the entire population directly. A critical assumption was that recurrent excitatory synapses were powerful enough so that bursting in one cell would evoke bursting in a connected postsynaptic cell, provided the postsynaptic cell was not simultaneously inhibited or refractory from a recent burst. The model could account for several features of the electrophysiological data, such as the 50- to 100-msec latency from a local stimulus to a population burst. The model was also predictive; for example, it suggested that activation of a single CA3 pyramidal cell should—in some cases—initiate a synchronous population burst. Subsequent studies in picrotoxin-treated slices indeed showed that in about one of three cells, an evoked spike burst in a single cell could trigger a burst from the entire CA3 population (Miles and Wong, 1983). Furthermore, dual intracellular recordings in CA3 have directly shown that excitatory synapses are indeed powerful enough for burst transmission to occur between monosynaptically connected cells (Miles and Wong, 1987a). These and other data provided overwhelming evidence in favor of a critical role for chemical synapses in synchronizing the activity of CA3 pyramidal cells. This model did not require any form of electrical or ionic interaction to reproduce—at least qualitatively—several well-established electrophysiological observations.

-------------------- **II. Results** --------------------

A. Synchronization through Electrical Interactions Alone

1. Electrophysiological Data

a. Synchronous Bursting in Low-[Ca^{2+}] Solutions.   Exposure of hippocampal slices to low-[Ca^{2+}] solutions, which demonstrably block chemical synaptic transmission, can lead to evoked and spontaneous bursts of population spikes (Taylor and Dudek, 1982b; Jefferys and Haas, 1982; Konnerth et al., 1984). Although *spontaneous* release of synaptic "quanta" can still occur in this solution, spontaneous release that is not coupled to action potentials cannot be an effective synchronizing mechanism. These electrophysiological data therefore provide strong evidence that mechanisms other than chemical synapses can synchronize the firing of CA1 pyramidal cells. With further reductions in the concentration of divalent cations, the dentate granule cells and CA3 pyramidal cells can also fire synchronous action potentials (i.e., population spikes) with chemical synaptic transmission blocked (Snow and Dudek, 1984a). Although an important contribution by shifts in extracellular K$^+$ has been proposed, particularly for the spread of these synchronized bursts (Konnerth et al., 1984, 1986; Yaari et al., 1986), electrical interactions between neurons almost certainly play a critical role as a synchronizing mechanism to generate the large population spikes in low-[Ca^{2+}] solutions.

b. Electrotonic Coupling versus Electrical Field Effects.   Either electrotonic junctions or electrical field effects could in principle synchronize hippocampal pyramidal cells when chemical synapses are blocked in low-[Ca^{2+}] solution. Two types of evidence suggest that electrotonic coupling via gap junctions cannot by itself account for the synchronization. First, all experimental measures of electrotonic coupling suggest that the cells do not form the interconnected syncytium that would be necessary for extensive synchronization to occur. The available data argue that many hippocampal neurons are not coupled, and that those that are coupled are only connected to a few other cells to generate small groups or clusters. Second, although events similar to what one would expect of electrotonic coupling potentials (i.e., fast prepotentials, see Fig. 1B) can be observed in some pyramidal cells when chemical synapses are blocked, in most neurons these events are rare and it is difficult to reveal them during spontaneous discharges. Although particularly strong or particularly weak electrotonic junctions to an impaled neuron might not lead to coupling potentials after presynaptic spikes, these observations strongly argue that electrotonic coupling alone cannot account for the profound synchronization of action potentials routinely observed in low-$[Ca^{2+}]$ solutions.

Although electrical field effects have long been considered a possible mechanism for synchronizing cortical neurons (see Dudek *et al.*, 1986, for discussion), this hypothesis fell into considerable disfavor throughout the 1970's. However, studies in other neuronal systems, particularly the Mauthner cell in goldfish (e.g., see Korn and Faber, 1979), clearly showed that the electrical field from an action potential in one neuron can influence the excitability of other neurons if certain morphological considerations are applicable. Because of the particular anatomical arrangement in the Mauthner cell system of the goldfish, action potentials can produce inhibitory field effects. Differential recording (intracellular minus extracellular) of transmembrane potential during synchronous firing (i.e., population spikes) of hippocampal neurons has revealed field-effect depolarizations when chemical synapses were blocked (Fig. 1C and D). In fact, whenever the criteria for accurate measurement of transmembrane potential with differential recording techniques are met, field-effect depolarizations can be detected during population spikes and are associated with an increase in membrane excitability (Taylor and Dudek, 1984a,b). Thus, hippocampal population spikes can have an excitatory influence on inactive cells in the population, but it is unclear how small a group of hippocampal neurons must fire synchronously to cause a nearby inactive neuron close to threshold to fire an action potential. The fact that the previously reported field effects are inhibitory in the Mauthner cell system and excitatory in the hippocampus is readily explained by the different geometrical arrangements of the interacting neurons. The existence of field-effect depolarizations during differential recording and simultaneous negativities during single-ended intracellular recording, combined with the general lack of intracellularly recorded positive transients (i.e., electrotonic potentials), implies that field effects are more likely to synchronize action potentials in this structure than is electrotonic coupling (Taylor and Dudek, 1984a,b; Taylor *et al.*, 1984; Yim *et al.*, 1986).

2. Computer Modeling

The observation of synchronous firing without chemical synapses suggested that electrical interactions, particularly field effects, need to be included in models of synchronous firing by hippocampal pyramidal cells. Although incorporation of electrotonic junctions into the computer

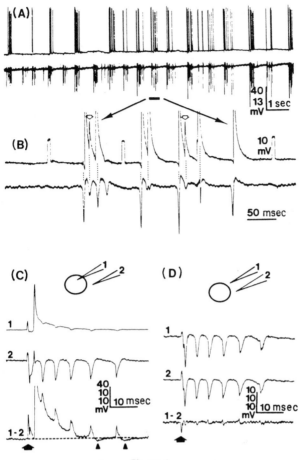

Figure 1.
Synchronous bursting of hippocampal pyramidal cells in low-$[Ca^{2+}]$
solutions that block chemical synapses. (A) Spontaneous bursts of
synchronous action potentials recorded from CA1 pyramidal cells in a
hippocampal slice bathed 4 hr in a solution containing 2.3 mM Mn^{2+} and
0.5 mM Ca^{2+}. The solution rapidly blocked chemical synaptic transmission
to CA1 pyramidal cells. Intracellularly recorded action potentials (top
trace) occurred synchronously with population spikes in the extracellular
record (lower trace). (B) Part of the records from (A) are expanded, as
indicated by the bar and arrows. Open arrows point to subthreshold
depolarizations, which resemble fast prepotentials. (C) Differential
recording of transmembrane potential. As indicated in the inset, the
intracellular trace (1) minus the extracellular trace (2) represents a measure
of transmembrane potential (1 − 2). Field-effect depolarizations, which
were only apparent in the differential recording, occurred synchronously
with population spikes in the extracellular record. The dashed line shows
resting potential. (D) Extracellular control. The intracellular electrode was
withdrawn about 5 μm to provide evidence that the extracellular electrode
in (C) was close to the impaled cell. Differential recording under these
conditions revealed no depolarization during the population spikes
(bottom trace), thus indicating that the differential recording in (C)
accurately measured transmembrane potential. [Reproduced from Taylor
and Dudek (1982), with permission. Copyright 1982 by the AAAS.]

simulations was comparatively simple, since they can be represented electrically as simple low-resistance pathways between neurons, the addition of field effects was considerably more difficult. An analytical approach—for example, calculating extracellular potentials from Poisson's equation applied to an idealized set of current sources—was rejected because it did not allow appropriate interplay between transmembrane currents and extracellular currents. The algorithm must allow for the possibility that transmembrane currents flowing through the extracellular medium will alter transmembrane potentials, which in turn will affect voltage-dependent transmembrane currents (Fig. 2). A network of neurons with electrical field effects between individual elements will therefore possess "cooperative" properties, since extracellular current flow and the electrical behavior of the neurons continuously affect each other. An approach is required, therefore, in which neuronal behavior and extracellular current flow are coupled together on the time scale over which such properties actually change. We have produced such an approach (Traub *et al.*, 1985a,b) wherein the differential equations for the neurons and the linear equations for extracellular current flows are coupled every integration step (i.e., every 50 μsec).

   a. Structure of the Model.   The initial network for analyzing electrical field effects was an extrapolation of the 100-cell model used to study synaptic interactions. It is necessary that the model of each cell include dendrites, so that current loops can form across different regions of cell membrane. The extracellular space is simulated as a resistive three-dimensional lattice where two dimensions represent a layer of pyramidal cells, and the third dimension is for vertical layers corresponding to dendritic compartments. Although the initial model contained 100 neurons with a branched apical dendrite and 27 compartments at 19 levels, the most recent one contains 2000 cells with unbranched apical and basilar dendrites (Fig. 3). Each dendritic compartment is 0.1 space constant in electrotonic length. The different levels in the extracellular lattice are not evenly spaced, in order to match the physical coordinates of the lattice and the electrotonic coordinates of the model neurons (Rall, 1962). Because of dendritic branching in hippocampal neurons, the length of a segment of dendritic cylinder corresponds to a smaller length of actual space as one moves away from the soma (Rall, 1962). Currents flow inside the neurons and across membranes to corresponding points in the extracellular lattice and through the lattice. Two opposite faces of the lattice are grounded (i.e., are connected to points fixed at zero potential) to represent a slice with two faces in contact with a medium whose resistivity is small compared to tissue resistivity and whose other faces are closed to current flow. Extracellular resistivity is increased in the vicinity of the cell body layer in accord with the results of Jefferys (1984). In present implementations, there are two cells for each section through

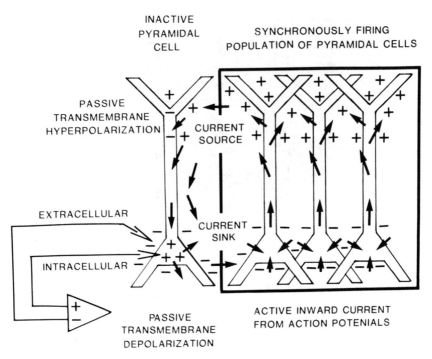

Figure 2.
Hypothetical mechanism of electrical field effects. The square (at right)
represents a population of synchronously firing pyramidal cells. Inward
current at the cell bodies from a population spike by these neurons causes
a current sink or extracellular negativity at the soma of the inactive
pyramidal cell (left). The sink in the cell body layer and the source in the
dendrites are associated with current flow (indicated by arrows).
Differential recordings from the intracellular and extracellular
microelectrodes show field-effect depolarizations in the cell body of an
inactive hippocampal neuron (i.e., one that is not firing when the
population is active). [Reproduced from Dudek *et al.* (1986). Role of
electrical interactions in synchronization of epileptiform bursts. *In* "Basic
Mechanisms of the Epilepsies" (A. V. Delgado-Escueta *et al.*, ed.). Raven
Press, New York.]

the lattice, thus allowing for the fact that pyramidal neurons are layered
two or more deep in the hippocampal slice.

This general approach to modeling electrical field effects is similar
to that described by Traub and co-workers (1985a,b), except that we are
now using a larger, and hence more realistic, system (i.e., more cells
and more lattice points). We have been able to undertake larger field
computations because of certain simplifications in model structure (i.e.,
no branching dendrites, no dendritic bursting sites) and because we have
been able to use the vector facility of the IBM 3090 computer to speed

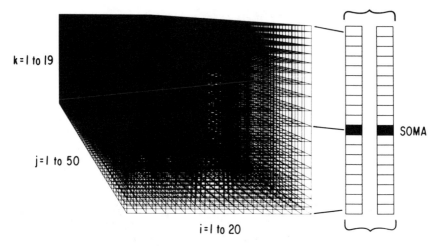

Figure 3.
Schematic diagram indicating structure of computer model. The population of hippocampal neurons consists of 2000 pyramidal cells. A lattice with dimensions 20 × 50 × 19 is used to calculate extracellular potentials. Each neuron in the 20 × 50 population contains 19 compartments, including the soma (shaded). The 19,000 lattice points represent extracellular locations throughout the network of neurons. The lines between each lattice point are extracellular resistors. Each vertical line in the extracellular lattice corresponds to two model pyramidal cells, thus yielding a total of 2000 neurons. The soma of each neuron has active currents, and is attached to two equivalent cylinders (one each for the basilar and apical dendrites). Excitatory synapses connect the pyramidal cells in some versions of the model. A separate population of neurons is excited by pyramidal cells, and in turn inhibits pyramidal cells, thus simulating the recurrent inhibitory circuit.

up the calculations. We briefly note that the differential equations for neuronal membrane behavior are solved using an explicit Taylor series method. The 19,000 linear equations for the extracellular potentials, equivalent to a discrete version of Poisson's differential equation, are solved with an iterative overrelaxation method (Varga, 1962). Other technical considerations concerning methods have been or will be given elsewhere (Traub *et al.*, 1985a,b, 1987).

  b. Simulation of Synchronous Bursting with Electrical Interactions.   The experimental observations with low-[Ca^{2+}] solutions revealed several specific phenomena (Taylor and Dudek, 1982b; Jefferys and Haas, 1982; Konnerth *et al.*, 1984), and an accurate model would be expected to replicate these electrophysiological characteristics. First, repetitive large population spikes in the field potential recording occurred synchronously with action potentials recorded intracellularly in nearby neurons. Action potentials in a particular cell, however, did not always occur one-to-one with population spikes, since individual cells sometimes failed to fire during particular population spikes. However, when a cell did fire, it was almost always in phase with a population spike. Furthermore, spike synchrony, or near-synchrony, could occur over large areas (hundreds of micrometers or more). Several experimental observations also indicated that the synchronized firing did not result simply because of perfectly identical kinetics for voltage-dependent conductances across the population. For example, if an individual cell was hyperpolarized by injected current, it rapidly resumed firing in phase with the population upon terminating the current injection (Taylor and Dudek, 1984b). Methods were used in the model to ensure that this type of artifactual synchrony was not present. Finally, the electrical field effect from a population spike yields a somatic transmembrane depolarization during differential recording, whereas intracellular recordings referenced to ground often show a brief negativity in phase with the population spike. These were key features of the electrophysiological data that we felt needed to be present in any accurate simulation of this experimental situation.

In the early simulations of electrical interactions with the 100-cell model, Ca^{2+} currents and Ca^{2+}-dependent currents were blocked (Traub et al., 1985a). The cells were made hyperexcitable by effectively lowering threshold, and spontaneous, repetitive firing was induced with depolarizing currents injected into the somata of 16 cells in the middle of the array. Similar to the data shown in Fig. 4 from a 2000-cell model (see below), it was possible to produce synchronous firing with field effects alone, as long as extracellular resistance was made large enough. These simulations had many of the properties characteristic of the electrophysiological recordings in low-$[Ca^{2+}]$ solutions. For example, transmembrane recordings showed field-effect depolarizations, while single-ended intracellular recordings (i.e., with respect to ground) showed small, brief negativities synchronous with the population spikes. When the extracellular resistance was low, a variety of plausible arrangements of electrotonic junctions did not by themselves cause synchronous firing. When field effects were of intermediate strength, however, electrotonic junctions tended to enhance synchronization. These initial simulations emphasized the importance of electrical field effects and provided a theoretical framework for understanding how they operate. The simulations also suggested that, at least under the conditions studied, electrotonic junctions had relatively little effect on synchronization of the population activity.

Recent preliminary studies on electrical field effects have now been undertaken with a 2000-cell model after some simplifications. Although it is possible to simulate population bursting with field effects alone in this model, the initial studies suggest—surprisingly—that the model is less robust when more cells are present; that is, synchronized firing is only observed under rather specific circumstances. Because of boundary

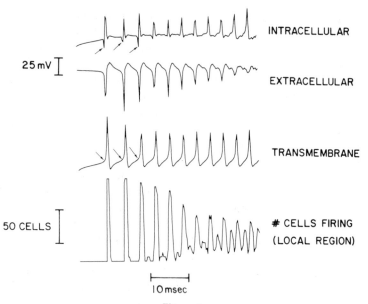

Figure 4.
Computer simulation of synchronous burst in a low-[Ca^{2+}] solution.
Intracellular, extracellular (both relative to ground and recorded from the
cell body layer), and transmembrane (intracellular minus extracellular)
potentials are shown for a typical hippocampal neuron in the model. The
bottom trace shows the number of cells that are depolarized > 20 mV in a
local region (120 cells) around the illustrated neuron. Chemical synapses
and Ca^{2+} conductance are blocked. Note that the intracellularly recorded
action potentials are synchronized with the population spikes. The brief
negativity preceding each action potential in the single-ended intracellular
recording (upper trace, arrows) corresponds to a field-effect depolarization
in the differential recording of transmembrane potential (third trace,
arrows).

conditions, the extracellular fields are not homogeneous in space and
field effects may actually tend to desynchronize spikes in neurons at
different locations. Nevertheless, if the intrinsic membrane properties
of the cells are similar enough, the basic features of field-induced synchrony (as outlined above) are still observed in a model with 2000 cells
(Fig. 4). It is interesting to speculate that electrotonic junctions might
compensate for the dispersant tendencies seen in the 2000-cell model,
and might act to maintain synchrony.

B. Electrical Field Effects with Chemical Synapses

1. Differential Recording of Field-Effect Depolarizations

Although electrical field effects appear to be important for synchronizing neuronal activity in low-[Ca^{2+}] solutions, a critical issue is
whether they are effective during convulsant-induced synchronous

bursting, when ionic constituents are normal or nearly normal. Based on the hypothetical mechanism for their occurrence (Fig. 2), one would intuitively expect that the electrical field associated with the population spike would tend to excite inactive cells under any conditions. Differential recording of transmembrane potentials (Fig. 5) during synchronized bursting in the presence of the $GABA_A/Cl^-$ channel-blocker, picrotoxin, combined with intracellular hyperpolarizing current or injection of QX314 to block action potentials in the impaled cell, has clearly revealed field-effect depolarizations on the peak of depolarization shifts (Snow and Dudek, 1984b). Similarly, orthodromic stimulation of afferents to hippocampal pyramidal cells in normal media revealed field-effect depolarizations, and these events could be larger than chemically mediated synaptic potentials under some conditions (Snow and Dudek, 1986). These data raised the issue of how electrical field effects influence the convulsant-induced epileptiform field potential and also how they might operate in the normal brain.

2. Contribution of Field Effects to the Shape of the Epileptiform Field Potential

Since large field potential transients are known to occur during epileptiform bursting, we undertook computer simulations of this situation using both recurrent excitation via chemical synapses and also electrical field effects in the model. An analysis of the interactions between chemical synaptic and electrical mechanisms was obtained by combining the two models described above (Traub et al., 1985b). Under these conditions it was possible to simulate the extracellular, intracellular, and transmembrane recordings during synchronous bursting in picrotoxin (Fig. 6). Again, when extracellular resistance was low, the field potential revealed relatively little action potential synchronization. However, clear population spikes were present when extracellular resistance was increased. These initial data supported the hypothesis that chemical synaptic mechanisms synchronized neurons over the time scale of tens and hundreds of milliseconds, whereas electrical field effects synchronized cells in the millisecond time range, thus producing the "teeth" in the "comb-shaped" epileptiform field potential. More recent studies concerning propagation of synchronized bursts in the CA3 area suggest that the properties of local excitatory chemical synapses and axonal conduction, rather than electrical field effects, determine propagation rate (Traub et al., 1987a; Miles et al., in press).

Although these simulations have been able to reproduce experimental observations, a major effort continues to be directed toward increasing the precision of important parameters in the model and toward including different physiological effects. Several types of recently obtained data have been incorporated into the latest versions of the model (Traub et al. 1987, 1988, Miles et al., in press), such as the spatial distribution of excitatory synaptic connections, the existence of slow inhib-

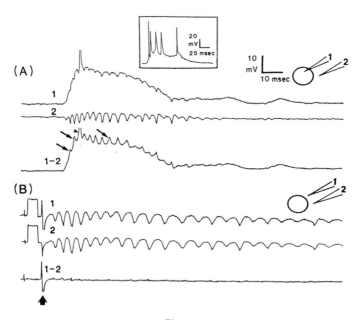

Figure 5.
Differential recording of transmembrane potential during a synchronous burst by pyramidal cells in a picrotoxin-treated hippocampal slice. The enclosed inset shows a spontaneous spike burst at resting potential. (A) Field-effect depolarizations were revealed with differential recording when steady hyperpolarizing current was injected through the intracellular microelectrode to block most of the action potentials in the impaled neuron. The top trace (1) is a single-ended intracellular recording (i.e., with respect to a remote bath ground), the middle trace (2) is an extracellular recording (also with respect to a remote bath ground), and the bottom trace (1 −2) is a recording of transmembrane potential. At resting potential, spikes were synchronous on both electrodes, but slightly inactivated during the large, slow depolarization. In the differential recording (1 −2), field-effect depolarizations (arrows) could be seen during the spike burst when hyperpolarizing current was injected and only one spike (arrowhead) was generated in the impaled neuron. (B) Extracellular control recordings after loss of the impalement. The electrode that had been intracellular (electrode 1, see diagrams) recorded the extracellular field potential immediately outside the neuron in response to orthodromic stimulation (at arrow). Differential recording (1 −2) under these conditions showed that the electrodes had been electrically close. A 10-mV, 5-msec calibration pulse preceded the stimulus. [Reproduced from Dudek *et al.* (1986). Role of Electrical Interactions in Synchronization of Epileptiform Bursts. *In* "Basic Mechanisms of the Epilepsies" (A. V. Delgado-Escueta *et al.*, ed.). Raven Press, New York.]

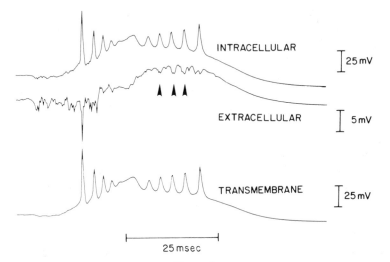

Figure 6.

Simulation of synchronized burst. The model for this simulation had 2000 pyramidal cells with 10 excitatory synaptic inputs per cell. Fast inhibition was blocked, excitatory synapses were functional, and Ca^{2+} conductance and Ca^{2+}-dependent K^+ conductance were present (i.e., conditions corresponding to Fig. 5). Stimulation of a single cell elicited the event. Arrowheads indicate synchronization of action potentials in individual cells with population spikes in the local field potential.

itory postsynaptic potentials (IPSPs) during and after synchronized bursts, and the possibility of developing synchrony when some degree of fast inhibition is present. Careful consideration is now being directed to the magnitude of unitary (Miles and Wong, 1986) and synchronized synaptic currents (Johnston and Brown, 1981), together with anatomical (Boss *et al.*, 1987) and physiological (Miles and Wong, 1986) data on cell density and connection probability. We anticipate that attention to all of these matters will be important for an accurate temporal and spatial synthesis of epileptiform field potentials (Swann *et al.*, 1986). An example of a simulation with 2000 pyramidal cells and slow inhibition from 100 additional neurons is shown in Fig. 6.

III. Discussion

A. Contribution of Local Interactions to Burst Synchronization

1. Chemical Synapses

Several lines of evidence suggest that local excitatory chemical synapses are important for synchronous bursting in hippocampus, but they are not essential for all types of synchrony. Previous studies have shown that synchronous bursting in the presence of penicillin or picrotoxin is blocked with low-[Ca^{2+}], high-[Mg^{2+}] solutions. Miles *et al.* (1984), moreover, showed that low-[Ca^{2+}], high-[Mg^{2+}] solutions and solutions containing an excitatory amino acid antagonist (γ-D-glutamylglycine or D-2-amino-5 phosphonovalerate) could block synchronous bursting without a significant decrease in membrane excitability. However, several studies have now shown that synchronous bursts of action potentials can also occur in low-[Ca^{2+}] solutions that block chemical synapses (Taylor and Dudek, 1982; Jefferys and Haas, 1982; Konnerth *et al.*, 1984). Different mechanisms pertain in the two conditions. For the condition where synaptic inhibition is blocked and synaptic excitation is still functional, a cascade of neuronal activation appears to be necessary: bursting in a small population of neurons causes an ever-expanding recruitment of other pyramidal cells. Although the available data are limited, the particular susceptibility of the CA3 area for synchronous bursting is likely due to the presence of a larger number or more powerful recurrent excitatory connections in CA3 than in other areas (i.e., CA1 and dentate gyrus). Furthermore, the pronounced intrinsic burst-generating properties of the CA3 pyramidal cells will facilitate transmission of excitatory activity from cell to cell. Two important features of the model are excitatory synaptic connectivity and intrinsic burst generation, which in turn are responsible for burst propagation and synchronization. The computer model with chemical synapses alone not only predicts the previously established observation of a relatively long burst latency to a localized stimulus, but also that intracellular stimulation of a single cell with a depolarizing current pulse should evoke population bursts. Further experimental and modeling work is still required to account quantitatively for burst synchronization and spread in terms of the measured number and strength of excitatory synaptic connections in the hippocampus.

2. Electrical Field Effects

The computer models that incorporate only electrical field effects—without chemical synapses—can also generate synchronous population spikes similar in some respects to models with only chemical synapses as a mechanism for local communication. The parameters used in this model are reasonably realistic. Like the models with only chemical synapses, action potentials in active cells must be able to recruit inactive cells or at least influence the timing of their action potentials. This will happen in low-[Ca^{2+}] solutions because inactive cells are close to firing threshold and because inactive cells will "see" fields generated by large numbers of simultaneously firing cells. Simulations with relatively small neuronal networks (i.e., hundreds of cells) indicate that spontaneous activity in a few cells can activate a sufficiently excitable population to fire synchronously. Models with electrical field effects and those with chemical synapses alone are most likely to fire population bursts if a *group* of synchronously firing cells acts as the initiator of the activity. It is tempting to speculate that these are electrically coupled clusters (see below), but synchronous afferent input from some other structure or the "chance" synchronization of a small group of adjacent cells could also start the cascade of bursting neurons. A single cell thus can activate the whole population if it first excites a small group or cluster of cells, which in turn start the cascade. Presently most modeling and experimental data argue that the primary effect of electrical fields is to synchronize neurons on a fast time scale, thus leading to the relatively smooth waveform often observed for spontaneous population spikes. Slower effects of electrical fields are also possible, but they will require both difficult experiments and computer simulations to test their feasibility (see below).

3. Electrotonic Coupling

Evidence for electrotonic coupling via gap junctions in hippocampus and elsewhere in the mammalian brain has long been controversial. Virtually all of the computer modeling has suggested a minor or nonexistent role for electrotonic coupling in the generation, synchronization, and spread of hippocampal bursts. As indicated above, both the model with chemical synapses alone and the one with electrical field effects alone suggest that synchronous activity within a small group or cluster of neurons, such as would be expected of a small coupled network, is a particularly effective means for initiating the synchronization process in a hippocampal network. Several studies in both hippocampus and neocortex have shown significant (if not dramatic) blockage of dye coupling with treatments that cause intracellular acidification (Connors et al., 1984; Gutnick and Lobel-Yaakov, 1983; MacVicar and Jahnsen, 1985). These data argue that gap junctions mediate dye coupling, and for our purposes here they also open up experimental avenues for exploring the importance of coupling to synchronization and spread of epileptiform bursts. Similarly, the data of Gutnick and co-workers (1985) suggest that the slice procedure and associated dendrotomy may increase junctionally mediated coupling in some systems. This observation implies that coupling may be quite sensitive to external influences. On the one hand, a more direct and quantitative assessment of the number of junctions and the strength of coupling is necessary; that is, it is important to know why different methods of assessing coupling give different measures of strength and numbers of coupled cells (see Dudek et al., 1983, 1986, for discussion). It would be valuable to determine whether altering the amount of coupling causes changes in the synchronization of hippocampal activity. To be specific, is it possible to block electrotonic coupling and still obtain synchronous activity? It is somewhat surprising that electrotonic coupling is classically considered a mechanism for synchronizing electrical activity (e.g., in mammalian inferior olive, and in the pattern-generation networks of invertebrates), but it does not appear to be important for synchronization in hippocampus. This is probably a direct function of the limited amount of coupling thought to be present in cortical structures.

4. Ionic Changes

We have not discussed any of the experimental data that involve alterations in extracelluar $[K^+]$ and $[Ca^{2+}]$ during synchronous bursting, and the possible role that these alterations in ionic concentrations might play in synchronizing and recruiting cells. The main reason for this is that ionic shifts have not yet been incorporated into computer models in a direct sense. Recent experimental data argue that increases in extracellular $[K^+]$ are responsible for the slow spread of synchronous bursts in low-$[Ca^{2+}]$ solutions (Konnerth et al., 1986; Yaari et al., 1986). The available data suggest that K^+ acts on a very slow time scale, generally increasing the excitability of the neuronal population and ultimately causing an overall increase in spontaneous firing rates. The propagation rate (1 mm/sec) for this excitability increase is much slower than the propagation velocity of epileptiform events seen in convulsant-treated slices (about 100 mm/sec) (Knowles et al., 1987). It is interesting, however, that increases in extracellular $[K^+]$ can cause synchronized bursts resembling those that occur with picrotoxin, although these shifts in $[K^+]$ merely diminish IPSPs without blocking them entirely (Rutecki et al., 1985; Korn et al., 1987).

5. Cooperativity

The issue of cooperativity of mechanisms of local interaction is critical, and this would be particularly difficult to assess with experiments alone. A reasonable approach has been to ask the question, "Which mechanism(s) of local communication can synchronize neurons by itself, and which one is most important?" But in a normally functioning physiological system, more than one system can be operative at a time and the importance of a particular mechanism of neuronal interaction may not be apparent under some conditions. For example, chemical synaptic potentials may be necessary to bring cells close enough to threshold in order for electrical field effects to be significant. In a system with low excitability where membrane potential of most neurons is well below threshold, chemical synaptic mechanisms would be expected to be more important since EPSP amplitude is enhanced when a cell is hyperpolarized and no other activity is occurring. Electrical field effects, at least from action potentials, would be ineffective for cells with low excitability. In another example, as indicated earlier, increasing the amount of coupling in a network could conceivably create a cluster of synchronously firing cells that would be particularly capable of evoking population bursts. The importance of this phenomenon may not be apparent until the population of cells in the model is large enough and the coupled cluster is of appropriate size. With regard to changes in extracellular $[K^+]$, it is conceivable that intense activity and the associated alterations in ionic concentrations could lead to cellular swelling, as well as cellular depolarization, which would then increase the effectiveness of electrical fields as a synchronizing mechanism. One extremely important benefit of computer models is the ability to explore the ramifications of these cooperative interactions quantitatively as a means of aiding experimental interpretations.

B. Local Interactions and Hippocampal Potentiation

Several situations may exist where local neuronal interactions in the hippocampus could be involved in phenomena associated with long-term potentiation (LTP) and other forms of synaptic plasticity. One example involves recurrent excitation. It is known that repetitive stimulation leads to a decrease in GABA-mediated inhibition and that removal of this inhibitory system tends to reveal local excitatory synapses (Miles and Wong, 1987a; Christian and Dudek, 1988). Miles and Wong (1987b) have shown that after repetitive stimulation of afferent input to CA3 pyramidal cells, the strength of interaction between weakly connected neurons can be enhanced. Another possible mechanism for alterations in effective synaptic strength involves electrical interactions and the "dissociation" phenomenon that often occurs in LTP experiments (see Dudek et al., 1988). After LTP, there is often a disproportionate enhancement of the population spike; that is, the population spike is substantially larger for a population excitatory postsynaptic potential (EPSP) of a particular amplitude (e.g., Abraham et al., 1985). Repetitive stimulation is known to cause an increase in extracellular resistance (Dietzel et al., 1980, 1982a,b), and this could in turn enhance electrical field effects, thus increasing population spike amplitude. This mechanism would be particularly effective in those LTP experiments where extracellular recordings are used, and extracellular stimulus intensity is adjusted so that a small population spike is evoked for each stimulus before the tetanizing train. Under these conditions, nearly all cells in the population would be expected to have a large EPSP that is close to (but below) threshold, while only a small fraction of the cells actually fire action potentials to each test stimulus. Repetitive stimulation would then increase the amplitude of the EPSP in some cells and cause them to fire, thus leading to a larger population spike, which would in turn cause a larger field-effect depolarization in the cells that were below threshold. Since the large EPSPs have depolarized the neurons *close* to threshold, field-effect depolarizations alone may recruit additional neurons. As more neurons are activated, a larger population spike would occur, and this would in turn recruit additional cells through electrical field effects. It has been argued that this would not explain the decrease in latency that has been observed under these conditions (see Abraham *et al.*, 1985); however, field effects directly depolarize cells, and they could in principle cause a decrease in spike latency. It has also been argued that this mechanism is unlikely because the phenomenon of "dissociation" has not been seen after antidromic activation; however, repetitive antidromic stimulation would not necessarily cause the same alterations in extracellular space and resistance seen with synaptic activation. More importantly, during orthodromic activation of hippocampal neurons, virtually all neurons are close to threshold during the peak of the EPSP at the soma, where spikes are initiated and where field effects are most prominent. During antidromic stimulation, neurons whose axons are not activated by the stimulus are well below threshold, so slight increases in field-effect depolarizations at the soma would generally not recruit additional cells. Therefore, one would not expect this mechanism to be operative during antidromic stimulation, but rather only during orthodromic activation. Unfortunately, experiments to address this issue *directly* will be extremely difficult. The reason is technical in nature. Although one can reveal larger field-effect depolarizations with differential recording during orthodromic activation (Turner *et al.*, 1984), it is extremely difficult to conduct *independent* tests of enhanced excitability (e.g., see Taylor and Dudek, 1984a) under these conditions. Computer simulations, however, might provide a means for evaluating this hypothesis. In essence, it is possible to conduct experiments with the computer model that are impossible or extremely difficult to perform in a physiological system.

C. Electrical Field Effects from Synaptic Potentials

Another situation where electrical field effects could be extremely important, and yet where experimental analyses alone would be difficult and inconclusive, involves population EPSPs and their associated sinks and sources. Virtually all of the studies on electrical field effects have dealt with action potentials. Field effects might also occur when synchronous chemical EPSPs occur in a population of hippocampal neurons. Two situations where these are known to be prominent are during (1) spontaneous epileptiform bursts and (2) certain LTP experiments, where synchronous activation of neuronal populations with electrical stimuli are used. The rationale underlying this hypothetical mechanism is that synchronous activation of excitatory synapses at distal dendritic zones, for example, would cause a current sink in the extracellular space at the level of the active synapses and a source or positivity in surrounding

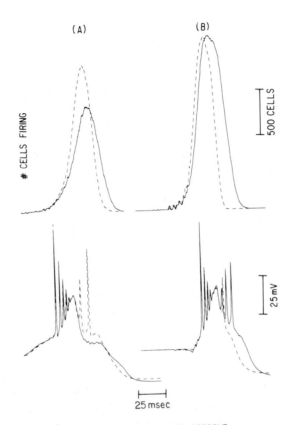

Figure 7.
Preliminary evidence from computer simulations that electrical field effects
have complex actions on population bursting. Bursts similar to those
shown in Fig. 6 were analyzed either with a low level of inhibition present
(A) or with inhibition completely blocked (B). Each cell had 20 excitatory
synaptic inputs in (A) and 10 inputs in (B). The number of neurons firing
in the 2000-cell model as a function of time is indicated with field effects
present (solid line) and absent (dashed line) in the upper set of traces. The
intracellular responses of typical cells in the population are shown in the
lower traces for each condition. In (A), the slow positivity underlying the
epileptiform field potential produces a transmembrane hyperpolarization,
which has a net inhibitory effect on the population. In (B), the enhanced
generation of action potentials when field effects are present offsets this
inhibitory effect.

inactive regions, including the somatic area. In fact, differential recordings during orthodromic activation of hippocampal neurons have shown that EPSPs appear reduced when recorded differentially under these conditions (e.g., compare Fig. 1A1 with Fig. 1A3 in Snow and Dudek, 1986). Unfortunately, it is impossible to prove experimentally that the extracellular somatic positivity arising from distal dentritic input has an inhibitory effect on spike generation. One simply cannot perform real experiments with and without electrical field effects. However, preliminary computer simulations (which were actually aimed at the "dissociation" questioned above) did reveal an inhibitory effect from the population EPSP. When this was incorporated into a model where both recurrent excitation and electrical field effects were present, preliminary simulations indicated that electrical field effects could either enhance or depress synchronous bursting, depending on the details of parameter choices (Fig. 7). A large body of data suggests that synaptic currents substantially contribute to extracellular recordings from large ensembles of neurons (such as the electroencephalogram). Yet, so far, little consideration has been given to the synchronizing or desynchronizing effects of the fields themselves under these conditions. A balance of electrophysiological experimentation and computer simulation will provide new information on this potentially important, but rather difficult, issue.

IV. Conclusion

The aim of this chapter has been to review recent work combining intracellular and extracellular recordings from hippocampal slices with computer simulations of complex neuronal networks. This strategy has revealed numerous insights into the function of neuronal populations that would not have been clear from just one or the other approach alone. The strength of previous modeling research of this nature has been its use of electrophysiological data as the critical input for deriving parameters, and its ability to predict future experimental outcomes. On the other hand, the value of the model for future electrophysiological experimentation will be that tentative priorities can be assigned to certain types of data; that is, some parameters in the model greatly affect the behavior of the system, whereas other parameters appear to have little or no effect. As the model continues to become more detailed, it will allow us to answer questions that are not amenable to experimentation, at least with available techniques. Nonetheless, a constant interplay between electrophysiological experimentation and the quantitative theoretical framework associated with computer models of neuronal networks will be essential for understanding the dynamic behavior of large neuronal ensembles characteristic of the mammalian brain.

Acknowledgments

We are grateful to Dr. R. K. S. Wong and Dr. R. Miles for useful discussions and to Dr. A. Rossi for important help in using the 3090 vector facility. We also thank A. Bienvenu and B. Farmer (Tulane Medical School, New Orleans, Louisiana) for secretarial assistance. This work was supported in part by National Institutes of Health grant NS 16683 and Air Force Office of Scientific Research grant 85-0317 to F. E. Dudek and by IBM.

References

Abraham, W. C., Bliss, T. V. P., and Goddard, G. V. (1985). *J. Physiol. (London)* **363**, 335–349.

Ayala, G. F., Dichter, M., Gumnit, R. J., Matsumoto, H., and Spencer, W. A. (1973). *Brain Res.* **52**, 1–17.

Boss, B. D., Turlejski, K., Stanfield, B. B., and Cowan, W. M. (1987). *Brain Res.* **406**, 280–287.

Brown, D. A., and Griffith, W. H. (1983). *J. Physiol. (London)* **337**, 287–301.

Brown, T. H., and Johnston D. (1982). *J. Neurophysiol.* **50**, 487–507.

Christian, E. P., and Dudek, F. E. (1988). *J. Neurophysiol* **59**, 90–109.

Connors, B. W., Benardo, L. S., and Prince, D. A. (1984). *J. Neurosci.* **4**, 1324–1330.

Dietzel, I., Heinemann, U., Hofmeier, G., and Lux, H. D. (1980). *Exp. Brain Res.* **40**, 432–439.

Dietzel, I., Heinemann, U., Hofmeier, G., and Lux, H. D. (1982a). In "Physiology and Pharmacology of Epileptogenic Phenomena" (M. R. Klee, H. D. Lux, and E.-J. Speckman, eds.), pp. 5–12. Raven Press, New York.

Dietzel, I., Heinemann, U., Hofmeier, G., and Lux, H. D. (1982b). *Exp. Brain Res.* **46**, 73–84.

Dudek, F. E., Andrew, R. D., MacVicar, B. A., Snow, R. W., and Taylor, C. P. (1983). In "Basic Mechanisms of Neuronal Hyperexcitability" (H. H. Jasper and N. M. van Gelder, eds.), pp. 31–73. Alan R. Liss, New York.

Dudek, F. E., Snow, R. W., and Taylor, C. P. (1986). In "Basic Mechanisms of the Epilepsies" (A. V. Delgado-Escueta, A. A. Ward, Jr., D. M. Woodbury, and R. J. Porter, eds.), pp. 593–617. Raven Press, New York.

Dudek, F. E., Gribkoff, V. G., and Christian, E. P. (1988). In "Long-Term Potentiation: From Biophysics to Behavior" (P. W. Landfield and S. A. Deadwyler, eds.), pp. 439–464. Alan R. Liss, New York.

Gutnick, M. J., and Lobel-Yaakov, R. (1983). *Neurosci. Lett.* **42**, 197–200.

Gutnick, M. J., Lobel-Yaakov, R., and Rimon, G. (1985). *Neuroscience* **15**, 659–666.

Jefferys, J. G. R. (1984). *Soc. Neurosci. Abstr.* **10**, 1074.

Jefferys, J. G. R. and Haas, H. L. (1982). *Nature (London)* **300**, 448–450.

Johnston, D., and Brown, T. H. (1981). *Science* **211**, 294–297.

Johnston, D., and Brown, T. H. (1982). *J. Neurophysiol.* **50**, 464–486.

Kay, A. R., and Wong, R. K. S. (1987) *J. Physiol. (London)* **392**, 603–613.

Knowles, W. D., Traub, R. D., and Strowbridge, B. W. (1987). *Neuroscience* **21**, 441–455.

Konnerth, A., Heinemann, U., and Yaari, Y. (1984). *Nature (London)* **307**, 69–71.

Konnerth, A., Heinemann, U., and Yaari, Y. (1986). *J. Neurophysiol.* **56**, 409–423.

Korn, H., and Faber, D. S. (1979). In "The Neurosciences: Fourth Study Program" (F. O. Schmitt and F. G. Worden, eds.), pp. 333–358. MIT Press, Cambridge, Massachusetts.

Korn, S. J., Giacchino, J. L., Chamberlin, N. L., and Dingledine, R. (1987). *J. Neurophysiol.* **57**, 325–340.

MacVicar, B. A., and Dudek, F. E. (1980). *Brain Res.* **184,** 220–223.

MacVicar, B. A., and Jahnsen, H. (1985). *Brain Res.* **330,** 141–145.

Miles, R., and Wong, R. K. S. (1983). *Nature (London)* **306,** 371–373.

Miles, R., and Wong, R. K. S. (1986). *J. Physiol. (London)* **373,** 397–418.

Miles, R., and Wong, R. K. S. (1987a). *J. Physiol. (London)* **388,** 611–629.

Miles, R., and Wong, R. K. S. (1987b). *Nature (London)* **329,** 724–726.

Miles, R., Wong, R. K. S., and Traub, R. D. (1984). *Neuroscience* **12,** 1179–1189.

Miles, R., Traub, R. D., Wong, R. K. S. (1988). *J. Neurophysiol.* (in press).

Numann, R. E., Wadman, W. J., and Wong, R. K. S. (1987). *J. Physiol. (London)* **393,** 331–353.

Rall, W. (1962). *Ann. N. Y. Acad. Sci.* **96,** 1071–1092.

Rutecki, P. A., Lebeda, F. J., and Johnston, D. (1985). *J. Neurophysiol.* **54,** 1363–1374.

Snow, R. W., and Dudek, F. E. (1984a). *Brain Res.* **298,** 382–385.

Snow, R. W., and Dudek, F. E. (1984b). *Brain Res.* **323,** 114–118.

Snow, R. W., and Dudek, F. E. (1986). *Brain Res.* **367,** 292–295.

Swann, J. W., Brady, R. J., Friedman, R. J., and Smith, E. J. (1986). *J. Neurophysiol.* **56,** 1718–1738.

Taylor, C. P., and Dudek, F. E. (1982). *Science* **218,** 810–812.

Taylor, C. P., and Dudek, F. E. (1984a). *J. Neurophysiol.* **52,** 126–142.

Taylor, C. P., and Dudek, F. E. (1984b). *J. Neurophysiol.* **52,** 143–155.

Taylor, C. P., Krnjevic, K., and Ropert, N. (1984). *Neuroscience* **11,** 101–109.

Traub, R. D. (1982). *Neuroscience* **7,** 1233–1242.

Traub, R. D., and Wong, R. K. S. (1982). *Science* **216,** 745–747.

Traub, R. D., Dudek, F. E., Taylor, C. P., and Knowles, W. D. (1985a). *Neuroscience* **14,** 1033–1038.

Traub, R. D., Dudek, F. E., Snow, R. W., and Knowles, W. D. (1985b). *Neuroscience* **15,** 947–958.

Traub, R. D., Knowles, W. D., Miles, R., and Wong, R. K. S. (1987a). *Neuroscience* **21,** 457–470.

Traub, R. D., Miles, R., and Wong, R. K. S. (1987b). *J. Neurophysiol.* **58,** 752–764.

Traub, R. D., Miles, R., and Wong, R. K. S. (1988). *Soc. Neurosci. Abstr.* **14,** 260.

Turner, R. W., Richardson, T. L., and Miller, J. J. (1984). *Exp. Brain Res.* **54,** 567–570.

Varga, R. S. (1962). "Matrix Iterative Analysis." Prentice-Hall, Englewood Cliffs, New Jersey.

Wong, R. K. S., and Prince, D. A. (1981). *J. Neurophysiol.* **45,** 86–97.

Wong, R. K. S., Prince, D. A., and Basbaum, A. I. (1979). *Proc. Natl. Acad. Sci. U.S.A.* **76,** 986–990.

Yaari, Y., Konnerth, A., and Heinemann, U. (1986). *J. Neurophysiol.* **56,** 424–438.

Yim, C. C., Krnjevic, K., and Dalkara, T. (1986). *J. Neurophysiol.* **56,** 99–122.

19

Models of Calcium Regulation in Neurons

Robert S. Zucker

I. Introduction

It is becoming increasingly clear that calcium is a critical second messenger involved in the regulation of synaptic plasticity (see Chapters 4, 10, 14, 15, and 18, this volume). Consequently, in order to understand fully the plastic capabilities of neurons it is necessary to understand in detail the mechanisms by which calcium enters cells, its subsequent subcellular effects, and its subcellular distribution and regulation.

Calcium acts as an intracellular trigger of many important processes in neurons. The two most familiar examples are regulation of electrical activity and activation of synaptic transmitter release. In neurons, the primary source of intracellular calcium is influx through voltage-dependent membrane channels. Calcium is initially highly localized to calcium channel mouths, and must reach nearby or distant sites of action by diffusion in cytoplasm, where it is also rapidly bound to native buffers. To maintain homeostasis, the calcium that has entered a neuron during a depolarization must be removed, first from cytoplasm and eventually from the cell as a whole. This is accomplished by a variety of mechanisms, including uptake into intracellular organelles and extrusion by surface membrane pumps. In order to understand how calcium operates to regulate neuronal function, it has become necessary to construct models of intracellular calcium diffusion, binding, uptake, and extrusion. In this chapter, I shall describe several of these models, including tests of their validity and their application to control of electrical activity and transmitter release.

II. Calcium-Dependent Currents and Electrical Activity

Calcium-dependent potassium currents ($I_{K(Ca)}$) are present in a variety of cell types (Petersen and Maruyama, 1984). In neurons, this current is often activated by action potentials, and contributes to spike repolarization, after-hyperpolarization, and neuronal adaptation (Meech, 1978). Calcium-activated nonspecific cationic current ($I_{NS(Ca)}$) has also been observed in several types of cells (Petersen and Maruyama, 1984). Its function is less clear. Finally, calcium current itself is subject to regulation by intracellular calcium in many neurons, whereby internal calcium accumulation leads to inactivation of the channels admitting calcium (Eckert and Chad, 1984).

A. Three Distinct Currents Regulate Bursting

I have concentrated on molluscan neurons in which all three calcium-dependent currents operate—bursting pacemaker neurons in the dorsal upper left quadrant of the abdominal ganglion of *Aplysia californica*. Figure 1 illustrates these currents after a depolarizing pulse, and the normal pattern of bursting in left upper quadrant neurons of *Aplysia*. Each current plays a role in shaping the endogenous action potential bursts in these cells:

1. An external tetraethylammonium (TEA) sensitive form of $I_{K(Ca)}$ is the dominant current for the first 50–100 msec following spikes in a burst and the end of the burst (Kramer and Zucker, 1985b). This early outward current, along with the voltage-dependent delayed-rectifier potassium current, repolarizes each action potential and generates a 50- to 100-msec hyperpolarizing after-

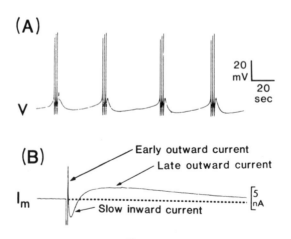

Figure 1.
(A) Endogenously generated action potential bursts in a dorsal upper left quadrant bursting pacemaker neuron in an *Aplysia* abdominal ganglion. (B) Current following a 50msec depolarizing voltage-clamp pulse to 0 mV from a holding potential of −35 mV. [Adapted from Kramer and Zucker (1985a).]

potential. At low temperatures and in some other molluscan bursting neurons (Deitmer and Eckert, 1985; Thompson et al., 1986; Smith and Thompson, 1987), a TEA-insensitive form of $I_{K(Ca)}$ persists for seconds and contributes to the late outward current that hyperpolarizes cells between bursts. At temperatures near the intertidal water temperature in Southern California where our animals are collected, we do not see a prolonged form of $I_{K(Ca)}$.

2. After $I_{K(Ca)}$ decays to low levels, $I_{NS(Ca)}$ is the dominant current for about 1 sec after each spike and the end of the burst (Kramer and Zucker, 1985a). This slow inward current generates a depolarizing afterpotential, which helps trigger subsequent spikes and serves to accelerate firing during the early part of the burst (Thompson and Smith, 1976; Adams, 1985; Smith and Thompson, 1987). In R15, a different bursting pacemaker neuron from the ones we have studied, this current is triggered partially by axonal spikes even in voltage-clamp studies (Adams and Levitan, 1985).

3. Finally, calcium-dependent inactivation of resting calcium current dominates during the late interburst interval (Adams and Levitan, 1985; Kramer and Zucker, 1985b). The calcium-dependent block of this inward current appears as a late outward current after a depolarization in voltage-clamp records. As this inactivation decays, the low-threshold calcium pacemaker current resumes and the neuron is depolarized until the next burst begins.

The roles played by these currents in shaping electrical neuronal activity depend critically on their time courses. Why should three calcium-activated or inactivated currents have such different durations? If each is dependent on submembrane calcium following influx through calcium channels, why do they decay at different rates? To answer these questions, we must know how submembrane calcium varies as a function of time after an influx, and we must know how each current depends on intracellular calcium.

B. Time Course of Submembrane Calcium Activity Following Influx

The measurement of submembrane calcium activity is no trivial matter. Calcium indicators such as aequorin, arsenazo III, quin-2, and fura-2 provide measures of average calcium activity throughout cytoplasm. Two-dimensional imaging of absorbance or fluorescence signals still produces results affected by calcium all along a line through the cell.

Calcium-sensitive microelectrodes respond too slowly to follow changes in submembrane activity following a burst. Thus no method presently exists to measure unequivocally the calcium activity beneath the membrane.

One approach to this problem is to compare signals generated by aequorin and arsenazo III injected into neurons that are depolarized to admit calcium. Depolarizing pulses of equal duration and different amplitude should lead to similar spatial distributions of intracellular calcium with different magnitude, if the processes governing calcium movement in cells (diffusion and pumps) are roughly linear. The absorbance of arsenazo III is linearly related to local calcium concentration, while aequorin photoemission varies as the 2.5 power of local calcium. For any given spatial distribution of calcium in a neuron, the aequorin signal should be proportional to the arsenazo III signal raised to the 2.5 power. This prediction was readily confirmed (Fig. 2A). However, after calcium influx, changes in the spatial distribution of calcium should be reflected by a more rapid drop in the nonlinear indicator aequorin signal than in the linear indicator arsenazo III signal as calcium diffuses away from the membrane (Smith and Zucker, 1980). This prediction was also confirmed (Fig. 2B), and provides direct evidence for diffusional redistribution of calcium in cytoplasm after entry at the surface.

Although confirming the existance of intracellular calcium gradients that change with time, the above results still did not permit the direct estimation of submembrane calcium concentration. For this purpose, we were forced to turn to a model of calcium movements in cytoplasm (Smith and Zucker, 1980). We solved the diffusion equation for cytoplasmic calcium in spherical coordinates, with influx at the surface determined by the magnitude and time course of calcium currents during voltage-clamp pulses. Calcium diffused inward with rapid binding to a fixed cytoplasmic buffer, with a measured binding ratio determined by the ratio of total calcium influx to average calcium concentration change measured with arsenazo III. Calcium was removed in the model either by surface pumps or uptake into organelles at rates measured independently in neuronal tissue (Blaustein et al., 1978; Requena and Mullins, 1979). This model, run with all parameters constrained to narrow ranges determined by independent measurement, successfully predicted the different time courses of aequorin and arsenazo III responses to depolarizing pulses (Fig. 2C). Such simulations, then, are as close as we have come to being able to "measure" submembrane calcium activity after influx through calcium channels.

C. Calcium Removal Mechanisms

The simulations of calcium diffusion away from the membrane showed that the rapid fall of aequorin signals reflected the diffusional dilution of submembrane calcium. The slower decay of arsenazo III absorbance

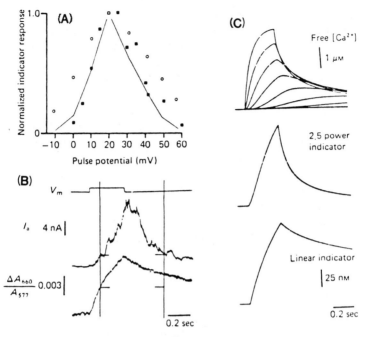

Figure 2.
(A) Normalized arsenazo III absorbance changes (circles) and aequorin photoemissions (squares) as functions of pulse amplitude, for 0.3-sec pulses in a bursting pacemaker neuron. The line plots arsenazo III responses raised to the 2.5 power. (B) Photomultiplier current (I_a) indicating aequorin photoemissions and arsenazo III absorbance changes ($\Delta A_{660}/A_{577}$) from two bursting pacemaker neurons, in response to a +20-mV, 0.3-sec pulse from a holding potential of −45 mV. (C) Theoretical predictions from the Smith and Zucker (1980) model: top trace, predicted calcium concentration changes at depths of 0.2, 0.6, 1.2, 1.8, 2.8, 4.3, 6.5, and 10.8 μm beneath the membrane (from the top), in response to a depolarization to +15 mV for 0.3 sec. The predicted aequorin and arsenazo III signals are shown in the middle and bottom traces respectively. [Adapted from Smith and Zucker (1980).]

reflected true removal of calcium from cytoplasm. What is the mechanism of this removal? A number of possibilities exist: (1) surface extrusion by Na/Ca exchange or an ATP-driven pump (Requena, 1983), (2) uptake into organelles such as endoplasmic reticulum (Blaustein et al., 1978; Henkart et al., 1978), and (3) diffusion past saturated buffers with subsequent additional buffering (Connor and Nikolakopoulou, 1982). Simulations with the diffusion equation indicated that any of these three mechanisms operating with parameters within measured ranges could account for the decay of arsenazo III signals.

To begin to distinguish these possibilities, we have looked at the effects of depolarizations of different amplitude and duration, and compared them to simulations based on different removal processes. For example, the highly saturated buffer model of Connor and Nikolako-poulou (1982) predicts that larger influxes of similar time courses will be removed much more slowly than smaller ones. This prediction was not confirmed (Smith, 1980). If cytoplasmic calcium is taken up into or-ganelles, then the calcium entering during depolarizations of different amplitude or duration will be removed at the same rate. Since removal is slowed by binding to a buffer, saturation of the buffer with large pulses might even cause removal to occur more quickly. We have not observed this (R. S. Zucker, unpublished data). If calcium is removed primarily by surface membrane extrusion, then calcium entering during long pulses, which permit diffusion further from the membrane during influx, will be pumped out more slowly. We have observed such an effect (R. S. Zucker, unpublished data), suggesting an important role for surface pumps, which are present in *Aplysia* neurons (Satin, 1984).

D. Photodynamic Chelators for Control of Cytoplasmic Calcium

We have recently turned to nitr-5, a photolabile calcium chelator (Adams *et al.*, 1988), as a tool for manipulating intracellular calcium and studying calcium regulatory mechanisms. This substance may be loaded with cal-cium and injected into neurons as a high-affinity buffer. When exposed to a bright flash of ultraviolet light, nitr-5 is photolyzed to a low-affinity form, releasing "caged" calcium into cytoplasm (Tsien and Zucker, 1986).

Figure 3A illustrates the effect of a flash of light on the calcium concentration in a neuron filled with 10 mM nitr-5. Because light is ab-sorbed from the front surface of the cell (facing the light) to the back surface, calcium is released nonuniformly, with the greatest increment occurring at the front surface. Subsequently, calcium and the various buffer species diffuse until equilibrium is reached. In order to estimate the time course of surface calcium concentration after a flash, we de-veloped a model (Landò and Zucker, 1989) of nitr-5 photolysis, buffer equilibration, and diffusion that is diagrammed in Fig. 3B. In this model, we represent the cell as a cube, and calculate the light intensity as a function of distance from the front of the cell. Photolysis converts a per-centage of nitr-5 proportional to the light intensity at each point. The buffer equations for the high- and low-affinity forms of nitr-5 and the native cell buffer are solved simultaneously at each point, and the re-sulting free calcium and free and calcium-bound forms of both nitr-5 species and the native cytoplasmic buffer are all allowed to diffuse in-dependently between the front and back of the cell. The free calcium concentration at points on the surface may be related to calcium-de-pendent membrane currents.

In order to convert submembrane calcium activities to membrane

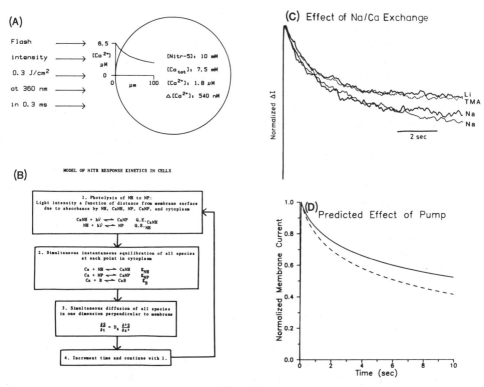

Figure 3.
(A) Effect of light flash on free calcium concentration in a neuron filled with nitr-5. The circle represents the cell, and the curve at its left surface shows the spatial gradient of free calcium at the moment of the flash, whose properties are indicated on the left. The concentrations of nitr-5, total calcium, and free calcium, and the increment in volume-average free calcium caused by the flash, are shown inside the cell. (B) Outline of computational model used to simulate the effect of a flash on calcium concentration in a cell filled with nitr-5. Abbreviations: NH, nitrobenzhydrol (the high-affinity form of nitr-5); NP, nitrosobenzophenone (the low-affinity form of nitr-5); B, native buffer; Q.E.$_s$, quantum efficiency of species s; K_s, dissociation constant of species s; D_s, diffusion constant of species s. (C) The $I_{K(Ca)}$ currents in a cell filled with 5mM nitr-5 and 3.75 mM calcium caused by 100 J of electrical energy discharged through a flashlamp focussed on the neuron. The traces marked "Na" were recorded in normal-sodium-containing seawater at the beginning and end of the experiment. The traces marked "Li" and "TMA" indicate responses in seawater with sodium replaced by lithium or tetramethylammonium, respectively, to block Na/Ca exchange. (D) Predicted flash responses in a neuron filled with nitr-5, with (dashed line) and without (solid line) a surface calcium extrusion pump (pump rate 0.001 cm/sec). [Adapted from Tsien and Zucker (1986) and Landò and Zucker, 1989.]

currents, we must know the relationship between calcium concentration and current level. We determined this by isolating $I_{K(Ca)}$ by recording it at the reversal potential for $I_{NS(Ca)}$ (about -25 mV), and by isolating $I_{NS(Ca)}$ by recording current at the reversal potential for $I_{K(Ca)}$ (about -75 mV). We could also block $I_{K(Ca)}$ with external TEA to measure $I_{NS(Ca)}$. When $I_{K(Ca)}$ was blocked with TEA and $I_{NS(Ca)}$ was eliminated by recording at its reversal potential, light evoked no response at all. When calcium current was isolated in a sodium-free, TEA-substituted medium, and enhanced with barium substituted for calcium, elevation of calcium by release from nitr-5 had little or no effect on subsequent calcium currents. Thus we were unable to elicit the calcium-dependent inactivation of calcium current by elevating calcium with nitr-5, and could not use this method to study the late outward current. This suggests that this effect of calcium on calcium channels occurs only at very high calcium levels, such as are likely to be present at calcium channel mouths (Chad and Eckert, 1984), or in regions of the cell shaded from the light, such as the axon hillock. We were, however, able to selectively activate $I_{K(Ca)}$ or $I_{NS(Ca)}$ using nitr-5.

By using increasing flash intensities, and causing larger and larger increments of calcium activity, we could determine the relationship between calcium concentration and membrane current for these two currents. Both of them depended linearly on the magnitude of a calcium concentration jump, even when the increment in calcium was several times the previous resting calcium level. Neither current showed saturation at calcium concentrations reaching 20 μM. Therefore, both membrane currents should be linearly related to the average submembrane calcium concentration.

E. Evidence for Na/Ca Extrusion

Figure 3C shows flash responses of $I_{K(Ca)}$ in a left upper quadrant bursting pacemaker neuron. The upper two traces show responses in media with lithium or tetramethylammonium in place of sodium to block Na/Ca exchange. These responses are similar to the predicted response time course (upper trace in Fig. 3D) using the model of Fig. 3B. When the cell was bathed in normal-sodium sea water, the nitr-5 response decayed somewhat more rapidly. When we added a surface membrane pump to our model, and adjusted it to remove calcium at a rate of 1 pmol/cm^2 sec per micromolar free calcium (Requena, 1983), we obtained the lower trace of Fig. 3D, which is similar to the experimental records in Fig. 3C. Apparently, Na/Ca exchange affects the decay of nitr-5 signals by removing some of the calcium formed near the surface. This and the preliminary result described in Section II,C suggest that Na/Ca exchange is one important mechanism involved in restoring calcium homeostasis following nervous activity. Whether ATP-dependent extrusion and uptake into organelles such as endoplasmic reticulum are also important for removing calcium during electrical activity in *Aplysia* neurons remains to be determined.

F. Kinetics of Calcium-Dependent Currents

We still need to explain the origin of the different decay rates of $I_{K(Ca)}$ and $I_{NS(Ca)}$ after a burst or depolarizing pulse. We initially thought these currents were activated by calcium with different stoichiometries, but the results mentioned in Section II,D and other results to be published soon (Landò and Zucker, 1989) indicate that both currents are activated by calcium with a simple first-order stoichiometry. We would then expect them to decay with the same time course as average submembrane calcium. In fact, Fig. 4A shows that the decay of $I_{NS(Ca)}$ after a pulse follows very closely the decay of average submembrane calcium concentration following influx predicted by the Smith and Zucker (1980) model (Section II,B).

Why does $I_{K(Ca)}$ (shown in Fig. 4B) decay faster? The answer is that the conductance underlying $I_{NS(Ca)}$ is not sensitive to voltage (Kramer and Zucker, 1985a; Swandulla and Lux, 1985), while that underlying $I_{K(Ca)}$ is highly voltage-dependent (Gorman and Thomas, 1980). Since calcium activates $I_{K(Ca)}$ linearly (Section II,D), we represented the interaction of calcium with the receptor activating $I_{K(Ca)}$ as a simple first-order binding reaction with voltage-dependent forward and backward rate constants. These rate constants can be determined from measurements of the relaxation time constant of $I_{K(Ca)}$ in response to voltage steps, and steady-state conductance versus voltage measurements. We used nitr-5 photolysis to activate $I_{K(Ca)}$, and measured the responses to a voltage step at potentials near the reversal potential for $I_{NS(Ca)}$. The responses to a voltage step before a light flash were subtracted from those after a flash to obtain relaxations of $I_{K(Ca)}$ to steady-state levels caused by an increment of calcium concentration and change in voltage. These data allowed us to calculate the rate constants for our $I_{K(Ca)}$ reaction scheme (Landò and Zucker, 1989). From this we could predict how $I_{K(Ca)}$ should decay after a depolarizing pulse in a cell containing nitr-5, where submembrane calcium decays according to Fig. 4A. The $I_{K(Ca)}$ experiences both voltage- and calcium-dependent relaxations, and decays somewhat faster than $I_{NS(Ca)}$. Our model fits experimental observations (Fig. 4B). The sum of early outward and slow inward currents gives the characteristic outward–inward tail current sequence normally observed after a voltage-clamp depolarization (Fig. 4C).

To summarize Section II, we developed a model of calcium diffusing radially inward from the cell membrane, which includes provisions for influx, binding, and extrusion at the surface or uptake into organelles. This model accounts for the time courses of aequorin and arsenazo III

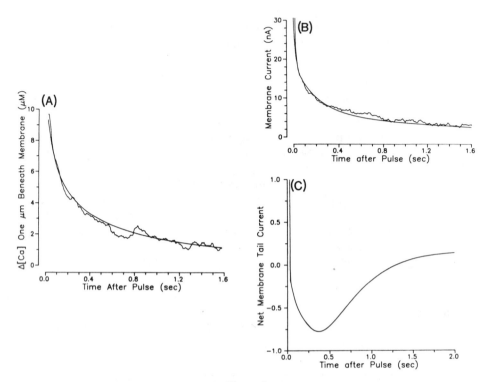

Figure 4.
(A) Predicted decay of submembrane calcium concentration (smooth curve)
for a −10-mV, 100-msec pulse, using the Smith and Zucker (1980) model.
The noisy curve is normalized $I_{NS(Ca)}$ tail current (inward current plotted
upward) following a −10-mV, 100-msec pulse and returning to −77 mV
to eliminate potassium currents. The bath also contained 50 mM TEA. (B)
Predicted decay of $I_{K(Ca)}$ (smooth curve) for a −10-mV, 100-msec pulse,
based on the change in submembrane calcium shown in (A) and
measurements of the calcium- and voltage dependence of $I_{K(Ca)}$. The noisy
curve is normalized $I_{K(Ca)}$ following such a pulse, obtained as the difference
current before and after adding 3 mM TEA to the bath. (C) Expected net
tail current obtained by scaling and mixing predicted currents from (A)
and (B). [From Landò and Zucker, 1989].

signals following depolarizing pulses, and the time course of $I_{NS(Ca)}$ after
a depolarization. Preliminary results suggest that surface extrusion of
calcium entering during electrical activity is more important than internal
sequestration into organelles. Nitr-5 experiments indicate that both $I_{K(Ca)}$
and $I_{NS(Ca)}$ depend linearly on submembrane calcium concentration. A
model of nitr-5 and calcium diffusion in cells explained the time course
of currents evoked by release of "caged" calcium from nitr-5, and also
simulated the effect of Na/Ca exchange in speeding the decay of flash
responses. Finally, we found that the voltage-dependent relaxation of

$I_{K(Ca)}$ following a depolarization is responsible for its decaying faster than $I_{NS(Ca)}$ and submembrane calcium activity, leading to the characteristic sequence of early outward and slow inward currents following a burst. The reason for the very slow kinetics of late outward current, caused by calcium-dependent inactivation of the calcium pacemaker current, remains to be determined.

III. Presynaptic Calcium and Transmitter Release

My laboratory has also been interested in the effect of presynaptic calcium on transmitter release. One synapse that is amenable to the sorts of biophysical manipulations used in *Aplysia* cell bodies is the giant synapse in the squid stellate ganglion. A great deal is known about this unusually large glutaminergic contact, and it has been a popular preparation in synaptic physiology since its discovery by J. Z. Young (Zucker, 1989).

A. Experiments on the Squid Giant Synapse

My experimental work on this synapse focussed on the role of calcium in synaptic facilitation. During repeated action potentials, successive excitatory postsynaptic potentials (EPSPs) grow as phasic transmitter release by individual action potentials increases (Charlton and Bittner, 1978a). Not due to changes in action potentials, afterpotentials, or calcium currents (Charlton and Bittner, 1978b; Charlton et al., 1982), facilitation was proposed to be a consequence of residual calcium in nerve terminals from prior activity summating with calcium influx during subsequent spikes to evoke more release of transmitter, which is nonlinearly dependent on calcium activity (Katz and Miledi, 1968; Miledi and Thies, 1971). We found that raising presynaptic calcium does facilitate release by spikes, and that residual calcium can be detected in nerve terminals following activity (Charlton et al., 1982).

Just as in *Aplysia* cell bodies, we observed several different calcium-dependent processes and measurements with very different time courses. Presynaptic calcium is supposed to activate phasic transmission directly (Katz, 1969), and this process lasts only 1–2 msec. Yet residual calcium is supposed to cause facilitation, which lasts tens to hundreds of milliseconds. And our measurement of presynaptic calcium activity using arsenazo III microspectrophotometry showed free calcium concentration to remain high for seconds after electrical activity. How can these differences in time course of calcium-dependent events be reconciled?

First of all, again just as in *Aplysia* cell bodies, arsenazo III absorbance reports average cytoplasmic calcium activity, not its concentration at membrane sites where transmitter is released. The brief synaptic delay (< 0.5 msec) allows calcium to diffuse with binding only about 50 nm from channel mouths before causing transmitter release (Fogelson and Zucker, 1985). Arsenazo III absorbance does not report these local high calcium concentrations responsible for triggering neurosecretion, and this explains the huge difference in time courses of phasic release and pre-synaptic calcium measurements. As to facilitation, the highly nonlinear relation between transmitter release and calcium would cause a small residual amount of calcium at release sites to have very little effect on transmitter release, which will therefore terminate quickly as residual calcium decays. But its summation with peak calcium in the next spike can greatly facilitate release, as a consequence of the same nonlinearity.

B. One-Dimensional Model of Presynaptic Calcium Diffusion

Although these arguments are qualitatively plausible, it must be shown that the time courses of phasic transmitter release, synaptic facilitation, and presynaptic arsenazo III absorbance changes can be explained quan-titatively by what we expect to happen to calcium at presynaptic ter-minals. As a first approximation, the nerve terminal can be treated as a cylinder with calcium entering uniformly at the surface and diffusing radially inward. We solved the diffusion equation in cylindrical coor-dinates (Zucker and Stockbridge, 1983), with influx determined by volt-age-clamp experiments, and cytoplasmic buffering, uptake into organ-elles, and extrusion at the surface included with parameters set within the range of reported values (Fig. 5A). Simulations with this model pro-vided a good fit to the arsenazo III absorbance signal (Fig. 5B), and pre-dicted that submembrane calcium would decay rapidly enough to account for phasic transmitter release even with only a square law relating release to presynaptic calcium (Fig. 5C). Facilitation expressed by a second spike

---

Figure 5.
The one-dimensional model of presynaptic calcium diffusion. (A) Schematic of the model used to predict the effects of spikes on presynaptic calcium concentration. (B) Predicted average calcium concentration change, and observed absorbance change (from Charlton *et al.*, 1982) from a presynaptic terminal injected with arsenazo III, in response to 66 spikes at 33 Hz, ending at time 0. (C) Predicted square of submembrane calcium concentration and observed excitatory postsynaptic current (EPSC). Transmitter release should be somewhat faster than the EPSC, and somewhat slower than the submembrane calcium raised to a power reflecting calcium cooperativity in releasing transmitter. (D) Predicted facilitation of a second response as a function of the interval between it and the first response, and data from two preparations (from Charlton and Bittner, 1978a). (E) Predicted facilitation following a single spike and during and after a 5-sec tetanus at 20 Hz. (F) Predicted square of submembrane calcium for the first and last spikes in the 5-sec train. Transmitter release should be similar to (but somewhat slower than) these curves. [Adapted from Zucker (1987b).]

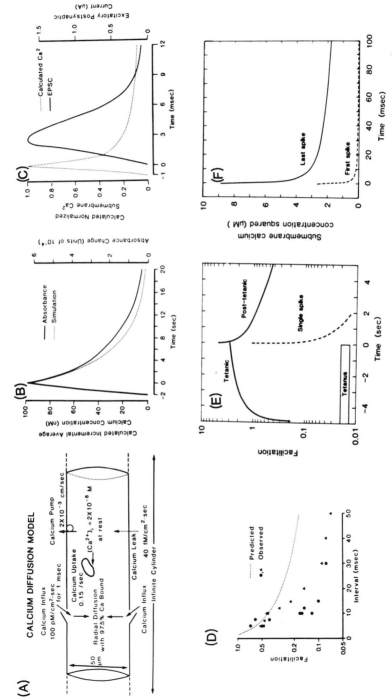

CALCIUM DIFFUSION MODEL

Calcium Influx
100 pM/cm²·sec
for 1 msec

Calcium Pump
2X10⁻³ cm/sec

$[Ca^{2+}]_i = 2X10^{-8}$ M
at rest

Calcium Uptake
0.15 /sec

Radial Diffusion
with 97.5% Ca Bound

Calcium Leak
40 fM/cm²·sec

Calcium Influx
Infinite Cylinder

50 µm

(A)

(B)

Calculated Incremental Average
Calcium Concentration (nM)

— Absorbance
...... Simulation

Absorbance Change (Units of 10⁻⁴)

Time (sec)

(C)

Calculated Normalized
Submembrane Ca²

...... Calculated Ca²
— EPSC

Excitatory Postsynaptic
Current (nA)

Time (msec)

(D)

Facilitation

...... Predicted
•▲ Observed

Interval (msec)

(E)

Facilitation

Tetanic

Post-tetanic

Single spike

Tetanus

Time (sec)

(F)

Submembrane calcium
concentration squared (µM)

Last spike

First spike

Time (msec)

was also predicted to be roughly similar to measured values (Fig. 5D). However, when the model was driven by repeated calcium influxes to simulate a tetanus of 100 spikes at 20 Hz (Fogelson and Zucker, 1985), a serious problem developed. Facilitation accumulated during the tetanus and decayed afterward with fast and slow components (Fig. 5E), as observed experimentally at other preparations (Magleby and Zengel, 1982). But the simulations predicted that late spikes in the train would continue to release transmitter at high rates for more than 100 msec (Fig. 5E), clearly contradicting what the synapse actually does.

C. Three-Dimensional Model of Presynaptic Calcium Diffusion

The trouble with the one-dimensional calcium diffusion model is that posttetanic residual calcium is too large a fraction of peak calcium at release sites, and decays too slowly (Fig. 6B). This leads to the critical error of transmitter release lasting a long time for late spikes in a tetanus (Fig. 5F), and to a predicted facilitation after one spike declining too slowly (Fig. 5D). These problems could be reduced somewhat by increasing the cooperativity of calcium action in releasing transmitter, consistent with accumulating experimental evidence (Katz and Miledi, 1970; Lester, 1970; Charlton et al., 1982; Augustine et al., 1985; Augustine and Charlton, 1986). But then our simulations predicted a facilitation that was much larger than observed. Somehow, our simulations were indicating too high a residual calcium compared to the peak at an action potential, or, equivalently, too low a peak calcium at each spike.

This is precisely the error that should occur by representing calcium entry as a spatially uniform flux across the membrane. Calcium actually enters through discrete calcium channels and releases transmitter in their immediate vicinity. Each calcium channel will be surrounded by a cloud of calcium ions, or a "calcium domain," at the end of an action potential and when transmitter release occurs (Fig. 6A). Only after release does each calcium domain collapse by diffusion in three dimensions, with subsequent one-dimensional radial diffusion of residual calcium. Thus a more realistic model would simulate calcium entering at discrete points and diffusing away from each channel in three dimensions into the axoplasm. This would naturally predict larger local calcium concentration peaks that would dissipate more rapidly than in the one-dimensional model (Fig. 6B).

Such a model was constructed by considering calcium diffusion into the presynaptic terminal from arrays of calcium channels (Fogelson and Zucker, 1985). The model included the usual provisions for calcium binding and extrusion. Transmitter release was considered to occur approximately 50 nm from calcium channel mouths, limited on the low side by requiring exocytosis not to obliterate calcium channels, and on

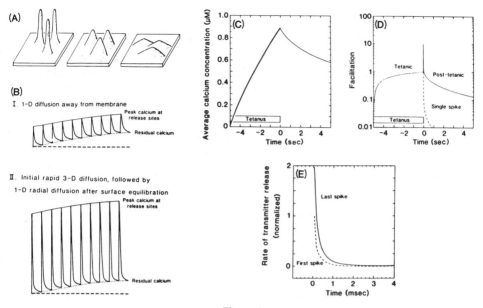

Figure 6.
The three-dimensional model of presynaptic calcium diffusion. (A) Schematic drawing of the collapse of calcium domains surrounding single calcium channel mouths inside the nerve terminal at the end of the spike and short times later. (B) Comparison of the relative calcium magnitudes of peaks of calcium activity during spikes, and residual calcium activity after spikes, for one- and three-dimensional models. (C) Predicted average free calcium concentration during and after a 5-sec 20 Hz tetanus. (D) Predicted facilitation evoked by one spike or the tetanus. (E) Predicted rate of transmitter release, if this is assumed to follow the fifth power of calcium at release sites 50 nm from calcium channel mouths, for the first and last spike in the train. [Adapted from Zucker (1987b).]

the high side by the time available for calcium diffusion during the synaptic delay. Various arrays of calcium channels were considered, but the one most successful in fitting the data had the channels clustered into active zones, as suggested by ultrastructural studies (Pumplin *et al.*, 1981). Simulations with this model successfully predicted not only the changes in arsenazo absorbance in a tetanus (Fig. 6C), and tetanic and posttetanic facilitation (Fig. 6D), but also the rapid termination of transmitter release after late spikes in a tetanus (Fig. 6E). The latter result in particular required calcium channels to be clustered, leading to two phases of three-dimensional diffusion, away from single channel mouths and then away from each cluster. Spreading channels uniformly on the presynaptic surface led to only one phase of three-dimensional diffusion (away from each calcium channel), and transmitter release still lasted too long after a tetanus.

D. Voltage Dependence of Transmitter Release

Llinás *et al.* (1981) reported a curious characteristic in the relation between transmitter release and presynaptic calcium current at the squid giant synapse. As larger depolarizations are used, calcium influx and transmitter release both increase, and then decline as the calcium equilibrium potential is approached. One would expect equal currents on the rising and falling limbs of the calcium current versus voltage curve to release equal amounts of transmitter. Instead, Llinás *et al.* found that the current caused by the larger depolarization always evoked more transmitter release. Even when calcium tail currents were eliminated by considering only calcium current and release before the end of the pulse, some hysteresis usually persisted in these measurements (Smith *et al.*, 1985; Augustine *et al.*, 1985). To account for this result, Llinás *et al.* (1981) proposed that some of the steps involved in calcium-dependent exocytosis were voltage-dependent.

However, consideration of the effects of voltage on calcium domains leads to a different conclusion (Simon and Llinás, 1985; Zucker and Fogelson, 1986). Large depolarizations open more calcium channels than small pulses, with less calcium entering each channel as the calcium equilibrium potential is approached. This means that synaptic vesicles are exposed to calcium entering several calcium channels. This increases the overlap of adjacent calcium domains: multiple calcium-sensitive sites on vesicles are more likely to be activated, and the peak calcium concentration at release sites will be higher due to domain overlap, despite the fact that less calcium enters each channel (Fig. 7A and B). This leads immediately to a hysteresis in the relationship between transmitter release and calcium current, depending on whether large or small depolarizations are used (Fig. 7C). Calcium diffusion models predict this form of hysteresis without the need to invoke any voltage-dependent steps in neurosecretion.

This result parallels recent work on neuromuscular junctions, in which a number of experiments were interpreted as indicating a voltage dependence of transmitter release (reviewed in Parnas and Parnas, 1986). We have shown that all of these experiments can be explained by a conventional calcium hypothesis of transmitter release, with no need to invoke voltage-dependent steps in the release process (Landò *et al.*, 1986; Zucker and Landò, 1986; Zucker *et al.*, 1986; Zucker, 1987a).

To summarize Section III, we have been able to measure changes in presynaptic calcium activity during synaptic transmission with calcium-sensitive dyes. Theoretical simulations of calcium movements allow us to relate these measurements to calcium-dependent processes such as transmitter release and synaptic facilitation. Improved models of calcium diffusion explain an otherwise surprising relationship between calcium influx and transmitter release at low and high voltages.

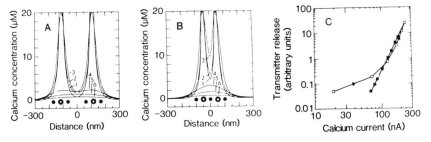

Figure 7.
(A) Predicted spatial profile of free calcium concentration when the average spacing of open calcium channels is 218 nm for a 2.5 msec depolarization to −20 mV. Open circles denote open calcium channels, and closed circles nearby release sites. The single-channel current is 490 fA. Traces 1–6 are for 1.0, 2.0, 2.4, 3.4, 4.4, and 6.5 msec after the beginning of the pulse. Calcium domains show very little overlap. (B) A similar plot for a 2.5-msec depolarization to 0 mV, where open calcium channels are 101 nm apart and the single-channel current is 350 fA. Calcium domains now display significant overlap. (C) Predicted relationship between peak rate of transmitter release and macroscopic presynaptic calcium current at the end of 2.5-msec pulses. Transmitter release is proportional to the number of open calcium channels times calcium concentration 50 nm away raised to the fifth power. Calcium current is proprotional to the number of open calcium channels times the single-channel current. Open squares represent pulse potentials of −25 to 0 mV (when all channels are open), and filled squares represent pulse potentials from +10 to +60 mV. The arrowheads point in the direction of increasing pulse potential. [Adapted from Zucker and Fogelson (1986).]

IV. Conclusion

Calcium is at the center of a neuron's electrical activity and means of communication. Understanding neural function demands close attention to the movements of calcium within cells. Recent technological innovation permits the measurement and control of intracellular calcium with a precision not even dreamed of 10 years ago. While designing experiments based on new technology, we must constantly revise and refine our formulations of cellular mechanisms under control of calcium. Theoretical modeling and computer simulation have provided as much insight into neural function as have new experimental results. Together the two approaches provide a symbiotic power that dwarfs what can be accomplished with either alone. And fortunately, theoretical and experimental developments seem if anything to be accelerating, promising a good deal more progress and excitement to come in the near future.

Acknowledgments

This chapter summarizes the work of many exceptional colleagues, including Roger Tsien, Norman Stockbridge, Stephen Smith, Luca Landò, Richard Kramer, Aaron Fogelson, and Milton Charlton. The research has been funded by National Institutes of Health grant NS 15114.

References

Adams, S. R., Kao, J. P. Y., Grynkiewicz, G., Minta, A., and Tsien, R. Y. (1988). Biologically useful chelators that release Ca^{2+} upon illumination. *J. Am. Chem. Soc.* **110**, 3212–3220.

Adams, W. B. (1985). Slow depolarizing and hyperpolarizing currents which mediate bursting in *Aplysia* neurone R15. *J. Physiol. (London)* **360**, 51–68.

Adams, W. B., and Levitan, I. B. (1985). Voltage and ion dependences of the slow currents which mediate bursting in *Aplysia* neurone R15. *J. Physiol. (London)* **360**, 69–93.

Augustine, G. J., and Charlton, M. P. (1986). Calcium-dependence of presynaptic calcium current and post-synaptic response at the squid giant synapse. *J. Physiol. (London)* **381**, 619–640.

Augustine, G. J., Charlton, M. P., and Smith, S. J. (1985). Calcium entry and transmitter release at voltage-clamped nerve terminals of squid *J. Physiol. (London)* **367**, 163–181.

Blaustein, M. P., Ratzlaff, R. W., and Schweitzer, E. S. (1978). Calcium buffering in presynaptic nerve terminals. II. Kinetic properties of the nonmitochondrial Ca sequestration mechanism. *J. Gen. Physiol.* **72**, 43–66.

Chad, J. E., and Eckert, R. (1984). Calcium domains associated with individual channels can account for anomalous voltage relations of Ca-dependent responses. *Biophys. J.* **45**, 993–999.

Charlton, M. P., and Bittner, G. D. (1978a). Facilitation of transmitter release at squid synapses. *J. Gen. Physiol.* **72**, 471–486.

Charlton, M. P., and Bittner, G. D. (1978b). Presynaptic potentials and facilitation of transmitter release in the squid giant synapse. *J. Gen. Physiol.* **72**, 487–511.

Charlton, M. P., Smith, S. J., and Zucker, R. S. (1982). Role of presynaptic calcium ions and channels in synaptic facilitation and depression at the squid giant synapse. *J. Physiol. (London)* **323**, 173–193.

Connor, J. A., and Nikolakopoulou, G. (1982). Calcium diffusion and buffering in nerve cytoplasm. *Lect. Math. Life Sci.* **15**, 79–101.

Deitmer, J. W., and Eckert, R. (1985). Two components of Ca-dependent potassium current in identified neurones of *Aplysia californica*. *Pfluegers Arch.* **403**, 353–359.

Eckert, R., and Chad, J. E. (1984). Inactivation of Ca channels. *Prog. Biophys. Mol. Biol.* **44**, 215–267.

Fogelson, A. L., and Zucker, R. S. (1985). Presynaptic calcium diffusion from various arrays of single channels: Implications for transmitter release and synaptic facilitation. *Biophys. J.* **48**, 1003–1017.

Gorman, A. L. F., and Thomas, M. V. (1980). Potassium conductance and internal calcium accumulation in a molluscan neurone. *J. Physiol. (London)* **308**, 287–313.

Henkart, M. P., Reese, T. S., and Brinley, F. J., Jr. (1978). Endoplasmic reticulum sequesters calcium in the squid giant axon. *Science* **202**, 1300–1303.

Katz, B. (1969). "The Release of Neural Transmitter Substances." Thomas, Springfield, Illinois.

Katz, B., and Miledi, R. (1968). The role of calcium in neuromuscular facilitation. *J. Physiol. (London)* **195**, 481–492.

Katz, B., and Miledi, R. (1970). Further study of the role of calcium in synaptic transmission. *J. Physiol. (London)* **207**, 789–801.

Kramer, R. H., and Zucker, R. S. (1985a). Calcium-dependent inward current in *Aplysia* bursting pacemaker neurones. *J. Physiol. (London)* **362**, 107–130.

Kramer, R. H., and Zucker, R. S. (1985b). Calcium-induced inactivation of calcium current causes the inter-burst hyperpolarization of *Aplysia* bursting neurones. *J. Physiol. (London)* **362**, 131–160.

Landò, L., and Zucker, R. S. (1989). "Caged calcium" in *Aplysia* pacemaker neurons. Characterization of calcium-activated potassium and nonspecific cation currents. *J. Gen. Physiol.*, in press.

Landò, L., Giovannini, J., and Zucker, R. S. (1986). Cobalt blocks the increase in MEPSP frequency on depolarization in calcium-free hypertonic media. *J. Neurobiol.* **17**, 707–712.

Lester, H. A. (1970). Transmitter release by presynaptic impulses in the squid stellate ganglion. *Nature (London)* **227**, 493–496.

Llinás, R., Steinberg, I. Z., and Walton, K. (1981). Relationship between presynaptic calcium current and postsynaptic potential in squid giant synapse. *Biophys. J.* **33**, 323–352.

Magleby, K. L., and Zengel, J. E. (1982). A quantitative description of stimulation-induced changes in transmitter release at the frog neuromuscular junction. *J. Gen. Physiol.* **30**, 613–638.

Meech, R. W. (1978). Calcium-dependent potassium activation in nervous tissues. *Annu. Rev. Biophys. Bioeng.* **7**, 1–18.

Miledi, R., and Thies, R. (1971). Tetanic and post-tetanic rise in frequency of miniature end-plate potentials in low-calcium solutions. *J. Physiol. (London)* **212**, 245–257.

Parnas, I., and Parnas, H. (1986). Calcium is essential but insufficient for neurotransmitter release: The calcium-voltage hypothesis. *J. Physiol. (Paris)* **81**, 289–305.

Petersen, O. H., and Maruyama, Y. (1984). Calcium-activated potassium channels and their role in secretion. *Nature (London)* **307**, 693–696.

Pumplin, D. W., Reese, T. S., and Llinás, R. (1981). Are the presynaptic membrane particles the calcium channels? *Proc. Natl. Acad. Sci. U.S.A.* **78**, 7210–7213.

Requena, J. (1983). Calcium transport and regulation in nerve fibers. *Annu. Rev. Biophys. Bioeng.* **12**, 237–257.

Requena, J., and Mullins, L. J. (1979). Calcium movement in nerve fibres. *Q. Rev. Biophys.* **12**, 371–460.

Satin, L. (1984). Sodium-dependent calcium efflux from single *Aplysia* neurons. *Brain Res.* **300**, 392–395.

Simon, S. M., and Llinás, R. R. (1985). Compartmentalization of the submembrane calcium activity during calcium influx and its significance in transmitter release. *Biophys. J.* **48**, 485–498.

Smith, S. J. (1980). Calcium regulation in gastropod nerve cell bodies. In "Molluscan Nerve Cells: From Biophysics to Behavior" (J. Koester and J. H. Byrne, eds.), pp. 81–91. Cold Spring Harbor Lab., Cold Spring Harbor, New York.

Smith, S. J., and Thompson, S. H. (1987). Slow membrane currents in bursting pacemaker neurones of *Tritonia*. *J. Physiol. (London)* **382**, 425–448.

Smith, S. J., and Zucker, R. S. (1980). Aequorin response facilitation and intracellular calcium accumulation in molluscan neurones. *J. Physiol. (London)* **300**, 167–196.

Smith, S. J., Augustine, G. J., and Charlton, M. P. (1985). Transmission at voltage-clamped giant synapse of the squid: Evidence for cooperativity of presynaptic calcium action. *Proc. Natl. Acad. Sci. U.S.A.* **82**, 622–625.

Swandulla, D., and Lux, H. D. (1985). Activation of a nonspecific cation conductance by intracellular Ca^{2+} elevation in bursting pacemaker neurons of *Helix pomatia*. *J. Neurophysiol.* **54**, 1430–1443.

Thompson, S. H., and Smith, S. J. (1976). Depolarizing afterpotentials and burst production in molluscan pacemaker neurons. *J. Neurophysiol.* **39**, 153–157.

Thompson, S. H., Smith, S. J., and Johnson, J. W. (1986). Slow outward tail currents in molluscan bursting pacemaker neurons: Two components differing in temperature sensitivity. *J. Neurosci.* **6,** 3169–3176.

Tsien, R., and Zucker, R. S. (1986). Control of cytoplasmic calcium with photolabile 2-nitrobenzhydrol tetracarboxylate chelators. *Biophys. J.* **50,** 843–853.

Zucker, R. S. (1987a). The calcium hypothesis and modulation of transmitter release by hyperpolarizing pulses. *Biophys. J.* **52,** 347–350.

Zucker, R. S. (1987b). Neurotransmitter release and its modulation. *In* "Neuromodulation: The Biochemical Control of Neuronal Excitability" (L. K. Kaczmarek and I. B. Levitan, eds.), pp. 243–263. Oxford Univ. Press, London and New York.

Zucker, R. S. (1989). The role of calcium in regulating neurotransmitter release in the squid giant synapse. *In* "Presynaptic Regulation of Neurotransmitter Release" (J. Feigenbaum and M. Hanani, eds.). Freund, Tel Aviv (in press).

Zucker, R. S., and Fogelson, A. L. (1986). Relationship between transmitter release and presynaptic calcium influx when calcium enters through discrete channels. *Proc. Natl. Acad. Sci. U.S.A.* **83,** 3032–3036.

Zucker, R. S., and Landò, L. (1986). Mechanism of transmitter release: Voltage hypothesis and calcium hypothesis. *Science* **231,** 574–579.

Zucker, R. S., and Stockbridge, N. (1983). Presynaptic calcium diffusion and the time courses of transmitter release and synaptic facilitation at the squid giant synapse. *J. Neurosci.* **3,** 1263–1269.

Zucker, R. S., Landò, L., and Fogelson, A. L. (1986). Can presynaptic depolarization release transmitter without calcium influx? *J. Physiol. (Paris)* **81,** 237–245.

Index